£60, 027
HIF

*BRITISH FOREIGN POLICY
IN THE AGE OF THE
AMERICAN REVOLUTION*

BRITISH FOREIGN POLICY IN THE AGE OF THE AMERICAN REVOLUTION

H. M. Scott

CLARENDON PRESS · OXFORD
1990

Oxford University Press, Walton Street, Oxford OX2 6DP
Oxford New York Toronto
Delhi Bombay Calcutta Madras Karachi
Petaling Jaya Singapore Hong Kong Tokyo
Nairobi Dar es Salaam Cape Town
Melbourne Auckland
and associated companies in
Berlin Ibadan

Oxford is a trade mark of Oxford Univerisity Press

Published in the United States
by Oxford University Press, New York

British Library Cataloguing in Publication Data
Scott, H. M. (Hamish M), 1946–
British foreign policy in the age of the American
revolution.
1. Great Britain. Foreign relations. Policies of
government, history
I. Title
327.41
ISBN 0–19–820195–8

Library of Congress Cataloging in Publication Data
Scott, H. M. (Hamish M.), 1946–
British foreign policy in the age of the American Revolution/
H. M. Scott.
p.   cm.
Includes bibliographical references (p.
1. Great Britain—Foreign relations—1760–1789.   2. United States—
History—Revolution, 1775–1783.   I. Title.
DA510.S26   1990
327.41'009'033—dc20   90–6886
ISBN 0–19–820195–8

Typeset by Cambrian Typesetters, Frimley, Surrey
Printed in Great Britain by
Courier International Ltd,
Tiptree, Essex

*To my mother
and to the memory
of my father*

Acknowledgements

IN the research and writing of this book I have incurred a large number of obligations, which I happily acknowledge here. Archival research in Britain and abroad has been made possible by generous grants from the British Academy, the Carnegie Trust for the Universities of Scotland, the Twenty-Seven Foundation, the Wolfson Trust, and the Travel Fund of the University of St Andrews: I am grateful to them all. For permission to consult and cite papers in private possession, I have to thank the Earl of Buckinghamshire, the Earl Cathcart, the Duke of Grafton, the Earl of Mansfield, and the Marquess of Weymouth. I am grateful for the assistance and unfailing co-operation of staff in all the archives and libraries in which I have worked. I am particularly indebted to the Inter-Library Loans Librarian at the University of St Andrews, Ms Sue Rowe, who has uncomplainingly obtained material for me, and also to Mrs Joan Auld of the University of Dundee Library, who facilitated access to the Mansfield Papers. For specific permission to cite unpublished doctoral theses I have to thank Professor M. S. Anderson, Dr Robert R. Crout, Dr Margaret M. Escott, Dr John Hardman, and Dr Michael Hamer; I am also grateful to the authors of the other dissertations listed in the bibliography.

The initial research from which this book has evolved was undertaken under the inspirational supervision of Professor Ragnhild M. Hatton, who has been a continuing source of guidance and encouragement. Professor Michael Roberts, the doyen of historians of eighteenth-century British foreign policy, very kindly sent me copies of important material from Swedish archives. Dr M. J. Rodriguez-Salgado most generously translated material in Spanish and also undertook research at Simancas on my behalf: my debt to her is particularly great. Dr Thomas Munck of the University of Glasgow kindly translated material from Danish, and my colleague Professor A. F. Upton from Swedish. Professor Derek Beales read an early version of the text: his incisive comments made me realize what I should be trying to do. G. C. Gibbs and Dr Derek McKay both commented extensively on a final draft: their suggestions and encouragement are only a small part of my obligation to them over many years. I am grateful to Mrs Margaret Smith and especially to Mrs Nancy Bailey, who typed and retyped successive versions of this book. Mr Anthony Morris provided essential support and advice, and the skill of his colleagues at Oxford University Press smoothed the transition from manuscript to printed text. My wife has assisted at all stages, and also proved an exacting critic of style and substance: without her assistance and enthusiasm this book would not have been completed. But neither she, nor any of the other scholars mentioned, are to be held responsible for the remaining defects. My greatest obligation is inadequately acknowledged elsewhere.

H.M.S.

St Andrews
August 1989

Contents

Abbreviations

Add. MSS	British Library (London), Additional Manuscripts
ADM	Public Record Office (London), Admiralty series
AM	Archives Nationales (Paris), Archives de la Marine
Archives . . . Orange-Nassau	*Archives ou correspondance inédite de la Maison d'Orange-Nassau*, ed. G. Groen van Prinsterer: 4th series (Leiden, 1909–14), 5th series (Leiden, 1910–15)
BDI	*British Diplomatic Instructions 1689–1789*, ed. J. F. Chance and L. G. Wickham Legg (7 vols.; London, 1922–34)
BDR	D. B. Horn, ed., *British Diplomatic Representatives 1689–1789* (London, 1932)
Bancroft/Circourt	George Bancroft, *Histoire de l'action commune de la France et de l'Amérique pour l'indépendance des États-Unis*, ed. and trans. A. Circourt (3 vols.; Paris, 1876)
Bedford Corr.	*Correspondence of John, Fourth Duke of Bedford*, ed. Lord John Russell (3 vols.; London, 1842–6)
Bernstorff Corr.	*Correspondance ministérielle du comte J. H. E. von Bernstorff 1751–1770*, ed. P. Vedel (2 vols.; Copenhagen, 1882)
Bernstorffsche Papiere	*Bernstorffsche Papiere*, ed. Aage Friis (3 vols.; Copenhagen, 1904–13)
Black, *Natural and Necessary Enemies*	Jeremy Black, *Natural and Necessary Enemies: Anglo-French Relations in the Eighteenth Century* (London, 1986)
Buckinghamshire Papers	Papers of John, 2nd Earl Buckinghamshire, Norfolk County Record Office, Norwich
Burke Corr.	*The Correspondence of Edmund Burke*, ed. Thomas W. Copeland (9 vols.; Cambridge, 1958–70)
CP	Archives des Relations Extérieures (Paris), Correspondance Politique
Cal. HO Papers	*Calendar of Home Office Papers of the Reign of George III*, ed. J. Redington and R. A. Roberts (4 vols.; London, 1878–99)
Cathcart Papers	Papers of the 9th Baron Cathcart

Cavendish Debates	*Sir Henry Cavendish's Debates of the House of Commons, during the Thirteenth Parliament of Great Britain*, ed. J. Wright (2 vols.; London, 1841–3)
Chatham Corr.	*Correspondence of William Pitt, Earl of Chatham*, ed. W. S. Taylor and J. H. Pringle (4 vols.; London, 1838–40)
Conn, *Gibraltar*	Stetson Conn, *Gibraltar in British Diplomacy in the Eighteenth Century* (New Haven, Conn., 1942)
Corney, *Tahiti*	*The Quest and Occupation of Tahiti by Emissaries of Spain during the Years 1772–1776*, ed. B. G. Corney (3 vols.; London, 1913–15)
Corr. Geo. III	*The Correspondence of King George III from 1760 to December 1783*, ed. Sir John Fortescue (6 vols.; London, 1927–8)
Dépêches van Thulemeyer	*Dépêches van Thulemeyer 1763–1788*, ed. H. T. Colenbrander (Werken uitgegeven door het Historische Genootschap, 3rd series, vol. 30; Amsterdam, 1930)
Die Politischen Testamente ed. Volz	*Die Politischen Testamente Friedrichs des Grossen*, ed. G. B. Volz (Berlin, 1920)
Documents of the American Revolution	*Documents of the American Revolution 1770–1783 (Colonial Office Series)* ed. K. G. Davies (21 vols.; Shannon, 1972–81)
Doniol, *Participation*	Henri Doniol, *Histoire de la participation de la France à l'établissement des États-Unis d'Amérique* (5 vols.; Paris, 1886–92)
Dull, *French Navy*	J. R. Dull, *The French Navy and American Independence: A Study of Arms and Diplomacy 1774–87* (Princeton, NJ, 1975)
E	Archivo General de Simancas (Simancas), series Estado
Egerton	British Library (London), Egerton MS
FO	Public Record Office (London), Foreign Office series
Fitzmaurice, *Life of Shelburne*	Lord Fitzmaurice, *Life of William, Earl of Shelburne* (2nd rev. edn., 2 vols.; London, 1912)
Franklin Papers	*The Papers of Benjamin Franklin*, ed. L. W. Labaree, W. B. Willcox, *et al.* (27 vols. to date; New Haven, Conn. 1959–)
Grafton Autobiography	*The Autobiography and Political Correspondence of Augustus Henry, Third Duke of Grafton*, ed. Sir William R. Anson (London, 1898)

Grafton Papers	The Papers of the Third Duke of Grafton, Suffolk Record Office, Bury St Edmunds
Grenville Papers	*The Grenville Papers*, ed. W. J. Smith (4 vols.; London, 1852–3)
HHStA	Haus-, Hof- und Staatsarchiv (Vienna)
HMC	*Historical Manuscripts Commission*, Reports
Horn, *British Diplomatic Service*	D. B. Horn, *The British Diplomatic Service 1689–1789* (Oxford, 1961)
Journal de l'abbé de Véri	*Journal de l'abbé de Véri*, ed. Baron Jehan de Witte (2 vols.; Paris, 1928–30)
Keith Memoirs	*Memoirs and Correspondence of Sir Robert Murray Keith*, ed. Mrs Gillespie Smyth (2 vols.; London, 1849)
KP	Kanslipresidenten
Lalaguna Lasala, 'England, Spain and the Family Compact'	J. A. Lalaguna Lasala, 'England, Spain and the Family Compact, 1763–1783' (Ph.D. thesis, University of London, 1968)
MD	Archives des Relations Extérieures (Paris), Mémoires et Documents
Mackesy, *War for America*	P. Mackesy, *The War or America 1775–1783* (London, 1964)
Madariaga, *Armed Neutrality*	Isabel de Madariaga, *Britain, Russia and the Armed Neutrality of 1780* (London, 1962)
Madariaga, *Russia*	Isabel de Madariaga, *Russia in the Age of Catherine the Great* (London, 1981)
Malmesbury Diaries	*Diaries and Correspondence of James Harris, First Earl of Malmesbury*, ed. Earl of Malmesbury (4 vols.; London, 1844)
Martens, *Recueil des traités*	F. von Martens, *Recueil des traités et conventions conclus par la Russie avec les puissances étrangères* (15 vols.; St Petersburg, 1874–1909)
Mémoires de Reverdil	*Struensée et la Cour de Copenhague 1760–1772: Mémoires de Reverdil*, ed. Alexandre Roger (Paris, 1858)
Œuvres	*Œuvres de Frédéric le Grand*, ed J. D. E. Preuss (30 vols.; Berlin, 1846–56)
O'Gorman, *Rise of Party*	Frank O'Gorman, *The Rise of Party in England: The Rockingham Whigs 1760–82* (London, 1975)
Parl. Hist.	*The Parliamentary History of England from the Earliest Period to the Year 1803* (36 vols.; London, 1806–20)
Pol. Corr.	*Politische Correspondenz Friedrichs des Grossen*, ed. J. G. Droysen *et al.* (46 vols.; Berlin etc., 1879–1939)
PRO	Public Record Office (London)

Proceedings and Debates	*Proceedings and Debates of the British Parliaments Respecting North America 1754–1783*, ed. R. C. Simmons and P. D. G. Thomas (6 vols. to date; New York, 1982–)
Recueil	*Recueil des instructions données aux ambassadeurs et ministres de France, depuis les traités de Westphalie jusqu'à la Révolution française* (30 vols. to date; Paris, 1884–)
Roberts, *British Diplomacy*	Michael Roberts, *British Diplomacy and Swedish Politics 1758–1773* (London, 1980)
Roberts Transcripts	Copies of documents made by Professor Michael Roberts in the Riksarkivet (Stockholm) and generously communicated by him
Rockingham Memoirs	*Memoirs of the Marquis of Rockingham and his Contemporaries*, ed. Earl of Albemarle (2 vols.; London, 1852)
St. Paul of Ewart	*Colonel St. Paul of Ewart, Soldier and Diplomat*, ed. George Grey Butler (2 vols.; London, 1911)
Sandwich Papers	*The Sandwich Papers*, ed. G. R. Barnes and J. H. Owen (4 vols.; London, 1932–8)
Sbornik	*Sbornik imperatorskogo russkogo istorischeskogo obshchestva* (148 vols.; St Petersburg, 1867–1916)
SP	Public Record Office (London), State Papers (Foreign) series
Spencer, *Sandwich Corr.*	*The Fourth Earl of Sandwich: Diplomatic Correspondence 1763–1765*, ed. Frank Spencer (Manchester, 1961)
Stevens, *Facsimiles*	Benjamin F. Stevens, *Facsimiles of Manuscripts in European Archives Relating to America 1773–1783* (25 vols.; London, 1889–98)
Stormont Papers	Papers of David Murray, Viscount Stormont and Second Earl of Mansfield, Scone Palace, Perthshire
Stowe	British Library (London), Stowe MS
Thynne Papers	Papers of the Third Viscount Weymouth, Longleat House, Wiltshire
Walpole Corr.	*Horace Walpole's Correspondence*, ed. W. S. Lewis (48 vols.; New Haven, Conn., 1937–83)
Walpole, *Last Journals*	*The Last Journals of Horace Walpole during the Reign of King George III, from 1771–1783* ed. A. F. Steuart (2 vols.; London, 1910)
Walpole, *Memoirs*	*Horace Walpole: Memoirs of the Reign of King George III*, ed. G. F. R. Barker (4 vols.; London, 1894)

A Note on Dates

Unless otherwise indicated, all dates in this study are given in the New Style. During the second half of the eighteenth century, the Russian calendar was still eleven days behind that in use throughout the rest of Europe, and any such dates are indicated by OS.

The Study of British Foreign Policy in the Age of the American Revolution

UNTIL recently, the study of Britain's foreign policy in the age of the American Revolution suffered from neglect and from Sir Lewis Namier. None of the scholars who established the subject of eighteenth-century British diplomacy—Sir Richard Lodge, J. F. Chance, Basil Williams, D. B. Horn—carried out detailed research on the two decades after 1763.[1] Indeed, Lodge proclaimed that these years were 'largely a blank' in Britain's foreign relations.[2] Sir Adolphus Ward, when he wrote the relevant sections of the *Cambridge History of British Foreign Policy*, also appeared to doubt whether London at this point actually conducted diplomacy.[3] Devoting only a few paragraphs to relations with Europe, he concentrated instead on colonial matters and on Britain's problems in North America.

The Namier-inspired revival of interest in George III's reign did not extend to its diplomacy. Curiously, the Duke of Newcastle's lifelong concern with continental diplomacy was not echoed by Sir Lewis, whose one inadequate excursion into eighteenth-century foreign policy was the essay on the Peace of Paris in *England in the Age of the American Revolution*.[4] His disciples were equally unconcerned with foreign affairs. It is possible to read John Brooke's study of *The Chatham Administration 1766–1768*[5] without realizing that Pitt's first political objective on taking office was to conclude alliances with Prussia and Russia, and that the fiasco which followed did nothing to improve his ministry's stability or its prospects of survival. The Namierite preoccupation with political intrigue led to the neglect of larger questions of policy, foreign as well as domestic. When, a quarter of a century ago, Sir Herbert Butterfield reviewed British diplomacy after 1763, the only substantial work available to

---

[1] Although Horn did publish a short study of *British Public Opinion and the First Partition of Poland* (Edinburgh, 1945).

[2] *Great Britain and Prussia in the Eighteenth Century* (Oxford, 1923), 139.

[3] (Cambridge, 1922), i. 127–31.

[4] (London, 1963 edn.), 283–403 *passim*.

[5] (London, 1956).

him was Frank Spencer's edition of the Sandwich correspondence, which was the sole study of foreign policy sponsored by Namier.[6]

Some justification for this neglect can be found in the attitude of contemporaries. For much of the eighteenth century, questions of foreign policy and military and naval strategy had dominated domestic politics, but this was no longer the case after the Seven Years War. In the 1760s and early 1770s successive governments were preoccupied with internal and colonial problems. They were confronted by Wilkes and by the emergence of political radicalism, by the problems of the East India Company and of Canada, and by unrest and ultimately rebellion in Britain's North American colonies. These, and their own political survival, periodically relegated foreign policy to a subsidiary position. The old Duke of Newcastle complained in 1767 of 'the total neglect of foreign affairs'; the elder Pitt had done the same thing two years earlier.[7] Such strictures were exaggerated. Diplomacy became a lower priority for British governments after 1763, but it did not cease to exist. And in the later 1770s, with the outbreak of the American rebellion and then a world war with the Bourbon powers, foreign policy once again became important and even pre-eminent. There is thus little justification for the almost complete neglect, until the 1960s, of Britain's diplomacy during the age of the American Revolution.

During the last two decades this situation has been transformed.[8] In the same way that the study of eighteenth-century politics has been emancipated from Namier's grip,[9] British diplomacy has been rescued from near oblivion. A series of scholarly and important studies has opened up the 1760s and 1770s. By a curious paradox, we are now far better informed about foreign policy after the Seven Years War than about almost any other period in the eighteenth century.[10] Frank Spencer, in a challenging introduction to the Earl of Sandwich's diplomatic correspondence, provided the first overall survey of the early years of peace. M. S. Anderson and Isabel de Madariaga have illuminated Anglo-Russian relations. P. F. Doran

[6] 'British Foreign Policy 1762–65', *Cambridge Historical Journal*, 6 (1963), 131–40, reviewing *The Fourth Earl of Sandwich: Diplomatic Correspondence 1763–1765*, ed. F. Spencer (Manchester, 1961).

[7] *A Narrative of Changes in the Ministry*, ed. M. Bateson (London, 1898), 113–14; *Memoirs of the Marquis of Rockingham and his Contemporaries*, ed. Earl of Albemarle (2 vols., London, 1852), i. 193.

[8] A comprehensive survey is provided by J. Black, 'British Foreign Policy in the Eighteenth Century: A Survey'. *Journal of British Studies*, 26 (1987), 26–53.

[9] Cf. H. T. Dickinson, 'Party, Principle and Public Opinion in Eighteenth Century Politics', *History*, 61 (1976), 231–7.

[10] The works of the authors mentioned in the remainder of this paragraph are listed in the Bibliography.

and K. W. Schweizer have cleared up the vexed question of Anglo-Prussian diplomacy during the Seven Years War and Bute's alleged 'desertion' of Frederick the Great. Nicholas Tracy has explored the naval dimension of foreign policy and its crucial role in relations with France. Geoffrey Rice has studied Anglo-Bourbon relations and the career of Lord Rochford, while Michael Metcalf has charted British policy in Sweden in the early years of peace. But this renaissance has been primarily the work of Michael Roberts, to whom we owe both our overall picture of Britain's diplomacy and our detailed knowledge of one of its most important dimensions: the search for a Russian alliance.

British foreign policy after 1763 is no longer *terra incognita*, as it was even two decades ago.[11] Yet this recent scholarship has its limitations. Most studies have been restricted to relations with one continental state, and this has made it difficult to formulate a clear picture of overall diplomatic strategy. One by-product is that Russia's importance within the broad framework of British policy may have been exaggerated. The chronological development of Britain's diplomacy has also been lost. The successes and failures of the 1760s and 1770s do not emerge clearly from existing studies, which have tended to generalize from an examination of relations with one particular state or group of states. Above all existing research has not been evenly distributed: it has concentrated almost exclusively on the years up to the great Anglo-Bourbon confrontation in 1770–1 over the Falkland Islands. The few studies of British diplomacy during the 1770s are often unsatisfactory.[12]

It is unfortunate for the overall reputation of Britain's diplomacy during the age of the American Revolution that the early years when its shortcomings were all too apparent have been studied in some detail, while the decade when it fared better has, until now, been comparatively neglected. Many of the familiar strictures are in reality comments on the undoubted deficiencies of British foreign policy during the 1760s.[13] Then its wounds were largely self-inflicted, through incompetence, conflicting political priorities, and, at times, simple bad luck. By contrast Britain's diplomacy during the 1770s was rather more realistic, her ministers provided more secure direction, and their successes were more apparent. The foreign policy problems of Lord North's Ministry owed less to the failings of Britain's own statesmen than to circumstances outside her control.

[11] M. Roberts, *Splendid Isolation 1763–1780* (Reading, 1970), 3.
[12] The only work which can be completely relied on for the period after 1773 is I. de Madariaga's magisterial *Britain, Russia and the Armed Neutrality of 1780* (London, 1962).
[13] This is true, for example, of the most familiar survey, M. Roberts's *Splendid Isolation*.

British diplomacy was to be undermined principally by a fundamental shift in the pattern of European alliances and by the outbreak of rebellion in the North American colonies.

This preoccupation with the first decade of peace is particularly surprising since after 1775 foreign policy became far more important. The American rebellion, and the resulting struggle with the Bourbons, made it a matter of permanent and vital concern to ministers. To a surprising extent, however, Britain's diplomacy during the American War has been ignored, and where it has been studied it has all too often been viewed through a false and distorting perspective. A sizeable, though not altogether satisfactory, literature exists on the peace negotiations of 1782–3, and Professor de Madariaga has written a remarkable and definitive study of the Armed Neutrality and of Anglo-Russian relations. Yet large areas of British foreign policy after 1775 have been studied superficially or neglected altogether, above all relations with France, Spain, and the Dutch Republic. Even Piers Mackesy's magnificent study of Britain's American War deals with diplomacy tangentially.[14]

Existing studies of British foreign policy after 1775 have tended to distort it. They have treated it incidentally as part of the general subject of the diplomacy of the American Revolution and viewed it in an American, rather than the more correct Anglo-French perspective. To a remarkable extent, writing about the international dimension of the American Revolution continues to be dominated by the prejudices and assumptions of nineteenth-century American Patriot historians. This is evident in the works of the dean of American diplomatic history, S. F. Bemis, and more recently the writings of historians such as R. B. Morris.[15] Their view is firmly patriotic and, at times, strongly nationalistic, assuming the inevitability of American independence and British defeat. In the writings of Bemis there is also an implied and even explicit contrast between the political morality of the new American Republic and the corrupt Machiavellian diplomacy of the old European states.

The deficiencies of such a perspective can easily be recognized and corrected. Less easy to eradicate has been the accompanying preference for an American, rather than a European, framework. Belief in the absolute primacy of the American struggle has proved

---

[14] *The War for America 1775–1783* (London, 1964).

[15] The assumptions behind historical writing on this subject have been explored by A. de Conde in his somewhat pessimistic surveys, 'Historians, the War of American Independence, and the Persistence of the Exceptionalist Ideal', *International History Review*, 5 (1983), 399–430, and 'The French Alliance in Historical Speculation', in R. Hoffman and P. J. Albert, eds., *Diplomacy and Revolution: The Franco-American Alliance of 1778* (Charlottesville, Va., 1981).

remarkably tenacious and has led to an exaggeration of the conflict as a factor both in European diplomacy and in British policy. But the traditional picture is now coming under increasing and effective attack. The studies of Richard Van Alstyne, Jonathan R. Dull, and James Hutson in particular have done much to substitute the correct European perspective for the familiar American one.[16] Until now British diplomacy during the American War has not received sufficiently detailed examination. This is rectified in the second half of this book, which is intended to reinforce these revisionist studies.[17] The perspective of these chapters, like that of the whole book, is firmly European. Their principal conclusion is that the cabinet was always more concerned with Britain's relations with France, and to a lesser extent, Spain—and less preoccupied with the war across the Atlantic—than has generally been recognized.

The two decades between 1763 and 1783 possess an essential unity. Britain's problems in foreign policy during the American War resulted in part from developments during the dozen years after the Peace of Paris. The struggle against the rebel colonists and then against the Bourbons as well was fundamentally affected by the earlier course of British diplomacy. At the same time, it is clear that 1775 was a significant date. During the years of peace after 1763 diplomacy had been a matter of intermittent concern. The periodic initiatives in the search for a continental alliance, together with occasional if sometimes acute crises with the Bourbons and in 1773 with Denmark, had ensured that Britain's foreign policy from time to time spluttered into life. It was not a permanent source of concern to ministers as it was to be after 1775. During the American War foreign affairs were in the forefront of British politics as they had not been since 1763.

In a second, and quite distinct way, the mid-1770s were a watershed. For a decade after the Seven Years War Britain had remained an element in the political calculations of the major continental states. Her reputation might be tarnished and her influence was certainly declining, but it survived until the early 1770s. By the time of the American War this was no longer true. One important theme of this study is the way in which Britain was inexorably squeezed out of European politics. She was the victim of her own political failures and, more fundamentally, of a major realignment of the continental states. By the later 1770s this transformation was complete and Britain's diplomatic influence in Europe was very slight. This was to be a factor of considerable

[16] These are listed in the Bibliography.   [17] Below, chs. 9–12.

importance during the American War, and it provides one major justification for an extended study of the period between 1763 and 1783.

This study is distinctive in one particular respect: it views Britain as an integral part of the continental states-system and examines her foreign policy in a European and international perspective, and not merely a purely British one.[18] Her failure to secure an ally and her resulting isolation are explained not only in terms of the deficiencies of British policy but also of a fundamental change in European diplomacy. Hitherto Britain's negotiations with continental powers have been studied from a narrowly English perspective.[19] Historians, like British statesmen at the time, have seen the question of alliances in an exclusively English light and have not always recognized that continental states had priorities of their own and that these did not necessarily coincide with Britain's interests. Yet the progress and eventual failure of the Anglo-Russian alliance negotiations reflected Catherine II's changing objectives and her diminishing interest in an alliance as well as Britain's refusal to pay a subsidy or to accept the 'Turkish clause'. Russia's changed attitude by the early 1770s paralleled that of other states. In 1763 Britain, after her decisive victory in the Seven Years War, appeared the leading European power. Her unique wealth and strength were widely recognized and made her an attractive ally. This admiration was soon to be undermined, and by the early 1770s it had been destroyed. Immediately after the Peace of Paris, however, continental observers expected Britain to play a prominent European role and they were surprised when this did not happen. One theme of this study is the decline of Britain's importance in European diplomacy and of her standing in the eyes of the continental states: developments which together undermined her own foreign policy. In 1763 Britain appeared to be more a part of the European states-system than at any time since the early 1720s. No doubt this position was in part illusory, the result of an unusual degree of British involvement in continental diplomacy and warfare during the preceding two decades, but it was to be an important factor for some years after the Peace of Paris.

[18]   This is exactly the approach advocated for a slightly later period by P. W. Schroeder, 'Old Wine in Old Bottles: Recent Contributions to British Foreign Policy and European International Politics, 1789–1848', *Journal of British Studies*, 26 (1987), 1–25: see esp. p. 21.

[19]   The one partial exception to this was Frank Spencer, in his ed. of *Sandwich Correspondence*, but he concentrated on 1763–4 and did not follow up his initial insight. Michael Roberts, the leading historian of British foreign policy at this period, is certainly aware of the vital importance of shifts in the patterns of continental alliances, but these are not crucial for his various studies.

A second emphasis in this present study which may be found surprising is the attention given to naval matters. The navy's importance in Anglo-Bourbon relations was revealed in a significant series of studies by Nicholas Tracy and, from a French perspective, by Jonathan R. Dull.[20] Dr Tracy has demonstrated that after 1763 ministers were determined to uphold Britain's supremacy at sea, the basis of her victories during the Seven Years War, and that this influenced and at times even dictated their policy towards France. His arguments, however, are not entirely convincing: he makes insufficient use of French material for comparative purposes. Naval strength was essentially relative. French and even Spanish weakness at sea was at least as important a source of Britain's supremacy as the strength of her own fleet. Consequently the present study devotes considerable attention to the condition and state of readiness of the navies of all three states. The course of Anglo-Bourbon relations for at least a decade after 1763 was determined principally by the failure of French and Spanish efforts to rebuild their shattered fleets. There is a more serious flaw in Dr Tracy's work: at times he appears to see only the naval dimension of foreign policy, and the fleet from being an instrument of policy becomes the determinant of that policy. His viewpoint can seem that of the Admiralty or the Navy Board rather than the Secretary of State's office.[21] The present study accepts the central significance of sea power for British foreign policy and, in particular, emphasizes the importance of detailed calculations of relative naval strength. But it insists on the primacy of purely political calculations.[22] Brandishing the fleet was always the means rather than the end of Britain's diplomacy.

One final problem concerns the actual scope and focus of a study of British foreign policy. In recent years a significant series of works by Jeremy Black has emphasized the domestic dimensions of foreign policy and has pointed to the importance of factors such as the press and parliament and to the role of the king in the making of British diplomacy.[23] Perspectives such as these are certainly valid for the reigns of George I and George II, and they achieve the important purpose of restoring an awareness of foreign policy to the study of domestic developments. But such an approach cannot be applied to

[20] Their major publications are listed in the Bibliography.

[21] This is partly a matter of the sources exploited: Dr Tracy relies very heavily on Admiralty material.

[22] See below, Ch. 5, for some detailed criticisms of Dr Tracy's work on the British response to the French annexation of Corsica.

[23] See, in particular, *British Foreign Policy in the Age of Walpole* (Edinburgh, 1985), *Natural and Necessary Enemies: Anglo-French Relations in the Eighteenth Century* (London, 1986), and his numerous articles.

the two decades after 1763, when the situation was very different from that which had earlier prevailed. Above all, George III's accession in 1760 signalled a dramatic reduction in Hanover's importance in British politics and in Britain's diplomacy.[24] The implications were considerable. Under the first two Hanoverians royal efforts to throw Britain's weight behind the Electorate had inevitably kept foreign affairs at the centre of political debate, but this was no longer so after 1760. The disappearance of the Hanoverian factor was part of the eclipse of foreign policy until the later 1770s.

Throughout the age of the American Revolution—as perhaps throughout the eighteenth century—'foreign policy' could mean very different things to different people. 'Foreign affairs'—that is to say the importance of foreign policy as a factor in domestic politics—were only of intermittent importance after 1763 and they were also viewed in the narrow perspective of relations with the Bourbon powers. Most members of the political and commercial classes were only interested in foreign policy when relations with France or Spain appeared critical. There were moments when this narrow viewpoint was shared by the ministers who controlled British diplomacy and certainly relations with the Bourbons were always central to the cabinet's deliberations. But the two secretaries of state were usually obliged to take a broader view. Though they were not infrequently distracted by other duties, they necessarily gave more consistent attention to European affairs than most of their colleagues.

This present study emphasizes the international rather than the internal dimension of British diplomacy. Domestic factors were certainly important, but the principal emphasis is on Britain's relations with the major continental states. It is thus a study of foreign policy rather than of foreign affairs, and it examines internal developments only where they directly influenced Britain's relations with the European powers: as they did, most strikingly, in 1768 when the French annexed Corsica.[25] In one further respect this study may be found to be rather traditional, and that is in the emphasis on personalities. Though such attention to individuals in the study of the past is currently unfashionable, personalities intruded at every point in the formulation and execution of foreign policy. In the second half of the eighteenth century, Britain's administration remained pre-modern. In the language of Max Weber, government had not yet been 'routinized'. If a secretary of state was too busy, or too lazy, or even too drunk, to reply to the dispatches sent to him, then diplomats

---

[24] See below, Ch. 3, for this fundamental change.   [25] Below, Ch. 5.

abroad could remain in limbo for weeks or months on end. In a similar way the shortcomings of Britain's diplomats were transferred to her foreign policy. The successes and failures of British diplomacy after 1763 were, to a significant extent, related to the strengths and weaknesses of the men who controlled and executed it.

2

The Making of British Foreign Policy

IN the eighteenth century, foreign diplomats were frequently at a loss to fathom who controlled Britain's diplomacy. Most were used to continental-style absolutisms where policy was determined by the sovereign, usually helped by one all-powerful minister. No such clear-cut pattern was evident in London. In strict constitutional theory foreign policy remained the crown's exclusive prerogative, but by the 1760s the practice was very different. The complex ways in which British diplomacy was formulated and executed puzzled and sometimes exasperated European observers. This was both a comment on Britain's distinctive constitution and a response to the complicated manner in which her foreign relations were conducted.[1]

Formal responsibility for day-to-day control lay with the Northern and Southern Secretaries, who divided foreign policy between them on a geographical basis.[2] The Secretary of State for the Southern Department was still recognized to be the senior minister and handled relations with France, Spain, Portugal, the Italian states, Switzerland, and the Ottoman Empire.[3] His seniority reflected the pre-eminent position of the two leading Bourbon powers, France and Spain, within the overall framework of British policy. The Northern Secretary dealt with the remaining continental countries: the Dutch Republic, Prussia, Austria, the smaller German states, Denmark, Sweden, Poland, and Russia. Assisted only by two under-secretaries and a handful of clerks and decipherers, the two secretaries were responsible for conducting a regular correspondence with British diplomats abroad.[4] This establishment was decidedly small: in the

[1] There are valuable introductions to the machinery by D. B. Horn, *Great Britain and Europe in the Eighteenth Century* (Oxford, 1967), 6–21, and by P. Langford, *The Eighteenth Century 1688–1815* (London, 1976), 3–15. Though mainly concerned with a later period, there are some important insights in C. R. Middleton, *The Administration of British Foreign Policy 1782–1846* (Durham, NC, 1977).

[2] The standard work is M. A. Thomson, *The Secretaries of State, 1681–1782* (Oxford, 1932).

[3] This argument differs from the established view (e.g., Horn, *Great Britain and Europe*, 13); during the 1760s and 1770s, however, the Southern Secretary was senior in prestige and political importance. For a similar conclusion, see M. M. Escott, 'Britain's Relations with France and Spain, 1763–1771' (unpublished Ph.D. thesis; University of Wales, 1988), 14.

[4] Strictly speaking, there were three secretaries after 1768 when the American Secretaryship was established, but only two dealt with foreign affairs. Leslie Scott, 'Under-Secretaries of State, 1755–1775' (unpublished MA thesis, University of Manchester, 1950) provides basic biographical information on the under-secretaries, some of whom were extremely influential.

mid-1780s the French foreign office had over seventy permanent officials when its British counterpart probably still numbered less than twenty.[5] The responsibilities of the two secretaries were also far wider than the conduct of British diplomacy: they were the principal executors of all government policy and, as such, responsible for implementing cabinet decisions and maintaining the routine correspondence in almost every area of domestic and colonial affairs. Only the armed forces lay partially outside their orbit.

This dual responsibility for diplomacy and for a wide area of internal and colonial policy was not, in itself, unique to Britain. In the later eighteenth century, purely functional departments of state were still emerging and many continental ministers retained formal or informal responsibility for domestic policy. France's leading minister throughout the 1760s, the Duc de Choiseul, nominally administered one-quarter of the French provinces as well as conducting Louis XV's official diplomacy,[6] while the Austrian Chancellor Kaunitz was actively involved in Habsburg internal policy. But the British system of Northern and Southern Secretaries was unique in two important respects. The scale of the other responsibilities on the two senior secretaries was far greater than that shouldered by Kaunitz or even by the notably hard-working Choiseul. Secondly, Britain's ministers frequently had the extra and unique burden imposed by her parliamentary system: that of introducing or defending government policy in either the House of Lords or the House of Commons when parliament was in session.[7]

Inevitably, Britain's diplomacy could often be pushed into the background or even squeezed out altogether by the competing problems faced by the government and its secretaries of state. The importance of this during the age of the American Revolution was considerable. After 1763 foreign affairs competed for ministerial attention with a new and ever-increasing range of problems, and this militated against the emergence of any coherent policy, whether for America or for Europe. Instead problems increasingly were dealt with on an *ad hoc* basis. The sustained attention to continental issues necessary if a successful diplomacy were to be conducted was to

[5] A. Cobban, *Ambassadors and Secret Agents: The Diplomacy of the First Earl of Malmesbury at The Hague* (London, 1954), 17. In the 1760s, the Southern Secretary had a staff of around 13: Escott, 'Britain's Relations with France and Spain', 17.

[6] Amédeé Outrey, *L'Administration française des affaires étrangères: Histoire et principes* (Paris, 1954), 20.

[7] Foreign diplomats often complained it was difficult to persuade the two secretaries to attend to foreign affairs when parliament was meeting: e.g. CP (Angleterre) 503, fo. 283; cf. Nolcken to KP, 28 Apr. 1767, Roberts Transcripts. The ministry's need to report on foreign policy when the session began towards the end of the year may have made negotiations easier in the autumn: Black, *Natural and Necessary Enemies*, 111.

prove very difficult during the 1760s and 1770s. Domestic radicalism, proto-industrial disorder, Ireland, India, Canada, above all the North American colonies: each of these issues at times dwarfed foreign affairs. During the Chatham Administration the Southern Department was simply unable to cope with the mountains of colonial business, and this was one reason for the creation of an American Secretaryship in 1768. The frequent changes in British colonial policy generated so much paper that, as the Duke of Grafton remarked in 1767, neither Solomon nor a horse could cope with it.[8] Even after the creation of a separate American department, diplomacy was frequently neglected in order to deal with Canadian or Indian or domestic affairs. The official diplomatic correspondence contains many half-apologies for dispatches ignored or belatedly answered by beleaguered ministers. Equally important, the secretaries were frequently obliged to neglect their regular meetings with the diplomatic corps in London. Their periodic absences were a source of irritation and complaint to foreign ambassadors and strengthened the notion that Britain was becoming indifferent to continental affairs. The familiar emphasis on Britain's 'neglect' of Europe immediately after the Peace of Paris is, at one level, a comment on the unusual way her foreign policy was controlled. The competing demands on a secretary's time were first apparent during the winter of 1763–4 when the Northern Secretary Sandwich's pursuit of alliances with Russia and Austria was deflected by his involvement in the Wilkes affair; this was to be even more evident at the time of the French annexation of Corsica in 1768 when the government was all but paralysed by the rioting in London.

The British system was unique in its geographical division of responsibility. In every other major European state one individual controlled foreign policy. This was not the case in Britain until the establishment of the Foreign Office in 1782. The division between the Northern and Southern Secretaries amazed foreign diplomats, to whom the resulting drawbacks were most clearly evident. But at various times during the 1760s and 1770s British statesmen were also forced to recognize the disadvantages. These deficiencies were sometimes concealed by one secretary assuming a leading role. This dominance could even extend to that minister handling issues that properly lay within the other province. Sandwich was to dominate foreign policy in 1763–4, during the first year of the Grenville Ministry, while in the final years of Lord North's government

---

[8] P. D. G. Thomas, *The Townshend Duties Crisis: The Second Phase of the American Revolution 1767–1773* (Oxford, 1987), 47; M. M. Spector, *The American Department of the British Government, 1768–1782* (New York, 1940), 18–19.

Stormont was *de facto* Foreign Secretary, exercising overall control of Britain's diplomacy. Suffolk was to enjoy a similar position of pre-eminence after Rochford's resignation late in 1775, though his supremacy was periodically interrupted by his own ill-health.

The difficulties which could arise when one secretary did not take control were all too obvious. Foremost among these was the danger that their views might diverge and even be diametrically opposed. A particularly striking example came in 1768 over Corsica. Then Shelburne as Southern Secretary was prepared to fight France to prevent Choiseul annexing the island, while his brother Secretary, Weymouth, was determined on peace. A similar conflict was apparent in the early years of the American rebellion. Weymouth, by now Southern Secretary, appeared to be pursuing an aggressive policy towards the Bourbon powers when his colleague Suffolk wanted to preserve peace so as to reconquer the colonies. The most glaring example of a split came in 1772–3. The then Northern Secretary, Suffolk, was following an orthodox, anti-French strategy but subsequently discovered that the Southern Secretary, Rochford, was negotiating secretly for an alliance with France![9]

Such instances of two contradictory policies being pursued simultaneously were important but relatively infrequent. They highlighted a much more common problem: that of ensuring that the two ministers spoke with one voice, or at least did not contradict each other too blatantly. Periodically, foreign diplomats in London would be startled to receive different and even opposite views on the same issue from the two secretaries, and the resulting confusion did nothing to improve Britain's standing abroad.[10] Occasional and sometimes spectacular disagreements over policy did occur and they could be crucial: as over Corsica. Indeed there is only one example of completely satisfactory co-operation between two active and con-scientious secretaries, and even that was transient. In the early 1770s, immediately after the great crisis over the Falklands, Rochford and Suffolk for a time worked harmoniously together, until this partnership was destroyed by the secret Anglo-French negotiations.

Such tensions and contradictions made clear the difficulties which ministers could encounter in synchronizing the various strands in Britain's diplomacy. British ministers in foreign courts could find themselves left in ignorance of initiatives being pursued not by their own superior but by the other secretary, though these would be vital for the state to which they were accredited or even for their own

[9] This was first established by M. Roberts: 'Great Britain and the Swedish Revolution, 1772–3' in his *Essays in Swedish History* (London, 1967), 286–347.
[10] e.g. CP (Angleterre) 515, fo. 360.

negotiations. Just as important, Britain's diplomats often complained that they were not informed of the general objectives of policy, even where these involved their own court. The contrast with continental states was striking and certainly not to Britain's advantage. Too much should not be made of Kaunitz's 'political algebra', of his mathematical and symmetrical view of the workings of the European states-system and of the place of each individual country within it. Yet Austrian foreign policy—like that of Russia, or Prussia, or Spain—did not suffer from divided control and, as a result, had clearer objectives than Britain's diplomacy. In the two decades after 1763 British ministers frequently appeared to be pursuing one policy towards France and another towards Russia, rather than conducting a coherent strategy which embraced the whole continent.

The problems from having two secretaries were evident to successive British governments, particularly during the 1770s, and this contributed to the establishment in 1782 of the Foreign Secretaryship.[11] It was the most important administrative legacy of this period and seemed a clear improvement on the old pattern. It finally gave Britain what all major continental states had long possessed: a single person responsible for foreign policy. But the undoubted benefits were only to become apparent in the years of peace after 1783. The first Foreign Secretary was Charles James Fox, whose rivalry with the Home Secretary, Shelburne, over the peace settlement in 1782 certainly equalled and may even have eclipsed any earlier clash between two secretaries of state. Fox's successor Grantham played little part in the actual peace negotiations, though they should have been largely in his hands.

Shelburne's monopoly of peace-making during his short-lived ministry illustrated another perennial problem, the intervention of other ministers in the day-to-day running of diplomacy. Once again the contrast with the major continental states was striking. Kaunitz or Panin would usually discuss foreign affairs with their sovereign and no one else; but a British secretary of state had to take into account the views not merely of the king but of his cabinet colleagues. The Northern and Southern Secretaries were formally responsible only for the execution of policy. Though they obviously played a prominent part in formulating a diplomatic strategy, this could also reflect and even be determined by the wishes of others. They also had to consider the two additional factors unique to Britain's distinctive eighteenth-century constitution: parliament, and what may be styled 'public opinion'. There were thus five factors

---

[11] The precise circumstances surrounding the creation of the Foreign Office remain elusive, though some light is thrown by Middleton, *Administration of British Foreign Policy*, ch. 1.

which could influence foreign policy in varying degrees: the king's wishes; the discussions and decisions of cabinet; intervention by individual ministers; the attitude of the House of Commons and, to a lesser extent, of the House of Lords; and the views of the political nation at large.

Foremost among these was the role of the king. George III was probably the most consistent influence on British diplomacy throughout the age of the American Revolution.[12] This reflects both the frequent changes of secretary of state and the King's enduring importance. The monarchy's political role between the 1760s and the 1780s is a familiar battleground for historians, though emphasis has traditionally been concentrated on George III's constitutional conduct rather than on his importance for the workings of the executive. It is clear that, whatever its political implications, the institutional and personal role of the monarchy was still considerable, particularly where foreign policy was concerned. The king, at least in constitutional theory, concluded treaties and signed alliances, made peace and declared war. The growth of parliament's role in the decades after 1688 had extended to securing a say in foreign policy, but in the 1760s and 1770s it was universally recognized that Britain's diplomacy remained the prerogative of the crown. This was tacitly acknowledged in the contemporary doctrine, which Granville enunciated formally in 1761, that a secretary of state could 'take a foreign measure' with the approval of the king alone.[13]

George III was always actively involved in the conduct of foreign policy. He made his views known, and these preferences were usually respected by the ministers of the day. He saw all important dispatches as they arrived and was shown the drafts of replies before they were sent off.[14] This permanent scrutiny occasionally enabled

[12] The principal evidence for the King's involvement in the making of policy is to be found in *Corr. Geo. III*, i–vi *passim*, and in such collections of his letters to secretaries of state as have survived: there is a particularly extensive series of these in Stormont Papers, Boxes 14 and 16, and some smaller collections, such as his letters to Conway in 1765–6, in Egerton 982, fos. 1–38. From a rather different perspective, I. R. Christie has recently emphasized the King's involvement in major policy decisions, especially over diplomatic strategy: 'George III and the Historians—Thirty Years On', *History*, 71 (1986), 218. P. D. G. Thomas, however, has shown that the King had limited influence on American policy in 1763–75: 'George III and the American Revolution', *History* 70 (1985), 16–31. For an interpretation of the King's role which accords with that advanced here, see T. C. W. Blanning, ' "That Horrid Electorate" or "Ma Patrie Germanique"? George III, Hanover and the *Fürstenbund* of 1785', *Historical Journal*, 20 (1977), 311–44.
[13] Richard Middleton, *The Bells of Victory: The Pitt–Newcastle Ministry and the Conduct of the Seven Years' War 1757–1762* (Cambridge, 1985), 197. Granville was Lord President of the Council.
[14] See, e.g., the paper drawn up by Charles Jenkinson in the final stages of the Seven Years War on 'The Business of a Secretary of State' and printed in *The Jenkinson Papers 1760–1766*,

the King to intervene decisively, as he did most dramatically in 1770 when he was the first to resist Weymouth's attempts to involve Britain in war over the Falkland Islands. There are also very few instances of the cabinet overcoming George III's declared views. Two instances of ministers imposing their policy on the crown can be given. In 1781 George III had initially opposed the offer of Minorca to Russia, but was brought round by the cabinet's arguments. In 1766 Chatham's ill-fated approach to Prussia went ahead despite the King's renowned animosity towards Frederick the Great. Yet this initiative did not prevent George III from pursuing an active anti-Prussian policy in the Dutch Republic where Britain's ambassador Sir Joseph Yorke, acting on the King's private instructions, unsuccessfully tried to prevent the Stadtholder marrying a Prussian princess. With these two exceptions, however, official diplomacy usually accorded with royal wishes.

George III's views were distinct and firmly held. He was one of the most acute observers of British foreign policy and of the new problems it faced.[15] Two overlapping papers drawn up by the King in 1772–3 provide a judicious analysis of the difficulties created for Britain by the novel dominance of the three eastern powers.[16] This made him sympathetic to a *rapprochement* with France and he was certainly involved in the secret Anglo-French negotiations of 1772–3. At other times his views were more orthodox. He believed that Britain's diplomacy should be based on opposition to France and that this required alliances with continental states. In particular he favoured the revival of the traditional links with Austria and even with the Dutch Republic; he seems in general to have been less committed to a Russian alliance than many of his ministers, though he was certainly not opposed to one on the right terms.[17] His Francophobia, which had been significantly modified in the early 1770s by events in eastern Europe, was reawakened after 1775 by France's assistance to the American rebels and by her eventual

---

ed. N. S. Jucker (London, 1949), esp. pp. 4–5; cf. CP (Angleterre) 479, fo. 26. Suffolk warned one incautious British diplomat to 'recollect always that your letters are for the Royal eye': Countess of Minto, ed., *A Memoir of the Rt. Hon. Hugh Elliot* (Edinburgh, 1868), 118.

[15]   For Hans Stanley's testimony, see *Chatham Corr.* iii. 64–5.

[16]   See below, Ch. 7, for these.

[17]   'My political Creed', George III declared at the beginning of the 1770s, 'is formed on the system of King William, England in conjunction with the House of Austria and the [Dutch] Republic seems the most secure barrier against the Family Compact': *Corr. Geo. III*, ii. 204. The King's interest in a Dutch alliance, at a time when this was discounted by most British statesmen, perhaps came from Electoral considerations: ibid. ii. 110. For his views on the Russian alliance, see *Chatham Corr.* iii. 66. George III was resolutely opposed to granting the 'Turkish clause'.

intervention in the war. His opposition to the final peace settlement was only overcome with difficulty by Shelburne.

The King's involvement was strengthened by two circumstances. As Elector of Hanover he was naturally informed about and interested in diplomacy within the *Reich*. The 'German Chancery' in London received a steady stream of information, often more expert and informed than that provided by British diplomats in Germany. Similarly, the protean Hanoverian diplomatic service had always allowed private initiatives by the British monarch, though there were far fewer of these after 1760 and the network of electoral agents may have been smaller than before.[18] More important under George III was the information, expertise, and wider perspective which the King received from the connection with Hanover. Royal influence was also strengthened by the rapid turnover of secretaries of state. Particularly during the 1760s the succession of short-lived ministries, and the youth and inexperience of many of them, ensured that the King soon had more experience of government and greater knowledge and interest in foreign affairs than many of the men responsible for Britain's diplomacy. There were moments when the secretaries of state actually appeared to be looking towards the King for guidance and they were usually anxious not to adopt a line of policy at variance with royal wishes.[19]

George III's influence was strengthened by his personality. Whatever view may be taken of the political role and conduct of the King, it is clear that he took full advantage of the prevailing constitutional conventions to play an active part in government. George III was certainly not the man to underplay his hand, and he always intervened over foreign policy when he believed this was essential. During the 1770s he was even prepared to work against official diplomacy. The existence of an inner group of ministers in 1772–3, which explored the possibilities of Anglo-French reconciliation and even an alliance, was first revealed by Michael Roberts.[20] What has not been appreciated is that this shadowy alignment reappeared after 1775 and was important during the American War. At certain points there was a full-blown *secret du roi*, and this inner group was prepared to pursue a diplomatic strategy at variance with official policy and even diametrically opposed to it. The King was always centrally involved and was probably the

[18] See below, Ch. 3, for the virtual disappearance of Hanoverian influences on British foreign policy after George III's accession.

[19] Cf. P. D. G. Thomas, 'George III and the American Revolution', 31, and, more generally, pp. 16–31 *passim*, for the way successive ministries unsuccessfully looked to the King for a lead in American policy.   [20] In the article cited above, n. 9.

principal influence; the other important members of the *secret* were North and Mansfield.

George III's role in foreign policy underlines the importance of personalities. This was equally true of the periodic interventions by other ministers. Formally the two senior secretaries only executed policy and were responsible for the day-to-day conduct of diplomacy. In practice they enjoyed significant freedom of action and in untroubled times effectively ran British foreign policy, sometimes with the King's help. But a very different pattern emerged at periods of crisis, especially if one or both of the Bourbon powers were involved, as they usually were. In such circumstances it was normal for the rest of the ministry to become involved and for foreign affairs to be brought before the cabinet.[21] Questions of foreign policy could also come to cabinet when alliance negotiations were at an advanced stage, particularly if they involved concessions by Britain or a subsidy. During the 1760s the cabinet was consulted periodically over Russia's terms for an alliance and always reaffirmed established policy: that of refusing concessions. But the cabinet was principally anxious about the state of Anglo-Bourbon relations and formally considered these when the situation appeared critical.

There is an important but difficult distinction between the full cabinet and smaller, less formal discussions. The full cabinet was normally consulted over the question of peace and war. It frequently considered foreign policy, or rather the state of Britain's relations with France and at times Spain, after the outbreak of the American rebellion in 1775. More routine matters were handled by a smaller *ad hoc* group of ministers. During the Grenville Ministry immediately after 1763 the habit became established of discussing foreign policy after Tuesday evening cabinet dinners.[22] Once the plates and glasses—or perhaps merely the plates—had been cleared away, those present would discuss matters of foreign affairs demanding attention and might even approve particular dispatches.[23] This custom seems to have continued throughout the period, but the evidence is very scanty. In any case, a clear distinction between such informal gatherings and formal meetings of the entire cabinet is difficult to

[21] The cabinet's role is elusive, partly because of the small number of surviving minutes which deal with foreign policy, at least before the American War. For the cabinet at this period, see I. R. Christie, 'The Cabinet in the reign of George III, to 1790' in his *Myth and Reality in Late Eighteenth-Century British Politics* (London, 1970), 55–108.

[22] For the origins of this practice, see *Grenville Papers*, ii. 489.

[23] During George Grenville's administration, four ministers were normally involved: Grenville himself, the two Secretaries of State, and the Duke of Bedford who, though Lord President of the Council, had considerable experience of foreign affairs and had negotiated the Peace of Paris: see below, Ch. 4.

draw. The most that can be said is that the cabinet scrutinized foreign policy and occasionally intervened directly in its formulation. There was considerable variation between different ministries and its role varied according to political circumstances and to the personalities involved. During its discussions secretaries of state were expected to take a leading part, to introduce the business and apparently to propose distinct lines of policy which other ministers might accept or, occasionally, modify.[24] These discussions were seldom profound and a secretary of state was very seldom overruled by his colleagues.

The forum of cabinet was not the only way other ministers might influence foreign policy. The First Lord of the Admiralty was necessarily involved in any crisis with the Bourbons, for after 1763 the navy was all-important in relations with France and Spain. The law officers of the Crown were periodically consulted, for example when a proposed treaty involved a change in Britain's domestic legislation, and more consistently after 1778, when the Anglo-French War once again posed the notoriously tricky problem of neutral rights. Much more frequent and important were interventions by the leader of the ministry. His pre-eminence among the king's ministers always gave him potential and decisive influence in foreign policy. In 1764–5, for example, George Grenville was responsible for the hard-line stance adopted towards the Bourbon powers. More surprising are Lord North's periodic and vital interventions, which are only fully apparent from foreign sources and have not been appreciated by historians of his premiership. Over the Falkland Islands in 1770–1, briefly during the Anglo-French negotiations in 1772–3, and more consistently during the American War, Lord North was engaged in a wide variety of unofficial and semi-official diplomatic initiatives. Even in early 1782, in the final weeks of his ministry, he was secretly involved in peace overtures to France and to the Dutch Republic. North's precise responsibility for these initiatives is more problematical. Since he was part of the *secret du roi* he may simply have been responding to royal pressure or even implementing the King's wishes.

One reason why North, like Grenville before him, intervened was an appreciation of parliament's importance for foreign policy. Both men led their ministry in the Commons and therefore understood the

[24] Few secretaries of state were as conscientious as the persevering Stormont, who treated the cabinet to long reviews of the state of British diplomacy (for examples of the kind of lengthy papers which he read out, see Stormont Papers, Box 64). These had a predictably soporific impact on his colleagues: see e.g. *HMC Knox*, 271–2, for the difficulty some ministers had in staying awake at the cabinet meeting in Dec. 1780 which decided on war with the Dutch Republic.

necessity of pursuing an acceptable diplomatic strategy and defending it against opposition attack. But parliament exerted a more direct influence.[25] Any treaty concluded during the parliamentary session, or which involved either a change in the law of Great Britain or a financial charge, had to be 'laid' before both Houses.[26] This obligation was less important after 1763 than during the previous half-century, principally because Britain concluded far fewer treaties. During the entire age of the American Revolution, Britain only signed four significant treaties: the peace settlements concluded in 1763 and 1783, an Anglo-Russian commercial agreement signed in 1766, and an Anglo-Swedish treaty of friendship two years later. There was also a series of subsidy treaties for mercenaries with German states during the American War. No political alliances were concluded at this time, and this inevitably reduced the importance of communicating treaties to both Houses.

Parliament's importance arose from two principal factors: its own constitutional role and the political situation during the 1760s and 1770s. After 1688 it had come to assume a general supervisory role over Britain's diplomacy. Foreign policy was an important part of government business and, as such, ministers expected to defend it in parliament, especially their conduct of Anglo-Bourbon relations. This was of particular importance during the 1760s, and even to some extent during the 1770s, when the parliamentary position of many ministries was fragile.[27] Only Lord North, during the first half of his ministry, possessed a secure Commons majority. Their vulnerability ensured that ministers tried to pursue a foreign policy that was defensible and that did not too obviously challenge the prejudices of parliament and the political nation. Their difficulties were increased by the development of the practice of 'calling' for papers.[28] Opposition motions requesting that all the correspondence relating to a particular negotiation or diplomatic crisis should be laid before the Commons became an established parliamentary tactic and, in the eyes of the government of the day, a threat to the secrecy of diplomatic

[25] More work is needed on this topic. The fundamental article, though for an earlier period, is G. C. Gibbs, 'Parliament and Foreign Policy in the Age of Stanhope and Walpole', *English Historical Review*, 77 (1962), 18–37; its conclusions are confirmed by J. Black, *British Foreign Policy in the Age of Walpole* (Edinburgh, 1985), 75–89.

[26] G. C. Gibbs, 'Laying Treaties Before Parliament in the Eighteenth Century', in R. Hatton and M. S. Anderson, eds., *Studies in Diplomatic History: Essays in Memory of David Bayne Horn* (London, 1970), 116–37.

[27] Cf. P. Langford, *The First Rockingham Administration, 1765–1766* (Oxford, 1973), 85, for the ministry's awareness of the need to secure parliamentary approval for its 'patriot' foreign policy.

[28] For this, see P. D. G. Thomas, *The House of Commons in the Eighteenth Century* (Oxford, 1971), 24–5 and 38–9.

negotiations. Such motions almost always failed; but ministers sometimes found it expedient to anticipate such demands by laying a carefully selected series of papers of dispatches before both Houses.

Parliament's interest in foreign affairs was sporadic, at least in the period up to 1775: thereafter the American War gave it permanent importance and it secured more attention. Corsica and the great Anglo-Bourbon confrontation over the Falklands produced lively debates, but the interest which these episodes created was not sustained. The standard of parliamentary discussion about foreign affairs was very low: a reading of the debates indicates that there was less knowledge of Europe and less concern with the state of British diplomacy than during the reigns of the first two Hanoverians. This reflects both the diminished importance of foreign policy after 1763 and the disappearance of Hanover as a factor in British politics and diplomacy for two decades after George III's accession.[29] The opposition was always prepared to attack ministers for their handling of foreign policy, but its onslaughts were opportunistic rather than consistent: 'roasting a minister', in North's evocative description.[30] Yet parliament was always a latent and, occasionally, an active influence on diplomacy: the threat that some dispatches might have to be made available to the House of Commons encouraged secretaries of state to issue verbal instructions to ambassadors before they left England or, more usually, to correspond privately with diplomats abroad, as Shelburne did with Rochford in 1766 and Stormont with Yorke in 1779–80.[31] Fear of parliamentary scrutiny also can be seen in the drafting of official dispatches. In 1766 the ambassador-designate to Russia, Hans Stanley, after an extensive reading of the Russian correspondence, complained that ministers too often drew up their dispatches not to instruct British diplomats but to serve as a defence of their own actions if and when these were attacked in parliament.[32]

Parliament's influence after the Seven Years War was fundamentally negative. It inhibited and, on occasions, actually prevented ministers from adopting novel policies, particularly towards the Bourbons. In 1772–3 Rochford abandoned attempts at Anglo-French reconciliation, principally because of his fear of a hostile

[29] Cf. the comments of R. Pares, *King George III and the Politicians* (Oxford, 1967 edn.), 4–5.

[30] *The Writings and Speeches of Edmund Burke*, ed. P. Langford, ii: *Party, Parliament and the American crisis 1766–1774* (Oxford, 1981), 20–1; Egerton 215, fo. 171.

[31] The resulting problems for the researcher are obvious: significant gaps in the State Papers (Foreign) series, which cannot always be filled, even from private correspondence.

[32] Stanley to Buckinghamshire, 18 Aug. 1766, Add. MSS 22359, fo. 52. In the event, Stanley quickly withdrew from the embassy: see below, Ch. 5.

reaction from the House of Commons. Even relatively minor concessions to France, for example over the fortifications at Dunkirk or the Newfoundland Fisheries, were made all but impossible by the hostility of the Commons towards the national enemy.[33] This was even more true of the major Anglo-Bourbon dispute of the first decade of peace over the Falkland Islands.[34] Parliament's influence on diplomacy should not be exaggerated: ministers sometimes exploited and exaggerated their own difficulties with the Commons as a tactic against credulous foreign ambassadors. Yet its importance was real. It confirmed ministers in their pursuit of an essentially traditional and orthodox diplomatic strategy and was a major obstacle to innovation. In addition the tone of parliamentary debates and the divisions revealed, together with their wide circulation on the continent, contributed to Britain's decline in the eyes of Europe.[35]

This was equally true of the final influence on British foreign policy, that of public opinion. It is dangerous and perhaps inaccurate to talk of 'public opinion' in the eighteenth century, even in the 1760s and 1770s. Yet there was clearly significant interest in foreign affairs outside Whitehall and Westminster, especially among the commercial classes in the City and in the provinces. Newspapers and periodicals printed considerable amounts of foreign news, not least because continental events affected business confidence.[36] While the interest is undoubted, it is much more difficult to prove that the public at large exerted any real influence.[37] Popular concern was once again restricted to relations with France and, to a lesser extent, Spain, and its influence was essentially negative. There are occasional instances of vested interests being consulted: as the Russian Company was, for example, over the renewal of the commercial

[33] See, e.g., *Proceedings and Debates*, ii. 43, 44, 46, for pressure on the ministry in Apr. 1765 from merchants (mainly from the West Country) over the Newfoundland Fisheries.

[34] In the winter of 1770–1, Parliament was to be an important influence on the dispute with Spain, and for several years thereafter it was a reason—or perhaps merely an excuse—for Britain's refusal to abandon Port Egmont: see below, Ch. 6.

[35] See Stormont's interesting testimony to this: *Parl. Hist.* xxi, cols. 641–2.

[36] J. Brewer, 'Commercialization and Politics' in N. McKendrick *et al.*, *The Birth of a Consumer Society* (London, 1983 edn.), 215–16. For a sound brief survey of foreign affairs in the press, see Escott, 'Britain's Relations with France and Spain', 53–65.

[37] Black, 'British Foreign Policy in the Eighteenth Century: A Survey', *Journal of British Studies*, 26 (1987), 46–7, has some wise words. His conclusion is that 'public opinion [is] of questionable importance in the formulation of foreign policy' (p. 47); cf. Black, *Natural and Necessary Enemies*, 114. The limited influence of newspapers and 'public opinion' in the making of foreign policy in the period 1763–71 has now been demonstrated by Dr. Escott's careful researches: 'Britain's Relations with France and Spain', 517 and *passim*. From the perspective of American policy, Peter Thomas concluded that official attitudes were similarly uninfluenced by newspapers and self-interested journalism: *The Townshend Duties Crisis*, 16–17.

treaty in the mid-1760s. But such examples of direct influence on foreign policy are very rare. The importance of 'public opinion', like that of parliament, lay in confirming ministers in their hard-line attitude towards the Bourbons and in preventing concessions: official policy now coincided with parliamentary and popular hostility towards France in particular.[38] The influence of such factors should not be exaggerated. The Gallophobia of the newspapers and of most MPs was undoubted and could not be disregarded by any ministry. Yet the combined forces of the press and of James Boswell could not avert the humiliating acceptance of France's annexation of Corsica. The freedom of the British press periodically caused problems and was a minor source of irritation in relations with certain states. Ministers were forced from time to time to apologize to Catherine II of Russia when suggestions appeared in newspapers or periodicals that she had murdered her husband Peter III or the young Ivan VI.

Parliament's oversight of foreign policy partly explains why negotiations were transacted through Britain's ambassadors and ministers abroad.[39] Occasionally, important discussions were conducted or even initiated in London, either at a moment of particularly acute crisis or, more usually, to evade parliament's scrutiny. But secretaries of state believed, not unreasonably, that Britain's point of view would be more vigorously and more accurately represented to a foreign government by one of her own diplomats. This had the additional advantage of ensuring that British policy was encapsulated in formal written instructions which could be laid before parliament should the ministry's conduct come under attack. This 'English plan' of conducting diplomacy meant that Britain's diplomatic service was crucial for success.[40]

To speak of a 'diplomatic service', even by this relatively late period, may give a misleading impression of the degree of professionalization and coherent organization possessed by the assembled ranks of British ambassadors, envoys, and ministers plenipotentiary. Diplomatic vacancies that arose were usually filled on a casual *ad hoc* basis, and political influence was at least as important as previous experience or relevant expertise. Many posts were difficult to fill, and this may have been exacerbated by the acute ministerial instability of the 1760s: this appeared to increase the opportunities for an ambitious man to secure preferment at home rather than

[38] Black, *Natural and Necessary Enemies*, 72, 207.
[39] For the reasons, see D. B. Horn, *The British Diplomatic Service 1689–1789* (Oxford, 1961), 5–8; cf. K. L. Ellis, 'British Communications and Diplomacy in the Eighteenth Century', *Bulletin of the Institute of Historical Research*, 31 (1958), 159–67.
[40] The standard work is Horn, *British Diplomatic Service*.

accepting a spell abroad as a necessary stage in a political career. Particular problems always arose in filling embassies to remote parts of Europe: few candidates came forward for posts in the inhospitable towns and backward courts of eastern Europe and especially for those at Warsaw, St Petersburg, and Constantinople. This was partly a matter of finance: the expenses of such postings were considerable and they were only belatedly and sometimes partially repaid. No such problems arose in filling the Paris embassy, which was the apex of the British diplomatic service and in standing the equivalent of a cabinet post.[41] The problem here was appointing a suitable ambassador for the key position within Britain's diplomacy. Traditionally the embassy had been occupied by noblemen with little or no diplomatic experience but whose rank and prestige gave lustre to the British crown. This was an important reminder that diplomacy was still about honour and reputation. Several such gilded amateurs were appointed to Paris during the age of the American Revolution. Neither the Earl of Hertford (ambassador 1763–5) nor the Duke of Richmond (1765–6) had any previous diplomatic experience, while that of the Earl Harcourt (1768–72) was limited to a month's embassy to Mecklenburg-Strelitz to conclude a marriage treaty on George III's behalf.[42] They conformed to the established pattern, but, unusually enough, professional diplomats held this key post for over half of the fifteen years (1763–78) when Britain and France were at peace. Lord Rochford was ambassador from 1766–8, and Lord Stormont from 1772 to 1778.

Stormont and Rochford were also extremely unusual in that they had made a career in diplomacy and had risen through the ranks of ministers and envoys to the pre-eminent position at Paris. The most important embassies, and particularly those in western and southern Europe, still tended to be dominated by amateur diplomats, often noblemen who took only one embassy. There was also a distinctive professional element. Men such as Sir Joseph Yorke, the long-serving ambassador at The Hague, and Sir John Goodricke, at Stockholm for a decade after the Seven Years War, were largely content to serve their country abroad. Their motives were mixed: a combination of duty, the hope of subsequent preferment at home, or simply because other doors were closed to them. This applied with particular force to the pronounced Scottish component in the diplomatic service.[43]

[41] Cf. J. S. Bromley, 'The Second Hundred Years' War (1689–1815)', in D. Johnson, *et al.*, eds., *Britain and France: Ten Centuries* (Folkestone, 1980), 171.   [42] *BDR* 61.

[43] The standard discussion is D. B. Horn, *Scottish Diplomatists 1689–1789* (London, 1944), partly reprinted in Horn, *British Diplomatic Service*, 115–22; see also K. W. Schweizer, 'Scotsmen and the British Diplomatic Service, 1714–1789', *Scottish Tradition*, 7–8 (1977–8), 115–36.

The influence of Scotsmen on British diplomacy was at its peak in the generation after 1763, particularly in the less fashionable European courts. Men such as Sir Andrew Mitchell and subsequently Hugh Elliot at Berlin, Stormont and Sir Robert Murray Keith at Vienna, together with several lesser figures, formed the backbone of the diplomatic service and provided such professionalism as it possessed. The reasons for this Scottish diaspora are well known. The mid-eighteenth century was the heyday of anti-Scottish prejudice in England, which was powerfully boosted by the career of Lord Bute in the early 1760s.[44] Diplomacy, the armed forces, and service in the colonies were the principal careers open to ambitious Scotsmen.[45] Most filled—and were content to fill—middle-rank posts in Britain's diplomatic service, but only one Scottish diplomat used it as a stepping-stone to high political office in London: Stormont not merely rose to be ambassador to France but finally became Secretary of State (1779–82). His rise was quite exceptional, and it was principally a testimony to the support of his uncle, the distinguished lawyer Lord Mansfield.

The recruitment of British diplomats could be, and often was, remarkably haphazard. The Duke of Leeds was startled to be offered the French embassy in 1783 while he was listening to a debate in the House of Lords, though his surprise did not prevent his accepting with alacrity.[46] For the most part ministries filled diplomatic posts as best they could, and there was very little sign of a career structure within the ranks of ministers and ambassadors. The same was true of the continental states with the sole exception of France, where there was a rudimentary hierarchy and professional habits of mind. The British diplomatic service was at least as good as that of any other major state except France, and it was probably better than most. The only area where the selection of diplomats seriously hindered official policy was over the Russian alliance.

Russia was central to British strategy throughout this period, yet the quality of diplomats sent to Catherine II's court hardly matched the important negotiations they had to transact. Horace Walpole spoke with feeling in 1770 of 'such simpletons as we have sent to

[44] H. M. Atherton, *Political Prints in the Age of Hogarth* (Oxford, 1974), 209–16; cf. J. Brewer, 'The Misfortunes of Lord Bute: A Case-Study of Eighteenth-Century Political Argument and Public Opinion', *Historical Journal*, 16 (1973), 19–22.

[45] Horace Walpole's remarks were characteristically pungent: 'In fact, [colonial] governments and embassies were showered on the Scotch [sic] as less ostensible and invidious, while offers and private men of that nation crowded, or were crowded into, the army and the navy': *Last Journals*, i. 268.

[46] *The Political Memoranda of Francis, Fifth Duke of Leeds*, ed. O. Browning (London, 1884), 77–8. In the event, he did not go to Paris.

Petersburgh' and, while the persevering yet limited Cathcart was the main target for his strictures, his comments have a more general applicability.[47] The Russian Court was unpopular with aspiring diplomats and the embassy was notoriously difficult to fill. As a result the ambassadors who made the long and difficult journey to St Petersburg were seldom of the first rank. Buckinghamshire, Cathcart, and Gunning were all inadequate diplomats and, in the latter case, this was compounded by behaviour that was frequently erratic and impulsive. Macartney and Harris were certainly more able, but they were youthful, inexperienced, and at times naïve. Britain's failure to conclude the desired alliance certainly owed something to the limitations of her diplomats; but it owed far more to the premisses of British policy and to the attitude of Catherine II and her ministers. Elsewhere British objectives were not seriously affected by the shortcomings of the diplomats employed. Even at Paris the noble amateurs who held the embassy from 1763 to 1766 and 1768 to 1772 exerted little direct influence on Anglo-French diplomacy.[48]

British diplomats received minimal training before taking up their posts. Some had served briefly as attachés to a British mission; but most did no more than look through their predecessors' dispatches in the Secretary of State's office before setting out.[49] Though few were as conscientious as the indefatigable Cathcart,[50] most made some attempts to familiarize themselves with the broad contours of past and present British policy towards their accredited state. This, together with the copies of their predecessors' dispatches which they received on arrival at the foreign court, inevitably reinforced the static thinking which bedevilled British diplomacy throughout the age of the American Revolution. The preparations and instructions of British diplomats were deficient in one further respect. The formal instructions which they received at the outset of their mission were more narrowly conceived, and also far briefer, than those given to French or Austrian or even Russian ambassadors. They often merely repeated the instructions given to previous British diplomats and were drawn up in a rather routine and sometimes casual way. Britain's ambassadors seldom—if ever—received the wide-ranging

---

[47] *Walpole Corr.* xxiii. 208; cf. below, Chs. 6–7, *passim*, for some account of Cathcart in Russia.

[48] Though Hertford subsequently contributed to a significant misunderstanding in Anglo-French relations: see below, Ch. 5.

[49] For the assumption that they would do so, see *BDI* v: *Sweden 1727–1789*, ed. J. F. Chance (London, 1928), 229. In Feb. 1783, the Duke of Leeds prepared for his abortive embassy to Paris by a daily stint at the Foreign Office reading the 'former correspondence, as well as those down to the present time': *Political Memoranda*, ed. Browning, 78.

[50] Cf. below, Ch. 6, for his efforts.

and extensive instructions given to their continental counterparts. Crucially they were usually not told the broader objectives of British diplomacy or the significance of their own mission within the overall framework of policy. The absence of such guidance, partly the result of the geographical division between the Southern and Northern Departments, was a frequent source of complaint to diplomats during the age of the American Revolution and did something to undermine British policy.

Britain's envoys and ambassadors exerted a limited measure of influence on official policy. The conventional verdict that they did not must be severely modified, at least for the 1760s and 1770s.[51] In a general sense the reports of envoys and ambassadors established the framework within which official policy was discussed and formulated, and to this extent they always influenced policy. After 1763 their role was on occasions far greater than has been realized. In the early years of peace Sir John Goodricke was able to create a distinct British strategy at Stockholm and to convince his superiors of Sweden's potential importance for Anglo-Russian relations and for Britain's overall policy.[52] Subsequently Rochford, while he was Secretary of State (1768–75), deferred in some matters to the greater knowledge of Stormont as ambassador first at Vienna and then at Paris. Stormont himself remained an important influence on British diplomacy after Rochford's resignation, while Sir Joseph Yorke at The Hague exerted similar influence particularly after the outbreak of the American rebellion. Britain's overall diplomatic strategy was devised by the ministry of the day and principally by the Northern and Southern Secretaries. Its contents, the tactics to be employed, the precise policy to be pursued at particular courts, were often filled in by senior diplomats abroad, many of whom had far greater experience of diplomacy and knowledge of European affairs than their political masters in London. The influence of senior diplomats in part reflected the frequent preoccupation of their superiors with domestic and colonial policy and the inexperience of many of the secretaries of state.

The principal conclusion which emerges from this survey of the formulation and execution of official policy is the central importance of personalities. A formal administrative framework existed, but to a significant extent it was at the mercy of the individuals who controlled Britain's diplomacy. It needed men to make it work, and these same men could make or wreck foreign policy. The skill or

---

[51] See, e.g., Horn, *British Diplomatic Service*, 183–4.
[52] This has been demonstrated by Michael Roberts: *British Diplomacy and Swedish Politics 1758–1773* (London, 1980), chs. 2–4; see below, Ch. 4.

incompetence of an ambassador, the foresight, experience or inexperience, and preoccupations of a secretary of state, the wishes of the king or the prime minister: variables such as these were fundamental to the success or failure of British foreign policy after 1763. This is why personalities occupy a prominent, though not pre-eminent, place in the study of diplomacy during the age of the American Revolution. The shortcomings of British diplomacy apparent immediately after 1763, and the subsequent recovery, are both to a significant extent to be explained in terms of personalities. More fundamentally, however, British foreign policy was shaped by the legacies of the Seven Years War.

3

The Legacies of the Seven Years War

IN autumn 1763 two Venetian diplomats sat down to compose their
relazione.[1] Their embassy to England had only lasted a year, but they
had witnessed the triumphant Peace of Paris which had concluded
the Seven Years War in the previous February. Their final report to
the Venetian Senate was dominated by admiration for the elder Pitt
and for the victories won under his leadership. This panegyric of
Britain's power and greatness concluded with a brief review of the
factors which had brought her fortunes to their zenith. Foremost
among them were her financial strength, commercial mastery, and
naval power, coupled with social harmony and political stability.
Together these factors, directed by Pitt's leadership, energy, and
strategic flair, had brought Britain a commanding position in Europe
and overseas. Though modern scholarship is less certain of Pitt's role,
and more aware of the vital contributions of Anson, Ligonier, and
even Newcastle, the analysis of the two Venetians was remarkably
prescient.[2] Britain in 1763 appeared to dominate Europe in the same
way that *La Serenissima* had been supreme among the states of the
Italian Peninsula and even the Mediterranean in the age of Venetian
power.

Their unrestrained admiration was widely held at the end of the
Seven Years War. Yet only twenty years later Britain was to emerge
from another conflict, the American War of 1775–83, amidst
prophecies of her final decline. The contrast between the two peace
settlements, Paris in 1763 and Versailles in 1783, is striking. With
hindsight it is clear that the Seven Years War was a solvent of Anglo-
American links and the source of subsequent clashes between the
government and its colonial subjects. In a similar way Britain's
diplomacy throughout the age of the American Revolution was
influenced directly and indirectly by the legacies of the Seven Years
War.

It had been a prolonged and intensive conflict with two distinct,
though not totally separate, dimensions. It was one of a series of

---

[1] It is printed in *Ambasciatori veneti in Inghilterra*, ed. L. Firpo (Turin, 1978), 155–7; ibid.,
pp. xxix–xxi places the embassy in context and provides basic biographical information on the
two diplomats, Tommaso Querini and Francesco Morosini II.
[2] All previous studies have been superseded by Richard Middleton, *The Bells of Victory:
The Pitt–Newcastle Ministry and the Conduct of the Seven Years' War 1757–1762*
(Cambridge, 1985).

Anglo-French wars which had begun in 1688 and would continue until 1815. Britain had won the latest round through a strategy which Pitt subsequently described as conquering America in Germany. France had been tied down in Europe by British subsidies to Prussia and a British-financed 'Army of Observation' operating in western Germany. The consequent division of French resources produced a decisive British victory overseas. The Peace of Paris brought Britain substantial territorial gains, principally at Louis XV's expense. France's position in India was all but destroyed; the loss of Canada and part of Louisiana, together with the subsequent cession of the rest of Louisiana to Spain, meant that she was completely excluded from the North American mainland, though she retained a foothold in the Newfoundland Fisheries. Only in the West Indies did the French avoid serious losses of territory, and even here she ceded Grenada and the Grenadines and gave up her claims to the so-called 'neutral islands'. This was, however, balanced by France's retention of Martinique and Guadeloupe, the two principal West Indian sugar islands, occupied by Britain during the fighting but handed back at the peace. In West Africa the French recovered their trading post at Goree but were forced to cede their settlement on the Senegal river. In the final stages of the conflict Bourbon Spain had concluded an alliance with France (August 1761) and had gone to war with Britain. This intervention had been short-lived and totally unsuccessful: Cuba and Manila had both been captured by British forces. In 1763 Spain had to cede Florida to Britain, receiving most of Louisiana from France as compensation. The scale of Britain's triumph, measured by her gains at the Peace of Paris, was to be the principal factor in Anglo-Bourbon relations throughout the 1760s and 1770s.

The Seven Years War on the European continent produced no such decisive territorial changes. Prussia, with some aid from Britain, had managed to resist the seemingly overwhelming coalition brought together by the Austrian Chancellor, Kaunitz. In 1756–7 an alliance of Austria, Russia, and France, supported by Sweden and soldiers from the *Reich*, had emerged. It had been assembled and directed from Vienna and had aimed to defeat Prussia and to recover the former Habsburg province of Silesia, seized by Frederick II in 1740. Prussia's survival was due in part to shortcomings in this coalition. In particular France's enthusiasm for the continental war had diminished, especially after her shattering defeat by Frederick's army at Rossbach (November 1757); she had concentrated instead on the conflict overseas, where she was suffering major losses at Britain's hands. The burden of the continental struggle had fallen increasingly on

Austria and on Russia. By 1760, however, Austria's administration and her finances were close to collapse and Vienna was dependent for military victory on the Russians, who nearly defeated Frederick II. The complete reversal of St Petersburg's policy in 1762, following the death of the Empress Elizabeth in January, finally saved Prussia. Russia's new ruler was the ardent Prussophile Peter III who withdrew from the coalition and set about aligning himself with Berlin. In the event, his deposition in July 1762 prevented this alliance being finalized but his six-month reign was crucial for the outcome of the continental war.

Russia's withdrawal prevented Frederick's defeat. Prussia's survival also owed much to her own exertions. Her army and her administration had proved superior to those of her enemies, while Frederick the Great had shown himself to be a ruler of genius. He was not merely a talented general but an inspiring war leader whose indomitable courage had sustained his state in the darkest hours of the struggle. The extent of Prussia's success became apparent when peace was concluded in 1763. Seven years of intensive and destructive warfare had apparently failed to produce a decisive result. Frederick forced Austria to accept a settlement based on the *status quo ante bellum* at Hubertusburg (February 1763), an outcome which had seemed improbable for most of the war. In sharp contrast to the Peace of Paris no territory changed hands. Prussia had survived and the 'miracle of the house of Hohenzollern', as Frederick termed it, was complete. The Seven Years War on the continent seemed a draw. It was really a victory for Prussia and a serious defeat for Austria and for France, while in the longer term Russia gained most from the fighting.

The relative position of the major states had been decisively affected and this was of fundamental importance for Britain. In several significant respects European international relations throughout the 1760s and 1770s were dominated by the legacies of the struggle against Prussia. In the first place, the European states-system had itself been transformed. In the century after the Peace of Westphalia (1648) three great powers had emerged and had together dominated Europe. During the late seventeenth and most of the first half of the eighteenth century, diplomacy had revolved around the struggle of Britain and Austria against France, while the second-rank states had attached themselves to one side or the other. The Seven Years War had converted this system of three great powers into one of five leading states. By the 1760s Prussia and Russia had decisively entered the ranks of the major powers. Prussia had risen to prominence very rapidly after Frederick II's accession in 1740 and by

the end of the Seven Years War she had become a great power,
perhaps even the leading continental state. The conflict had also
given Russia a new political importance. Though she had gained no
territory, her prestige had been significantly increased by her
victories over Prussia's formidable army. Russia had been the leading
member of the coalition during the second half of the war and she
could never again be ignored by the other continental states.

The emergence of Russia and Prussia was decisive in two distinct
ways. The five great powers together dominated Europe more
completely than ever before. In the 1760s and 1770s there was a
larger gap between the major powers and the other states, which
were often political clients lacking a fully independent foreign policy
of their own: Spain was largely dependent on France for a decade
after the Peace of Paris, as Denmark was on Russia. Secondly, the
emergence of two new powers on Europe's eastern periphery gave
this region a wholly new importance after 1763. This was apparent
in the major political issues which arose during the next generation.
Sweden, Poland, and the Ottoman Empire proved to be the focus of
most concern, and in the settlement of these problems the eastern
powers played the dominant part.

Anglo-French rivalry continued and even intensified after 1763,
but it was rapidly ceasing to be the main factor in European
diplomacy. Though British and French statesmen recognized the new
and puzzling pattern in international relations only slowly and with
difficulty, the change was fundamental and irrevocable. Its implications for British foreign policy were particularly serious. Britain's
victory in her eighteenth-century struggle with France had been
based largely on manipulating the European states-system and
exploiting the established Habsburg-Bourbon rivalry. This strategy
had depended on the threat which the powerful French state
seemingly represented to the rest of Europe. By 1763, however, it
was Britain and not France which appeared predominant. The Seven
Years War had been the first full-scale conflict since 1648 (with the
single exception of the Great Northern War of 1700–21) which had
not been primarily about France's place in Europe. Even the War of
the Austrian Succession (1740–8) had been dominated by France's
attempt to recover her former pre-eminence. The fighting on the
continent after 1756, however, had centred on Prussia's ambitions
and status, and it had revealed, for the first time, the extent of French
decline. Britain's traditional diplomatic strategy had been undermined,
though it would be the 1770s before this was fully appreciated in
London.

The Seven Years War had four principal consequences for British foreign policy, and these proved to be enduring. It poisoned Anglo-Prussian relations for a quarter of a century; it substantially reduced Hanover's importance for British diplomacy; it completed the process by which Britain's traditional European perspective came to be supplemented by an imperial and world-view, which complicated the task facing ministers; and it decisively affected Britain's attitude to continental alliances and her ability to conclude them. Individually each development significantly influenced British foreign policy; cumulatively their impact was even greater.

The most notorious legacy was the enduring damage to Anglo-Prussian diplomacy. This resulted from the troubled and frequently acrimonious partnership after 1756.[3] Relations between London and Berlin had traditionally been rather distant and their wartime co-operation had been accidental and unexpected, and proved to be transient. The political transformation which had preceded the Seven Years War (the celebrated 'Diplomatic Revolution' of 1756) had left Prussia isolated in the face of a coalition headed by Austria, France, and Russia. Simultaneously Britain, already engaged in a maritime and colonial war with France, had found herself lacking the continental ally ministers believed essential. Mutual isolation led to a brief partnership during the Seven Years War. Britain had earlier concluded a neutrality convention with Frederick II (Convention of Westminster, January 1756), which aimed to exclude an Anglo-French war from Germany. After some initial—and considerable—hesitation, ministers had used this tenuous link to forge a temporary wartime partnership with Prussia. At Pitt's instigation a firmer bond was provided by a Subsidy Convention first signed in April 1758 and renewed annually until 1761, but no formal alliance was ever concluded.

Britain's partnership with Prussia had been popular among the public at large because Frederick the Great won some notable military victories and could plausibly be portrayed as a 'Protestant Hero'.[4] Yet it rested on insecure foundations. Britain's only enemy for much of the war was France and there was never a formal British declaration of war against either Austria or Russia. To Frederick, however, Maria Theresa and the Empress Elizabeth were his

---

[3] See the definitive study by P. F. Doran, *Andrew Mitchell and Anglo-Prussian Diplomatic Relations during the Seven Years War* (New York and London, 1986), on which the following paragraphs are largely based.

[4] There is a pioneering, though not totally convincing, study by M. Schlenke, *England und das friderizianische Preussen 1740–1763* (Freiburg and Munich, 1963): see especially pp. 225–65.

principal foes. In a very real sense Britain and Prussia were fighting different enemies and their partnership reflected this. British help to Frederick was considerable. In addition to an annual subsidy of £670,000 for four years, Prussia obtained more significant assistance in the British-financed 'Army of Observation' in Westphalia, which protected Frederick's vulnerable western flank. There was also the less tangible, but no less important, psychological support which came from the knowledge that Prussia was not fighting alone.

Britain, for her part, obtained significant strategic advantages and did so at a bargain price. Her spectacular victories overseas were facilitated by the division of French resources which resulted from Louis XV's commitments to the anti-Prussian alliance. Finally, the partnership with Prussia—and this was perhaps Pitt's masterstroke—provided a means of protecting Hanover without appearing to do so. Politicians and the public in Britain were extremely sensitive and resolutely opposed to anything which smacked of British resources being expended on the King's electoral dominions. But for several years they accepted with scarcely a murmur substantial support for Frederick II which achieved precisely the same purpose. The King of Prussia became for Pitt 'a kind of Trojan Horse which could be trundled through the Commons on appropriate occasions to the plaudits of a near-unanimous house. But hidden inside were the Hanover estimates.'[5] Pitt's attitude was always fundamentally opportunistic, despite all the fine rhetoric he lavished on the Prussian king.[6]

For Britain, the partnership was a question of expediency. For Prussia it was increasingly a matter of necessity. This mutual need kept the two states together for several years, though the relationship was never harmonious. As it weakened, so also did Anglo-Prussian co-operation. Britain, victorious overseas, saw less and less need for an expensive commitment to the continental war. Public opposition was focused by Israel Mauduit's celebrated pamphlet, *Considerations on the Present German War* (1760), and this, together with the general war-weariness, found political expression after George III's accession in the efforts of the new King and his minister-favourite, Bute, to bring a speedy end to the fighting. Pitt's resignation (October 1761) opened the way to ending the commitment to Prussia; the Subsidy Convention was not renewed; and the partnership dissolved acrimoniously in 1762.

These events quickly assumed, and long retained, a considerable

---

[5]   Doran, *Andrew Mitchell*, 212–3.
[6]   See, e.g., *Parl. Hist.* xv, col. 1270.

notoriety.[7] Frederick II, aware that Prussia had been exploited by Britain during the Seven Years War, immediately proclaimed he had been 'deserted' and most German historians, for whom the writings of the greatest Prussian King were Holy Writ, endorsed this verdict. The myth of Britain's betrayal of her faithful Prussian ally was established and proved remarkably tenacious. In fact there was never a clear-cut 'breach' in relations. Instead, in the final years of the war, both states pursued their own objectives regardless of their partner's wishes, in the way that European powers had always done. Britain, buttressed by huge victories overseas, enjoyed a freedom of action which Frederick, struggling for his very survival, could never possess. After Pitt's resignation Bute presided over a change in British policy, which became particularly evident in the early months of 1762. Peace now became an infinitely higher priority in London than support for the Prussian cause, especially with the simultaneous outbreak of an Anglo-Spanish war. In a similar way, Frederick's behaviour after the accession of the pro-Prussian Peter III implicitly accepted that wartime co-operation was at an end. The Anglo-Prussian links had never been strong and the events of 1762 merely acknowledged this; yet it was unfortunate for future relations that the partnership's ending had been so acrimonious. Britain's indifference (as it seemed to Frederick) to Prussian interests was reinforced by her failure to ensure that the Anglo-French peace preliminaries of November 1762 provided for the return to Prussia of her territories in western Germany, occupied by French troops since the early stages of the war. The second half of 1762 saw a bitter 'paper war' between the two states during which the embers of past resentment were vigorously raked over. It was an unedifying, if appropriate, end to a temporary partnership.

The events of 1762 set the tone for relations over the next two decades. Frederick II's celebrated resentment is notorious: he conceived an obsessional hatred of Bute which he carried to the grave, and he also long blamed George III and the Duke of Bedford for their roles in the supposed 'desertion'. For the next ten years the

---

[7] F. Spencer, 'The Anglo-Prussian Breach of 1762: An Historical Revision', *History*, 41 (1956), 100–12, is useful but marred by a desire to transfer guilt from Bute to Frederick; W. L. Dorn, 'Frederick the Great and Lord Bute', *Journal of Modern History*, 1 (1929), 529–60, is one of the earliest attempts to defend Bute, though not wholly convincing; Doran, *Andrew Mitchell*, 295–381, is an admirable detailed treatment; see also the important articles by K. W. Schweizer: 'The Non-Renewal of the Anglo-Prussian Subsidy Treaty, 1761–62: A Historical Revision', *Canadian Journal of History*, 13 (1978), 383–96; 'Lord Bute, Newcastle, Prussia and the Hague Overtures: A Re-examination', *Albion*, 9 (1977), 72–97; and (with Carol S. Leonard), 'Britain, Prussia, Russia and the Galitzin Letter: A Reassessment', *Historical Journal*, 26 (1983), 531–56.

Prussian King pursued an unrelenting campaign against successive British ministries, concentrating on the personality and supposed influence of Bute. It was waged principally by his agents in London, whose activities further soured relations. His resentment was reinforced by sound political calculation and, above all, by a determination not to be dragged into any future Anglo-Bourbon conflict. Frederick's foreign policy after 1763 sought to avoid war and this objective would be imperilled by any future links with Britain, whose peace with France and Spain he believed temporary. Viewed in this light the events of 1762 became a convenient pretext for a policy which Frederick's political instinct convinced him was essential. Had Lord Bute not existed, it would have been necessary to invent him.

Britain's resentment proved even more enduring. Ministers had disliked Frederick's behaviour during the war, and they had been outraged by his actions in its final stages and by his subsequent propaganda campaign against Britain. George III long remained personally hostile to the Prussian King, and this reinforced British ill will. For over two decades after 1763 there was very little official interest in an alliance: only Pitt, his disciple Shelburne, Charles James Fox, and—very briefly—Suffolk envisaged new links with Prussia.

The wartime partnership had been a means of protecting Hanover. Yet the Seven Years War closed an era in Anglo-Hanoverian relations. George II's death in 1760 was a turning-point in the history of the personal union between Kingdom and Electorate.[8] It brought to an end more than four decades when Electoral interests had directly influenced and occasionally determined British policy. This influence, at its peak during the 1740s and 1750s, vanished for almost twenty years after George III's accession. Britain's official position, repeated *ad nauseam* to foreign diplomats, was always that 'George King of England' and 'Georg Kurfürst von Hannover' were two distinct beings. The age of the American Revolution was the one period between 1714 and 1815 when this political fiction appeared to have some basis in fact.

Between 1760 and 1783 Britain's diplomacy was far less affected by Electoral considerations than before the Seven Years War.[9]

---

[8] R. M. Hatton, *The Anglo-Hanoverian Connection 1714–1760* (The Creighton Trust Lecture, 1982; London, 1983), 1. Prof. Hatton's lecture provides an incisive discussion of relations. The institutional aspects are outlined by K. L. Ellis, 'The Administrative Connections between Britain and Hanover', *Journal of the Society of Archivists*, 3 (1969), 546–66. See now J. Black, 'The Crown, Hanover and the Shift in British Foreign Policy in the 1760s', in Black, ed., *Knights Errant and True Englishmen: British Foreign Policy 1660–1800* (Edinburgh, 1989), 113–34.

[9] There is a good recent study by U. Dann, *Hannover und England 1740–1760: Diplomatie und Selbsterhaltung* (Hildesheim, 1986).

George III did not at first exploit his undoubted influence over British policy to promote the interests of his Electorate. By 1785–7, over the issue of the Bavarian exchange, the King would seize the initiative from his British ministers and would seek to throw Britain's weight behind Hanoverian policy within the *Reich*.[10] There is only one similar example of the strategy of subordinating British policy to Electoral interests in the entire age of the American Revolution. This was also over Bavaria: in the spring of 1778 George III briefly and unsuccessfully attempted to align British and Hanoverian policy to resist Austrian annexation of Bavarian territory. In the later 1770s concern at Vienna's expansionist policy within the *Reich*, for which Joseph II was widely believed responsible, was alarming George III and his Electoral ministers, and this was the origin of Hanover's subsequent participation in the *Fürstenbund* ('League of Princes') in 1785. But this anxiety did not exert permanent influence on Britain's diplomacy before the end of the American War: on the contrary, during this conflict George III subordinated his Electoral fears of Austria to the wider interests of British policy, which looked towards Vienna for a pro-British mediation and even an alliance. This subordination of Hanoverian to British interests was particularly evident in 1780 when Austria tried to elect a Habsburg to the coadjutorship of Cologne.[11] It was accompanied by a strict distinction between the two spheres in which George III moved.[12] The King would not allow his British ministers to play any part in the affairs of the Electorate, and they in turn upheld this clear distinction between the interests of Hanover and those of Great Britain.[13]

The explanation for the Electorate's diminished importance is to be found principally in George III's personality and policies. He was the first Hanoverian king to have been born in England: as he proclaimed, 'Born and educated in this country, I glory in the name

[10] For this episode, see the excellent article by T. C. W. Blanning, ' "That Horrid Electorate" or "Ma Patrie Germanique"? George III, Hanover and the *Fürstenbund* of 1785', *Historical Journal*, 20 (1977), 311–44.

[11] See, in particular, George III to Stormont, 1 July 1780, Stormont Papers, Box 16.

[12] The King was able to distinguish between his British and Hanoverian roles to a remarkable extent. See e.g. his letter to Stormont of 19 Dec. 1779: 'I will certainly be very cautious that from my German Dominions no transactions with the *Emperor Joseph* shall be but full of civility but his views on the Empire are to be the *Master* not the most *Exalted Character*; consequently I should not do my duty towards the Empire if I did not carefully watch so dangerous an object; in short as King of Great Britain I wish amity with the House of Austria; but no consideration shall make me as Elector betray the trust reposed in me' (ibid., Box 16).

[13] For a particularly clear statement of this, written when Hanoverian-British relations were being complicated by the affair of the Rhineland Bishoprics, see Stormont to R. M. Keith, 23 June 1780, SP 80/222, fo. 201.

of Britain.'[14] His political education had implanted strong anti-
Hanoverian sentiments, for the new ruler had grown up in the
entourage of his father the Prince of Wales in an atmosphere of fierce
hostility to all George II's policies, particularly his active concern for
Electoral interests. Only the year before George III came to the
throne he had spoken of 'that horrid Electorate which had always
lived upon the very vitals of this poor Country'.[15] These sentiments
were clearly apparent in the first years of his reign. The King's efforts
to end the 'German War', which he saw as both costly and futile,
were a rejection of his grandfather's policies. These, he believed, had
taken Britain into the continental Seven Years War to defend the
Electorate. The role of George III and of Bute during the final stages
of that conflict immediately made clear that the new King was a very
different ruler from the first two Hanoverians.[16] His British subjects
were convinced that the 'Hanover rudder' was a thing of the past and
that they now had an English king and not a German elector on the
throne. Political and parliamentary debate during the age of the
American Revolution was remarkably free of hostility towards
Hanover and of accusations that the King was exploiting Britain in
the interests of the Electorate. This would have been inconceivable
only a few years before.[17]

It was assisted by circumstances within Germany. Politics were
quiescent there for at least a decade after 1763. France's wish to
pursue her struggle with Britain overseas was crucial, though not
immediately apparent, and this meant that there was no longer a
French threat to the Electorate, while Austria and Prussia were war-
weary and preoccupied with internal reconstruction. Until the
emergence of a more aggressive Habsburg strategy, particularly
towards Bavaria, during the later 1770s, there were few challenges
to the German *status quo* to alarm Hanover's rulers, and by then
Britain was preoccupied with the American War. Frederick II's more
restrained policy also contributed significantly to Hanover's tranquillity. During the 1740s and 1750s it had been primarily fear of the
rising power of Prussia, Hanover's neighbour both to the east and to
the south-west and the ally of her old enemy France, which had led
electoral ministers to exert influence on British policy through

[14] See J. Brooke, *King George III* (London, 1974 edn.), 156, 612, for the correct version of
this famous remark in the King's Speech to his first parliament.
[15] *Letters from George III to Lord Bute 1756–1766*, ed. R. R. Sedgwick (London, 1939),
28 (letter of 5 Aug. 1759).
[16] Walpole, *Memoirs*, i. 3–4; Add. MSS 32921, fo. 341.
[17] See most recently G. C. Gibbs, 'English Attitudes towards Hanover and the Hanoverian
Succession in the First Half of the Eighteenth Century', A. M. Birke and K. Kluxen, eds.,
England und Hannover: England and Hanover (Munich, 1986), 33–50.

George II and the Duke of Newcastle.[18] After 1763, however, the Prussian King supported the political and territorial *status quo*. Secondly the Hanoverian ministers themselves recognized the decisive change brought about by George II's death and acknowledged their own reduced influence in London,[19] and they made no real attempt to influence British policy as they periodically had done before 1760.

This did not lead George III to neglect his German territories. On the contrary he was to be a conscientious, if absentee, ruler of Hanover.[20] Though he never visited the Electorate, he married a German princess, learned to speak German, and corresponded regularly with his Electoral ministers on the internal government of Hanover, where he pursued a mildly reformist policy and even abolished labour service on the domain lands in 1775. As time passed, the King's outlook changed. In the later 1770s and early 1780s, under the pressure of defeat in America and mounting political conflict at home, George III became increasingly disillusioned with his position as King of Britain.[21] This led him to look with rather more favour on Hanover: that 'horrid Electorate' became his 'patrie Germanique', he sent his sons to study at the University of Göttingen, and at one moment of acute constitutional crisis even dreamed of abdication and of exchanging the British throne and its party strife for a happy life as the absolutist Elector of Hanover. Though the King's changing outlook was undoubtedly significant for the future, it had no impact on British foreign policy before 1783.

Despite George III's views, his British ministers continued to take some account of Hanover's position in their foreign policy. In one sense a clear-cut distinction between 'British' and 'Electoral' interests was false. The simple fact that George III also ruled German territories forced ministers to provide for the Electorate's defence: as their predecessors had usually done since 1714. Britain's search for allies during the first decade after 1763 was partly motivated by the familiar desire to protect Hanover, while in 1778 Suffolk's renewed efforts to conclude an alliance reflected his fear that France might once again make it a hostage when war broke out. Ministers differed from their predecessors before 1760, or from their successors during the 1780s and 1790s, in one significant respect. They were almost entirely free from direct royal intervention on Hanover's behalf, and

[18] W. Mediger, 'Great Britain, Hanover and the Rise of Prussia' in R. Hatton and M. S. Anderson, eds., *Studies in Diplomatic History: Essays in Memory of David Bayne Horn* (London, 1970), 199–213.
[19] Dann, *England und Hannover*, 167–8.
[20] See the important and well-documented article by S. Conrady, 'Die Wirksamkeit König Georgs III. für die hannoverschen Kurlande', *Niedersächsisches Jahrbuch für Landesgeschichte*, 39 (1967), 150–91.   [21] Blanning, ' "That Horrid Electorate" ', 338.

this makes the age of the American Revolution unique in the history of Britain's eighteenth-century foreign relations.

Britain's interest in European diplomacy after 1763 was weakened by the wider imperial horizons created by her victories during the Seven Years War. The precise importance of the newly enlarged empire remains elusive. The considerable problems involved in ruling it certainly distracted attention from foreign affairs. The Southern Secretary in particular came to be squeezed between the competing demands of Europe and empire. He was formally responsible both for relations with France and Spain, still the heart of British diplomacy, and for the administration of the colonies. Though the establishment of the American Secretaryship in 1768 nominally removed one major area of concern, the urgent problems which arose in India, Canada, and Ireland during the 1760s and 1770s continued to compete for his attention with policy towards the Bourbons.

Britain's territorial gains and the continuing vitality of her empire after 1763 came to complicate relations with France, Spain, and the Dutch Republic. Anglo-Bourbon diplomacy in particular was dominated by colonial issues to an even greater extent than before the Seven Years War. Local disputes originating in Africa or, more especially, in the American hemisphere periodically disrupted relations in Europe. Within this established framework Spain was now more prominent than France. The British and Spanish empires were the two largest colonial powers, and in North America and around the Caribbean they were often neighbours as well as rivals.

This was part of a larger transformation. During the age of the American Revolution Britain was usually to face not simply France or Spain but a united Bourbon front. Here too the Seven Years War was crucial. British statesmen had feared the potential might of the united House of Bourbon ever since the accession of a French prince to the Spanish throne in the early eighteenth century, but the Franco-Spanish connection had proved less secure, and usually less menacing, than anticipated. The co-operation embodied in the two Family Compacts of 1733 and 1743 had been interspersed with periods of distant and even acrimonious relations. Indeed, the reign of Ferdinand VI after 1746 had seen the Family Compact in abeyance. His death in 1759 was a turning-point in Spanish foreign policy. The new King, Charles III, was always implacably hostile towards Britain. Within two years he had signed a firm anti-British alliance with France, the Third Family Compact of August 1761, and for the next generation this was a fixed point of European diplomacy. Charles III had previously ruled the Bourbon Kingdom of Naples and Sicily, and always resented how he had been coerced by a British naval bombardment during the War of the Austrian Succession. This resentment had been increased by the severe defeats inflicted on Spain after she entered the Seven Years War in 1762.

Except for a few years during the 1770s, opposition to Britain was the principal and at times only motive of Spanish foreign policy thoughout the age of the American Revolution. This was both a matter of revenge for past defeats and of anxiety at further British encroachments on Spain's vulnerable empire. There was always fear and suspicion, and sometimes real tension as well, in Anglo-Spanish relations in the colonial sphere after 1763. Both states saw peace as precarious. The potential for conflict in North America in particular was considerable, though at first it was restrained by local British and Spanish officials, aware of the vulnerability of their own defences and also anxious to safeguard the fragile economic development of their territories.[22]

Spain's position was considerably weaker in 1763 than it had been at Charles III's accession. Her disastrous intervention in the Seven Years War had revealed military, naval, and financial inadequacies. Yet the peace settlement, and the cession of Louisiana from France, placed Spain's ramshackle and sprawling territories in the front line against the expanding British empire in America. It was a role which Charles III's state was unfit to discharge, a fact recognized in Madrid. Immediately after 1763 the Spanish government began the immense task of reviving the empire's economic power and, more urgently, strengthening its defences. Spain was clearly on the defensive and her foreign policy took account of this.

Though British ministers were certainly aware of Spanish weakness after 1763, they were forced to take seriously the threat posed by joint Bourbon action. Charles III's state might not be a formidable military power, but its navy was not negligible and, though in poor condition, it was being rebuilt. The obvious danger was that Spain might deflect sufficient British resources to weaken any future effort against France. Yet Spanish feebleness, and Charles III's subordinate position within the Family Compact, were apparent to the cabinet. Britain's contempt was evident in her assumption that France spoke for the Bourbon powers: ministers usually approached the French government directly in any dispute, believing that Madrid barely had an independent foreign policy.[23]

The central place of continental alliances in British foreign policy was also strengthened by the Seven Years War. This is at first sight

---

[22] J. P. Moore, 'Anglo-Spanish Rivalry on the Louisiana Frontier 1763–68' in *The Spanish in the Mississippi Valley, 1762–1804*, ed. J. F. McDermott (Urbana, Ill., 1974), 72–86.
[23] See e.g. CP (Angleterre) 462, fo. 33.

paradoxical, since the wider imperial horizons, Hanover's diminished importance, and even the poor relations with Prussia would all appear to weaken Britain's concern with Europe, while her own military involvement on the continent after 1756 had been far less than in previous Anglo-French conflicts. In the longer perspective, however, Pitt's war for empire was crucial in fixing official attitudes for the next generation about the necessity of allies. Throughout the age of the American Revolution ministers sought to conclude alliances, principally with Austria and Russia, believing that their predecessors had always done so and that Britain's interests could best be protected by such treaties. The precedents were in fact considerably more ambiguous than was realized. During the wars of 1688–1713, the fledgling British state had concluded treaties with France's principal opponents, Austria and the Dutch Republic, and had sent soldiers to fight on the battlefields of the Low Countries and Germany. This intervention had been successful in restraining the power and ambitions of Louis XIV, but the principles behind it were not usually followed in the years of peace after 1713.

The wars of William III and Marlborough gave birth to two distinctive attitudes to strategy and diplomacy, and these were to be the principal strands in Britain's eighteenth-century foreign policy. The first, which had generally prevailed during that struggle, was the Whig or interventionist doctrine. This emphasized the importance of opposition to France, pursued by means of alliances with European states and military operations on the continent during wartime. By contrast the Tory approach was hostile to such military and diplomatic intervention and instead urged a 'blue-water' strategy based on the navy and on attacks on French colonies and commerce. After 1713 the idea of a Tory foreign policy came to be associated with isolationism and with friendship with France. With some significant exceptions, this was the view which had prevailed between the 1710s and the early 1740s. During this generation France had more often been conciliated than opposed, and indeed the Anglo-French Entente of 1716–31 had provided a period of good relations and even examples of effective diplomatic co-operation. By contrast the age of Stanhope and Walpole had seen not merely a weakening of the historic ties with the Dutch Republic and Austria but considerable tension between the former partners in the Grand Alliance. After 1740, however, British foreign policy came to be dominated once again by active opposition to France pursued principally through Austrian and Dutch alliances. Whig ideas, in the doldrums for a generation, returned to prominence, particularly after Walpole's fall in 1742, and they continued to shape official policy at least until the 1780s. Their renewed importance owed something to the revival of French military expansion on the European continent after 1740 and rather more to Newcastle's distinctive ideas and enduring influence.[24] The broad lines of British foreign policy throughout the age of the American Revolution were those established by the Duke while he ran Britain's diplomacy during the 1740 and 1750s.

France's moderation and indeed pacifism had been a major source of improved relations after 1713. With the Emperor Charles VI's death in 1740 this was replaced by renewed military expansion. The Duc de Belle-Isle's motive in attacking Austria was to destroy Habsburg power once and for all, and there were moments during the 1740s when it seemed as if this might actually be achieved, particularly as France was now in alliance with the rising power of Prussia, with her youthful and ambitious King and formidable army. During the final stages of the War of the Austrian Succession the Maréchal de Saxe won a startling series of victories which all but destroyed the legendary 'Barrier' in the Southern Netherlands. France's spectacular military successes recalled the great days of her armies under Louis XIV and were a major source of Newcastle's anxieties. The Duke had been in office as Secretary of State since 1724, though always in a subordinate position, and his own ideas about foreign policy were far less consistent than he later proclaimed. From the early 1740s, however, he asserted the enduring validity of Whig ideas, and these were to guide his own foreign policy when he secured actual control after Carteret's fall late in 1744.

Newcastle ran British foreign policy between 1744 and 1756, and he remained influential until the final stages of the Seven Years War. His importance was twofold: he fixed Britain's diplomacy securely into its anti-French groove, which was to endure until 1815 and beyond,[25] and he established the doctrine that this rivalry demanded alliances with leading continental states. The Duke's ideas amalgamated established Whig thinking with his own response to developments during the 1740s. France's re-emergence as a military power and as a direct threat to Britain was exacerbated by the new importance of Prussia, a French ally capable of winning victories of her own, by the reinvigorated Bourbon alliance, and finally by the Jacobite rebellion in 1745. Newcastle was alarmed less by the Highland clans than by the opportunity which their invasion of England offered for France to deliver a decisive blow. His recurring

---

[24] See H. M. Scott, ' "The True Principles of the Revolution": The Duke of Newcastle and the Idea of the Old System' in Black, ed., *Knights Errant and True Englishmen*, 55–91, on which the following paragraphs are based.

[25] Black, *Natural and Necessary Enemies*, 56.

anxiety was that if the French ever became dominant on the continent, they would strangle Britain's trade, invade the British Isles, and even topple the Hanoverian dynasty and with it the Protestant succession and Whig ascendancy.

Newcastle's response was a reassertion of the fundamental Whig doctrine that France must be fought on the European continent. The Duke always saw the generation after 1688 not merely as the origin of Britain's greatness but as a storehouse of precedents to guide later generations. The idiom in which he thought and acted was always that of the age of William III and Marlborough. His first important action on taking control of British policy was to restore the alliance which had defeated Louis XIV: in 1745 a Quadruple Alliance was signed between Britain, the Dutch Republic, Austria, and Savoy-Sardinia. More important for the future course of British foreign policy was Newcastle's relentless advocacy of a restored Grand Alliance to contain France. By the end of the 1740s the Duke's ideas had hardened into a doctrine, in response to events during the War of Austrian Succession and to the new influences on him at this time. His thinking owed most to the similar views advanced by his Dutch friend, the leading Orangist statesman William Bentinck, by the principal Hanoverian minister G. A. von Münchhausen, and by George II. The three visits which Newcastle made to the continent between 1748 and 1752 provided ample opportunities for long discussions with Bentinck and Münchhausen and for the King to exert an unusual degree of influence over his minister. The first such trip, in the year peace was signed, also furnished the distinctive label by which this interventionist style of diplomacy was henceforth known: the Old System, a term which came into general use from summer 1748 onwards.

The Old System aimed to secure as many allies as possible to contain France on the continent and to protect vital British interests, above all the Low Countries and Hanover. It was given a special flavour by the distinctive language in which this aim was expressed and by the questionable historical precedents upon which it rested. Though Newcastle always proclaimed his aim was to restore the 'true principles of the Revolution', the Old System was in reality a means of securing the maximum number of allies against France. This was the Duke's aim between 1748 and 1756, when he sought to breathe new life into the Austrian and Dutch alliances and eventually to add one with Russia, with her abundant military manpower.

By the mid-1750s the failure of his schemes was evident. The Diplomatic Revolution of 1756 appeared to sound the death-knell of Newcastle's vision. The centrepiece of the Old System, the hinge on which it turned, was the Barrier in the Low Countries. The Franco-Austrian alliance signed in that year made this all but redundant. Austria was now France's ally, rather than her enemy, and this exposed the Dutch Republic to direct French attack. This, coupled with the Republic's political and even economic decline, removed the final element in the Old System: the Dutch were to remain neutral in the war that followed. Yet, if the Old System had apparently ceased to be practical politics, its basic ideas seemed to be validated by the Seven Years War. This was because it was essentially a means of opposing France, which was accomplished with spectacular success after 1756.

The Old System was always a search for armies as well as allies. Britain sought to find continental states to put their own soldiers into the field against France and in this way to reduce her own military commitments in Europe, enabling resources to be concentrated on the Anglo-French struggle overseas. The contemporary distinction between 'American' and 'continental' warfare was—at one level—a false antithesis.[26] Pitt's celebrated ideas resembled Newcastle's more muddy formulation of the strategic imperatives more closely than might be imagined. The Duke gave a higher priority to the war in Germany, but this was a matter of emphasis. Pitt also saw the necessity of continental operations, both to protect Hanover and to divert France. Indeed, in November 1761 Newcastle explicitly endorsed Pitt's famous remarks about conquering America in Germany.[27] The Duke went on to argue that colonial conquests would also have to be defended on the banks of the Elbe. This was not merely a plea for the continuation of the 'German war', then coming under increasing attack, but was also an assertion of the necessity of continued diplomatic involvement on the continent once peace had been concluded. Newcastle believed that this was the principal lesson of the Seven Years War, and his ideas now determined official policy.

The fundamental idea of the Old System, that of fighting France in Europe, appeared to be vindicated by the war. The costs of such continental operations after 1756 were strikingly low when compared to earlier conflicts. Precise figures are hard to find, but it seems as if the 'German war' never consumed more than 25 per cent of annual expenditure.[28] Prussia received a subsidy of £670,000 for four years,

---

[26] Middleton, *Bells of Victory*, 23. For the debate over strategy, see R. Pares, 'American Versus Continental Warfare 1739–63', repr. in his *The Historian's Business and Other Essays* (Oxford, 1961), 130–72.   [27] Add. MSS 32931, fos. 46–7; 32919, fo. 133.

[28] This is suggested by the figures in R. Browning, *The Duke of Newcastle* (New Haven, Conn. 1975), 276.

while the 'Army of Observation' in western Germany cost considerably more. Far greater sums were spent on the navy and the fighting
overseas. This reversed the pattern in earlier wars, when the principal
outlay had been on military operations on the continent. The same
reversal was apparent where manpower was concerned. British
soldiers were sent to fight in the 'Army of Observation', but far fewer
than in the wars of 1688–1713 and 1740–8: in 1761 only 18,000
British soldiers were fighting in Westphalia, and this was the highest
figure in the war.[29] Indeed, early in 1758 Newcastle advanced the
remarkable proposition that 'money has always been looked upon as
the proper and most effective contribution that England could make
to a war upon the Continent'.[30] This may have accorded with the
Duke's own experiences during the 1740s and 1750s, but it would
have startled William III and Marlborough. Nevertheless it remains
true that, in terms of British soldiers and even British gold, the
'German war' provided value for money, despite the storm it
provoked after 1760.

This was one reason why Britain's wartime partnership with
Prussia was defended and justified in terms strongly reminiscent of
the Old System.[31] Support for any major continental state against
France was coming to be seen as validating its basic ideas. Indeed,
Prussia's Protestantism and the victories won by her armies made her
a more attractive partner against Catholic France than Catholic
Austria had ever been. Though Newcastle's own preference remained
the traditional Austrian and Dutch alliances, supplemented by new
links with Russia, he accepted and defended co-operation with
Prussia after 1756. The Seven Years War followed the precedents of
earlier conflicts with France more closely than might be imagined
and—at one level—confirmed the Old System's basic principles.

This was evident in the renewed search for allies in the final stages
of the war. In the early months of 1762 George III, Bute, and
Newcastle were involved in a remarkable though unsuccessful
attempt to restore Britain's links with Vienna and The Hague.[32]
Their efforts foundered on the refusal of the Habsburgs to give up
their French alliance and of the Dutch to abandon their neutrality. In
the final winter of the war a new British ambassador, the Earl of
Buckinghamshire, was sent to St Petersburg to open negotiations for
a Russian alliance.[33] All three initiatives were couched in the

---

[29] Sir R. Savory, *His Britannic Majesty's Army in Germany during the Seven Years War*
(Oxford, 1966), 311.   [30] Quoted by Middleton, *Bells of Victory*, 60.
[31] Schlenke, *England und das friderizianische Preussen*, 218–25.
[32] Schweizer, 'Lord Bute, Newcastle, Prussia and the Hague Overtures', 72–97.
[33] His 'Instructions', dated 13 Aug. 1762, are printed in *Sbornik*, xii. 16–22.

language, and embodied the ideas, of the Old System. Each prospective partner was pursued in terms of the threat posed by France, now reunited to Spain by the Third Family Compact of 1761, to the 'liberties of Europe' and the 'balance of power'. The problem was that such rhetoric no longer corresponded to the actual political situation.

The Seven Years War had not merely confirmed Britain's belief in the importance of allies; it had simultaneously undermined the basis on which such partners had usually been secured. The threat of French hegemony, whether real or imaginary, had been the foundation on which British ministers sought to build alliances, and as late as the 1740s such talk had some basis in reality. By 1763 France's decline was more evident than her power. The Seven Years War, and in particular the humiliating defeat at Rossbach, destroyed her army's reputation for a generation, while her navy was no match for Britain's superior fleet and had been reduced to a very poor state. The conflict had finally demonstrated that even France's great resources could not sustain a military role on the European continent and simultaneously fight Britain overseas.

This was soon apparent to the able and hard-working Duc de Choiseul, who was Louis XV's leading minister from 1758 until the very end of 1770. From his early months in office, Choiseul set out to reduce substantially France's commitments to the struggle against Prussia and instead to concentrate on the more important conflict with Britain. The shift in French strategy from a primarily 'continental' approach to a 'colonial' one, apparent during the next generation, had its origins in the Seven Years War and was becoming evident by the end of that conflict. France's continental interests were now subordinated to the struggle with Britain overseas and to the desire for revenge for the defeats suffered at Pitt's hands. After 1763 French foreign policy aimed only to neutralize Europe in a future conflict with Britain, and this was to be accomplished by Vergennes during the American War.

These changed priorities were evident in Choiseul's decision to move from the foreign office in 1761 and assume personal responsibility, as minister for the navy and for the army, for the rebuilding of France's armed forces, after the shattering defeats they had suffered during the Seven Years War. This was to preoccupy him during the next few years. His cousin, the Duc de Choiseul-Praslin, became foreign minister, though Choiseul retained overall direction and personally handled the all-important relations with Spain. Only in spring 1766 did he return to the foreign office, exchanging the naval portfolio with Praslin.

France's political decline and her changed strategic priorities were two important legacies of the Seven Years War for British foreign policy. They were not immediately evident to Britain's ministers, who long believed and acted as if French power still threatened Europe, as it had done under Louis XIV. Throughout the age of the American Revolution the search for allies was conducted in terms of the French threat to the 'liberties of Europe' or the 'balance of power'. The problem was that if any state threatened hegemony by 1763 it was Britain and not France. This was occasionally glimpsed by British observers during the next two decades, but the implications were never fully appreciated, far less integrated into official policy. It was partly a matter of ingrained attitudes. Many and probably most of the men who controlled Britain's diplomacy after the Peace of Paris had grown up during the acute phase of Anglo-Bourbon rivalry between 1739 and 1763, and some had been in the diplomatic and even military front line against France and Spain.[34] Two future Secretaries of State, the Earl of Sandwich and Lord Stormont, together with the influential ambassador at The Hague, Sir Joseph Yorke, had all occupied their first diplomatic posts during the 1740s and 1750s. All three men had owed their initial appointments to Newcastle's influence, and his distinctive ideas had been part of their political education. Another post-war Secretary of State, H. S. Conway, had had a distinguished military career, while the Scottish diplomat Sir Robert Murray Keith had also fought in the Seven Years War and Yorke had taken part in the campaigns against France in the Low Countries during the 1740s. To such men belief in France's enduring hostility came naturally. They always thought in terms of Anglo-Bourbon rivalry, and assumed that this should be pursued by an anti-French alliance system and by continental military operations as well as by a strong navy.

More important than such assumptions, however, was the continuation and, indeed, intensification of Anglo-French rivalry after 1763. Choiseul aimed to prepare France for a future war of revenge and sought to rebuild the navy. This was appreciated in London, where the French threat appeared more serious because of the existence of a firm Bourbon alliance, the Third Family Compact of 1761. The Spanish King, Charles III, was hostile towards Britain and, at least until the great confrontation over the Falklands in 1770–1, Bourbon unity was complete. Indeed, this alliance was one reason why observers in London, and George III and Bute in particular, were already afraid of a new conflict even before the

---

[34] Black, *Natural and Necessary Enemies*, 68–9.

Seven Years War had been concluded.[35] In order to secure a settlement, Britain had been forced to make a series of concessions during the peace negotiations of 1761–2. The final terms restored to Louis XV not merely the West Indian sugar islands but a share in the Newfoundland Fisheries, which were crucial for France's re-emergence as a naval power since they were the principal source of sailors: this was why Pitt had wished to exclude the French totally. France thus retained the naval and commercial potential to be a powerful state and could recover very quickly. She also remained a strategic threat in the Caribbean and even against British North America. Such fears were exaggerated, but it was not unreasonable for Britain's ministers in 1762–3 to fear an early attack and to believe a new war might soon begin.

These anxieties were increased by a report received in London at the end of 1762, shortly after preliminaries were signed, which suggested that France's future financial problems were likely to be far less serious than those of Britain herself.[36] With hindsight it is clear that the reverse was true. France's decision to pay for the Seven Years War through borrowing rather than by taxation saddled her with a large peacetime debt and a permanent annual deficit.[37] After 1763 the cost to the French treasury of servicing Louis XV's loans was twice what it had been before 1756 and consumed the massive figure of 60 per cent of annual revenue. France's finances were now in a critical situation and this proved to be a formidable obstacle to her recovery. In particular the shortage of funds hindered naval reconstruction, since ships could not be repaired and constructed with the speed Choiseul's plans demanded, and this forced him to pursue a moderate policy towards Britain throughout the rest of his ministry. At the time the report about France's fiscal strength appeared only too plausible, particularly to ministers already worried about Britain's own national debt. This had almost doubled as a result of the Seven Years War, from around £74 million to some £133 million, and was alarming contemporaries.[38] After 1763 there was real fear of a national bankruptcy. In retrospect this was clearly exaggerated, but at the time men believed that the capacity to raise taxes had been overtaken by the vast cost of servicing the national

[35] See the important article by J. L. Bullion, 'Securing the Peace: Lord Bute, the Plan for the Army, and the Origins of the American Revolution', in K. W. Schweizer, ed., *Lord Bute: Essays in Re-interpretation* (Leicester, 1988), 17–35.   [36] Ibid. 33–4.

[37] J. C. Riley, *The Seven Years War and the Old Regime in France: The Economic and Financial Toll* (Princeton, 1986), 231–2, 236, and *passim*.

[38] J. Brewer, *The Sinews of Power: War, Money and the English State* (London, 1989), 114. Prof. Bullion quotes an even higher contemporary figure of £140 million: 'Securing the Peace', 24.

debt. Taxation in the first year of peace was perhaps twice the level it had been before the fighting began, and for the next dozen years a policy of strict financial retrenchment was usually pursued.[39]

This provided another legacy of the war for British foreign policy and hindered the search for an alliance. The swollen national debt confirmed ministers in their refusal to consider a peacetime subsidy. By the mid-eighteenth century the idea that such payments were wasteful of money and seldom produced tangible benefits for Britain had been elevated into an inviolable principle. It was to be a central tenet of British policy throughout the age of the American Revolution that subsidies should not be paid in peacetime. The Seven Years War had ended amidst a torrent of criticism for the whole idea of subsidies.[40] The attack on the 'German war' was by implication also an attack on the principle of sending English men and English money to support the fighting on the European continent, and until the outbreak of the American rebellion ministers resolutely refused any subsidy.[41] Britain's wealth had been one principal attraction to potential partners, and the refusal of peacetime subsidies hindered her efforts to find an ally. But though this contributed to her failure, it was less important than the new international alignments created by the Seven Years War.

When viewed from London, the Bourbon threat dominated the diplomatic horizon, but Anglo-French rivalry was no longer Europe's main political preoccupation. France's decline and changed priorities, along with the rise of Prussia and Russia, ended Britain's ability to manipulate continental alliances in her own interest. Although British ministers remained wedded to the Old System, it was rapidly ceasing to be practical. This is more striking with hindsight than it was at the time. A central theme of British policy throughout the age of the American Revolution was Britain's failure to appreciate fully the consequences of the Seven Years War.

Other legacies are less easy to establish. It would be fundamentally misleading to see the conflict as the point at which Britain turned her back on Europe in favour of empire.[42] There was no such clear-cut

---

[39] Brewer, *Sinews of Power*, 124; J. Steven Watson, *The Reign of George III 1760–1815* (Oxford, 1960), 91.

[40] C. W. Eldon, *England's Subsidy Policy towards the Continent during the Seven Years' War* (Philadelphia, 1938), 141–60; Schlenke, *England und das friderizianische Preussen*, 249–65.

[41] See Rochford's revealing remarks to Maltzan: *Pol. Corr.* xxvii. 508.

[42] This would seem to be one implication, though never fully developed, of G. Niedhart, *Handel und Krieg in der britischen Weltpolitik 1738–1763* (Munich, 1979); such an interpretation also occasionally surfaces in Pares's fundamental article, 'American Versus Continental Warfare 1739–63', 130–72: see especially p. 172.

break; on the contrary British foreign policy remained traditional in its pursuit of continental alliances at least until 1815. The wider imperial perspective which ministers were gradually forced to adopt after the Peace of Paris may have weakened their established concern with continental diplomacy. This was especially true during two decades when the major issues arose in distant eastern Europe, in which Britain had seldom shown much interest. At first this strengthened British insularity rather than suggesting isolationism.

The triumphant Seven Years War influenced Britain's diplomacy in one other respect. In a very real sense the scale of these victories encouraged her to assume the role of conqueror. During the war neutral states had been outraged at Britain's rough handling of their shipping, and after 1763 there was widespread resentment at this brutal behaviour over maritime rights. British ministers were not restrained by such condemnation or by the protests of the commercial states. Their ready resort to naval muscle in order to impose their view of neutral rights was accompanied after 1763 by a new willingness to coerce any country which dared to resist Britain's will. The Bourbons throughout the first decade of peace, like the small state of Denmark in 1773, were to be intimidated into submission by *force majeure* in the shape of Britain's dominant navy: in the estimation of many contemporaries, Britain had become the bully of Europe. Admiration for British power and wealth after 1763 was mingled with resentment of Britain's overweening conduct, and this was soon to be accompanied by *Schadenfreude* at her mounting internal and colonial difficulties.[43]

The Seven Years War was the principal source of this new domineering attitude. It was apparent in Britain's dealings both with her own colonists in North America and in her foreign policy. In the heady aftermath of the Peace of Paris Britain was generally less willing to be conciliatory: whether over the Dunkirk fortifications, the ditch at Chandernagore, or the demand for the 'Turkish clause' in Anglo-Russian alliance negotiations. Not all ministries were to uphold British interests as decisively as that of George Grenville, who viewed and treated France as a 'conquered nation'.[44] But throughout the 1760s and 1770s British foreign policy was to be characterized by intransigence, overconfidence, and an unwillingness to treat potential allies on a basis of equality. These tendencies, long present in Britain's diplomacy, had been significantly strengthened by recent victories. Henceforth one characteristic of foreign policy was an

[43] See, e.g. CP (Angleterre) 456, fo. 81; cf. Madariaga, *Armed Neutrality*, 109. For a similar Swedish fear of Britain's commercial dominance, see the 'Circular Instructions' of 12 Mar. 1770, Roberts Transcripts; cf. *Bernstorffsche Papiere*, iii. 557.   [44] See below, Ch. 4.

unwillingness to compromise; yet compromise remained the very essence of negotiations and, frequently, a precondition for success.

The legacies of the Seven Years War were considerable and in some measure contradictory. The emphasis upon the changes, however necessary, is only one side of the story. The fundamental continuities in British diplomacy were still more important than the discontinuities created by the fighting which had ended in 1763. To a significant extent the war's principal impact was to confirm and even reinforce established assumptions. British foreign policy sought to protect certain areas of particular strategic or commercial importance: above all the Low Countries, out of a historic fear of invasion from across the 'narrow seas'; the King's Electorate of Hanover; and the Baltic, the main source of the naval stores on which Britain's maritime supremacy was increasingly based. After 1763 ministers recognized an obligation to support their two traditional and surviving allies: the faded states of Portugal and the Dutch Republic. In the latter case, this had been strengthened by the Revolution of 1747 and by William IV's early death in 1751, which had together underlined the belief that Britain's support for the House of Orange and for the Dutch alliance was a historic duty.

In a more general sense, foreign policy continued to uphold the reputation of the King and to defend the interests of his subjects. It also aimed to preserve peace, not merely between Britain and her Bourbon enemies but more generally among the continental states. This objective was strengthened by the cabinet's awareness of the enlarged national debt after the costly Seven Years War. Religion was no longer an important factor in British policy or in international relations generally. After 1763 ministers did profess a vestigial concern with the Pretender, though they had ceased to fear a Jacobite restoration.[45] In any case, Britain's diplomacy was still dominated by strategic and political concerns. Principal among these was an enduring fear of France, as soon became clear once peace had been signed.

[45] See, e.g., Suffolk to Grantham, 20 Sept. 1771, Add. MSS 24157. For this change, and the earlier concern, see J. Black, 'Jacobitism and British Foreign Policy under the First Two Georges 1714–1760', *Royal Stuart Papers*, 32 (1988), 1–18.

4

The Failure of the Old System, 1763–1765

BRITAIN'S Seven Years War was formally ended by the signature of the definitive treaty in February 1763. Immediately, foreign policy ceased to be the principal issue for government and in domestic politics.[1] Diplomacy and military strategy, which had dominated political debate throughout the reigns of the first two Hanoverians, were relegated to subordinate positions. The pattern of the next decade quickly became established: the attention given to Europe was considerably reduced by competing, and more immediate, problems. Foremost among these in 1763–4 was the Grenville Ministry's very survival.

Bute's resignation in April 1763 threw British politics into turmoil.[2] The King appointed George Grenville to head the government, but withheld his complete support and continued to consult Bute. The hiatus continued until late August when, with the breakdown of negotiations with Pitt, George III had to give Grenville full backing. A stable ministry required not merely the king's confidence, but also parliament's support. Grenville's first parliament, which met in November 1763, was dominated by the Wilkes affair. In the previous April, issue no. 45 of the *North Briton* had denounced the peace settlement and the men who had negotiated it; more importantly, it had also personally attacked the King. The author was widely known to be an MP, John Wilkes, who was first arrested on a general warrant and then released. This raised two questions: the legality of general warrants and the issue of parliamentary privilege. These dominated the early weeks of the new session and it was not until mid-February 1764, when the government narrowly won a famous vote on general warrants, that the Grenville Ministry could feel secure.

These upheavals inevitably affected the conduct of British diplomacy. Grenville, the ministry's leader, was preoccupied with domestic

---

[1] R. Pares, *King George III and the Politicians* (Oxford, 1967 edn.), 4.
[2] P. D. G. Thomas, *British Politics and the Stamp Act Crisis: The First Phase of the American Revolution, 1763–1767* (Oxford, 1975), 1–20; P. Lawson, *George Grenville: A Political Life* (Oxford, 1984), 154–80.

affairs and his parliamentary majority.[3] He limited his involvement
in foreign policy to rejecting any idea of a subsidy and to urging a
hard-line attitude towards France.[4] Diplomacy was handled by the
two Secretaries of State. The senior was the Earl of Halifax, Southern
Secretary after September 1763, who was already notorious for his
laziness; 'dead and rotten before his body actually died' was
Rockingham's subsequent verdict.[5] Halifax's earlier zeal at the
Board of Trade had evaporated and he allowed his brother Secretary
to take the initiative. After September 1763, the Northern Secretary
was the Earl of Sandwich, who effectively controlled foreign policy
during the first half of the Grenville Ministry.[6] Sandwich had some
previous diplomatic experience: he had negotiated the peace settlement at the end of the War of the Austrian Succession. His views on
foreign policy were clear, and they were a legacy of early exposure to
Newcastle's distinctive ideas, particularly in 1746–8. Sandwich
always supported the Old System, believing Britain must oppose
France and Spain and should do so through continental alliances. He
himself favoured treaties with Britain's old ally Austria and the new
power of Russia: two states he regarded as natural partners who
would one day resume their traditional alliance.[7]

These two dimensions of British foreign policy throughout the age
of the American Revolution became established in the early months
of peace: continuing rivalry with the Bourbons, and the search for
one or more allies to provide security against this established threat.
Ministers recognized that British victories in the Seven Years War
had increased France's resentment, and after 1763 they maintained
an anxious and close watch over her activities.[8] Their policy was
based on a conviction that France would try, sooner or later, to
regain some of her losses and would be assisted by Spain. The French

[3] See e.g. *Grenville Papers*, ii. 186.   [4] Ibid. ii. 240.
[5] CP (Angleterre) 450, fo. 494; *Burke Corr.* ii. 219.
[6] For one example of him transacting business outside his own province, see *Grenville Papers*, ii. 344–5.
[7] The account of Sandwich's policy owes much to the exemplary edition of *The Fourth Earl of Sandwich: Diplomatic Correspondence 1763–1765* by F. Spencer (Manchester, 1961). Though the essential starting-point, many of the ideas put forward in the introduction are more challenging than convincing: see the penetrating remarks of Sir H. Butterfield, 'British Foreign Policy, 1762–65', *Cambridge Historical Journal*, 6 (1963), 131–40. In particular, Dr Spencer may exaggerate the importance of the Russian alliance for ministers and thereby underestimate the attachment to the old alliance with Austria. He is also too isolationist: his views that all that was needed was naval superiority over the Bourbons was not the attitude of the Grenville Ministry as a whole.
[8] The 'Separate and Private Instructions for Hertford', 29 Sept. 1763, printed in *BDI* vii: *France 1745–1789*, ed. L. G. Wickham Legg (London, 1934), 85–90, provide a good introduction to the official attitude; France's naval preparations were worrying the Earl of Egmont (First Lord of the Admiralty) as early as Dec. 1763: *Grenville Papers*, ii. 171–5.

state was always viewed as the greater threat, and Louis XV's energetic minister, Choiseul, was recognized to be Britain's most implacable foe. Immediately after the Peace of Paris, however, there was little to create alarm. Relations were now founded on mutual fear rather than mutual aggression. Though French hostility was assumed, some minor disputes demonstrated Choiseul's moderation and wish for peace. Anglo-Spanish relations were similarly harmonious.[9] The only dispute was over the Manila Ransom, a sum allegedly due to Britain for not sacking the capital of the Spanish Philippines when it had been captured in 1762. Although this subsequently caused serious friction, the British government did not at first pursue it vigorously. Instead, the Grenville Ministry aimed during its first year in power to strengthen Britain's international position by concluding defensive alliances, first with Russia and then with Austria.

The quest for a Russian alliance was a central thread throughout the 1760s and 1770s. Even before peace had been signed, Britain had opened negotiations, and these continued intermittently during the next decade. The discussions went on infinitely longer than any comparable ones and were pursued with considerably more vigour. This demonstrated the alliance's very real attractions for British ministers.[10] Russia had emerged from the Seven Years War with her resources seemingly unimpaired and her political standing enhanced. Her victories over the formidable Prussian forces completed the process by which Britain came to regard her as a desirable ally: indeed, in British eyes, Russia was for long an army rather than a state. Russian military power, however exaggerated London's view of this, appeared to complement British naval and financial strength. The distance separating the two states prevented serious political rivalry, while mutual hostility towards France offered that common political interest essential for a stable partnership. France's struggle with Britain had its counterpart in her contest with Russia in eastern Europe.

There was also a long-established and mutually advantageous trading connection, enshrined in the Commercial Treaty of 1734,

[9] The best study is Lalaguna Lasala, 'England, Spain and the Family Compact', 120 ff.

[10] M. S. Anderson, *Britain's Discovery of Russia 1553–1815* (London, 1958), 108–42, provides a valuable discussion of British attitudes. Though its principal focus lies outside this period, there are some incisive general comments in D. Gerhard, *England und der Aufstieg Russlands* (Munich and Berlin, 1933): see, in particular, pp. 17–30. An interesting contemporary view is provided by the anonymous (though officially inspired) 'State of the Negotiation for a Treaty of Alliance between Great Britain and Russia, from 1763 to 1771' in SP 103/63, fos. 37–62.

and this certainly provided a basis for closer political contacts, though whether it actually advanced alliance negotiations is uncertain.[11] Close economic ties were essential since Russia, by her victories in the Great Northern War (1700–21), had secured control over the crucial Baltic naval stores. These links had been followed by a growing British awareness of Russia's potential utility. The idea that she could provide mercenary soldiers gradually gained ground. This notion, central to the British view until the late 1770s, had produced a defensive alliance in 1742 and further agreements in 1746 and 1755, though the latter was never ratified. The burgeoning friendship had not been interrupted by the Seven Years War. Though on different sides, the two states had not formally been at war, diplomatic relations had been maintained, and trade had reached new levels. British ministers had repeatedly declined to send a fleet to the Baltic to protect the Prussian coastline, partly in order not to offend Russia. Catherine II, sole ruler after July 1762, was personally Anglophile. She had received British subsidies in her needy days as Grand Duchess and was renowned for her hostility towards France.

In 1763, it seemed an alliance would soon be signed. But earlier relations revealed possible difficulties. Previous agreements had been one-sided: in return for a subsidy, St Petersburg agreed to hire out soldiers but secured no reciprocal aid. Indeed, Britain was specifically exempted from having to provide assistance should Russia be attacked by her most dangerous enemy, the Ottoman Empire. This one-sidedness reflected Britain's political ascendancy and Russia's relative backwardness in the 1740s and 1750s. By the 1760s, Russia had entered the ranks of the great powers and Catherine II was determined this should be acknowledged by other states. These new aspirations immediately clashed with Britain's old assumptions. In particular, ministers still wanted to model any treaty on that of 1742 and refused to provide support where only Russian interests were involved. Specifically, they would not include Turkish wars in any treaty, since these had been excluded in 1742. Russia, however, was determined on complete equality.[12] Russian aid if Britain were attacked must be matched by a British promise of assistance. This so-called 'Turkish clause' was central to the negotiations' eventual failure.

In the early months of peace, Russia's own problems in foreign affairs led her to look for co-operation and even an alliance.

---

[11] Gerhard, *England und der Aufstieg Russlands*, 15.
[12] See e.g. Buckinghamshire to Sir Joseph Yorke, 27 Nov. 1764, Buckinghamshire Papers.

Catherine II's initial diplomatic strategy was to avoid commitments until she had secured her regime at home and until the European situation became clearer. This was balanced by her need for support in any Polish election. By the early 1760s, Augustus III's ill health threatened an early vacancy on Poland's elective throne. Since the beginning of the eighteenth century, Russia's rulers had played an increasingly dominant role in Poland, which they regarded as a satellite. Poland was an invaluable buffer-state which protected the Russian empire from direct attack while allowing Russia's own troops to move westwards. The continuation of this invisible empire demanded the election of another Russian puppet. Catherine intended that this should be her former lover, the Polish nobleman Stanislas Poniatowski, though as yet she refused to announce her candidate.

Recent Polish elections had all been accompanied by fighting and by foreign intervention. The Saxon royal family, rulers since 1697, was unlikely to give up this position, and the royal title it brought, without a struggle and might be supported by France and Austria. Catherine was particularly afraid the French would incite the Turks to attack her when she was already committed in Poland: as Choiseul attempted in 1763–4. Russia herself was dangerously isolated should other states oppose Poniatowski's imposition. Prussia was already offering support in return for an alliance, but though her renowned army was an attraction, Frederick II had his own ambitions in Poland and was altogether too much of a rival to be an ideal partner. The other possible source of assistance was Britain, pre-eminent after the Seven Years War. To the Empress, the attractions of such co-operation were very real. Russia hoped to use Britain's wealth from her colonies and commerce, and also believed Anglo-French hostility could be exploited to neutralize Louis XV's opposition. These hopes dictated the Empress's policy in the early months of peace and influenced discussions about an alliance.

Britain had first approached Russia during the final stages of the Seven Years War. Buckinghamshire, who arrived in St Petersburg in late September 1762, had immediately proposed that the 1742 treaty should be renewed. Catherine, though sympathetic to Britain, was determined to avoid commitments and rejected this approach. The ambassador instead tried to renew the Commercial Treaty. This had lapsed, but its provisions still operated pending renegotiation. These parallel talks, which were to bulk large in Buckinghamshire's duties during the next two years, at first made no progress. The confused situation at the Russian court and the Empress's reluctance to commit herself were significant obstacles to any negotiations. It was only the Polish King's deteriorating health which forced Catherine to attend to foreign affairs.[13]

In the closing weeks of 1762, Russia had raised the possibility of British support for her candidate in any election. London's reply was favourable but non-commital.[14] Now, as in the months to come, Augustus III's health was a barometer of Anglo-Russian negotiations. The Empress's coyness over naming her choice, together with the King's sudden recovery in early spring 1763, ensured that negotiations did not proceed beyond generalities, but the possibilities were clear. To leave Britain in no doubt, Catherine explicitly declared that her attitude to any alliance would depend on a favourable response over Poland.

These terms went far beyond anything Britain would contemplate. Ministers believed such concessions were unnecessary and any self-respecting state should jump at the chance of a British alliance.[15] Russia's demands also challenged Britain's traditional indifference to events in Poland.[16] Many Englishmen were hostile to a country substantially Catholic and long viewed as a French puppet, part of the famous *barrière de l'est*. This reinforced London's determination to reject Catherine II's demands. Active support at Warsaw or against the Turks was always out of the question, and this was a formidable obstacle to any alliance. This attitude rested less on the proclaimed desire not to endanger Britain's declining Levant trade than on a determination to avoid distant quarrels where no vital British interest appeared to be involved. From Britain's point of view,

[13] The account of negotiations immediately after the Seven Years War which follows differs significantly from that in Roberts, *British Diplomacy*, 61–3 and 428 n. 95, and in M. F. Metcalf, *Russia, England and Swedish Party Politics 1762–1766* (Stockholm and Totowa, 1977), 39–42. Both authors give too much emphasis to Sweden and too little to Poland, and thereby underestimate the decisive impact on Russian policy of Augustus III's death. I also believe Prof. Roberts is wrong to dismiss Britain's opportunity of an alliance on reasonable terms as lightly as he does. Though he rightly emphasizes Panin's stiff terms, he gives insufficient weight to Russia's problems in the final months of 1763 which would probably have forced the Russian minister to modify his initial demands. It was British intransigence, rather than Russian terms, which prevented these negotiations from getting off the ground. For a view which accords with that put forward here, see Madariaga, *Russia*, 189–90.

[14] For a fuller account of Anglo–Russian negotiations in 1762–4, see H. M. Scott, 'Great Britain, Poland and the Russian Alliance, 1763–1767', *Historical Journal*, 19 (1976), 62–9, on which the following paragraphs are based. The article by J. Black, 'Anglo-Russian Relations after the Seven Years' War', *Scottish Slavonic Review*, 9 (1987), 27–37, covers similar ground and adds only some curious and misleading *obiter dicta*.

[15] Cf. M. Roberts, 'Great Britain, Denmark and Russia, 1763–70' in R. Hatton and M. S. Anderson, eds., *Studies in Diplomatic History: Essays in Memory of David Bayne Horn* (London, 1970), 236–67, at p. 250, for a similar conclusion.

[16] See e.g. the later view of George III: *BDI* vii: *France 1745–1789*, ed. Wickham Legg, 91–2 n. 2.

this was credible and even commendable except that she was seeking an alliance and might have recognized that some concessions were essential to conclude it. This stance was also a poor recommendation to a prospective ally. The pattern persisted throughout the next decade, as Britain refused to base negotiations on anything approaching equal obligations and sought to limit concessions.

Russian diplomacy was proverbially slow, and this, together with the distance involved, ensured no progress was made in the months after Augustus III's recovery. The King's survival made foreign policy less urgent for St Petersburg and Catherine became absorbed in internal problems. The severe court crisis in summer 1763 effectively suspended diplomatic activity and it was early autumn before things returned to normal. By late August, however, Buckinghamshire's persistence had prised a draft alliance from the Russian ministers. This was essentially the 1742 defensive treaty with several minor and one major alteration: war with the Ottoman Empire was not specifically excluded from qualifying Russia for aid. Britain would be obliged to assist Catherine II if she were attacked by the Turks. This was the first mention, and origin, of the 'Turkish clause', that refrain of relations in the years to come. Its implications were a major stumbling block throughout the next decade. Worse still, from Britain's point of view, the Russian draft contained two secret articles. The first provided that in any future vacancy in Poland, Britain would work with Russia to elect a mutually acceptable candidate. The British government would defray electioneering expenses and, if fighting broke out, would pay 500,000 roubles (approximately £100,000) towards the cost of Russian operations. Britain was thus to underwrite a policy over which Catherine II would retain complete control. A second secret article provided, in general terms, for co-operation and particularly financial assistance in Sweden. Though this anticipated later Russian demands, it had little immediate significance.

Poland was Russia's real object. The provisions for British money reflected her financial exhaustion, a potentially debilitating weakness in the political market-place of Warsaw. For Russia, moreover, the 'Turkish clause' was intimately connected with Poland. Russia's activities in the Balkans and the Crimea irritated Constantinople, but were unlikely to provoke fighting. Her Polish policy was quite another matter. The Ottoman Empire had watched the growth of Russian power at Warsaw with increasing fear and suspicion, and this resentment was fanned continually by French diplomacy. Catherine II feared success in Poland might be jeopardized by Turkish intervention. The spectre of war on two fronts was frightening: hence the 'Turkish clause', which was inserted in her later alliances with Prussia and Denmark.

These proposals were quite unacceptable to Britain.[17] The Grenville Ministry confirmed traditional indifference to Poland and refused assistance. After a long and expensive war, ministers wanted to avoid any commitments that might lead to more fighting. A cabinet meeting on 16 September 1763 summarily rejected the Russian draft on grounds that became familiar.[18] The 'Turkish clause' was refused, ostensibly because it might damage British trade in the Levant, while the demand for aid in Poland and even Sweden was deemed 'utterly inadmissible' since it involved a peacetime subsidy. The Grenville Ministry instead returned to that most enduring of British delusions, the idea that a treaty could be modelled on that of 1742.

This disappointed Russia, but by the time the British reply had been received, the situation had changed dramatically. Augustus III's death on 5 October 1763 was unexpected in its suddenness, and it revived the negotiations. It brought all Catherine's fears of France and the Turks into the open and made her even more anxious for British support. Nikita Panin, emerging as Russia's foreign minister, no longer insisted on the 'Turkish clause' and instead offered a treaty for support in Poland and, specifically, a subsidy of 500,000 roubles. Russia's desperate need for ready cash meant that, in effect, her alliance was for sale, particularly as parallel negotiations with Prussia had made little progress.[19] Panin's discussions with Buckinghamshire reveal London's opportunity. The problem was still the price demanded, for Britain would not agree to a peacetime subsidy. Bland and useless expressions of goodwill were the extent of British support, and the negotiations were doomed to failure. Panin appreciated that nothing could be secured from Britain and turned his attention fully towards Prussia. Frederick II's anxiety for a treaty enabled rapid progress to be made and, in April 1764, a Russo-Prussian defensive alliance was concluded. Prussia provided the help in Poland and assistance against a Turkish attack refused by London, and this increased Russia's price for a future alliance with Britain.

[17] *Sbornik*, xii. 119.

[18] See the cabinet minute in *Additional Grenville Papers 1763–1765*, ed. J. R. G. Tomlinson (Manchester, 1962), 318.

[19] It would be wrong to deny that, for Panin at least, Frederick II was the more valued political partner; but, equally, the British and Prussian alliances were not seen as alternatives in St Petersburg. At the beginning of Dec., Panin was still thinking in terms of a triple alliance of Russia, Prussia, and Britain (*Sbornik*, xii. 168) and though the Prussian King's distaste for any such links was duly expressed (ibid. xxii. 174–5), it seems clear his need for a Russian alliance would have forced him to accept Britain's inclusion in the 'Northern System'.

Panin later made no secret that 500,000 roubles would have concluded the Anglo-Russian alliance immediately after Augustus III's death.[20] Russia's terms would seldom be lower than in the final weeks of 1763, when her more extreme demands would have been abandoned in exchange for one thing: a British subsidy. This was precisely the thing no British ministry could contemplate, particularly when convinced that France would not intervene over Poland. The automatic opposition to French schemes which was the basis of British policy, and on which Russian calculations had been founded, also implied Britain would not become involved if France abstained. When, early in November, French assurances were received in London, a potential motive for British intervention was removed.

Ministers were preoccupied with internal problems in the final months of 1763. The opening of parliament and the Wilkes affair monopolized the government's time and, more importantly, consumed the attention of the minister responsible for foreign policy, as Sandwich was also in charge of Wilkes's prosecution in parliament. The impact of financial and domestic problems upon British diplomacy became very clear at this time. A government concerned at the swollen national debt and haunted by Wilkes and by possible parliamentary defeat easily confirmed established thinking about foreign affairs: no subsidy in peacetime; no meddling in Polish politics. There was little sign that any minister, and certainly not Sandwich, appreciated the opportunity created by Augustus III's death. This first round of Anglo-Russian negotiations had revealed the considerable gap between the two states and suggested attitudes would be hard to reconcile. Even Russia's lowest price—a peacetime subsidy of £100,000—was still far too high for ministers, and the opportunity was lost.

Even before these negotiations collapsed, Britain had also tried to restore the alliance with the Habsburgs.[21] Now and for some years to come, a majority of British statesmen viewed Austria as the most desirable ally. The approach, however, was initially delayed by the need to restore formal diplomatic relations. Once this had been done events moved with a speed unusual in the slow-moving world of eighteenth-century diplomacy, which demonstrated Britain's wish for a treaty. Austria was France's ally and had fought the Seven Years War in partnership with her. This alignment appeared secure in the

---

[20] See e.g. ibid. xxii. 271–2. Cf. Buckinghamshire's later view: *HMC Lothian*, 371.

[21] For a fuller account of relations in 1763–4 see H. M. Scott, 'Anglo-Austrian Relations after the Seven Years War: Lord Stormont in Vienna, 1763–1772' (unpublished Ph.D. thesis, University of London, 1977), 46–89, on which the following section is based.

early months of peace, yet British ministers did not at first view it as an insuperable obstacle.

During the conflict, the two states had not formally been at war and each had simply fought on the side of the other's enemy: Austria as France's ally, Britain as Prussia's partner. Diplomatic relations had been severed in 1757 at Vienna's instigation. Most British ministers were unreconciled to losing the traditional Austrian alliance. They regarded the Diplomatic Revolution as temporary and looked towards the Old System's swift revival. Such expectations had inspired an unsuccessful approach to Vienna early in 1762 and were little diminished by the rejection on that occasion. Even while peace was being concluded, London's wish for an Austrian alliance had been emphasized.

Relations were formally restored in late autumn 1763. The instructions given to Britain's ambassador, Lord Stormont, testified both to London's desire to restore the old alliance and to her optimism that this could be done, though there was to be no immediate approach. This was also apparent in the very friendly reception accorded to the new Austrian ambassador, Seilern, when he reached England. Even before he had been accredited, George III, during his first, and private, audience, had stressed the Old System's advantages to both states and made clear his own wish to see it restored. Several ministers, during their initial meetings with the ambassador, also underlined Britain's desire for an alliance. This contrasted with the more muted reception given to Stormont in Vienna. It embodied Austria's attitude towards Britain after the Seven Years War. Friendly relations and, in time, a good political understanding were certainly sought by Kaunitz; but there was no interest in a new alliance. This was soon appreciated by Stormont, but his realism did not prevent him inadvertently setting in motion a formal approach late in 1763.

In mid-November, Sandwich had sent all British diplomats details of the ministry's successes in early divisions in the new parliamentary session. This was an attempt to discredit the wild rumours on the continent of ministerial instability, largely produced by the Wilkes affair. The Northern Secretary appreciated the damage political upheavals could do to Britain's standing abroad. Stormont duly passed on this information to Kaunitz, who expressed polite satisfaction. This was genuine, but inspired less by regard for Britain than by fear her weakness might tempt Choiseul to attack.

Stormont reported these rather formal statements to Sandwich and also passed on a rumour that Seilern had instructions to say nothing until it was clear the Grenville Ministry would survive. He was then to initiate an Austro-British *rapprochement*. Britain's ambassador was rightly sceptical about this tale. Seilern was certainly interested in English politics, but under no such instructions. His silence simply expressed Kaunitz's belief there was nothing to discuss. But Sandwich interpreted this as a favourable opportunity. His own devotion to the Old System here overcame his political judgement:[22] Stormont's dispatches contained nothing to suggest the time was ripe for a new alliance. The Northern Secretary believed otherwise and launched a formal approach. He employed the pretext of a supposed Prussian threat to Hanover. A dispute over debts contracted by the British commissariat in Germany during the Seven Years War had been inflamed by Frederick II, who had seized some British military magazines as insurance against the compensation he claimed was due to his subjects. There was no likelihood of a Prussian attack, but Sandwich used the imagined threat as the pretext for a long discussion with the Austrian ambassador on Christmas Eve.

He began by emphasizing his desire for restored links and declaring the two states to be 'natural allies'. He then asked what would be Vienna's attitude if Frederick II attacked Hanover. Seilern was unable to give any formal answer, but he was indiscreet enough to say, 'as a private man', he believed Austria would provide assistance. This was an early indication that the ambassador was far more favourable towards Britain and towards a new alliance than his government, and it encouraged Sandwich to make a formal approach in Vienna. But when Stormont spoke to the Austrian Chancellor in mid-January 1764, Kaunitz dispelled once and for all British hopes of a swift revival of the Old System. While making clear his wish for good relations, he declared Austria would adhere to her established French alliance.

British ministers had hoped that Austria would immediately abandon France and return to the fold, but Kaunitz's rejection forced them to accept this would take some time. Though they remained preoccupied with an Austrian alliance, they realized it could be several years before it was restored. This led to the development of a more realistic strategy. Yet the greater realism over timing did not prevent a nostalgic yearning from remaining central to British thinking. It is remarkable that, in 1763–4 and in the years ahead, there was so little understanding in London of the strength of the Austro-French alliance, though this was the rock on which approaches to Vienna foundered. Ministers also failed to appreciate

---

[22] For the strength of his desire for an Austrian alliance, see the comments of an expatriate Irishman in the Imperial service who visited England for 2 months in spring 1764: 'O'Flannagan's Relation', 11 July 1764, HHStA, England-Varia 11, fos. 23–4.

the extent of Habsburg decline after the costly and destructive Seven Years War. Austria, by 1763, was clearly the weakest great power and this might have made British statesmen question an alliance's value.

The Grenville Ministry was not seriously concerned with the failure to secure allies. This was accepted with some equanimity and rather more pique. It was easy, in the heady aftermath of the Seven Years War, to shrug off the failure to sign treaties. Ministers assumed alliances with Russia and even Austria would eventually be concluded, and were convinced no concessions were needed. They were still operating within a blinkered and outdated view of the European states-system, believing that since Britain and France 'were the two great Powers of Europe, peace or war depended upon their measures'. They assumed Anglo-French rivalry was still the continent's dominant concern and that, in any emergency, alliances would be there for the taking.[23]

This insular approach embodied established patterns of thought. During the Seven Years War, however, with the emergence of Russia and Prussia, the centre of political gravity moved sharply east. Britain had traditionally been indifferent to Europe's distant edge, and in 1763–4 she again ignored a Polish king's death. Ministers were more concerned, as the Russian ambassador sourly remarked, with the election in Essex than with the vacancy in Warsaw.[24] They failed to appreciate the importance of the Polish election for post-war alliances, though this had been made clear during the Anglo-Russian negotiations.[25] Its implications could not be conjured away by pretending eastern Europe did not exist. Britain's foreign policy and, in particular, her search for an ally were decisively affected by events over Poland in 1763–4.

The most obvious consequence was the Russo-Prussian alliance of April 1764. This enabled Catherine II to make Poniatowski King of Poland and determined Russia's diplomatic strategy for the first half of her reign. The Prussian alliance was the foundation of the 'Northern System' associated with Nikita Panin, now clearly the Empress's principal adviser. It was the late 1770s before this was superseded by Potemkin's more aggressive plans for southern expansion. The 'Northern System' reflected both Russia's ambitions and her anxieties. The Polish election had been an unwelcome, if crucial, diversion from domestic problems. Once Poniatowski had been safely elected king in September 1764, Catherine was able to

[23] *Grenville Papers*, ii. 344, 533.
[24] Michael Roberts, *Macartney in Russia* (*English Historical Review*, Supplement 7; London, 1974), 38.   [25] See e.g. CP (Angleterre) 457, fos. 124, 134.

return to her pressing internal concerns, and this preoccupation was apparent in the 'Northern System' itself.

Panin aimed to secure the tranquillity of the Russian empire's three critical border zones: Poland, Sweden, and the Black Sea region. France's influence there since the seventeenth century appeared to be Russia's major threat, and this made the 'Northern System' essentially anti-French. The Empress was at least as hostile towards France as her minister, and for the next decade endorsed his strategy. Panin aimed at combating French influence and preserving peace on Russia's western frontier by means of a series of alliances. It was originally envisaged that, in addition to Prussia, the 'Northern System' would include Denmark, Sweden, Poland, and Britain. Treaties were concluded with Copenhagen in 1765 and 1767, but its other intended members proved elusive. Panin wanted to exploit British gold and British sea power against France, and he intended London to be one of the founder members of the 'Northern System'. This favoured a Russo-British alliance, and for several years he tried to conclude one. But there were now two significant obstacles. The 'Turkish clause' had become a precondition for any treaty with Russia, since Prussia had promised aid against an Ottoman attack in April 1764 and Denmark was to do so a year later. Secondly, Britain henceforth had to reckon with Prussian hostility at St Petersburg.

The Russo-Prussian alliance was the foundation of the 'Northern System'. Yet Frederick II was always fundamentally opposed to Panin's grandiose plans. He wanted a Russian alliance but was also determined to be Catherine II's only important partner. After April 1764, Prussia's influence in St Petersburg was directed against any extension to include either Denmark or Britain. Frederick was unable to prevent the Russo-Danish alliance, which demonstrated his limited influence. But Prussia's treaty with Catherine II did not in itself make an Anglo-Russian alliance impossible, or even unlikely. More important was Frederick's campaign against Britain in St Petersburg during the next few years, and his continual harping on her weakness and irresolution certainly did nothing to increase London's prospects. It contributed to Russia's diminishing belief in the value of formal British links by the later 1760s.

Malice was one element in Frederick's propaganda, but far more important was shrewd political calculation. The Prussian King intended to avoid commitments to either western power, since he had no wish to be dragged into the new Anglo-French war he believed inevitable. He also appreciated that his control over Russia, and therefore the alliance's value, would be increased if he remained Catherine's only major ally. This was principally why he devoted so much time and energy to preventing any extension of the 'Northern System', particularly to include Britain. The Russian alliance had been Frederick II's main objective since 1762 and after April 1764 he tenaciously defended it. He believed this treaty would deter the Habsburgs from any future attack, for he appreciated that Russia now held the balance between the two German powers.[26]

After April 1764, Frederick had no further use for relations with Britain, and in the summer a complete breach took place. Anglo-Prussian diplomacy had been distant and acrimonious after the celebrated breakup of the wartime partnership in 1762. This was exacerbated by the interference in domestic British politics of Prussia's agent in London, Michell. At the end of the Seven Years War, Frederick II had ordered his ministers in England to intrigue with the parliamentary opposition, in the hope that Bute and Bedford might be turned out of office. Michell continued this campaign in the early months of peace. His links with opposition politicians, especially Pitt, were immediately known to British ministers through interception of Prussian correspondence.[27] His intrigues, and his malevolent reports, were naturally resented.[28] Already in May 1763, Britain's representative in Berlin, Andrew Mitchell, had been ordered to work for Michell's recall, but his representations had been ignored. In December, Britain formally requested his withdrawal, but Frederick's ministers still proved obdurate.[29] Eventually, however, the Grenville Ministry had enough of Michell's activities.[30] Sandwich ordered the British minister in Berlin to press the recall. Frederick II grudgingly agreed, with the barbed remark that 'it is me not my Minister you are angry with'.[31] Prussian business in London was handled by an inexperienced secretary of embassy, and in summer 1764, Britain similarly downgraded her representation in Berlin. The breach between the wartime partners was complete.

The Russo-Prussian alliance in April 1764 also focused and stabilized international relations. The fluidity apparent after the Seven Years War was gradually replaced by a more stable and definable international scene. The earlier fluidity had itself largely reflected contemporary uncertainty over Russia's role and this was

---

[26] See e.g. *Pol. Corr.* xxiv. 253.   [27] See e.g. *HMC Eglinton*, 354–5.

[28] Michell's links with the opposition were particularly blatant: CP (Angleterre) 457, fo. 113.

[29] Spencer, *Sandwich Corr.* 111. Sandwich may have been trying to demonstrate the bad state of Anglo-Prussian relations to Austria, whose alliance he was actively seeking: see above, pp. 61–4.

[30] According to the Swedish minister, Nolcken, Michell's comments on the Wilkes affair were one reason for his recall: to KP, 8 June 1764, Roberts Transcripts.

[31] Spencer, *Sandwich Corr.* 151–3, 163–5.

resolved by Catherine's alliance with Prussia. This partnership confronted the other fixed point of the international constellation, the Franco-Spanish alliance. Austria was most affected by this political division of Europe into two mutually antagonistic systems. She was bound by treaty to France but inclined by logic towards Russia. Habsburg ambitions after 1763, whether in south-eastern Europe against the Turks or in Germany against Prussia, could only be realized with St Petersburg's support. While it would be too strong to say that Austria actively sought a Russian alliance, Kaunitz at least appreciated its value. The Russo-Prussian treaty of April 1764 ended any such ideas. Vienna, whose hostility towards Frederick was considerable, had to consolidate her own links with Versailles. This, in turn, made any British *rapprochement* with Vienna even less likely.

The clarification of continental politics and Europe's division into two rival 'systems' had serious implications for London, though these were only slowly and with difficulty perceived there. Britain's struggle with the Bourbons was now of secondary importance. By the 1760s, continental observers no longer saw the western powers as diplomatic pacemakers. To them, the Prusso-Austrian conflict in Germany (though this was temporarily in abeyance) and Franco-Russian rivalry on Europe's northern and eastern fringes, were more fundamental than an Anglo-French struggle increasingly waged overseas.

The Seven Years War, and the Peace of Paris, had created several significant problems for Anglo-French diplomacy. Two of these were, and remained, hardy perennials: Dunkirk and the Newfoundland Fisheries. Dunkirk's historic role as the lair of privateers and pirates, and its potential as a wartime naval base, had made eighteenth-century British statesmen anxious to remove its threat. By the peace settlements at Utrecht (1713) and Aix-la-Chapelle (1748) France had promised to fill in the harbour and demolish the fortifications, but she had found means not to implement these obligations in full. In 1763 the French had agreed to destroy the remaining fortifications and to fill in the *cunette* (ditch), though this prevented Dunkirk's port facilities from silting up. As soon as full diplomatic relations had been restored, British ministers began to insist that this time Louis XV should keep his word.

The French government, naturally enough, was anxious not to implement the peace terms fully, for Choiseul appreciated Dunkirk's value. France was too weak to reject British demands outright. She therefore sought to spin out discussions by agreeing to British and

French commissioners reporting on the actual situation at Dunkirk. The peace terms provided considerable scope for prevarication. Article XIII had laid down that, though the *cunette* and fortifications should immediately be destroyed, 'provision shall be made, at the same time, for the wholesomeness of the air, and for the health of the inhabitants, by some other means, to the satisfaction of the King of Great Britain'.[32] Choiseul seized on this provision and insisted that since the *cunette* was an integral part of the port's sanitation it could not be filled in until alternative provision had been made for the inhabitants' health. Britain's reaction was predictably unsympathetic. Dunkirk's destruction was seen both as a test of France's future intentions and as a symbol of her defeat and political decline. Fear of parliamentary and public opinion prevented even the most minor concessions. But no vigorous action was taken to enforce the treaty. Halifax's handling of the dispute was indecisive, and Britain was further restrained by a concern not to offend Austria: the neighbouring area of Furnes, in the Austrian Netherlands, might be flooded if the *cunette* were totally destroyed.[33] By the beginning of 1764, Britain and France had begun the long and inconclusive diplomatic *pas de deux* which was to continue until the outbreak of the next war, while little was done to reduce Dunkirk's value as a base for privateering.

Anglo-French discussions over the Newfoundland Fisheries were similarly lengthy and inconclusive.[34] The problem was the limited access to the all-important cod-fisheries given to the French by the Peace of Paris. France retained the islands of St Pierre and Miquelon for drying catches. She was also permitted to fish in the Gulf of St Lawrence, but only at a distance of three leagues from the British coasts. Such provisions were easier to draw up on paper than to enforce, and matters were also inflamed by the vigorous action of Britain's local representative, Commander Palliser, who became governor in 1764 and who strove to reduce still further France's share in the Fisheries. French fishermen, who had been expelled during the Seven Years War, encountered considerable difficulties in

---

[32] Z. E. Rashed, *The Peace of Paris 1763* (Liverpool, 1951), 221.

[33] Black, *Natural and Necessary Enemies*, 116–9; P. Coquelle, 'Le Comte de Guerchy, ambassadeur de France à Londres (1763–1767)', *Revue des études historiques*, 64 (1908), 457–8.

[34] The best introduction is G. O. Rothney, 'British Policy in the North American Cod Fisheries with Special Reference to Foreign Competition 1775–1819' (unpublished Ph.D. thesis, University of London, 1939), 1–52. There is a detailed, if rather prolix and Francocentric, account in C. de la Morandière, *Histoire de la pêche française de la morue dans l'Amérique septentrionale* (3 vols.; Paris, 1962–6), ii. 732–932. For the British position see, e.g. *Cal. HO Papers 1760–5*, nos. 1267, 1295, 1395, and 1471.

re-establishing themselves after the peace. Local clashes inevitably followed, which were taken up by the respective governments. Successive British ministries were aware that even the limited access given to France was widely seen as an unwarranted concession and they were also pressed in parliament to take firm action.[35] Both states recognized the broader issue involved. The Fisheries were the principal source of sailors for France's fleet, and Choiseul's plans for naval reconstruction and an eventual war of revenge demanded that her rights should be pushed beyond the letter of the treaty. A restrictive interpretation of the peace by Britain would therefore be a blow against French naval recovery. Strategy thus combined with economics to produce considerable friction and intermittent negotiations over the Newfoundland Banks. The first round took place in 1763–4 but was inconclusive. Thereafter the Fisheries continued to occupy diplomats and their governments, but nothing was achieved as each side successfully evaded the other's demands.

The Seven Years War had created two further problems: the question of the 'Canada Bills', and the cost of maintaining French prisoners of war.[36] These were essentially financial issues, and both states were anxious to reduce the war's immense cost. The Canada Bills occupied both governments on and off throughout the next decade. This peculiarly complex and particularly intractable dispute concerned France's responsibility to compensate stockholders, and particularly British merchants, in the Canada Bills. These were debts owed by Canada's former French government, which had financed its expenditure by issuing and then redeeming paper money. The cost of the Seven Years War had enormously increased the number and value of Canada Bills in circulation, but in the emergency of the British conquest, payments had been suspended in 1759. When France had formally ceded Canada in the peace settlement, she had promised compensation to holders of Canada Bills. The relevant clause was ambiguous and it soon became clear many investors faced considerable losses. Ministers were pressed by merchants in Britain and Canada and by the parliamentary opposition to secure more generous treatment for British stockholders than the French were offering their own subjects. Prolonged discussions produced a settlement, signed in spring 1766, but the issues were too complex to be resolved by a simple convention and diplomatic representations continued over the next ten years.

The final problem was the compensation due to the British

---

[35] See e.g. *Proceedings and Debates*, ii. 43, 44, 46.

[36] A convenient, if rather nationalistic, summary of these two issues is provided by Coquelle, 'Le Comte de Guerchy', 437–47.

government for the maintenance of the relatively large numbers of French prisoners captured during the fighting and only returned at the peace. Two points were at issue: the total sum involved and the time-scale of the repayments. Choiseul wanted to limit any such payment and to spread it over as many years as possible. This was both because of France's straitened financial circumstances and, interestingly enough, because if repayment could be made in stages, Britain would have an incentive to remain at peace while France would gain an essential breathing space.[37] The figures involved were intricate, and at first the British government—as in the parallel negotiations over the Manila Ransom—did not pursue the matter very vigorously. The decisive intervention of the ministry's leader, George Grenville, in summer 1764 gave impetus to these discussions and in the following February a convention was signed, by which France agreed to pay £670,000 spread over four years. This was rather less than Britain had demanded, and it was a minor success for French diplomacy and, in particular, for the ambassador in London, Guerchy.[38]

These four issues, mainly legacies of the Seven Years War, occupied diplomats and caused undoubted bad feeling, but they were not really vital. These exchanges were a consequence, rather than a cause, of Anglo-French rivalry and never led to a major confrontation. Disputes over Dunkirk or the Canada Bills always remained directly controlled by the respective governments, which were careful not to allow the diplomatic temperature to rise too high. Both Britain and France, though for rather different reasons, wished for a period of peace and did not press minor questions too hard. They were less able to control events outside Europe, and the first serious Anglo-Bourbon confrontation after 1763 was brought on by separate incidents at the Bay of Honduras and on Turks Island. The first of these arose between Britain and Spain; the second involved relations with France. The fact that they emerged at almost the same time, together with British assumptions about Bourbon unity, ensured that they soon coalesced into a single quarrel.

The Honduras Bay dispute was a legacy of the peace settlement with Spain.[39] Both governments had been anxious, by the end of

[37] CP (Angleterre) 458, fo. 80.

[38] A separate, though broadly similar, dispute over the English East India Company's claims to be compensated for maintaining French prisoners in India dragged on for several years.

[39] There are several useful accounts of this dispute: see, in particular, V. L. Brown, 'Anglo-Spanish Relations in America in the Closing Years of the Colonial Era', *Hispanic American Historical Review*, 5 (1922), 358–67; Lalaguna Lasala, 'England, Spain and the Family Compact', 120–47, which is particularly valuable for the Spanish side of the story; and N. Tracy, 'The Gunboat Diplomacy of the Government of George Grenville, 1764–1765: The

1762, to conclude a final agreement and this had been largely responsible for the very loose wording of Article XVII of the Peace of Paris which recognized, in general terms and for the first time, Britain's right to cut logwood in return for the destruction of British fortifications in Honduras. At issue was British access to Yucatan and the Bay of Honduras. There had been English settlements here since the second half of the seventeenth century, and over the following two generations logwood cutting had replaced piracy as the main occupation of these outposts. Logwood yielded a vegetable dye essential in the manufacture of British woollen goods, and its price had been pushed down by the breaking of the Spanish monopoly. But by the 1760s logwood had become less important than mahogany cut in the same region. The rapid expansion of English furniture-making had created an increasing demand for this hard wood, and logwood was now cut principally to disguise the illegal cargoes of mahogany, for the export of which Spain never gave permission. This was one foundation of the considerable prosperity of the British settlements, particularly after 1763, whose well-being depended on contraband trade with the nearby Spanish colonies.

Article XVII of the Peace of Paris was ambiguous, and Madrid hoped to interpret it very narrowly and restrict the cutters to as few locations as possible. The Spanish government also argued that the destruction of fortifications implied the evacuation of settlements, but this view of the peace terms was rejected by the British settlers and by the Grenville Ministry as well. Spain feared less the logwood cutting itself than the potential opportunity to expand illegal British trade with her colonies, and she was even worried that Britain might incite unrest among the native Indian population, who were already the target of Protestant missionary activities by the English. At the beginning of February 1764 the Spanish governor of Yucatan, acting on Madrid's instructions, expelled a party of logwood cutters from the River Hondo on the pretext that it had not obtained a formal licence from the Spanish or British authorities. When news of this reached London in mid-June, it was immediately and vigorously

Honduras, Turks' Island and Gambian Incidents', *Historical Journal*, 17 (1974), 711–22, which is essential for the naval dimension; see now his shorter account in N. Tracy, *Navies, Deterrence and American Independence: Britain and Seapower in the 1760s and 1770s* (Vancouver, 1988), 42–8. The complex and confusing situation on the Mosquito Shore is studied by W. S. Sorsby, 'The British Superintendency of the Mosquito Shore, 1749–1787' (unpublished Ph.D. thesis, University of London, 1969), especially pp. 124–55, and F. G. Dawson, 'William Pitt's Settlement of Black River on the Mosquito Shore: A Challenge to Spain in Central America, 1732–87', *Hispanic American Historical Review*, 63 (1983), 677–706. I have also used material from the French archives not consulted by these scholars.

taken up with the Spanish government. This reflected Britain's awareness of Spain's weakness. It was hoped an easy diplomatic victory would boost the Grenville Ministry's domestic prestige.[40] Britain's ambassador in Madrid was the volatile Earl of Rochford, and his bellicose handling of the affair even exceeded the threatening intentions of his superiors. Though Spain did not wish for a serious confrontation, Grimaldi wanted the peace treaty clarified and sought to avoid any immediate settlement. In early August the Spanish foreign minister, alarmed by Rochford's menacing tone, tried to switch discussions to London, but by then the issue of logwood cutting had become linked to, and even dwarfed by, an Anglo-French clash over Turks Island.

Its origins were rather similar. Turks Island was part of a small archipelago lying to the south of the Bahamas and the north of St Dominique. On 1 June 1764 the French governor-general of the Antilles, d'Estaing, had expelled a party collecting salt there, as British subjects from Bermuda had been doing since the later seventeenth century. Turks Island possessed a broader significance than its salt, however. Lying between Jamaica and the American colonies, its good harbours were important commercially. It also offered strategic advantages, both as a base for wartime operations against French colonies and trade and for securing peacetime intelligence about French shipping.[41] When news of d'Estaing's actions reached London at the very beginning of August, diplomatic protests were immediately made to France.

Britain's representations were from the outset shaped by George Grenville's greater role in foreign policy. Hitherto he had been preoccupied with parliament and with internal politics. By the summer of 1764, with the more stable domestic scene, he was beginning to give more attention to Britain's international position. Grenville had been hostile to what he regarded as Bute's lenient peace in 1762–3 and he knew how unpopular the final treaty was in the country at large.[42] He believed the best way to preserve peace was by firm and prompt action to uphold the settlement and to deter Choiseul from launching his war of revenge.[43] His hard-line approach contrasted sharply with his colleagues' moderation. British foreign policy was largely in the hands of Grenville, the two Secretaries of State, and the Duke of Bedford, Lord President of the Council. Bedford was the most moderate, anxious not to press

---

[40] See Nolcken to KP, 3 July 1764, Roberts Transcripts; *Grenville Papers*, ii. 418.
[41] Lalaguna Lasala, 'England, Spain and the Family Compact', 137; cf. *Cal. HO Papers 1760–5*, no. 1398.   [42] Thomas, *British Politics and the Stamp Act Crisis*, 3.
[43] *Grenville Papers*, ii. 423, 510; Lawson, *George Grenville*, 207.

France too hard for fear of provoking a war and believing her re-establishment as a European power a prerequisite of any secure peace.[44] His unusual sympathy for the national enemy led many contemporaries to regard him as pro-French, and throughout the 1760s he certainly maintained the links with France forged during the peace negotiations.[45] Halifax was similarly moderate, though from lethargy rather than from principle, while Sandwich's firmness had been weakened by groundless fears about the navy's fitness for any war. The arguments of his colleagues did lead Grenville to adopt a slightly more moderate stance. By late July 1764, however, he had concluded that the cabinet's firm line was not being upheld by Sandwich and especially Halifax in their discussions with Bourbon diplomats, and it was the leading minister who dictated the vigorous response over Turks Island.[46]

Honduras Bay and Turks Island were close enough for one naval force to be used for both incidents. On 17 August orders were sent to prepare two ships of the line. Simultaneously diplomatic pressure on France and Spain was increased. When Grimaldi refused to give way, the British government immediately ordered two more ships to be fitted out. This show of strength was massive given the limited Bourbon naval forces in the New World and, while Spain appeared impervious, France immediately caved in. Even before news had been received from d'Estaing, the French government had effectively disavowed him and conceded all Britain's demands.[47] D'Estaing was ordered to return British property and France promised reparations. Two British ships were sent to central America, but naval action proved unnecessary, for in mid-September Madrid also capitulated, promising to re-establish the logwood cutters and not to molest them in the future.

Britain's naval might had been decisive in this first test of strength. The mobilization of capital ships was intended less as outright coercion than as a reminder to the Bourbons of their inferiority at sea. This was something ministers took every opportunity to emphasize: in June 1764 the French ambassador was shown round Portsmouth dockyard to underline the strength and preparedness of

[44] For example, over the prisoner of war debts: *Additional Grenville Papers*, ed. Tomlinson, 159–60. The Duke had been equally moderate towards France after the previous war, during his spell as Southern Secretary (1748–51): Black, *Natural and Necessary Enemies*, 54.

[45] *Bedford Corr.* iii. 242, 255–6; cf. below, Ch. 5 for Bedford's continuing links with French diplomats. For France's awareness of the Duke's unusual Francophilia and hopes that this could be exploited, see *Recueil . . . Angleterre, iii*, ed. P. Vaucher, 415–6.

[46] *Grenville Papers*, ii. 511.

[47] CP (Angleterre) 458, fos. 260–1, 264–6; *HMC Eglinton*, 233–5.

the British fleet.[48] Grenville's 'gunboat diplomacy' proved effective against two states that recognized Britain's naval dominance and their own need of peace. The episode set the tone of Anglo-Bourbon relations until at least 1770. Britain, confident and aggressive after her victories in the Seven Years War, was on the offensive and confronted the vulnerable and exposed Spanish American empire and the few remaining French possessions in the New World. Further clashes were to be expected, and it was probable that such confrontations would arise locally. In 1764 France had been drawn into an unwanted confrontation by an enthusiastic subordinate. This emphasized how governments in Europe were not completely in control of diplomatic relations. They were often forced to react to unexpected disputes between official or semi-official local representatives, in the Indian subcontinent as well as in America and, to a lesser extent, in Africa. The fact that the Anglo-Bourbon struggle was, more than ever before, a world-wide one increased the likelihood of such clashes, and metropolitan governments had to decide whether to support or to disavow their agents' actions. Colonial disputes did not determine Anglo-Bourbon relations after 1763; but they provided an unpredictable and potentially unstable element in diplomacy.[49] The considerable initiative local British, French, or Spanish representatives enjoyed in practice was the real origin of several of the most serious diplomatic crises of this period.

The disputes over the logwood cutters and over Turks Island had, above all, demonstrated the decisive importance of naval strength. Between 1763 and 1783 sea power was largely to determine Anglo-Bourbon relations. Naval supremacy had always been important, and it became decisive during and after the Seven Years War.[50] This was inevitable because of the global nature of the struggle; but the three governments became even more aware of the importance of sea power after the Seven Years War. For the first time in peace, Britain and France kept a close watch on their enemy's dockyards.[51] On both sides of the Channel, foreign policy was coming to be based on up-to-date assessments of the size, condition, and state of readiness of the opposing fleets.

This intelligence was collected in various ways. Diplomats and

[48] CP (Angleterre) 457, fos. 204–5. He was not, of course, allowed to see vessels under construction or being repaired.

[49] A particularly clear acknowledgement of this is in Praslin to Choiseul, 11 Feb. 1765, CP (Angleterre) 462, fo. 277.

[50] There are some valuable general comments in the contributions on 'The Second Hundred Years' War (1689–1815)', by J. Meyer and especially by J. Bromley in D. Johnson, F. Bédarida, and F. Crouzet, eds., *Britain and France: Ten Centuries* (London, 1980), 139–72.

[51] Bromley, ibid. 166.

consuls habitually reported any scraps of naval information which came their way, as did merchant captains who visited enemy ports. Occasionally, Britain would send a frigate to 'look into' a French or Spanish port and this could provide a general impression of the condition of the opponents' navies. The more precise information needed could only be collected by systematic espionage. Britain benefited from minor intelligence networks run from the consulates at Turin and Hamburg, but depended principally on the Wolters' agency in Rotterdam.[52] Robert Wolters maintained an impressive network of agents scattered throughout the continental ports and his information was remarkably accurate. Ministers relied increasingly on his agency, particularly after the execution in 1768 of a British agent caught spying in a French dockyard. This discouraged such direct methods. Wolters died in 1771, but his network was continued by his wife and his chief clerk and it remained an important source of naval intelligence until the mid-1780s.

Choiseul's intelligence gathering was even more extensive, and its results were remarkably accurate. Detailed and precise information was provided firstly by the close examination of British newspapers, carried out from 1759 onwards.[53] These furnished regular and surprisingly exact details of the movement and construction of ships, while additional information came from the annual parliamentary vote for the navy. During the 1760s, E.-J. Genet emerged as the French government's expert on the British navy, maintaining up-to-date tables of the location and condition of Britain's entire fleet.[54] His information was considerably increased by the spy network controlled from the French embassy in London and formalized in 1768.[55] This was a remarkably wide-ranging affair. In the 1760s it had agents in the navy board and at Portsmouth and Plymouth, and it was considerably expanded during the 1770s. This network was soon supplying abundant and up-to-date intelligence and was to be active until 1778 and beyond.

The detailed figures for relative naval strength available to both

---

[52] The Turin consulate was particularly important because of its proximity to the great French naval base at Toulon: for examples of the information it could supply, see T. Potter to Shelburne, 20 Apr., 21 May, and 28 May 1768, all in SP 92/73. There is a good study of the Wolters' agency by N. Tracy, 'British Assessments of French and Spanish Naval Reconstruction 1763–1768 [*sic*: for 1778]', *The Mariner's Mirror*, 61 (1975), 73–85. For a slightly later period, there is a useful account by F.-P. Renaut, *Le Secret Service de l'Amirauté britannique au temps de la guerre d'Amérique 1776–1783 (L'espionnage naval au XVIIIᵉ siècle*, i) (Paris, 1936).

[53] For this, see CP (Angleterre) 492, fos. 440–2; cf. AM B⁷ 475, for further evidence of the way newspapers were being used.

[54] See e.g. the remarkably detailed 'État de la Marine Anglaise' [1767], AM B⁷ 473 Pièce 44.

[55] The best introduction is CP (Angleterre) 508, fos. 241–50.

governments gave a new precision to their political calculations.[56] Choiseul's moderation was based on his appreciation of Bourbon naval inferiority; conversely Britain knew her superiority enabled her to intimidate France with comparative safety. Britain maintained her naval lead, in terms of ships of the line, at least until the mid-1770s. Contemporary calculations of naval strength principally took account of 'capital ships' (i.e. mounting fifty guns or more and therefore able to fight in the usual eighteenth-century 'line ahead' formation) which were ready for service or could be made ready within a relatively short period.[57] By this yardstick, Britain enjoyed an enormous lead. Her navy had reached an unprecedented size during the Seven Years War: it was half as big again in 1763 as it had been in 1756.[58] After the Peace of Paris its strength on paper was at least 120 ships of the line and may even have reached 140 or 150.[59] Throughout the 1760s and 1770s ministers adopted a two-power naval standard: the size of the British fleet should equal and preferably exceed the combined strength of the French and Spanish navies.[60] Until the entry of France and Spain into the American War in 1778–9, Britain retained her mathematical superiority and, to a significant extent, based her policy towards the Bourbons on this.

Britain's navy, while certainly not starved of funds, did not have enough to prevent a decline in readiness and effectiveness and this gradually undermined her dominance. The enlarged navy inherited from the Seven Years War would obviously cost more to maintain, but instead the naval budget was an immediate target for Grenvillite economies and it was to be the early 1770s, after the scare of the second Falklands crisis, before it was substantially increased.[61] The income enjoyed by the Earl of Egmont, Sir Charles Saunders, and Sir

[56] This becomes apparent when the figures in Tracy, 'British Assessments', 73–85, are compared with those in H. M. Scott, 'The Importance of Bourbon Naval Reconstruction to the Strategy of Choiseul after the Seven Years' War', *International History Review*, 1 (1979), 17–35.

[57] There is a problem over the definition of 'ship of the line': to the French this meant any vessel mounting 50 guns or more, but to the British it meant *more* than 50 guns. For purposes of comparison, I have adopted the French practice and have tried to adjust the British figures accordingly. There was, in reality, more to it than mere numbers. Both the weight of shot (a British '74' was barely equal to a French '52') and the tasks performed should have been taken into account (J. S. Bromley in Johnson *et al.*, *Britain and France*, 165, 168). But these factors seem to have been ignored at the time.

[58] R. F. Mackay, *Admiral Hawke* (Oxford, 1965), 308.

[59] P. M. Kennedy, *The Rise and Fall of British Naval Mastery* (London, 1976), 106; N. Tracy, 'The Falkland Islands' Crisis of 1770: Use of Naval Force', *English Historical Review*, 90 (1975), 40, where a paper strength of as many as 157 is suggested.

[60] *Grafton Autobiography*, 168, for a characteristic statement of this doctrine.

[61] See the very valuable table setting out expenditure on the navy 1763–81 in Mackay, *Admiral Hawke*, 305.

Edward Hawke, successively First Lords of the Admiralty between 1763 and 1771, was insufficient, and economies were soon being introduced.[62] Some of these were inevitable with the ending of hostilities. Most officers were placed on half-pay and by September 1765 the peacetime establishment had been reduced to 16,000 men. Most ships of the line, and many other vessels, were laid up in 'ordinary', that is they were provided with only skeleton crews and were not provisioned or armed. Financial considerations dictated that smaller, and therefore cheaper, vessels were kept in commission at home or in the West Indies and elsewhere: this was why the Grenville Ministry's decision to arm four capital ships in autumn 1764 showed they were in earnest. Britain's security against surprise attack was entrusted to the system of 'guardships'.[63] These were ships of the line kept permanently, if partially, provisioned, armed, and manned: they had perhaps one-third of their full complement on board. In an emergency the guardships would be ready for action far more quickly than ships kept in 'ordinary', yet they were far cheaper to maintain than vessels fully in commission and offered a means of unobtrusively expanding the fleet during any crisis with the Bourbons. After July 1765 twenty guardships were maintained, and the system was a commendable and successful means of reconciling the financial constraints on the Admiralty with Britain's need for defence. These economies were essential, given the financial regime imposed on the navy after 1763, and, despite the shrill denunciations of the parliamentary opposition, did not seriously weaken British power.

The long-term damage inflicted by governmental economy was more serious. Money was simply not available to remedy the bad conditions in the dockyards, which had inevitably been neglected during the Seven Years War, or to carry out the substantial repairs necessary by 1763. The magnitude of these problems was further increased by the fifty per cent rise in the size of the navy during the war. One result had been that ships were built with 'green wood' (unseasoned timber) and their life expectancy was considerably less than that of vessels built of properly seasoned timber, which might last for twenty years without a major refit. The cumulative impact was felt by the 1770s, when the new First Lord of the Admiralty, the Earl of Sandwich, was confronted with a very serious situation. Even this did not immediately destroy Britain's lead over the Bourbons,

[62] There is room for a full-scale study of the navy and its administration after the Seven Years War: there is a brief account in N. Tracy, *Navies, Deterrence and American Independence: Britain and Seapower in the 1760s and 1770s* (Vancouver, 1988), Ch. 2.
[63] For which see ibid. 10–11.

though. Naval strength was always relative, and the problems of the British navy paled almost into insignificance when placed alongside those of their Bourbon counterparts.

French strategy after 1763 aimed at neutralizing Europe while eventually attacking Britain overseas. This demanded a navy strong enough to defeat the formidable British fleet.[64] Shortly after the Peace of Paris, Choiseul calculated that France would need 80 ships of the line and Spain 60 before their united fleets could challenge Britain: since the British navy was believed to have around 140 or 150 capital ships, the doctrine of naval parity demanded the combined Bourbon navies should be roughly equal. Choiseul, as navy minister in the early years of peace, devoted his energy to constructing a powerful French fleet. The task was formidable, though he initially believed it could be accomplished in four or five years. By the end of the Seven Years War, the French navy was in a lamentable condition. France also lacked the shore facilities essential if new ships were to be built and existing vessels repaired and overhauled. Choiseul introduced some important administrative reforms and brought about a real improvement in the principal ports. But France never possessed the *matériel* (particularly timber), manpower, and, above all, money essential to realize his plans. Though considerable progress was made, the initial target of eighty of the line remained a distant prospect. Choiseul did bring about a notable improvement in the fleet's effective strength and readiness, and in the long term his work increased the naval threat which Britain had to face by the later 1770s. In the short term his grandiose schemes were a failure.

Spain's parallel attempts to rebuild her shattered navy were even less successful. In the early years of peace Choiseul repeatedly urged the Spanish government to embark on a massive naval programme. Madrid was uncomfortably aware of her scattered empire's vulnerability to British attacks and gave colonial defence a higher priority than naval reconstruction. In any case, the funds available were extremely limited and little progress was made at first towards remedying the poor condition of the Spanish fleet. As with France, naval reconstruction was not a total failure. By the later 1760s the enlarged Spanish navy was beginning to become a significant factor in Anglo-Bourbon relations and one which British ministers were forced to take increasingly seriously.

The Bourbons' inability to rebuild their shattered fleets with any

---

[64] Cf. Scott, 'The Importance of Bourbon Naval Reconstruction', 17–35, for this and the following two paragraphs.

speed was the decisive factor in relations until the very end of the 1760s and even beyond. This failure obliged Choiseul repeatedly to put back his date for the war of revenge. In the final stages of the Seven Years War he had believed France and Spain would be in a position to fight by 1767, but within a year this date became 1768. It was once again put back in 1767, this time until 1770; yet in 1770 Choiseul still believed that France at least was not yet fully prepared to fight Britain. Aware of the risk of exposing the Bourbons to another humiliating defeat, the French foreign minister was obliged to pursue a moderate and generally pacific policy towards Britain at least until the final months of his ministry. Though his deep hostility was never in doubt, he quickly accepted that his war of revenge could not be launched until France and Spain had rebuilt their navies. These efforts were quickly known to British ministers through their intelligence network and did cause the cabinet some superficial concern. But reports of French and Spanish activity soon emphasized the slow progress being made and the continuing and considerable inferiority of the Bourbon fleets.[65]

Britain's supremacy at sea had been the principal reason for Bourbon moderation over Honduras Bay and Turks Island. A further illustration of this basic fact of political life and a striking example of the effectiveness of Britain's 'gunboat diplomacy' was provided in early 1765 by an Anglo-French dispute over the Gambia.[66] During the Seven Years War the French had been expelled from their post at Albreda on the river Gambia, but they returned at the peace and began to fortify it. Though Senegal had been handed over to Britain by the settlement, no mention had been made of the Gambia. The river Gambia was important principally because of the trade in negro slaves, and Britain may have wanted to use its acquisition of Senegal to enforce a commercial monopoly. The British settlement located up river from Albreda immediately protested to London at French actions. Nothing was done until early in October 1764 when, shortly after Spain's capitulation over the logwood cutters, the cabinet decided that the small squadron usually sent to West Africa each year should simply eject the French from Fort Albreda. The squadron was strengthened by the replacement of one of its ships by a capital vessel, and at the beginning of January 1765 it sailed with highly ambiguous orders on how to deal with any French resistance.

Britain's intention had been to present France with a *fait accompli*: no diplomatic representations had been made, though the British

[65] Tracy, 'British Assessments', 73–85.
[66] For this incident, see Tracy, 'The Gunboat Diplomacy . . . of George Grenville', 722–8, Tracy, *Navies, Deterrence and American Independence*, 48–53, and CP (Angleterre) 462.

ambassador in Paris had been informed of the plan to expel the French. In early January 1765 the French embassy in London heard of the expedition. Guerchy's resulting enquiries were met by some bland assurances from Halifax and on the 20th the ambassador formally requested clarification. Secrecy was now replaced by bravado. Flushed by recent successes over the logwood cutters and Turks Island, Britain announced that France must concede all her demands *before* the orders given to the squadron sent to West Africa would be countermanded. The French government was outraged and the foreign minister, Praslin, bluntly told Britain's ambassador Hertford that 'this method of proceeding was not well calculated to support the present amicable disposition which prevailed between the two courts'.[67] The French ministry also recognized they had to comply with Britain's request. Denying any intention of forcibly trading on the Gambia or fortifying Albreda, France conceded the essential British demands and peace was preserved.

These three incidents were relatively minor, but they were a reminder—if any was needed—of the extent of Anglo-Bourbon rivalry. The first disputes in summer 1764 had been accompanied by a new diplomatic initiative in Sweden. This inaugurated a period when northern Europe assumed an unusual importance for British foreign policy. This was initially a move against France's growing influence at Stockholm, part of that reflex which ensured Choiseul's intrigues would everywhere be opposed. It quickly became a factor in Anglo-Russian diplomacy as well, as both states came to view Sweden as a testing ground for future intentions.

Relations had swiftly deteriorated after the collapse of alliance negotiations at the end of 1763. Russia's disappointment and resentment were made very clear and, particularly after the conclusion of the Prussian treaty in spring 1764, Panin considerably increased his terms for an alliance. These became both the 'Turkish clause' and effective British support, in Poland and in the Baltic generally.[68] It was on these points that future talks foundered. Secure in the alliance with Prussia, Catherine II and Panin now had less reason to make the concessions they had been prepared for immediately after Augustus III's death. In particular they were resolved Britain would not secure a treaty without promising assistance in any Turkish war. Frederick II was also determined no future Russian ally would pay a lower price than he had. There was still a place for Britain in the 'Northern

---

[67] Quoted by Tracy, 'The Gunboat Diplomacy ... of George Grenville', 726; cf. CP (Angleterre) 462, fo. 111.

[68] Martens, *Recueil des traités*, ix(x). 225–6; cf. Add. MSS 6826, fo. 81.

System', but the terms for admission were higher and would be dictated by Russia.

The British government, for its part, showed no sign of abandoning its position over alliances in general and subsidies in particular. After the negotiations collapsed in 1763, ministers believed the next move was up to Russia. Discussions between the two states quickly became little more than the mindless reiteration of entrenched positions. This coolness spread to the commercial negotiations, and Sandwich was soon admitting nothing would be accomplished until Britain's ineffective and, by now, discredited ambassador was replaced. Contemporaries found Buckinghamshire pompous and boring.[69] He had compounded this limited competence by a tiresome pursuit of detail which exasperated most people, and in particular Sandwich. His principal offence had been a clumsy attempt in summer 1763 to bribe the Russian Vice-Chancellor, M. L. Vorontsov.[70] The ambassador had been so inept as to put this offer in writing, for which he had been sharply rebuked by the British government.

By early 1764 it was obvious that Buckinghamshire would have to leave St Petersburg. His successor, Sir George Macartney, was offered the post in May 1764, but it was October before he was formally appointed Envoy Extraordinary and the end of December before he reached Russia.[71] These months saw a shift in attitudes. Each state continued to want an alliance, but insisted it should be concluded on its own terms. Both also came to see Sweden, rather than Poland, as the testing ground. Co-operation in Stockholm might be a way round the impasse represented by the 'Turkish clause' and Britain's refusal of a peacetime subsidy, though at first the situation there merely revealed the distance separating the two states.

During her 'Age of Liberty' Sweden had become an arena for great-power rivalry, and this reached its peak in the 1760s. After Charles XII's death in 1718, the monarch became the prisoner of the Estates and Swedish domestic politics developed into a party dogfight. Since the end of the 1730s the Hats had been in the ascendant. They wanted revenge on Russia and were therefore supported by France. They aimed to recover some of the lands lost at the end of the Great Northern War, though their attack on Russia in 1741 had led to defeat and further territorial losses. By the 1760s, their ascendancy was coming to an end. The Hats' ill-judged foreign policy had led to the unsuccessful and expensive intervention against

[69] For example, Bérenger's verdict, quoted by W. F. Reddaway, 'Macartney in Russia, 1765–67', *Cambridge Historical Journal*, 3 (1929–31), 260–94, at p. 264.
[70] Roberts, *Macartney in Russia*, 12.
[71] Ibid. 3–4.

Prussia in the Seven Years War. At the same time, their corruption further weakened their hold on power.

Their principal domestic opponents were the Caps, who had been supported since the 1740s by Russia and, briefly, by Britain. After the Diet of 1760–2, they appeared about to take power. The third element was the monarchy, and the court was to play an increasingly important role during the 1760s. The Constitution of 1720 had placed the monarch in fetters. A pensioner king merely approved the Estates' decisions. After an attempted royalist coup in 1756, further restrictions were placed on Adolf Frederik's authority. These were unacceptable to the resourceful and ambitious Queen, the Prussian King's sister, Lovisa Ulrika. Her complex ambitions were the most puzzling component in Sweden's confused domestic strife.

During this period, Russia, France, and Britain were all prepared to expend much energy and resources in Stockholm. Russia's concern was rooted in her vulnerable north-western frontier, and it was increased by Catherine's preoccupation with Poland and her anxieties about the Turks. Russia's policy since the 1740s had been to support the Caps and to uphold the Constitution of 1720, which seemed to make Sweden less of a threat by restricting royal authority and making foreign initiatives more difficult. Her permanent enemy, in Sweden as throughout northern and eastern Europe, was France. In the 1760s Stockholm assumed a higher place in French priorities. The collapse of the French position in Poland, which resulted from her indifference at the time of Poniatowski's election, and the seeming lethargy of the Turks, led Choiseul to view Sweden as the most promising arena for his anti-Russian initiatives. Though its objectives were to change periodically, French diplomacy aimed in the early years of peace to support the Hats, to align them with the court, and to increase royal power. France's involvement furnished one important reason for British ministers to interest themselves in Swedish politics, particularly since they knew of Choiseul's policy through interception of French correspondence in Hanover.[72]

The Baltic was important as the principal source of the naval stores on which British maritime supremacy was based. This made Britain a supporter of the 'Tranquillity of the North' and in the 1740s it had led her to support the Caps. The Seven Years War had demonstrated both the extent and the dangers of French influence in the north. France's client, Sweden, had joined the anti-Prussian coalition in 1757, and a real threat to Britain's vital naval stores had been posed

[72] For which see B. Petersson, ' "The Correspondent in Paris": En engelsk informationskälla under 1700-talet', *Scandia*, 28 (1962), 387–99; and H. Stiegung, *Den engelska underrättelseverksamheten rörande Sverige under 1700-talet* (Stockholm, 1961).

by the embryonic Scandinavian Armed Neutrality of 1759. The Hats' disarray at the end of the war also offered Britain the opportunity to overthrow French influence once and for all. A further reason for involvement came to be the desire to improve relations with Russia.

This strategy emerged in 1764–5 and was principally the creation of a remarkable diplomat, Sir John Goodricke.[73] He had been appointed to Stockholm in March 1758, to help Prussia by encouraging Sweden to make peace. The Swedish Hat government, fearing an English minister might aid the court to repeat the coup of 1756, refused to admit him. Goodricke had spent the next six years in the uncongenial surroundings of Copenhagen. He put this time to very good use and acquired a thorough knowledge of Sweden's language and institutions, accomplishments probably unique among eighteenth-century British diplomats. By 1763–4 Sweden's chronically bad financial position and the hope that Britain might make up for the deficiencies caused by France's failure to pay the subsidy arrears promptly, encouraged the Hats to re-establish diplomatic relations. Goodricke arrived in Stockholm in April 1764, as party strife was approaching boiling point. The chaotic state of Swedish finances, tottering on the edge of outright bankruptcy, suggested an extraordinary Diet might have to be called. The ruling Hats, aware of their unpopularity, naturally resisted this, but in September 1764 they were forced to summon one for the following January.

The calling of this Diet ended British indecision. The resumption of normal relations did not commit London to an active policy. Nor, despite Sandwich's later attempts to argue the contrary, had Goodricke been sent to oblige Catherine II. Britain's attitude to Russia remained cool, after the failure of negotiations in 1763–4 and the conclusion of the Russo-Prussian treaty, and this inevitably affected British policy in Sweden. Ministers accepted the need to oppose France wherever her influence was manifest, but Sandwich was not initially inclined to meddle at Stockholm, particularly since this would cost money: not merely for bribery but perhaps for a subsidy as well. By degrees Goodricke persuaded his superiors French power might be toppled and it was even worth expending money to achieve this. During the summer and autumn of 1764 Goodricke convinced the Northern Secretary that a further Franco-Swedish treaty might put Sweden's fleet at Choiseul's disposal. This was a more potent argument to a navy-minded minister such as Sandwich than the vague prospect of an improvement in the balance of trade also held out as bait. By autumn 1764 the Northern

[73] Roberts, *British Diplomacy*, chs. 1 and 2. This is essentially a political biography of Goodricke.

Secretary was moving towards intervention, and he was forced to a decision by the calling of the Diet in September for the following year. Britain now agreed to spend money on an equal basis with Russia and to send £4,000 to Goodricke, though in the event Panin sent three times as much to Osterman.

The partnership between Goodricke and the shrewd and resourceful Osterman was an important factor in Anglo-Russian relations. Their co-operation was unusually close and extremely harmonious, and it survived the baffling vicissitudes of British policy at Stockholm. This was all the more remarkable since Goodricke was often kept short of funds in a capital where money was all-important; on occasions he depended on Osterman's private credit. Panin always realized Russia could not intervene too openly, because she was a close and apparently menacing neighbour. He therefore viewed Britain as a convenient proxy, capable of playing a role St Petersburg could not publicly adopt. Britain should provide a subsidy to keep Sweden out of the French camp, while Russia provided significant funds for bribery. Panin's strategy, however, convinced British ministers that Russia wanted to throw the entire expense on them, and this worsened relations.[74] Even in 1764–5, at the height of the Goodricke–Osterman co-operation, Sandwich was suspicious of Russian intentions.[75]

The Cap triumph in the Diet of 1765 was not simply due to the money paid out by Goodricke and Osterman; the French ambassador, Breteuil, spent more to support the defeated Hats.[76] The two ministers played a significant part in counselling and supporting the Caps, and Goodricke established the successful strategy of concentrating on the Estate of Burghers. Yet this triumph was not followed up by Sandwich. British suspicions, and specifically the fear they might be called on to provide a subsidy to Sweden, now surfaced. Ministers refused funds to consolidate the initial Cap triumph in the Diet elections and, for much of 1765, Goodricke was critically short of money, though he skilfully kept his friends together. The successful co-operation in Stockholm, however, at first had little impact on the broader course of Anglo-Russian diplomacy.

The second half of the Grenville Ministry also saw significant changes in the official attitude towards Vienna.[77] Britain's policy during the next generation took shape in the aftermath of the

---

[74] Buckinghamshire had reported late in 1764 that Panin was 'determined to throw . . . much of the expense [of the Northern System] upon England': 6 Nov. 1764, *Sbornik*, xii. 188.

[75] Ibid. xii. 196–7.

[76] Roberts, *British Diplomacy*, 436–7 n. 213, endorsing M. Metcalf's verdict in *Russia, England and Swedish Party Politics*, 140–1.

[77] The analysis which follows is based on the official diplomatic dispatches in SP 80/199 ff.

Austrian rebuff in 1763–4. Though the seriousness of this was not admitted, a more realistic approach did emerge. Ministers still expected new links, but accepted they would take several years. However, their faith in the Old System had not been seriously weakened. The thought that the Austro-French alliance might have destroyed it for the foreseeable future does not seem to have occurred to them.

These assumptions were based on a false premiss. Kaunitz's undoubted desire for good relations was viewed too optimistically in London. After the Seven Years War, Britain was usually a minor factor in Habsburg policy. Until Joseph II's accession to sole power in late 1780, that strategy was largely determined by the Chancellor. Kaunitz's view was remarkably consistent.[78] He was pursuing essentially the same policy for the same reasons in the 1770s as in the 1760s or even the 1750s. It was the corollary of his loyalty to Versailles. He had made his choice between 1749 and 1756 and saw no reason to reverse it. Alliance with Britain had nothing to recommend it, given that Austria's principal enemies were now Prussia and the Turks, and London would not help against either. As long as the Russian alliance was out of reach, France was Vienna's only possible partner.

Kaunitz maintained this alignment during the generation after the Seven Years War. Its original purpose (French aid to defeat Prussia) had not been achieved; yet France contributed far more to the Habsburg war effort between 1756 and 1763 than Britain had done during the War of the Austrian Succession, and her alliance also strengthened Vienna's position in Italy and in the Low Countries. France remained permanently involved on the continent after 1763 by political tradition and geography. This contrasted sharply with London's increasingly insular policies, which were a poor recommendation to any prospective partner. Kaunitz also believed Britain's parliamentary system, with its inherent instability, made her a less reliable ally than absolutist states, and this concern was increased by the political upheavals during the first decade of George III's reign.[79] But these were always minor considerations. Austria's Chancellor maintained the French alliance as the best available guarantee of peace and security.

[78] The principal sources for his attitude are the immensely detailed 'Instructions' for Seilern, 3 Sept. 1763, HHStA England-Korrespondenz, 109, and the rather less illuminating 'Instructions' for Belgioioso, 22 Sept. 1770, ibid. 115, and it is on these that the succeeding analysis is based.

[79] After 1763, Austrian diplomats had instructions to be particularly attentive to possible ministerial changes and they reported—and speculated—on these at length, which in turn confirmed Kaunitz's suspicions about parliamentary government: see their reports in HHStA England-Korrespondenz 109 ff.

This determined his attitude towards Britain. Anglo-French rivalry precluded close relations between Vienna and London, and this was accepted by Kaunitz, determined not to compromise his fundamental links with France. But whereas British ministers saw relations largely in terms of an alliance, the Chancellor took a broader view, believing they could contribute to his overall aims. Though architect of the Diplomatic Revolution, he was not fundamentally hostile towards Britain. He certainly resented London's control over Austrian policy during the first half of the eighteenth century and believed the British alliance was now redundant. This had not blinded him to the value of continued good relations, which he had tried to cultivate during the 1750s, always hoping for Britain's neutrality in the continental war. This remained his objective after 1763. There were two main reasons for this. Kaunitz wanted to keep Britain out of the Prussian camp, because he could never forget she had fought the Seven Years War in partnership with Austria's deadly enemy. His rigidly symmetrical approach led him to conclude Britain would ally with the German power not aligned with France. It suggested his own French alliance would encourage new Anglo-Prussian links. This became even more serious after the Russo–Prussian alliance in April 1764, for he believed Britain to be Russia's natural ally. There was far less danger of an Anglo-Prussian *rapprochement* than Kaunitz feared, yet this anxiety influencd the Chancellor's policy towards London. Kaunitz also wanted good relations in order to retain the option—and it was never more than this—of a future English alliance, which might be forced on Austria should the French alignment collapse. It was an insurance policy on which the premiums were strikingly low: all that was needed was British friendship. Given London's preoccupation with the Old System, Anglo-Austrian diplomacy quickly became and long remained remarkably harmonious. Both states also wished for peace in Europe and this encouraged good relations. British ministers, however, interpreted these as further proof of the Old System's inevitability. This, in turn, reinforced Britain's new strategy. It was announced in embryonic form by Sandwich in late January 1764 and was to be echoed by every Northern Secretary for the next decade and more. It did not emerge overnight: the principles laid down by Sandwich and elaborated by Stormont gradually hardened into a doctrine.[80] The new policy was first fully expressed early in

[80] The earliest complete statement is two dispatches written from the Austrian capital in summer 1764: Stormont to Sandwich, 18 July and 24 Aug. 1764, SP 80/201. There is an obvious analogy here with Goodricke's role in the evolution of British policy in Sweden: cf. above, pp. 83–4.

1765. Any resumption of the Old System, the Northern Secretary declared,

must be a work of time, and depend upon events; it would be a great indiscretion in us were we not to do everything that prudence requires to pave the way for a reunion of measures with the House of Austria and to remain in a situation to profit of those events, whenever they happen.[81]

This represented a coherent attempt to adjust to Austria's refusal to consider any new links, and also sheds light on British thinking about alliances.

Britain believed she should be 'reserved' in negotiation and, after an initial approach, any further initiative must come from the prospective ally.[82] This doctrine was apparent in Anglo-Russian negotiations during the early years of peace, and it was central to the view of the Austrian alliance. Though Britain continued to hope for new links, the next formal overtures were delayed until 1780–1. George III and his ministers continually stressed the merits of the Old System to the Austrian ambassador in London, and similar hints were dropped in Vienna, but Britain's strategy did not go beyond this. It was not primarily political realism. The Austro-French alliance was never seen as more than a transient barrier. Ministers actually believed Austria would, sooner or later, be anxious to conclude a new treaty. All Britain should do was to be prepared to receive the Habsburgs back when they abandoned, in the current diplomatic refrain, their 'unhappy system', their 'unnatural alliance', in favour of the 'old and natural alliance'. Ministers had demonstrated goodwill; it was up to Austria to make the next move.

Britain believed the Old System's revival would be facilitated by a political upheaval in Vienna. Since ministers assumed the alliance was 'natural', they concluded the alignment which had replaced it in 1756 had resulted from Kaunitz's malign influence,[83] and that his retirement would lead to a speedy revival of the old links. The Chancellor was always threatening to resign. It encouraged Stormont and his superiors to believe he would soon leave office, and this would be followed by the triumph of the Old System's many friends at Vienna, an exiguous group that existed largely in the ambassador's

[81] Sandwich to Stormont, Most Secret, 8 Jan. 1765, printed in Spencer, *Sandwich Corr.* 264.
[82] Stowe 259, fos. 1–2.
[83] This had been exactly Newcastle's response to the Franco-Austrian alliance in 1756: M. Schlenke, *England und das friderizianische Preussen 1740–1763* (Freiburg and Munich, 1963), 195; Britain's minister in Vienna had responded similarly: R. Waddington, *Louis XV et le renversement des alliances* (Paris, 1896), 346.

imagination.[84] Advocates of an English alliance were singularly lacking within Vienna's corridors of power.

Kaunitz's failure to resign gradually convinced Britain he would never retire. Indeed, in time, Stormont appreciated he might be preferable to any alternative. Implict was a recognition that the new alliance would be longer delayed than first anticipated, and this modified British thinking. London's hopes came to be focused on Joseph II, who became Emperor and Co-Regent on the death of Francis Stephen of Lorraine in August 1765. Ministers realized nothing could be expected from Maria Theresa, who retained painful memories of her treatment in the 1740s, when London had coerced Austria into following a largely British policy. In any case, the Empress-Queen, as Stormont continually pointed out, was dominated by Kaunitz and his French ways. Joseph II was a rather different matter, and it was on the Emperor Britain's hopes came to rest.

This policy was once again based on a false premiss. Stormont and his superiors rapidly concluded Joseph was the son of his Lorraine father and therefore anti-French: Francis Stephen had never forgiven Louis XV's state for the way it had forced him to leave his beloved Duchy for Tuscany at the end of the 1730s. Though in the 1760s at least Joseph II was an orthodox supporter of the French alliance, he was always potentially antagonistic towards France.[85] By the 1770s, French opposition, particularly within the *Reich*, together with his own appreciation of the value of a Russian alliance, were turning the Emperor away from Versailles. British ministers, accustomed to view all diplomacy through the lens of their own struggle with France, mistakenly assumed he was therefore pro-English. Though they recognized that, at least during the early years of the co-regency, Joseph II's influence would not be sufficient to reverse Habsburg policy, they believed—or simply hoped—it would be a different matter when he secured full power: then, they expected, he would immediately break with France and unite with Britain. These expectations were apparent in the Northern Secretary's remarks in 1769 that Austro-French friendship was very precarious and only hung on Maria Theresa's life, and that the Emperor was a sworn enemy of all things French.[86] That Joseph II might be pro-Austrian never seems to have occurred to British observers.

---

[84]   For which see e.g. Stormont to Sandwich, 4 Jan. 1764, SP 80/200, and the more extreme statement in the ambassador's secret letter of 23 Jan. 1765, Stormont Papers, Letter-Book 506, fo. 45.
[85]   See e.g. his views in the 'Tableau Générale' of 1768: HHStA Familienarchiv Sammelbände, 88, fos. 121–5. I am grateful to Prof. Derek Beales for drawing this document to my attention and for generously loaning me his copy.   [86]   *Pol. Corr.* xxix. 8 n. 5.

The mid-1760s witnessed this modification of British strategy which became that of joining the 'reversionary interest' at the Habsburg court, abandoning present chances for future expectations. The continuing faith in the Old System was part of a central problem of foreign policy during the 1760s and 1770s. In retrospect, this dedication to the Austrian alliance, together with the language in which it was clothed, appear anachronistic, part of the outdated thinking which lay behind Britain's diplomacy.[87] At the time, it seemed perfectly logical to look towards the Habsburgs. The Old System had sought to restrain France. The need for such restraint was more apparent than ever after 1763, particularly now the Dutch Republic had ceased to be an effective political force. Britain remained menaced by France, and also feared Spain's hostility. She, therefore, looked for an Austrian alliance against the Bourbons. The problem, as ministers came dimly and belatedly to realize, was that European diplomacy was coming to revolve around the eastern powers and not the Anglo-French struggle. The burden under which British diplomacy now laboured was that alliances still appeared essential, but the capacity of traditional policies to produce them was vanishing.

[87] In 1767, for example, Britain's Northern Secretary could write of his dread of seeing 'the liberties of Europe left, as it were, at the mercy of the House of Bourbon'; while as late as 1780, one of his successors could refer to the need for 'an effectual Barrier against the encroachments of the House of Bourbon': Conway to Stormont, 13 Jan. 1767, SP 80/204; Stormont to Sir R. M. Keith, Most Confidential, 12 Dec. 1780, SP 80/223.

5

The Decline of British Diplomacy, 1765–1768

THE Grenville Ministry's modest record in foreign affairs proved far superior to that of their political successors. During the next three years, acute ministerial instability and serious problems in America and over the East India Company helped to undermine British diplomacy. But the main reason for the decline was the weakness, irresolution, ignorance, and at times incompetence of the ministers responsible for foreign policy. In Europe, as at home and in the American colonies, Britain lost her way primarily because of the limitations of her statesmen.[1]

Between the fall of the Grenville Ministry in summer 1765 and the appointment of the Earl of Rochford to the Northern Department in October 1768, five men passed through the Secretaries' office: the Duke of Grafton, H. S. Conway, the Duke of Richmond, the Earl of Shelburne, and Viscount Weymouth. Only one possessed any previous diplomatic experience, and that was very limited: Richmond had been ambassador in Paris for three months in 1765–6. None had held a major government post and they were, by the standards of eighteenth-century ministries, unusually young: their average age on assuming office as Secretary of State was thirty-four, while that of the other ministers directly responsible for foreign policy between 1763 and 1783 was forty-four upon entering office.[2] Their inexperience was soon apparent to foreign diplomats and this certainly helped to lower Britain's prestige abroad.[3] But it was their growing indifference to Europe, together with the feebleness with which foreign policy was conducted, which did most to undermine Britain's international position.

The Grenville Ministry's death-throes finally ended in July 1765.

[1] P. Langford, *The First Rockingham Administration 1765–1766* (Oxford, 1973), 3. This study also contains (pp. 84–92) a very efficient summary of the Rockingham–Cumberland Ministry's foreign policy.

[2] Grafton had been born in 1735, Conway in 1719, Richmond in 1735, Shelburne in 1737, and Weymouth in 1734.

[3] See e.g. Seilern's cool verdict: to Kaunitz, 19 July 1765, HHStA, England-Korrespondenz III.

An administration headed by Lord Rockingham and, until his death at the end of October 1765, the Duke of Cumberland came into power determined to expose the supposed failings of their predecessors. The two Secretaries of State were the Duke of Grafton, who held the Northern Department, and H. S. Conway, and they were far from an ideal team. Grafton was energetic, but young, inexperienced, and nervous, while Conway was notoriously indecisive. This was also the only occasion during the dozen years of peace after 1763 when two inexperienced newcomers became Secretaries of State simultaneously.[4] However, they set to work with a will to remedy the neglect of foreign affairs during the Grenville Ministry's final months, when the Regency Bill had monopolized the cabinet's attention.

Their gaze fell first on relations with the Bourbons and, in particular, on the Manila Ransom. This complex dispute had languished during the second half of the Grenville Ministry, principally because an integral part of it, the case of the ship the *Santissima Trinidad*, was before the Lords of Appeal. The origin of the so-called Manila Ransom was Britain's capture of the capital of the Spanish Philippines in early October 1762.[5] This expedition had been mounted from India, and its target had been Manila's fabled bullion. The acting Spanish governor, Archbishop Rojo, had promised the British captors (who had a financial interest in the expedition's success) a ransom of four million Spanish dollars, in order to prevent the town being looted. Half of this was to be paid in cash and the rest from the cargo of the *Filipino*, which belonged to the city's inhabitants and was expected to arrive from Acapulco with their goods and bullion on board. In fact the *Filipino* escaped capture and the British instead took the *Santissima Trinidad*, which they claimed was not part of the ransom but lawful prize.

It proved impossible to collect the two million dollars due from Manila's inhabitants, or even the reduced figure of one million which was agreed when these difficulties became apparent: six months after the city's surrender only some 600,000 dollars had been collected. In February 1763 the commander of the departing British fleet, Admiral

---

[4] See Roberts, *British Diplomacy*, 179–212 *passim*; cf. *Sbornik*, lviii. 472; *Rockingham Memoirs*, i. 224; M. M. Escott, 'Britain's Relations with France and Spain, 1763–1771' (unpublished Ph.D., University of Wales, 1988), 32.

[5] For the Manila Ransom and the Rockinghams' handling of it, see G. W. Rice, 'Great Britain, the Manila Ransom and the First Falkland Islands Dispute with Spain, 1766', *International History Review*, 2 (1980), 389–94; E. A. Julian, 'British Projects and Activities in the Philippines: 1759–1805' (unpublished Ph.D. thesis, University of London, 1963), which corrects the usual version of how the ransom originated; and Lalaguna Lasala, 'England, Spain and the Family Compact', 155–246 *passim*.

Cornish, threatened to plunder the city a second time if the outstanding ransom was not paid immediately. Archbishop Rojo now signed bills drawn on the Spanish treasury for the two million expected from the *Filipino*: these were the origin of the Manila Ransom. The British claim for the half of the ransom which Rojo had promised Madrid would pay was complicated by three further issues. The original agreement signed in October 1762 had stipulated that the four million dollars was in return for the captors' not sacking the town, but the British commander had been unable to prevent his men looting and it had been almost two days before order had been restored. Secondly, the *Santissima Trinidad* became the subject of a prolonged legal dispute. The British captors argued that she was lawful prize and therefore quite separate from the ransom issue. Spain denied this, asserting that the October agreement had also provided for freedom of commerce on the high seas after Manila's capitulation; the matter was soon being fought out in the British courts. Finally, Archbishop Rojo's conduct came under close scrutiny by Madrid. His authority to act as governor-general of the Philippines after the death of the official Spanish administrator was not clear, and this could be used to question Spain's obligation to pay the ransom, particularly since the Archbishop appeared to have collaborated with the British after the city's capture. There was ample scope for prevarication when the already complex question of the Manila Ransom was taken up between the two courts.

Britain's claim for the ransom dominated relations in the mid-1760s. The first formal demand had been made as long ago as December 1763. Madrid's reply was that Rojo had no authority whatsoever to draw on the Spanish crown, which would not pay the two million dollars. But the Spanish foreign minister Grimaldi was aware of Spain's inability to resist if Britain pressed the claim, and he therefore played for time. The case of the *Santissima Trinidad* provided an admirable way of prolonging the dispute. Spain contended that this galleon was not lawful prize, since it had been taken on the high seas after the capitulation had been signed. When the British High Court of Admiralty pronounced in November 1763 that its seizure had been legal, the Spanish ambassador put in an appeal.[6] This began a year later, in November 1764, and it was not dismissed until August 1765, the month after the formation of the Rockingham Ministry.

Britain now returned to the issue of the ransom and in September

---

[6] Britain's position is set out in a long opinion by the Advocate-General, James Marriott, 23 Oct. 1764, *Cal. HO Papers 1760–5*, no. 1486.

1765 vigorous representations were made in Madrid for the payment of the full sum.[7] Spain again refused and now produced an additional argument: that the continued looting for forty hours after the capitulation's signature broke its terms and therefore invalidated the ransom itself. In fact, Britain had a good case for repayment and, crucially, had the actual bills signed by Rojo.[8] This was the measure of the British reply, delayed until December 1765, because Conway was seriously ill. In the interim the ambassador in Madrid, on his own initiative, had made considerable progress towards securing payment. The Earl of Rochford was a career diplomat, yet he lacked political connections at home and therefore needed a triumph to make his reputation. In the closing months of 1765 he pursued the ransom as vigorously as he dared.[9] His role in the earlier dispute over the logwood cutters had convinced him that Madrid would yield to the threat of war, and he knew from his considerable intelligence network that Spain could not fight, given the wretched state of her armed forces. His rough handling of Spanish ministers and his periodic hints of Britain's willingness to use force certainly went beyond the intentions of his superiors, but they were remarkably effective.[10] Rochford's belligerent stance had been reported to Choiseul, who immediately warned Grimaldi that the Bourbons were not yet ready for a war and that Madrid would probably have to pay the ransom. In January 1766 the Spanish foreign minister was driven to acknowledge Spain's responsibility for the debt, provided that it could be authenticated. But he continued to play for time, alleging his ignorance of the details of the capitulation and using Rojo's death in January 1764 as the excuse for a further delay.

Grimaldi, at Choiseul's suggestion, now produced an unexpected trump from Spain's feeble diplomatic hand: the idea that the whole dispute should go to arbitration. The suggestion of the Prussian King, Frederick II, as arbiter, was similarly inspired. Behind this proposal lay a broader purpose. Choiseul had been alarmed by signs of an Anglo-Prussian *rapprochement* during the second half of 1765. Relations between London and Potsdam were distant and periodically acrimonious, when the Rockingham Ministry took power. The outgoing Northern Secretary, Sandwich, had recently ordered Andrew Mitchell to send his formal letters of recall to Berlin to be

[7] *Grenville Papers*, iii. 88; cf. *HMC Eglinton*, 396.

[8] Rice, 'Great Britain, the Manila Ransom', 391.

[9] G. W. Rice, 'An Aspect of European Diplomacy in the Mid-Eighteenth Century: The Diplomatic Career of the Fourth Earl of Rochford at Turin, Madrid and Paris, 1749–1768' (unpublished Ph.D. thesis, University of Canterbury, New Zealand, 1973), 290–309.

[10] CP (Espagne) 544, fos. 101–2, 112, 131–2; for Spain's resentment, see *HMC Eglinton*, 398.

presented by Britain's chargé d'affaires, instead of returning in person to take his leave. This petty and spiteful act completed the breach between the two courts, begun in the final stages of the war and continued by the withdrawal of Michell from London in 1764. The Rockinghams, however, wanted Pitt's continued support and were also anxious to demonstrate Britain's improved international position to parliament when it reassembled.[11] This ensured that the idea of *rapprochement* with Frederick II, to be followed by a triple alliance of Britain, Prussia, and Russia, was pursued during the second half of 1765. The alliance proposed by Pitt proved elusive: Frederick had no intention of concluding any treaty with either of the western powers, and would only agree to resume full diplomatic relations.[12] But these attempts, and Pitt's clear influence to which they testified, alarmed Choiseul. Any such alliance threatened his plans for an eventual war of revenge. These demanded Britain's diplomatic isolation in order that the fighting should not spread to Europe.

Choiseul's idea of arbitration by Frederick II was designed both to test Britain's resolve and, by worsening Anglo-Prussian relations, to remove any threat of a northern alliance. He appreciated that Britain was bound to reject arbitration, since she believed the matter to be clear-cut, but this would risk offending the Prussian King.[13] The mounting political problems facing the Rockingham Administration by the beginning of 1766 and Conway's lack of resolution had already weakened Britain's position, and the proposed mediation totally discomfited the ministry, now rapidly disintegrating.[14] After some hesitation, Conway secured cabinet approval to attempt a quick settlement with Spain: in mid-June, following Madrid's blunt rejection of a demand for the whole ransom (something over £500,000), Britain indicated that she would now settle for a mere £300,000. This simply revealed to Grimaldi that Britain's earlier firmness had been temporary, and principally due to Rochford's initiative. The Spanish foreign minister now began to insist even more vigorously on arbitration. Since Britain was uncertain how to react to this proposal, a complete impasse had been reached by the

---

[11]   Nolcken to KP, 27 Nov. 1765, Roberts Transcripts.

[12]   Cf. the correspondence in SP 90/84.

[13]   Since Prussia was at this point unsuccessfully pursuing a commercial treaty with Spain, the Bourbon ministers rightly calculated that Frederick II would have to accept the role of arbitrator.

[14]   George III is said to have poured scorn on the Southern Secretary's conduct, remarking to Rochford on his return from Spain that he must have had 'difficulty to know how to act, as they [i.e. Conway's dispatches] were sometimes warm, sometimes cold': Walpole, *Memoirs*, ii. 338.

final stages of the Rockingham Ministry. Conway's uncertain handling of the dispute had done much to undermine the advantageous position which Rochford had created. Grenville's brutal treatment of the Bourbons might not be very attractive, but it was certainly preferable to the weakness and confusion apparent during the second half of the Rockingham Administration.

A similar pattern was apparent in relations with Russia. Initially, the new Northern Secretary, Grafton, had seemed disposed to abandon the Grenville Ministry's economy, and during autumn 1765, Goodricke in Stockholm was liberally supplied with funds. The resulting improvement in Anglo-Russian diplomacy was not sustained and the payments were soon cut off, as British policy in Sweden quickly came to reflect a further deterioration in relations with St Petersburg.[15] The principal focus of Anglo-Russian diplomacy was now the commercial negotiations and over these, as over continued co-operation at Stockholm, the Rockingham cabinet came to display a stubbornness that bordered on immobility. In the early months of 1766, as acute American and domestic political problems preoccupied ministers, relations with Russia and foreign policy generally were pushed into the background, to the detriment of Britain's fading hopes for an alliance.

The arrival of Sir George Macartney in St Petersburg at the end of 1764 had opened a new era in Anglo-Russian relations.[16] Britain's new envoy was young and inexperienced, but he was energetic and a definite improvement on the discredited Buckinghamshire. The emphasis of his mission was now firmly on the renewal of the commercial treaty. Britain had responded to the breakdown of discussions for an alliance at the end of 1763 by insisting, as usual, that the next move was up to Russia. Macartney's formal instructions laid down that he was to take no further initiative over the alliance, but was simply to transmit any Russian approach for consideration in London.[17] The British cabinet was clearly looking for and expecting Russian concessions over any treaty: when Panin attempted to reopen these negotiations in August 1765, his overtures immediately foundered on the 'Turkish clause'.[18] For the first eighteen months of his mission, therefore, Macartney was preoccupied with the renewal of the commercial treaty.

---

[15] Roberts, *British Diplomacy*, 181–6.
[16] See M. Roberts, *Macartney in Russia* (*English Historical Review*, Supplement 7 (London, 1974)), and the less satisfactory W. F. Reddaway, 'Macartney in Russia, 1765–67', *Cambridge Historical Journal*, 3 (1929–31), 260–94.
[17] These are dated 24 Oct. 1764, SP 91/74, fos. 86–93; excerpts are printed in *Sbornik*, xii. 184–6.   [18] Ibid. xii. 210–21.

The problems he encountered were broadly similar to those in the political negotiations.[19] Britain's desire to model any new alliance on that of 1742 was paralleled by her wish to renew the 1734 commercial treaty as far as possible. The same assumptions of superiority evident in both sets of discussions were resented by a Russia conscious of her new status as a great power and of a rapidly developing economy. Catherine II and her ministers were determined to avoid anything which smacked of subordination, political or economic. These and other difficulties were overcome by Macartney's vigour, and progress was now surprisingly fast, particularly after the envoy persuaded Panin to take the commercial negotiations into his own hands.[20]

In the middle of August 1765 Britain's envoy signed the new commercial treaty, which actually extended some of the advantages Britain and her merchants had enjoyed since 1734.[21] Macartney accepted too a provision (Article IV) which seemed to leave the door open for subsequent action by Russia to protect her commerce and manufactures, and also invoked that holiest of holies, the English Navigation Act, to justify this. These provisions were unacceptable to the Russian Company and to ministers in London.[22] Since Macartney had flouted his express instructions both in signing the treaty and in accepting Article IV, he was immediately rebuked and his conduct disavowed. There followed an interval of almost a year, during which Panin repeatedly threatened an end to all negotiations and Britain obstinately refused to accept the Russian terms. Only in summer 1766 was a settlement reached and the commercial treaty finally signed.

This treaty was certainly a considerable triumph for Macartney, the one positive achievement of his mission, but it was achieved at the cost of further damage to political relations. Even at the last minute, Russia had insisted on some trifling changes in the wording of the final treaty, simply to express her resentment at Britain's apparent indifference to Russian interests in Stockholm and Warsaw. This resentment was increased by London's obstinacy in the

[19] A good brief study is P. H. Clendenning, 'The Background and Negotiations for the Anglo-Russian Commercial Treaty of 1766', in A. G. Cross, ed., *Great Britain and Russia in the Eighteenth Century: Contacts and Comparisons* (Newtonville, Mass., 1979), 145–63.

[20] *Sbornik*, xii. 207–8.

[21] For this and the dispute which followed, see Roberts, *Macartney in Russia*, 22 ff.

[22] *Sbornik*, xii. 221–6. There is an interesting exchange of letters between Grafton and the Lord Chancellor, Northington, between 23 and 28 Sept. (in Grafton Papers) which confirm that Northington was the origin of the objection over Article IV (as Michael Roberts suggested: *Macartney in Russia*, 24). For the Russian Company's objections, see the correspondence between its secretary and Grafton in late Sept. 1765, Grafton Papers; cf. *Grenville Papers*, iii. 90–1.

commercial negotiations which, together with lukewarm support in Sweden, was beginning to drive the two states apart. Britain's parsimony, evident in the small sums grudgingly given to Goodricke, was more resented in St Petersburg simply because it contrasted so obviously with her evident prosperity. London's stated view that she only acted in Stockholm to oblige Russia, though not without foundation, was as Goodricke said 'not engaging'.[23] For the first eighteen months of Macartney's mission, there was absolute deadlock in the alliance negotiations.

From late in 1765 onwards foreign policy had been pushed into the background. Two issues preoccupied the Rockingham Administration during the first half of 1766: the repeal of the Stamp Act and its own political survival. By spring its position had become precarious and by the summer its short period in office was over. It was succeeded by a ministry headed by William Pitt, but British diplomacy was to be one of the earliest casualties of the Great Commoner's unswerving faith in his own superior genius.

Pitt's return to office in July 1766 brought foreign affairs back to the forefront of British politics. He was associated with a more interventionist style of diplomacy[24] and he certainly had strong and highly original views on foreign policy. Almost alone among British politicians, he believed the wartime partnership with Prussia could be revived and an alliance with Russia added to this to provide security against the Bourbons. There was, he said, '*a great cloud of power in the north*, which should not be neglected'.[25] A northern system had been an *idée fixe* with Pitt since the closing stages of the Seven Years War, when the death of the implacably anti-Prussian Empress Elizabeth had appeared to make such a realignment possible. The acrimonious breach with Prussia in 1762 had seemed a fatal blow to any prompt reconciliation, as Pitt himself had recognized. During his famous speech to the House of Commons on the peace preliminaries (9 December 1762), he had denounced what he regarded as the abandonment of Frederick II as being likely to destroy any prospect of such a system.[26] Such realism, however, had little permanent appeal. His old belief that British security should be based on a league of the northern powers soon reasserted itself.[27] In autumn

[23] Roberts, *Macartney in Russia*, 43 n. 3.
[24] *Bernstorff Corr.* ii. 263; cf. *Walpole Corr.* xxii. 436.
[25] *Bedford Corr.* iii. 349.
[26] B. Williams, *The Life of William Pitt, Earl of Chatham* (2 vols.; London, 1913), ii. 138, 142–3, 146–7.
[27] A. von Ruville, *William Pitt, Earl of Chatham* (English trans., 3 vols.; London, 1907), iii. 389–90; cf. Williams, *Life of Pitt*, ii. 225.

1763, and again in summer 1765, when his return to office was seriously discussed, the creation of a 'triple alliance' was one of the points insisted on by Pitt and equally firmly rejected by the King.[28] George III's hostility towards Prussia and its ruler was renowned: a decade later the French ambassador in London noted his 'personal animosity' towards Frederick II.[29] In July 1766, however, the King's antipathy towards Prussia, and his own preference for an Austrian alliance, were temporarily overcome by his belief that only Pitt could restore political stability and give direction to government policy.[30]

Pitt's first objective on taking office was to create his 'northern league'. Alliances were to be sought with Prussia and Russia, and the cabinet also envisaged future treaties with Denmark, Sweden, the Dutch Republic, and even some of the smaller German states.[31] Relations with Prussia had been patched up at the end of the previous year, and in June 1766 Andrew Mitchell, newly knighted and with the enhanced status of Envoy Extraordinary, returned to Berlin. Before his departure he had had two interviews with Pitt which left him in no doubt of the latter's desire to create a northern alliance, though Mitchell himself was rightly sceptical of the prospect of success, at least at the Prussian court.[32] Nevertheless, the creation of this wide-ranging alliance became Britain's principal objective during the second half of 1766. The way this plan was to be realized was characteristically imaginative. A special envoy was to be sent to Berlin and St Petersburg where, Pitt assumed, all difficulties would simply evaporate at the very mention of his name: a name which had recently been transformed into the Earl of Chatham by a peerage in the early days of his ministry. Less than two weeks after the formation of the Chatham Administration a bewildered and decidedly reluctant Hans Stanley was named for the mission.[33]

This 'northern league' was, at first sight, logical enough. It aimed to unite Britain with the two strongest continental states after 1763 and it mirrored Panin's diplomatic objectives. The problem, which Chatham never appreciated, was that it took no account of Britain's

---

[28] *Grenville Papers*, ii. 199; *Grafton Autobiography*, 45–6, 83–5; *Corr. Geo. III*, i. 120 124–5; cf. J. Brewer, *Party Ideology and Popular Politics at the Accession of George III* (Cambridge, 1976), 123–5.

[29] This had emerged at the time of the Anglo-Prussian breach of 1762: see *Letters from George III to Lord Bute, 1756–1766*, ed. R. R. Sedgwick (London, 1939), 81, 86, 95, 107, 149; CP (Angleterre) 498, fo. 334; cf. ibid. 499, fo. 204.

[30] George III's hostility towards Prussia was only shelved: it was apparent in summer 1766 when he tried unsuccessfully to persuade the Prince of Orange to marry either the King's own sister or another princess rather than Frederick the Great's niece: *Corr. Geo. III*, i. 261–70 *passim*.   [31] *Chatham Corr.* iii. 31 n. 1.

[32] Williams, *Life of Pitt*, ii. 225; Cobenzl to Kaunitz, 13 May 1766, HHStA, DD.B 113, Belgien.   [33] *Grenville Papers*, iii. 284–5.

relations with either state, or of her diminished role in the new political pattern which had emerged since the last war. Pitt's 'Northern System', like the parallel dreams of a revived Austrian alliance, was no longer practical politics. A Russian alliance might have been concluded, though at the price of considerable British concessions over terms. But instead of concentrating on direct negotiations with St Petersburg, Chatham determined to conclude his league by way of Berlin, where the door was firmly bolted against Britain. His plans also presented several significant practical problems and attention came to be focused on these.[34] Any approach to Prussia would undoubtedly antagonize Austria, with whom Britain was cultivating friendly relations. The Habsburg ambassador, Seilern, had recently been assured that no such overture was contemplated.[35] Conway, the Austrophile Northern Secretary, was characteristically anxious about the damage this initiative would do to Britain's good relations with Vienna, and he resented the way in which the initiative had been decided on without his knowledge, though it lay within his department.[36] The nomination of Hans Stanley also presented difficulties. Macartney had for some time been seeking to return to England and so Stanley could reasonably be named ambassador to Russia, though Sir George's recent success in signing the Commercial Treaty certainly made it an inopportune moment to recall him.[37] The nomination of a new ambassador to Frederick II, when Mitchell had so recently returned to Berlin, posed a further problem. There was, above all, the small matter of whether such a mission actually had any chance of success. Such doubts and procedural difficulties did not much trouble Chatham, who remained confident of his own ability to conjure away barriers which, to lesser men, appeared insurmountable obstacles. They sorely vexed Conway, in whose province as Northern Secretary the matter lay, and they also troubled the ambassador-designate, Stanley. Between them the two men managed to introduce a welcome breath of realism into the proceedings.

Chatham's original scheme had not considered Britain's present relations with either Prussia or Russia.[38] It might, Stanley suggested (and Conway agreed), be prudent to enquire as to the prospects at the Prussian court before he set out. Sir Andrew Mitchell was therefore instructed to inform Frederick of the proposed mission and

---

[34] *Chatham Corr.* iii. 15–9.

[35] Cf. Seilern's dispatches for June and July 1766, HHStA, England-Korrespondenz 113.

[36] Walpole, *Memoirs*, ii. 364, 463.

[37] Roberts, *Macartney in Russia*, 33, 61.

[38] Stanley, after he had spoken to Pitt, was surprised to discover just how bad Britain's relations with Prussia actually were: *Chatham Corr.* iii. 19–20.

to discover his reaction.[39] The experienced Mitchell was considerably
more realistic. Even before he formally broached the scheme with the
Prussian King, he predicted not only its impossibility, but even the
actual arguments with which he would be confronted.[40] Frederick's
absence in Silesia delayed the inevitable, but when, early in
September, the King returned, he gave Mitchell an interview which
left Britain's envoy in no doubt as to the futility of a formal approach
by Stanley.[41] Arguments about the need to form 'a firm and solid
system in the North, to counter-balance the formidable alliance of
the House of Bourbon', made little or no impression on a monarch
resolved to avoid any danger of involvement in a future Anglo-
French war. Indeed, in view of Chatham's bellicose reputation, his
return to power appeared to bring such a conflict closer. Frederick
was also unable to resist some playful recriminations on Britain's
past conduct and present situation. 'He then hinted to me,' reported
Mitchell, 'the treatment he had met with from us when the late peace
was made, and talked of the instability of our measures and sudden
changes in our administrations, which made it almost impossible to
transact business with us with any sort of security.' Not even the
magical name of Pitt made any impression on the Prussian King and
by the end of the interview it was evident to Mitchell that no alliance
was possible.[42]

Ministers in London, however, were by now firmly under the spell
of Chatham, who could not recognize a refusal when he received one
and urged that the approach should be pursued.[43] Mitchell, for his
part, was sensible enough to let the matter rest there, but this realism
only earned him the irritation of his superiors and in November he
was told to try again. The second interview on 1 December 1766 was
a carbon copy of the first.[44] This new rejection finally convinced
British ministers that the Prussian alliance was not available. As
American policy was beginning to consume more and more of the
ministry's attention, the scheme was abandoned early in 1767.[45]

This fiasco merely demonstrated the obvious: an Anglo-Prussian
alliance was impossible. In his first formal interview, Mitchell had
countered Frederick's comment that 'Chi sta bene non se muove'

[39] Ibid. iii. 29–32.
[40] Ibid. iii. 46–50; cf. Mitchell to Yorke, 13 Sept. 1766 (but written before he saw the King),
Add. MSS 6810, fo. 57.   [41] *Chatham Corr.* iii. 67–71.
[42] Frederick was quick to note the danger done to Pitt's reputation and to his ministry by
assuming the title 'earl of Chatham': *Pol. Corr.* xxv. 197, 241.
[43] Only Chatham could have written apropos of Mitchell's first interview that 'there
appears to be sufficient opening already for Mr. Stanley to go to Berlin'! To Grafton, 27 Sept.
1766, Grafton Papers.
[44] SP 90/85, fos. 223–7; *Chatham Corr.* iii. 139–43.   [45] SP 90/86, fo. 1.

with the instant reply that 'Chi sta solo non sta bene.'[46] His retort was in reality a comment on Britain's isolation and not (as he intended) applicable to Prussia, secure in her Russian alliance. When first informed of Chatham's scheme by his agent in London, Frederick had declared that he would have nothing to do with it 'because a scalded cat fears even lukewarm water'.[47] He inevitably professed to see the hated hand of Bute behind the Chatham Administration, and this certainly did nothing to increase Britain's prospects of success. But it was his fear of being dragged into a further war, perhaps by a French attack on Hanover, which principally determined him to refuse Chatham's alliance. The King was, in these months, increasingly preoccupied with the problem of Poland and the Dissidents, and Britain could not further Prussian interests there.[48] His rejection of Britain's overtures was thus founded on a firm grasp of political reality, unlike Chatham's scheme, which revealed only his ignorance of contemporary continental politics and his disregard for the new problems which confronted British diplomacy. 'Mr. Pitt's plan', Grafton sourly remarked, 'was Utopian . . . he lived too much out of the world to have a right knowledge of mankind.'[49] This comment is as appropriate to the failure of Chatham's foreign policy as of his ministry as a whole. The Great Commoner was as outdated and unrealistic in his thinking about diplomacy as the majority of his contemporaries, though—characteristically—his delusions were sometimes original.

Chatham's initial interest in foreign policy had not been sustained and the second approach to Prussia had principally reflected his colleagues' complete deference to his views. By late September 1766 he was at Bath, the victim of a mental and physical collapse. Though he returned to London for the parliamentary session in November, in January he returned to Bath, where he was to remain until March. His subordinates proved unequal to the task of directing the King's government. Foreign policy was an early victim of the confused ministerial politics of these months and of the competing issues, above all America and India, which crowded in on the bedraggled remnants of the Chatham Administration from the end of 1766 onwards.

Formal control of British diplomacy was in the hands of H. S. Conway, Northern Secretary after May 1766, and the Earl of Shelburne, who had occupied the Southern Department since

---

[46] *Chatham Corr.* iii. 68.
[48] Ibid. xxv. 197, 245, 261, 265.

[47] *Pol. Corr.* xxv. 198.
[49] *Grafton Autobiography*, 91.

August. Their collective inadequacy soon became apparent. Shelburne's undoubted intelligence did not make up for his youth and inexperience, and above all his temperamental failings. The abrasive edge to his character, which was to dog him all his political life, quickly alienated his ministerial colleagues and he was soon an isolated figure in the cabinet.[50] His aloofness, coupled with his total lack of diplomatic experience, was reflected in his handling of the all-important relations with France and Spain. His brother Secretary, Conway, had already been in office for a year, but he had acquired little understanding of European politics, and, crucially, had already shown irresolution in his conduct of business. He was also distracted by his duties as leader of the House of Commons.[51] The two Secretaries bore considerable responsibility for the collapse of British diplomacy during the first year of the Chatham Ministry.

They were soon faced by a serious deterioration in relations with the Bourbons. The origin of this was not the long-running dispute over the Manila Ransom, which had been in limbo since June 1766 and would remain so until the following winter. It was rather produced by British exploration in the South Atlantic and, in particular, by the settlement at Port Egmont on West Falkland.[52] The English had discovered and named the Falkland Islands in the later seventeenth century, but neither they nor the French fishermen from St Malo who frequented them in the early 1700s had established a permanent settlement, though the latter had named them the 'Îles Malouines'. British interest in the islands was principally the result of Anson's famous circumnavigation in the 1740s. In 1749 the Admiralty had decided to establish a base there and prepared an expedition. Spain heard of these preparations and immediately protested that any such settlement would be a clear breach of Article VIII of the Treaty of Utrecht, which effectively forbade access to any part of her South American empire. Britain rejected such a restrictive interpretation of the 1713 settlement, but ministers wanted to preserve the recent peace and therefore abandoned the project in 1750.

British interest in a South Atlantic base revived after the Seven

---

[50] For a recent, sympathetic portrait, see C. Stuart, 'Lord Shelburne', in H. Lloyd-Jones, V. Pearl, and B. Worden, eds., *History and Imagination: Essays in Honour of H. R. Trevor-Roper* (London, 1981), 243–53.

[51] P. D. G. Thomas, *The Townshend Duties Crisis: The Second Phase of the American Revolution 1767–1773* (Oxford, 1987), 4.

[52] See the excellent study by Rice, 'Great Britain, the Manila Ransom', 386–409; and Lalaguna Lasala, 'England, Spain and the Family Compact', 192–246, for the Spanish side; J. Goebel, *The Struggle for the Falkland Islands* (New Haven, 1927; repr. 1982), 225–61, is less satisfactory.

Years War. This was linked to a fundamental shift in Britain's imperial and commercial objectives.[53] A determined attempt was made to exploit the commanding position secured at the Peace of Paris. In particular, Britain aimed at a trading empire stretching across the Pacific and Indian Oceans and into the South China Sea, which would absorb the increasing volume of manufactured goods produced by her industries. The principal target was the massive potential markets of Japan and China, and an attempt was soon to be made to establish commercial bases in the Malay Archipelago, as entrepôts for this trade. Linked to these ambitions was a plan to break into the Pacific, both to find the supposed undiscovered continent in the southern seas and to develop a western route to the Far East. Such ambitions had lain at the heart of the maritime enterprises of the Elizabethans almost two centuries before, and British expansion in the 1760s and 1770s was a conscious emulation of their Tudor forebears. This expansion inevitably brought Britain into conflict with Spain, who wished to maintain her monopoly over the Pacific. The focus of this collision came to be the Falkland Islands. These lay to the east of the Straits of Magellan and would be an excellent base for a British push into the Pacific. Indeed Egmont, the First Lord of the Admiralty in the early years of peace, believed the Falklands to be

undoubtedly *the Key to the whole Pacifick Ocean*. This Island must command the Ports and Trade of Chili, Peru, Panama, Acapulco, and in one word to all the Spanish Territory upon that Sea. It will render all our Expeditions to those parts most lucrative to ourselves, most fatal to Spain, and no longer formidable, tedious or uncertain in a future War.[54]

Strategic and economic considerations thus merged to produce British expansion into the Pacific, which began in 1764 when Commodore Byron was sent principally to take possession of the Falkland Islands.[55]

Byron arrived in January 1765 and, before continuing on his circumnavigation, he explored the islands and duly declared them British territory, though he established no settlement.[56] Rumours of

[53] The fundamental, if occasionally controversial and overdrawn, statement of this hypothesis is V. T. Harlow, *The Founding of the Second British Empire 1763–1793* (2 vols.; London, 1952–64); see, in particular, vol. i, chs. 1 and 2.

[54] *Byron's Journal of his Circumnavigation 1764–1766*, ed. R. E. Gallagher (Cambridge, 1964), 161.

[55] His secret instructions, which consciously echoed Drake's in 1577, are printed ibid. 3–9.

[56] The account of Byron's expedition in Harlow, *Founding*, i. 22–6, must now be modified in the light of the introduction to *Byron's Journal*, ed. Gallagher, pp. xix–lxxxii, despite its surprising confusions over British history in the 1760s.

a parallel French settlement on East Falkland (Byron had landed only on West Falkland) alarmed the British government and in September 1765 a second expedition was sent out. It was commanded by Captain McBride, who established a blockhouse and a small settlement on West Falkland at Port Egmont in January 1766.[57] The French explorer Bougainville had in fact founded a small colony at present-day Berkeley Sound (on East Falkland) early in 1764, but two years later Choiseul's determination to maintain the Family Compact led France to abandon this colony and to acknowledge Spain's territorial monopoly in the South Atlantic. By then, McBride had carried out his instructions to locate the French settlement and to order the colonists to leave. In spring 1766 the British government was becoming seriously alarmed at the supposed scale of the French settlement on East Falkland and considered reinforcing McBride. The cabinet hesitated for several months before taking such a step, and matters were further delayed by the ministerial upheavals of summer 1766. But at the end of August the Chatham Administration, initially determined to take a firm line against the Bourbons, decided to reinforce McBride's expedition. It was this decision which prompted Spain to protest vigorously that the British settlement was illegal and that the islands were Spanish territory, and this produced a serious diplomatic confrontation. Spain feared that Britain was also trying to form a settlement on the South American continent and perhaps even to the west of the Straits of Magellan. For Madrid, it was not only the Falkland Islands, but the whole Pacific that was now at stake.

The Spanish ambassador in London, Masserano, had been carefully watching Britain's attitude since the previous spring and had lodged an initial protest about the settlement at Port Egmont in May 1766. Byron's return after his circumnavigation alerted Masserano to the full extent of British activities in the Falklands: despite the stringent security precautions which had surrounded the whole voyage, the ambassador was able to obtain considerable information, principally from the French embassy's intelligence network.[58] Masserano's initial attempts to question British ministers were rebuffed, and it was the early months of the Chatham Administration before these representations assumed serious proportions. Matters were initially delayed by the inexperience of the new Southern Secretary, Shelburne,[59] and by his belief (apparently

[57] McBride's secret orders, dated 26 Sept. 1765, are printed in Corney, *Tahiti*, ii. 441–5.

[58] Some of Masserano's dispatches for these months can be found ibid. i. 24–51.

[59] This is apparent, e.g., from Masserano to Grimaldi, 26 Sept. 1766, abstracted in *Carteret's Voyage Round the World 1766–1769*, ed. H. Wallis (2 vols.; Cambridge, 1965), ii. 309–10.

shared by the Admiralty) that the Falklands and the Malouines were two separate groups of islands! Once this confusion had been removed, Britain adopted a firm line towards Spain. But this firmness was not accompanied by any initiative designed to resolve the dispute. The Chatham Administration, by now effectively deprived of its leader, never attempted the kind of bold stroke which the Grenville Ministry had employed so successfully in 1764–5.

From August until October 1766, Anglo-Spanish diplomacy consisted solely of protests and counter-protests. Madrid's claims that the region was part of Charles III's territories and had been reserved to Spain by the Treaty of Utrecht were countered by Britain's insistence that the Spanish could not reserve such vast territories and that in any case the English had discovered the islands first. Such exchanges pushed up the diplomatic temperature, but they did nothing to bring a settlement any closer. The opportunity for another British triumph over the Bourbons was certainly apparent, if not to ministers then to the Earl of Rochford, formerly ambassador in Madrid and from early November 1766 Britain's representative at the French court.[60] Bourbon strategy remained essentially pacific. Choiseul believed France and Spain were not yet prepared for a war and he was, in any case, now deep in the series of anti-Russian initiatives which he began immediately after returning to the foreign office in April 1766. For the next few years France pursued a markedly anti-Russian policy, trying to incite the Turks to attack Catherine II and supporting the Empress's opponents in Poland and in Sweden. A reorientation of French diplomacy was under way, and Choiseul did not wish to see these initiatives undermined by a war in the west. Though both Bourbon powers wanted peace, they still feared that Pitt's return to power several months before might plunge them into a new conflict. Choiseul regarded the Chatham Administration's initial firmness over the Falklands as menacing and feared the dispute might well produce the war he dreaded. As British firmness was not reinforced by any decisive action or diplomatic initiative, the French foreign minister grew in confidence. In the second half of October, Choiseul initiated moves to circumvent the impasse created by Britain's immobility.

Rochford's illness had delayed his arrival in France. In any case he already enjoyed something of a reputation as a Francophobe, principally because of his rough handling of Spanish ministers while in Madrid.[61] Instead, Choiseul approached the former British ambassador to France, the Earl of Hertford, who was in Paris on

---

[60] See his letter to Chatham, Private, 28 Nov. 1766, *Chatham Corr.* iii. 131–4.
[61] Cf. above, p. 93.

holiday. In several private conversations during the final week of October, Choiseul gradually worked round to his new initiative, which linked the Falklands to the question of the Manila Ransom. This latter dispute had also become bogged down: since the previous June Spain had been waiting for London to reply. The French foreign minister now proposed that if the British would evacuate Port Egmont, France would mediate over the Manila Ransom and ensure a prompt settlement favourable to Britain. Choiseul hoped in this way to remove the threat of war which the Anglo-Spanish impasse appeared to bring nearer.

British diplomacy had already been weakened by the political upheavals which followed Pitt's return to power, and the further problems which intervened towards the close of 1766 brought it close to collapse. Matters were not helped by Hertford's bungling of Choiseul's proposals: he reported the offer to settle the Manila dispute in return for an evacuation of Port Egmont, but not, crucially, the idea that Britain should accept France's mediation over the ransom. But it was principally the Chatham Administration's internal problem which weakened and ultimately destroyed British diplomacy towards Spain in the winter of 1766–7. The opening of the parliamentary session in November and the question of the East India Company's charter were difficulties enough, but later in the same month the rump of the Rockinghams resigned, threatening the ministry with extinction. Though negotiations with the Bedfords failed, the administration was patched up towards the end of the year. After an initial parliamentary defeat in December, Chatham had a fit of the sulks and went off to Bath to nurse his gout and his wounded pride. His second withdrawal, and the serious breakdown which he suffered in January 1767, threw the ministry into total confusion and for a time all but stopped government business.[62] Shelburne, the Southern Secretary, was forced meanwhile to tackle the worsening situation in the British colonies in North America, where a new political initiative was urgently needed.

The winter of 1766–7 provides a clear illustration of how Britain's standing could be lowered and her foreign policy virtually destroyed by internal political strife and by the more pressing domestic and colonial problems. There was little risk of a Bourbon attack, given Britain's naval predominance, but a ministry as unsure of its parliamentary majority as were Chatham and his colleagues had to avoid any sign of weakness in its dealings with France and Spain. One reason why part of Shelburne's correspondence with Rochford

[62] Nolcken to KP, 10 Feb. 1767, Roberts Transcripts.

in Paris is not in the official State Papers was the cabinet's fear that
the opposition would call for the relevant dispatches in parliament.[63]
Consequently Britain hesitated, prevaricated, and then simply
allowed the dispute with Spain to drop. Shelburne initially sent
Rochford contradictory instructions. Britain agreed to combine the
two issues, but rejected mediation by France.[64] Scarcely had the
ambassador begun to grapple with this intractable problem than he
was magisterially rebuked for his ignorance of something which had
not been communicated to him.[65] The British cabinet, misled by
Hertford and now anxious for the speedy triumph which Choiseul's
offer seemed to promise, believed by December 1766 that they could
secure the full and prompt payment of the Ransom by evacuating the
Falklands and were prepared to consider this. But when the French
ambassador explained that it would involve Choiseul's mediation,
the cabinet rejected this outright. It took no further initiative over
either the Manila Ransom or the Falklands settlement. Britain
demanded the two million dollars on several occasions during the
next few years, but could never overcome Madrid's insistence on
arbitration, and her claim was never to be met.

The settlement at Port Egmont could not so easily be swept under
the diplomatic carpet. Spain was certainly unreconciled to any British
presence in the islands and, when its extent became clear, she acted to
expel the colonists. This was to produce a far more serious
confrontation in the second half of 1770. The episode was to prove a
turning-point in Anglo-Bourbon relations. Choiseul had earlier
concluded that the failure of naval reconstruction forced France and
Spain to pursue a moderate line. The opportunity for naval blackmail
by Britain in 1766 was considerable, but the Chatham Administration's lack of consistent purpose reduced British diplomacy to a
new low point and encouraged Choiseul to adopt a more adventurous
strategy. The ministry's instability and other pressing political
problems were part of the explanation, but the principal cause was
the personal failings of the men responsible for British foreign policy:
Conway, Shelburne, Grafton, and Chatham himself.

The first months of the Chatham Administration also saw a
further deterioration in Anglo-Russian diplomacy. The acceptance
of the modified commercial treaty in summer 1766 had not been
followed by the improved political relations for which both sides still
hoped and which they had earlier expected would result. Stanley's
mission had been intended to include Russia, and the ambassador-

[63] Cf. Rice, 'Great Britain, the Manila Ransom', 409.
[64] Add. MSS 9242, fos. 1–5.   [65] Ibid., fos. 10–14.

designate had, laudably enough, prepared for it by studying the relevant correspondence in the Secretary of State's office. Even more unusually, Stanley had produced a digest of these dispatches. After reviewing negotiations since Catherine II's accession, he concluded the Britain would have to concede the 'Turkish clause' if she wanted an alliance and was not prepared to pay a peacetime subsidy. This was immediately denounced by the King, because of the supposed potential damage to British trade in the Levant and, more generally, because no such concession was necessary for the conclusion of any alliance by Britain.[66] Ministerial orthodoxy continued to reject any sacrifices, either over help against the Turks, or over a peacetime subsidy, though the need for them was by now apparent to everyone except ministers in London.[67] Instead, in the winter of 1766–7, Britain again tried to circumvent the barrier to any alliance, this time by way of Copenhagen.

This latest initiative followed a persistent failure to exploit the opportunity presented by the situation in Sweden, and it soon foundered on the same basic obstacle encountered there, Britain's enduring parsimony. For two decades before 1763, ministers had dismissed Denmark as a French puppet. But the initial Russo-Danish *rapprochement* in 1765 and the move towards a final settlement of the Holstein exchange represented a decisive move out of the French camp. The idea of Copenhagen as a path to a Russian alliance seems to have originated with Grafton. In the winter of 1766–7 Britain took tentative steps to conclude an Anglo-Danish alliance.[68] Ministers as usual rejected any thought of a peacetime subsidy and, in any case, the leading Danish statesman, J. H. E. von Bernstorff, was immersed in the last stages of the Holstein negotiations. Denmark's provisional treaty with Russia was signed in April 1767 and Bernstorff refused to be diverted from the incomparably more important matter. By May, Britain had abandoned all thought of an alliance with Denmark and predictably blamed St Petersburg for this failure.[69]

This latest half-initiative further damaged relations. Panin resented British attempts to teach Russia her business as far as the situation in Copenhagen was concerned, particularly when Britain, relying on Gunning's notably erroneous reports from the Danish capital,

---

[66] *Corr. Geo. III*, i. 392; *Bedford Corr.* iii. 349.

[67] Roberts, *Macartney in Russia*, 59; Add. MSS 37054, fo. 1; *Sbornik*, xii. 310.

[68] For this fiasco, see M. Roberts, 'Great Britain, Denmark and Russia, 1763–1770' in *Studies in Diplomatic History: Essays in Memory of David Bayne Horn* ed. R. Hatton and M. S. Anderson, 248–52.

[69] Ibid. 252; Nolcken to KP, 28 May 1767, Roberts Transcripts.

suggested opposing and, eventually, overthrowing Bernstorff: Bernstorff the architect of Denmark's *rapprochement* with Russia! This brief and ill-starred episode was simply another blind alley into which British foreign policy stumbled in these years and it provided a clear illustration of Britain's insularity. That Denmark might have objectives of her own never seems to have dawned on ministers in London, who remained convinced of the supreme value of a British alliance and continued to react with blind incomprehension when continental states ignored this basic truth.

Relations with St Petersburg were further damaged by the débâcle of Chatham's 'northern alliance'. When Russia had been notified of Stanley's original nomination, Catherine II had responded in February 1767 by naming Ivan Chernyshev as her ambassador in London. This was a significant concession by the Empress, who always tried to economize by maintaining diplomatic relations below the ambassadorial level. It illustrates Catherine's own Anglophilia and her enduring hopes for an alliance. The abandonment of Stanley's mission, and the desultory way this was notified to St Petersburg, therefore caused bad feeling. When, in April 1767, Russia was formally told he would not now be coming, Panin reacted with cold indifference. Britain at first hoped to avoid matching Chernyshev's ambassadorial status in a new appointment to Russia.[70] When Panin made clear that reciprocity was essential, the British government could not find an appropriate candidate willing to go to St Petersburg and, after Macartney's departure, came to be represented merely by a chargé d'affaires.[71] This in itself hindered good relations, and it provided an opportunity for Prussian diplomacy to create further obstacles to any improvement in the future.[72] From spring 1767 Anglo-Russian diplomacy became distant and sometimes acrimonious.[73]

Stanley's initial nomination had completely undermined Macartney's position at the Russian court.[74] He was doubly compromised: by the behaviour of his government and by his own indiscretions. His principal offence had been to seduce Mademoiselle Khitrov, one of Catherine's ladies-in-waiting and Panin's cousin. This had resulted in the lady's pregnancy and banishment from

[70] Even as late as Aug. 1767, Conway, though forced to accept that an ambassador would have to be sent, was still trying to back out: Add. MSS 37054, fo. 8.

[71] CP (Angleterre) 477, fo. 172.

[72] For the problems facing British diplomacy during these 18 months, see Add. MSS 37054, fos. 80–1.

[73] Relations were not helped when Conway, oblivious of Catherine's sensitivity over the imperial title, styled her 'Czarina' and had to apologize formally: ibid., fo. 9.

[74] Add. MSS 6826, fo. 74.

court, and the Empress had been outraged, not on grounds of morality but of etiquette.[75] In late 1767 (after his return to England) he was again nominated ambassador to Russia when the ministry could not find a candidate prepared to go to St Petersburg, Panin wrote directly to him bluntly warning that he would not be accepted at the Russian court if he tried to return.[76]

The spring of 1767 was the end of an era in Anglo-Russian relations.[77] Macartney's formal recall reached St Petersburg in mid-April, a few days before the news that Stanley's mission had been abandoned. The conclusion of the Russo-Danish treaty in the same month strengthened Panin's position in the Baltic, at the same time as Conway admitted that an Anglo-Danish alliance was impossible. All the doors which might have led to a Russian alliance were now closed, for ministers had effectively discounted the Swedish route. There were no further negotiations until a new British ambassador reached St Petersburg in August 1768. Macartney's mission had seen the two states moving so much apart, that Britain's envoy in his final months in St Petersburg could write that he believed 'a treaty of alliance . . . as distant and unlikely to be brought about, as a league with Prester John, or the King of Bantam'.[78] This exaggerated judgement was certainly coloured by Macartney's humiliation and resentment, yet it was near the mark. By 1767 Russia had begun to move out of the orbit of potential British allies.

Britain's failure, at one level, simply expressed Panin's growing doubts about such links.[79] Inflexibility over terms tells its own story about the anticipated benefits. A subsidy was out of the question; in Russian eyes the early years of peace had also revealed Britain's unwillingness to give effective support at Warsaw, Stockholm, or Copenhagen. The one other thing Britain had to offer was also a point on which London was inflexible: the 'Turkish clause'. As Panin made clear, with one eye on possible future difficulties in Poland, it was principally the 'Turkish clause' which made Russia value the alliance.[80] This impasse merely reflected a far more fundamental

---

[75] Though Macartney's predecessor believed that the Swedish minister (probably C. F. von Düben) had also enjoyed the lady's favours: 'England and Sweden were equally concerned in the negotiation, but . . . Sweden had prudently withdrawn before the secret Article was made public' (Buckinghamshire to his wife, the Countess of Buckinghamshire, 7 Feb. 1767, Buckinghamshire Papers).

[76] *Sbornik*, lxvii. 546; for the hostility towards Macartney in Russia, see ibid. cxli. 388–9.

[77] Roberts, *British Diplomacy*, 240.

[78] Macartney to Conway, 6 Feb. 1767, printed in J. Barrow, *Some Account of the Public Life and a Selection from the Unpublished Writings, of the Earl of Macartney* (2 vols.; London, 1807), i. 424.   [79] See, e.g. his remarks to Solms early in 1766: *Sbornik*, xxii. 427.

[80] Panin to Gross, 29 Jan. 1765 (OS), Martens, *Recueil des traités*, ix(x). 226; see also Panin to Gross, 8 Feb. 1765 (OS), *Sbornik*, lviii. 177; cf. Panin's remark to Macartney that the British

division. The years since 1764 had seen a decline in Russia's belief in
the value of an English alliance. This can be traced to two
interrelated factors: St Petersburg's growing strength and diplomatic
self-confidence, and the decline of British power which became
visible from the mid-1760s.

By 1767 the situation was changing; and changing to London's
disadvantage. In 1763, a British alliance had much to commend it to
a continental state. The Peace of Paris had seen Britain at the height
of her power, her commercial and colonial pre-eminence unquestioned,
her financial strength unmatched in Europe, her prestige as yet
undimmed. It was a different story a few years later. Britain's
problems at home and abroad during the mid-1760s lowered her
standing in the eyes of Catherine and Panin, as of Europe generally.[81]
This decline was highlighted by a simultaneous transformation in
Russia's position, for Britain's problems contrasted unhappily with
the growing stability and success of Catherine's government at home
and abroad. The Russia Macartney left in spring 1767 was a far cry
from the troubled country which a few years before had appre-
hensively confronted Augustus III's death. Though Britain's chance
of an alliance did not disappear completely after the Russo-Prussian
treaty of April 1764, the fact that Catherine II did have a secure ally
in Prussia could only reduce the opportunity to conclude an alliance
without a significant British concession, particularly since Frederick
II spent considerable time and effort trying to convince Russia of the
decline of British power and the depreciation of an alliance with
London.[82] His influence at St Petersburg was uncertain but undoubted,
and he was determined to be Catherine's only major ally. Though the
Anglo-Russian negotiations did not fail because of a Prussian veto,
Frederick's anti-British propaganda did confirm Russia's doubts
about the value of an alliance.[83]

Russia's new-found confidence was inevitably reflected in her
negotiations with foreign states, and Britain suffered with the rest.
Russian arrogance and pretensions are an endless, if overstated,
theme in Macartney's dispatches. Panin, who had sought financial
aid over Poland in 1763, was three years later demanding a subsidy
in Sweden on pain of an immediate end to all negotiations if this was
not forthcoming.[84] His threat was not carried out, but its message is

'alliance could be of no use to Russia except in case of a war with the Ottoman Porte; for what
other power dared to attack her?': ibid. xii. 295.

[81] Cf. SP 91/77, fo. 302.
[82] For a good example of his tactics, see *Sbornik*, xx. 232–3.
[83] Cf. Roberts, *Macartney in Russia*, 36.
[84] *Sbornik*, xii. 280.

clear. Russia's growing awareness of her own strength and a parallel recognition of Britain's decline were combining by the later 1760s to make an alliance increasingly unlikely, particularly as its attraction also came to be undermined by continued Anglo-Bourbon hostility after 1763 and by the apparent inevitability of more fighting between the western powers.[85] By the later 1760s it was apparent that Russia had far less to gain from a treaty than did the British government. Britain's near-dependence on Russia for vital naval stores guaranteed harmonious trading relations, while as long as British policy was anti-French (and this orientation seemed permanent), then it was bound to be pro-Russian.[86] Panin, moreover, like many other observers, doubted whether Britain could now play a political role on the continent, in view of her insular diplomacy.[87] He therefore insisted on a price beyond anything which London would contemplate. This attitude was strengthened by his appreciation that Russia was the only power Britain could court with any prospect of success.[88] His oft-remembered remark to Macartney that 'We wanted Russia more than Russia could ever want us'[89] enshrined a basic truth, but it was also a comment on the changed, and changing, situation of the two states. In one sense, the problem was that they *were* such natural allies.[90] Neither government had been prepared to make the kind of concessions which had smoothed the path to the signature of other alliances.

The lack of progress in Anglo-Russian negotiations in 1767–8 also demonstrated the absence of a foreign policy at this time.[91] Ministers were preoccupied with India, with the serious opposition in the American colonies, particularly to the Townshend duties, and with attempts to prolong the political life of the crumbling Chatham Administration. Deprived of their nominal leader, Grafton and his colleagues were swept along on the tide of events. They saw little immediate threat from France and therefore no apparent need for an

---

[85] As early as autumn 1764, Panin was professing to believe that a new Anglo-Bourbon war would soon break out: SP 91/74, fo. 46.

[86] British ministers made exactly the same calculation in reverse. See e.g. *BDI* iii: *Denmark 1689–1789*, ed. J. F. Chance (London, 1926), 178.

[87] He professed to be concerned about this as early as Oct. 1764: SP 91/74, fo. 113.

[88] See e.g. *Sbornik*, xii. 295–6.

[89] That it was Panin and not (as is usually said) Macartney who was the real originator of this famous phrase is evident from SP 91/77, fo. 189.

[90] As early as Mar. 1765, Nolcken had pointed out that British ministers were so sure of a community of policy with Russia against France that they were prepared to wait for a treaty (to KP, 5 Mar. 1765, Roberts Transcripts). The Russian government, of course, made the same calculation in reverse: *Sbornik*, lxvii. 76.

[91] See e.g. the complaints of the Austrian ambassador: Seilern to Kaunitz, 13 Mar. 1767, HHStA, England-Korrespondenz 113.

active diplomacy.[92] It was symptomatic of these other political priorities that a project for a treaty with Sweden, produced by the government in Stockholm in spring 1767, should lie in the Northern Secretary's office unanswered for eighteen months.[93] Grafton later wrote that 'What was then passing in Poland and between Russia and the Porte, were undoubtedly important events, and were neither overlooked nor unlamented by the British cabinet: but the distant situations of these countries, rendered all active interference on our parts, except by our good offices, preposterous'.[94] These good offices were exerted on behalf of Poland's Dissidents: Catherine II was seeking to force the Polish King to alleviate the situation of his Protestant and Greek Orthodox subjects, and Britain was quick to put her diplomatic weight behind the Empress at Warsaw.[95] Here again ministers sought, by minor concessions over relatively trivial matters, to avoid a major concession over either the 'Turkish clause' or a peacetime subsidy. But, as Grafton recognized, the growing dominance and independence of Russia and Prussia were making it difficult for Britain to exert real influence in Europe.

Parliamentary and American problems preoccupied ministers, and Shelburne and Conway were becoming notorious for their neglect of diplomacy and of diplomats. 'The Secretaries of State', Nolcken complained in July 1767, 'are so busy in Parliament that they conduct their offices like a secondary business.'[96] In that summer Conway's inability to decide whether to resign paralysed the Northern Department for six weeks.[97] Both Secretaries made a bad impression on foreign diplomats, who censured their ignorance and their insularity. By the beginning of 1768 there are hints that the diplomatic corps were starting to boycott the weekly conferences which British ministers continued to hold. This was partly because of the frequent and prolonged absence of senior ministers from town, and

partly because of the obstruction and delays that any business one wants to bring up generally meet with . . . [English ministers] preferably fasten their attention on the domestic scene and as much as possible turn away from foreign affairs, which can be noted on every occasion when they come into question.[98]

[92] See Nolcken's very full analysis: G. A. von Nolckens riksdagsberättelse, 1769, Roberts Transcripts; cf. Roberts, *British Diplomacy*, 242–3, and *Grafton Autobiography*, 168.
[93] Roberts, *British Diplomacy*, 235–6.　　[94] *Grafton Autobiography*, 168.
[95] See e.g. Conway to Wroughton, 7 Oct. 1766, SP 88/92.
[96] Nolcken to KP, 3 July 1767, Roberts Transcripts; cf. the duke of Newcastle's complaint in spring 1767 about 'the total neglect of foreign affairs', cited above, p. 2.
[97] *Pol. Corr.* xxvi. 221 n. 4; cf. *Grenville Papers*, iv. 97, 109.
[98] Nolcken to KP, 5 Jan. 1768, Roberts Transcripts.

This neglect was principally due to the very real difficulties which confronted the ailing Chatham Administration. By the winter of 1767–8, the serious problems in Ireland and the American colonies, along with their own political survival, were far more immediate priorities for ministers than the intricacies of Polish politics. The death of Charles Townshend in autumn 1767 had made Grafton the effective leader of the ministry, and in December he tried to strengthen his parliamentary position by an alliance with the Bedfords. Their leader, the Duke of Bedford, was old and in failing health, and had no wish to return to office. But he succesfully insisted on important posts for two of his principal lieutenants: the Earl of Gower became Lord President of the Council in December 1767, while in the following month Viscount Weymouth entered the government as Northern Secretary. The replacement of the ineffective Conway did nothing to strengthen British diplomacy; indeed, Weymouth was to prove even less capable than his discredited predecessor.[99]

The new Northern Secretary was a man of undoubted intelligence but with a flawed personality. Devoted to the gaming table, frequently drunk, and habitually indolent, he depended heavily on his loyal Under-Secretary, the experienced Robert Wood, to transact official business.[100] Weymouth's neglect of the routine correspondence was soon notorious: during the entire nine months that he controlled the northern department, the minister in Sweden received only four letters.[101] The new Secretary tried to hide his total ignorance of continental affairs behind a proverbial taciturnity, but foreign diplomats in London were not deceived and his shortcomings were soon notorious all over Europe. Within a few months the French ambassador had proclaimed him to be 'usually badly informed and always very ignorant'.[102] The Southern Secretary, Shelburne, was little better and in any case effectively isolated in the cabinet.[103] His relations with Weymouth in particular were very

[99] Roberts, *British Diplomacy*, 264–5. Weymouth omitted to send the secret intelligence (derived from interception in Hanover) on which British policy in Sweden was substantially dependent throughout the entire 9 months that he was Northern Secretary.
[100] M. Roberts, *Splendid Isolation 1763–1780* (Reading, 1970), 6; Walpole, *Memoirs*, iii. 96–7, 159–60; cf. Junius's sneer about Weymouth and 'the bewitching smiles of Burgundy': *The Letters of Junius*, ed. J. Cannon (Oxford, 1978), 31; Tony Hayter, *The Army and the Crowd in Mid-Georgian England* (London, 1978), 137. Sir Nathaniel Wraxall discreetly commented that 'His application to business by no means kept pace with his abilities, nor was he ever a popular Minister': *Historical Memoirs of My Own Time (1772–1784)* (2 vols.; London, 1815), ii. 198.
[101] Roberts, *British Diplomacy*, 236.
[102] CP (Angleterre) 478, fo. 47.
[103] *Grafton Autobiography*, 154; J. Norris, *Shelburne and Reform* (London, 1963), 52–3.

poor: it was said that the two men had never exchanged a visit.[104]
The shortcomings of the Secretaries and the divisions within the
ministry were to contribute to the weak handling of a serious crisis
with France, which blew up in spring 1768 over Corsica.

For a generation, the decaying Italian republic of Genoa had been
struggling to retain the island of Corsica, where a formidable
separatist movement had emerged. Since the 1730s Genoa had come
to depend on France's financial and military support to sustain this
struggle, but by the 1760s the rebels were clearly gaining the upper
hand. Acknowledging this defeat, the Genoese Republic began to
negotiate the formal cession of the island to France at the very
beginning of 1768. Corsica's location in the western Mediterranean,
close to the great southern naval base at Toulon, gave it considerable
strategic importance for France. Choiseul had always shown an
interest in securing some form of control over the island and, in
particular, over the strategically vital ports.[105] He had been
emboldened by British weakness, particularly over the Manila
Ransom and the Falklands in 1766. He also feared that Britain
would oppose any annexation and might even launch a preventive
war. Choiseul therefore tried to maintain absolute secrecy during the
intensive negotiations with Genoa which led, by the Treaty of
Versailles signed on 15 May 1768, to France's thinly disguised
purchase of the island at a bargain price.

It proved impossible to keep these discussions completely secret.
Rumours had reached British ministers in the previous year that
Genoa might try to hand over Corsica to France, and in the early
months of 1768 reports of Franco-Genoese negotiations did arrive in
London.[106] These were vague and at times contradictory, and it was
early April before British ministers began to realise that French
reinforcements might be sent to the island.[107] Even then the
ambassador in Paris, Rochford, was uncertain about the truth of
these rumours. He also reported that Choiseul had vigorously denied
any decision had been taken and had told him that only the extension
of an existing convention (providing for French military aid) was
under consideration. Rochford concluded that while France might

---

[104] P. Durrant, 'A Political Life of Henry Fitzroy, Third Duke of Grafton (1735–1811)'
(unpublished Ph.D. thesis, University of Manchester, 1978), 194.

[105] T. E. Hall, *France and the Eighteenth-Century Corsican Question* (New York, 1971),
119–81.

[106] See e.g. James Hollford to Shelburne, 6 Feb. 1768, SP 79/24.

[107] Rochford to Shelburne, 31 Mar. 1768 (received 4 Apr. 1768), SP 78/274, fos. 119–21.
This was the first occasion on which Rochford had mentioned Corsica.

have some long-term aim of annexing Corsica, for the moment she was not in a position to risk war with Britain. This assessment was accepted by Shelburne, who merely told the ambassador to keep a close watch on the situation.[108]

During the next month, the British government gradually realized the full extent of Choiseul's plans. In April reports began to be received in London that the outright cession of Corsica was being arranged.[109] Although Shelburne was alarmed, the official British response was notably weak:[110] observation remained the extent of Britain's reaction. There were several reasons for this. Relations with France had improved considerably during the past year and Britain was anxious that this improvement should be maintained.[111] Secondly, Corsica was not generally viewed as a vital British interest. James Boswell, who had visited the island in 1765, had tried to arouse sympathy for the Corsicans and for their remarkable leader, Pasquale Paoli, and his celebrated *Account of Corsica* (1768) introduced the conflict to the British public. But his energetic campaign had little impact on official circles in London.[112] The island was of negligible economic importance and was regarded as irrelevant to Britain's declining trade in the Mediterranean.[113] Its potential strategic importance was dimly recognized, but ministers believed that possession of Gibraltar and Minorca secured their naval position in the western Mediterranean, and there was certainly no interest in official circles in acquiring the island.[114] Above all, the British response was fatally weakened by the simultaneous emergence of serious internal problems. The spring of 1768 demonstrated how Britain's weak diplomacy could be wrecked by competing domestic difficulties. During these weeks, as Choiseul's intentions became clear, the cabinet's attention was consumed by the general election in March, by continuing ministerial upheavals, by another round in the

---

[108] SP 78/274, fo. 123.

[109] Mann to Shelburne, 26 Mar. 1768, SP 98/73; Hollford to Shelburne, 9 Apr. 1768, SP 79/24; Rochford to Shelburne, 21 Apr. 1768, SP 78/274, fos. 106–7.

[110] See, in particular, Shelburne to Rochford, Secret, 29 Apr. 1768, ibid., fos. 210–11.

[111] For Shelburne's testimony to this, see SP 78/274, fos. 52, 78–80. Shelburne's moderation was probably confirmed by a rumour in mid-Apr. 1768 that France was prepared for war: see *HMC III*, 143.

[112] F. A. Pottle, *James Boswell: The Earlier Years 1740–1769* (London, 1966), 250–61, 266–8 and 303–8. There was considerable public sympathy for the Corsicans and in the following year, the defeated Paoli came to London and was received by George III, but this was a response to the Corsican struggle against France rather than to the French annexation: Black, *Natural and Necessary Enemies*, 120–1.

[113] M. S. Anderson, 'British Diplomatic Relations with the Mediterranean, 1763–1778' (unpublished Ph.D. thesis, University of Edinburgh, 1952), 233–4; cf. 1–67 *passim* for British trade in the region.

[114] Nolcken to KP, 24 May 1768, Roberts Transcripts.

Wilkes affair, and, above all, by very serious popular unrest.[115]

Riots had begun in January, the result of an usually severe winter and of several successive bad harvests, and the unrest was greatly intensified by Wilkes's victory in the Middlesex election at the end of March.[116] John Wilkes had only recently returned from exile in France. He remained legally an outlaw and also awaited sentence for his original conviction in 1764 for blasphemy and seditious libel. This confronted the cabinet with the question of whether Wilkes, as a convicted outlaw, should be allowed to take his seat when the new parliament met in May. By 20 April, shortly before news was received from Paris that Franco-Genoese agreement over Corsica was almost complete, ministers decided to exclude Wilkes from the Commons.[117] Even more immediate and serious was the intensification of the rioting which followed the Middlesex election. For the next six weeks unrest was all but continuous in the capital, and this culminated in the notorious 'Massacre of St George's Fields' (10 May 1768) when troops fired on a crowd, killing a number of rioters. The situation remained tense until Wilkes's two appearances in court (8 and 18 June 1768). This serious unrest understandably preoccupied the cabinet. Shelburne, responsible for relations with France, was still isolated in the government. He found it extremely difficult to persuade ministers to give full attention to France's shadowy negotiations with Genoa, when they faced a far more immediate threat from the London mob.[118]

The British ambassador in Paris had launched some vigorous, though unofficial protests, as soon as it became clear that additional French troops were to be sent to Corsica, but his official dispatches were more muted and cautious in tone.[119] Britain was relying

[115] The article by N. Tracy, 'The Administration of the Duke of Grafton and the French Invasion of Corsica', *Eighteenth-Century Studies*, 8 (1974–5), 169–82, provides a careful examination of this episode based on material in the Public Record Office. But it neglects the all-important domestic political context (neither Wilkes nor the rioters are mentioned) and, since Dr Tracy has not used the French archives, it says very little about the divisions within the cabinet and the importance of these for France. This is equally true of his subsequent account in *Navies, Deterrence and American Independence: Britain and Seapower in the 1760s and 1770s* (Vancouver, 1988), 62–8. The best available study is Anderson, 'Britain's Diplomatic Relations', 228–83.

[116] For these events, see G. Rudé. *Wilkes and Liberty: A Social Study of 1763–1774* (Oxford, 1965), 37–56, and Hayter, *Army and the Crowd*, 136–45 and 178–80. The government's total preoccupation with the riots is apparent from *Cal. HO Papers 1766–9*, pp. 320 ff.

[117] J. Brooke, *The Chatham Administration 1766–1768* (London, 1956), 354.

[118] In mid-May, Shelburne was finding it difficult to secure a cabinet meeting to discuss Corsica because of the preoccupation with internal affairs: SP 78/275, fo. 12.

[119] CP (Angleterre) 478, fos. 8–9 and 63–4; SP 78/274–5. Dr Rice very plausibly suggests that this moderation was due to Rochford's unwillingness to cry wolf again after his unhappy experiences in 1766: 'Great Britain, the Manila Ransom', 408.

principally on Rochford's judgement, and until well into May he emphasized that no immediate territorial cession was in prospect.[120] A further complication was the ambassador's serious illness at this point. The rumours about the Franco-Genoese treaty continued to be very vague, and even at the end of April Shelburne still professed to believe that France merely intended to send reinforcements to Corsica.[121] Early in May he finally spoke to the French ambassador about the reports of a Franco-Genoese agreement. But Châtelet had been well briefed before he left France (he had arrived in London as recently as February 1768) and he was ready with a very straight diplomatic bat.[122] Denying all knowledge of any such agreement, Châtelet himself protested that France had no obligation to inform Britain before undertaking negotiations with other powers. He also rebuffed Shelburne's rather half-hearted attempts to argue that any such cession would be a clear breach of the peace of Aix-la-Chapelle which had guaranteed the status quo in Italy and would also upset the European balance of power.

Despite Châtelet's denials, British ministers now grasped that some form of French control over Corsica was being negotiated.[123] It is not clear whether they appreciated that outright cession had already been arranged. The cabinet was deeply divided over whether Britain could, or even should, do anything to oppose the annexation, and in the aftermath of the 'Massacre of St George's Fields' it was preoccupied with the tense situation in London. Ministers did discuss Corsica on several occasions in May and June, and remarkably enough their divisions and the arguments employed were fully known to the French ambassador.[124]

Two conflicting attitudes largely followed the political divisions in the expiring Chatham Administration. Grafton, the *de facto* leader

---

[120] On 10 May 1768, Shelburne still doubted rumours of a French take-over of the island: to Hollford, SP 79/24.

[121] On 21 Apr., Rochford reported that France had actually *refused* Genoa's offer to sell the island: to Shelburne, SP 78/274, fos. 206–7; CP (Angleterre) 478, fos. 127–40; in his dispatch of 29 Apr. to Rochford, Shelburne spoke in terms of a future agreement to transfer the island to France: SP 78/274, fos. 210–11.

[122] His formal instructions (*Recueil . . . Angleterre*, iii. 436–49) contain no mention of Corsica, but the ambassador was clearly given secret, and verbal, instructions: CP (Angleterre) 478, fos. 166–88; cf. SP 78/275, fo. 2.

[123] Early in May, Shelburne sent an agent, John Stewart, to investigate France's readiness for hostilities and Paoli's capacity to mount serious resistance (Tracy, 'Grafton and the French Invasion of Corsica', 174; Fitzmaurice, *Life of Shelburne*, i. 364). But neither Stewart's mission nor the subsequent and rather similar mission mounted by Grafton affected the outcome: *Grafton Autobiography*, 203 ff.; *Corr. Geo. III*, ii. 38–40.

[124] CP (Angleterre) 478, fos. 345–7; 479, fos. 62–4 and 112–43. The reports of the Neapolitan envoy, Caracciolo, confirm this split: see Fitzmaurice, *Life of Shelburne*, i. 365, and *HMC III*, 140.

of the ministry, Shelburne, Lord Camden, and Sir Edward Hawke were all alarmed by the threat to British naval interests.[125] They urged a vigorous response and were prepared for war: many contemporaries believed they were here following the lead of their political mentor, Chatham. This faction was opposed by Lord Gower, Lord North, Weymouth, and the Earl of Hillsborough, a group that was usually, though inaccurately referred to at the time, as the 'Bedfords'. They argued that Corsica was not worth a war, and they had, for some time, been anxious to drive Shelburne from office. This debate, and Choiseul's knowledge of these divisions, severely weakened Britain's diplomacy.[126] Shelburne continued to complain to Châtelet and lodged a more formal protest in Paris, but France's knowledge of the sharp split in London enabled Choiseul to ignore him, confident that Britain would not go to war.[127] The principal source of these leaks was clearly Bedford, not himself in the cabinet, but whose supporters had recently joined the ministry. The Bedfords were known at the time as the 'French party'; they favoured peace with France in order to concentrate on coercion of the American colonists; and their leader had long been the principal Francophile in British public life.[128] Bedford had revisited France as recently as 1765 and maintained close personal contacts with successive French ambassadors: at the height of the crisis in June, Châtelet caused a sensation by going to stay with the Duke for three days.[129] The French ambassador was also careful to maintain close contacts with Gower and Weymouth, and to provide each with information and arguments to strengthen the case for peace.[130]

Britain's response was also undermined by other factors. Remarkably enough, at the beginning of June the Duke of Grafton made a determined effort to force Shelburne, whom he had long disliked, out of the ministry: this at a time when both were arguing within the cabinet for a vigorous response over Corsica![131] Shelburne was unwilling to go without a fight and set about defending his own

[125] Camden was Lord Chancellor; Hawke, First Lord of the Admiralty.
[126] See Nolcken to KP, 24 May 1768, Roberts Transcripts. Rochford received surprisingly few official dispatches in these weeks, given the importance of Corsica: SP 78/275 *passim*. There is only one apparent gap, No. 18.
[127] *BDI* vii: *France 1745–89*, ed. L. G. Wickham Legg, 101–4. The French embassy's intelligence network was soon reporting that no naval or military preparations had been set on foot and this increased French confidence: CP (Angleterre) 478–9 *passim*.
[128] Nolcken to KP, 29 Dec. 1767, Roberts Transcripts. Choiseul frequently testified to the importance of the friendship of Bedford and his followers for France: see e.g. CP (Angleterre) 477, fo. 268.
[129] *Bedford Corr.* iii. 313 ff; CP (Angleterre) 457, fo. 135; 464, fo. 130, 184; 479, fos. 136–7.   [130] CP (Angleterre) 479, fo. 62.
[131] For this, see Brooke, *Chatham Administration*, 363 ff.

position.[132] Grafton's attack had the effect of pushing the Southern Secretary into a more moderate stance towards France.[133] In addition, Weymouth's repeated and uncharacteristic outbursts to members of the diplomatic corps, that Britain would never fight over Corsica, further undermined Shelburne's strategy in the critical weeks of May and June.[134] Ministers were also troubled that opposition to France would mean supporting the Corsicans, whom they regarded as rebels.[135] The argument of political legitimacy was one which most governments still found it difficult to resist.

The continuing uncertainty over the precise nature of the Franco-Genoese treaty also encouraged inaction: until shortly before this convention was formally communicated, most ministers believed— or feigned to believe—that it principally concerned further French reinforcements and a French lease over the island. British statesmen certainly suspected that greater French control over Corsica would be the outcome, but they failed to grasp that its formal transfer had already been arranged. Above all, ministers were aware of Britain's dangerous diplomatic isolation. This was particularly apparent in the context of France's stable alliances with Madrid and Vienna. Shelburne remarked on one occasion that when Châtelet came to see him, he had Spain in one pocket and Austria in the other.[136] These considerations were important and they added fuel to the cabinet debate. But Britain's diplomacy was paralysed principally by the serious internal problems in spring 1768 and by the deep divisions within the Grafton Ministry itself.[137]

Choiseul's strategy of presenting Britain with a *fait accompli* secured a notable success. At the end of June he communicated the

---

[132] Cf. CP (Angleterre) 479, fos. 112–43.

[133] This change became apparent shortly after Grafton went on the offensive: compare Châtelet's judgement on Shelburne's conduct as being 'spirited and tenacious' (10 June 1768) with his emphasis on the Secretary's 'very moderate and very mild' conduct (18 June 1768): ibid. 479, fos. 64, 122.

[134] Fitzmaurice, *Life of Shelburne*, i. 374.

[135] Nolcken to KP, 31 May 1768, Roberts Transcripts. As recently as 1763, the British government had attempted, by means of an Order in Council, to prevent munitions and other supplies being sent from Britain to the Corsican rebels.

[136] Châtelet to Choiseul, 18 July 1768, CP (Angleterre) 479, fo. 132. In a notably indiscreet outburst, the Southern Secretary went on (fos. 133–34) to censure the conduct of the 'iniquitous' ministers who had caused the breach with Frederick II in 1762 and made clear his own wish for an alliance with Prussia. In this, as in his hard-line attitude towards France, Shelburne was following the lead of his mentor, Chatham.

[137] Cf. Shelburne's later claim that he had been 'left alone, and deserted by all his colleagues in office and brethren in cabinet': *Parl. Hist.* xviii, col. 1390. Britain also resisted some sustained attempts by the Savoyard state and by its ambassador in London to persuade it to resist the French annexation. The Turin government believed that this would weaken its own position in the western Mediterranean and hoped for British support: Thomas Potter (chargé d'affaires in Turin) to Shelburne, 21 May and 11 June 1768, SP 92/73.

formal Franco-Genoese treaty to Britain, confident that the French annexation would not be opposed. When Châtelet presented Shelburne with this, the Southern Secretary simply showed Britain's resentment at France's striking gain.[138] A few days later the cabinet formally considered the treaty. Ministers were content to note that it was 'a departure from the system hitherto professed by His Most Christian Majesty and must endanger the confidence that has hitherto subsisted between the Two Crowns'.[139] There was nothing Britain could do now, and in summer 1768 the French take-over went ahead.[140] Paoli's spirited and remarkably successful resistance, and James Boswell's success in popularizing the Corsican cause in Britain, induced the government to provide some belated, and secret, aid to the rebels.[141] This was principally munitions, and it may have sustained Corsican resistance: it was to be summer 1769 before the French conquest was completed.[142] But all attempts by Paoli to secure greater support foundered on the Grafton Ministry's fear of war.

Shelburne's belated and distinctly half-hearted attempts to salvage something out of the wreckage failed completely. Choiseul calmly ignored his suggestions that in return for Britain's tacit acceptance of French annexation, France should either encourage Spain to pay the Manila Ransom, or herself make some concessions in the long-running dispute over Dunkirk.[143] The annexation of Corsica was a considerable boost to France's flagging international reputation and to Choiseul's own position, which was coming under attack. It was also a further severe blow to Britain's political standing in Europe and seemed, to many observers, conclusive proof of Britain's decline. The point was not that the Grafton cabinet should have gone to war over Corsica: there was much to be said for the conclusion that no vital British strategic interests were involved. But it should not have

[138] The French ambassador's account of this notably bad-tempered discussion is in CP (Angleterre) 479, fos. 203–5.

[139] Cabinet Minute, 27 June 1768, cited by Tracy, 'Grafton and the French Invasion of Corsica', 178. This phrase was incorporated almost verbatim into Shelburne's dispatch to Rochford of 1 July 1768 (*BDI* vii: *France 1745–89*, ed. L. G. Wickham Legg, 104), but the ambassador was not instructed to make any further representations.

[140] As Shelburne tacitly admitted: to Sir James Gray, Secret, 18 June 1768, SP 94/179. The fact that both Châtelet and Rochford returned home on leave in the late summer of 1768 was seen as tacit recognition by Britain of France's gain: Lalaguna Lasala, 'England, Spain and the Family Compact', 251.

[141] Tracy, 'Grafton and the French Invasion of Corsica', 179–81; Pottle, *Boswell*, 390, 394–7; George III to Grafton, 14 Aug. and 16 Sept. 1768, Grafton Papers.

[142] George III was promised repayment by ministers, but almost 20 years later the King was still complaining that he had received none: M. Roberts, 'Great Britain and the Swedish Revolution, 1772–3', *Essays in Swedish History* (London, 1967), 332 n. 9.

[143] Lalaguna Lasala, 'England, Spain and the Family Compact', 255.

dithered for two months and then done nothing.[144] At the height of its indecision, a shrewd English observer had noted that 'our supineness, it is said, makes us contemptible all over Europe'.[145] This, rather than the French gain of Corsica, gave the episode its importance at the time.

Britain's hesitant and ultimately feeble conduct strengthened the belief that, distracted by internal and American problems, she had ceased to have a foreign policy. In July 1768 the perceptive and well-informed Swedish minister, Baron Nolcken, noted Britain's 'extraordinary reserve about all matters concerning foreign powers' and added the amazing comment that, in the six months since Weymouth entered office, he had not managed to have a single decent discussion with the Northern Secretary.[146] Weymouth's celebrated taciturnity was no doubt part of the explanation, but the impression was growing that London was indifferent to Europe.[147] Frederick II professed to believe Britain had resumed a 'Tory' foreign policy: her ministers, he declared, only thought of the benefits of trade and aimed to avoid either a European war or any continental alliance.[148] Panin agreed, noting that Britain could no longer be considered a 'land power', while Bernstorff remarked that since 1763 Britain's European role had been less than at any time since the Revolution of 1688.[149] Horace Walpole concurred: ministers, he declared, 'endeavoured to doze over all thoughts of the continent'.[150]

Many European observers had concluded by the later 1760s that Britain had lost her way.[151] Her growing insularity, inept handling of foreign affairs, and proclaimed indifference to the continent, were additional obstacles to any alliance. The continuation of Anglo-Bourbon rivalry was also a formidable barrier. This meant, as Bernstorff shrewdly pointed out, that any power signing a treaty with London immediately brought Bourbon hostility on to itself and secured very little in return, in view of Britain's refusal to pay peacetime subsidies.[152] In these circumstances the British insistence on equality had a hollow ring, given the stability of France's alliances

---

[144] Whether diplomatic representations, or even the kind of naval demonstration envisaged by Dr Tracy ('Grafton and the French Invasion of Corsica', 169, 173, and *passim*), would have deflected Choiseul must be doubtful.   [145] *Grenville Papers*, iv. 306.

[146] Nolcken to KP, 12 July 1768, Roberts Transcripts; cf CP (Angleterre) 478, fo. 347.

[147] *Pol. Corr.* xxvii. 349 n. 5; cf CP (Angleterre) 478, fo. 47. This was also a frequent theme of the Austrian ambassador in these months: see his dispatches in HHStA, England-Korrespondenz 114.   [148] *Die Politischen Testamente*, ed. Volz, 206.

[149] Martens, *Recueil des traités*, ix (x). 274; *Bernstorff Corr.* ii. 329.

[150] *Memoirs*, iii. 216; cf. Nolcken to KP, 4 Oct. 1768, Roberts Transcripts.

[151] In mid-1767, Kaunitz noted this decline and prophesied that it would probably accelerate: to Seilern, 6 June 1767, HHStA, England-Korrespondenz 113.

[152] *Bernstorff Corr.* ii. 391–2.

with Spain and Austria and the dominance of this system in the southern half of the continent.

Britain's lack of purpose, highlighted by the Corsican episode, was more damaging still. It undermined her reputation, which remained the basis of a successful diplomacy.[153] This was further lowered by ministerial instability and by the accompanying publicity. British diplomats regularly complained about the bad impression these upheavals made in foreign courts, where such frequent changes of personnel were quite unusual. Macartney's characteristically outspoken verdict, that 'however wise-judged or necessary the frequent changes in the Administration may be supposed at home, it is certain that they render us ridiculous nay despicable abroad', expressed the exasperation of his fellow envoys.[154] These complaints were at their peak in the later 1760s, and they testified to one element in Britain's decline.

British pride, after the intoxicating victories of the Seven Years War, was also recognized to be part of the explanation. Britain still wanted alliances, declared Bernstorff, provided they cost her nothing in money or trouble.[155] The failure to conclude treaties, particularly with Russia, was also recognized to have contributed to this. The principal reason for Britain's growing insularity was widely recognized to be her serious internal and colonial problems.[156] Continental statesmen were accustomed to view foreign policy as the principal, and indeed, unique concern of government, and they were generally unsympathetic to the other British problems.[157] London's diplomacy appeared to be drifting along no particular course. This, together with the high tone in which Britain's growing insularity was expressed, only reinforced the view that she was ceasing to be part of the European states-system.

John Wilkes's personal contribution to this was considerable. The failure to act effectively against him on his return in 1768, and his renewed importance as a focus for unrest, were seen as conclusive evidence of Britain's decline.[158] One particular episode increased his impact. Early in April 1768, when rioting in London was at its peak, the Austrian ambassador was detained by a Wilkite mob. The price of his release was nominal enough: to join in a cry of 'Wilkes and

---

[153] See, e.g. the devastating comments of Bernstorff, himself sympathetic to England: *Bernstorff Corr.* ii. 330.

[154] Add. MSS 6826, fo. 118.   [155] *Bernstorff Corr.* ii. 331.

[156] e.g. Frederick II's view in Nov. 1768: *Pol. Corr.* xxvii. 426; cf. *Bernstorff Corr.* ii. 271, and the views of the Austrian ambassador: to Kaunitz, 13 Mar. 1767, HHStA, England-Korrespondenz 113.   [157] *Bernstorff Corr.* ii. 425; cf. HMC *Eglinton*, 414.

[158] Roberts, *Splendid Isolation*, 12. British diplomats were continually complaining about the damage done to Britain's prestige by Wilkes's career: see e.g. SP 90/87, fo. 65.

Liberty'. The haughty and aristocratic Seilern refused and he was saved only by the bravery of his coachman.[159] Seilern was outraged and protested vigorously. For a time there was even talk of lowering Austria's diplomatic representation in London to the level of chargé d'affaires. Although this episode had no such serious repercussions, it was the talk of the diplomatic corps for several weeks. By suggesting the British government was even powerless to protect the diplomats accredited to it, the ambassador's adventure further lowered Britain's flagging international standing. In fact, the nadir was reached in spring and summer 1768. Britain's diplomatic recovery, like the parallel emergence of stability at home, began with the final dissolution of the Chatham Administration in that autumn.

[159] For this episode, see Seilern's dispatches for early Apr. (HHStA, England-Korrespondenz 114) and CP (Angleterre) 478, fos. 17–18. To judge by the Austrian diplomatic dispatches, Horace Walpole's celebrated story (*Memoirs*, iii. 189–90) that Seilern was dragged out of his coach, held upside down, and had 'No. 45' chalked on the soles of his feet, would seem to be apocryphal.

6

The Beginnings of Recovery, 1768–1771

SHELBURNE left the Southern Department in October 1768. His resignation, along with his mentor, Chatham, led to a reshuffle in which the Northern Secretary Weymouth switched to the senior southern province.[1] Towards the end of October 1768 Weymouth was succeeded by the Earl of Rochford at the Northern Department. A career diplomat, having served at Turin, Madrid, and Paris, the new Northern Secretary had more diplomatic experience when he entered office than any other secretary of state during the age of the American Revolution, with the single exception of Stormont.[2]

Rochford's promotion strengthened British diplomacy in several ways. As a former ambassador he was actually aware of European issues and prepared to discuss them with foreign diplomats. The contrast with the evasive and taciturn Weymouth was soon apparent: Nolcken noted after his very first interview that, unlike his predecessor, Rochford did not try to cut short any discussion.[3] In itself this helped to boost Britain's flagging reputation abroad. Rochford as an ambassador had also experienced at first hand the periodic neglect of British diplomacy by ministers at home. He himself was to be particularly scrupulous in his conduct of the routine correspondence, until distracted by overwhelming American problems and weakened by ill health in 1774–5. The benefit to Britain's foreign policy was considerable: after 1768 there is a significant decline in complaints by diplomats of being left in ignorance over the objectives of official policy. Unlike his immediate predecessors, Rochford entered office principally because of his own

---

[1] Curiously enough in view of his reputation for neglecting business, Weymouth requested and was given the senior Southern Department specifically because 'the most material business to this country must go through the hands of him who has the Southern correspondence' (J. Brooke, *The Chatham Administration 1766–1768* (London, 1956), 375), but this request seems to have been motivated entirely by personal pride and political prestige, and not by any new-found zeal for foreign affairs. Rochford's appointment as Southern Secretary, though it would have made excellent sense in view of his diplomatic service at Turin, Madrid, and Paris, would have appeared a slight to Weymouth: hence the change of province.

[2] Stormont was Northern Secretary from 1779 until 1782.

[3] Nolcken to KP, 11 Nov. 1768, Roberts Transcripts.

merits as an ambassador. This independence, together with the fact that he had not been a member of any previous administration, enabled him to stand aloof from another round of the Wilkes affair.[4] During the next eighteen months British politics were dominated by John Wilkes and by the petitioning movement, but Rochford continued to give all his attention to foreign affairs. Throughout most of his secretaryship—he was to remain in office until 1775[5]— he concentrated on Britain's diplomacy, and he was certainly to be far less distracted by internal and colonial problems than any of his predecessors since 1763. This was assisted by the creation of a third secretaryship for the American colonies in January 1768.

Rochford's appointment created greater unity in the control of British diplomacy than there had been since the early stages of the Grenville Ministry. Weymouth's ignorance and neglect of his official duties, together with his obvious distaste for his job,[6] made him at first only too glad to abandon the initiative to his brother Secretary, and as a result, Rochford acquired considerable control over both provinces and was at times *de facto* 'Foreign Secretary'.[7] The unity which this gave to British diplomacy was significant during the next few years and contributed to Britain's revival. But this recovery was primarily a matter of the greater realism and vigour of British policy from autumn 1768 onwards, together with the growing regard in which Britain slowly came to be viewed abroad.

By autumn 1768 British diplomacy had drifted dangerously close to the rocks. Rochford, who proved to be an imaginative foreign minister,[8] immediately set about trying to avert the impending shipwreck. His success was to be incomplete, but he did try to strengthen Britain's position by a series of initiatives. These were principally concerned with a renewed search for a continental ally. During the next eighteen months relations with the Bourbon powers were relatively untroubled. Choiseul was preoccupied with the conquest of Corsica and, in any case, remained convinced that a war with Britain could still not be won. In 1768–9 Rochford concentrated

---

[4] See Nolcken's remarks: to KP, 30 Dec. 1768, ibid.

[5] Rochford switched to the Southern Department in Dec. 1770.

[6] At no other time, perhaps, could a secretary of state have declared that British diplomats 'should *hear* as much and *say* as little as possible', and certainly Weymouth reinforced precept with example: *Sbornik*, xii. 369.

[7] There are even indications that unity of control extended to Rochford conducting negotiations with countries in the Southern province, but the evidence is far from clear. During the second half of 1770, however, Weymouth reasserted himself and for a time played a decisive role in Anglo-Bourbon relations: see below, pp. 139/52.

[8] M. Roberts, *Splendid Isolation 1763–1780* (Reading, 1970), 7. George III thought that Rochford was guilty of 'too much precipitation' and added that his 'zeal makes him rather in a hurry': *Corr. Geo. III*, ii. 370–1.

instead upon eastern and south-eastern Europe, where a Russo-Turkish War broke out shortly before he took office.

Rochford's first aim was to end Britain's dangerous diplomatic isolation, which he recognized had been highlighted during the crisis over Corsica.[9] The three eastern powers remained the only potential allies. By the later 1760s, however, the choice was even narrower. The fiasco of 1766 had demonstrated very clearly that, unless circumstances should change dramatically, Frederick II was unwilling to contemplate new links with Britain. His immediate and blunt rejection of Pitt's overtures had widened the gap separating the two states and, after Chatham's effective disappearance in spring 1767, relations with Prussia received little attention in London. Ministers always tended to regard Britain's alliance as a not-to-be-missed opportunity and they responded to the Prussian rebuff with characteristic pique.[10] Sir Andrew Mitchell, the British envoy to Prussia, was now politically redundant. His last five years in Berlin were a period of honourable semi-retirement. He maintained his cordial relations with the Prussian ministers and even with the King himself, enjoyed the company of his friends, and reported such news as he could discover, which was little enough.[11] Relations with the Habsburgs were considerably better, and more was certainly expected from Vienna, although the desired revival of the Old System was now recognized to be a distant event.[12] Only Russia remained, and it was there that Britain was to look for an alliance during the next three years. Rochford himself favoured such links, and in autumn 1768 circumstances once again appeared to bring the two states together.

Moves to revive the negotiations with Catherine II had in fact begun during the final months of the Chatham Administration. The search for a suitable ambassador for St Petersburg had ended late in February 1768 when Lord Cathcart accepted the mission: principally, it would seem, because he had a large family to support and came to an agreement that he would continue to enjoy the emoluments of his post on his return to England.[13] Though his wife's pregnancy delayed his departure for several months, the new ambassador immediately set to work with the energy and enthusiasm which were to characterize his mission. After a detailed perusal of his predecessors' dispatches, from which he clearly derived some fixed ideas, Cathcart

[9] Black, *Natural and Necessary Enemies*, 90.
[10] See e.g. SP 90/85, fos. 175–7; 90/86, fo. 1.
[11] Add. MSS 6810, fo. 206.
[12] CP (Angleterre) 479, fo. 134.
[13] CP (Angleterre) 477, fo. 242.

set out for St Petersburg in summer 1768. His determination was apparent in his decision to travel by sea, rather than by the more usual, slower, overland route, and he arrived early in August.[14] If Macartney's recall had seemed a political full stop, Cathcart's arrival opened a new paragraph in relations.

The ambassador's formal instructions underlined that, though there should be no immediate attempt to revive the alliance negotiations, an early initiative was clearly intended.[15] Yet they were also a formidable obstacle to any treaty. The 1742 treaty was to remain the basis of any alliance and, even more remarkable, Cathcart was actually told to regard the instructions previously given to Buckinghamshire and to Macartney as his 'Rule of Conduct', yet the failure of these was obvious. This was not an auspicious beginning, though the next few years were to see considerable activity. Both the new and resolute Northern Secretary and the new and energetic ambassador played a part in reviving Anglo-Russian diplomacy; but the principal reason was the outbreak of a Russo-Turkish war in autumn 1768. The fighting in the Balkans continued until 1774 and transformed both Britain's foreign policy and the general shape of European diplomacy.

The Sultan's declaration of war in October 1768 was the culmination of a steady deterioration in Russo-Turkish relations which went back several years. Its principal cause was Ottoman resentment at Russia's increasingly direct intervention in Poland and the measure of control which she appeared to be securing in Warsaw. This hegemony was a direct threat to the Turks. In any future war, a Polish auxiliary army would be an important diversion and might do something to replace Russia's lost ally, Austria. By the summer of 1768 the Ottoman Empire was determined to fight: all that was needed was a pretext, which was provided by a double violation of Ottoman territory by Russian troops. On 6 October Obreskov, the Russian Resident in Constantinople, was imprisoned in the Castle of the Seven Towers, an action the Porte had always regarded as equivalent to a formal declaration of war. This was an extremely serious matter for Catherine II and her advisers. Russia was already deeply committed in Poland, where a guerilla war tied up a significant number of Russian troops, and now faced a full-scale conflict with the Turks as well.

The Empress's difficulties were increased by a new crisis in Sweden, late in 1768. Catherine II's recurring nightmare was of

---

[14] *Sbornik*, cxli. 447; BDR, 117.
[15] Cathcart's 'Instructions', dated 21 July 1768, are in SP 104/240, pp. 27–34; an extract is in *Sbornik*, xii. 333–4.

simultaneous problems at three points on her western frontier, and this was what now threatened. In Stockholm the Caps, the party of Russia and Britain which had been so triumphant in 1765-6, were on the defensive against an alliance of the Hats and the court. Choiseul, aware of Russia's difficulties in Poland and encouraged by the Turkish declaration of war, sought to increase the Empress's problems through a political revolution in Sweden. The arrival of a new French ambassador in Stockholm signalled the opening of a French offensive in the final weeks of 1768.[16] The climax to some shadowy and complex manœuvring came in mid-December. The Swedish King, Adolf Frederik, refused to exercise his functions, thereby precipitating a constitutional crisis, and demanded the calling of a Diet which would probably sweep the Hats to power. The civil service also went on strike and forced the summoning of a Diet for spring 1769.

The outcome was certainly less than Choiseul had hoped for, but the success of the Hat–court alliance was a heavy defeat for Anglo-Russian diplomacy, and it intensified Russia's anxieties about her vulnerable position around the Baltic. Panin saw the threatened restoration of absolute monarchy as the prelude to a Swedish attack from Finland. The Empress and her minister were also concerned that the new elections would involve considerable extra expenditure, when Russia was already short of money.[17] This ensured that a central theme in Russo-British diplomacy, particularly during the winter of 1768-9, was sustained Russian attempts to persuade Britain to bear a large part of the cost. Choiseul was viewed in St Petersburg as the architect of Russia's difficulties.[18] His anti-Russian strategy appeared to be reaching fruition. France's role at Stockholm was evident; in Poland she was believed to be assisting Russia's opponents; while the Empress and her advisers, exaggerating French influence at Constantinople, attributed the Ottoman declaration of war principally to Choiseul's intrigues.[19]

It is against this background that the renewed alliance negotiations must be seen. Already, by late summer 1768, the threatening situation in the Balkans had led Catherine II and Panin to look towards Britain, the enemy of France and a possible source of financial aid. Cathcart's unusually friendly reception in August revealed Russia's wish to revive the negotiations.[20] The desire for an

---

[16] For these events, see Roberts, *British Diplomacy*, 265–74.
[17] *Sbornik*, cxli. 466.   [18] *Sbornik*, xxxvii. 184, 239–40.
[19] See e.g. Panin's comments, reported in Cathcart to Stormont, 12 Nov. 1768, *Sbornik*, xii. 398–9; cf. Madariaga, *Russia*, 204.
[20] This is apparent from the French diplomatic dispatches in *Sbornik*, cxli.

alliance, greater than at any time since 1763, increased during the next few months, with the Turkish declaration of war and then the crisis in Sweden. The breach with the Ottoman Empire in October also removed the formidable barrier of the 'Turkish clause'. Russian ministers soon accepted that Britain could not now be expected to provide assistance against the Turks, since a state could not promise aid against a third party, once a war had actually broken out, without itself becoming a belligerent. Panin hoped, however, that Britain would provide support against France, particularly in Stockholm.

St Petersburg was also encouraged by the behaviour of the new British ambassador. Cathcart was certainly eager to succeed where Buckinghamshire and Macartney had failed, and he was none too careful to keep within his instructions in the attempt.[21] At the beginning of his mission, he had been warned to have nothing to do with any Russian proposals to circumvent difficulties over the 'Turkish clause'.[22] But Cathcart immediately and enthusiastically indulged in some diplomatic horse-trading with Panin, in order to revive the alliance negotiations. Above all, he flouted his orders by encouraging the Russian government to believe that Britain was now prepared to give what she had hitherto always refused: a subsidy.[23] Within a few weeks of his arrival Cathcart had, in effect, offered a subsidy of £100,000 in the event of a Turkish war.[24] Panin appears to have taken this complete reversal of Britain's stance at face value and to have believed that vital financial aid could now be expected.[25] St Petersburg's willingness for an alliance in the winter of 1768–9 reflected both Russia's growing problems in foreign affairs and her belief that Britain's attitude had been transformed.[26]

[21] Cathcart had made clear his intentions before leaving London. His detailed study of the Russian correspondence in the Secretary of State's office made him 'the better judge of my instructions . . . as I hold it to be much better to settle matters of that importance and detail in conversation and upon the spot than by corresponding from so immense a distance': to Sir William Hamilton, 10 June 1768, Cathcart Papers, F I.
[22] Weymouth to Cathcart, 30 Sept. 1768, excerpts in *Sbornik*, ii. 365–9, and *in extenso* in SP 91/79, fos. 18–24; cf. Roberts, *British Diplomacy*, 291.
[23] By mid-Sept., the Swedish envoy in St Petersburg, Baron Ribbing, was reporting that Cathcart had proposed a subsidy treaty to Panin: KP to Ribbing and KP to Nolcken, 6 Oct. 1768 and 8 Oct. 1768, Roberts Transcripts.
[24] Roberts, *British Diplomacy*, 291 and 470 n. 87. It seems likely that the figure of £100,000 (approximately 500,000 roubles) was selected by Cathcart because he knew, from his detailed study of the Russian correspondence before he left Britain, that this was the sum which Panin had demanded for an alliance in the closing weeks of 1763: cf. above, Ch. 4.
[25] This is suggested by Martens, *Recueil des traités*, ix(x), 270–1; cf. *Sbornik*, cxli. 459, 469, 491, 502.
[26] This is not the only evidence of Cathcart's deficiencies. He was careless over cipher security (Roberts, *British Diplomacy*, 290–1); he became involved early in 1769 in Panin's attempts to

Negotiations were formally opened by an extended note given to the British ambassador on 10 October 1768. This recapitulated Russian thinking about an alliance and asked the British government to send a treaty project for formal consideration.[27] Even before news of Obreskov's imprisonment had reached St Petersburg, Panin had significantly modified his earlier insistence on the 'Turkish clause'.[28] Instead, prompted by Cathcart, he suggested a British subsidy of 500,000 roubles (approximately £100,000) in the event of a Turkish attack, to be balanced by the offer of 12,000 Russian soldiers in any Anglo-Bourbon war. If this was not acceptable, Panin would have been prepared to abandon the 'Turkish clause' entirely, in return for an annual subsidy of £50,000 to Sweden. Both proposals were completely unacceptable, as the Russian ambassador Chernyshev soon discovered in London.[29] Rochford, though he emphasized his own wish for an alliance, made clear the impossibility of a peacetime subsidy. Cathcart endeavoured meanwhile to keep Russia's interest in the alliance alive during frequent meetings with Catherine's ministers, and ceaselessly tried to persuade his superiors in London that they should provide the subsidy to Russia which he himself had proposed.[30]

This was always too stiff a price for the British government to pay. Rochford was anxious for an alliance but, though he welcomed the abandonment of the 'Turkish clause', he saw in the new Russian terms a further stumbling block in the substantial shape of the sacred cow of 'no subsidies in peacetime'. Panin's proposals were immediately rejected by Britain on the familiar grounds that subsidies had proved useless in the past and would in any case be rejected by parliament.[31] Though they would not provide a subsidy, British ministers were prepared for further expenditure in Sweden and still

intimidate Sweden without instructions (ibid. 281 ff.), though Rochford subsequently gave hesitant approval to his behaviour; while it was, to say the least, tactless of him to tell the Prussian minister Solms of British dissatisfaction with Frederick II at exactly the moment Britain was trying to conclude an alliance with Prussia's ally, Russia (*Sbornik*, cxli. 478). In general, Cathcart lacked judgement; his enthusiasm too often outran his discretion; and, critically, he had no previous diplomatic experience. But he was devoted to the quest of a Russian alliance and was certainly not lacking in common sense, though this was too often obscured by his verbosity.

[27] *Sbornik*, xii. 371–9.

[28] Ibid. 388–90; cf. Martens, *Recueil des traités*, ix(x). 271.

[29] Ibid. 273, 275.

[30] *Sbornik*, cxli. 484, 526. See, in particular, Cathcart's lengthy private letter to Weymouth, 18 Oct. 1768, Thynne Papers Box B. This makes clear Cathcart had frequently been seeing that shifty operator, Caspar von Saldern, and there are hints that the Holsteiner (at Panin's suggestion?) was encouraging his conviction that a subsidy would make the alliance: *Sbornik*, xii. 382–4, 414, 415–17.

[31] Ibid. xii. 404–5.

wanted to co-operate there.[32] An offer of such co-operation was included in the formal British reply, the treaty-project given to Chernyshev in mid-February 1769.[33] This offered a conventional defensive alliance to last for twenty years. Britain would not pay the demanded subsidy, and the nearest thing to a concession to Russia's viewpoint was the proviso—to balance the 'Turkish clause'—that Britain should not be entitled to aid in the event of a colonial or Mediterranean war.

Rochford's proposal, and especially the refusal of a subsidy, were the more resented by St Petersburg precisely because of Cathcart's frequent promises of financial assistance. This latest British project was full of all the ideas and attitudes which Russian ministers had found so offensive before: Catherine II's agent in Copenhagen, Filosoffof, put the point very fairly when he complained to Britain's minister there of 'our persisting to treat Russia in the same manner as we did, forty years ago, which she was too sensible of her force and superiority to bear'.[34] Neither Russia's need of diplomatic and financial support, nor the offer to co-operate in Sweden, could make Rochford's proposals acceptable to Panin. In mid-April 1769 the Russian minister rejected the treaty-project out of hand and three weeks later ended all negotiations.[35] Not surprisingly, after this breakdown Cathcart noted that his reception at the Russian court became much cooler.[36] But the ambassador would not admit failure. He still tried to keep the alliance negotiations alive by means of a series of private, and strictly unofficial, initiatives in late spring and early summer 1769. These were to no avail, and in July Rochford pronounced the discussions 'entirely at an end'.[37]

Britain's failure to honour Cathcart's promises inevitably cooled relations and the whole episode reawakened Panin's resentment over British assumptions of superiority. But this was not the end of the matter for Britain. Rochford had been impressed by Russia's seeming willingness for an alliance and by the exaggerated reports of this he was receiving from the gullible and inexperienced Cathcart.[38] The Northern Secretary did not appreciate that Russia's flexibility was partly based on the ambassador's own promise of a subsidy, and he now set about trying to find an alternative path to a formal treaty.[39]

[32] Though Rochford, with characteristic indiscretion, told the Russian ambassador that the cabinet believed Goodricke dishonest and were therefore reluctant to send money to him! Martens, *Recueil des traités*, ix(x). 276.   [33] *Sbornik*, xii. 422–5.

[34] Roberts, *British Diplomacy*, 293.   [35] *Sbornik*, xii. 432–3, 436–41.

[36] Ibid. xii. 463–5; cf. ibid. cxli. 558.   [37] Roberts, *British Diplomacy*, 293–5.

[38] Only the ambassador could have pronounced Panin 'veracity itself': *Sbornik*, xii. 380.

[39] The well-informed Nolcken reported in July 1769 that Rochford was privately more prepared for concessions to Russia than his colleagues: to KP, 7 July 1769, Roberts Transcripts.

Not for the first time a secretary of state sought to escape from a political cul-de-sac which had been created by Britain's own inflexibility. During the next two years Rochford pursued a series of initiatives which he hoped would induce Catherine and Panin to conclude an alliance on Britain's terms. The most promising avenues appeared to be Sweden, where since 1763 co-operation had probably been most harmonious and certainly most successful, and the Russo-Turkish War.

Rochford would not consider a subsidy to Sweden, but he was prepared for significant expenditure in Stockholm which became essential with the calling of the Diet for spring 1769. By the late 1760s Sweden's domestic politics were a particularly complex triangular struggle.[40] The Diet elections had produced the expected Hat victory, but within a few months the Hat–court alliance looked shaky. The Hats and the Caps were both more suspicious of the court, and in particular of the resolute and ambitious Crown Prince Gustav, than they were of each other. The terrain in Stockholm was still recognizable, though the battle-lines were now drawn somewhat differently. The knowledge of Choiseul's plans for a political revolution had also transformed Russian policy, which now aimed simply at preventing any political change. This did not seriously damage Anglo-Russian co-operation in Sweden, which continued to rest more on the remarkable partnership of Goodricke and Osterman than on the policies of their governments. Britain's minister continued the struggle, though his effectiveness was undermined by Rochford's increasingly parsimonious attitude. Together the two diplomats ensured that the Diet of 1769 ended in a 'modified triumph' for Britain and Russia: an outcome which had not seemed likely at the beginning of the year.[41] This welcome success did nothing to further an alliance. Co-operation in Stockholm in fact demonstrated both the possibilities and the limitations of the emergent Anglo-Russian *entente*. Where their interests coincided, as in Sweden, the two states worked together to some purpose. Yet this co-operation was never wholehearted. Both sides suspected that the other was dragging its feet. The most that can be said for Anglo-Russian diplomacy in Sweden in 1769–70, is that it did nothing to make an eventual alliance less likely, in spite of serious and recurring disputes over money. Even this negative verdict is impossible where relations over the Russo-Turkish War were concerned.

The second, and more important way by which Britain hoped to secure an eventual alliance on her own terms, was through a

[40] Roberts, *British Diplomacy*, Ch. 9, provides an authoritative survey.
[41] Ibid. 323.

successful mediation of Catherine's war with the Turks.[42] Such an outcome was always unlikely, and wholly improbable once Russia overcame her initial problems; but from late in 1768 until the end of 1770 British diplomacy sought to persuade the Porte to make peace. Ministers hoped that this initiative would consolidate the good relations with Austria: Vienna's dread of a new and widening war was well known. Britain was also motivated by an established desire to preserve peace in Europe and, once this proved impossible, to make the war in the Balkans as brief and as limited as possible. Ministers saw France as the real instigator of the conflict and this added to their anxieties. In the later 1760s Choiseul appeared more active and intriguing than in the early years of peace and this, together with the growing tension on the continent, aroused British suspicion of France and did something to undermine the detachment with which European issues had come to be viewed in London.[43]

In the early stages of the war Russia was certainly prepared for a prompt and peaceful settlement, given her problems in Poland and her anxieties over Sweden. There were always very considerable barriers, however, to any mediation. Foremost among these was the Empress's diminishing willingness to submit to any imposed settlement, as the extent of Turkish weakness became clear. Another formidable obstacle was the volatile and xenophobic public opinion in the Turkish capital. The Sultan and his advisers were, in a very real sense, the prisoners of the mob in Constantinople and dared not make peace, even after a series of major defeats in 1769–70. The Ottoman Empire was also profoundly unwilling to hand back any of its earlier conquests; but the Russian victories ensured that such concessions became the price of peace. Ottoman intransigence was encouraged and perhaps intensified by French diplomacy. Choiseul wanted to prolong the war in the Balkans, in order to assist his anti-Russian policies in Sweden and Poland, and his strategy was pursued by the new French ambassador in Constantinople, the able and energetic Saint-Priest.

Britain's desired role as mediator also presented problems of its own. The negotiations had to pass through the hands of Sir John Murray, the British ambassador to the Porte, who had only recently arrived from Venice and was intent on leaving Constantinople as

---

[42] M. S. Anderson, 'Britain's Diplomatic Relations with the Mediterranean, 1763–1778' (unpublished Ph.D. thesis, University of Edinburgh, 1952), provides an admirable account of British policy and served as the basis of two important articles: 'Great Britain and the Russo-Turkish War of 1768–74', *English Historical Review*, 69 (1954), 39–58, and 'Great Britain and the Russian Fleet, 1769–70', *Slavonic and East European Review*, 31 (1952–3), 148–63.

[43] See Nolcken's very acute analysis: G. A. von Nolckens riksdagsberättelse, 1769, Roberts Transcripts.

soon as possible. He was inexperienced in the confusing byways of diplomacy in the Ottoman capital, personally unpopular, and, crucially, a mediocre diplomat, without the vision or initiative to seize the very slender chance of success presented by events. In any case, Britain's traditional friendship with Russia made her suspect in Ottoman eyes, and the Turks were likely to insist on their traditional friend and patron, France, being included in any mediation. This was anathema to Russia, since Catherine II regarded Choiseul as the principal source of her problems.

The prospects for a successful mediation, or even for a settlement involving British diplomacy, never very great, were destroyed by Britain's assistance to the Russian fleet in 1769–70.[44] The transfer of two Baltic squadrons to the Mediterranean led to Russia's spectacular naval victory at Chesmé (July 1770), where the Sultan's fleet was all but destroyed. The Russian ships had received supplies and undergone necessary repairs in British ports: without such help they might not have completed the voyage south. Moreover, British subjects in Russian service, and in particular John Elphinstone and Samuel Greig, had played a prominent part in these naval operations.

The assistance given to the Russian fleet destroyed Britain's position at the Porte. Ministers believed that nothing they had done transgressed the bounds of neutrality, but their actions appeared in a very different light in Constantinople. French diplomacy needed no second bidding to inflame the Porte's anti-British sentiments and in June 1770, before the disaster at Chesmé, Britain was told that her mediation was unacceptable because of the aid to the Empress's ships. It was another six months, and much futile diplomacy later, before ministers abandoned their efforts. By the end of 1770 British diplomacy at the Porte had returned to its usual immobility. Britain had always looked less likely to mediate in the war than Prussia or Austria. Both German states had quickly emerged as potential mediators. They were anxious that the fighting might spread and involve them directly, and also determined to prevent Russia from making too great territorial gains from a weakened Ottoman Empire. It was to this Prusso-Austrian alignment, a *rapprochement* which had emerged during the later 1760s, that the Porte turned after the shattering defeats of summer 1770. In August the Ottoman government requested Prusso-Austrian diplomatic intervention and in December 1770 it promised to accept only their mediation. Catherine II, who had never been much inclined to submit to British mediation once her initial difficulties were resolved, was to find the

---

[44] For this episode, see Anderson, 'Great Britain and the Russian Fleet, 1769–70', 148–63.

more formidable intervention of the two other eastern powers more difficult to elude.

Britain's pursuit of a Russian alliance and her novel concern with south-eastern Europe in 1768–70 for a time had been more important than relations with the Bourbons. This was possible because ministers, though concerned at Choiseul's increasingly active policy, remained confident that an early French attack was unlikely,[45] and because intelligence reports still emphasized Britain's mastery at sea. France also wanted peace in western Europe. Though there were moments when Choiseul professed to fear that a war would be started by British ministers anxious to strengthen their own positions, he remained convinced in 1768–9 that this was improbable and that peace would be preserved by the political upheavals in England and by the unrest in the American colonies.[46] He believed peace to be essential, given continuing Bourbon inferiority at sea and his own preoccupation with containing Russia in eastern Europe, and this conviction was apparent in his satisfaction at the consolidation of North's Ministry in early 1770.[47] In January Grafton resigned, his nerve and his administration broken by the petitioning movement of the previous year. North now became the ministry's leader, though for the moment there were few changes in personnel.

Anglo-French diplomacy therefore remained relatively untroubled from autumn 1768 until mid-1770.[48] Fundamental hostility had not been seriously weakened, far less removed, but both states now had different priorities and this improved relations. Britain's desire for peace and her search for financial economies presupposed better relations with the Bourbons. Diplomats remained preoccupied with the seemingly intractable disputes over Dunkirk, the Newfoundland Fisheries, the Canada Bills, and the British East India Company's claim over French prisoners captured during the Seven Years War. Little progress was made on any of these issues, which in itself indicates both governments had other priorities in these years. In the early months of 1770, however, there was a noticeable deterioration in relations produced by events in India.

The Seven Years War had established British supremacy in the subcontinent and after 1763 France's position was precarious. But

---

[45] For this confidence, see G. A. von Nolckens riksdagsberättelse, 1769, Roberts Transcripts.

[46] e.g. CP (Angleterre) 485, fo. 42; 486, fos. 85, 416.

[47] For example, ibid. 490, fo. 366; 491, fo. 14.

[48] A brief account of these minor disputes is provided by P. Coquelle, 'Le Comte Duchâtelet, ambassadeur de France à Londres (1768–1770)', *Bulletin historique et philologique* (1909), 313–26.

the British, mindful of the narrow margin of their own victory in the 1740s and 1750s, exaggerated the remaining French threat in India.[49] Although French weakness initially led to a period of fairly harmonious relations, in the later 1760s this gradually gave way to confrontation. After the inevitable time-lag imposed by the distances involved, this came to be reflected in Anglo-French diplomacy in Europe.

The growing confrontation in the subcontinent had several dimensions. It was linked to a shift in France's priorities which became apparent around 1767. In the early years of peace, the French, both in Bengal and in the Carnatic, were on the defensive and were preoccupied with restoring their shattered position. The British Company's assumption of the *Diwani* (right to raise revenue) in Bengal in 1765, had been followed by disputes between rival merchants. The French traders resented attempts to restrict their commercial opportunities, while they themselves were suspected, by the British, of clandestine trade and of illegally exporting gold from Bengal. The resulting tension simply confirmed the basic British assumption that the French wished to destroy their power in India. By the later 1760s a more forward French policy can be glimpsed, with the arrival of the young and ambitious Jean-Baptiste Chevalier in July 1767 as governor of Chandernagore.[50] Chevalier dreamed of carving out a new area of influence for France in northern India; he certainly had plans to destroy Britain's position in Bengal; and the French government was interested in his schemes. In the same year the French crown assumed responsibility for the islands of Mauritius (Île de France) and Réunion (Île de Bourbon) and immediately began to strengthen their defences and garrisons. These islands lay in the Indian Ocean, to the east of Madagascar, and were important staging posts on the route to India.

Reports of French reinforcements at Mauritius were worrying the Madras Council from 1768 onwards. Ignorance of the precise numbers of troops involved inevitably led to the threat being exaggerated.[51] The spectre of a French invasion was particularly serious, because of the first Mysore War of 1767–9. This was

[49] A good introduction is B. E. Kennedy, 'Anglo-French Rivalry in India and in the Eastern Seas 1763–93: A Study of Anglo-French Tensions and of their Impact on the Consolidation of British Power in the Region' (unpublished Ph.D. thesis, Australian National University, 1969). A detailed examination of France's position after 1763 is S. P. Sen, *The French in India, 1763–1816* (Calcutta, 1958), ch. 1–4.

[50] This was seriously worrying the Court of Directors in London by the closing months of 1768: *Fort William – India House Correspondence*, v: *1767–1769*, ed. N. K. Sinha (Delhi, 1949), 143.

[51] These anxieties are clearly apparent ibid. 420–1, 470, 494.

initially indecisive, but at the very end of 1768 Hyder Ali invaded and devastated the Carnatic, and in the following March dictated peace to the Madras Council. Throughout 1768 the Council had been growing more and more alarmed about the threat of a French seaborne invasion and had pleaded for help from London. Simultaneously, a serious Anglo-French confrontation was developing in Bengal.

At the centre of the dispute was the ditch at Chandernagore.[52] The town was the principal French settlement and trading post in Bengal, some twenty miles north of Calcutta. Its fortifications had been destroyed during the Seven Years War and the Peace of Paris had forbidden either any rebuilding of these or the establishment of any garrison. Soon after his arrival, Chevalier requested permission to construct a ditch to improve its sanitation. The local East India Company representative initially agreed. But towards the end of April 1769 the British authorities became concerned by reports of vast excavation works which could easily be turned into fortifications.[53] The authorities at Calcutta were also alarmed that new barracks and gun carriages were being constructed, apparent further evidence that the French intended to fortify Chandernagore.[54] Its military potential had been demonstrated during the Seven Years War, when it had only been captured after a long and difficult siege. Any fortification would directly violate the Peace of Paris, and the French excavations appeared to confirm British fears about Chevalier's intentions, and indeed, French activities throughout India. The Bengal Secret Committee ordered the ditch to be filled in and this was done in July 1769. But the local British authorities remained apprehensive about French intentions, while the vastly outnumbered French in Bengal resented the way in which they had been forced to submit to *force majeure*.[55] Both sides made their anxieties clear to their metropolitan governments, and from the end of 1769 onwards the ditch at Chandernagore became an issue in Anglo-French diplomacy in Europe.

The British government's response was tempered by its desire to secure greater control over the East India Company. The cabinet was undoubtedly alarmed by the apparent French offensive in the East: Chandernagore and the threat from Mauritius were seen as two sides of the same coin. At first ministers in London had taken a less serious

[52] There is a good account in Kennedy, 'Anglo-French Rivalry in India', 96–128.

[53] The map of Chandernagore and its ditch in *Fort William – India House Correspondence*, v: *1767–1769*, opposite p. 420, suggests that the British were correct to be alarmed by these excavations.

[54] Ibid. v. 596–7.   [55] The connection is clearly made ibid. v. 609–10.

view of France's activities than did the East India Company and its agents,[56] but by December 1769 the matter had been taken up with the French government.[57] Britain's representations embodied the Grafton Ministry's moderate approach to relations. France was assured that the filling in of the ditch at Chandernagore had been entirely the response of the local British authorities: there was no wish for a war. Rochford also demanded that Choiseul should accept the ditch's destruction and explain the reinforcements apparently sent to Mauritius. The French foreign minister was equally anxious to preserve peace, and he recognized that fighting was unlikely over these issues. He also resented the actions of the British East India Company, and for this reason vigorously rebuffed Rochford's protests with some grievances of his own. During the first half of 1770 these exchanges pushed up the political temperature, but relations did not deteriorate until the summer. Then two separate issues inflamed Anglo-French diplomacy and, by the closing months of the year, war was to be closer than at any time since 1763.

The first was the appearance of the Russian fleet in the Mediterranean in 1770, after its spectacular passage from the Baltic. In autumn 1769 there had been a false alarm when it had briefly seemed that France might attack it as it passed through the Channel, and in the following summer similar British fears sharply worsened relations.[58] In May 1770 the British cabinet heard reports of naval preparations at Toulon, and these rumours continued throughout June, probably encouraged by the Russian agent in London.[59] Diplomatic representations were made in Paris, but France was evasive. Britain therefore prepared to reinforce her own Mediterranean squadron, believing Choiseul was contemplating naval action to support the Turks: the episode focused British anxieties about France's actively anti-Russian strategy.[60] Ministers, and in particular the Southern Secretary Weymouth, saw the French threat to the Russian fleet almost as an act of hostility against Britain herself.[61] The failure to conclude a formal alliance had not yet weakened the assumption that Catherine II was a natural ally; more important Britain felt obliged to respond immediately to any French naval

---

[56] N. Tracy, 'Parry of a Threat to India, 1768–1774', *The Mariner's Mirror*, 59 (1973), 36–7; cf. *BDI*, vii: *France 1745–1789*, ed. L. G. Wickham Legg, 109, for Britain's muted response.

[57] Ibid. 110–11.

[58] There is a brief account in N. Tracy, *Navies, Deterrence and American Independence: Britain and Seapower in the 1760s and 1770s* (Vancouver, 1988), 75–8.

[59] G. A. von Nolckens riksdagsberättelse, 1771, Roberts Transcripts.

[60] *BDI* vii: *France 1745–1789*, ed. Wickham Legg, 111–12.

[61] G. A. von Nolckens riksdagsberättelse, 1771, Roberts Transcripts.

initiative. Throughout the summer of 1770 preparations increased on both sides of the Channel, as the familiar pattern in periods of tension became established.

This dispute never actually came to a head. Britain's response, though swift, was always essentially moderate. She wanted to prevent the Russo-Turkish War spreading and therefore to stop France intervening in the eastern Mediterranean, but she was also aware that a too vigorous response might actually widen the conflict.[62] Choiseul seems to have been unable to obtain royal support for his planned attack, while the scope for effective French intervention was greatly reduced by the shattering Turkish defeat early in July at Chesmé. Britain certainly contemplated naval action to protect the Russian ships, and the episode demonstrated her intense suspicion of France and particularly of Choiseul.[63] Its principal importance was its revelation of Weymouth's willingness for vigorous action to defend British interests.[64] Even at this stage it went beyond the intentions of his cabinet colleagues and it was to be still more apparent during the second half of 1770, when events in the Mediterranean were overtaken by a far more significant dispute.

This concerned the Falkland Islands, and within a few months was to bring Britain and the Bourbons to the brink of war.[65] It was the most serious crisis for British foreign policy between the Peace of Paris and the outbreak of the American rebellion, and it proved a turning-point. This confrontation began as an Anglo-Spanish dispute, but British assumptions about Choiseul's leadership of the

---

[62] This fear is particularly apparent from Weymouth's 2 letters of 6 July: SP 78/281, fos. 14, 16. Part of the first is printed in *BDI*. vii: *France 1745–1789*, 113; but not the key passages or the all-important second, and private, letter.

[63] See Weymouth's secret instructions to Commodore Proby, 18 Aug. 1770, *Cal. HO Papers 1770–2*, no. 225. Proby was in command of the British Mediterranean squadron.

[64] This is suggested by the strong emphasis on secrecy and by the orders given to Proby to correspond only with Weymouth himself: ibid., no. 225.

[65] This account of the Falklands' crisis is principally based on the British and French diplomatic correspondence: SP 78/281–2, and SP 94/184–6; CP (Angleterre) 492–5, and CP (Espagne) 561–2. Among the numerous secondary studies, N. Tracy, 'The Falkland Islands Crisis of 1770; Use of Naval Force', *English Historical Review*, 90 (1975), 40–75, and his more recent account in *Navies, Deterrence and American Independence*, 69–99, are fundamental; Lalaguna Lasala, 'England, Spain and the Family Compact', 259–323, is valuable for the Spanish perspective; while useful accounts from the French side are provided by E. Daubigny, *Choiseul et la France d'outre-mer, après le Traité de Paris* (Paris, 1897), 252–84, and by L. Blart, *Les Rapports de la France et de l'Espagne après le pacte de famille, jusqu'à la fin du ministère du duc de Choiseul* (Paris, 1915), 143–202. The best-known study of this episode is J. Goebel, *The Struggle for the Falkland Islands* (New Haven, Conn., 1927; repr. 1982), 271–410, but this is written from the standpoint of the international lawyer rather than the historian; it is misleading in some of its broader arguments and naïve in its use of diplomatic correspondence; and it is throughout mildly anti-British. It does, however, furnish important detail.

Bourbons and Spain's dependence on France's support ensured it soon acquired a French dimension.[66]

The problem of the British settlement on West Falkland had merely been shelved in 1767.[67] Spain was not reconciled to a British presence, and the wooden blockhouse at Port Egmont had become a time bomb in relations.[68] At first the Spanish government was uncertain about the settlement's precise location and even wondered if there might be an additional British outpost to the west of the Straits of Magellan. These anxieties were intensified by Madrid's knowledge of continuing British interest in the Pacific and by the re-emergence, in the later 1760s, of the question of the right of British merchants to trade freely with Old and New Spain. It was the settlement at Port Egmont, however, which was most resented, and Madrid was determined to destroy it.

By the winter of 1767–8 Spain had located the British blockhouse on West Falkland. The Spanish foreign minister, Grimaldi, was even then fully prepared to fight Britain and he now responded vigorously. Orders for the eviction of the tiny garrison were drawn up.[69] Before these were sent out to South America, they were communicated to the French government and personally approved by Louis XV.[70] Grimaldi also reminded Choiseul in March 1768 and again in July of the same year, that the French minister's own timetable envisaged that the Bourbons would be ready for war in 1770 and emphasized that the time taken to send orders to Spain's colonial governors would delay any confrontation for two years.[71] At this stage the Spanish foreign minister accepted the considerable risk of war, because he was prepared to begin the *revanche* and believed he would enjoy France's full support in any dispute. His vigorous policy was also encouraged by the evident weakness of British diplomacy in the second half of the 1760s, and Grimaldi even hoped London might not resist a Spanish *fait accompli*.

The orders to destroy Port Egmont were delayed by the need to send out an expedition to South America to enforce them. By the beginning of 1769 naval reinforcements had reached Bucareli, the energetic Spanish governor ('captain-general') of Buenos Aires. Matters were further put back by necessary repairs to this expedition and by the local Spanish authorities' shortage of money to carry these

---

[66] Nolcken believed that British ministers saw the attack as part of a more general Bourbon offensive gathering pace since the later 1760s and orchestrated by Choiseul: G. A. von Nolckens riksdagsberättelse, 1771, Roberts Transcripts.   [67] Cf. above, Ch. 5.

[68] Madrid's concern with Port Egmont can be followed in Corney, *Tahiti*, i. 51–178 *passim*.

[69] Ibid. i. 108–10.

[70] Lalaguna Lasala, 'England, Spain and the Family Compact', 244.

[71] Ibid. 243, 254.

out. By the end of 1769, however, Bucareli was preparing a squadron to sail to Port Egmont. Simultaneously, events in the Falklands were moving towards a crisis. The British settlement and the Spanish base at Puerto Soledad (the former French colony Port St Louis which Choiseul had handed over to Spain) had hitherto existed in isolation. In December 1769 ships from each base had a chance encounter and an exchange of letters followed. In this the British naval commander in the Falklands, Captain Hunt, not merely rejected Spain's assertion of sovereignty, but proclaimed Britain's undisputed right to the region and threatened to expel the Spaniards by force if they did not leave within six months. This represented Britain's established position, but it provided a pretext for Bucareli. In February 1770 two Spanish frigates visited Port Egmont and requested that the British settlers should leave. Hunt refused and vigorously asserted Britain's own claim to the islands. Bucareli's response was to send a second and much larger Spanish force which evicted the tiny British garrison in June. Reports of these events in the South Atlantic began to reach Europe by the middle of 1770 and, within a few months, produced a serious Anglo-Bourbon confrontation.

News of the first Spanish visit to Port Egmont arrived in London early in June.[72] Britain's initial response was muted: naval preparedness was marginally, though covertly, increased by adding men to two guardships; in July they were formally mobilized. At this stage, the seriousness of these developments was not apparent and no formal protest was made. Relations with the Bourbon powers were the responsibility of the Southern Secretary, Weymouth, who, at this point, was willing to compromise. He tried to convince Choiseul that, while Britain regarded Port Egmont as unimportant in itself, the ministry could not publicly abandon it since this would alarm the business community and antagonize parliamentary and public opinion, and he clearly hoped that France would persuade Spain to make some kind of apology to preserve peace.

The moderation of the Bourbon powers was becoming apparent. In 1768–9, when the expedition was being planned, Grimaldi had been prepared to fight. By 1770 his priorities were rather different and his attitude was certainly more pacific. He was preoccupied with some delicate negotiations with Rome over the Jesuits. His willingness for war had been undermined both by his own awareness of Bourbon weakness and by Choiseul's insistent emphasis on a further postponement of the *revanche*. Grimaldi's bellicose stance

---

[72] Thomas Coleman to George Grenville, 4 Mar. 1770 (but received in June), *Grenville Papers*, iv. 505–9. (Coleman was in command of the small British military detachment at Port Egmont.) Cf. *Burke Corr.* ii. 142.

was finally abandoned when he heard, on 17 August 1770, of the departure of the Spanish squadron from Buenos Aires.[73] The opportunity for a successful war against Britain still had its supporters, notably the influential Spanish ambassador in Paris, Aranda, and the minister of war, Arriaga, but they were unable to secure control of policy. From the beginning of the diplomatic confrontation over the Falklands, Grimaldi worked for a negotiated settlement, and he was prepared to disown Bucareli, though the latter had simply carried out his orders. At the end of August, the Bourbon governments informed Britain that an expedition against Port Egmont had sailed in the previous spring and blamed this initiative on the governor in Buenos Aires, and they redoubled their diplomatic efforts when news of the actual expulsion arrived early in September.

The British government received a separate report of this expedition, though not of its outcome, on 8 September.[74] This was a much more serious matter, since a British base had been destroyed and force had been used against the British flag. It was immediately answered by a considerable naval mobilization: the sixteen available guardships were ordered to be prepared for service.[75] Britain's response was shaped by the Southern Secretary and it marked a return to the spirit of George Grenville's 'gunboat diplomacy', so successful in 1764–5. Weymouth exploited the considerable freedom of action allowed by the constitutional conventions of the day and during the next three months British policy principally reflected his attitudes. He aimed to force Spain into an early and complete surrender, believing naval and financial weakness would ensure the Bourbons would not fight: diplomacy, backed by naval preparations, would force Madrid to accept the British demands.[76] Weymouth therefore brushed aside attempts by Masserano, the Spanish ambassador in London, to promote a negotiated settlement and instead set out Britain's terms: Spain was not merely to disavow Bucareli, but was to re-establish the British settlers at Port Egmont. This was not to be matched by any British disavowal of Captain Hunt, which the Spanish government was seeking. Spain believed that Hunt's conduct had inflamed the situation, but his actions were upheld by London throughout the dispute, to Madrid's annoyance. To reinforce these British demands, twenty-four additional ships of the line were ordered to be got ready, and by the end of September Britain had no less than forty capital

[73] Lalaguna Lasala, 'England, Spain and the Family Compact', 292–4.

[74] V. L. Brown, 'Anglo-Spanish Relations in America in the Closing Years of the Colonial Era', *Hispanic American Historical Review*, 5 (1922), 408 n. 172.

[75] Tracy, 'The Falkland Islands Crisis', 52–7, for Britain's vigorous response in Sept.

[76] This was also the main theme of the reports of the chargé d'affaires in Madrid, James Harris: see e.g. *Malmesbury Diaries*, i. 63–4, 65.

ships in preparation, at a time when Bourbon naval mobilization had barely begun.[77]

The immediate and massive response alarmed both Bourbon governments. Choiseul in particular made determined efforts to bring about an early settlement.[78] Though he appreciated that war might be inevitable and also accepted that France had to support Spain in any conflict, he hoped to settle the dispute peacefully. In the second Falklands crisis, as indeed throughout his ministry, Choiseul was generally less bellicose than either Britain or even Spain.[79] His warlike reputation depends more on his rhetoric and on his preparations for a future war than on his actual policies, which were usually remarkably moderate, at least towards Britain.

His pacific attitude until the closing weeks of 1770 was based on three considerations: his preoccupation with Russian expansion, his recognition of Bourbon weakness, and his own crumbling authority. French foreign policy continued to be directed primarily against Catherine II, as since 1766. Choiseul had been alarmed by Russia's sweeping successes against the Turks and regarded the Falklands dispute as an untimely distraction from his efforts to check her expansion, to encourage Turkish resistance and to give material aid to the Sultan. He feared an Anglo-Bourbon war might enable the Russian Empress to consolidate her dominance over eastern Europe.[80] His intelligence network continued to supply precise and accurate information on Britain's naval strength and this revealed Bourbon inferiority in the all-important matter of ships of the line.[81] In 1770 France's increasing financial difficulties, which Choiseul acknowledged to be in sharp contrast to the stability of British credit, culminated in a serious financial and economic crisis, which gave an

[77] Even by mid-Oct., Weymouth was clearly thinking of trying to accelerate these preparations and 'to collect the greatest naval force in the shortest time possible': *Cal. HO Papers 1770–2*, no. 290.

[78] CP (Angleterre) 493, fo. 64, 72; SP 78/281, fos. 133, 137–8.

[79] This is clear from his dispatches to Ossun (French ambassador in Madrid) in these months: CP (Espagne) 560–1 *passim*. The fact that Ossun was Choiseul's old friend and political ally makes this correspondence a particularly instructive source.

[80] This concern is apparent, e.g., in CP (Autriche) 314, fos. 32–3; cf. *Sbornik*, cxli. 191.

[81] Though precise figures for relative naval strength in 1770 cannot be given with any confidence, Britain still enjoyed a considerable lead in ships of the line and Choiseul knew this. The latest authority believes that Britain had a paper strength of 157 of the line (Tracy, 'Falkland Islands Crisis', 40); in Aug. 1770, Choiseul thought Britain's current strength was 143 (CP (Angleterre) 492, fos. 403–8, 443–4). Against that, the Bourbon navies totalled only between 110 and 120, depending on which figure for French strength is taken: AM B⁵ 5; AM B⁵ 7; CP (Angleterre) 494, fo. 463; H. M. Scott, 'The Importance of Bourbon Naval Reconstruction to the Strategy of Choiseul after the Seven Years' War', *International History Review*, 1 (1979), 30.

additional incentive for peace.[82] It was not that this would have deterred him from going to war: on the contrary, he believed that a great power must find the necessary resources. But these financial difficulties focused the existing divisions within the French ministry and limited his freedom of action. In particular the opposition of Terray (who had become Controller-General in December 1769), to French naval mobilization during the final months of 1770, and his ability to delay essential funds, intensified the rivalry within the King's council, and indirectly contributed to Choiseul's fall.

During the second half of 1770 Choiseul's position as a minister was coming under increasing pressure.[83] His domestic enemies were numerous: Madame du Barry and her supporters, the members of the *secret du roi*, the *dévots*, the opponents of the *parlements*, whose friend Choiseul was said to be. In particular, he now faced formidable opposition from within the ministry: from the Chancellor, Maupeou, and from Terray. The impact of this challenge was ambiguous. By the final weeks of 1770, his weakening hold on power and his growing conviction that war was becoming inevitable, made him more willing to fight: particularly as he realized that his own position would be stronger if hostilities began.[84] Until then Choiseul seems to have concluded that any early conflict would be more likely to give his opponents their chance, and this reinforced his desire for peace.[85] He believed, however, that firmness was more likely to avert war than to bring it about, and he adopted a defiant, though not bellicose, tone during the second half of 1770.[86]

Choiseul initially hoped for a prompt settlement, which he tried to sponsor by diplomacy in Madrid and in London. He believed Spain was in the wrong and would have to make some kind of restitution, but he found the Spanish government surprisingly resistant to such ideas. During the second half of 1770 Madrid pursued a more independent line than in the earlier confrontations with Britain, and this provided a new and unstable element in the dispute. Since 1763 Choiseul had enjoyed considerable control over Spanish foreign policy, but at this critical point he suddenly found that he no longer spoke for both Bourbon powers and that events were slipping out of

[82] CP (Angleterre) 492, fo. 49; cf. Daubigny, *Choiseul et la France d'outre-mer*, 258. See also the illuminating article of J. F. Bosher, 'The French Crisis of 1770', *History*, 57 (1972), 17–30.
[83] Blart, *Les Rapports de la France et de l'Espagne*, 143–62, and Daubigny, *Choiseul et la France d'outremer*, 262–84, are probably the best available accounts of his decline and fall.
[84] CP (Angleterre) 494, fo. 19. This change is particularly evident in his dispatch of 3 Dec. 1770, ibid. 494, fos. 274–5; cf. CP (Espagne) 561, fo. 361.
[85] Louis XV was already alarmed by his forward policy in eastern Europe: Blart, *Les Rapports de la France et de l'Espagne*, 175.   [86] CP (Espagne) 561, fo. 285.

his control.[87] He realized that he was trapped by Madrid's greater independence, and that the Family Compact could operate against its senior partner. The fact that Choiseul was to fall from power because of this crisis should not disguise France's limited impact on the diplomacy of these months.

The confrontation was more a purely Anglo-Spanish one than might seem likely, and indeed than it appeared to British ministers at the time. Spain had at first been prepared for some concessions and had hoped that both sides could agree to abandon the Falklands. But Britain's massive response in September, the scale of her demands, and refusal to disavow Captain Hunt, soon hardened Madrid's attitude. Weymouth believed that Britain's naval superiority enabled him to impose his own terms, and the arrival on 23 September of a British account of the events at Port Egmont in June stiffened his resolve.[88] His price for a settlement was a full restoration of the British post on West Falkland and compensation for the 'insult' caused by the Spanish expulsion.[89] This amounted to a complete Spanish surrender, and it was unacceptable to Madrid.[90] As in the previous confrontation over the Falklands in 1766–7, Spain believed that nothing less than the future of her monopoly of the Pacific, as a *mare clausum*, was at stake. When it became apparent that the re-establishment of the British base was part of London's terms, Madrid's hopes for a settlement ended. The Pacific Ocean was to be maintained as a Spanish lake, and the risk of a war involved was more readily accepted, since Spanish ministers calculated France had to support them in any conflict.

Spain's attitude had become intransigent rather than deliberately bellicose. It contributed significantly to the impasse which had emerged by mid-October and which was to last for three months, when war was widely believed likely and perhaps inevitable.[91] The gulf between the satisfaction which Britain was demanding and the

[87] Immediately after the news of the British expulsion from Port Egmont reached Europe, Choiseul told Walpole that 'he could answer for the Court of Spain, that she did not mean to go to war': SP 78/281, fo. 137. The clearest acknowledgement of this loss is in Choiseul's despatch to Ossun on the day before he was dismissed: 23 Dec. 1770, CP (Espagne) 561, fos. 466–7; cf. F.-P. Renaut, *Le Pacte de famille et l'Amérique: La politique franco-espagnole de 1760 à 1792* (Paris, 1922), 191.

[88] Lalaguna Lasala, 'England, Spain and the Family Compact', 297.

[89] See e.g. Weymouth to Harris, 17 Oct. 1770, SP 94/185.

[90] Lalaguna Lasala, 'England, Spain and the Family Compact', 298–9.

[91] By mid-Oct. 1770, Frederick II was pronouncing war 'inevitable', though he later changed his mind: *Pol. Corr.* xxx. 200, 219; cf. *Archives . . . Orange-Nassau*, 4th series, iv. 228, 230–5, for W. Bentinck's view that fighting was extremely likely. In Britain, war was generally believed probable: see e.g. *Documents of the American Revolution*, i. nos. 621, 624, 626, *etc.*

concessions which Spain was prepared to make was considerable. This became apparent during extended negotiations in September, October, and November between Weymouth and Masserano.[92] The Southern Secretary started from the premiss that Spain was entirely to blame. It therefore followed that Britain could not make any concessions. Such reasoning might be faultless logic to a British secretary of state; but to a Spanish ambassador, charged with negotiating a settlement which protected Charles III's honour and reputation, it appeared in a very different light. Weymouth's notorious intransigence, and his high-handed behaviour towards Masserano, were further obstacles to any agreement.[93] By mid-November a negotiated settlement appeared as distant as ever.

This impasse was not the principal cause of the widespread belief that war was becoming inevitable. The diplomatic stalemate was primarily important because of the extensive naval mobilization which accompanied it and which itself was widely seen as the harbinger of war. This mobilization was accelerated by the precise knowledge, which both Britain and France possessed, of the state of their opponents' fleets. Their extensive and efficient intelligence networks, revealing the scale of enemy preparations, encouraged further mobilization. The rapid escalation which could result was apparent in the closing months of 1770. Throughout the age of the American Revolution, France was also haunted by memories of Britain's decisive onslaught on her fleet in 1755, which had done much to weaken the French naval effort during the Seven Years War, and was resolved she would never again be caught unprepared. These naval preparations created their own momentum for war.[94] A decision for war or peace became unavoidable, as capital vessels could not be kept fully crewed and armed in port for very long. Naval mobilization begun to reinforce diplomacy came, within two or three months, to overtake negotiations: the first state to mobilize had either to employ her fleet or throw away her advantage. By the second half of November 1770 the British government, having won the race to commission its ships, could no longer escape the choice between peace and war. A negotiated settlement appeared more distant than ever, and two formidable obstacles to any agreement had also emerged at this time. Both lay within domestic British politics, a dimension of the Falklands crisis which has not received sufficient attention.

[92] These can be followed in Goebel, *Struggle for the Falkland Islands*, 285–306.
[93] The American Secretary, Hillsborough, later declared that the Southern Secretary's discussions with the Spanish ambassador were 'rough and hostile': *HMC Various VI*, 264.
[94] Tracy, 'The Falkland Islands Crisis', 61–2.

The first was the influence which parliament, and in particular the House of Commons, had on the dispute.[95] Choiseul understood very well that parliamentary supervision of British policy could be an obstacle and had initially suggested a prompt agreement before the new session opened in mid-November.[96] British ministers were reluctant to meet parliament before a settlement had been secured. They also knew that any agreement formally signed after the session opened would have to be laid before both Houses. This made substantial concessions by Britain very difficult, since the opposition would inevitably attack any sign of weakness.[97] Similarly, with their usual opportunism the ministry's opponents would have been the first to condemn the government if it had gone to war over the Falklands. The capacity of the North Ministry to control the lower house was still uncertain. The French chargé d'affaires believed that its political survival depended on the preservation of peace, and Lord North appears to have agreed.[98] As soon as parliament reassembled (13 November) the ministry's handling of the dispute came under scrutiny and before long its conduct was being attacked.[99] During the next two and a half months fear of parliamentary censure, and perhaps defeat, influenced British policy and helped to shape the final settlement with the Bourbons.[100] The importance of the House of Commons was reinforced by the role which the renowned parliamentarian, Lord North, was to play in the dispute's final stages. This episode provides one of the clearest illustrations during the two decades after 1763 of parliament's enduring ability to influence British diplomacy, though in an essentially negative way.

A second and rather more serious obstacle was Weymouth's stubborn and eventually belligerent attitude which determined

[95] See, in particular, the emphatic testimony of the French chargé d'affaires: CP (Angleterre) 495, fos. 8, 13, 15, 21; cf. G. A. von Nolckens riksdagsberättelse, 1771, Roberts Transcripts.

[96] CP (Angleterre) 493, fos. 132–5, 159–60; cf. Lalaguna Lasala, 'England, Spain and the Family Compact', 296.

[97] In Nov., at Mansfield's suggestion, consideration was given to delaying the new session in the hope that a settlement could first be reached; ministers were clearly expecting trouble. But this expedient was quickly rejected by the King on the grounds that France and Spain 'would upon it augur that we are resolved at all events to accommodate the present dispute, and consequently would encourage them to raise perhaps so much in their demands as would make War absolutely necessary': *Corr. Geo. III*, ii. 166.

[98] CP (Angleterre) 495, fo. 21.

[99] These were particularly fierce on 29 Nov. 1770, during a debate to increase the naval establishment: Egerton 223, fos. 3–25.

[100] This fear proved to be unjustified. In the event, the North Ministry had very little serious trouble with parliament in 1770–1. The opposition was vocal in its criticism but, principally due to North's skilful handling of the Commons, the ministry won all the divisions easily enough. Nevertheless, fear of parliamentary censure was a significant element in the cabinet's handling of the dispute.

British policy from early September until the very end of November. The Southern Secretary had previously advocated peaceful co-existence with France, and in 1768 he had been one of the leaders of the peace party within the cabinet at the time of Choiseul's annexation of Corsica. His attitude in 1770 was very different. From the outset he was firm, vigorous, and apparently bellicose. Throughout these months British policy principally embodied his wish for a hard line against the Bourbons. Weymouth certainly informed, and perhaps consulted, the King,[101] but he did not keep his cabinet colleagues abreast of developments and particularly of his negotiations with the Spanish ambassador.

This neglect was initially aided by the absence of senior ministers: both North and Rochford (the Northern Secretary) were out of town when news of the expulsion from West Falkland arrived in September and Weymouth himself left for the country shortly afterwards.[102] The continuing lack of consultation throughout the next two months was essentially a matter of the Southern Secretary's habitual secrecy, his isolated position within the cabinet, and the distrust which many of his colleagues felt for the overbearing and ambitious man.[103] This animosity was intensified by a sharp exchange late in September between Weymouth and the American Secretary, the Earl of Hillsborough, over their respective spheres of influence in the event of war.[104] This very dispute suggested that, even at this early stage, Weymouth was prepared to fight. His abrasive conduct during the quarrel intensified the suspicion and hostility which many ministers felt towards him and also earned him the lasting enmity of Hillsborough and, more significantly, of Lord North. Weymouth was the principal obstacle to North's total ascendancy in the cabinet, and this was to be a significant and hitherto overlooked dimension of the later stages of the Falklands crisis.

Until the final week of November the cabinet supported, or at least acquiesced in, the Southern Secretary's inflexible stance. There was some suspicion of Weymouth's motives, and rather more of his secrecy, but general agreement that financial and naval weakness

---

[101] This can be implied from George III to Weymouth, 15 Oct. 1770, Thynne Papers, vol. xxxviii, fo. 35.

[102] CP (Angleterre) 493, fos. 56–7; *Burke Corr.* ii. 161.

[103] The only satisfactory treatment is M. T. Hamer, 'From the Grafton Administration to the Ministry of North 1768–1772' (unpublished Ph.D. thesis, University of Cambridge, 1970), Ch. 7.

[104] Ibid. 217; cf. *Corr. Geo. III*, ii. 161; some light is thrown on Weymouth's passage at arms with Hillsborough by the similar discussion two years later: see ibid. i. 379–80. (This later exchange is misdated by the editor.)

would eventually force Spain to submit to Britain's terms.[105] This confidence was apparent in the King's Speech when parliament reassembled on 13 November: significantly this looked to a prompt settlement by adopting the earlier Spanish view that the entire blame should be shouldered by Bucareli.[106] But the continuing diplomatic impasse, together with the scale of naval preparations, were bringing war ever closer.[107] By the second half of November, Britain's mobilization was getting out of control. Preparations were so far advanced that a final decision between peace and war was becoming imperative. Faced with this choice many ministers doubted whether the distant Falkland Islands were actually worth fighting for, particularly as they appreciated that war might bring down the North government.

Weymouth's growing isolation was as much a matter of personalities as of policies. He was not the only hawk in a cabinet of doves: on the contrary, the ministry and the King favoured firm handling of the dispute and recognized war might be unavoidable. They did not wish to force Spain to fight, though increasingly this appeared to be Weymouth's objective. The Southern Secretary's real intentions remain elusive. His handling of foreign policy subordinated Britain's interests to his own personal and political advantage. The most plausible interpretation of his conduct in the final months of 1770, one endorsed by contemporaries, is that he aimed to provoke a war, at the instigation of his influential Under-Secretary, Wood, in order to destroy the North Ministry. Chatham would then be swept back to power, but he would be little more than a figurehead. In such an administration Weymouth could hope to exercise more authority than in any government headed by his political rival, Lord North.[108]

The crisis came to a head at the end of November. War appeared inevitable and, at Weymouth's instigation, the British government took a series of measures which seemed the prelude to actual fighting. A vote for 40,000 seamen was passed by the House of Commons and the pace of impressment was stepped up; grain exports were prohibited; officers in the Gibraltar garrison were ordered back to their post; and British merchants were advised to leave Spain. But the imminence of war now led to the overthrow of

---

[105] Cf. Hamer, 'From the Grafton Administration', 215 n. 2, for North's view on 31 Oct. that 'Spain would comply with our demands'.

[106] *Journal of the House of Commons*, xxxiii. 3.

[107] In mid-Nov., North was said to be anxious for peace, but apprehensive that war could not be averted: *Chatham Corr.* iii. 479.

[108] *HMC Knox*, 264. William Knox believed that in such a ministry Weymouth would be 'the acting minister': cf. Walpole, *Memoirs*, iv. 185–6, 242–3. Both Knox and Walpole alleged that Wood's stockjobbing affected his conduct.

Weymouth's policy.[109] The leading parts in this revolution were played by the King and by North. George III had been monitoring the Southern Secretary's conduct of negotiations with Spain.[110] He increasingly feared that Weymouth's action were designed to make fighting inevitable, and this led him, on 23 November, to reject the Southern Secretary's requests for an augmentation of the army and for the appointment of an admiral to the Mediterranean squadron. Instead, in a clear attempt to keep negotiations with Spain alive and thus avert a formal breach, the King referred these matters to a cabinet meeting. Before this met on 28 November, Lord North had the first two in a series of meetings with Francès, the influential French chargé d'affaires.

North had until now played little part in foreign policy, about which he proclaimed himself to be entirely ignorant, and he even refused to discuss European issues with the diplomatic corps in London, though he spoke good French and could converse freely with them.[111] But his distrust and dislike of Weymouth, and his fear that war would destroy his planned financial recovery and his ministry, made him intervene decisively. He was quick to take up Francès's suggestion of a private interview; the Bourbon diplomats in London, under Choiseul's direction, were by now seeking to circumvent the Southern Secretary in their search for a settlement. During two secret meetings (on 27 and 28 November) between the Prime Minister and the chargé d'affaires, the basis of a settlement emerged.[112] Developing an idea put forward earlier by Choiseul, North suggested that in return for Spain apologizing for the expulsion and reinstating the British garrison on West Falkland, Britain would undertake to abandon Port Egmont at some future date: this amounted to a tacit recognition of Spanish sovereignty, and it overturned Weymouth's previous attitude which had upheld the British claim to the islands. Fear of parliamentary disapproval led North to insist that this agreement should be merely verbal. This suggestion was quickly seized on by Francès, under clear instructions from Choiseul to secure a settlement at almost any price, and transmitted by Masserano.

North's initiative, which was supported and perhaps inspired by George III, was a flagrant intervention in the affairs of the Southern

---

[109] These events can be followed in *Corr. Geo. III*, ii. 172–4.

[110] Thynne Papers, vol. xxxviii, fos. 35, 36.

[111] N. W. Wraxall, *Historical Memoirs of My Own Time (1772–1784)* (2 vols.; London, 1815), i. 499; CP (Angleterre) 497, fo. 45; 493, fo. 57.

[112] Francès' dispatch of 3 Dec., giving an account of these interviews, has not survived; but the discussions can be reconstructed from CP (Angleterre) 494, fos. 311–16; cf. the account based on Spanish sources in Goebel, *Struggle for the Falkland Islands*, 307 ff.

Department.[113] Weymouth was totally isolated and the cabinet quickly approved North's actions. The Prime Minister now set about securing Spain's acceptance. Significantly he himself handled the negotiations, until the contours of a final settlement were fixed in mid-January.[114] Weymouth's policy had thus been overturned, to his unconcealed fury. At a cabinet meeting on 7 December the Southern Secretary made a final attempt to recover the initiative, proposing in effect a surprise attack on the French in India and the Spanish in the Philippines, and also reviving his earlier suggestion that Harris should be recalled from Madrid.[115] These proposals were rejected by his colleagues. Opposition was led by Weymouth's sworn enemy, Hillsborough, and perhaps inspired by the King. The Southern Secretary then resigned, declaring that the cabinet had opposed him 'on five occasions and where his own Department was immediately concerned'.[116] North's intervention marked a significant stage in his growing political maturity and confidence. He was henceforth master of his cabinet. Rochford was immediately transferred to the Southern Department and, after a short delay, the Earl of Sandwich returned to office as caretaker Northern Secretary on 19 December 1770.

Weymouth's resignation removed a formidable barrier to a peaceful settlement, but it did not dispel the threat of war. His departure had modified rather than transformed British policy, which remained menacing in tone. Throughout December Britain continued to press for an early settlement. Rochford, who came to the Southern Department with a record of implacable hostility towards the Bourbons, repeatedly threatened Masserano that if no settlement were concluded by the reopening of parliament in January, war would be inevitable.[117] On one occasion the new Southern Secretary melodramatically claimed that without an agreement the North Ministry would be forced to resign and implied this would open the way for the formation of a more bellicose government.[118] The new British terms put forward by North still required Spain to make significant concessions and Madrid's agreement could not be assumed: a Land Tax of four shillings in the

[113] For the emerging axis between King and minister, see *Corr. Geo. III*, ii. 172, 174.

[114] Ibid. ii. 174, 185–6, 210–11: this last letter is misdated by Fortescue and clearly belongs to mid-Jan. 1771.

[115] For this decisive cabinet meeting, see ibid. ii. 174–7, 179–80; cf. *HMC Various VI*, 264, for the scheme to attack Spain in the Far East, which Hillsborough attributed to Wood. The constitutional significance of the King's intervention is taken up by I. R. Christie, *Myth and Reality in Late Eighteenth-Century British Politics and Other Papers* (London, 1970), 99–102.

[116] *Corr. Geo. III*, ii. 182.

[117] SP 78/282, fo. 5; British anxieties about a war were very real: see *Documents of the American Revolution*, i, no. 21–2.   [118] CP (Angleterre) 495, fo. 18.

pound was voted on 12 December; North told the Commons that *'war was too probable'*; and naval preparations continued.[119]

While Charles III and his ministers were considering their reply, the whole issue was decided by Choiseul's dismissal on Christmas Eve. Peace was preserved principally by the revolution at the French court. This may seem paradoxical: until his final month in office, France's foreign minister had pursued a moderate and pacific policy and had continually urged Spain to make the concessions needed to maintain peace; but he was now dismissed by Louis XV in an attempt to avert fighting. The explanation is twofold. There were signs that in the last weeks of his ministry, as his enemies made deeper inroads into his position, Choiseul had become resigned to war. This reflected both his pessimism about the scope for a negotiated settlement and his belief that a conflict might retrieve his own crumbling position. France's extensive naval preparations, however, and the secrecy with which Choiseul conducted French policy, had convinced the pacific French king that his minister was about to lead the country into war with Britain.[120] This was the occasion, if not the fundamental cause, for Louis XV's decision to dismiss Choiseul and his cousin Praslin on 24 December 1770.

The exiling of France's leading minister to his estates at Chanteloup was the turning-point in the Falklands crisis. It was decisive because the French King simultaneously notified his Spanish relative that France needed peace and, by implication, would not support him if fighting broke out.[121] Deprived of the support on which Madrid had previously counted, Spain had little alternative but to come to terms.[122] On 31 December the news of Choiseul's fall reached the Spanish capital. It was widely interpreted as an indication that France would not fight. The Spanish King, Charles III, now gave his support to the moderate policies championed by his foreign minister, Grimaldi, and rejected the bellicose line still urged by Arriaga and by Aranda. Madrid accepted that a negotiated settlement was essential and that concessions were unavoidable. On 2 January 1771 instructions to this effect were sent to Masserano. Spain announced her acceptance of the peace proposals put forward by North and championed by the fallen Choiseul.

[119] Tracy, 'Falkland Islands Crisis', 61; *Chatham Corr.* iv. 57. British expectations of war were confirmed by the arrival, on or shortly before 26 Dec., of an intercepted French dispatch from Hanover which appeared to confirm Choiseul's determination to fight: *Corr. Geo. III*, ii. 190–1.

[120] Daubigny, *Choiseul et la France d'outre-mer*, 275.

[121] CP (Espagne) 561, fos. 451–2; cf. ibid. 562, fo. 7.

[122] The final stages of the dispute can be followed in Lalaguna Lasala, 'England, Spain and the Family Compact', 310–23, and in CP (Angleterre) 495 *passim*.

The path to a final settlement was still a troubled one. The recall of Britain's chargé d'affaires in Madrid, James Harris, had created a serious obstacle to any agreement. This had been decided on at a cabinet meeting on 19 December 1770, principally as an attempt to placate the opposition in parliament, but it only became public early in January.[123] Both Francès and Masserano weré outraged by this provocative action and they demanded that full diplomatic relations should be restored before negotiations commenced.[124] Rochford was predictably obdurate, but George III and Lord North were rather more flexible, and the Prime Minister and the Spanish ambassador were soon able to sort out a compromise.[125] This paved the way for formal negotiations between Rochford and the French chargé d'affaires Francès, for the Spanish government was not prepared to allow its ambassador to become involved in the talks until it was clear that the suggested formula was acceptable to Britain.

These negotiations quickly produced an agreement, signed on 22 January 1771, one hour before parliament reassembled.[126] Spain disavowed Bucareli's action and promised to restore Port Egmont to a British garrison. The Spanish government also declared that these concessions in no way affected its fundamental claim to sovereignty over the Falkland Islands. Rochford, for his part, assured the Spanish ambassador that Britain would abandon Port Egmont at a future date. These assurances were verbal and secret, but they were a significant modification of Britain's earlier attitude and, together with North's tacit recognition of Spanish sovereignty, they reveal her desire for a settlement. Spain naturally tried to capitalize on Rochford's promises, but her attempts now, and during the next few years, to persuade Britain to evacuate West Falkland were unsuccessful. British ministers, though concerned at the cost of the Falklands, vigorously resisted such demands because Rochford's assurances had by now leaked out.[127] Evacuation of Port Egmont would confirm British concessions to secure a settlement, which ministers had denied when the issue was debated in parliament in January 1771. Though the government had won the division with

[123] *Cal. HO Papers 1770–2*, no. 383; cf. Rochford to Harris, 21 Dec. 1770, SP 94/185: the British chargé d'affaires' departure was not a signal for war but a crude attempt to put pressure on the Spanish government: CP (Angleterre) 495, fos. 7–8.

[124] *Corr. Geo. III*, ii. 202; *Chatham Corr.* iv. 67.

[125] Harris duly left Madrid, but he had lingered some 60 miles north of the Spanish capital and was able to return very rapidly when his instructions were countermanded on 18 Jan. The reason for this convenient delay was not diplomatic finesse but Harris's pursuit of a Spanish lady! Madariaga, *Armed Neutrality*, 3; *Malmesbury Diaries*, i. 73.

[126] *BDI* vii: *France 1745–1789*, 119; cf. Rochford to Harris, 25 Jan. 1771, SP 94/186.

[127] *Cal. HO Papers 1770–2*, no. 1112.

some ease, it had been attacked for weak handling of the dispute, and it was sensitive to any suggestions of secret concessions to Spain. Parliament was henceforth an important obstacle to any withdrawal. Port Egmont was restored by the Spanish authorities in September 1771, but its garrison was reduced and the decision to abandon it was taken, on the grounds of simple economy, in 1774.

In the longer view the Falklands crisis was significant because it marked the beginning of North's involvement in foreign affairs.[128] His decisive intervention was the means by which he established his supremacy within the cabinet, and it was also important for future British diplomacy. Throughout the next decade he continued to exert considerable influence on foreign policy and on occasions intervened personally in negotiations. This involvement was based on close co-operation with George III which had emerged over the Falklands.[129] In the troubled years that lay ahead this partnership was to be an important influence on foreign policy as well as on domestic and colonial issues. It would, at times, even operate against Britain's official diplomacy.

North's own ideas on foreign policy were never very profound. In 1770–1 his principal objective had been to avoid the war which Weymouth appeared to have brought on. His motives related principally to domestic British politics. He wanted to strengthen his own political position and that of his ministry, and he was anxious not to endanger his planned financial measures. Peace was to remain North's overriding aim. Yet he was careful to uphold British interests. He was liked and trusted by foreign envoys, and his bluff and friendly manner quickly won him the respect of the diplomatic corps in London.[130]

The Falklands crisis also strengthened Britain's diplomatic recovery. Paradoxically, Weymouth's contribution to this was considerable. The vigour he had imparted to British policy impressed foreign observers, for it was generally believed the Bourbons had backed down when faced with Britain's show of strength.[131] Choiseul's

[128] This has not hitherto received the detailed attention it merits, principally because it only becomes fully apparent from foreign sources. The account in P. D. G. Thomas, *Lord North* (London, 1976), 46–51, emphasizes the domestic political repercussions. Contemporaries were more aware of North's significant contribution to a settlement. Junius, for example, during his outburst against 'the treachery of the King's servants' during the dispute singled out North 'who takes the whole upon himself' for particular censure: *The Letters of Junius*, ed. J. Cannon (Oxford, 1978), 222.

[129] It seems likely that the King at the very least encouraged North to intervene directly against Weymouth in late Nov. 1770, but the evidence for this is circumstantial.

[130] See, in particular, Escarano's later comments: E 6998, fo. 13.

[131] See e.g. G. A. von Nolckens riksdagsberättelse, 1771, Roberts Transcripts.

dismissal was viewed as the consequence of this firmness. But the Falklands crisis did not in itself re-establish Britain's political credit. It reinforced a recovery that was already under way, but would only be completed by 1773, and it did nothing to assist in the search for a continental alliance.

Britain's success in western Europe in 1770–1 contrasted sharply with her continuing ineffectiveness further east. The months that had seen the confrontation over the Falklands also witnessed another unsuccessful initiative over the Russian alliance. The failure of earlier British attempts to mediate in the Russo-Turkish war had not discouraged Rochford, who again approached St Petersburg in autumn 1770.[132] This aimed to exploit Catherine II's renowned hostility towards France, recently intensified by Choiseul's threat to send a French fleet to the eastern Mediterranean. Britain pointed to the way French influence at the Porte had supposedly brought about the Turkish declaration of war in October 1768, to recent attempts to conclude a formal alliance with the Turks, and to Choiseul's continuing aid to the Polish Confederates as evidence of France's aggressively anti-Russian strategy. Though the treaty-project which was forwarded to Cathcart on 15 August 1770 retained the 'Turkish clause', it was significantly modified in a way that reveals both Britain's longing for an alliance and her belated and partial recognition that a price would have to be paid. It was not Britain, however, but the Sultan who was to pay it. Rochford offered to guarantee Russia's gains at any future peace with the Turks. Even more remarkable was Britain's promise that if this settlement were concluded under her mediation, she would press Constantinople to satisfy Russia's territorial demands, particularly over Azov, the Kuban, and the navigation of the Black Sea. Alliance and mediation were for the first time formally linked.

Rochford's proposals shed interesting light on his view of the role of an impartial mediator and they also reveal his willingness to sacrifice the Turks on the altar of Britain's Russian alliance. But his initiative led nowhere. Though the formal approach was made in September 1770, no reply was received for nine months. Neither Cathcart's habitual enthusiasm and unshaken belief that a treaty was just around the corner, nor his pursuit of Panin, could prise a definite answer out of the Russian government.[133] Only at the end of June

---

[132] *Sbornik*, xix. 55–61.
[133] Ibid. xix. 103–5, 141–5, 158–60, 160–2; and, in full detail, in SP 91/85–8. For the ambassador's meetings with the Russian minister, *Sbornik*, cxliii. 218.

1771 was an explicit refusal given to this latest approach, ostensibly because of British parsimony over Sweden.[134]

This initiative was, significantly, Britain's last attempt to conclude a Russian alliance before the American revolt. Panin's frank indifference was symptomatic both of St Petersburg's new political priorities and of a fundamental change in Anglo-Russian relations. His unconcern was more remarkable in view of Russia's new problems around the Baltic, which emerged in the winter of 1770–1: the very months during which the British approach languished. In September 1770 a coup against Bernstorff resulted in the dismissal of Denmark's leading minister and his replacement by Struensee. Denmark had been an important part of the 'Northern System'. Her fleet was significant in a purely Baltic context and her alliance was a useful check on Sweden. The fall of Bernstorff, the architect of the Russo-Danish *rapprochement*, was followed three months later by a formal breach in relations. To Catherine II the events in Copenhagen were the work of France. Early the next year the death of the Swedish king, Adolf Frederik, increased Russia's difficulties. This brought the resolute Crown Prince Gustav to the throne. With his accession Russian anxieties about the restoration of absolutism in Stockholm and a Swedish attack from Finland surfaced. It was symptomatic that, when his father died (February 1771), Gustav III was in France, discussing his plans for a coup and his hopes of French support. This serious deterioration in Russia's position around the Baltic came at a time when Catherine II's government was already fully committed in Poland and against the Turks. Yet the Empress showed herself wholly uninterested in Rochford's proferred alliance. In 1768–9 a similar, if rather more serious crisis had for a time revived the negotiations. Now it was a different story, and not even Cathcart could overcome Russia's indifference or conceal this from his superiors.

Britain's latest initiative was partly undermined by its timing.[135] It coincided with the remarkable Russian victories of summer and autumn 1770 and also with the emergence of the serious dispute over the Falkland Islands. Her victories made Catherine II believe that she could dictate her own terms to the Turks, while the real threat of an Anglo-Bourbon war was an obvious barrier to any alliance. Russia's coolness, however, had far more fundamental causes. Catherine was certainly grateful for Britain's assistance to her fleet, but this was not enough to overcome her growing doubts about the value of an alliance. The Empress and Panin were more than ever convinced of

[134] Ibid. xix. 215–6.
[135] As Rochford tacitly admitted it might be: SP 91/85, fos. 102–3.

Britain's decline. Ths conviction, already apparent by the close of Macartney's mission, had been strengthened by Britain's evident weakness abroad and her continuing political strife at home. The shambles of British diplomacy over Corsica in 1768 was particularly significant, since the Empress was an enthusiastic supporter of Paoli, while the eventual triumph over the Bourbons in 1770–1 came too late to repair Britain's standing at the Russian court.[136] Britain's continuing domestic upheavals, and the exaggerated reports of these which were received from the ambassador in London, Chernyshev, were particularly important: Cathcart later complained that 'the Empress and her ministers have always been, and still are with respect to English politics, *in the Opposition*'.[137] Significantly, Chernyshev had stopped off at the Prussian court on his way to London and had been regaled by Frederick II with stories of Britain's political instability, and these clearly influenced the ambassador's view of British politics.[138]

Relations with Britain had in any case assumed a much lower priority in St Petersburg.[139] The Turkish war and the Polish situation were now becoming increasingly complex and inextricably linked. The winter of 1770–1 had seen not only Rochford's final bid for the Russian alliance, but the far more significant visit of Prince Henry of Prussia to the Russian court, when Catherine was converted to the idea of partitioning Poland. Panin had also been having to face the problems for Russia created by the Austro-Prussian *rapprochement* of the later 1760s. The pressing offer of mediation in the Turkish war made by the two German powers could not easily be eluded, and in the complex diplomacy which resulted was to be found the origins of the first partition of Poland, which dominated European politics from 1771 onwards. These preoccupations contrasted sharply with Britain's apparent indifference to eastern Europe and her inability to influence events there.

British attempts to conclude the Russian alliance in 1768–71 had completely failed. Ministers continued to hope a treaty would be concluded, though characteristically they emphasized the next move was up to Russia.[140] Cathcart, distressed by his wife's death and by his own failure, returned home in August 1772. The finale to his

---

[136] D. M. Griffiths, 'Catherine the Great, the British Opposition and the American Revolution', in L. S. Kaplan, ed., *The American Revolution and a 'Candid World'* (Kent, Oh, 1977), 87–8.　　　　　　　　　　　　　　　　　　　　　　　　　[137] *Sbornik*, xix. 228.

[138] Martens, *Recueil des traités*, ix(x). 272–3. British ministers believed that the Russian ambassador was not a supporter of the alliance: SP 91/80, fos. 74–5.

[139] As British observers occasionally recognized: see, e.g. ibid. 91/87, fo. 235.

[140] See the 'Instructions' for Gunning, 27 May 1772, *Sbornik*, xix. 265–7; SP 91/87, fo. 235; cf. 91/88, fo. 63.

embassy was in keeping with the past four years. He lingered in the Russian capital after the arrival of his successor, Sir Robert Gunning, to pass on his accumulated wisdom to the new ambassador during a series of political tutorials. In a quite extraordinary and wholly unprecedented step, he also asked Panin for a signed account of Russo-British diplomacy since 1768 and for a certificate that he had behaved properly at the Russian court, no doubt to exculpate himself with his superiors. What he received was a familiar and withering recapitulation of Russian grievances over the alliance negotiations, and even Cathcart found it prudent to suppress this.[141] Even now his follies were not complete. After he returned to Britain he sought to present the Empress, whom he so admired, with a bust of Peter the Great, happily ignorant that it was a copy of a famous original.[142]

Cathcart and his wife had secured the personal affection of Catherine II, not least for the way in which he styled her his 'chère Impératrice' in formal correspondence in defiance of all the diplomatic conventions of the day.[143] Russia's alliance continued to elude all Britain's efforts. Cathcart had been an inadequate ambassador and had himself contributed to the cooler tone of Anglo-Russian diplomacy after 1768–9.[144] But the fast diminishing prospects for an alliance owed less to his deficiencies than to Russia's changed priorities and to the new diplomatic pattern. As Panin very sensibly pointed out to the Empress, there was no need for Russia to assume the obligations of a formal treaty with London when she could secure most of the advantages from the *entente* which already existed: he now talked of harmony, not of alliance. As long as Britain's policy was anti-French then it was necessarily also pro-Russian. In one sense, Cathcart had been right when he declared that 'the common interests of the two courts and their sense of them unite them closer than treaties are able to do'.[145] The failure to conclude a formal alliance did not irrevocably damage relations, which remained fairly harmonious until the later 1770s, though it was significant in the wider framework of British foreign policy. By 1771 Britain's recovery was becoming apparent. But so too was a transformation of the European states-system that would soon undermine traditional British diplomacy almost completely.

[141] *Sbornik*, cxliii. 482.   [142] Ibid. xvii. 189, 195–6, and 197 for these efforts.
[143] See ibid. xiii. 188, 209, 302.
[144] See e.g. ibid. cxliii. 471, for the way he was still being duped by Panin during his embassy's final days: cf. ibid. cxliii. 303, 426.
[145] Cathcart to Sir William Hamilton, 16 Dec. 1769, Cathcart Papers A 75, fo. 654.

7

The Ascendancy of the Eastern Powers,
1771–1773

BY the mid-point of the Russo-Turkish War, the division of the continent into two separate diplomatic systems was well advanced and would soon reach its full extent. Russia, Prussia, and Austria were preoccupied with the fighting in the Balkans and with plans to partition Poland. By contrast, Anglo-Bourbon rivalry was now conducted overseas, as the Falklands episode had confirmed. The eastern powers would not be dragged into this world-wide struggle: significantly, at the height of the crisis, Austria and Prussia had agreed to remain neutral in any war over Port Egmont. This agreement at Neustadt in 1770 marked a further stage in the breakdown of Anglo-French leadership of the continent. It underlined that the other powers would no longer be drawn into each and every conflict between Britain and the Bourbons, as had often been the case in the eighteenth century, and that they had their own political priorities. By the second half of 1771 the growing independence and predominance of the three eastern powers were evident. The corollary was the weakening hold of the western states on European affairs.

Britain's isolation since 1763 contributed to this, but more fundamental was the growing political maturity of the eastern powers. Two interrelated developments came together in the first partition of Poland, concluded in 1772. Russia and Prussia now enjoyed complete ascendancy in eastern Europe and, together with Austria, formed a separate and distinct diplomatic system there. The western states, preoccupied with their own rivalry, no longer shaped the continent's political destiny. Britain's unsuccessful attempts to mediate in the Russo-Turkish War in 1768–71 symbolized their growing ineffectiveness, yet at first London exhibited little concern.[1] It was to be several years before ministers appreciated the serious

---

[1] Though in Nov. 1772, Britain's isolation was tentatively noted by the cabinet: *HMC Dartmouth*, 107. The *Annual Register* for 1772 pronounced the partition of Poland to be 'the first very great breach in the modern political system of Europe' (p. 2) and went on to provide a full and acute analysis of its implications and those of the coup in Sweden in Aug. 1772 (pp. 2–8).

implications of developments in eastern Europe. The Russo-Turkish War and the Polish partition appeared very remote issues to British observers in the early 1770s. During Lord North's early years in power, foreign affairs were a low political priority, though Britain's international position was never neglected as completely as at times during the 1760s. Apart from a crisis with Denmark in spring 1772 and a brief confrontation with France a year later, the cabinet was to give little sustained attention to foreign policy until the outbreak of the American rebellion in 1775. This neglect was facilitated by the diminished threat from the Bourbons after 1770–1 and by the growing confidence which resulted from Britain's victory over Port Egmont.

One delayed consequence of this crisis was the entry to office of the Earl of Suffolk, who became Northern Secretary in June 1771. Suffolk has been roughly handled by historians and his contribution to British diplomacy has been disparaged. He is usually remembered for his supposed ignorance of French, his gouty constitution, and his equally gouty foreign policy.[2] This is undeserved, and his conduct of British foreign policy during the difficult years of the 1770s deserves more credit than it has received.[3] Principal among the myths that still surround him is the notion that he knew no French, the established language of diplomacy, with the implication that this hindered his discussions with foreign envoys in London.[4] This was clearly the case when he entered office: six months before he described himself as a 'very bad Frenchman'.[5] But in June 1771 he immediately set to work to learn the language. Though a poor linguist, within a few years he was able to converse quite fluently in French with members of the diplomatic corps.[6]

These successful efforts epitomized the way Suffolk grew into his post. Diligent application turned him into a capable and respected Northern Secretary.[7] He was certainly ignorant of foreign affairs when he entered office.[8] His appointment was an attempt by North to strengthen the government's position in parliament and his own

---

[2] He was, for example, traduced by H. W. V. Temperley, *Frederic the Great and Kaiser Joseph* (London, 1915; repr. 1968), 263; cf. Madariaga, *Armed Neutrality*, 9.
[3] See Roberts, *British Diplomacy*, 363–4 and ch. 9 *passim*, for an important reassessment.
[4] See e.g. M. Roberts, *Splendid Isolation 1763–1780* (Reading, 1970), 7.
[5] *Corr. Geo. III*, ii. 206.
[6] Masserano to Grimaldi, 21 June 1771, E 6980; Add. MSS 34412, fo. 177.
[7] See e.g. Yorke's comments: Add. MSS 35370, fo. 77.
[8] See, e.g. Masserano to Grimaldi, 21 June 1771, E 6980; cf. the scathing comments of the French chargé d'affaires: CP (Angleterre) 497, fos. 46–7; the Austrian envoy, Belgioioso, indignantly complained that he was so ignorant he had to explain Austria's diplomatic outlook to him *ab initio*: to Kaunitz, 14 June 1771, HHStA England-Korrespondenz 116.

authority in the cabinet.[9] Suffolk initially demonstrated a measure of exasperation with the complexities of European politics and the importunities of foreign diplomats.[10] But he always had a good grasp of Britain's essential interests and was prepared to work to master the business of his office. Though his views on foreign policy were essentially traditional, he was to become a shrewd, realistic, and highly capable Secretary of State, with a stock of sound common sense and a resilience that served Britain well as she struggled to adjust to the new diplomatic constellation of the 1770s.[11]

Suffolk remained Northern Secretary until 1779, though he was frequently to be handicapped by ill health: while still a relatively young man, he was cruelly afflicted by gout. He was notably conscientious, and he soon acquired the respect of foreign envoys for his friendly and straightforward manner and for the regularity of his meetings with the diplomatic corps. His secretaryship, at least until the outbreak of the American rebellion, contrasted sharply with the neglect that had earlier been notorious.[12] For several years it was also marked by unusually close co-operation between the Northern and Southern Departments. By the mid-1770s, Suffolk was to quarrel very seriously with his brother Secretary, Rochford, but the two men initially worked well together.[13] One Secretary might be an active and able minister, but it was unusual for both to be so concerned with European issues as was the case in the early 1770s. This was not without its dangers, as would become particularly evident in 1772–3 at the time of the secret Anglo-French negotiations. But the partnership of Suffolk and Rochford was at first relatively untroubled, and it helped to smooth the transition to the new international situation which Britain now faced. The two Secretaries also enjoyed considerable freedom, for the cabinet was preoccupied with domestic and colonial problems and only concerned itself with diplomacy when war threatened.

In the early 1770s Lord North was primarily concerned to consolidate his own political authority. Domestic policy was dominated by his efforts to reduce the National Debt and to implement financial retrenchment. The cabinet's major problems arose in Britain's overseas possessions, although they did not at first

[9] CP (Angleterre) 497, fos. 46–7.
[10] See, e.g. Suffolk to Keith, 30 July 1771, SP 75/125, for his ignorance and uncertainty over Denmark; cf. Egerton 2701, fos. 169–70.
[11] See e.g. the assessment of the Danish foreign minister, A. P. von Bernstorff, which was particularly remarkable in view of the deterioration in relations between London and Copenhagen under Suffolk: *Bernstorffsche Papiere*, iii. 591.
[12] His businesslike approach is clear from his letters to his Under-Secretary, William Eden: Add. MSS 34412 *passim*; see esp. fos. 172, 182; cf. Roberts, *British Diplomacy*, 364.
[13] See e.g. Add. MSS 34412, fo. 182.

include the American colonies, where a relative calm prevailed in the early 1770s. Instead, ministers were forced to turn their attention to Ireland, India, and Canada. Convinced they would not face an early Bourbon attack, North and his hard-pressed colleagues were usually content to leave foreign affairs to the two senior Secretaries of State. In western Europe at least, peace appeared secure and this remained Britain's overriding aim. Nevertheless the early 1770s were of considerable significance. The recovery that had begun in the later 1760s continued and, assisted by triumphs over the Bourbons in 1770–1 and France in spring 1773, Britain's reputation revived in Europe's capitals. Simultaneously, the ascendancy of Russia and Prussia in particular was undermining the whole basis of British diplomacy. The implications of the new political pattern on the continent came to be recognized, if not fully understood, in London. This in turn contributed to a gradual reassessment of Britain's foreign policy, in which alliances were viewed as less important than naval power for her security.

This concern with the fleet also emphasized that Britain's diplomacy was coming to be seen mainly in terms of policy towards France and Spain.[14] In the aftermath of the Falklands crisis the Bourbon threat appeared to diminish and for a time relations improved. Few British statesmen believed that this would be other than temporary, and a close watch continued to be kept on the enemy fleets, yet the early 1770s did see a marked reduction of tension.[15] This had two obvious sources: an improvement in Britain's relations with France, and a significant weakening of the Family Compact, which in turn contributed to an Anglo-Spanish *détente*. But the determining factor was Britain's increasing lead at sea, revealed to ministers by their intelligence network. Before long her absolute mastery was even recognized at Versailles. This further shift in the naval balance was crucial in the broader context of Anglo-French diplomacy. It resulted from the diametrically opposite achievements of the two new naval ministers who came to power after the Falklands crisis, Sandwich and Boynes. Sandwich's energetic work strengthened the British fleet exactly at the point that his counterpart was actually weakening France's navy, and this handed the initiative to Britain for several years to come.

The Earl of Sandwich became First Lord of the Admiralty in January 1771.[16] During the next few years his undoubted interest

[14] As Nolcken pointed out: G. A. von Nolckens riksdagsberättelse 1771, Roberts Transcripts.   [15] *Corr. Geo. III*, ii. 429–35; *Cal. HO Papers 1770–2*, no. 1399.
[16] Sandwich's reputation was for long blighted by the fact that his years at the Admiralty (1771–82) saw serious naval defeats and the loss of the American colonies; the charges of his

and knowledge of naval matters (he had served at the Admiralty immediately after the War of the Austrian Succession and had also, very briefly, been First Lord in 1763), together with his administrative ability, brought about a significant improvement in Britain's navy. His success was apparent in his major rebuilding programme: between 1771 and 1777 twenty-two new ships of the line were constructed and forty-two were repaired.[17] This was facilitated by North's appreciation of the importance of a strong fleet and willingness to provide some of the necessary funds. Sandwich was a political ally of the Prime Minister, and the navy was largely exempted from the prevailing financial retrenchment. Indeed expenditure on the fleet was substantially increased in the early 1770s and, though later reduced, it remained far higher during the years of peace up to 1775, than it had been throughout the previous decade.[18] Though some shortcomings in Britain's naval mobilization had been apparent, the confrontation over Port Egmont had principally confirmed her continuing superiority at sea. However, the crisis was exploited by North and Sandwich to increase the naval budget. In 1770 the government's parliamentary critics had attacked the fleet's poor condition and had loudly censured the stewardship of the then First Lord, the elderly and ailing Hawke. Once the emergency was over, the House of Commons appeared more willing to spend money on the navy.[19] This expenditure was also linked to the growing insularity of British foreign policy. Funds were provided, in part, because a strong navy was coming to be seen as a better basis for Britain's security than uncertain foreign alliances, particularly given the upheavals in the European states-system in the early 1770s.[20]

The serious situation which Sandwich inherited originated during the Seven Years War.[21] The ships that had then been built with unseasoned timber were decaying rapidly and many were urgently in

political opponents were too readily believed by credulous historians in search of a scapegoat. But during the past half-century, his reputation had steadily risen. This was begun by the ed. of *The Sandwich Papers*, ed. G. R. Barnes and J. H. Owen (4 vols.; London, 1932–8; Navy Records Society), established by the important D.Phil. thesis of M. J. Williams, 'The Naval Administration of the Fourth Earl of Sandwich, 1771–82' (University of Oxford, 1962), and completed by P. Mackesy's *The War for America 1775–1783*. The brief account of Sandwich's work which follows is based on these authorities and on the useful summary in N. Tracy, *Navies, Deterrence and American Independence: Britain and Seapower in the 1760s and 1770s* (Vancouver, 1988), 31–41.

[17] Williams, 'Naval Administration', 428, 443.
[18] See the valuable table setting out naval expenditure in R. F. Mackay, *Admiral Hawke* (Oxford, 1965), 305.
[19] G. A. von Nolckens riksdagsberättelse 1771, Roberts Transcripts.
[20] See North's revealing remarks about alliances and naval power: Egerton 232, fos. 59–60, 67; cf. *Parl. Hist.* xvii, col. 241.   [21] See above, Ch. 4.

need of repair and rebuilding. This situation had been exacerbated by the naval economies after 1763, which had prevented a full programme of reconstruction. Sandwich soon discovered that neither the timber stocks nor dockyard facilities were adequate for the work now essential. The shortage of timber and other naval stores was particularly acute. Economies after 1763 had prevented the replenishment of stocks and had actually led to a further depletion. This had been made worse by a serious fire at Portsmouth in July 1770, which destroyed one of the few substantial stores of ship's timber.[22] In the dockyards the situation was equally bad, and shore facilities were inadequate to handle essential refitting. Sandwich's attempts to improve this situation were not immediately successful. Real progress only began to be made in the dockyards during the American War. But within a few years Sandwich did bring about a significant improvement in the stocks and supply of timber, which in turn made possible a major programme of rebuilding and refitting. The navy's condition and state of readiness both increased during his early years at the Admiralty. This reinforced Britain's lead at sea, particularly given the simultaneous damage Boynes was inflicting on the French fleet.

The condition and even the numerical strength of France's navy declined in the early 1770s, while in the dockyards the situation was even worse.[23] French sea power was undermined by its lower priority after Choiseul's fall, by the prevailing financial retrenchment, and above all by the eccentric reforms introduced by the new naval minister, Bourgeois de Boynes. These changes were in theory attractive, but in practice disastrous. Boynes's efforts to reform naval administration set the 'pen' (civilian administrators) against the 'sword' (professional captains); his creation of a naval academy and his introduction of training cruises alienated a naval establishment that prided itself on training 'before the mast'; while his introduction of army-style 'brigades' and other innovations from land service were not only widely unpopular but also failed to work. Before long the situation was chaotic. Boynes's reforms effectively disabled the French navy for three years and were abandoned by his successor. Their disastrous impact was gradually revealed to British ministers by their naval intelligence network.

British confidence was further strengthened by the priorities of the new French government and by the policy pursued by Choiseul's

---

[22] One contemporary estimate put the damage as high as £500,000 (*Walpole Corr.* xxiii. 228 n. 26), which was almost a quarter of the naval budget for 1770.

[23] See Dull, *French Navy*, 11–14, and J. Tramond, 'La Marine et les réformes de M. de Boynes', *La Revue maritime*, 61 (1925), 153–80.

eventual successor, the Duc d'Aiguillon. The 'Triumvirate' that ruled during the final three years of Louis XV's reign (1771–4) sought peace abroad, in order to make possible financial retrenchment and a solution of the problem of the *parlements* at home. These domestic priorities reinforced the North Ministry's belief that it would be several years before Britain would have to face another French attack.[24] This was also encouraged by a simultaneous and significant improvement in relations with France.

The crisis over the Falklands and the political revolution at Louis XV's court, by which it had been resolved, marked a turning-point. Choiseul's considerable antagonism had made relations tense and often acrimonious during his ministry. His recognition of Britain's naval supremacy, however, had produced a limited *détente* during his final years in power and had prevented him from launching a war of revenge. Choiseul's dismissal was followed by an interval of six months (December 1770–June 1771) during which France's diplomacy almost ground to a halt, before d'Aiguillon emerged as his successor. It is difficult to disentangle d'Aiguillon's conduct of France's diplomacy from his unenviable reputation in French court politics as a ruthless intriguer and an obstinate opponent. His foreign policy certainly deserves more credit than it has received. It constituted a realistic and intelligent attempt to adapt to the dramatic eastern realignment of the early 1770s. He aimed to prevent further Russian expansion westwards and avert the partition of Poland. His policy here continued Choiseul's anti-Russian initiatives of the later 1760s; it differed in attempting not merely to produce a temporary Franco-British *détente* but also to establish co-operation and even an alliance between the traditional enemies.

D'Aiguillon recognized that neither France nor Britain on her own could exert much influence in eastern Europe. He believed that Anglo-French co-operation might be able to check, and even to reverse, the new-found dominance of the eastern powers, and was convinced that this was the most promising way to restore France's vanishing influence in Europe. As a first step a significant improvement in relations with Britain was achieved. Louis XV's love of peace was now echoed by his foreign minister, as Choiseul's firm line was replaced by an almost obliging tone.[25] D'Aiguillon's friendly and open conduct towards the British representative in Paris was at one level a matter of political and economic necessity: King and ministry were united in their determination to avoid an early war with Britain.

---

[24] In May 1772, North told the Commons that there was 'the fairest prospect of the continuance of peace that I have known in my time': *Parl. Hist.* xvii, col. 489.

[25] Rochford explicitly testified to this: Add. MSS 24158, fo. 145.

France's desire for better relations was evident in some minor colonial concessions and by a general willingness to defer to Britain's wishes: as, for example, in the way the Young Pretender was immediately ordered out of France when he travelled to Paris in autumn 1771.[26] The reversal of traditional policy was apparent in French diplomatic correspondence. D'Aiguillon was soon praising Sandwich's efforts to build up Britain's navy—a remarkable sentiment for the minister of a state which had been the principal victim of British sea power—and commenting favourably on North's attempts at financial retrenchment.[27]

By the winter of 1771–2, ministers recognized a marked improvement had taken place in relations. In March 1772 a well-placed British observer noted that 'The present situation of the two Courts is favourable. The tone of one [France] is much fallen,' while Britain 'wishes not to pick a quarrel'.[28] Significant sources of tension remained, particularly British anxieties about French ambitions in India and Canada, but the North cabinet recognized that France had become less hostile.[29] This improvement was believed to be transient. Most British ministers recognized that rivalry was inevitable, but they welcomed a respite in the struggle.

Britain's sense of security was aided by a significant weakening of the Bourbon Family Compact in the early 1770s and by a related improvement in Anglo-Spanish diplomacy. The confrontation over Port Egmont had demonstrated that even a weakened Spanish empire could pose a threat to the neighbouring British colonies in North America and this was one reason why ministers sought better relations with Madrid. The Falklands crisis was clearly a turning-point in Franco-Spanish diplomacy. Since its inception in 1761 France had dominated the Third Family Compact, and in the 1760s Choiseul had exerted considerable influence on Madrid's foreign policy. In the early 1770s the balance of political power within this alliance shifted towards Spain, as Charles III and his ministers adopted a more independent line.[30] This transformation resulted principally from Spain's resentment at being abandoned by France at

[26] For this affair, see SP 78/283.
[27] CP (Angleterre) 497, fo. 224; 499, fos. 30–6, 47, 132.
[28] Mansfield to Stormont, 27 Mar. 1772, Stormont Papers, Box 52. Mansfield was Lord Chief Justice and a political confidant of the King.
[29] H. Richmond, *The Navy in India 1763–1783* (London, 1931), 52–5, 62–3; N. Tracy, 'Parry of a Threat to India, 1768–1774', *The Mariner's Mirror*, 59 (1973), 38–42; id., *Navies, Deterrence and American Independence*, 100–5; *Fort William—India House Correspondence*, vi, pp. xxix–xxx, 315–6, 435; *Documents of the American Revolution*, v. no. 63.
[30] A useful, if somewhat overdrawn account is A. S. Aiton, 'Spain and the Family Compact, 1770–1773' in A. Curtis Wilgus, ed., *Hispanic American Essays* (North Carolina, 1942; repr. New York, 1970), 135–49.

the height of the dispute. Thereafter, Madrid was always less prepared to follow Louis XV's lead, and a new, essentially self-interested view of the Family Compact emerged south of the Pyrenees. In the early 1770s France continued to expect Spanish support: not only against Britain, but also against Russia.[31] This was not always forthcoming; indeed the French government's apparent willingness for war, particularly in 1772–3 over Sweden, was unpopular in Madrid and further weakened the Family Compact. By the mid-1770s relations with Britain, though still significant, had lost the absolute priority which they had possessed for Charles III and ideas of a *revanche* were being shelved. Spain was instead coming to devote more attention to relations with Portugal in South America and to the perennial problem of the North African corsairs.

The waning of the Family Compact was certainly recognized in London. Britain now faced a weakened Bourbon challenge with a fleet that was being strengthened all the time.[32] Immediately after the Falklands débâcle, Rochford tried to exploit Madrid's resentment, in an attempt to undermine the Family Compact, to divide the Bourbon powers, and to inaugurate a new era of Anglo-Spanish friendship.[33] This diplomatic strategy was first signalled by George III. In a remarkable interview with the Spanish ambassador shortly after the joint disarmament which finally ended the confrontation over Port Egmont, the King described the recent crisis as 'like a lovers' quarrel; The lovers quarrel so that they will have the pleasure of making up and re-affirming their love'![34] This was an astonishing remark in view of the tense relations ever since Charles III's accession, but it does reveal Britain's new aims.[35] Though these hopes proved rather too ambitious, the early 1770s did see a gradual improvement in relations.[36] The basis of this was Britain's recognition that the Bourbon powers were not a single political force and that Madrid was becoming independent of Versailles. In the 1760s ministers had treated relations with Spain simply as a minor dimension of their policy towards France; but they were now coming to recognize that Anglo-Spanish diplomacy was a distinct subject and offered considerable scope for a political initiative.

[31] Lalaguna Lasala, 'England, Spain and the Family Compact', 346–95.

[32] Egerton 232, fo. 67, for North's confidence.

[33] See the 'Separate and Secret Instructions' for Lord Grantham, the new ambassador to Spain, 23 May 1771, Add. MSS 24157, fos. 7–14, esp. Articles 3 and 4, fos. 9–10.

[34] Masserano to Grimaldi, 26 Apr. 1771, E 6978.

[35] This was certainly appreciated by the Spanish ambassador in London (see e.g. his dispatch of 21 June 1771, E 6980). But Masserano was a firm supporter of the Bourbon alliance as the basis of Spain's security, and he rejected all Rochford's entreaties (Masserano to Grimaldi, 1 Aug. 1771, E 6981).

[36] See Grantham's important analysis of this: 12 Dec. 1771, Add. MSS 24174, fos. 34–8.

This was apparent in Britain's new-found desire not to offend the Spanish government. It was signalled over the right of British warships to enter Spanish ports and especially Cadiz. This had long been a source of minor disputes, ostensibly because Madrid believed the privilege was being abused to cover the illegal export of silver from Spain. In spring 1771 Charles III's government issued a decree prohibiting the future entry of warships. This was immediately accepted by Britain, which had hitherto refused any concessions on the issue.[37] Even more surprising were the cabinet's attempts in the following summer to calm Madrid's fears over British intentions in the Pacific. Though the return of Captain James Cook in July, after his celebrated first voyage, reawakened Spanish anxieties, ministers assured Masserano they would prevent any British attempts to colonize the South Seas in order to preserve friendly relations.[38] Remarkable evidence of this new-found desire not to offend Madrid came in December 1771, when Rochford and George III intervened to prevent Sandwich naming two ships the *Raleigh* and the *Drake* on the grounds that these names 'will give great offence to the Spaniards'.[39] The Southern Secretary also displayed considerable moderation in the minor colonial disputes which still arose. In 1771 Rochford tried to restrain the East India Company from any provocative action against the Spanish in the Far East.[40] Even more surprising was his moderation over Crab Island.[41]

This tiny and uninhabited island lay three miles off the coast of Puerto Rico and was an obvious base for smuggling, which the Spanish colonial authorities were determined to stamp out. In October 1771 they arrested an English schooner which was cutting the abundant timber on Crab Island. On several previous occasions incidents of this kind had produced considerable diplomatic tension. The exchanges over Crab Island, though they dragged on until 1774, were notable for the moderation of both governments. In particular Rochford's restrained approach contrasted sharply with Britain's vigorous and at times intransigent stance in 1770–1. The fundamental issue in each dispute was broadly similar: action by the Spanish authorities against British subjects. But over Crab Island the Southern Secretary went out of his way to avoid any serious

---

[37] See, in particular, Masserano to Grimaldi, 24 Apr. 1771, E 6978.
[38] See Masserano's correspondence for these months in E 6980.
[39] *Sandwich Papers*, i. 381.
[40] Lalaguna Lasala, 'England, Spain and the Family Compact', 338.
[41] For this, see V. L. Brown, 'Anglo-Spanish Relations in America in the Closing Years of the Colonial Era', *Hispanic American Historical Review*, 5 (1922), 470–3, and Lalaguna Lasala, 'England, Spain and the Family Compact', 328–36. It is detailed in Grantham's correspondence for 1771–4: Add. MSS 24157–9 and 24174 *passim*.

confrontation and never seriously questioned Spain's right to the island. British diplomacy aimed simply to secure the release of the ship and its crew. Even these representations were suspended in 1772–3, during a period of considerable tension produced by France's threatened naval intervention in the Baltic, and they seem to have been abandoned in 1774.

Improved relations were welcomed in Madrid as well as in London.[42] Spain's new-found independence and changed political priorities, together with her recognition of France's weakness and unreliability, made her grateful for any breathing space in the struggle with Britain. However, the extent of this *détente* should not be exaggerated. Both states understood that old enmities would not simply evaporate, and sources of tension remained. Spain's foreign minister, Grimaldi, was viewed in London as irrevocably anti-British and therefore a considerable barrier to good relations.[43] With France's collapse after Choiseul's fall, British ministers actually believed Spain more likely to attack than the stricken French state.[44] Madrid viewed the Falkland Islands as the major source of continuing friction. To Spanish observers the British settlement at Port Egmont was a 'thorn in their side'.[45] Spanish diplomacy and particularly the ambassador in London, Masserano, pressed for Britain to honour the verbal undertakings of January 1771 to evacuate the base.[46] The North Ministry dragged its feet, fearful that any early abandonment of Port Egmont would confirm rumours of secret concessions in 1770–1 to secure a settlement and thereby expose it to further attacks in parliament.

The potential for serious tension remained, particularly overseas, where Britain's dynamic and expanding empire was bound to collide with Spain's extensive remaining territories.[47] The limited control which metropolitan governments could exert over events in the colonies increased the danger that such local clashes might produce a larger confrontation.[48] Yet in the first half of the 1770s there was a significant improvement in relations, and this strengthened Britain's growing confidence. Indeed, by the winter of 1771–2 the North Ministry faced few apparent problems in foreign affairs. Relations

[42] As Grimaldi made clear: Add MSS 24174, fos. 32–3.

[43] Add. MSS 24157, fo. 288. From being in Madrid (1763–6), Rochford was an old foe of Grimaldi who was, in any case, regarded in London as Choiseul's creature and therefore anxious for war against England.

[44] This was certainly Sandwich's view: *Cal. HO Papers 1770–2*, no. 883.

[45] Masserano to Grimaldi, 24 Apr. 1771, E 6978.

[46] J. Goebel, *The Struggle for the Falkland Islands* (New Haven, Conn., 1927; repr. 1982), 377–410.

[47] *Documents of the American Revolution*, iv, nos. 204, 631, 633, 673; v, no. 137.

[48] For Grimaldi's very clear recognition of this, see Add. MSS 24174, fos. 32–3.

with the Bourbons were better than at any time since 1763, while events in eastern Europe appeared to be of little concern to Britain. Ministers were free to concentrate on internal and colonial questions. But these preoccupations were deflected during the first half of 1772 by an unexpected and, for a time, extremely serious diplomatic crisis. Remarkably, this did not involve the Bourbon powers, or even a new initiative over an alliance, but the small and relatively unimportant state of Denmark.

The origin of this rapid deterioration in relations with Copenhagen was the compromising and ultimately dangerous situation of George III's youngest sister. Caroline Mathilda had married King Christian VII of Denmark in November 1766, when she was only fifteen and in the same year that the young bridegroom ascended the throne.[49] Their marriage had not been a happy one, and before long the Queen was being treated by her husband with a mixture of indifference and open contempt. Christian VII was weak, dissolute, and mentally unstable: he was already advancing into the schizophrenia that would soon disable him almost completely. In the later 1760s the royal couple was falling under the sway of a German doctor, Johann Friedrich Struensee, who became the court physician. By 1770 Struensee effectively controlled royal policy and had also become the Queen's lover. Though the complaisant and increasingly unstable King appeared unconcerned, the Queen's English relatives were alarmed and outraged. In August 1770 the Princess of Wales (mother of George III and Caroline Mathilda) travelled to Germany. She met the royal couple at Lüneburg, and tried to promote a reconciliation and also to persuade her daughter of the error of her ways.[50] This initiative was unsuccessful, and thereafter events in Copenhagen moved very rapidly.

During the second half of 1770 a faction of younger courtiers, headed by Struensee and his accomplice Brandt, supplanted the old ministers of the Danish King. Even the distinguished and by now veteran statesman, J. H. E. von Bernstorff, was ousted by a coup in September. By December 1770 the conspirators had secured complete control over the King and the government. Struensee's power, already considerable, increased during 1771 and he created a virtual

---

[49] S. P. Oakley, *The Story of Denmark* (London, 1972), 152–5, provides a clear summary of these complex events. The old study by W. H. Wilkins, *A Queen of Tears: Caroline Mathilda, Queen of Denmark* (2 vols.; London, 1904) must be used with caution. It does contain much useful information, but is uncritical, romantic in tone, and inaccurate over detail. For the Danish perspective, see in particular, E. Holm, *Danmarks Riges Historie*, v: *1699–1814* (Copenhagen, 1897), 343–85.

[50] Roberts, *British Diplomacy*, 333–4; cf. *Bernstorffsche Papiere*, ii. 114.

personal dictatorship. Christian VII, by now completely disabled by schizophrenia, had effectively been supplanted by the favourite and his royal mistress. The King's mental breakdown, however, was not known outside the royal palace and it was widely believed that he was simply a prisoner of Struensee and the Queen. Struensee used his total authority to introduce a series of enlightened reforms at breakneck speed. But these, together with the scandalous origin of his power and the fact that he and the Queen were widely seen as the gaolers of the unfortunate King, made him increasingly unpopular, as did his arrogant refusal to learn Danish. During the second half of 1771 formidable opposition began to emerge, both at court and in the country at large.[51] Before long Struensee was himself overthrown by a further coup (17 January 1772) and imprisoned, as was the Queen. A leading part in these upheavals was played by the Queen Mother, Juliana Maria, Christian VII's stepmother, and by her influential adviser Ove Høegh Guldberg. Juliana Maria was anxious that her own son (Frederick) should one day supplant his stepbrother on the throne, though the two children of Christian VII and Caroline Mathilda were an obvious barrier to these ambitions. The Queen Mother had also deeply resented her treatment during Struensee's ascendancy, and Caroline Mathilda's fate, like that of the fallen minister, was now largely in Juliana Maria's hands.

Bernstorff's overthrow and the resulting uncertainty in Danish foreign policy were serious developments for Russia. Britain, by contrast, had come to view Denmark as no more than a pawn in the search for a Russian alliance. No fundamental British objectives were affected, but the interests and reputation of the royal family were at stake, and these could not be ignored by the King's ministers. While Caroline Mathilda's behaviour had been indiscreet and probably culpable, she was still George III's sister. During the first six months of 1772 British diplomacy was guided almost entirely by the King's wishes in a way that was unique in the age of the American Revolution. The King's puritan morality and his strong sense of family and majesty were outraged. Denmark's proximity to his Hanoverian Electorate was perhaps an additional reason for his anxious defence of the family's honour. Royal reputation was at least as important a motive for British intervention as concern for Caroline Mathilda's fate. Throughout the episode the King maintained an extensive secret correspondence with his sister, but his pleas that she should mend her ways went unheeded.[52]

[51] Struensee's security measures are vividly described in SP 75/125, fos. 116–21.
[52] For one such admonitory letter, written immediately after Bernstorff's fall, see Roberts, *British Diplomacy*, 334; for the continuing correspondence, SP 75/126, fo. 3.

By the closing weeks of 1771 developments in Denmark were seriously worrying George III and his ministers, and the situation became critical with the overthrow of Struensee in January 1772.[53] During the next six months the principal objective of Britain's foreign policy was the release of Caroline Mathilda. The central role in the drama which now unfolded was played by a Scottish soldier and diplomat, Robert Murray Keith, who had been minister in Copenhagen since June 1771.[54] From the outset Keith adopted a firm and even threatening tone towards the new Danish government, and his actions were endorsed by his superiors in London, who followed his lead.[55] On the same day that Struensee was overthrown and the Queen imprisoned, Keith is said to have burst in on a meeting of the Danish Council, which was discussing Caroline Mathilda's fate, and melodramatically threatened 'war against Denmark, if a hair of her head were touched'.[56] Britain's representative demanded that the Queen should be treated with all the respect due to her rank, and his representations did produce some amelioration in the circumstances of her imprisonment, as well as alarming the new regime in Copenhagen.[57]

Keith's prompt intervention at first seemed likely to lead to Caroline Mathilda's safe release. This was certainly the view of

---

[53] *BDI* iii: *Denmark 1689–1789*, ed. J. F. Chance (London, 1926), 183; SP 75/125, fos. 95–6, 97. The first news of the Danish revolution caused 'great consternation' in London: *Pol. Corr.* xxxi. 749–50; cf. *Walpole Corr.* xxiii. 373–4, 380.

[54] There is a serious and very revealing gap in Keith's dispatches. His correspondence for June 1771–Jan. 1772 in SP 75/125–6 contains only a few insignificant letters after 17 Jan. 1772 and his dispatches end abruptly with that of 11 Feb. 1772 (SP 75/126, fo. 33), and Suffolk's with that of 28 Feb. 1772 (ibid. fos. 35–6). No letters for the crucial months from Feb. to May are to be found in SP 75/126, or in SP 110/1 (which contains deciphered copies of Keith's dispatches for 1771), or in the relevant volumes of his papers in the British Library: Add. MSS 35503 and 35547. In fact, the relevant correspondence was largely destroyed on George III's specific orders: Wilkins, *A Queen of Tears*, ii. 101–2 n. 1; cf. SP 82/90, fos. 262, 288. These gaps are to be explained by the extreme sensitivity of Keith's negotiations: for the minister's own testimony, see *Keith Memoirs*, i. 285, 288. Unusual security precautions already surrounded his correspondence and its deciphering (SP 75/126, fo. 18) and while the crisis in Copenhagen was at its peak, couriers were regularly used (e.g. *Corr. Geo. III*, ii. 330, 340). Important material not available elsewhere is contained in *Keith Memoirs*, i. 154–345, and the other major sources are Frederick II's correspondence in *Pol. Corr.* xxxii, and the reports of the French minister in CP (Danemark) 157. The reports of the British minister in Hamburg, Woodford, contain a little additional information (SP 82/90).

[55] Suffolk, who clearly found the situation in Copenhagen both confused and confusing, had on several earlier occasions given Keith *carte blanche*: SP 75/125, fos. 26, 40–1; *BDI* iii: *Denmark 1689–1789*, 183. The winter of 1771–2 was unusually severe and the British envoy was forced to rely on his own initiative in the aftermath of the coup; during the next 2 months, communications with London were particularly slow and unreliable.

[56] *Keith Memoirs*, i. 250; Wilkins, *A Queen of Tears*, ii. 100–1.

[57] Ibid. ii. 129; Keith's threats, and Danish concern at these, are apparent in Juliana Maria's letter to Frederick II, 18 Feb. 1772, *Pol. Corr.* xxxi. 789.

George III and his ministers.[58] The new Danish foreign minister, Count Osten, suggested that the delicate situation could best be resolved as a private matter between sovereigns rather than as a public cause between states. In the weeks after Struensee's fall, a private letter from (nominally) Christian VII to George III did much to remove British anxieties.[59] By the second half of February, Britain believed that Caroline Mathilda would soon be released and was, in the mean time, being treated with every consideration. Crucially, there seemed no reason to fear that the Queen would be implicated in the judicial proceedings against Struensee and his supporters. Keith's 'most spirited and proper representations' (as Rochford described them) were believed to have saved the day. George III's approval and gratitude for his minister's conduct at Copenhagen were signalled by the immediate award of a KB, exceptionally at a time when there was no vacancy.[60] This success, however, was more apparent than real. By the final week of February Caroline Mathilda had been decisively drawn into the judicial enquiries that were under way.

The commission of enquiry set up after the January revolution only began to interrogate its chief target on 20 February 1772. Struensee's rapid confession, whatever its intentions, conclusively implicated Queen Caroline in the events of the past two years.[61] In particular his public avowal that he had been her lover posed the tricky problem of how royal adultery should be handled: under Danish law this was high treason and subject to the death penalty. A special tribunal was set up to investigate the Queen's conduct and, on 9 March, Caroline Mathilda was interrogated and admitted her adultery. Despite Keith's vigorous protests, the tribunal proceeded to consider the question of a divorce during March and early April.[62] It had become apparent by the end of February, after Struensee's confession, that it would be impossible to keep the Queen out of the judicial aftermath of the coup. The refusal of the Queen Mother to allow Keith to present a letter from George III to the Danish King in person had meanwhile revealed the fiction that Christian VII had returned to power, and suggested that Caroline Mathilda might indeed be in danger from the faction in control in Copenhagen.[63] The new Danish regime, aware that its actions were technically

[58] Add. MSS 24158, fo. 53; cf. Walpole, *Last Journals*, i. 16.
[59] *Mémoires de Reverdil*, 387; Add. MSS 24158, fo. 53.
[60] SP 75/126, fos. 35–6.
[61] This is in *Mémoires de Reverdil*, 396–400. The fallen favourite's confession confirmed what had already been discovered by the careful questioning of the Queen's female servants: Holm, *Danmarks Riges Historie*, 373.
[62] *Keith Memoirs*, i. 284; *Mémoires de Reverdil*, 407.
[63] Wilkins, *A Queen of Tears*, ii. 120–2.

illegal and fearful of a counter-coup, was anxious to press ahead with the trial of Struensee.[64] The divorce and imprisonment of Caroline Mathilda were a precondition for this, yet this was exactly what the British government was anxious to prevent. Relations between the two states now deteriorated very rapidly.

By early March the British government feared Caroline Mathilda would not be released.[65] These anxieties were fuelled by the abundant rumours that she might actually suffer the same fate as Struensee, who was to be executed. This was always improbable, but it was a possibility which Britain had to take seriously. Ministers recognized that at the very least George III's sister would have to submit to the dishonour of divorce and perhaps formal deposition and would then be imprisoned in Denmark. British resentment increased in the face of Copenhagen's continuing refusal to accede to Keith's demands, and by the second half of March matters were clearly coming to a head.[66] In response to what was viewed in London as another unsatisfactory Danish reply, Britain formalized her demands. At the beginning of April Keith requested that the divorce proceedings should be suspended, that the royal couple should instead merely separate, and that the Queen should be allowed to leave Denmark.[67] This last request was acceptable, but the other two were now definitely not. Ostensibly this was because they would have prevented Christian VII from remarrying, but more likely these demands were viewed as a threat to the stability of the new regime in Copenhagen and as interference in Denmark's internal affairs.[68]

Keith's demands were backed by a blatant threat of *force majeure*. Britain had already announced that a squadron was assembled in the Thames and, if necessary, would sail to enforce her will.[69] In particular, the British minister in Copenhagen declared that if the Queen were imprisoned, she would be forcibly released by a British

[64] S. Cedergreen Bech, *Struensee og hans tid* (Copenhagen, 1972), 392.

[65] *Walpole Corr.* xxiii. 386–7.

[66] On 17 Mar., George III commented that 'great rancour and inclination to blacken the affair as much as possible is not wanting, therefore the decision must now finally be taken': *Corr. Geo. III*, ii. 330; cf. Walpole, *Last Journals*, i. 71.

[67] Juliana Maria to Frederick II, 4 Apr. 1772, *Pol. Corr.* xxxii. 101. This makes clear Denmark's inability to resist Britain's demands.

[68] E. Holm, *Danmark-Norges Historie 1720–1814*, iv: ii (Copenhagen, 1902), 374–5. In an attempt to placate George III, the Danish authorities proposed the royal divorce would not be made public and this was done, but it did not deflect Britain's mounting pressure on Copenhagen.

[69] *Pol. Corr.* xxxii. 60. This 'squadron' was simply those few ships that were located in the Thames. No vessels appear to have been mobilized specifically for use against Denmark before mid-Apr., though a storeship was sent to the Thames on 18 Feb.: ADM 2/97 and 241 *passim*.

fleet.[70] When news reached London that Keith's latest representations had been ignored and the formal divorce would soon be pronounced, the full weight of Britain's massive naval superiority was brought to bear. In mid-April, eleven ships of the line, two bomb vessels, and a fireship were mobilized and Denmark was threatened with war unless the Queen was released.[71] Denmark's navy was respectable by Baltic standards, but it could not hope to resist such a substantial and well-armed British fleet.

This mobilization was countermanded within forty-eight hours, for Britain's earlier threats had forced the Danish government to surrender. Unable to resist Britain's mighty navy, the Queen Mother and her advisers had to allow Caroline Mathilda to go into exile.[72] The divorce had by now been finalized, but it was not published, and the Queen was to be allowed to leave the country. In the crucial area of reputation Caroline Mathilda had neither been publicly divorced nor deposed as Queen, while George III had refused to give the assurance demanded by Copenhagen that his sister would never return to Denmark.[73] The Queen was reluctant to leave and may even have been dreaming of a political come-back.[74] It took all Keith's persuasion to overcome her stubbornness, and on 1 June 1772 she finally left Denmark aboard a Royal Navy ship for exile in Hanover.[75] Britain's high-handed behaviour continued to the end: the Danish authorities were forced to salute the vessel in which Caroline Mathilda was conveyed into exile, and subsequently were obliged to return all the Queen's dowry.[76]

Suffolk announced the Queen's release to British diplomats in terms appropriate to a fairy-tale rescue, with Keith cast as knight errant. The reality was rather different. Caroline Mathilda exchanged imprisonment in Denmark for an equally restrictive custody in Hanover. The French minister in Copenhagen had shrewdly predicted that George III would not wish his sister to return to England.[77] That would have emphasized the dishonour brought on the royal family

---

[70] *Pol. Corr.* xxxii. 157 n. 1. At the end of Mar., Blosset had reported that the castle at Ålborg in Jutland was being prepared for the Queen: CP (Danemark) 157, fo. 161.

[71] Tracy, *Navies, Deterrence and American Independence*, 103; *Corr. Geo. III*, ii. 337–9; *Walpole Corr.* xxiii. 401; *Keith Memoirs*, i. 286. For the mobilization on 16 Apr. and its countermanding on the 18th, see ADM 2/241, fos. 236–40, 248–9 and ADM 2/97, fos. 417–21, 424, 433–4.

[72] The effectiveness of Britain's naval blackmail is suggested by Juliana Maria's letter to Frederick II, 18 Apr. 1772, quoted in *Pol. Corr.* xxxii. 146 n. 4.

[73] Holm, *Danmark-Norges Historie 1720–1814*, iv:ii. 433.

[74] This was certainly Blosset's view: CP (Danemark) 157, fo. 200.

[75] Ibid. 157, fos. 188–9, 192, 200.

[76] *Corr. Geo. III*, ii. 352, 360; *Bernstorffsche Papiere*, iii. 177.

[77] CP (Danemark) 157, fo. 189.

and might, in a country with a parliamentary system and an inquisitive press, cause the King even more embarrassment. Instead, Caroline Mathilda was held under house arrest in Hanover, where she died three years later. George III's behaviour, and in particular his subsequent treatment of his sister, are unattractive.[78] The upheavals in Denmark had created a difficult situation, but it had been inflamed by the menacing stance immediately assumed by Keith and later reinforced by his government. Britain's diplomatic representations had amounted to direct intervention in Denmark's internal affairs and were throughout couched in threatening terms. Suffolk's distinction between British demands which were not negotiable and the matters which London was prepared to discuss with Copenhagen was very revealing. The release of Caroline Mathilda and her retention of the royal title were both a 'claim of right' and only the fine print of the settlement was open to negotiation.[79] London's willingness to use main force against a minor state, and the threatening tone of her diplomacy, were important reminders that Britain's reputation after the Seven Years War as the bully of Europe was not wholly undeserved.

Although the episode did considerable, though not permanent damage to Anglo-Danish relations, it did not involve any major British interests.[80] The principal importance of these events is in their timing. From the closing weeks of 1771 until the middle of 1772, Britain was preoccupied with Caroline Mathilda's fate, while Poland was being partitioned.

The diplomatic origins of the first partition were complex. The tripartite division of Poland finalized in August 1772 resulted principally from Frederick II's long-standing interest in securing strategically important Polish Prussia, subsequently the Hohenzollern province of West Prussia. The King knew this would unite Brandenburg, the core of his state, with the distant yet important province of East Prussia. He was able to realize this aim by exploiting the situation in the Balkans. By 1770–1 both Austria and Prussia were alarmed by the scale of Russia's victories and by her likely territorial gains once peace was concluded. Yet with the failure of all attempts to mediate in the war, there was no obvious way to restrict Catherine II's annexations from the Turks.

[78] The brief and rather misleading account by J. Brooke, *King George III* (London, 1974 edn.), 427–30, is too indulgent to the King; cf. *Bernstorffsche Papiere*, iii. 180, 312.

[79] Suffolk to Keith, 1 May 1772, *Keith Memoirs*, i. 287.

[80] For Danish testimony to this, see the comments of A. P. von Bernstorff (who became foreign minister in 1773): *Bernstorffsche Papiere*, iii. 291, 313; British ill will is apparent from *BDI* iii: *Denmark 1689–1789*, 185–7.

Austria was inevitably hostile to the growth of Russian power on the lower Danube, and in the first half of 1771 Vienna appeared to be preparing for military intervention to support the Ottoman Empire, which might also be backed by its traditional ally, France. This frightened Frederick II. His principal objective was still to avoid any war, yet if the fighting spread he might be forced to join in on the side of his Russian ally. He therefore manœuvred with great skill to secure Russian and eventually Austrian support for his plan. Catherine II was to make her territorial gains at the expense of the Poles rather than the Turks, while the balance of power would be preserved by allowing the other two eastern monarchies to make equivalent gains from the defenceless Polish state. In this way peace would be preserved, Frederick would secure West Prussia, and it was hoped the Russian Empress's thirst for Turkish territory would be quenched elsewhere.

Catherine II's support was secured by the Prussian King's brother, Prince Henry, during a visit to the Russian Court in the winter of 1770–1. Thereafter Frederick II worked on a broad diplomatic front. Austrian reluctance was the major obstacle, and he overcame this by first arranging the partition with Russia and then forcing the Habsburgs either to join in, or to accept a further deterioration of their relative position in eastern Europe. In February 1772, Frederick and Catherine signed a convention agreeing to seize areas of Polish territory. Austria soon signalled her acceptance, and in August a series of treaties signed in St Petersburg laid down each state's precise share. This represented the end of the diplomatic negotiations, and the three eastern powers set about imposing their annexations on Poland.

This frenzied diplomatic activity was conducted in strict secrecy, out of a fear that one or both the western powers would discover its object and would then try to prevent the partition: France's traditional links with Poland made her particularly feared. This strategy was largely successful. It was March 1772 before either of the western states fully appreciated what was being arranged. Such fears were in any case exaggerated. The schemes of the eastern powers were to be facilitated by Britain's withdrawal from continental diplomacy and by France's declining influence in eastern Europe.

Britain's traditional indifference to the eastern half of the continent reached its apogee in the chorus of silence which greeted the first partition.[81] A handful of pamphleteers, among whom the enthusiastic Polonophile John Lind occupied pride of place, sought to lay the

[81]   D. B. Horn, *British Public Opinion and the First Partition of Poland* (Edinburgh, 1945).

matter before British eyes, but to no avail. Politicians and public alike showed little interest in the fate of a state about which most Englishmen knew very little and cared rather less. This indifference was reinforced by strong hostility towards a country that was substantially Catholic and that had long been accounted a French puppet. In the early 1770s there appeared to be no reason why this traditional neglect should be questioned, far less overturned. British foreign policy was preoccupied with relations with the Bourbons and with Denmark, and the partition appeared as irrelevant as events in far-away Poland had usually been. Horace Walpole lamented 'the most impudent association of robbers that ever existed', while David Hume found further evidence for his fear that 'the two most civilised nations, the English and the French, should be on the decline, and the barbarians, the Goths and Vandals of Germany and Russia, should be rising in power and renown', but these were atolls of concern set in a sea of indifference.[82] London did no more than reiterate those hopes for peace on the continent which had been its constant litany since 1768.

Britain's official response was both belated and incomplete.[83] In some degree this was a tribute to the absolute secrecy surrounding the partition negotiations, which had been successfully concealed from British diplomats. This first positive evidence was only obtained by James Harris, the envoy in Berlin, a fortnight after the Prusso-Russian convention had been signed.[84] Even then British ministers showed little interest in Poland's fate.[85] Suffolk's long-remembered reference to the first partition as 'this curious transaction' was the measure of Britain's official response.[86] During the first half of 1772 the fate of Caroline Mathilda appeared a more immediate concern than that of Poland. 'It is in vain', Suffolk concluded, 'to form conjectures on this strange transaction', and the Northern Secretary certainly reinforced precept with example.[87] There is no sign of anything approaching an official attitude, far less a coherent policy, in the six months between partition becoming an open secret in March 1772 and the public announcement of the annexations in the

---

[82] *Last Journals*, i. 159; Horn, *British Public Opinion*, 18–9.

[83] W. Konopczynski, 'England and the First Partition of Poland', *Journal of Central European Affairs*, 8 (1948–9), 1–23, deals with the British response, but is marred by a belief that Britain was implicated by virtue of her indifference; W. Michael, *Englands Stellung zur ersten Teilung Polens* (Hamburg and Leipzig, 1890) is more concerned with Danzig, though pp. 3–11 outlines the official attitude to the partition itself.

[84] *Malmesbury Diaries*, i. 79–80; SP 90/91, fos. 53–5.

[85] See e.g. Suffolk to Stormont, 24 Mar. 1772, SP 80/211.

[86] *Malmesbury Diaries*, i. 82. Rochford concurred, styling the partition 'this extraordinary transaction': *St. Paul of Ewart*, i. 38.   [87] *Malmesbury Diaries*, i. 82.

autumn. Suffolk expressed no more than polite curiosity about the actual intentions of the three eastern courts, while Polish appeals for help were calmly brushed aside by ministers, with the honest excuse that there was nothing they could do to stop the partition.[88] Britain's lingering hopes of Austrian and Russian alliances ensured that the full odium was heaped on the King of Prussia,[89] and there is no sign that official attitudes towards either Vienna or St Petersburg were permanently affected by their involvement.[90]

There was, in fact, very little Britain could have done to prevent partition. Horace Walpole put the point very well when he remarked that the British fleet could not easily sail to Warsaw.[91] Diplomatic representations by Britain alone were unlikely to have any impact, while Poland was certainly not worth a war. It was not clear that any vital British interests were involved, until Frederick II's menaces towards Danzig (Gdańsk) became so blatant that ministers were stirred into some belated and unsuccessful diplomacy, in an attempt to protect Britain's trade.[92] Most British observers viewed the partition as a further and very welcome example of France's decline.[93] The tendency of ministers to see events uniquely in terms of Anglo-French rivalry was undiminished in the early 1770s: the very fact that France was so obviously embarrassed and ignored, confirmed Britain's passive attitude.[94]

Ministers could ignore the first partition, but they could not conjure away its profound implications for Britain's diplomacy. The three partitioning powers were also the states upon which London had traditionally depended for continental alliances. Their rivalry, and their willingness, and at times need to conclude treaties with the western powers, had been the basis of Britain's periodic alignments with one or more of the eastern states. But now these powers were partners, rather than rivals, and scope for alliances was considerably reduced.[95] The partition also signalled that the eastern powers were no longer the political dependants of the more advanced western states, but were willing to act independently. In this context the

---

[88] Michael, *Englands Stellung*, 9–10; *Malmesbury Diaries*, i. 85.

[89] See, in particular, Suffolk to Stormont, 10 Sept. 1772, SP 80/212, partially printed in Horn, *British Public Opinion*, 5–7.

[90] Though in the short term ministers did resent how Russia and Austria had concluded the partition: CP (Angleterre) 499, fos. 334–5; Suffolk to Stormont, Private, 13 Jan. 1773, Stormont Papers, Box 38; Add. MSS 61860, fo. 115.

[91] Cf. *Walpole Corr.* xxiii. 475.   [92] This is examined below, pp. 197–202.

[93] *Walpole Corr.* xxiii. 419–20.   [94] e.g. Walpole, *Last Journals*, i. 119.

[95] See e.g. the report of Guines that the new Prusso-Austrian alignment was seen in London as 'un monstre en politique' and that both Secretaries of State feared its political consequences: 1 May 1772, CP (Angleterre) 499, fo. 306.

partition and in particular the Prusso-Austrian *rapprochement*, were a further blow to traditional British assumptions.

Before long the implications of this realignment were being tentatively noted in London, but they were mainly interpreted in a stubbornly insular way. The Northern Secretary, Suffolk, was always alert for any hint of a revival of the Anglo-Austrian alliance and he saw the resolution of the eastern crisis in terms of the Old System. Insularity in a secretary of state could go no further. The new diplomatic alignment he believed would emerge, he saw as an opportunity for Britain to renew her links with the Habsburgs. This miraculous transformation would be facilitated by Joseph II's emergence as a figure of real authority in Vienna and by the consequent decline of the malign influence of Kaunitz.[96] The Southern Secretary, Rochford, was also of the opinion that the moment might be opportune to recover the Austrian alliance.[97] But he possessed a deeper understanding of European events and of their implications for Britain.[98] The partition, Rochford remarked on one occasion, 'had completely changed the political system of Europe'.[99] He was prepared to adjust British diplomacy quite radically to take account of this new situation, and there were moments in 1772–3 when it appeared that he might be about to undertake what had usually been unthinkable: reconciliation and even an alliance with the national enemy, France.

Britain's predicament had its counterpart on the other side of the Channel. Alarmed by the menacing turn of events in eastern Europe in 1772, d'Aiguillon sought to build on the existing good relations and to establish some form of political co-operation with Britain directed against the dominance of the eastern powers, and in particular of Russia. Almost from the moment he took office he had been suggesting, unsuccessfully, that Britain and France should work together to prevent Catherine II from securing a foothold in the Mediterranean when peace was concluded with the Turks.[100] In mid-February 1772, before news of the partition had leaked out, he had tried to persuade the North Ministry to play a more active European role, but his ideas and his emphasis on the danger to British trade of Prussian designs on Danzig as yet found no echo in London.[101] Towards the end of March, soon after the French government

---

[96] Suffolk to Stormont, 6 Apr. 1772, SP 80/211; this was, of course, an established theme: cf. above, pp. 87–8.   [97] *Sandwich Papers*, i. 32.
[98] See e.g. his illuminating analysis of European affairs, produced in Nov. 1772 apparently for the cabinet: ibid. i. 30–3.   [99] CP (Angleterre) 500, fo. 142.
[100] M. S. Anderson, 'Great Britain and the Russo-Turkish War of 1768–74', *English Historical Review*, 69 (1954), 55.   [101] SP 78/284, fos. 91–2.

became aware that the partition had been arranged, d'Aiguillon made a secret approach to London for a joint diplomatic initiative designed to frustrate it.[102] His plan envisaged a combination of French pressure in Vienna and British influence in St Petersburg which would isolate Prussia and force the partition's abandonment. Though Rochford half-heartedly and unsuccessfully did try to dissuade Russia, Britain gave no effective support to the French scheme.

D'Aiguillon had until this point provided all the impetus for a *rapprochement*.[103] Indeed his overtures had received no encouragement from the North Ministry, which appeared completely hostile. At the end of May 1772, the perenially indiscreet Rochford revealed his interest in co-operation with France. During a long discussion with her ambassador, he told Guines that, if he were master of British deliberations, he would combine with d'Aiguillon to put pressure on the eastern powers to prevent the partition being implemented.[104] He also admitted that Britain's efforts to persuade Russia to explain what was going on over Poland had been ignored. This was the first time Rochford had revealed his sympathies so openly, though he was, for the moment, thinking of no more than diplomatic support for a French initiative. D'Aiguillon, however, was certainly encouraged by these disclosures.[105] A further sign of potential British interest came in July 1772 when George III, in a mysterious piece of secret diplomacy, hinted to France that he personally would be glad to act as a channel for the conclusion of an alliance.[106] Yet in both capitals there was still understandable suspicion that the other ministry might not be genuine and, though d'Aiguillon continued to press co-operation on the British ambassador, nothing further had been done by the autumn.[107]

Two events combined to force the issue. In mid-August 1772 the eastern powers signed the final partition treaties, which were formally communicated to Britain and France in September. Previous

---

[102] *Recueil . . . Angleterre, iii*, ed. P. Vaucher, 466–7; d'Aiguillon's secret letter to Rochford of 23 Mar. 1772 is substantially printed by B. du Fraguier, 'Le Duc d'Aiguillon et l'Angleterre', *Revue d'histoire diplomatique*, 26 (1912), 610–12; cf. Roberts, *British Diplomacy*, 371.

[103] He was handicapped throughout by the scepticism and, at times, hostility to d'Aiguillon's schemes of the ambassador in London, the Comte de Guines, nephew of the fallen Choiseul: Fraguier, 'Le Duc d'Aiguillon', 613.

[104] CP (Angleterre) 499, fos. 335–6.   [105] Ibid. 500, fos. 3–4.

[106] Fraguier, 'Le Duc d'Aiguillon', 615. George III used Lord Holderness as an intermediary in his approach to the French ambassador in London. For the King's interest in reconciliation, see *Corr. Geo. III*, ii. 428–9.

[107] In July, d'Aiguillon went as far as to suggest the idea of a triple alliance of Britain, France, and Spain as a 'means of keeping the troublesome Northern Powers in order': SP 78/285, fo. 294.

uncertainties as to the scale of the proposed territorial changes were now swept aside, as were hopes that partition might be prevented by disagreements among the partners.[108] The extent of the annexations and their implications were now clear and could no longer be ignored. A more immediate problem was Gustav III's *coup d'état* on 19 August which restored royal authority in Sweden. These two events inevitably focused attention, in London and in Versailles, on the situation in the North and on the menacing power of the eastern monarchies and, in particular, Russia. While the completion of the Polish partition drew Britain and France together, the Swedish revolution ultimately destroyed any prospect of a *rapprochement*.

London's quest for the Russian alliance had made the preservation of Sweden's constitutional settlement of 1720 into a British objective. Gustav III's action not only destroyed this settlement; it also posed a real threat to European peace.[109] In St Petersburg memories of Charles XII's expansionist policies made Russia fearful of a stronger monarchy in Stockholm. In the winter of 1772–3 there appeared a genuine danger that Russia would attack Sweden and forcibly restore the 'Age of Liberty'. There was also a risk, particularly in the autumn of 1772, that Gustav III might seek to consolidate his new regime by seizing Norway from Denmark. Both in Stockholm and in St Petersburg there was considerable nervousness in these months, and each side saw the other's defensive measures as aggressive, which increased tension. These developments could also provoke a wider conflict. France had signed a defensive alliance with Gustav III shortly after his accession in 1771, and proclaimed her intention to support him in the event of a Russian attack. A new treaty was concluded late in February 1773 by which Louis XV committed himself to send 12,000 men if Sweden were attacked.

The system of defensive alliances which now covered most of Europe meant that any Baltic conflict could lead to a general war. Russia's ally, Frederick II, had the bait of Swedish Pomerania to draw him into the conflict, while for a time it seemed as if Denmark might unilaterally attack Sweden. In the winter of 1772–3 the Baltic appeared as great a threat to Europe's peace as the Balkans had been a few years before. In the event, Catherine II and Panin considered attacking Sweden, but concluded that Russia was in no position to begin a war in Northern Europe. The bulk of Catherine's army was already committed against the Turks and in Poland, and the greater part of her fleet was operating in the Mediterranean. The Empress

[108] CP (Angleterre) 500, fo. 54; cf. SP 91/90, fo. 45.
[109] *HMC Dartmouth*, iii. 196–7.

and her advisers always recognized that peace in the Balkans must precede an attack on Sweden, and extended negotiations with the Turks in 1772–3 failed to produce a settlement.[110] Russia had the inclination, but not the resources, to fight Gustav III and so peace was preserved. It is against the threat of general war that British and French actions must be viewed.

Developments around the Baltic highlighted the growing inability of Britain's traditional foreign policy to deal with the new political alignments of the early 1770s. By inclination, and by past practice, Britain should co-operate with Russia; but this path—though it might produce the long-desired alliance—led straight to a possible war against Sweden and France.[111] Any war was anathema to British ministers, while the prospect of fighting on the same side as Britain's old antagonist, Prussia, and her new enemy, Denmark—which was now reconciled with Russia—could not be described as compelling.[112] Yet the alternatives were no more appealing. Though co-operation with France to restrain Russia might avert the threatened conflict, it was a powerful challenge to British assumptions. In the event, Britain determined, or perhaps merely stumbled, on an ingenious mixture of these options. Russia was warned that France would not be restrained, while Versailles was threatened with prompt reprisals if she supported Gustav III.[113] In particular, ministers confirmed their established position, that any French naval activity would immediately be answered by an equivalent British squadron being sent to sea.[114] This compromise proved successful, but it did not rest on a unanimous view among ministers. The situation around the Baltic in 1772–3 gave added force to those in official circles prepared for a radical *rapprochement* with France.

The principal member of this shadowy group was Rochford; it also contained the Earl of Mansfield, Lord Hillsborough, probably Lord North, and perhaps the Earl of Shelburne; while the King, the most clear-sighted observer of British foreign policy at this moment,

---

[110] Madariaga, *Russia*, 226–31.

[111] Sandwich believed that the Baltic situation would produce an Anglo-Russian alliance (*Sandwich Papers*, i. 24); Suffolk thought this no more than a possibility (*HMC Dartmouth*, iii. 197).

[112] For Britain's dilemma, Egerton 2701, fos. 169–70.

[113] There is a masterly account by M. Roberts, 'Great Britain and the Swedish Revolution, 1772–3', *Essays in Swedish History* (London, 1967), 286–347; cf. Tracy, *Navies, Deterrence and American Independence*, 105–10, for a rather different view.

[114] In early Oct. 1772, the cabinet had reaffirmed that if any French fleet came out of port, Britain would put a fleet of her own to sea, and the number of seamen voted for 1773 had been increased to 20,000: PRO 30/29/1/14, fos. 667, 669. This attitude was maintained into spring 1773.

was for a time an enthusiastic supporter of co-operation with France.[115] For North, whose understanding of European politics rested chiefly on a Treasuryman's desire to avoid a war and its expense, it was principally a matter of money.[116] George III and Rochford both possessed a broader view of British diplomacy and were aware of the new problems which it faced. King and minister also appreciated the profound obstacles to such a major change in foreign policy and ultimately each proved unwilling, or simply unable, to surmount them.

George III's personal diplomacy in July 1772 had given fresh life to the negotiations. He had suggested a commercial treaty between the two countries and this was enthusiastically taken up by d'Aiguillon, partly out of a genuine interest in the possible benefits to French trade, but also in the hope that it might lead to an alliance. A French agent was sent to discuss a trade treaty and reached London in November. By now George III's interest in an Anglo-French *rapprochement* had disappeared. The developing Baltic crisis, and perhaps a concern for Hanover's security now that its three traditional guardians were united, had undermined his enthusiasm and forced him back into the old familiar assumption, that opposition to France was essential.[117] In the winter of 1772–3 Rochford was the only active British supporter of reconciliation, though he was never wholehearted. Political instinct always dictated the avoidance of any intimacy, and though the logic of d'Aiguillon's proposals was considerable, exactly how France could aid Poland was not immediately clear.[118] But Rochford's volatile temperament carried him further than he wished, and his periodic indiscretions kept French hopes alive. Towards the end of October his natural 'vivacity' led him into an extremely indiscreet conversation with Garnier, the French chargé d'affaires.[119]

Garnier had suggested an Anglo-French agreement not to assist an aggressor (be it Russia or Sweden) in the Baltic, in the hope of preventing a war in the North. Rochford's initial reply was encouraging, though fear of popular censure and parliamentary defeat led him to favour an informal understanding, rather than a

[115] See the two overlapping memoranda drawn up by the King at this time: the first was written in the summer or early autumn of 1772 and is in *Corr. Geo. III*, ii. 428–9; the second, which belongs to the late autumn of 1772 or even the winter of 1772–3, is in Add. MSS 61860, fo. 115.

[116] See e.g. his proposal on 5 Sept. 1772 to reduce the expenditure on the navy and Sandwich's tart response: *Sandwich Papers*, i. 19–26.

[117] The King's change of heart cannot be dated with absolute certainty; yet it can be implied from CP (Angleterre) 500, fos. 208–11 and 217–20, that by the end of Oct., George III had effectively abandoned his thoughts of a reconciliation; Black, *Natural and Necessary Enemies*, 78.   [118] Ibid. 78.   [119] CP (Angleterre) 500, fos. 199–203.

formal and therefore public convention. This approval was strictly unofficial; yet the garrulous Rochford compounded the indiscretion by telling Garnier that the King also believed that such an agreement would be useful and that North would also support it. A little reflection, and a discussion with George III, convinced Rochford of the inadvisability of this conversation and, the very next day, he saw Garnier again.[120] Mingling ministerial threats of naval reprisals with secret assurances that Russia would not attack Sweden and that Britain would ensure this, he effectively reversed his position of the previous day and rejected all idea of an Anglo-French agreement. Garnier's response to this somersault was predictably disparaging.[121] D'Aiguillon had a deeper understanding of the constraints on Rochford and he was not discouraged, instead noting with pleasure how far the Southern Secretary's views coincided with his own. The French minister was content to watch the progress of the commercial negotiations, hopeful of a future political understanding.[122]

These hopes were finally dashed in spring 1773. D'Aiguillon had been sufficiently encouraged to send the Chevalier de Martange on a secret mission to London.[123] At the very end of March and in early April, Martange had a series of discussions with Rochford, which finally revealed Britain's refusal even to consider an alliance.[124] Though Rochford continued to profess support for this, he frankly told d'Aiguillon's agent that a treaty was now out of the question.[125] The Southern Secretary's previous ambivalence was replaced by the orthodoxy of British ministers for generations: France was Britain's enemy, her actions were everywhere to be watched and where necessary resisted, her alliance was rejected outright.

The episode ended with an old-style Anglo-French crisis.[126] In the second half of March reports reached Paris of Russian troop

---

[120] CP (Angleterre) 500, fos. 208–11, 217–18. There may also have been a cabinet meeting: Roberts, 'Great Britain and the Swedish Revolution', 307.

[121] CP (Angleterre) 500, fos. 209–11, for his tart comments.

[122] Ibid., fos. 241, 307–8.

[123] CP (Angleterre) 501, fo. 31; Guines was recalled for consultations and sent back to propose an alliance, to be widened to include Spain and Sweden, but nothing came of this initiative: *Correspondance secrète du comte de Broglie avec Louis XV 1756–74*, ed. D. Ozanam and M. Antoine (2 vols.; Paris, 1956–61), ii. 396 n. 2. For Martange, see ibid. i. 200 n. 1; his real mission was kept secret from the French ambassador in London, Guines, who was openly hostile to the idea.

[124] His dispatches are printed in *Correspondance inédite du général-major de Martange*, ed. C. Bréard (Paris, 1898), 508–34.   [125] Ibid. 512.

[126] There are contrasting accounts of the Anglo-French naval confrontation of Apr.–May 1773 by Roberts, 'Great Britain and the Swedish Revolution', 312–22, and by Tracy, *Navies, Deterrence and American Independence*, 110–7. As Prof. Roberts demonstrates, Rochford was prepared to connive at French aid to Sweden by delaying British naval preparations and thus avoid an Anglo-French war. The brief account which follows draws on both these

concentrations near the Finnish border. It was widely assumed this was a prelude to a Russian attack on Gustav III and France would soon receive a formal demand for assistance. D'Aiguillon was anxious to assist France's protégé, but he had no wish for a general war, which he appreciated might be provoked by sending a fleet to the Baltic.[127] He therefore toyed with indirect assistance to Sweden by an attack on the Russian naval squadron still operating in the Mediterranean. This was now in a rather dilapidated condition and would be an easy target for a French fleet. While such measures were being considered, France mobilized twelve ships of the line at Toulon. These preparations were soon known to British ministers through their intelligence network and in mid-April an already serious situation became critical.

Rochford's role in the war-scare which now emerged was significant, yet it remains problematical. By the second half of March he was in full retreat over the secret negotiations with France and anxiously covering his tracks. This was due to his recognition that an immediate *rapprochement* was impossible and to the fact that his discussions with French agents were no longer secret.[128] Rochford now fell back on orthodox opposition to France, and indeed himself sought to inflame relations. Britain's new ambassador in Paris, Lord Stormont, was a protégé of the Southern Secretary, who had played an important part in his appointment.[129] Stormont's firm and vigorous stance on his return to the French court at the end of March was probably encouraged, and perhaps dictated, by Rochford, now anxious to pose as the determined opponent of France.[130] By early April, when he met Martange, Rochford was running scared and on the 8th, having written privately to the ambassador in Paris, encouraging his hard line, he disappeared to his country estate for nearly a fortnight, during which time he was incommunicado.

By the time Rochford returned the crisis had reached its peak.[131]

accounts, on the British dispatches in SP 78/287–8 and in Stormont Papers, Boxes 38 and 39, and on the material in *Corr. Geo. III*, ii. 467 ff.

[127] Martange's secondary purpose had been to discover whether Britain would remain neutral if France were to aid Gustav III: *Correspondance secrète*, ed. Ozanam and Antoine, ii. 386–7 n. 3. [128] Walpole, *Last Journals*, i. 188; *Burke Corr*. ii. 429.

[129] See Mansfield to Stormont, 31 Mar. and 14 Apr. 1772, Stormont Papers, Box 52.

[130] Rochford and Stormont clearly met during the latter's leave in England in Feb. and Mar. 1773 (SP 78/287, fo. 1). The ambassador's unusually firm response from the end of Mar. onwards was partly inspired by rumours of French naval preparations, but was also dictated by his discussions with Rochford, who clearly deceived him. Verbal instructions to diplomats were very much in character for Rochford.

[131] Walpole, *Last Journals*, i. 188, 190–1. Walpole believed that there was no danger of war at this point, but his confidence owes much to hindsight. In the spring of 1773, the threat was very real, though the crisis was considerably less acute than that of 1770–1.

Stormont was not disposed to accept d'Aiguillon's repeated assurances that the ships at Toulon were merely intended for the kind of training cruise which the naval minister Boynes had pioneered the year before. The fact that these vessels were being victualled for eight months suggested to British observers that actual operations were contemplated.[132] During Rochford's absence Suffolk took complete control of foreign policy, and by mid-April he and the King were greatly alarmed by France's preparations. On the 21st, fifteen guardships were put into commission. Britain's own mobilization effectively decided the issue, since d'Aiguillon was not prepared to risk war and backed down. The time taken to send orders to Toulon, together with Britain's suspicions of the old enemy, delayed the final settlement until mid-May, when a mutual disarmament was arranged.

Rochford had come back to London for a cabinet meeting on 21 April, and he spent the next few weeks enforcing and then saluting this latest British triumph. Though his own secret negotiations with France were public knowledge, his position was for the moment secure. Yet his relations with his brother Secretary, Suffolk, were henceforth to be noticeably cooler. The origins of the serious tension between the two ministers which was to emerge by the mid-1770s and of Rochford's growing isolation within the cabinet are to be found in the repercussions of the Polish partition and the Swedish coup. The difficulties which the system of two secretaries, each responsible for part of Britain's diplomacy, could cause, were certainly fully evident. Rochford's brave new direction in foreign affairs was diametrically opposed to Suffolk's more traditional stance.

The extended Anglo-French discussions in 1772–3 did not lead to a political alliance, which superficially seemed to offer a promising way out of the impasse facing both powers. The radical nature of the proposal was, in itself, a powerful challenge to established assumptions about Franco-British rivalry, and this was one reason for its failure. D'Aiguillon's commitment to the scheme was more consistent and whole-hearted, but he did not have to reckon with a hostile House of Commons. Even France's foreign minister was tentative, at times doubtful of British goodwill.[133]

Rochford's political foresight was considerable. Yet he and George III both believed the partitioning powers were unlikely to remain united for very long, and this reduced the attractions of a French

---

[132] See, in particular, Suffolk to Stormont, 16 Apr. 1773, Stormont Papers, Box 38.
[133] CP (Angleterre) 500, fo. 4, 172.

alliance.[134] So too did the risk of committing Britain against—and exposing Hanover to—the formidable eastern powers. Both men also recognized that public opinion, parliament, and probably a majority in the cabinet, would never sanction an alliance with Louis XV. The one point on which most ministers and their political opponents were in full agreement was that automatic opposition to France should be the basis of British foreign policy. Indeed, Rochford went as far as to suggest to Martange that the publication of an Anglo-French treaty might well bring down the North Ministry.[135] He well remembered the unpopularity of the Falklands settlement early in 1771, which to the ministry's more extreme parliamentary critics had smacked of appeasement. With his taste for melodrama, he was in no doubt about the fate of a minister who sought to defend Anglo-French alliance negotiations in parliament.[136]

Another reason why Rochford stepped back from the brink can be suggested. A *rapprochement* required considerable mutual trust, yet trust was not in abundant supply in Anglo-French diplomacy at this point. This was partly the legacy of past conflicts and present rivalries. Relations had certainly improved in the early 1770s, but this was generally viewed as temporary, and it had done nothing to weaken the widespread belief that the two states were natural rivals, if not actually enemies. Rochford remained suspicions of d'Aiguillon and, in particular, of French activities in India and Africa.[137] Recent events also contributed. Gustav III's coup, while drawing the two states closer together, also emphasized, and probably heightened, existing suspicions. For the Swedish revolution had been, in part, brought about by France, where the events of 19 August 1772 were celebrated as a triumph for Louis XV's diplomacy.[138] In Britain Gustav III's actions were interpreted and condemned as a product of French intrigue, and Rochford was particularly loud in his condemnation. D'Aiguillon denied any such responsibility to British diplomats, but his disclaimers had a hollow ring in London, where ministers knew of French intrigues in Stockholm through the usual Hanoverian interceptions and were also inclined to attribute the collapse of the Russo-Turkish negotiations in spring 1773 to

---

[134] Black, *Natural and Necessary Enemies*, 78.

[135] *Correspondance inédite de Martange*, ed. Bréard, 512, 518.

[136] The clearest statement of this fear is perhaps Rochford's remarks reported in CP (Angleterre) 500, fo. 201.

[137] For British concern in 1772–3 at renewed French expansion in Senegambia, see *Documents of the American Revolution*, iv, nos. 247, 286, 1199, 1212, 1348, 1367, 1428, 1435–6, and 1542; cf. Black, *Natural and Necessary Enemies*, 77.

[138] *St. Paul of Ewart*, i. 8–10.

France's malign influence.[139] French responsibility for Gustav III's success—however exaggerated Britain's view of this—was a serious barrier to any *rapprochement*. It could only reinforce assumptions about the permanence of French hostility at exactly the moment when d'Aiguillon was trying to persuade London that such prejudices belonged to the past.[140]

The final rejection of France's overtures in spring 1773 underlined the predicament which faced British policy-makers. The new situation revealed by the Polish partition seriously weakened the established premiss of Britain's diplomacy: that the quarrels of the continental powers would always provide an ally against the French. In particular, it had been assumed that one of the German powers—usually Austria, but briefly Prussia—would be glad of Britain's alliance against France and her clients in the *Reich*. The partition of Poland, and the triple alliance which it appeared to represent, destroyed this assumption. The ally, which circumstances now made available, was none other than the national enemy, France. Politically, such a realignment was too dramatic a step for British ministers, as the events of 1772–3 showed. The first partition highlighted Britain's new problems and also revealed that one possible solution was unacceptable.

The assumption that at least one ally was essential was itself being questioned at this time. Britain's security was instead coming to be based on the navy. Predominance at sea had been the foundation of the triumph over the Bourbons in 1770–1, and this mastery had again been apparent during the most recent crisis with France. These two episodes had not merely demonstrated Britain's superiority in capital ships and speed of mobilization; they had also demonstrated that the Bourbons could be defeated without concluding continental alliances. Despite some British anxieties, Spain had played no part in the spring 1773 crisis, and Britain's improved relations with Madrid suggested the Family Compact was not an immediate threat. D'Aiguillon's moderation and his recognition of France's inability to fight any war suggested Britain would not have to fear a French attack as long as Louis XV lived. The shifts in the European states-system thus appeared to be of little immediate concern to Britain, whose security in the early 1770s was coming to depend on Sandwich's reconstructed fleet and on her predominance at sea.[141]

It was a supremacy which ministers took every opportunity to underline. In the second half of June 1773 George III and most of the

[139] Ibid. i. 43.
[140] Ibid. i. 13–5, 25; cf. CP (Angleterre) 500, fo. 145.
[141] See *Parl. Hist.* xvii, col. 948, for North's confidence in Jan. 1774.

cabinet went down to Portsmouth to attend a massive naval review.[142] Among the invited guests was none other than the French ambassador, the Comte de Guines, who saw with his own eyes the strength of British sea power:[143] once again the government was anxious to show off its naval strength to a French diplomat.[144] Guines's presence, and indeed the whole review, signified the new direction of British foreign policy. The ascendancy of the eastern powers was acknowledged in London, though its significance was only slowly being appreciated. Even before Britain's declining influence on the continent had been recognized, the navy had become the principal foundation of her security.[145] During the next two years this shift in priorities would give way to a full-blown acceptance of diplomatic isolation.

[142] H. S. Conway, who attended the review, thought that 'if half the powder had been spent in anything but salutes, it would probably have procured us half a dozen victories': *Keith Memoirs*, ii. 9.

[143] Guines appears to have dined on board the fleet with the King: Walpole, *Last Journals*, i. 239–40; Roberts, 'Great Britain and the Swedish Revolution', 321–2. But the French ambassador was not permitted (as he had hoped) to see work in progress in the yards: *Corr. Geo. III*, ii. 494.

[144] In May 1771, also at Sandwich's invitation, Guines had been shown round Portsmouth: CP (Angleterre) 496, fos. 220, 243, 260–1. For an earlier example of this, cf. above, Ch. 4.

[145] See, e.g., Suffolk to Gunning, Private, 11 June 1773, quoted by Roberts, 'Great Britain and the Swedish Revolution', 322.

8

Splendid Isolation, 1773–1775

RUSSIA and Prussia were now the driving forces in continental diplomacy, with Austria rather uneasily tagging on behind. It seemed as if Poland would be the political cement of a triple alliance. In fact, there were never such formal links: the partition treaties created no binding or permanent ties. But the joint implementation of the annexations, together with the novel unity of the eastern powers, understandably led western observers to talk in terms of a 'Triple Alliance'.

This realignment puzzled and alarmed British observers, and before long its implications were being pondered, though in a distinctly insular way. The influential ambassador in Paris, Lord Stormont, voiced the puzzled concern of many British diplomats when he noted that

the misfortune of the present moment is that there is no real System anywhere, no grand bond of Union, and therefore not knowing who is together, every Court stands upon his own bottom, and lives from hand to mouth without any great principle of Policy or carrying his views beyond the present hour.[1]

From The Hague, Sir Joseph Yorke echoed this view. 'Foreign affairs just now', he complained, 'are so confused and different from all old notions, that one is lost and in the Labyrinth', while two years later Suffolk bewailed 'the present want of system'.[2]

These and similar complaints testified to the puzzling new situation which confronted British diplomats and ministers.[3] References to the want of a 'system', or the 'unnatural' nature of European diplomacy, expressed their concern and their bewilderment. By 1773–4 there was some appreciation that continental alignments could no longer be exploited to Britain's advantage. Old assumptions had to be discarded. The new pattern revealed by the first partition was in some ways a more profound alteration than even the celebrated Diplomatic Revolution of 1756. In this unfamiliar political world there was no obvious niche for Britain. 'We are so

[1] Add. MSS 35505, fo. 206.
[2] Ibid. 35570, fo. 241; to Keith, Private and Confidential, 19 Oct. 1776, SP 80/218.
[3] See e.g. Add. MSS 35506, fo. 18.

uncontinental', lamented Yorke, 'and so hampered with the situation of all the Great Powers of Europe, that we hardly know which way to turn ourselves.'[4] The difficulty was not that there was an absence of definition but rather that the new pattern did not correspond to Britain's expectations. London's recognition of the new facts of diplomatic life was both belated and incomplete. Ministers long assumed that the 'Triple Alliance' would dissolve and a more familiar pattern re-emerge in Europe.[5] But between 1773 and 1775 they adjusted Britain's diplomacy to take account of the changes and adopted an outlook that can be described as one of splendid isolation.[6]

This strategy did not emerge overnight, and it was never to be fully articulated or even clearly defined. It was always an attitude of mind rather than a formal set of policies. Yet the new tone of Britain's diplomacy was unmistakable. For the first time since the Peace of Paris the search for a political alliance ceased to be a British objective. Events in Europe were largely ignored by the cabinet: no vital British interests appeared to be at stake in Poland or in the Balkans, though security demanded a close watch be kept on the Bourbons. Splendid isolation emerged in the aftermath of the first partition, but it was more than a simple response to the European realignment of the early 1770s. Britain's own failure to secure an ally during the previous decade contributed to it, as did her insular diplomacy since the Seven Years War. Another contributory factor was a hardening conviction, in the early 1770s, that a strong navy would provide better security against a French attack than uncertain foreign alliances.

The splendid isolation of these years was strengthened by Britain's renewed preoccupation with her North American colonies. In the second half of 1773 America returned to the forefront of British politics and remained there until the spring of 1775, when the rising tide of colonial opposition turned into open rebellion.[7] Though in the early 1770s there had been a significant reduction in Anglo-American tension, this improvement was superficial and always destined to be short-lived. From the beginning, the North Ministry was determined to enforce parliament's sovereignty over the colonies and to continue the duty on tea. Matters came to a head with the Boston Tea Party in December 1773. During the next four months

---

[4] Ibid. 35434, fo. 41.
[5] See e.g. Suffolk to Keith, 24 Sept. and 26 Nov. 1773, SP 80/214.
[6] For Frederick II's incisive analysis of this see e.g. *Pol. Corr.* xxxv. 14.
[7] For the political situation, see B. Donoughue, *British Politics and the American Revolution: the Path to War 1773–75* (London, 1964).

the cabinet was preoccupied with its response, the repressive legislation directed against Massachusetts, and with the separate issue of the Quebec Act. After a pause of several months, for American reaction to these measures, the final crisis began in late 1774. In addition, during the second half of that year North and his colleagues were distracted by a general election.

This preoccupation with North America served in two distinct ways to put British diplomacy into cold storage. It deflected ministerial attention from Europe: foreign policy was probably least important as a political issue from the middle of 1773 until the early summer of 1775.[8] The routine of diplomatic correspondence was maintained, but the minds of the two Secretaries were often elsewhere. Suffolk, in particular, came to be preoccupied with the situation on the other side of the Atlantic and indeed was a leading advocate of the military reconquest of the colonies. Rochford was less concerned with America but, like Suffolk, he was often called on to introduce and defend Britain's repressive legislation in the Lords.[9] In any case, neither of the senior secretaries enjoyed good health at this time. Suffolk was disabled by gout and was at times unable to carry out his official duties, while Rochford suffered from chronic ill health and was also depressed by his wife's death.[10] The only other member of the cabinet with substantial experience of European affairs was the Earl of Sandwich, First Lord of the Admiralty, but he concentrated on his own department and exerted no direct influence on foreign policy at this time.[11]

Success in the colonies also came to be regarded as essential for future credibility in foreign policy. After the Peace of Paris, internal divisions had contributed significantly to Britain's declining reputation in Europe. In recent years, the situation had improved: Britain's standing had been aided by the political stability provided by Lord North and particularly by the vigorous and successful naval

---

[8] It was significant that the King's Speech at the opening of the parliamentary session in Jan. 1774 declared that in the prevailing 'state of Foreign Affairs you will have full leisure to attend to the Improvement of our internal and domestic situation': *Journal of the House of Commons*, xxxiv. 391. This was the first speech from the throne to make such a connection; cf. SP 78/297, fo. 29, and *Burke Corr.* ii. 512.

[9] See e.g. *BDI* vii: *France 1745–1789*, ed. L. G. Wickham Legg, 139.

[10] Add. MSS 35508, fo. 109. In autumn 1774, Suffolk was unable to see a single foreign diplomat for 2 months and the French chargé d'affaires judged that poor health would force him to resign: CP (Angleterre) 507, fo. 170; G. W. Rice, 'An Aspect of European Diplomacy in the Mid-Eighteenth Century: The Diplomatic Career of the Fourth Earl of Rochford at Turin, Madrid and Paris, 1749–1768' (unpublished Ph.D. thesis, University of Canterbury, New Zealand, 1973), 542; P. D. G. Thomas, *Lord North* (London, 1976), 89; *Cal. HO Papers 1773–5*, no. 14.   [11] *Sandwich Papers*, i. 380.

mobilizations in 1770–1 and in 1773.[12] The emergence of serious colonial opposition, widely reported on the continent, once again damaged her credibility.[13] British observers were awake to this danger, and by the mid-1770s they viewed the situation with anxious concern. 'I don't see how the Government can give way,' commented Sir Joseph Yorke early in 1775, 'without losing the Colonies and becoming the scorn of Europe.'[14] The recovery of Britain's international prestige was believed to depend on the defeat of colonial opposition: as the King forcibly expressed it in 1774, 'we must get the colonies into order before we engage with our neighbours'.[15] One reason why Britain went to war with the Americans in 1775 was to be a conviction that her survival as a great power depended on recovering control over the colonies.[16]

The preoccupation with America strengthened Britain's isolationism and increased her indifference to events in Europe. The conclusion of the Russo-Turkish War by the Treaty of Kutchuk-Kainardji in July 1774 was the most important European event in these years, but it was largely ignored in London.[17] The cabinet was not called back from its summer holidays to consider the peace settlement, which was seen simply as another reverse for France.[18] This indifference embodied an awareness of Britain's diminished importance, but it primarily revealed the new isolationist spirit which guided her foreign policy.

The sea change was particularly apparent in Anglo-Russian diplomacy. Since 1763 ministers had repeatedly sought to ally with Catherine II. Yet in the early 1770s this quest was abandoned and contacts quickly became cooler and more distant. For Britain at least, this was deliberate policy. Sir Robert Gunning, formerly minister in Copenhagen, had been sent to St Petersburg in 1772 by his political patron, Suffolk, to impart a new spirit of realism to relations.[19] The Northern Secretary was concerned that the enthusiasm and frank

[12] *Sbornik*, xiii. 342; Martens, *Recueil des traités*, xiii. 146; *Sbornik*, xcccv. 240; *Pol. Corr.* xxxiii. 551, xxxiv. 6–7.

[13] The government was clearly aware of this danger and tried to publicize its own attempts to restore order in the colonies: see e.g. SP 78/292, fo. 61.

[14] Add. MSS 35571, fo. 9; cf. ibid. 35434, fo. 44.

[15] *Corr. Geo. III*, ii. 372, for the view of the King in 1774. (This letter is misdated by the editor.)

[16] R. W. Tucker and D. C. Hendrickson, *The Fall of the First British Empire: Origins of the War of American Independence* (Baltimore, Md., 1983), 356.

[17] Though characteristically the King noted its possible repercussions: *Corr. Geo. III*, iii. 121, 125.

[18] CP (Angleterre) 506, fo. 228. Here ministers endorsed the assessment of the influential ambassador to France, Stormont: SP 78/293, fos. 109–12.

[19] His 'Instructions', dated 27 May 1772, are in SP 104/240, pp. 87–95.

disregard for his instructions displayed by Gunning's predecessor, Cathcart, had conveyed the impression London might still agree to an alliance on Russia's terms, and Suffolk was anxious to dispel any such idea. British ministers were not yet completely indifferent to an alliance, though they doubted whether this could now be concluded on acceptable terms, and they were in addition becoming suspicious of Russia's territorial ambitions around the Black Sea.[20] They also recognized that formidable barriers now existed to the conclusion of any treaty and that, in the early 1770s, these were multiplying.

Britain attached little responsibility to Catherine II for the actual partition of Poland, but ministers did resent the way they had been deceived. They also recognized that the territorial changes in 1772 made an alliance less attractive, since an additional barrier to the westward march of Russian troops had been created by Frederick II's annexations from Poland.[21] In addition, the British government was not prepared to include Russia's gains in the reciprocal guarantee of territories which would be the basis of any defensive alliance. To have done so, ministers believed, would have amounted to formal and explicit approval of the partition and this they had always refused to give. Finally, Suffolk had been alarmed by Russia's menacing and even aggressive attitude towards Sweden in the winter of 1772–3 and thereafter he was wary of any alliance which might draw Britain into a Baltic war.[22]

The transformation of Britain's attitude in the early 1770s was striking. From being a 'natural ally', Catherine II's empire became in a few short years a state whose alliance involved unacceptable obligations and with whom no treaty would, for the moment at least, be contemplated. For a decade Britain had provided much of the momentum in the alliance negotiations; but in the spring of 1773 it was Russia who took the initiative. Catherine II and Panin were aware of their continuing problems around the Baltic and in the south. When news of the collapse of peace negotiations with the Turks arrived in April, they looked for a British alliance to buttress Russia's fragile international position. Now, as throughout the preceding decade, St Petersburg's desire for a formal treaty was

---

[20] SP 91/92, fo. 120; Suffolk to Keith, 11 June 1773, ibid. 80/213; N. Tracy, *Navies, Deterrence and American Independence: Britain and Seapower in the 1760s and 1770s* (Vancouver, 1988), 106.

[21] As Cathcart had pointed out at the time: Roberts, *British Diplomacy*, 407.

[22] M. Roberts, 'Great Britain and the Swedish Revolution', *Essays in Swedish History* (London, 1967), 298–9, demonstrates how the Northern Secretary gradually distanced himself from Russian policy in the autumn and winter of 1772–3; SP 91/92, fo. 120.

greatest during a critical period for Russian foreign policy.[23] But on this occasion the door was immediately slammed shut in the Empress's face.[24]

The new coldness which had fallen over Anglo-Russian diplomacy was particularly evident in the final months of 1773, when Britain deliberately did very little to assist a further Russian naval squadron making the long voyage from the Baltic to the eastern Mediterranean.[25] This contrasted sharply with events four years earlier. Now assistance was refused outright, in terms which made clear the poor state of relations.[26] Some Russian ships were allowed to enter Spithead, but little or no repair work was done on them in the naval dockyard. This was not entirely a question of Anglo-Russian relations. Sandwich was energetically trying to rebuild Britain's navy and all the available dockyard facilities and *matériel* were needed for this task. The episode principally revealed that, by the end of 1773, ministers were no longer prepared to do anything for the sake of good relations.[27]

This indifference reflected the growing isolationism in official circles in London.[28] 'About foreign affairs we are absolutely asleep', declared Burke in November 1773, adding the significant comment that 'His Prussian Majesty, God bless him, does all in his power to awaken us'.[29] One important exception to this lack of interest in European issues was a protracted diplomatic clash with Prussia in 1772–4. Its occasion was Frederick II's attempt to annex the Polish city of Danzig, whose independence British diplomacy sought to uphold. Paradoxically, however, these efforts merely demonstrated Britain's irrelevance for the eastern powers and thereby confirmed the strategy of splendid isolation.

Danzig was Poland's only substantial port. It had come to prominence during the second half of the fifteenth century and, at its peak, had been handling three-quarters of Poland's total foreign trade. It imported western manufactured goods and exported corn and raw materials: it was the obvious outlet for the produce of the Polish hinterland. Exports were transported down the river Vistula and then transhipped for the journey to the west. The city's

---

[23] Suffolk subsequently noted 'a disposition in Her Majesty [Catherine II] to resort to this country in the Hour of Distress': SP 91/93, fo. 194.   [24] *Sbornik*, xix. 354–5.

[25] For which see e.g. SP 91/93, fo. 194. For this episode, see the documents in SP 91/94; cf. *Corr. Geo. III*, iii. 42–4.   [26] SP 91/94, fos. 52–3.

[27] The most that can be said is that the government was anxious not to worsen relations. By the following spring, a new and much less favourable attitude to Russia was clearly apparent in London: see the comments of George III, North, and Rochford in *Corr. Geo. III*, iii. 89–91.

[28] This was certainly appreciated by the Russian government: *Sbornik*, cxxxv. 238.

[29] *Burke Corr.* ii. 490.

population was predominantly German and traditionally had enjoyed considerable autonomy within Poland: in particular, its transit trade was not subject to heavy customs dues. By the second half of the eighteenth century both the port and its commerce were in decline, but they still constituted an enticing target for Prussia.

After the destruction of the Seven Years War, Frederick II was more concerned than ever to strengthen the commercial and economic base of his state. He believed that Prussia's natural poverty could only be remedied by the income to be derived from industry and commerce, and in particular, from the transit trade through his territories: he hoped to dominate Polish commerce and thereby derive a substantial revenue from customs duties and other tolls. The Prussian King had always sought to exploit Poland's political weakness to his own economic advantage. At the time of the first partition he had tried unsuccessfully to include Danzig and Thorn (Toruń), an important entrepôt and fortress further up the Vistula, in Prussian annexations. At this point he was vigorously opposed by Russia: St Petersburg had guaranteed Danzig's privileged position earlier in the eighteenth century and Panin feared opposition from the commercial states of western Europe if Prussia captured it. In December 1771 Frederick, in order not to obstruct the partition's conclusion, had been forced to abandon his plan to annex Danzig. Nevertheless, Prussia's gains in 1772 enabled her to throttle the port's seaborne commerce and to impose tolls on trade on the Vistula. Ships that had already been taxed by the Polish authorities now faced a second demand for customs dues, from Prussian agents backed by troops. Thereafter Frederick II tried to divert trade away to Prussia's Baltic ports, especially Stettin (Szczecin). He hoped that this would eventually force Danzig to submit to annexation as the price for recovering its prosperity. During the next decade considerable economic damage was done to Danzig, though the Prussian campaign was eventually to fail.[30]

Frederick II's menacing posture, his military occupation of territory apparently belonging to Danzig, and his attempt to ruin the port economically, certainly alarmed Britain. The city's importance was twofold.[31] Danzig contained a sizeable colony of British traders, and their vigorous representations against the additional Prussian

---

[30] Frederick II's campaign appears to have halved the number of ships arriving annually: R. G. Albion, *Forests and Sea Power: The Timber Problem of the Royal Navy 1652–1862* (Cambridge, Mass., 1926), 163.

[31] A modern study of the dispute is still needed and research should be concentrated on the domestic and, in particular, commercial influences on British policy: this is one of the very few instances where such pressures were important. The best account is still W. Michael, *Englands Stellung zur ersten Teilung Polens* (Hamburg and Leipzig, 1890).

customs dues fuelled London's protests.[32] Danzig's Senate (city council) also tried to secure Britain's support by exploiting its own contacts among merchants in London.[33] In northern Europe, British trade with Poland was second in volume and importance only to that with Russia. The low tariffs had enabled this commerce to flourish, and Britain enjoyed a favourable, though modest, balance of trade: tobacco was the principal export to Poland. British merchants resented the duties which Prussia was trying to impose and feared that if the mercantilist-minded Frederick II were to annex the port, their traditional advantages would disappear. The dispute also had a broader significance. Trade with northern Europe was economically important and strategically vital for Britain and in the eighteenth century her share of this had increased. The Baltic region was the principal source of the crucial naval stores and, during the Seven Years War, Danzig itself had become a significant supplier of timber for the Royal Navy. [34] British ministers had no wish to see Prussia, with whom relations had been very poor for a decade, secure a dominant position in a region of such importance.[35] Though Britain was always aware that her representations had little chance of success, she took up the city's cause with considerable vigour;[36] in Frederick II's memorable phrase, George III became the 'Don Quixote of Danzig'.[37] Despite occasional Prussian anxieties, the efforts of Britain's King were to prove no more effective than those of the legendary Spanish knight.

British opposition to Frederick II's schemes can be divided into two phases. Initially, an attempt was made to persuade the other two eastern powers, and especially Russia, to restrain Prussia. By summer 1773 the failure of these representations was apparent and Britain now introduced economic sanctions against Silesian cloth imports.[38] Frederick countered this by threatening to disrupt trade with the Baltic. The danger to British naval stores was taken very seriously, since the situation in America was worsening and Sandwich was striving to improve the readiness of the fleet. By early 1774 Britain

[32] For glimpses of Sir Trevor Corry's role on behalf of the British factory at Danzig, see SP 104/224, pp. 68, 88–9, 108, 138.

[33] For these efforts, see SP 88/118. In Jan. 1774, the merchants' London agent, J. W. Anderson, presented a very informative 'Observations on the Distressed Situation of the Trade of Danzig', (see ibid); cf. *Cal. HO Papers 1773–5*, no. 458.

[34] Albion, *Forests and Sea Power*, 161, and more generally, 140–3 and 146–50.

[35] *Sbornik*, cxliii. 525.

[36] The cabinet had acknowledged this as early as Oct. 1772: PRO 30/29/1/14, fo. 669; in the following year, Rochford admitted that Frederick was as much master of Danzig as the King of Spain was of Madrid: *Pol. Corr.* xxxiv. 167–8.

[37] Ibid. xxxiii. 387; xxxiv. 16, 211, 216. Prussia's King never wasted a *bon mot*!

[38] Suffolk to Keith, 30 July 1773, SP 80/204; *Sbornik*, xix. 366.

had publicly acknowledged that it could do nothing effective against Prussia, though in the following spring Frederick II did grant British ships some concessions and these were welcomed in London.[39] In the event, Danzig managed to resist the Prussian offensive: the town's stubborn defence of its independence, together with Russia's evident unease, finally induced the Prussian King to abandon his plans for immediate annexation. He continued his economic campaign against the port and in 1782 went as far as a blockade, but it was not finally annexed until the second partition of Poland in 1793.

British diplomatic protests did little to restrain Frederick II over Danzig. Yet the confrontation had wider political significance. Anglo-Prussian relations had been very bad for a decade and the dispute caused a further deterioration. The behaviour of the Prussian agent in London contributed significantly to this. Maltzan had arrived there at the end of 1765. From the start he had filled his dispatches with the speculations and scandals of the day, and the flavour these imparted to his reports was certainly to Frederick II's taste. Sir Joseph Yorke, with one eye firmly on Maltzan's practice of reporting all rumours, as long as they discredited the British ministry of the day, declared that he was only 'the Echo of our Libels'.[40] Prussian diplomatic correspondence from London was, of course, regularly intercepted, and the style and content of Maltzan's reports were soon familiar to the British government.[41] Yet the tone of his dispatches, however much it might displease ministers, did not in itself furnish adequate grounds for his recall and for over a decade his reports nourished his master's established prejudices against Britain. His conduct during the Danzig episode further inflamed relations.

The lengthy diplomatic exchanges in 1772–4 inevitably involved Maltzan in frequent discussions with British ministers. After one particularly stormy interview with Suffolk on 5 April 1773, the Prussian agent simulated a total breach in relations by appearing to depart from London without formally taking leave.[42] Within two or three days, however, he had returned and was behaving as though nothing had happened. His conduct was immediately interpreted by British observers, and universally condemned, as an attempt to influence the stocks.[43] The sudden fall in the market which his actions were likely to produce could easily be exploited by his

[39] *Pol. Corr.* xxxv. 264–5, 331.
[40] Add. MSS 35371, fo. 38.
[41] SP 90/86, fo. 131; SP 90/88, fo. 4; *Corr. Geo. III*, iii. 469.
[42] SP 90/93, fos. 95–6, 97–9; cf. *Pol. Corr.* xxxiii. 462–3.
[43] Significantly, Suffolk was levelling this accusation against the Prussian agent *before* his feigned departure: SP 90/93, fo. 98. Maltzan's own explanation was that he had gone to Richmond to stay the night (*Pol. Corr.* xxxiii. 463).

associates to their, and his, profit.[44] Conclusive proof for this charge
is lacking, but the suspicion of stockjobbing was widespread and the
balance of available evidence, though circumstantial, is against
Maltzan.[45] His action was also that prescribed by his instructions. In
the early months of 1773, Frederick was briefly anxious that his
attempts to annex Danzig might be thwarted by combined pressure
from Britain and Russia.[46] To counteract this he adopted a strategy
of menaces towards London. Convinced that Britain would be cowed
by threats, he had instructed Maltzan that, if British ministers
rejected his undoubted 'rights' to Danzig, he was to depart from
London without formally taking leave and could make free use of
this threat to intimidate Suffolk. By the end of March 1773, the
possibility of Russian opposition to Frederick's schemes had faded,
but the King did not formally countermand his earlier instructions
and subsequently approved Maltzan's firm tone in his interview
with Suffolk on 5 April.[47] The details of these events, however, are
less important than the interpretation placed on them by British
ministers. The whole episode reinforced the low regard in which
Maltzan was held in London.[48] Britain's failure over Danzig
confirmed ministers in their hostility towards Frederick II and
ensured that relations with Prussia would remain acrimonious.[49]

Britain's attitude towards the second of the eastern powers,
Austria, was not seriously affected by the dispute. Ministers were
aware of Vienna's unease at further Prussian annexations, particularly
Danzig and its wealth. Any such unilateral gain would further
weaken Austria's relative position among the great powers. At the
end of November 1772 the Austrian Chancellor, Kaunitz had tried to
persuade the departing British ambassador, Stormont, that Britain
should intervene to protect her commerce: London's interest in
Europe was now seen by one perceptive observer as being primarily
economic in nature.[50] Kaunitz continued to press intervention on the
new minister in Vienna, Sir Robert Murray Keith, in the hope that
joint Anglo-Russian action might in some way restrain Prussia.[51]
These hopes were premature and proved unrealistic. Austria was
unwilling to oppose Frederick outright and in fact could not resist
Prussian encroachments on the city. Her own annexations rested on
the same basis as Prussian claims to Danzig. This was recognized by

---

[44] Add. MSS 35505, fo. 148.   [45] Ibid., fo. 213; Walpole, *Last Journals*, i. 186.
[46] See his correspondence in *Pol. Corr.* xxxiii.
[47] Ibid. xxxiii. 463.   [48] *Corr. Geo. III*, iii. 78.
[49] See e.g. Add. MSS 34412, fo. 242; cf. *BDI* vii: *France 1745–1789*, 148.
[50] Stormont to Suffolk, Private, 26 Nov. 1772, SP 80/212. Frederick II was rapidly coming
to the same view: *Pol Corr.* xxxiv. 116, 118.   [51] Michael, *Englands Stellung*, 42–4.

British ministers, who soon appreciated that the Habsburgs would give no real support.[52]

Britain was equally disappointed by Russia's attitude.[53] During the winter of 1772–3, Gunning had made some desultory representations at the Russian court, emphasizing the threat to British commerce.[54] He received no encouragement from Panin. Russia was certainly unhappy at the prospect of a Prussian Danzig but, beset by the problems of the Turks, in Poland, and around the Baltic, she needed Prussia's support. At this point Panin had no intention of losing this for the sake of a Polish port and British trade. His attitude inevitably confirmed the British view that Frederick II's influence still predominated in St Petersburg and thus contributed to the deterioration in Anglo-Russian relations apparent at this time.[55]

The principal significance of the dispute was to demonstrate that Britain's influence in eastern Europe had become negligible. Burke's remark at the time of the first partition, that 'Poland must be regarded as being situated on the moon', applied with equal force to the exchanges over Danzig.[56] There was nothing Britain could do to prevent Prussian annexation, as Suffolk honestly admitted: a naval blockade was unlikely to have affected Prussia and does not appear to have been considered.[57] London's protests were always rather half-hearted, and they were abandoned in the face of Frederick's obvious determination. This defeat revealed to British ministers, perhaps fully for the first time, the strength and coherence of the eastern alignment and their own diminished importance. Austria and Russia had both been unwilling, though for different reasons, to act against Prussia. The gains from Poland made by each state ultimately depended on the consent and support of the other partitioning powers: this, as the Danzig episode made clear to Britain, created considerable unity between the eastern powers. Britain, as Burke truly said, was now 'at the Circumference' of European politics.[58] Ministers in London consoled themselves that the new alignment was unlikely to be permanent and settled down to wait for its collapse: this, they believed, would come about when Austro-Prussian rivalry re-emerged. Until then, Britain could, and indeed should, do no more than keep a watching brief.

This strategy was also suggested by certain other factors. The French chargé d'affaires in London, Garnier, judged in 1774 that

[52] Suffolk to Keith, 26 Mar. and 16 Apr. 1773, SP 80/213.
[53] Add. MSS 34412, fo. 258.   [54] *Sbornik*, xix. 333–8.
[55] Suffolk to Keith, 30 July 1773, SP 80/214; cf SP 91/92, fo. 82.
[56] Quoted by N. Davies, *God's Playground: A History of Poland* (2 vols.; Oxford, 1981), i. 524.
[57] To Keith, 30 July 1773, SP 80/214.   [58] *Burke Corr.* ii. 513.

Britain would only renew her search for an alliance if she was confronted by aggression from France, and for the moment there was little sign of this.[59] The principal component in British foreign policy continued to be that of keeping a careful watch on the Bourbons. Indeed, Britain's mounting problems in America made peace more desirable than ever. Ministers still regarded Louis XV's state as Britain's main enemy and sources of tension remained. But in the mid-1770s relations continued to be surprisingly friendly and ministers saw no reason to fear an attack. Their confidence was apparent in the decision to reduce Britain's naval force in India in November 1773.[60]

The principal threat to this continuing *détente*, at least in British eyes, came with Louis XV's death in May 1774. The old King's fear of war had been renowned.[61] His heir was believed to be more aggressively inclined towards Britain, whose anxieties were increased by the simultaneous upheavals in the French ministry.[62] D'Aiguillon, who had contributed significantly to the improved relations, was forced to resign, along with the other members of the Triumvirate, and for a time there was considerable uncertainty over their successors. It was even feared that Britain's arch-enemy, Choiseul, might return to power.[63] Louis XVI's wife was the Austrian princess Marie Antoinette, whose marriage had been arranged by the exiled minister. The British government was anxious lest the new Queen might bring about the recall of its old foe.[64] Britain's attitude to Choiseul in the 1770s mirrored that of France to Chatham in the period after the Seven Years War. The bellicose reputations of both ministers were such that their return to high office was seen by the opposing government as the harbinger of a new conflict. At the beginning of Louis XVI's reign Choiseul was allowed to end his exile at Chanteloup and was even permitted to attend court again, but, though his spectre continued to haunt British ministers, his return to power was never seriously considered.[65] D'Aiguillon's eventual successor was a career diplomat, the Comte de Vergennes, who took

---

[59] CP (Angleterre) 506, fo. 229.

[60] H. Richmond, *The Navy in India 1763–1783* (London, 1931), 74–5.

[61] See e.g. Suffolk to Yorke, 17 May 1774, SP 84/542.

[62] BDI vii: *France 1745–1789*, 140.

[63] This was widely seen as a possible result of Louis XV's death: see e.g. *Bernstorffsche Papiere*, iii. 290–1.

[64] For a particularly clear statement of this concern, see Suffolk to Yorke, Private, 12 July 1774, SP 84/543.

[65] J. D. Hardman, 'Ministerial Politics from the Accession of Louis XVI to the Assembly of Notables, 1774–1787' (unpublished D.Phil thesis, University of Oxford, 1973), 163. As Dr Hardman makes clear, the new queen's flirtation with Choiseul was really an attempt to bait her enemy Maurepas.

up his post in July 1774. For the moment Vergennes was anxious to maintain good relations with Britain, and he was soon being viewed in London as the least unsatisfactory of all the potential candidates for the foreign ministry.[66] His appointment did not end the uncertainty at the French court, where ministerial upheavals continued until the autumn. These were welcomed in London, now that the threat of Choiseul's restoration had waned. 'The unsettled state of the French Ministry', as the King described it towards the end of August, was seen as a further guarantee of continued peace.[67] By autumn 1774 the growing stability of the government now headed by the ageing courtier Maurepas, and its evident pacifism, were both being welcomed in London.[68]

Britain's sense of security had two principal foundations. In the first place the cabinet appreciated that the French ministry was still preoccupied with internal and especially financial problems and that its foreign policy would therefore remain passive.[69] Financial reform and the resulting struggle with the *parlements* had contributed significantly to improved relations during the early 1770s. The preoccupation with domestic problems survived Louis XV's death. In particular the reforming schemes of the new financial minister, Turgot, aroused considerable opposition and the *parlements* were able to recover some influence. In the mid-1770s these struggles, and especially the monarchy's continuing financial difficulties, were a formidable obstacle to any aggressive foreign policy. This was certainly appreciated by the British cabinet: Lord North, who had a surprisingly detailed knowledge of French state finances, was particularly confident on this point.[70] France's internal difficulties were extensively reported and analysed by the British embassy in Paris. These reports reassured ministers that there was little danger of a French attack, and helped to make an active policy appear unnecessary.[71]

The second source of British confidence was the ministry's appreciation that it retained superiority at sea.[72] Here the cabinet was relying on Britain's intelligence network, which provided an accurate picture of the situation in the French naval dockyards.[73]

---

[66] BDI vii: *France 1745–1789*, 142. The new foreign minister's moderation was soon apparent in renewed discussions over the Newfoundland Fisheries: C. de la Morandière, *Histoire de la pêche française de la morue dans l'Amérique septentrionale* (3 vols.; Paris, 1962–6), ii. 937 ff.   [67] *Corr. Geo. III*, iii. 125.

[68] SP 78/293, fo. 270.   [69] See Suffolk to Yorke, 17 May 1774, SP 84/542.

[70] See e.g. SP 78/294, fo. 45. Cf. North's remarks in the Commons in May 1774: *Parl. Hist.* xvii, cols. 1330–4.   [71] *Documents of the American Revolution*, viii, no. 125.

[72] See Sandwich's remarks in the Lords in Feb. 1775: *Proceedings and Debates*, v. 397.

[73] See e.g. the material on the Bourbon navies provided by Mrs Wolters in 1774: SP 84/544–5 *passim*.

From time to time signs of activity were detected and crises erupted: as, for example, in spring 1774.[74] Such tension was always short-lived. These intelligence reports, when placed alongside the clear improvements in Britain's own navy, confirmed that France was quite unable to launch an attack. Even Sartine's efforts to rebuild the French fleet, after he became naval minister in August 1774, caused little immediate concern.

The very fact that relations were now viewed predominantly in terms of French intentions also contributed to Britain's sense of security. Though Franco-Spanish relations had been patched up in 1772–3, the Family Compact was always a less potent force after the Falklands episode than it had been under Choiseul, and Anglo-Spanish relations remained surprisingly good in the mid-1770s. Spain was now more independent of France than at any time during the previous decade, and she was also preoccupied with the activities of the Barbary corsairs in the western Mediterranean and with a serious boundary dispute in South America, with Portugal. Madrid's changed priorities were appreciated by the British government, which was careful not to inflame relations.[75] Britain's desire to remain on good terms with Spain was fully evident over the clash between Portugal and Spain in South America. Though formally Portugal's ally, Britain immediately made it clear that she would not support Lisbon in this dispute and tried to promote a peaceful settlement.[76]

Relations with France remained the motor nerve of British diplomacy. Though ministers occasionally demonstrated some unease about future French intentions, by 1774–5 they were for the most part confident about the present state of relations with Louis XVI.[77] This, in turn, further weakened their concern with foreign affairs, which by autumn 1774 had effectively disappeared from the political agenda.[78] The cabinet was instead preoccupied with the final crisis in America.[79] This opened early in October 1774 when news arrived that civil government in Massachusetts had finally collapsed. During

---

[74] For this brief crisis, see *Corr. Geo. III*, iii. 89–91, and SP 78/291.

[75] For a notable example of this concern, see Rochford to Lords Commissioners of the Admiralty, 12 May 1775, SP 94/198.

[76] *Cal. HO Papers 1773–5*, no. 693, for Britain's position; for Rochford's hopes of an early settlement, see SP 78/293, fo. 270; cf. below, Ch. 9, for more on this dispute and its repercussions.

[77] For example, in India: Richmond, *The Navy in India 1763–1783*, 75–6; cf. Rochford's remarks in the House of Lords in Feb. 1775: *Proceedings and Debates*, v. 394–5.

[78] *Burke Corr.* iii. 31.

[79] There is a convenient introduction by A. J. McCurry, 'The North Government and the Outbreak of the American Revolution', *Huntington Library Quarterly*, 34 (1970–1), 141–57, and a full account in Donoughue, *British Politics and the American Revolution*, 201–79.

the winter of 1774–5 the situation rapidly deteriorated. By November ministers realized they faced a colonial rebellion. They therefore responded by a further series of coercive measures designed to restore parliament's authority, but their actions merely strengthened American resistance. By the spring of 1775 it was clear that military repression was the only way to restore authority in the colonies, where fighting had already begun. The first news of the armed clashes at Concord and Lexington reached London on 29 May, and after some initial scepticism, was confirmed in mid-June.[80] By 25 July the costly engagement at Bunker Hill was known to ministers.[81] In the summer of 1775 Lord North's government was forced to recognize that Britain now faced nothing less than a full-scale war for America.

[80] Mackesy, *War for America*, 2; *St. Paul of Ewart*, ii. 156–7; CP (Angleterre) 510, fos. 258–62.   [81] Mackesy, *War for America*, 4.

9

Peace with the Bourbons, 1775–1777

FOREIGN policy was immediately subordinated to the American rebellion.[1] Britain's situation was unprecedented. Military operations had to be conducted on the other side of the Atlantic, 3,000 miles away, and the logistical problems dwarfed those in her other eighteenth-century wars. The fact that the fighting was in America and, until 1778, did not directly involve any European state made it unique. Britain's traditional strategy was to secure allies, to put their own armies into the field on the continent, but this was clearly impossible. During its early stages, the American campaign, together with the defence of the ministry's policies in parliament, preoccupied the two senior Secretaries of State. Suffolk in particular was prominent in organizing Britain's counter-offensive. Until the winter of 1777–8, the reconquest of the colonies was the cabinet's main priority. The fighting, however, also drew British diplomacy out of cold storage, into which it had been consigned in the years before 1775.

The American revolt forced ministers to give more attention to the Bourbon powers, particularly France, and relations with these states dominated British diplomacy until war began in Europe in 1778–9.[2] The rebellion made peace in Europe imperative. And this, in practice, meant peace with France. The real nightmare for ministers was a surprise attack when Britain was fully committed in America.

[1] In this and subsequent chapters, no attempt is made to provide a detailed account of the fighting, for which see the excellent study by Mackesy, *War for America*. Similarly, only a cursory examination of American diplomacy is possible. The best brief account of this is now J. R. Dull, *A Diplomatic History of the American Revolution* (New Haven, Conn., 1985), though S. F. Bemis's celebrated *The Diplomacy of the American Revolution* (1935; Bloomington, Ind., 1957 edn.) remains valuable. Some of the arguments of this chapter were anticipated by the important and unfairly neglected article by R. W. Van Alstyne, 'Great Britain, the War for Independence and the "Gathering Storm" in Europe 1775–1778', *Huntington Library Quarterly*, 27 (1964), 311–46.

[2] There is no adequate study of Anglo-Bourbon relations during the first half of the American War and the accounts in some otherwise reliable works can be seriously misleading: this is particularly true of Bemis, *Diplomacy of the American Revolution*. The most satisfactory account is R. W. Van Alstyne, *Empire and Independence: The International History of the American Revolution* (New York, 1965), 79–160 *passim*; the naval dimension is highlighted by N. Tracy, *Navies, Deterrence and American Independence: Britain and Seapower in the 1760s and 1770s* (Vancouver, 1988), 120–58, though the broader political context is at times treated rather sketchily.

Though France's intervention was not inevitable, there was always the danger that Britain's traditional enemy would exploit the colonial revolt and seek revenge for her defeat in the Seven Years War. A war in India and on the high seas against France, and on the other side of the Atlantic against a Franco-American alignment, was an alarming prospect. British strategists recognized the traditional eighteenth-century pattern might be reversed. Instead of France being tied down in a continental war and defeated overseas, Britain's military and naval forces could be committed to a world-wide struggle, with no European conflict to deflect the French. Good relations with France were essential if America was to be reconquered.

The study of Anglo-Bourbon relations during the American War can be distorted by hindsight. Britain was to go to war with France in 1778 and with Spain the following year. The wider conflict, together with eventual American independence, can create an air of inevitability. Three familiar assumptions must be avoided. First, there is a widespread belief that the Americans were bound to win. In fact, at least until the closing months of 1777 and Burgoyne's surrender at Saratoga, it appeared likely that Britain would defeat the rebel armies.[3] The eventual American victory resulted primarily from British resources being diverted after 1778–9 to the world-wide struggle with France and Spain. Bourbon intervention itself was far from inevitable. France's decisive contribution to American independence, together with her aid throughout the struggle, can make her entry appear preordained. Yet the French foreign minister, Vergennes, was surprisingly cautious and hesitant. He was conscious of the poor state of Louis XVI's navy and finances; he was uncertain of Spanish support and, more importantly, of American victory; and his ministerial colleagues were uncomfortably aware of France's domestic problems. Finally, the assumption that Spain was bound to assist France must also be avoided. Madrid had her own political priorities and was also less tied to the Family Compact than is sometimes assumed.

Spain was ambivalent about the rebellion. It was welcomed, since it weakened Britain and her expanding empire in America, viewed as a threat to Spanish dominance in the New World. But Spain had colonies of her own and was uncomfortably aware that this American empire could be imperilled by a successful colonial revolt, which might be copied further south. Although her leading minister, Grimaldi, was seen in London as irrevocably anti-British, he was

[3] Here I follow the arguments of Mackesy: *War for America, passim;* cf. the shorter statement of his views, 'British Strategy in the War of American Independence', *Yale Review,* 52 (1963), 539–57.

moderate and statesmanlike, and valued the good relations established during the early 1770s. Madrid came to be preoccupied with a Luso-Spanish dispute in South America, and was also unnerved by the humiliating failure of the expedition against Algiers in July 1775. This was a severe blow to Spain's confidence and prestige, and it reinforced her desire for good relations. Spanish policy during the first half of the American War was, therefore, cautious. Though he recognized the opportunity for revenge on Britain, Grimaldi preferred to wait on events and to explore what Spain might gain by diplomacy rather than by force.

The American War initially had little impact on Britain's relations with the Bourbons and the pattern established before 1775. Anglo-French diplomacy remained friendly for a year after the rebellion began, and only in 1776 did tension increase. Thereafter, relations deteriorated sharply until, by mid-1777, war was widely viewed as inevitable. There was no parallel decline in Anglo-Spanish diplomacy. In the early stages of the revolt and even after the formal ending of Anglo-French relations in March 1778, most ministers distinguished between the two Bourbon powers and hoped to maintain good relations with Madrid. Only during the winter of 1778–9 did the cabinet finally accept that Spain would fight alongside France.

Though relations had recently improved, France was still seen as Britain's major enemy. This was why ministers were concerned with Anglo-French diplomacy after 1775. Their analysis was at first reassuring: France was pacific and also in no condition to fight.[4] Her ministry was unstable and Turgot's financial reforms had led to a new struggle with the *parlements*. These domestic priorities were extensively analysed by British diplomats in Paris, and their reports reassured the cabinet.[5] Once again, Britain's confidence rested principally on her knowledge of the poor state of the French fleet. Since France's navy would be crucial in any war, its condition was seen as the best guide to her intentions. After Boynes's administration, it was certainly in no condition to challenge Britain at sea: as Rochford characteristically reminded the French ambassador in July 1775.[6] Any attempt to build up the French navy would quickly be apparent to Britain's intelligence network, as it was to be from 1776 onwards. The cabinet continued to be remarkably well informed about the French dockyards.[7] Up-to-date information was regularly

[4] *St. Paul of Ewart*, ii. 127; *Proceedings and Debates*, vi. 77; HMC *Stopford–Sackville*, i. 137. [5] See the correspondence for 1775 in SP 78/295–7.
[6] Doniol, *Participation*, i. 116; cf. *St. Paul of Ewart*, ii. 212.
[7] For the kind of information collected, *Cal. HO Papers 1773–5*, pp. 455–6 *passim*. There is a useful study of Britain's intelligence gathering by F.-P. Renaut, *Le Secret Service de*

provided by the embassy in Paris, by the Wolters' agency, and by other casual sources; indeed, such intelligence gathering may have increased after 1775.[8] Relations were not uniformly tranquil. There were occasional and short-lived periods of tension, caused by rumours of French naval preparations, notably in spring 1775 and in early 1776.[9] Though they were important reminders of the extent of suspicion and rivalry, they did not seriously disturb the surface calm of diplomacy. In March 1776, the French chargé d'affaires, Garnier, noted Britain's confidence, which had enabled her to concentrate on the rebellion from the summer of 1775 onwards.[10] This had been underlined when the ambassador in Paris, Stormont, was allowed to remain on leave when news came in of the first clashes in America.[11] When the King's Speech at the close of the parliamentary session (23 May 1776) announced the ministry's conviction that peace would continue in Europe, this confidence arose from France's pacific stance.[12]

Three new factors were beginning to complicate relations in 1775–6. One lay within domestic British politics: parliament's influence on diplomacy. Another had its origin in distant South America: the Luso-Spanish colonial confrontation and its wide-ranging repercussions. The third was a product of the revolt itself: the development of trade between the Americans and the Bourbon territories.

Parliament had always been a latent force in British foreign policy and had, at times, directly affected negotiations, notably in 1770–1 over the Falkland Islands. After 1775, it influenced relations with France. Ministers knew their actions would be closely scrutinized by their parliamentary opponents. In the winter of 1774–5, as the American crisis deepened, the government's critics had obliquely attacked its policy and preoccupation with the colonies by claiming it ignored French naval preparations and exposed the nation to a surprise French attack. The spectre of such a war was most

---

l'Amirauté britannique au temps de la guerre d'Amérique 1776–1783 (L'Espionnage naval au XVIIIᵉ siècle, i) (Paris, 1936).

[8] *St. Paul of Ewart*, ii. 38, 44–5, 45–7, 67, 78–80, 81–2, etc.; SP 84/548–51, *passim*.

[9] For the scare in Apr. 1775 caused by reports of naval preparations at Brest, see: *St. Paul of Ewart*, ii. 81–8; PRO 30/29/1/15, fos. 704–6, 708; and *Corr. Geo. III*, iii. 205–6; for that of early 1776 caused by erroneous reports of a fleet assembling at Toulon, which produced an immediate fall in the stocks, see: Walpole, *Last Journals*, i. 526; SP 78/298, fos. 41, 117.

[10] CP (Angleterre) 516, fos. 13–4; cf. North's view in Oct. 1775: *Corr. Geo III*, iii. 267.

[11] He had been absent since Mar., in order to avoid any disputes over diplomatic ceremonial at Louis XVI's coronation, and did not return until Oct., having been allowed to extend his leave because of illness: SP 78/295 *passim; St. Paul of Ewart*, ii. 249, 285, 301; CP (Angleterre) 511, fo. 73.

[12] *St. Paul of Ewart*, ii. 310; *Journal of the House of Commons*, xxxvi. 397.

effectively conjured up by the legendary Chatham, who for a time
early in 1775, re-emerged as a real force in the Lords, and his charge
was subsequently repeated and embellished by North's other
critics.[13] Ministers recognized the force of Burke's charge that he 'did
not choose to be caught by a foreign enemy at the end of this
exhausting conflict; and still less in the midst of it'.[14] The opposing
factions seized on this criticism, since it provided a means of
attacking the government and yet not appearing unpatriotic. For
several years the American War was extremely popular, both among
the political nation and among the public at large. This made it
difficult and dangerous for the opposition to criticize military
operations, especially in view of British successes in 1776.[15]

North's parliamentary position initially proved more secure than
anticipated. Only when Britain began to suffer defeats did his
majority come under any pressure. But ministers conducted relations
with the Bourbons with half an eye on possible parliamentary
criticism.[16] The consequences were, to some extent, contradictory. It
clearly kept the government up to the mark: by autumn 1776, the
timing of a naval reinforcement would be partly determined by the
new parliamentary session.[17] Yet parliament's concern indirectly
complicated Anglo-Bourbon diplomacy. French and Spanish diplomats in London sent back reports of debates, and their tone increased
fears of a preventive war.[18] Chatham's brief re-emergence revived
anxieties that he would be swept back to power, patch up a
settlement with the Americans, unite the nation, and secure his own
position, through a war with the Bourbons. These anxieties—which
were greatly exaggerated—also presented the British government
with a clear opening. Ministers skilfully exploited this fear to urge
moderate policies on France and Spain and in this way strengthen the
North Ministry, which was pacific and represented a barrier to the
dreaded war.

Britain's desire for peace in Europe, and her fear that this might
break down, were particularly apparent over the colonial confrontation between Spain and Portugal. This was viewed as a diplomatic
time bomb which could destroy British strategy in America. It also
came to be seen as an opportunity for London to demonstrate its
own pacifism and good faith. The quarrel arose from a complicated

[13] *Parl. Hist.* xviii, cols. 159, 207, 230–1, 251, 346, 442, etc.   [14] *Ibid.*, col. 491.
[15] P. D. G. Thomas, *Lord North* (London, 1976), 114–5; for the Rockinghams' predicament
in 1775–7, see O'Gorman, *Rise of Party*, 337–59.
[16] For Rochford's sensitivity to this, see E 6991, fo. 50.   [17] Cf. below, p. 239.
[18] e.g. Masserano to Grimaldi, 1 Aug. 1775, E 6991, fo. 2; ibid, fo. 23; cf. Doniol,
Participation, i. 60–2, 68, 84, for Vergennes's anxieties.

boundary dispute in South America.[19] Luso-Spanish rivalry for the no man's land between Portuguese Brazil and Spanish Rio de la Plata went back to the seventeenth century and reached its peak in the 1770s. During the brief Luso-Spanish War of 1762–3, Spain had made sweeping gains. After 1763, Madrid would not restore them, despite promising to do so in the Peace of Paris. This naturally produced tension, though Portugal's weakness ensured that she did not press Spain too hard on this issue in the following decade. By 1773, the boundary dispute had once again become a serious problem, as clashes in South America worsened relations in Europe.

Portugal's relative weakness meant that in any full-scale war with Spain she would come off worst. But her shrewd and unscrupulous leading minister, Pombal, played a weak hand with notable skill. While surreptitiously strengthening and expanding the Portuguese position in South America, he sought through pliant diplomacy to maintain peace with Spain in Europe. He aimed to provoke Madrid into open aggression. In Pombal's view, Lisbon's principal asset was the defensive alliance with Britain, included in the Methuen Treaties of 1703, and he believed Portugal was entitled to British aid should Spain attack. This could also be requested in terms of Britain's position as a guarantor of the Peace of Paris, which Madrid was infringing by its refusal to return the lands seized in 1762–3.

Britain denied any such obligation. Relations had been damaged by Pombal's protectionist commercial policies, though the enduring importance of Portugal's harbours to the British fleet, and the existing volume of trade, ensured these remained fairly harmonious. Britain resisted all Lisbon's pleas for aid and instead urged a negotiation primarily because she was preoccupied with America. By 1774–5, however, ministers were concerned not merely that colonial clashes would lead to war in Europe, but that Britain might be dragged into the struggle. This was not because of her formal treaty commitments to Portugal, which the cabinet decided could be ignored. However, ministers recognized that if France became involved, through the Family Compact, then it would be very difficult to ignore Pombal's pleas. In particular, they acknowledged Britain would have to fight if a Bourbon conquest of Portugal appeared likely.

[19] For this, see D. Alden, 'The Undeclared War of 1773–1777: Climax of Luso-Spanish Platine Rivalry', *Hispanic American Historical Review*, 41 (1961), 55–74, and the extended account in his *Royal Government in Colonial Brazil: With Special Reference to the Administration of the Marquis of Lavradio, Viceroy, 1769–1779* (Berkeley and Los Angeles, 1968), 59–278; see also Lalaguna Lasala, 'England, Spain and the Family Compact', 396–503 *passim*. The importance of this dispute and in particular its Anglo-Bourbon dimension for the diplomacy of the American War has not hitherto been fully recognized.

In 1774–5, Britain actively promoted a settlement. Ministers urged France to restrain Spain, while they themselves by turns cajoled and pleaded with Pombal to adopt more moderate policies. Their aims were defensive. They had no wish to be distracted from America and feared a wider conflict. The risk was acute when Britain began to match France's naval buildup in 1776–7 by commissioning more ships. The obvious danger was that Pombal would use these preparations as evidence of British support: as he, in fact, did. Ministers were, therefore, careful to emphasize to Madrid—and to Lisbon—that this was not so, and to make clear to Charles III that Britain would only aid Portugal if Spain invaded her Iberian neighbour. The mounting French pressure for Spanish intervention in the American War also made it imperative that Britain should not provoke Madrid by aiding the Portuguese. But if the dispute's dangers were evident, ministers recognized it also provided an opportunity to convince the Bourbons of Britain's pacifism. In this way, the cabinet's policy towards the Luso-Spanish confrontation reinforced its basic objective: preserving and consolidating peace in Europe.

This aim was threatened and eventually destroyed by the third new element in relations: the question of trade with the Americans. This was part of the larger problem of commerce and the existence of European colonies in the New World. Spain's empire was particularly large, sprawling across most of southern and central America and extending as far as the Mississippi—the frontier of the rebel colonies. The Spanish king also possessed Cuba, Hispaniola (Santo Domingo), and Puerto Rico, and these were all targets for American traders. Though some commerce did take place both in the New World and with metropolitan Spain, in the revolt's early stages it was not sufficient to alarm Britain.

Franco-American trade was considerably more important and caused more friction.[20] Already well established, it expanded rapidly after 1775. Though Britain's colonial commerce was legally reserved to British and North American ships, trading links had developed in defiance of these regulations. There was some direct trade with metropolitan France before the revolt, but the greater part was with French Caribbean colonies. Her major West Indian possessions were Saint Domingue (present-day Haiti), Martinique, and Guadeloupe,

[20] For this trade, see R. R. Crout, 'The Diplomacy of Trade: The Influence of Commercial Considerations on French Involvement in the Angloamerican War of Independence 1775–78' (unpublished Ph.D. thesis, University of Georgia, 1977), 22–32, 37–60, and 66–88; and the richly documented article by D. B. Goebel, 'The "New England Trade" and the French West Indies, 1763–1774: A Study in Trade Policies', *William and Mary Quarterly*, 3rd series, 20 (1963), 331–72.

and all had established trading links with British North America. In the 1770s these were being expanded and strengthened and they continued to grow after the revolt began, with the American search for munitions and trade. Commerce with France, usually through Dutch ports, also grew rapidly, since munitions were more readily available there. The Americans looked to her for support because she was Britain's established rival. Though this commerce was officially prohibited by the French ministry in 1775–6, such links were unofficially encouraged.

Britain was certainly aware of this trade, but her response was, at first, muted.[21] Indeed, in 1775–6, ministers tried to keep reports of Franco-American commerce secret, in sharp contrast to the glare of publicity directed on Dutch trade with the rebels. This had two purposes: the cabinet did not want to give credence to the claims of Chatham and his followers that France was secretly aiding the rebels, and was also anxious not to inflame relations with Versailles.[22] Mild diplomatic protests were made, but the matter was not pursued; in a similar way, British naval commanders were at first ordered not to detain French ships.[23]

In the revolt's early stages, ministers were walking a tightrope. They appreciated peace was essential and adopted a moderate stance in some minor disputes: as, for example, over the Newfoundland Fisheries in 1775.[24] They feared too evident weakness might encourage French aggression; firmness was believed to be the best way to uphold the peace, particularly when Louis XVI's navy was so weak. They therefore reminded France periodically of Britain's superiority at sea. In any case, they knew that French ministers were precisely informed about the British fleet through their spy-ring run from the embassy in London: remarkably enough, the cabinet was by now fully aware of this network.[25] Britain was also anxious not to push France into war and appreciated that her own considerable preparations for America might alarm the French government, which already feared a preventive strike. They were, therefore, careful to notify France of such preparations, and continually emphasized their pacifism to French diplomats in London, and to ministers at Versailles.

---

[21] *Cal. HO Papers 1773–5*, nos. 1045, 1253; *St. Paul of Ewart*, ii. 284, 292–3.

[22] Crout, 'Diplomacy of Trade', 70.

[23] Van Alstyne, *Empire and Independence*, 86; CP (Angleterre) 509, fos. 13–4.

[24] C. de la Morandière, *Histoire de la pêche française de la morue dans l'Amérique Septentrionale* (3 vols.; Paris, 1962–6), ii. 937–41.

[25] *HMC Dartmouth*, 367. The question arises, therefore, as to why the French agents were not rounded up. It may be that ministers were happy that their naval superiority should be fully known at Versailles, but I have been unable to discover any further information on this point.

A similar pattern was evident in Anglo-Spanish diplomacy, though here blandishments were more evident than threats. This was because ministers recognized it was less easy to intimidate Spain, since her fleet was in a better condition.[26] Britain's established policy of weakening the Family Compact was pursued for several years after 1775. Her hopes were apparent in the warm welcome given to the Spanish ambassador, Masserano, when he returned early in June.[27] The same strategy was evident in 1775 in the remarkable decision to spare Madrid embarrassment by not printing news of the Spanish disaster at Algiers in the official gazette.[28] Later that year, a minor dispute in the East Indies enabled Britain to give further evidence of her goodwill.[29] Madrid had been alarmed by the British East India Company's penetration into Balambangan (the eastern tip of Java), which seemed to threaten the Spanish trade monopoly with the Philippines. When Masserano raised this matter, Britain made concessions, and the dispute was settled amicably.[30]

London's wish for good relations was apparent in these exchanges and in the way ministers were careful to announce and explain naval preparations to Masserano.[31] Britain was aware rebel ships were entering the harbours of Old and New Spain, but as in the case of France, her representations were muted. Only when it became clear in October 1775 that the Americans were trying to buy munitions did ministers protest formally.[32] Spain's response was immediate and friendly. Orders were sent that such trade was to be prevented, and Britain accepted Madrid's good faith.[33] At this point, the interests of both states coincided. Britain's preoccupation with the American rebellion was matched by Spain's concern with the dispute with Portugal and with the Western Mediterranean.

Britain's desire for friendly relations with the Bourbons was clear when Rochford left office in November 1775.[34] North was anxious

---

[26] See Masserano's comments: E 6991, fo. 2.

[27] Masserano to Grimaldi, 2 June 1775, E 6990. Ministers had resorted to the transparent device of treating the returning ambassador very favourably at customs. They had earlier demonstrated their moderation in another round of the dispute over the right of British ships to enter Spanish ports: SP 94/198 *passim*. [28] E 6991, fo. 9.

[29] For the context, see V. T. Harlow, *The Founding of the Second British Empire 1763–1793* (2 vols.; London, 1952–64), i. 92–5. [30] E 6991, fos. 49–60.

[31] e.g. E 6990, fo. 22. This was, of course, essential because the ambassador would be aware of these preparations through the spy-ring run from the Bourbon embassies in London.

[32] *Cal. HO Papers 1773–5*, nos. 1074, 1191; Rochford to Grantham, 6 and 31 Oct. 1775, SP 94/199.

[33] Grimaldi to Masserano, 6 Nov. 1775, E 6991, fo. 53; cf. Grantham to Rochford, 2 and 9 Nov. 1775, SP 94/199.

[34] There are somewhat contradictory accounts of this cabinet reshuffle in B. D. Bargar, *Lord Dartmouth and the American Revolution* (Columbia, SC, 1965), 178–81; G. S. Brown, *The American Secretary: The Colonial Policy of Lord George Germain* (Ann Arbor, 1963),

to strengthen the ministry; there was widespread agreement that Lord George Germain should be brought into the cabinet; at the same time, the ambitious Northern Secretary, Suffolk, was attempting to increase his own power. The outcome was that Rochford, whose health had been poor, was prevailed upon to retire. The main reason was his bad relations with Suffolk.[35] In the early 1770s, the two men had co-operated closely, but their partnership had been weakened by Rochford's secret negotiations with France in 1772–3 and thereafter the Secretaries drifted apart.[36] This was a clash of personalities and of policies. Rochford disliked the ambitious Suffolk's growing influence and believed himself far more knowledgeable about foreign affairs.[37] The two men differed over America: Suffolk's renowned hard line contrasted sharply with Rochford's moderation and his willingness for a negotiated settlement.[38] They also clashed seriously over Suffolk's efforts to hire soldiers from Russia. Rochford subsequently claimed to have opposed this all along because Catherine II would never loan troops, and he certainly criticized the plan in cabinet.[39] By the autumn of 1775 he was isolated and willing to leave office.[40]

A leading candidate to replace him was Weymouth, Secretary of State from 1768 until 1770. His willingness for war over Port Egmont[41] had earned him the hostility of the Bourbons who, by contrast, now viewed Rochford as friendly and pacific.[42] This belligerent reputation made his reappearance in charge of relations with the Bourbon powers a difficult matter: as George III discreetly phrased it, 'Lord Weymouth and the Court of Spain cannot

31–2; O'Gorman, *Rise of Party*, 605 n. 10; and Thomas, *Lord North*, 88–9; the principal sources for these accounts are *Corr. Geo. III*, iii. 277–87, and *HMC Knox*, 256–7. French and Spanish diplomatic correspondence adds some further light and, in particular, reveals the considerable tension which existed between the two senior secretaries and suggest Suffolk's ambition extended to wanting to remove Rochford from office.

[35] E 6991, fo. 58.

[36] For one indication of this alienation, see Add. MSS 34412, fo. 290.

[37] With characteristic indiscretion, he made this claim to the French ambassador: CP (Angleterre) 511, fo. 100. Interestingly enough, Masserano agreed: E 6991, fo. 2. The occasion of this outburst was a minor *faux pas* committed by the British chargé d'affaires in Paris, over which Suffolk and Rochford clashed seriously.

[38] CP (Angleterre) 511, fo. 263; I. D. Gruber, *The Howe Brothers and the American Revolution* (Chapel Hill, NC, 1972), 36–7.

[39] Doniol, *Participation*, i. 192; E 6991, fo. 58. For the Anglo-Russian negotiations, see below, pp. 217–20.

[40] Doniol, *Participation*, i. 59; cf. CP (Angleterre) 511, fo. 18.

[41] Cf. above, Ch. 6. Weymouth had not been consistent in his antipathy towards the Bourbons (he had, notably, opposed war over Corsica in 1768: see above, Ch. 5) and he was equally unpredictable after 1775.

[42] See, e.g. E 6991, fo. 56: interestingly enough, the Spanish ambassador wheeled out the old charge of stockjobbing against Weymouth; cf. Doniol, *Participation*, i. 228–9, 238.

pleasantly transact business'.[43] This was why the King and North tried to make him Lord Privy Seal, with the American Secretary, Dartmouth, switching to the Southern Department. Their plans were wrecked by Dartmouth, who insisted on becoming Lord Privy Seal, and on 10 November Weymouth was appointed Southern Secretary.

Considerable efforts were made to reassure France and Spain that this did not signal any change in policy. These assurances, together with Weymouth's actual behaviour, ensured no serious damage was done. The new Southern Secretary's conduct was initially muted. The French ambassador was soon noting that the change had made little or no difference and Weymouth was not as hostile as he anticipated.[44]

One way by which diplomacy had immediately become involved in the American war was the attempt to find an army to defeat the insurgents. Britain's military establishment was, by continental standards, very small. Since the close of the seventeenth century, the emergency of a foreign war had been met either by securing European allies to fight England's enemies, or by hiring continental mercenaries. The first alternative was now impracticable, since the war was in America. By summer 1775, Britain's need for soldiers was very urgent.[45] In June and July, the cabinet had agreed to send 20,000 men to the colonies by the following spring.[46] Britain's own establishment was already over-stretched and could not provide all these troops. Reinforcements were soon dispatched from Ireland, and the King's Electoral army provided five regiments, to free the Gibraltar and Minorca garrisons for service in America. These measures, together with further recruitment within the British Isles, only nibbled at the problem, and the solution was thought to be troops from abroad.

The army for America was first sought in Russia. This is superficially rather surprising. Britain had usually recruited in Germany, either Hanoverians from the King's Electorate or mercenaries from the smaller German states. During the War of the Austrian Succession, and again in autumn 1755, ministers had envisaged hiring Russian troops, but for service in Europe. Both attempts had ultimately been unsuccessful, but they had demonstrated London's belief that Russia could supply soldiers. Although relations were now cooler than at any time since 1763, this did not deter

[43] *Corr. Geo. III*, iii. 283; cf. ibid., 281.
[44] CP (Angleterre) 513 *passim.* Masserano noted with some surprise that Weymouth had been 'affable and courteous' during their first interview: E 6991, fo. 60.
[45] Mackesy, *War for America*, 2–4, 39–40, 61–2; cf. Stevens, *Facsimiles*, no. 455.
[46] B. Donoughue, *British Politics and the American Revolution: The Path to War 1773–75* (London, 1964), 277.

Britain from a heavy-handed attempt to hire 20,000 Russians for service in America during the second half of 1775. This was the brainchild of Suffolk, who wanted prompt and vigorous military action against the rebels.[47] When the idea was first mooted, he had written ironically that these soldiers 'will be charming visitors at New York and civilize that part of America wonderfully'.[48] The Russian army had only recently suppressed the serious and large-scale Pugachev rising, and the Northern Secretary appears to have viewed the mutinous Bostonians as an American version of the Cossacks. The attractions were obvious. It would solve Britain's recruiting problems at a stroke, since the number sought from Russia was identical to that promised for North America, while Russian contingents might be expected to have fewer scruples than British troops, who could be restrained by a belief they were fighting fellow subjects.

Suffolk recognized that the coolness in relations since 1772–3 might hinder a subsidy treaty and therefore wrote privately to his protégé, Gunning, in St Petersburg, instructing him to probe Russia's attitude.[49] Unfortunately, the inexperienced and inadequate Gunning mishandled this approach twice over. Instead of briefly sounding Panin, he laid siege to the Russian minister, going to see him almost every day for a week.[50] This clearly indicated British hopes and enabled Russia to prepare her reply. Secondly, Gunning totally misinterpreted St Petersburg's response. Russia was still well disposed towards Britain; the recent coolness was largely on London's side.[51] Catherine II, and to a lesser extent her leading minister, hoped the colonial rebellion would soon be suppressed, though both already feared Britain might eventually lose America.[52] But they were unwilling to provide Russian troops, and Panin politely rebuffed Gunning's approach. The British envoy, however, became convinced that the Empress would actually provide soldiers.[53]

[47] These negotiations can be followed in Egerton 2703 and in SP 91/98–9; relevant documents are printed in *Sbornik*, xix. 463–505, and in Doniol, *Participation*, i. 210–29. The account in N. N. Bolkhovitinov, *Russia and the American Revolution* (Eng. trans., Tallahassee, Fla., 1976), 6–12 is useful, but incomplete and in places misleading.
[48] To William Eden, 20 June 1775, Stevens, *Facsimiles*, no. 851.
[49] Egerton 2703, fos. 257–8.   [50] CP (Russie) 98, fo. 408.
[51] Both in 1773 and in 1774, Catherine II had written apropos of Russo-British relations that 'our political views and interests are very closely interrelated, and lead by one path to the same goal': quoted by D. M. Griffiths 'Catherine the Great, the British Opposition and the American Revolution', in L. S. Kaplan, ed., *The American Revolution and 'A Candid World'* (Kent, Oh, 1977), 90; cf. *Sbornik*, cxxxv. 235.
[52] Ibid. xxvii. 44; CP (Russie) 98, fo. 398.
[53] Gunning's reply does not appear to have survived, but its optimism is apparent from Suffolk's letter of 1 Sept. 1775: Egerton 2703, fo. 279.

His enthusiasm and optimism in turn persuaded Suffolk Russia would send troops.[54]

The British cabinet immediately approved formal negotiations. Suffolk deceived his colleagues by disguising his own initiative, instead pretending that the Empress was offering troops.[55] When Gunning's initial reply arrived, ministers were summoned back from the country for a special cabinet meeting.[56] A courier was soon on his way to St Petersburg with several treaty projects and Catherine II was invited, in effect, to name her price. The remarkable urgency, and Britain's unique flexibility, made clear her predicament by autumn 1775. Ministers were determined a formal agreement should be concluded immediately. They hoped to use a Russian treaty to deflect the anticipated opposition onslaught when parliament reassembled on 24 October.[57] They were soon disappointed.[58] When Gunning submitted a formal request, he received an immediate and outright rejection: once again, several meetings were necessary before he would admit defeat.[59] By the beginning of November, failure was apparent.[60]

The episode did nothing to improve relations, which remained cool and distant for several years to come. This initiative also demonstrated how the greater political realism of the early 1770s might be an early casualty of the American War. Britain's initiative could be justified in terms of military necessity and political expediency, but it ignored a decade's diplomacy, which had made clear Catherine II was determined to be treated as a political equal by all the great powers. Instead, Suffolk presented her with an old-style troop-hiring treaty in the spirit of the Duke of Newcastle.[61] This

[54] This is particularly apparent from SP 91/99, fo. 72 (where the *command* of Russian contingents in America is discussed) and from *Documents of the American Revolution*, xi, no. 100.

[55] This allegation was subsequently made by Rochford to the French ambassador: Doniol, *Participation*, i. 192. It would seem to be confirmed by the unusual speed with which draft treaties were sent to Gunning and by George III's private letter to Catherine II written on 1 Sept. (Martens, *Recueil des traités*. ix (x). 288.) By Mid-Sept. moreover, it was rumoured in London that Russia had offered an alliance and the loan of ships as well as the 20,000 troops: E 6991, fo. 23.   [56] Ibid., fo. 23.

[57] SP 91/99, fo. 72. In the event, the new session was put back for 2 days by ministers who hoped for a final answer before it began: Walpole, *Last Journals*, i. 482–3 n. 1; HMC *Stopford–Sackville*, ii. 12.

[58] The cooler tone of Gunning's subsequent letters led the government to fear failure. By the beginning of Oct., it was rumoured that at most 5,000 troops would be secured and the whole negotiation might collapse (*Burke Corr.* iii. 225) and by the middle of the month, ministers expected a rejection: *Corr. Geo. III*, iii. 268.

[59] CP (Russie) 98, fo. 501.   [60] *Corr. Geo. III*, iii. 276.

[61] Though he tried to protect Russian sensibilities by proposing Britain should pay the expenses of Catherine's troops: Madariaga, *Armed Neutrality*, 9.

implied—perhaps correctly—that British ministers still saw her as a glorified German *Landgräfin* and Russia as a mercenary recruitment agency. The Empress resented the way her political sensibilities were trampled underfoot. This was why the British approach was rejected outright. It says much for Catherine's enduring friendship for England that the whole episode, and how it was mishandled by London, did not cause a formal breach in relations.

The unsuccessful attempt to secure Russian troops was an isolated example of active diplomacy towards the eastern powers. During the first half of the American War, ministers neglected this region, as they had done since the early 1770s, and instead concentrated on western Europe. The renewed concern with the Bourbon threat in 1775–6 was part of this broader reorientation. Foreign policy now focused on the maritime states along Europe's western periphery. Many of these states had their own colonies in the New World and this was one obvious reason for their importance after 1775.

This preoccupation with the maritime states was principally because of Britain's campaign against rebel trade, especially in munitions. During 1775, all commerce with the North American colonies was prohibited. Realizing that the Americans' financial position was weak, Britain tried to undermine it even further by a wider attack on all rebel trade, particularly after April 1776 when Congress opened its ports to the ships of all nations. This primitive economic warfare aimed to close Europe's ports, and, more importantly, European colonial harbours in the West Indies, to American shipping. It involved Britain's relations with six continental states: Denmark, Sweden, the Dutch Republic, and Portugal, as well as Spain and France. All had ports on, or near, the Atlantic seaboard, and all except Sweden had their own New World colonies: for this reason they were, in different degrees, American targets. In each case, Britain's relations with these states, after the war spread to Europe in 1778, came to be influenced by the initial discussions over trade with the insurgents.

The campaign was pursued by direct naval action. The British fleet blockaded the major areas in rebellion and intercepted American shipping on the high seas. Success was always incomplete. The length of the coastline to be blockaded and the Admiralty's refusal to weaken the Channel fleet, because of its fear of the Bourbons, ensured there were considerable limitations on British naval operations against the Americans in 1775–8.[62] Accurate intelligence of

[62] D. Syrett, 'Defeat at Sea: The Impact of American Naval Operations upon the British, 1775–1778', *Maritime Dimensions of the American Revolution* (Naval History Division, Department of the Navy; Washington, 1977), 14–5.

rebel shipping could, to some extent, assist these efforts and, after 1775, British diplomats, and especially consuls, were expected to provide information about commerce with America.[63]

Britain's aims were, at first, very limited. She sought only to secure the formal prohibition of trade, particularly in munitions. The campaign against American commerce in 1775–8 was intrinsically different from the severe problems which emerged after France's formal entry into the war. Until 1778, Britain largely respected other European shipping and concentrated the fleet against American or even British vessels trading on behalf of the insurgents.[64] Occasionally, merchant ships from continental states were seized by the British navy, or by privateers operating out of British ports, but though their cargoes might be confiscated, the vessels themselves were usually released quite quickly and compensation sometimes paid. The volume of European trade with America was initially quite small and this, together with Britain's acceptance that a total economic blockade was impossible, ensured that, until 1778, commercial questions produced little serious tension, except with the Dutch.[65]

Most European governments proved surprisingly co-operative. Though there was some public sympathy and even support for the American cause, the insurgents had few friends in official circles. Most rulers and their ministers disliked rebellion as such, and many also doubted if American resistance would last long. Britain might be temporarily embarrassed, but her vastly superior resources appeared to guarantee eventual victory. One further reason for the widespread reluctance to aid the Americans openly was that the legal position over trade was uncertain. Britain's view was that, in fact and in law, the rebellion was her own domestic concern, and it was difficult to challenge this stance.[66] It was not clear, even after the Declaration of Independence, that the former colonies were a sovereign state rather than unusually successful rebels. The theory of neutral trade was based on two or more independent states being at war and, until the summer of 1778, there was considerable doubt as to whether this was the case.

Britain, at first, achieved considerable success in closing Portuguese, Swedish, and Danish ports to American traders, but this must be set

---

[63] Britain was surprisingly well informed about American activities in Europe: Van Alstyne, 'Great Britain, the War for Independence', 311–46, *passim*.

[64] According to one contemporary estimate, only some 59 ships belonging to other European states were captured in the entire period up to Sept. 1778: F. C. Spooner, *Risks at Sea: Amsterdam Insurance and Maritime Europe 1766–1780* (Cambridge, 1983), 104.

[65] C. L. Roslund-Mercurio, 'The American Colonial Rebellion and Swedish-British Diplomacy, 1775–1778', [Swedish] *Historisk tidskrift*, 94 (1974), 475–89, at p. 480.

[66] See Suffolk's emphatic assertion of this: to Yorke, 30 July 1776, SP 84/553.

against a corresponding failure in the all-important case of the Dutch Republic.[67] Portugal proved unusually co-operative. Pombal wanted Britain's support in the dispute with Spain over colonial boundaries. Portugal was therefore first to prohibit trade, and in July 1776 closed all her ports to American shipping. Only after Pombal's fall in 1777 did Lisbon abandon this pro-English stance for a more even-handed neutrality.[68] Sweden's attitude was equally favourable because of Gustav III's hostility towards the Americans.[69] Until 1778, British diplomacy achieved its limited aims at Stockholm. Rigorous measures were taken, and usually enforced, though unarmed colonial vessels could trade in non-military goods, particularly at the new free port of Marstrand.[70] When, in 1777, the privateering war against British commerce assumed serious proportions, Gustav III prohibited American cruisers from entering Swedish harbours.

Relations with the other Scandinavian state, Denmark, were less harmonious, though once again Britain enjoyed significant co-operation.[71] Anglo-Danish diplomacy was complicated by a legacy of bitterness from the confrontation over Caroline Mathilda and also by the fact that Denmark had three colonies in the New World: St Thomas, St Croix, and St John. Before long, American ships were calling at these West Indian islands, and some Danish merchants seized the commercial opportunities offered by their search for trade and munitions. But the Danish government, anxious for good relations with London and mindful of its experiences in previous wars when its trade had suffered from British reprisals, was determined to avoid any similar confrontation with Britain's 'tyrannical empire of the seas'.[72] In autumn 1775, Denmark prohibited the export of military stores to her own colonies, to prevent them being re-exported to the rebels, and would not relax the existing mercantilist regulations which hindered any rapid expansion of trade. Britain was equally anxious to avoid provocative action,

---

[67] See below, pp. 223–33.

[68] Van Alstyne, 'Great Britain, the War for Independence', 317; C. R. Boxer, *The Portuguese Seaborne Empire, 1425–1815* (London, 1969), 196.

[69] There is a good study by C. L. Roslund-Mercurio. 'The Problem of Neutral Rights in Swedish Relations with Great Britain, 1775–1780' (unpublished Ph.D. thesis, Syracuse University, 1972), 29–95; this is effectively summarized in 'The American Colonial Rebellion', 475–82.

[70] This lay to the north of Gothenburg and opened in Jan. 1776; its creation was part of Gustav III's efforts to develop the Swedish economy.

[71] For a good general discussion, see O. Feldbaek, 'Eighteenth-Century Danish Neutrality: Its Diplomacy, Economics and Law', *Scandinavian Journal of History*, 8 (1983), 3–21; cf. id., *Dansk neutralitetspolitik under krigen 1778–1783* (Copenhagen, 1971), English Summary, 150.

[72] The phrase was A. P. von Bernstorff's: *Bernstorffsche Papiere*, iii. 541–2.

and was grateful for this co-operation. Some Danish vessels did trade with the enemy, and a few of these were seized by the British fleet, but they were released quite quickly and compensation sometimes paid to the Danish owners.[73] Such incidents, which revived memories of the Seven Years War, aroused resentment in Copenhagen, but there was little serious tension before the fighting spread to Europe.

Britain's new problems and changed priorities were most apparent in Anglo-Dutch relations. Since the mid-eighteenth century, ministers had largely ignored the Republic, but after 1775 it returned to the forefront of Britain's diplomacy. This came about principally because the Americans viewed the Dutch as the most promising source of munitions, especially gunpowder, and the best outlet for their own products. Britain's war against rebel trade also came to be a war against the Republic's commerce and this worsened relations. The American conflict inevitably revived unresolved disputes over neutral rights, and reawakened Dutch resentment at Britain's arrogant use of her naval might. Relations were also complicated by the ambiguous legacy of previous co-operation and by the Republic's distinctive constitution and complex domestic politics.

The Dutch Republic lived by trade and its merchants intended to exploit the commercial opportunities created by the revolt.[74] The towns of Holland, in particular, hoped that they would dominate the trade of an independent America. There was also some sympathy for the American cause, which to many resembled the Dutch struggle against Spain two centuries before. The Republic's merchants, and even its government, appreciated the new situation created by the revolt and adjusted their attitudes accordingly. In sharp contrast, British policy continued to be strongly influenced by past events and by an insular view of previous relations.[75] This blend of old assumptions and new opportunities proved an unstable and eventually explosive mixture during the American War.

For two generations after 1688, Britain had viewed the Republic as a natural friend and ally, one of the pillars of the Old System. In the

---

[73] For one such case, ibid. iii. 442, 445, 483. According to one contemporary estimate, only 8 Danish ships were taken in the period up to Sept. 1778: Spooner, *Risks at Sea*, 104.

[74] General accounts are provided by: J. W. Schulte Nordholt, *The Dutch Republic and American Independence* (1979; Eng. trans., Chapel Hill, NC, 1982); F. Edler, *The Dutch Republic and the American Revolution* (Baltimore, Md., 1911); F.-P. Renaut, *De la neutralité à la belligérance (1775–1780)* (Paris, 1924; vol. i. of *Les Provinces Uniés et la Guerre d'Amérique*); and S. Schama, *Patriots and Liberators: Revolution in the Netherlands 1780–1813* (London, 1977), chs. 2–3.

[75] For a particularly striking example, see Suffolk's remarks about the Barrier in the Southern Netherlands: to Yorke, 30 May 1775, SP 84/546.

1770s, the two states remained technically united by a treaty concluded a century before. The defensive alliance of 1678 had never been abrogated and its terms and applicability were debated during the American War; parallel discussions took place over the commercial treaty signed in 1674. The alliance had for long involved merely paper obligations and it exerted little direct influence on relations after 1775. Nevertheless, there was still a strong sense of community in Anglo-Dutch diplomacy and an awareness of the partnership's previous history. For a time, the two countries had actually been united in the person of the Stadtholder-King, William III, and they had fought together in the wars of 1689–1713. But the Republic had spent its power in the struggle against Louis XIV; after the Peace of Utrecht, it was never again the same political or commercial force as during its seventeenth-century Golden Age. In the eighteenth century, its slowly fading prosperity had come to depend principally on investment and finance, rather than on commercial enterprise. There had been a corresponding adjustment of Dutch foreign policy, which became explicitly neutralist. In the Seven Years War, for the first time in a European conflict, the Republic had formally declared itself neutral, and the maintenance of this position was its overriding aim after 1775.

In the mid-1770s, the Dutch government was less concerned with its international position than with domestic tensions. The Republic's unique constitutional structure, as a federation of seven sovereign provinces, created problems both for foreign diplomats and for the Stadtholder and his ministers. The need to consult not only the States-General, but also the States (representative assemblies) of all seven provinces, caused frequent and irritating delays and also provided scope for procrastination and opposition. Dutch internal politics were dominated by the struggle between the landward and the maritime provinces, and there had recently been another indecisive round in the contest over the Augmentation. The landward provinces urged the augmentation of the army, while the latter (and especially the principal province, Holland) demanded a stronger fleet to protect trade.

The Republic made little attempt to break out of the lethargy which had overtaken its foreign policy, and all initiative in relations now came from London. Since the 1750s, Britain had discounted it as a political force. Two decades later, ministers recognized the 'comparative weakness and insignificancy of the Republic' and believed this 'more likely to increase than diminish'.[76] They still

---

[76] Suffolk to Yorke, Private, 12 July 1774, SP 84/543.

assumed, however, that the Dutch were irrevocably yoked to Britain by family ties and by past history, and therefore viewed the Republic as a client and political dependant. They believed it would continue to do their bidding, particularly when ruled by the House of Orange, as it had been since 1747. The Republic's eighteenth-century neutrality had often been mildly pro-English in tone. By the 1770s, however, the traditional assumption that an Orangist regime would automatically be friendly towards Britain was coming into question.

William V had nominally been Stadtholder since 1751. His youth had, at first, made a regency essential and he had only assumed full authority in 1766, at the age of eighteen. William was weak and irresolute, and always strongly influenced by those around him. A well-meaning nonentity, 'my booby of a nephew' was Frederick the Great's damning verdict.[77] Considerable influence was wielded by three men: the venerable *Griffier* Heindrik Fagel, the Secretary of the States-General, and as a permanent official the man responsible for day-to-day foreign policy; the Grand Pensionary Pieter van Bleiswijk, first minister of the leading province, Holland, and *de facto* prime minister of the Republic; and Duke Louis Ernest of Brunswick, William V's old tutor and the Republic's Field Marshal. Fagel was resolutely pro-English, while Brunswick was broadly so, but also independent-minded, seeing the real dangers of any slavish dependence on London. The prudent and tactically shrewd van Bleiswijk was a trimmer who appreciated Holland's hostility towards Britain, and whose influence partly neutralized Fagel's Anglophile sentiments.[78] The Stadtholder was also pro-English, but his support was a dubious political asset. His wife, Wilhelmina, was more formidable, as befitted Frederick the Great's niece, and she exerted considerable influence on her husband. She believed that the Republic should look eastwards towards Prussia rather than remain tied to its traditional British alliance. George III, though not his British ministers, had tried unsuccessfully to prevent her marriage to the Stadtholder, and instead to marry him to the usual English princess. The Prussian marriage had weakened Britain's influence, though it was the mid-1770s before this became apparent. Relations had also been damaged by increasingly serious rivalry overseas. After the Seven Years War, Britain's dynamic empire pressed in on its gouty Dutch counterpart. The two countries were not simply competitors but often neighbours as well. By the eve of the American revolt, Britain's attempts to create a trading empire in the Far East were inflaming diplomacy in Europe.

[77] Quoted by A. Cobban, *Ambassadors and Secret Agents* (London, 1954), 22.
[78] *Dépêches van Thulemeyer*, 129: Renaut, *De la neutralité à la belligérance*, 51.

The Dutch seaborne empire, with outposts in Sumatra, Java, and the Moluccas, lay across the path of Britain's *Drang nach Osten*. Attempts in the 1770s to establish British factories in Borneo caused most tension: the neighbouring Malay archipelago was the heartland of Dutch economic power in the Far East. After the delay imposed by the distances involved, this friction transferred itself to diplomacy in Europe. Relations were further soured in 1773–4 by confrontations in West Africa and between the British East India Company and its Dutch counterpart, the Vereenigde Oost-Indische Compagnie (VOC), in India.[79]

These clashes were not serious in themselves and could have been resolved by diplomacy. But they were symptomatic of the deterioration in relations. Distant friendship was giving way to coolness, even before the American War created its own very considerable problems. These disputes assumed particular importance in Dutch domestic politics. The traditional opponents of the House of Orange and of Britain, as well, were the Regents: the party of the merchants and of the towns, above all Amsterdam. British encroachments on Dutch commerce and territory were especially resented by the mercantile sectors of the Republic. Even before the American revolt, anti-British sentiment was on the increase, particularly in Holland.

Anglo-Dutch diplomacy and the Republic's domestic politics were therefore intertwined. All these threads passed through the hands of Sir Joseph Yorke, Britain's representative at The Hague since 1751.[80] The ambassador was a man of rigid political outlook, little charm, and few social graces. He was a proud Hardwicke, and this impeccable Whig pedigree made him a staunch partisan of the Old System. Though he recognized the Republic's economic and political decline, he continued to view it as Britain's natural friend, and his views carried weight in London. Long residence at The Hague gave him enormous experience and knowledge of the Republic; yet his understanding of its politics could seem very superficial, and his judgements were often routine and inflexible. Above all, his personality was ill-suited to his post, and probably to a diplomatic career at all.[81] Yorke's habit of lecturing Dutch ministers and even

---

[79] *Cal. HO Papers 1773–5*, nos. 73, 114, 157, 285; SP 84/543 and 546, *passim*.

[80] A good study of Yorke and Anglo-Dutch relations, particularly during the American War, is urgently needed. The only existing account is D. A. Miller, *Sir Joseph Yorke and Anglo-Dutch Relations 1774–1780* (The Hague, 1970), but this is a mere sketch; based exclusively on printed material and on transcripts and facsimiles found in the USA, it provides a basic narrative, but is superficial and occasionally naïve and also contains some significant errors.

[81] The Prussian agent was predictably (and perhaps unfairly) disparaging: *Dépêches van Thulemeyer*, 56, 61, 130. R. Pares, who studied Yorke's conduct during the Seven Years War,

the Stadtholder himself was widely resented. His relations with the influential Brunswick had been soured by the Prussian marriage in 1767, which the ambassador, on George III's private instructions, had tried to prevent. The prince supported it, and never forgave him for his opposition. Dutch statesmen found Yorke proud, quick-tempered, prone to conduct official business through demands and threats rather than negotiation and compromise.[82] Yet if he was seen in the Republic as the personification of Britain's overbearing attitude, he was at the same time suspected in London of being 'too much a Dutchman'![83]

The Republic's importance had been signalled even before the rebellion began. The Americans looked towards their established contacts in the Netherlands and in the Dutch West Indian Islands for munitions. Dutch merchants were willing to supply powder, and in the second half of 1774 Yorke began to report this was being loaded on to American vessels at Amsterdam. When it became clear in October that cannons were to be supplied as well, Britain responded vigorously. A naval vessel was immediately sent to Dutch waters, and for the next six months it remained at the Texel (at the entrance to the Zuider Zee) ready to intercept any American ship trying to leave. In November, it forced a colonial vessel back into port, and it subsequently 'looked in' to Amsterdam itself, a visit which brought Dutch protests. At the same time, Yorke demanded the authorities should arrest the American ships.[84]

The Stadtholder and his ministers were sympathetic to this request. Since the colonists were still British subjects, any trade in munitions was probably illegal and certainly difficult to justify; it might, in particular, imperil the Republic's neutrality. British ministers initially declared themselves satisfied by the Dutch response and waited expectantly for decisive action. However, the Republic's federal structure made this slow and difficult, since individual provincial States had to consent. Relations between The Hague and Amsterdam had been inflamed by the Augmentation and Dutch ministers were anxious to conciliate Holland's leading town. After some delay, and

came to a similar conclusion: *Colonial Blockade and Neutral Rights 1739–1763* (Oxford, 1938), 246; cf. Renaut, *De la neutralité à la belligérance*, 152–3, and Edler, *Dutch Republic*, 14.

[82] *Archives . . . Orange-Nassau*, 5th series, i. 287; *Dépêches van Thulemeyer*, 103, 107; Schulte Nordholt, *Dutch Republic*, 21.
[83] Suffolk to [William Eden], (?July 1775), Stevens, *Facsimiles*, no. 455. Yorke was here suffering the fate of all British diplomats who resided at one particular post for a long period.
[84] SP 84/543, *passim*; *Cal. HO Papers 1773–5*, nos. 717, 732, 752; *Corr. Geo. III*, iii. 146–7.

with the arrival of three more American ships, the Republic finally prohibited munitions exports to America for six months in March 1775.[85]

Britain was apparently satisfied, yet the episode was also a portent of the likely difficulties. It indicated the Republic's problems in reconciling a neutral foreign policy with the new commercial opportunities. Britain's vigorous diplomacy in 1774–5 set the tone for the years ahead. Though ministers had professed moderation and their anxiety not to interfere with Dutch trade or to infringe the Republic's sovereignty, they had unhesitatingly used naval power to enforce their demands. Yorke had served at The Hague during the Seven Years War and his earlier experiences made him favour direct and vigorous measures from the outset.[86] He believed the Republic would be moved by action, not by mere words, and his discussions with Dutch ministers already contained an element of menace. The ambassador was continually urging exemplary action against American vessels on the high seas, believing that this 'would do more than fifty memorials' to discourage the Dutch from trading with the colonists.[87] Amsterdam's pre-eminence in American trade, and its role as leader of the opposition to Britain, became apparent in 1774–5. So, too, did the difficulties of enforcing the formal prohibition on the export of munitions, particularly in the towns of Holland. The weakness of Dutch central government was certainly becoming clear. These early exchanges, however, principally appeared to confirm both the established pattern of relations and Britain's traditional leadership. It was to be the first winter of the war before London's cherished belief in the Republic's client status was to be weakened by the affair of the Scots Brigade.

In autumn 1775, before Russia's formal refusal to supply troops was known in London, Britain had asked for the loan of the legendary Scots Brigade. This had been established in the second half of the sixteenth century during the Dutch revolt against Spain. From the beginning, it had consisted of Scottish volunteers and officers. During the Seven Years War, however, these links had been weakened when the British government, with its own manpower problems, had suspended the Brigade's traditional recruiting in Scotland. Though temporarily restored in 1764, it was again

[85] See Yorke's dispatches in the winter of 1774–5: SP 84/546, *passim*. Only at the end of Mar. did Britain withdraw her naval vessel from the Texel.

[86] For some account of his experiences, see Pares, *Colonial Blockade and Neutral Rights*, esp. pp. 242–79.

[87] Yorke to William Eden, 13 Jan. 1775, and Yorke to Suffolk, 14 Feb. 1775, both in SP 84/546; *Dépêches van Thulemeyer*, 138.

suspended the next year and this was confirmed in 1772–3.[88] This was an attempt to protect Britain's own recruitment in Scotland, where potential soldiers were in short supply. These developments inevitably diluted the national composition, and by the 1770s, the Scots Brigade consisted largely of foreign mercenaries who enjoyed a notably unmilitary existence in the sleepy Barrier towns of the Austrian Netherlands. Nominally 6,000 strong, it had fallen far below this establishment: one contemporary put its strength at around 1,800 and even Yorke believed there were fewer than 2,200 soldiers.[89] By autumn 1775, however, ministers recognized Britain's desperate need for troops. Though as recently as July the Brigade had been discounted, it was now central to British recruiting.[90] The Republic had twice refused to compromise its neutrality in the Seven Years War by allowing these troops to be taken into British pay, and it was no more co-operative in 1775–6.

At the very beginning of September, Suffolk raised the matter of its loan with Yorke.[91] This could not be demanded under the 1678 treaty, which applied only to Europe and excluded civil wars, and it was therefore requested in terms of Anglo-Dutch friendship. The Northern Secretary also held out the bait of renewed recruiting in Scotland. Initially, Yorke had considerable doubts. He recognized its limited military value, though he conceded it might be a useful stopgap. His first contacts with Dutch ministers, however, suggested the Republic could be persuaded to agree. At this point, Yorke believed the Brigade was to be stationed within the British Isles to free other units for service in America.

This encouraged Suffolk to make a formal approach on 10 October 1775. However, he now dropped his bombshell: the Brigade was to be sent to America. This placed Yorke in an impossible position, for he had assured the Republic's leaders of the opposite. This was an insuperable obstacle in the months ahead, but Britain's recruiting problems now demanded that any available troops be seized, particularly as it was now clear that Russian soldiers would not be available. Even though only 1,000 or so of its actual strength were fit for service, Britain continued to press for the loan of this meagre force from October 1775 until February 1776.

---

[88] *Papers Illustrating the History of the Scots Brigade in the Service of the United Netherlands 1572–1782*, ed. J. Ferguson (3 vols.; Scottish History Society, Edinburgh, 1899–1901), ii. 394; *Cal. HO Papers 1760–5*, nos. 1259, 1291, 1298; Spencer, *Sandwich Corr.* 83–4; Suffolk to Yorke, Private, 1 Sept. 1775, SP 84/547.

[89] *Dépêches van Thulemeyer*, 153; Yorke to Suffolk, Private, 5 Sept. 1775, SP 84/547.

[90] Suffolk to [?William Eden], (July 1775), Stevens, *Facsimiles*, no. 455.

[91] The negotiations can be followed in SP 84/547 and 552 *passim*, and in *Archives . . . Orange-Nassau*, 5th series, i. 407 ff.

The request was delayed by the cumbersome Dutch political system and finally defeated by the emergence of significant opposition. The refusal of the Brigade was viewed as reaffirming the Republic's strict neutrality, compromised by the seemingly pro-English stance over the earlier prohibition of munitions exports. William V, Fagel, and even van Bleiswijk initially believed Britain's request would have to be granted. But Brunswick, the Republic's Field Marshal and still a significant influence on the Stadtholder, was considerably more cautious.[92] He feared the loss of even these dubious soldiers in its precarious military position, and he was alarmed that Britain might be trying to compromise the Republic's cherished neutrality. This fear was widespread. The Brigade's release could be seen as a commitment to Britain's cause and was, therefore, opposed. Brunswick's reservations were influential, and they were soon supported by van Bleiswijk, who changed his views with characteristic ease when he appreciated the extent of public hostility. The matter dragged on through the winter of 1775–6. Holland's opposition resulted in an eventual decision to offer the Scots regiments on terms that amounted to a refusal. Thereafter, the question was allowed to drop, in part because of the success of British recruitment in Germany.[93] This episode made clear that Britain could not depend totally on the Dutch, and was a significant stage in relations.[94] It also revealed to Yorke, and less clearly to ministers in London, that the Republic's political structure could be exploited by England's enemies.

Problems were also emerging over Dutch trade with the Americans. The Republic's merchants soon came to dominate this commerce, since it was the principal source of munitions, and other products were re-exported through its ports.[95] Dutch West Indian islands were an obvious target for rebel ships, particularly when direct voyages between Europe and America became more difficult in 1776 and 1777 with the extension of the conflict and Britain's effective naval action. The turning-point in Anglo-Dutch diplomacy, as in

[92] For his views, see ibid., i. 409–17.

[93] R. Atwood, *The Hessians: Mercenaries from Hessen-Kassel in the American Revolution* (Cambridge, 1980), 24–8, for the success of Britain's recruitment in Germany; *Papers Illustrating the History of the Scots Brigade*, ed. Ferguson, ii. 478–9. During the second half of 1776, Yorke, on Suffolk's instructions, informally raised the Brigade's loan once again but met with significant opposition, and this ended Britain's interest in the regiments: Renaut, *De la neutralité à la belligérance*, 104–6.

[94] For Yorke's resentment, see *Dépêches van Thulemeyer*, 159; for the British government's, see Suffolk to Yorke, 27 Feb. 1776, SP 94/552.

[95] The majority of British captures in 1775–8 were Dutch ships. According to one estimate, of some 59 vessels taken before Sept. 1778, 35 were from the Republic: Spooner, *Risks at Sea*, 104.

Britain's relations with the other maritime states, was the outbreak of Anglo-French hostilities in 1778. But London's attempts to restrict trade, the actions of the British navy, and Yorke's high-handed behaviour all damaged relations in the early years of the war.[96]

The Dutch prohibition on munitions exports issued in March 1775 was renewed for a year on three subsequent occasions: August 1775, October 1776, and November 1777.[97] But it was easier to prohibit this trade than to prevent it, and the failure of these edicts soon became apparent. The profits from contraband trade were substantial. Dutch merchants expected to benefit from the Republic's habitual neutrality and trade with the insurgents was soon expanding rapidly. By spring 1776, Britain had begun to complain to The Hague, and also to stop and search Dutch shipping. Dutch complaints followed, and diplomacy settled down into an inconclusive exchange of protests and counter-protests familiar from the Seven Years War. The British government was determined to stop the supply of munitions, while the Dutch resented Britain's arbitrary use of her naval power. Despite Yorke's endless representations, there was very little that the Republic's government could do to prevent commerce with America. Its federal structure made decisive action extremely difficult, while the ambassador's heavy-handed diplomacy, together with the opposition of the towns led by Amsterdam, weakened the Anglophile sentiments of the Stadtholder and *Griffier*. Dutch commerce briefly recovered its former prosperity during the American War as the Republic's merchants, with the lure of extremely high profits, were prepared to run the risks involved in direct trade with the rebels. Though the greater part initially appears to have been carried on indirectly through the ports and in the ships of France and Spain, Britain's attention and soon her resentment focused on the direct trade conducted through Curaçao and, in particular, through St Eustatius.[98]

The tiny Dutch island of St Eustatius, lying to the north-east of the West Indies, was ideally located and quickly became a flourishing entrepôt. Governed by the aggressive de Graaf, it was suspected not merely of being the principal centre of contraband trade but also of sheltering American privateers, and it was therefore blockaded by the

---

[96] The brief account of Anglo-Dutch diplomacy which follows is based principally on SP 84/ 546–7 and 552–8 *passim*. [97] Edler, *Dutch Republic*, 27.
[98] Its importance was indicated by J. Franklin Jameson, 'St. Eustatius in the American Revolution', *American Historical Review*, 8 (1902–3), 683–708. Its role and that of Curaçao during the American Revolution are examined by C. Ch. Goslinga, *The Dutch in the Caribbean and in the Guianas 1680–1791* (Assen–Maastricht and Dover, NH, 1985), 120–1, 141–52, and 223–30. For the rapid expansion of trade after 1775, see the figures in Spooner, *Risks at Sea*, 101.

British navy.[99] Matters came to a head in November 1776. An American vessel exchanged salutes with the fort on St Eustatius, an action which implied formal Dutch recognition of colonial independence. Britain's response was immediate.[100] Her naval blockade was tightened, to the fury of local traders and the Republic's own merchants, and a strong diplomatic protest was handed to The Hague in February 1777. Though Dutch statesmen were, as usual, roughly handled by Yorke, their response was conciliatory.[101] Recognizing they could not defend de Graaf's actions, they soon determined to apologize. The governor was summoned back to Europe and his conduct was disavowed, though he was not dismissed as Britain was demanding; in the event, and after a delay of over two years, de Graaf was able to exonerate himself. The Republic's positive and rapid response satisfied the British government and at the very end of March 1777, the close blockade of the island was rescinded.[102]

This brief crisis exemplified the fragility of Anglo-Dutch diplomacy during the first half of the war. Significant sources of tension existed, principally due to the revolt, and Dutch resentment was increased by Yorke's behaviour. Many of the subsequent problems were already present in embryo.[103] Each state, though irritated and even wounded by its old friend's conduct, refused to push matters too far. This was partly because, at this stage, both had limited objectives. The Republic sought to uphold its cherished—and profitable—neutrality. Events in Europe were, in any case, reviving its need for British support. An apparent threat to the Barrier fortresses in the Austrian Netherlands, which nominally still defended the Republic's southern frontier against France, made The Hague anxious to reinvigorate the English alliance. In the mid-1770s, the Dutch became alarmed by Vienna's attempts to exchange the Austrian Netherlands for Bavaria. The poor health of the last Wittelsbach elector suggested that an opportunity might soon arise: the heir to Bavaria was rumoured to

---

[99] For a résumé of British complaints, see *Documents of the American Revolution*, xii, nos. 141–2.

[100] It can be followed in SP 84/555–6. For the implementation of the close blockade, see Suffolk to Lords Commissioners of the Admiralty, 15 Feb. 1777, ADM 1/4133. For the Dutch reply, see, in particular, *Archives . . . Orange-Nassau*, 5th series, i. 456–60.

[101] See ibid. 455–8 *passim*, and *Franklin Papers*, xxiii. 394, 460, for the ambassador's conduct; cf. Schulte Nordholt, *Dutch Republic*, 42, for the Grand Pensionary's resentment.

[102] Suffolk to Lords Commissioners of the Admiralty, 29 Mar. 1777, ADM 1/4133; cf. Suffolk to Yorke, 8 Apr. 1777, SP 84/556.

[103] For example, Dutch attempts to protect their trade by adopting convoys: for the hostile British response, see Suffolk to Yorke, 24 Sept. (Private) and 14 Oct. 1777, both in SP 84/557; for Yorke's outrage, see *Archives . . . Orange-Nassau*, 5th series, i. 484.

be close to an agreement with the Habsburgs. This would destroy the Barrier, still the psychological prop of the Republic's foreign policy, because its forts symbolized Austria's commitment to Dutch defence. British diplomatic support was desirable, as Brunswick saw particularly clearly.[104] This tempered Dutch antagonism towards Britain in 1776–7 and it contributed directly to the Republic's moderation over St Eustatius.

Britain, too, was anxious not to provoke a formal breach, and her attitude at this stage was considerably more moderate than during the Seven Years War.[105] This reflected her limited objectives. London was, in practice, prepared to accept Dutch neutrality, provided that the government at The Hague prohibited trade with the rebels and also allowed Britain's German mercenaries to embark from its ports. In the early stages of the revolt, Britain aimed only to hinder American commerce, to contribute to military victory across the Atlantic. Success was incomplete, but it was certainly not negligible: the insurgents found unexpected difficulties in trading with the smaller maritime states and even encountered some problems in that with the Dutch.

Britain's policy towards the Bourbons had also appeared successful at first. Both France and Spain seemed willing to place some barriers in the way of American trade and good relations were maintained. Yet this success was always something of an illusion. It rested less on British actions than on French and Spanish priorities. The outbreak of fighting in America gave the initiative to the Bourbons for the first time since the early 1770s. The growing tension after summer 1776 was similarly due to Spanish and especially French decisions. The key lay at Versailles. Vergennes was always aware of France's opportunity, though he also appreciated he had to move very cautiously. Louis XVI would be reluctant to sanction war; some ministers and notably Turgot argued that the main priority should be the pressing domestic problems; while Vergennes himself believed Britain's overwhelming superiority in resources would eventually give her victory in America. France's policy remained cautious and pacific until spring 1776, when it was transformed by a series of decisions which propelled her towards intervention.

This fundamental change was hammered out during highly secret

---

[104] Ibid. i. 441, 495.
[105] This was particularly apparent in the orders given to British naval commanders: see e.g. *Documents of the American Revolution*, xii, nos. 140–1. One of the best examples came in the winter of 1777–8, when no attempt was made to detain Bylandt's first convoy to St Eustatius: Miller, *Yorke*, 56–7; cf. *Dépêches van Thulemeyer*, 171.

meetings in March and April.[106] These saw a clash between two conflicting views of French political priorities. Turgot vigorously defended his belief that peace was essential to enable his wide-ranging financial reforms to mature. He was opposed by Vergennes, who had the influential support of Maurepas. The foreign minister urged that the opportunity presented by the colonial revolt to humble Britain should be seized. He hoped victory would not merely weaken British power; it would also restore France's diplomatic leadership in Europe, which had been undermined by the concentration of French resources overseas and by the simultaneous emergence of the three eastern powers. Vergennes advocated that aid should be secretly sent to the Americans and, eventually, France should openly intervene. He and his supporters accepted such assistance would soon become public and would eventually involve war with Britain. These arguments won the day. Vergennes's plans were in the mainstream of traditional French policy and appeared to involve few risks. By contrast, Turgot's alternative programme, which envisaged tackling France's domestic problems, was extremely radical and involved considerable dangers. Louis XVI's formal decision was announced on 2 May 1776 when he agreed to provide one million *livres* in secret aid for the Americans; Spain was to give a similar sum. Turgot's arguments had been completely rejected and he resigned on 12 May. Within a few weeks, French preparations for war were under way.

Only the King and a few senior ministers were involved in these secret discussions, and Britain had no opportunity to learn of the decision which had been taken. London's confidence in spring 1776 was apparent in the fact that the ambassador, Stormont, was again on leave. British diplomacy in Paris was handled by a chargé d'affaires who was unable to discover the switch in French strategy,[107] while, since the decision was never communicated to Louis XVI's ambassador in London, it could not be discovered by the interception of French diplomatic correspondence. Though the decision could be kept secret, however, the resulting preparations could not be disguised. A rapid buildup of France's fleet was essential.[108] Though the energetic Sartine had become naval minister in August 1774, reconstruction had barely begun and the navy was still in very poor condition, due to the continued financial restraint. Only in April and May 1776, as a result of Vergennes's victory, was

---

[106] Dull, *French Navy*, 30–48, provides an admirable short account.

[107] The ministerial changes were duly reported by Horace St. Paul, but he had no inkling of what lay behind Turgot's disgrace: *St. Paul of Ewart*, ii. 390, 398–400.

[108] The crucial importance of the state of the navy for the timing of France's intervention was established by Prof. Dull: *French Navy*, esp. chs. 3–4.

expenditure increased. Sartine set to work immediately, and from late spring there was a notable upsurge in activity in France's ports and dockyards. These efforts, together with the simultaneous and blatant increase in French aid to the insurgents, worsened relations. The honeymoon period in Anglo-French diplomacy ended with the adoption of Vergennes's strategy.

The naval preparations were quickly known to Britain's intelligence network and revealed the change in French strategy: by the end of May, both the government and the City had become alarmed.[109] The situation was so serious that, unusually, an entire cabinet was devoted to it.[110] At this meeting on 20 June, the First Lord of the Admiralty, Sandwich, made a determined, though only partially successful attempt to commit Britain to match France's naval buildup.[111] From the very beginning of the revolt, Sandwich had been particularly alarmed by the potential French threat, and his anxieties now reached a crescendo.[112] He secured considerable support from his cabinet colleagues. The number of guardships was increased from nineteen to twenty-four and efforts were made to increase the number of Marines, and to raise additional volunteers for the Royal Navy. Secret preparations were also made to carry out an immediate 'press' should the situation demand it. The cabinet was here responding to one of Sandwich's recurring, though exaggerated, anxieties: his fear that Britain's haphazard and inefficient recruitment of sailors for the Royal Navy by 'pressing' merchant seamen, as and when the need arose, placed her at a serious disadvantage when compared with France's practice of enrolling the *gens de mer* in the 'maritime classes', which he wrongly believed swifter and more efficient.

There was considerable agreement about the threat now posed by France: on the following day, Weymouth wrote that her naval preparations 'become a matter of very serious importance'.[113] The

---

[109] *St. Paul of Ewart*, ii. 420, 427, 429; *Sandwich Papers*, i. 212; *Walpole Corr.* xxiv. 213.

[110] Copies of the minutes of this meeting are in Thynne Papers, Box A; *Corr. Geo. III*, iii. 380; and *Sandwich Papers*, i. 212–3.

[111] The First Lord's anxieties, and his campaign to convince the cabinet, are apparent from the two papers which he drew up and which appear to have been circulated before the meeting. The first, a 'Précis of Advices and Intelligence received respecting the Equipment in the Ports of France and Spain' dated '20th June 1776' (this is in Thynne Papers, Box A; and in Add. MSS 61863, fos. 24–6; and is printed in *Corr. Geo. III*, iii. 380–2) assembled Britain's present knowledge of the Bourbon fleets. The second, a paper entitled 'Remarks on the State of His Majesty's fleet', also dated '20th June 1776' (this is in Thynne Papers, Box A, and also in *Corr. Geo. III*, iii. 378–80) outlined Britain's present naval dispositions and preparedness, and pleaded vigorously for an immediate and substantial increase in the number of ships in commission.   [112] *Sandwich Papers*, i. 205.

[113] *St. Paul of Ewart*, ii. 428.

cabinet, however, rejected two of Sandwich's key recommendations: to arm twelve of the line immediately (to match the preparations under way at Brest) and to sanction extra expenditure on the wages of dockyard workers, to speed up mobilization.[114] At this stage, a majority of ministers was not prepared to uphold the traditional doctrine of the 'two-power naval standard' in the rigorous way demanded by Sandwich. The explanation was partly financial: the cabinet rejected the two most expensive proposals, which would have involved asking parliament to increase the naval budget.[115] But the principal reason was the anxiety not to provoke France and thereby set in motion a naval race which could lead to war.[116] Most ministers still believed victory in America to be the first priority. Some clearly hoped French intervention could be delayed or even averted altogether by further successes there: already the idea was gaining ground that peace in Europe depended on military victory over the colonists.

The greater attention now given to Anglo-French relations was made clear by Stormont's return to Paris in June 1776.[117] He was to remain in France until the formal withdrawal of diplomats almost two years later. He immediately began to assess the changed French strategy.[118] The embassy's own intelligence network confirmed the naval buildup, and the ambassador believed this was on an unprecedented scale, in itself a significant verdict, since he had been in Paris during the naval crisis of spring 1773. Although the situation was now serious, however, it was not yet critical. Stormont correctly appreciated that French actions did not make war inevitable, far less imminent. He understood Vergennes's continuing caution and also placed these preparations in their proper context: there was certainly significant activity in the dockyards, but France was far from ready to fight.

The ambassador played an important part in Britain's foreign policy throughout the first half of the American War. His proximity

[114] The extent of the First Lord's reverse is apparent from the fact that the final cabinet minute even excluded a compromise proposal to secure further intelligence of Bourbon naval preparations 'and then to consider whether any more line of battle should be got in readiness for receiving men': this section was deleted from the minute printed in *Sandwich Papers*, i. 212–13 (since this edition was based on the family papers at Hinchingbrooke, it would seem likely that the deleted paragraph was inserted by Sandwich himself) but it does not appear in the copies in Thynne Papers, Box A, and in *Corr. Geo. III*, iii. 380.

[115] Sandwich mentioned the considerable cost in a rather defensive way at the end of his 'Remarks . . .': *Corr. Geo. III*, iii. 380.

[116] This was why diplomatic protests were not made over the French naval buildup: CP (Angleterre) 517, fos. 218–9.

[117] SP 78/299, fo. 216. He had been absent from Mar. until late Oct. 1775 and again from early Apr. until late June 1776.　　　　[118] SP 78/299, fos. 230–7 and 263–7.

to the French government, together with his wide experience, gave his opinions considerable influence. He was, by now, the leading British diplomat of his generation. Only Yorke, at The Hague, had longer service at a major post, and Stormont's experience was far broader. Though his views were conventional, his dedication and ability were unquestioned. British diplomats had always exerted indirect influence through their dispatches, which shaped the context within which foreign policy was determined. Stormont's influence was more direct and also extremely unusual. His relations with Weymouth were cooler than with his predecessor Rochford: the Southern Secretary's neglect of the routine correspondence irritated and finally exasperated the conscientious Stormont and, on several occasions, led him to complain.[119] Yet his influence survived Rochford's retirement. His reports from Paris had earlier been circulated as formal instructions to other British diplomats, and they continued to shape official thinking.[120] Many of the assumptions behind British policy towards France originate in his dispatches.[121]

Stormont always recognized that France might eventually declare war. But he correctly appreciated that, while she was pleased to see British resources consumed by the conflict in America and welcomed Britain's difficulties, an early attack was improbable. Only in one crucial respect was his analysis deficient: his belief that the leader of the French ministry, Maurepas, was pacific. This idea, established soon after Louis XVI's accession, was only abandoned during the winter of 1777–8, and it was fostered by private discussions between the two men. There is no evidence for Stormont's conclusion: on the contrary, Maurepas had supported Vergennes during the crucial debates in spring 1776. It seems probable the ambassador was deliberately deceived by the adroit Maurepas.[122]

Ministers claimed to be reassured by Stormont's reports in the summer of 1776.[123] These months, however, mark the opening of a new phase in relations: Britain's confidence now declined as she was

[119] e.g. ibid. 300, fos. 54–5.

[120] J. Flammermont, *Les Correspondances des agents diplomatiques étrangers en France avant la Révolution* (Paris, 1896), 502–3; cf. *BDI* vii: *France 1745–1789*, ed. L. G. Wickham Legg, 128.

[121] What became Britain's basic attitude is first set out in Stormont to Weymouth, Most Secret, 14 Feb. 1776, SP 78/298, fos. 117–8; cf. ibid. 299, fo. 306.

[122] There is no direct evidence for this hypothesis, but it is strongly suggested by the fact that Vergennes and Maurepas were usually fully aware of each other's discussions with Stormont and co-operated closely in determining their respective attitudes to the ambassador: there are numerous instances of this in Doniol, *Participation*, i–iii *passim*. The information which Forth supplied through his links with Maurepas (see below, p 250) helps to confirm Stormont's view of the comte as pacific.

[123] *BDI* vii: *France 1745–1789*, 150–1; cf. SP 78/299, fo. 280.

forced to give increasing attention to Anglo-French diplomacy. In particular, French naval preparations could no longer be ignored. The cabinet's concern increased in the months ahead, as France's conduct and the activity in her dockyards called into question Vergennes's repeated professions of peace and friendship. The meeting on 20 June was significant in a second respect: that of cabinet unity. During 1775 and the first half of 1776, there had been a measure of unanimity over Anglo-French relations. Though some ministers, headed by Sandwich, feared an eventual Bourbon attack, most agreed an early war was unlikely, and some even hoped it might be avoided altogether, by the swift defeat of the rebels.[124] In summer 1776, with the further buildup of French naval power, this unity began to crumble.

On 20 June 1776, the cabinet refused the Admiralty's demand to mobilize twelve of the line. Sandwich did not accept this decision. A month later, he used reports of increased French preparations to urge the commissioning of these ships.[125] He continued to plead for more capital vessels during the late summer and autumn of 1776 and, indeed, throughout the next two years. His arguments were Admiralty orthodoxy at least since the Seven Years War. French naval preparations had to be answered by an equivalent British mobilization. Failure to do this would imperil that touchstone of British security, the doctrine of the two-power naval standard. Sandwich appreciated—and probably exaggerated—the crucial advantage which the system of the 'classes' gave France in speed of mobilization. He also understood more clearly than his colleagues the tactical benefits France would derive in any war, if she secured a decisive lead in commissioning her fleet.[126]

The First Lord's arguments were based on a professional awareness of naval strategy, though he was not blind to the accompanying political dangers. He was prepared for this mobilization to be viewed as provocative and to worsen relations: he always believed war inevitable. His principal supporter was now Weymouth.[127] The Southern Secretary's attitude was erratic and probably inconsistent. At times, he voiced the official doctrine that France was still pacific.[128] But his established hostility towards both Bourbon powers, though not immediately apparent on his return to office, re-emerged during 1776. By that autumn, Weymouth was an obstacle to good relations with Spain.

[124] The Secretary at War, Barrington, also believed that France was still Britain's major enemy: C. R. Ritcheson, *British Politics and the American Revolution* (Norman, Okla., 1954), 171, 208.   [125] *Sandwich Papers*, i. 213–6.   [126] Ibid. i. 216.
[127] He also appears to have been supported by Gower: CP (Angleterre) 515, fos. 13–4.
[128] e.g. BDI vii: *France 1745–1789*, 157.

Suffolk was the principal spokesman for appeasement of the Bourbons.[129] The Northern Secretary had always favoured firm and even Draconian measures against the Americans, and he now looked confidently towards a total military victory. He was not indifferent to the French threat and his views on foreign policy had always been orthodox; but in 1776–7, he believed that diplomacy in Europe must be subordinated to the military struggle in America.[130] His most influential ally was North. The Prime Minister was alarmed that a European war, when Britain was already fighting in America, would be financially ruinous, and he was therefore reluctant to provoke France by naval preparations.[131]

These divisions were still matters of emphasis; it would be 1777–8 before serious splits arose. In 1776-7, with George III holding the ring, ministers compromised over British preparations. France's threat to reinforce her naval squadron in the West Indies aroused considerable foreboding.[132] This, together with the accelerated French naval buildup, produced a reassessment of British strategy.[133] Sandwich redoubled his pleas for more ships of the line and in late October 1776 the cabinet agreed.[134] The arrival of news of the British victory at Long Island, which boosted confidence, paved the way for a cabinet decision on 23 October to increase naval readiness.[135] The 'press', prepared in secret since June, was now carried out and the guardships were commissioned along with ten more capital vessels.[136] This was a considerable armament, amounting to some thirty-six ships of the line, and was obviously a response both to French preparations and to the increasing threat from American privateers.[137] It was also an attempt to placate the opposition in parliament:[138] significantly, these measures were implemented just before the new session began on 31 October, when

---

[129] Cf. Garnier to Vergennes, 16 Aug. 1776, printed though misdated in Doniol, *Participation*, i. 562.

[130] *Sandwich Papers*, i. 226; cf. *Grafton Autobiography*, 297.

[131] *Sandwich Papers*, i. 201.

[132] *HMC Knox*, 127; *BDI* vii: *France 1745–1789*, 153–4; Weymouth to Grantham, 29 Oct. 1776, SP 94/202; cf. Weymouth to Grantham, 6 Dec. 1776, ibid., and Germain to Lords of the Admiralty 4 Dec. 1776, ADM 1/4132.

[133] SP 78/299, fo. 528; in Oct., there were further reports: ibid. 300, fos. 50–5.

[134] *Sandwich Papers*, i. 216– 7; *Corr. Geo. III*, iii. 396–7.

[135] Gruber, *The Howe Brothers*, 162–5.

[136] *Walpole Corr.* xxiv. 252–3 and footnotes; *Corr. Geo. III*, iii. 296–7.

[137] E 6995, fo. 49: the Bourbon spy-ring makes this the most reliable figure; in addition, 5 ships were detailed to patrol the Channel. Syrett, 'Defeat at Sea', 18.

[138] As North was honest enough to tell Masserano: E 6995, fo. 49; for the circumstances of this meeting, see below, p. 247. Sandwich, in the debate in the Lords on the Address, clearly hinted at this rearmament during his defence of government policy towards France: *Parl. Hist.* xviii, cols. 1380–1.

ministers expected to be attacked over relations with France. Even this formidable mobilization was insufficient for Sandwich, who continued to worry about the lead France had secured.[139]

The First Lord's efforts had not been totally successful, but during 1776–7 Britain mobilized a significant number of capital ships and reinforced key stations. Ministers now put less emphasis in parliament on their confidence in French assurances and their anxieties were clear.[140] North even admitted that, while he believed France at present pacific, 'he would not answer for events six months' hence'.[141] War might not be imminent, but it was beginning to look inevitable. By March 1777, the Prime Minister had finally been won over by Sandwich's arguments that Britain should match the French buildup ship for ship.[142] France's preparations continued to be reported with considerable accuracy by Stormont, whose intelligence network was sophisticated and wide-ranging: on one occasion, Vergennes remarked that he was much better informed than the French ministers![143] The ambassador's detailed knowledge made him increasingly sceptical towards the foreign minister's claim that France's naval preparations were essential self-defence.[144] Contemporaries saw these developments as a naval race, familiar from earlier periods of Anglo-French tension.[145] On this occasion, the mobilization was on such a scale that, before long, war appeared probable.

The deterioration had three other causes, all of which were linked to the French decision to intervene. The first was the arrival of American agents in Paris during the second half of 1776.[146] Silas Deane reached there in July, to be followed by Arthur Lee and then by Benjamin Franklin, who arrived in December, and all received an enthusiastic welcome. Their objectives were to secure practical aid, principally munitions, and to work towards an eventual alliance.[147] Their activities were carefully monitored by the British government. Stormont reported what he could discover, and the American

[139] *Sandwich Papers*, i. 163.   [140] e.g. *Parl. Hist.* xviii, col. 1420.
[141] Ibid. col. 1426.   [142] *Corr. Geo. III*, iii. 429–30.
[143] SP 78/299, fo. 528; 300, fos. 50–5; *Beaumarchais Correspondance*, ed. B. N. Morton and D. C. Spinelli, (4 vols. to date; Paris, 1969–), ii. 187. For the quality of Stormont's intelligence: Van Alstyne, *Empire and Independence*, 96–7; for American and French testimony to this: *Franklin Papers*, xxiii. 354–5; *Beaumarchais Correspondance* ed. Morton and Spinelli, ii. 175–6; iii. 12.
[144] SP 78/300, fos. 149–51 and 227–32.   [145] See e.g. E 6996, fos. 16.
[146] By July 1776, Weymouth had begun to worry about this: SP 78/299, fos. 280–1; cf. *BDI* vii: *France 1745–1789*, 151–2.
[147] Brief introductions to their activities in Paris are provided by J. R. Dull, *Franklin the Diplomat: The French Mission* (Philadelphia: Transactions of the American Philosophical Society, 72: i (1982)), 11–32, and id., *Diplomatic History of the American Revolution*, 75–96.

mission was the target of significant British intelligence activity, directed from London.[148] The arrival of American agents in Paris and their enthusiastic reception—at the very least—raised serious doubts about France's real intentions. The Americans were simply rebels in British eyes; they found it very difficult in 1776–7 to establish contacts with any other European government. Yet at Paris they clearly received significant, if unofficial, aid and comfort from French ministers: ministers who nevertheless professed friendship towards Britain.

A second source of Britain's growing mistrust was the greater volume of French aid to the rebels and the increasingly blatant way this was sent.[149] France's decision to intervene had immediately led to an increase in the munitions and other supplies sent to the insurgents from her own ports and from her West Indian islands.[150] Though its precise extent was not known by the British government, intelligence reports, together with the Royal Navy's success in intercepting some cargoes in American and Caribbean waters, made it clear the volume of assistance increased significantly during 1776.[151] In the early stages of the revolt, Britain had been prepared to turn a blind eye to French aid—on such a small scale, it was not worth damaging relations to achieve a marginal reduction. It was less easy to ignore its increased volume in 1776–7, yet since it was still clandestine, it was difficult to do anything about it except by intercepting American and even French ships on the high seas.[152] This assistance, however, made clear Louis XVI's commitment to the American cause.[153]

The final source of tension, particularly important by summer 1777, was the increasing use made of France's ports by American privateers.[154] In 1776–7, Congress tried to extend the conflict by encouraging privateering in European waters. This campaign was

[148] This is why Weymouth at times seemed better informed on this subject than Britain's ambassador in Paris. Space does not permit any examination of the familiar and controversial question of British penetration of the American mission and who was (or was not) a British spy or American double-agent, a subject where the paucity of reliable evidence has in no way hindered speculation. The material gathered by Britain confirmed ministers in their belief in French duplicity.   [149] SP 78/299, fo. 306.
[150] Ibid. 300, fo. 231; Gruber, *The Howe Brothers*, 140.   [151] SP 78/301, fo. 430.
[152] See e.g. Weymouth's revealing comments in Feb. 1777: *BDI* vii: *France 1745–1789*, 160.
[153] *Sandwich Papers*, i. 287. Britain was also aware that officers in the French army were going to serve in American armies: see e.g. SP 78/302, fo. 7.
[154] A convenient introduction is provided by R. Y. Johnston, 'American Privateers in French Ports, 1776–1778', *Pennsylvania Magazine of History and Biography*, 53 (1929), 352–74, though this article fails to appreciate the measures ordered and sometimes implemented against the privateers by the French authorities.

remarkably successful. Considerable disruption was caused to Britain's coastal and European trade, particularly in 1777. This initiative always had broader objectives than mere commerce raiding. One important motive had been to increase Anglo-French tension. The kind of incidents which could easily result might exacerbate relations and thereby accelerate France's formal entry into the war.[155] During 1777, this aim was substantially realized.

France was seen as America's only friend and her ports were an obvious refuge for the privateers. Britain had succeeded in closing the harbours of most European states to American shipping, while the French coastline was adjacent to three principal areas for the privateering campaign: the Channel, the Bay of Biscay, and the Irish Sea. In early 1777, the American raiders were becoming a significant source of friction.[156] Britain increased her naval patrols and extended their scope into the Bay of Biscay.[157] France also stepped up her patrols, both to protect her own shipping and to ensure her territorial waters were not infringed by British warships pursuing Ameican raiders. There was an inevitable risk of clashes, and several incidents did occur. Britain also protested vigorously when American privateers sought sanctuary in France's Atlantic ports.[158] Their presence was legally indefensible, as even Vergennes immediately admitted. It had been clearly prohibited by the Treaty of Utrecht, and this prohibition had been specifically renewed by the Peace of Paris.[159] The French foreign minister was forced to bow to British pressure and ostensibly to prevent the harbours being used in this way.[160] The instructions sent to the French ports were unambiguous, but remedial action was slow and often incomplete.[161]

Britain could in practice do very little about the presence of privateers, the shipment of munitions, or the Franco-American negotiations. Ministers were forced to accept Vergennes's assurances, since the alternative was war, which Britain wanted to avoid or at least postpone. Far more vigorous representations were justified by France's flagrant support of the Americans, and the cabinet was certainly under no illusions about her duplicity.[162] The diplomatic protests lodged by Stormont up to summer 1777, in retrospect,

---

[155] Syrett, 'Defeat at Sea', 16.
[156] For instance, the activities of the *Reprisal*: SP 78/301 *passim*.
[157] Dull, *French Navy*, 70–3.
[158] SP 78/301–2, *passim*.   [159] Syrett, 'Defeat at Sea', 17.
[160] For Vergennes's duplicity on this point, see, in particular, *Franklin Papers*, xxiii. 468.
[161] The *Reprisal*, e.g., was able to sell its prizes and depart without action being taken against it.
[162] *BDI* vii: *France 1745–1789*, 159–60; cf. Suffolk to Keith, Private and Confidential, 11 Apr. 1777, SP 80/219.

appear surprisingly mild, but at the time this was realistic. Ministers believed that it would be 'a point gained if we can postpone, though we should not be able, ultimately, to prevent' war with France.[163]

At the heart of British policy lay an insoluble paradox. Britain was powerless to prevent France moving towards open intervention and sending significant aid to the rebels, except by herself launching a war. The cabinet might be divided over naval preparations, but no minister wanted to accelerate the war in Europe since this would multiply the government's difficulties. Nevertheless, a clear change was becoming apparent in Britain's priorities. In 1775–6, her diplomacy had aimed to preserve peace with the Bourbons in order to defeat the rebellion. By the first half of 1777, an early victory across the Atlantic was coming to be seen as the best—perhaps the only—way of averting a French attack.[164] Simultaneously, however, ministers were forced to recognize that the defeat of the rebels might take longer than they had calculated. They remained confident of victory, but were slowly recognizing the strength of colonial resistance.[165]

The deterioration in Anglo-French diplomacy focused attention on Spain. By the middle of 1776, there was less confidence that the Family Compact was in abeyance and that Britain would remain on good terms with Madrid during a period of tension and even war with France. A shift in the Spanish attitude to the American rebellion was under way.[166] In that summer, in response to France's request to match her own financial aid, one million *livres* was sent to Paris to support the American cause. Although some American vessels had obtained munitions in Spanish ports, hitherto direct assistance had been refused. In 1776–7, however, aid was sent to the Americans, at first through Paris and then directly. This represented an adjustment rather than a reversal of Spanish policy.[167] It was to prolong American resistance, not to secure their independence. Until the colonial dispute with Portugal was settled in October 1777, Spain

---

[163] North to Stormont, 15 Oct. 1777, Stormont Papers, Box 45. This letter contains an extremely interesting characterization of British policy towards France in 1776–7.

[164] SP 78/302, fo. 311.   [165] Gruber, *The Howe Brothers*, 188.

[166] B. P. Thomson, *Spain: Forgotten Ally of the American Revolution* (North Quincy, Mass., 1976), 23–69. This is an uneven and occasionally blinkered study, but it does contain important material.

[167] There was a similar adjustment in Spain's attitude to the entry of American ships into her ports: in the closing months of 1775, Madrid had prohibited this (above, p. 215), but by Sept. 1776, Grimaldi was arguing that it was difficult to distinguish between Englishmen and Americans and that this prohibition could not be enforced: E 6995, fo. 17.

would not consider any more than financial support. The Luso-Spanish settlement and the *rapprochement* which followed were the work of Spain's new foreign minister, Floridablanca, who had formally replaced Grimaldi in February 1777. Though a group at the Spanish court argued for intervention and had the influential support of the ambassador in Paris, Aranda, Spain's policy remained moderate. Madrid continued to use the Family Compact as a framework within which Spain's national interests could be pursued, rather than blindly accepting France's leadership under the banner of Bourbon unity. Floridablanca adopted the outlook of his predecessor and sought to preserve good relations with London.

Madrid's secret aid for the rebellion did not immediately damage Anglo-Spanish diplomacy. Though it was certainly apparent to British ministers, they refused to endanger relations and contented themselves with some half-hearted protests. Tension continued to grow and in 1776–7, particular difficulties arose in North America. Spanish Louisiana, with its Mississippi frontier with the American territories, was an established source of friction. It became a natural target for Americans seeking trade and even munitions: already in 1776 the insurgents were receiving powder from Spanish royal arsenals.[168] Further tension was caused by the attempts of the governor, Gálvez, to hinder English traders and by his open encouragement of American privateers, who were selling their prizes in New Orleans. By the middle of 1777, Britain's colonial governor of Florida was protesting vigorously, but this local friction was not at first transferred to Europe.[169] The cabinet continued to place good relations above aid to the Americans. Yet in 1776–7, clear divisions did become apparent among ministers.

Sandwich always seems to have been sceptical about an Anglo-Spanish reconciliation and he was now convinced that in any war, Britain would face the united forces of the Bourbon powers.[170] The naval buildup for which he was arguing in these months was directed against Spain as well as France. He came to be supported by Weymouth, who also believed war would involve both Bourbon states.[171] The two men were, at this stage, isolated. Most ministers

---

[168] J. W. Caughey, *Bernardo de Gálvez in Louisiana 1776–1783* (Berkeley, 1934), 87, and, more generally, chs. 5–7.

[169] *Documents of the American Revolution*, xv, nos. 107–10.

[170] This appears to have been the result of his unwavering belief in the threat posed by the combined Bourbon navies and by his championing of a two-power naval standard: see e.g. *Parl. Hist.* xviii, col. 285. It is striking that the First Lord always spoke of the Bourbons or France and Spain, never of France alone.

[171] This emerges, e.g., from his dispatch to Grantham of 26 Nov. 1776 (SP 94/202) and was the principal reason for his increasingly bad relations with Masserano: see below, p. 245.

clung to the hope that the Family Compact would not operate, and they were encouraged when French naval preparations in the early summer of 1776 were not accompanied by parallel Spanish ones.[172] Their hopes were especially apparent during the following winter.[173] They must be seen in the context of the serious divisions emerging over foreign policy both within the ministry and, crucially, between the two Secretaries of State.

Weymouth's difficult personality inevitably increased his isolation.[174] His relations with the Bourbon representatives in London were also poor: by August, Masserano was describing his attitude as 'very cold and reserved'.[175] This created considerable problems. By autumn 1776, the minister responsible for Anglo-Spanish diplomacy was distinctly hostile towards Madrid, while official policy was to maintain good relations. Weymouth's isolated position, and the increasing suspicion with which he was viewed by Bourbon diplomats, were a matter of personality as well as policy. His habitual reserve always made him a less trusted and popular figure than the bluff and friendly Suffolk with the diplomatic corps in London.[176] The two men now disagreed totally over policy. Whereas Suffolk endorsed the official strategy of cultivating Spain, Weymouth's anti-Bourbon sentiments were increasingly evident. The truth of George III's remark when he had returned to office was now clear:[177] the Southern Secretary had become an obstacle to the desired good relations.[178]

The solution proved remarkably simple: Weymouth was bypassed both by his own colleagues and by the Spanish ambassador. Already in August 1776, Masserano had side-stepped the Southern Secretary and had instead spoken to Suffolk.[179] Thereafter, discussions with Spain's ambassador were often conducted by other ministers.[180]

---

[172] BDI vii: *France 1745–1789*, 150–1. Some Spanish preparations were under way, but ministers recognized that these were uniquely concerned with the undeclared war with Portugal.

[173] For example, in the rejection of a scheme put forward in Dec. 1776 by the London agent of the English settlers on the Mosquito Shore, Robert White, for an assault on Spain's Central American territories: J. McLeish, 'British Activities in Yucatan and on the Moskito Shore in the Eighteenth Century' (unpublished MA thesis, University of London, 1926), 61, 127.

[174] CP (Angleterre) 517, fo. 331.

[175] E 6995, fo. 8; cf. Garnier's views: CP (Angleterre) 517, fo. 246; 518, fo. 291. As early as Mar. 1776, he was obstructing progress over the Newfoundland Fisheries and Suffolk was having to take these into his own hands: ibid. 515, fos. 7–8.

[176] Doniol, *Participation*, ii. 562–3; cf. CP (Angleterre) 515, fo. 360.

[177] For this, see above, pp. 216–7.

[178] By 8 Nov. 1776, Masserano was writing of the Southern Secretary's 'haughtiness' and his 'scant affection' for Spain: E 6995, fo. 49.   [179] Ibid., fo. 8.

[180] Though Weymouth continued to transact the routine diplomatic correspondence with Madrid: SP 94/202 *passim*.

Although this may have been against constitutional practice, it was politically vital. In late September, it was the Northern Secretary who reassured Masserano that Britain accepted Madrid's good faith over the American rebellion and even professed to believe that, unlike France, Spain was not sending aid.[181]

Britain's naval mobilization in late October made relations with Spain, and Weymouth's position, crucial. Since these preparations were a response to the recent buildup of France's fleet and to the deterioration in Anglo-French diplomacy, ministers could discount their impact at Versailles. However, they were anxious not to damage Anglo-Spanish relations and thereby reinvigorate the Family Compact. The timing of the naval preparations was unfortunate because it coincided with the climax of Luso-Spanish rivalry in South America. Britain was particularly concerned that this mobilization should not be seen in Lisbon and in Madrid as support for Portugal.[182] Ministers were anxious the colonial confrontation should not increase Spain's need for French support; they had also grown tired of Pombal's duplicity and reluctance to accept a negotiated settlement. During the winter of 1775–6, combined diplomatic pressure by Britain, France, and Spain had finally forced Portugal to order a suspension of hostilities in South America. But far from being settled, rivalry reached its peak in 1776.[183] In the middle of the year, while the diplomats were striving to convert their armistice into a permanent settlement, news arrived in Europe of a further crushing Portuguese victory which had forced Spain to abandon Rio Grande. Madrid's reaction was to prepare a massive expeditionary force for South America.

In the course of October and early November, Britain made strenuous and repeated efforts to convince Madrid that her naval preparations were directed only against France and that, far from supporting Portugal, she believed Spain's case just and recognized the situation had been inflamed by Pombal's conduct.[184] Madrid was told assistance would be sent only if Spain tried to conquer Portuguese territory and that Britain accepted that the Spanish

---

[181] E 6995, fo. 31. This was, of course, a pretence: the cabinet was perfectly well aware of Spain's assistance to the Americans.

[182] Britain's concern was well founded. Her limited mobilization in June 1776 (for which see above, pp. 235–6) had been viewed by Pombal as evidence that Britain was about to come to Lisbon's aid: Alden, *Royal Government in Colonial Brazil*, 192 n. 62.

[183] Alden, 'The Undeclared War of 1773–1777', 68–70; a fuller account can be found in his *Royal Government in Colonial Brazil*, chs. 7–8.

[184] Similar assurances had been given to Masserano in July: Alden, 'The Undeclared War of 1773–1777', 70.

government had no such intentions. Remarkably, these assurances were passed on not by Weymouth, the responsible minister, but by the Earl of Mansfield, then by the King himself, and finally by Suffolk, during a series of private discussions with Masserano in October 1776.[185] While the Northern Secretary in particular was openly critical of Pombal, Weymouth said nothing at all to the Spanish ambassador. And when, towards the end of October, ministers decided that Britain's new naval mobilization required further assurances to Spain, Weymouth refused outright to see Masserano as the cabinet had requested.[186]

No less a figure than Lord North, on George III's specific instructions, instead went twice to see Spain's ambassador.[187] On the second occasion, they talked for two hours. The very fact that such a conversation took place is itself doubly remarkable. North, as he frankly admitted, was preoccupied with the opening of the parliamentary session and was also recovering from illness.[188] In the second place, the Prime Minister habitually refused to discuss with foreign diplomats topics properly handled by the Secretaries of State. North had occasionally intervened in foreign policy, most notably during the final stages of the Falklands crisis in 1770–1. His conduct on that occasion, together with his renowned pacifism, had earned him Masserano's trust, and he was trying to exploit this. In the interview, North predictably sought to reassure Spain about the British naval buildup and emphasized the cabinet would not support Portugal. But the circumstances in which these talks took place reveal the urgency and, perhaps, the growing desperation of British policy and the obstacle which Weymouth represented to it.

The various approaches made to Masserano in October and early November marked the re-emergence of that shadowy alignment of

---

[185] For these, see Masserano to Grimaldi, 4 and 11 Oct. 1776, both in E 6995; Doniol, *Participation*, ii. 6. For the positive identification of the anonymous but highly placed nobleman in these and other dispatches from the Spanish ambassador as Mansfield, see CP (Angleterre) 522, fo. 38.

[186] Mansfield explicitly told the Spanish ambassador (who suspected this) that Weymouth had refused the cabinet's order to talk to Masserano: E 6995, fos. 49, 55; the Southern Secretary did send a dispatch to Grantham in Madrid after the cabinet meeting ordering him to reassure Grimaldi about the British naval preparations, but the tone of this letter was surprisingly low-key and fell short of the assurances given to Masserano: 29 Oct. 1776, SP 94/202.

[187] For these discussions, see E 6995, fos. 49–53; there is a French translation of this in CP (Angleterre) 519, fos. 38–48. Spain's ageing ambassador had been ill and was confined to his house by gout. When North first called on him, Masserano had just been purged and the Prime Minister was obliged to return later.

[188] See George III's letter to him of 28 Oct. 1776, *Corr. Geo. III*, iii. 398; for North's illness, see in general the correspondence ibid. iii. He had fallen from his horse and broken an arm.

George III, North, and Mansfield over foreign policy.[189] This had
come about in 1772–3 over the secret negotiations with France, and
it was to be of considerable importance during the next two years.[190]
Rochford had earlier been part of this group; this may have been one
reason for his growing alienation from Suffolk in his final years in
office. By the autumn of 1776, Rochford had retired and Suffolk had
been admitted to the inner circle.[191] It was not a full-blown *secret du
roi*, as it had been in 1772–3 and would be again in 1777–8. Indeed,
at this stage it aimed to promote and defend official policy against
Weymouth's maverick conduct. Nor was this alignment a fixed and
permanent influence on British diplomacy: it appears to have
emerged at critical moments in relations with the Bourbons.[192] By
the closing months of 1776, it had become the main force behind
foreign policy.

Throughout the winter of 1776–7, this group continued to
promote good relations with Spain.[193] In particular, Mansfield,
during a series of private discussions, often at the ailing Masserano's

[189] This grouping left few traces in British sources (Mansfield, in particular, was always
pathologically careful to cover his tracks) and it has to be reconstructed primarily from French
and Spanish diplomatic correspondence: its existence has not hitherto been noted. It is,
therefore, impossible to be certain about the respective roles of those involved. But the
mainspring appears to have been the King, who was resolved to reconquer America and
subordinate diplomacy in Europe to this objective. This is particularly suggested by Mansfield's
involvement, for he was a close confidant of George III and had frequently served as an
emissary for him (*Corr. Geo. III*, iii. 393; CP (Angleterre) 513, fos. 13–6, 55). Mansfield's
standing at court is suggested by the fact that exactly at this time (Sept. 1776) he was given an
earldom (see e.g. Walpole, *Last Journals*, i. 578). Lord North was unlikely to take any initiative
in foreign affairs without royal prodding (as e.g. over the Falklands in 1770–1: see above,
Ch. 6) and it was at the King's specific directions that he went to see Masserano in early Nov.
[190] Cf. above, Ch. 7; there are glimpses of unofficial co-operation over foreign policy even
earlier, notably in the final stages of the Falklands crisis (above, Ch. 6) but the Anglo-
French negotiations mark the real origin of this group.
[191] Though Rochford seems to have remained on the fringes of the inner group. In Apr.
1776, at the specific instructions of the King, Rochford delivered some clear warnings to the
playwright and enthusiast for the American cause Beaumarchais, who was in London, that
Britain resented France's increasing aid to the rebels: *Beaumarchais Correspondance*, ed.
Morton and Spinelli, ii. 177–82. Beaumarchais and Rochford were old friends (ibid. ii. 55, 56,
140), having first met when Rochford was ambassador in Madrid. (I owe this last point to Dr
G. W. Rice.)
[192] It is possible that Mansfield's private visit to France in Aug. 1774 had been part of these
private initiatives. According to Horace Walpole (*Last Journals*, i. 373), his aim was to
cultivate good relations and to persuade the French government not to exploit Britain's
difficulties in America. But Walpole's renowned animus against Mansfield makes his story
suspect, and I have been unable to discover anything more about this episode either from
British or French sources.
[193] North's desire for good relations with Madrid is apparent from his emollient remarks in
the Commons during a debate on alleged Spanish outrages on the Mosquito Shore: *Parl. Hist.*
xix, cols. 71–2. As North undoubtedly knew, the Spanish embassy received regular reports of
debates and his remarks would soon be known in Madrid.

house, repeatedly emphasized Britain's wish for peace.[194] Weymouth's relations with the Spanish ambassador became even cooler and more distant, while Suffolk's meetings with him multiplied and personal relations between the two men continued to improve.[195] Their discussions were the origin of a distinctive diplomatic initiative by Britain during the early months of 1777: the proposal for a mutual naval disarmament. This seems to have been Suffolk's brainchild; certainly the idea first emerged, though in a notably vague form, during three conversations with Masserano in December 1776.[196] Other ministers were, at first, slow to adopt the scheme, but in the early months of 1777, it became the cabinet's official policy.[197] Britain, Spain, Portugal, and—by implication—France were all to reduce their military and naval forces, thereby restoring peace between Madrid and Lisbon and reducing Anglo-French tension. This wide-ranging proposal narrowed considerably until, by April 1777, London was suggesting its naval forces and those of France should be reduced in stages. The attractions for Britain were obvious but, given the objectives of French strategy and, indeed, of Spanish policy towards Portugal, the proposal was bound to fail.[198] London's energetic pursuit of the mirage of naval disarmament revealed increasing desperation. By the first half of 1777, the continuing French naval buildup threatened war in Europe before victory had been secured in America. Simultaneously, ministers were being forced to recognize the strength of colonial resistance.[199]

The approach made to France in April 1777 also involved secret diplomacy. A private envoy, Nathaniel Parker Forth, was sent to work with the ambassador in Paris and, in particular, to cultivate the

---

[194] The Earl's principal aim was to convince Madrid of Britain's pacifism. But ministers were aware that Masserano's dispatches were forwarded to Spain via the Spanish embassy in Paris and that Aranda would pass on their contents to Vergennes. Mansfield's assurances were thus aimed indirectly at France as well, and he also emphasized Britain's desire for peace during discussions with the French ambassador in London (see Doniol, *Participation*, ii, *passim*). But British ministers were coming to recognize that it would be very difficult to preserve peace with France. The scale of French naval preparations and of French aid to the rebels made them hostile to the new ambassador Noailles and his deputy, the influential Garnier (E 6995, fo. 26), and they expected little from France. British assurances were always directed primarily towards Spain. For Mansfield's meetings with the Spanish ambassador, see E 6996, fos. 11–12, 16–17; cf. Doniol, *Participation*, ii. 327–8.

[195] Masserano to Grimaldi, 29 Nov. 1776, 6 Dec. 1776, and 7 Mar. 1777, E 6995, fos. 63–8 and 72–6; and E 6996; cf. Doniol, *Participation*, ii. 326.

[196] Ibid. ii. 145; Masserano to Grimaldi, 21 Feb. 1777, E 6996.

[197] Ibid., fo. 12; Doniol, *Participation*, ii. 200–10.

[198] See e.g. Masserano's shrewd scepticism: to Floridablanca, 21 Feb. 1777, E 6996; Spanish thinking is set out in an official paper of 5 Mar. 1777, ibid. For Vergennes's outright opposition, see Doniol, *Participation*, ii. 256–62.

[199] Gruber, *The Howe Brothers*, 177, 188.

leader of the French ministry, Maurepas, still viewed as a force for peace. Forth was to play a central, though often elusive, role in 1777–8.[200] He was one of the band of adventurers who sought to make a career out of the opportunities, for intelligence and unofficial diplomacy, created by the American War. By origin a member of the Anglo-Irish gentry, he had entered the world of Anglo-French finance and government loans in the mid-1760s. This had brought him to the attention of Mansfield, whom he had probably advised over investments, and therefore of his nephew Stormont, the ambassador in Paris. The importance of news and shipping movements had led Forth to build up a network of agents in the French ports, and this was the basis of his career in espionage after 1775, as part of Stormont's network of spies and informers. By 1777, Forth could move with some ease in French society. He was also on increasingly good terms with Maurepas: he was the anonymous figure with access to the leader of the French ministry from whom Stormont had earlier derived important information.[201] With the ambassador's influential backing, he now began a transient career as an unofficial agent of British diplomacy, and then as an emissary of Lord North.

Forth always possessed an exaggerated sense of his own importance and an ambition that outran his modest abilities. His personality was, in any case, ill-suited to the shadowy world of secret diplomacy. He was brash, dissolute, indiscreet, and unreliable: at a critical point, he undermined his own mission by disclosing two secret letters during an 'orgy'.[202] Inexperienced in the deception that was second nature to seasoned diplomats, Forth pursued the chimera of a negotiated settlement with enthusiasm and naïve good faith. All the signs are that, from the very beginning, he was led by the nose by the crafty Maurepas.[203] Ministers had hoped to exploit Forth's burgeoning friendship with the leader of the French ministry, but they were quickly undeceived.

Forth travelled back to Paris at the very end of March with orders

---

[200] M. Ward, *Forth* (Chichester, 1982) is a popular life of some merit and makes extensive use of Forth's own diary, but is occasionally uncritical and also contains some errors.

[201] This is clear from a comparison of Stormont's official dispatch of 9 Apr. 1777 (SP 78/302, fos. 37–51) with his private letter to Weymouth of the 10th: Thynne Papers, Box B; cf. Stormont to Weymouth, Private, 11 Feb. 1777, ibid.

[202] CP (Angleterre) 524, fo. 423; *Corr. Geo. III*, iii. 435; Doniol, *Participation*, ii. 774. George III was subsequently to describe Forth as 'a very dubious Negotiator': *Corr. Geo. III*, v. 105.

[203] This is strongly suggested by Vergennes to Ossun, 12 Apr. 1777, printed in Doniol, *Participation*, ii. 258. It may be that the entire Forth–Maurepas negotiation was an elaborate deception by the French ministry, designed to play for time while France completed her naval preparations, but I have been unable to discover any positive evidence to support such a theory.

to press the idea of a 'partial disarmament' (a staged, reciprocal reduction of capital ships in commission) on Maurepas.[204] He was aided by Stormont, who received verbal orders to work towards the same goal. The moment for such overtures appeared opportune. French ministers had been alarmed by the news that Britain had recently armed five more ships of the line and they had themselves promptly commissioned another seven.[205] Maurepas now faced a two-pronged assault.[206] First, he saw Forth and was given strong assurances of Britain's pacifism, together with a detailed explanation for her latest armament. Then he had an interview with Stormont, during which the idea of a staged demobilization took shape. The ambassador had been trying to suggest a 'partial disarmament' and according to his account this was formally proposed by Maurepas, though this seems improbable.[207] Stormont certainly left the meeting convinced there was a chance of an agreed demobilization. He submitted formal proposals on the same day and these were immediately and enthusiastically endorsed by the British government, by now grasping at straws.[208] But a little more than a week later, Stormont was forced to admit he had been duped and France would not agree to disarm.[209] Though the ambassador was quick to produce an ingenious explanation of how 'pacific' Maurepas and the French King had been overcome by more bellicose elements, Britain had been deceived all along. Forth continued to bombard Maurepas with professions of British pacifism, but these had no impact.[210] By the spring of 1777, the two states were on a collision course, and in the next few months tension increased sharply.

Britain's concern with the French naval buildup was strengthened by the collapse of these discussions.[211] The cabinet also knew France had moved on to the offensive in far-away India, where her agents were trying to build up support among the native princes.[212] The principal source of tension in May and June 1777 was the explosive question of American privateers, given an additional twist when it became clear French subjects were crewing the rebel vessels.[213]

[204] The instructions which he received are apparent from Stormont to Weymouth, Private, 10 Apr. 1777, Thynne Papers, Box B; for the discussions which preceded his return, *Corr. Geo. III*, iii. 432, 434–5. [205] SP 78/302, fo. 37.
[206] Ibid., fos. 38–41, 49–54; cf. Stormont to Weymouth, Private, 10 Apr. 1777, Thynne Papers, Box B.
[207] Particularly in the light of Vergennes's comments: to Ossun, 12 Apr. 1777, Doniol, *Participation*, ii. 258–9.
[208] SP 78/302, fo. 55; BDI vii: *France 1745–1789*, 160–1.
[209] SP 78/302, fo. 97. [210] Add. MSS 61863, fo. 28.
[211] HMC Knox, 129. [212] SP 78/302, fo. 25.
[213] Ibid., fos. 342–5; cf. BDI vii: *France 1745–1789*, 164–5.

France acknowledged it was contrary to treaties for her ports to be used in this way and her ministers ostensibly continued to make some efforts to prevent this. Unofficially, however, Vergennes and his colleagues were giving considerable support to the Americans. France's course between maintaining peace until her navy was in a condition to fight, and sustaining the American cause, was proving more and more difficult to chart. By the end of June, a deteriorating situation had become critical, due to the spectacular success of an American privateering cruise led by Lambert Wickes. Between 28 May and 27 June, his squadron had taken no fewer than eighteen British ships in the southern Irish Sea (St George's Channel). The Americans returned with their prizes to French ports, pursued by the British navy, and this precipitated a diplomatic crisis.

By July 1777, Britain and France were on the brink of war.[214] By March, the City expected hostilities and Sandwich secured more ships.[215] At the end of the parliamentary session in May, the situation was judged so serious that the cabinet decided to omit the customary sentence in the King's Speech about the preservation of peace in Europe.[216] A month later, ministers finally reacted to the expansion of Franco–American trade by ordering the navy to search any French ships found near the rebel colonies.[217] The sharp deterioration in relations with France was particularly serious in the context of the worsening news from America. By July, the cabinet was forced to recognize that its hopes for victory over the colonists were premature and that the campaign of 1777 would not end the rebellion.[218] In that same month, the Swedish minister, Nolcken, declared that Britain and France were in a state of 'half war', and the government itself was rapidly accepting peace in Europe would soon end.[219]

[214] Cf. Walpole's view: to Mann, 17 July 1777, *Walpole Corr.* xxiv. 316.

[215] *Walpole Corr.* xxiv. 282; *Corr. Geo III*, iii. 429–30; *Sandwich Papers*, ii. 16–17.

[216] *Journal of the House of Commons*, xxxvi. 540; cf. *Corr. Geo. III*, iii. 450, for the reasons for this. Every King's Speech until May 1777 had expressed confidence about the state of relations with France.

[217] Roslund-Mercurio, 'The Problem of Neutral Rights', 72–3.

[218] Gruber, *The Howe Brothers*, 198, 214, 216; cf. the stimulating survey by D. Syrett, 'The Failure of the British Effort in America, 1777', in J. Black and P. Woodfine, eds., *The British Navy and the Use of Naval Power in the Eighteenth Century* (Leicester, 1988), 171–90.

[219] Roslund-Mercurio, 'The Problem of Neutral Rights', 74; *Sandwich Papers*, i. 226; *Corr. Geo. III*, iii. 459–60.

10

War with the Bourbons, 1777–1779

THE acute crisis over privateering proved a turning-point in Anglo-French relations. During the previous twelve months war in Europe had become probable; in the summer of 1777 it became inevitable.[1] Throughout the second half of the year tension continued to grow, and both states speeded up their naval and military preparations. Formal diplomacy lost its surface politeness and neither government disguised its belief that war had become unavoidable.

Relations deteriorated because of decisions reached by the French council. Louis XVI's ministers had been convinced by the confrontation over privateering that a reassessment of their policy was essential. The strategy of 'limited intervention', designed to delay open hostilities until Sartine had rebuilt the navy, appeared instead to be about to involve them in war. By summer 1777 they recognized their clear choice: France must either abandon the Americans and remain at peace, or intervene openly and fight Britain. A preliminary decision to fight appears to have been taken by late July, when Vergennes began his campaign to enlist Spain in the coming struggle.[2] French naval preparations were accelerated and became increasingly blatant.[3] France was anxious to commission her fleet and reinforce her colonial defences before the fighting started, to prevent the kind of surprise attack which Britain had launched with such devastating effect two decades before. By August 1777 only the timing of France's war against Britain remained to be settled.

British ministers had also accepted fighting was about to spread to Europe. Their knowledge of France's increasing naval preparations reconciled them to her open intervention and a considerable expansion of the war. Britain's policy was now directed towards the timing of this attack. By mid-1777 ministers were clinging to the one remaining hope: that victory in America might still be achieved before the precarious peace with the Bourbons finally broke down.[4]

---

[1] See e.g. Germain's view early in Aug. 1777: *HMC Stopford-Sackville*, ii. 73; cf. Stormont to North, 23 Aug. 1777, Stormont Papers, Box 45, and Noailles's comments in CP (Angleterre) 524, fos. 164–5.   [2] Dull, *French Navy*, 74, 76; Doniol, *Participation*, ii. 460–9.

[3] A decision in principle to strengthen France's West Indian islands was finally taken in July: Dull, *French Navy*, 76.

[4] *HMC Stopford-Sackville*, ii. 73; *Sandwich Papers*, i. 226.

They rightly believed France would only fight if American resistance continued and, until the shattering news of Burgoyne's surrender at Saratoga arrived early in December, they still anticipated a military victory. By the second half of 1777 the cabinet aimed only to delay France's intervention. As part of this strategy Britain was now matching the French naval buildup ship for ship.[5] Simultaneously her foreign policy was being transformed. Peace had hitherto been pursued by moderation, but after July 1777 Britain switched to an aggressive diplomacy backed by the unambiguous threat of superior force. This was accompanied by Weymouth's return to full involvement in foreign policy, since his renowned hostility towards the Bourbons could more easily be accommodated within the new strategy.[6]

The pattern of Anglo-French relations during the decade after the Seven Years War re-emerged in July 1777: that of British bullying backed by naval preparations, the diplomacy of threats and menaces largely absent during the early stages of the American War and indeed since the confrontation in spring 1773.[7] France was explicitly told that if she did not abandon her support for the Americans, war would follow.[8] Ministers recognized that pliant diplomacy, supported by occasional reminders of British naval superiority—the policy pursued in 1775–77—would no longer restrain the French government.[9] Though this tougher stance was to worsen relations even more, its effectiveness, at first, appeared to be confirmed by Vergennes's response over privateering.

In July 1777 Stormont's protests about Wickes's return produced immediate concessions.[10] French ministers recognized that, since they were not yet willing to start fighting, they had to bow to British pressure, and they duly ordered that his squadron should be sequestered by the port authorities: this marked the real end of France's tolerant attitude towards the privateers.[11] It was far from being the end of the matter.[12] In mid-July another celebrated

[5] *Sandwich Papers*, i. 235–45, *passim*.

[6] This was also made necessary by Suffolk's serious illness in spring and early summer 1778; for over 4 months gout prevented him from seeing the diplomatic corps: E 7001, fos. 10, 23. But Weymouth had resumed his full role before the Northern Secretary became ill.

[7] SP 78/304, fo. 70; cf. George III's view: Add. MSS 37834, fo. 3. The change of tone is first apparent in Weymouth to Stormont, 4 July 1777, *BDI* vii: *France, 1745–1789*, ed. L. G. Wickham Legg, 166–7.

[8] SP 78/303, fos. 136–40, 142–9. In London, Weymouth went on to the offensive towards the French ambassador: Doniol, *Participation*, ii. 511–2.

[9] See Sandwich's professed confidence: *Parl. Hist.* xix, cols. 378, 479.

[10] SP 78/303, fos. 174–7. [11] *Franklin Papers*, xxiv. 287.

[12] For relations over privateering between July and Sept. see SP 78/303–4 *passim*; there is a good brief account in Dull, *French Navy*, 76–81.

American privateer, Gustavus Conyngham, slipped out of Dunkirk. Once again Stormont's protests were loud and immediate; once again France quickly caved in.[13] On this occasion, Vergennes took the ambassador to see Sartine, who showed him copies of the actual orders instructing the Dunkirk authorities to stop privateering cruises. In his discussions with Stormont, Vergennes poured all the blame on American bad faith, but neither the ambassador nor the British cabinet were disposed to believe him. Instead, Britain's diplomatic intimidation continued.[14] It reached its peak on 19 August when Stormont formally demanded that not only should Wickes's prizes be sequestered, but that he and his ships should be expelled from France's ports to the mercy of the British fleet ready to intercept them.

Britain had placed a time-limit of one week on her demand, and this provoked a particularly acute crisis during the second half of August. Vergennes recognized this was crude intimidation; he also believed the British government was trying to drive a wedge between France and the Americans and to discourage the French council from reinforcing the West Indies. He expected war and took measures to prepare for this, including the recall of the Newfoundland fishing fleet.[15] He also recognized that French preparations were incomplete and that it was still essential to delay the fighting. On 27 August, therefore, orders were again sent to the port authorities instructing them to prevent American privateers using French harbours, and in mid-September Wickes and his ships were finally expelled.

His departure, together with the other measures ordered by the French government, appeared a signal triumph for British diplomacy. In reality Stormont had won a pyrrhic victory. France's concessions merely sought to gain more time; simultaneously her military and naval preparations were accelerated. Though Britain's vigorous diplomacy had removed one point of tension, it could do nothing to halt the drift towards open war.[16] Britain's acceptance of this was apparent in the decision, towards the end of October, to intercept French and Spanish ships carrying supplies to the Americans, even though these vessels were ostensibly travelling to Bourbon possessions

[13] Cf. *Journal de l'abbé de Véri*, ii. 59–60.

[14] The tense state of relations did not prevent both Secretaries of State from taking their habitual holidays in Aug.: Weymouth went to his estate while Suffolk was on his honeymoon: CP (Angleterre) 524, fo. 309. There is some evidence that ministers did not expect that their demands would produce an immediate war: see e.g. *HMC Abergavenny*, 17.

[15] Dull, *French Navy*, 79–80; *Franklin Papers*, xxiv. 472; CP (Angleterre) 524, fo. 364.

[16] In Oct., Britain became fully aware of the extent of French commitments to the Americans from some papers on the captured privateer *Lexington*: North to Stormont, 17 Oct. 1777, Stormont Papers, Box 45.

in the New World.[17] Such action implied that peace was not expected to continue, and this was certainly the cabinet's view by the closing months of 1777.[18] During these months, however, Britain's firm stance was complicated, and at times imperilled by, the continuing shuttle diplomacy undertaken by N. P. Forth, who was still acting as a channel of communication between George III and North and the supposedly pacific Maurepas.[19] Forth's activities did not always weaken official policy. In August he was used to support the cabinet's offensive over privateering.[20] He reinforced Stormont's official protests by clear warnings to Maurepas that British public opinion was demanding war and that French concessions were essential. On this occasion his representations contributed to British success; they also confirmed ministers in their erroneous belief that Maurepas was pacific.[21] Forth's principal impact during the second half of 1777 was more damaging. His repeated journeys between London and Paris, and the assurances of Britain's pacifism which he carried, weakened official diplomacy. North's involvement in foreign policy in 1777–8 arose from a genuine dread of simultaneous wars in America and in Europe; he was beginning to lose heart and to doubt if victory were possible against the Americans alone, far less against the combined forces which now threatened.[22]

Both the inner group and Weymouth, as Southern Secretary, aimed to preserve peace as long as possible: by this stage even North had accepted war was inevitable and intended only to delay its outbreak.[23] But their methods were different and their messages

[17] SP 78/304, fo. 258.

[18] Significantly, the King's Speech at the beginning of the new parliamentary session (20 Nov. 1777) for the first time explicitly referred to the threat from the Bourbons and clearly looked towards an early war: *Journal of the House of Commons*, xxxvi. 541.

[19] Forth's importance is suggested by the fact that at this point he was put on the official payroll: *HMC Abergavenny*, 18. He continued to receive a secret service pension of £600 until 1810: C. R. Middleton, *The Administration of British Foreign Policy, 1782–1846* (Durham, NC, 1977), 337. The King's continued involvement is indicated by *Corr. Geo. III*, iii. 482; this refers to North's letter to Stormont of 15 Oct. 1777, Stormont Papers, Box 45. George III's participation is at this point to be explained by his absolute desire to reconquer America. The precise movements of Forth in 1777–8, and the negotiations which passed through his hands, cannot be reconstructed completely. The best source, which has not hitherto been exploited, is an important series of letters between North and Stormont which are in Stormont Papers, Box 45. In these private letters and in his official dispatches, Stormont continued to argue, though with diminishing conviction, that Maurepas was more pacific, or simply less bellicose, than the other French ministers, and this, no doubt, encouraged North's continuing approaches to him.

[20] See North's 3 letters to Stormont, 23 and 27 Aug. 1777, Stormont Papers, Box 45; CP (Angleterre) 524, fos. 430–3; *Corr. Geo. III*, iii. 467; cf. M. Ward, *Forth* (Chichester, 1982), 24–5.

[21] Though the peace overtures which he also carried were rejected outright: Doniol, *Participation*, ii. 527–9.

[22] C. R. Ritcheson, *British Politics and the American Revolution* (Norman, Okla., 1954), 216, 233.   [23] North to Stormont, 15 Oct. 1777, Stormont Papers, Box 45.

contradictory. Official diplomacy rammed home the message that Britain was arming and was at least as prepared as France to fight. Simultaneously, Forth was conveying the assurances of North and George III, that Britain was pacific and had no wish to see the conflict in America spread to Europe.[24] These contradictory viewpoints placed Stormont in a tricky situation. He was aware of Forth's private diplomacy, which involved not merely the King and the leader of the British ministry, but his own uncle and political mentor, Mansfield.[25] Simultaneously, he was receiving Weymouth's strongly worded dispatches prescribing a belligerent stance at Paris. The ambassador's own response to these divided counsels cannot be fixed with complete certainty. There are occasional signs that, particularly after August 1777, he softened the line prescribed by Weymouth, to accord more with the private diplomacy which was in action.[26] The impact of these fissures is clearer. They undermined British diplomacy towards France and can only have encouraged Vergennes.

The inner group was also active in Anglo-Spanish relations, though here its impact was less damaging. Britain's attitude towards Madrid was affected by the approach of war with France. During the 1770s Britain had separated Anglo-Spanish relations from Anglo-French diplomacy. From the late summer of 1777, however, these two dimensions coalesced, and before long ministers were viewing the Bourbon powers as a united and hostile force: as they had been throughout the 1760s.[27] The familiar assumptions re-emerged, largely because war in Europe was seen to be inevitable. Simultaneously, the cabinet began to be concerned at the enlarged Spanish navy: intelligence reports in August suggested that Charles III's fleet of around sixty ships of the line would be a major factor in any war.[28] Spain's importance to both Britain and France in 1777–9 reflected the success with which she had rebuilt her navy.

The effectiveness of British efforts to prevent the use of French harbours by American privateers created an additional problem. Barred from entering France's ports, American vessels increasingly began to put in to Spain's northern harbours, especially Bilbao and El Ferrol, where they tried to sell their prizes.[29] Britain was fully aware

---

[24] See e.g. North to Forth, 25 Sept. 1777, *HMC Abergavenny*, 18.
[25] For Mansfield's continuing desire for peace in Europe, see ibid. 17.
[26] This can be implied from CP (Angleterre) 524, fo. 423.
[27] e.g. SP 78/304, fos. 70–1.
[28] *Sandwich Papers*, i. 235–45 *passim*; SP 94/204, fo. 105. Information about the Spanish navy's strength was provided by two lists forwarded from Madrid at this time: SP 94/204, fos. 80–1 and 223–7. Its precise strength cannot be fixed with absolute certainty. British intelligence reports (ibid.) suggested an effective strength of 64 or 65 ships of the line in summer 1777, while Prof. Dull (*French Navy*, 363–4) gives a figure of 58 two years later.
[29] SP 94/204 *passim*.

of these developments, but her response was muted, and even though her protests were subsequently stepped up, her representations at Madrid were far less vigorous than at Paris. In a similar way, the British government did not at first complain about Spain's increasing aid to the Americans, though it certainly knew of this.[30] Good relations remained London's objective.[31] Indeed, the growing appreciation of Spanish naval strength reinforced established strategy. From the late summer of 1777 Spain's neutrality in an Anglo-French war was improbable, but it was still energetically pursued by ministers.

Official policy was reinforced by the continuing private diplomacy undertaken by George III and by North. Their hope of maintaining Anglo-Spanish friendship suffered a severe blow in September when the experienced Masserano, by now seriously ill, left Britain.[32] The easy personal relations which both North and Mansfield had established with him had been the basis of the efforts to retain and even reinforce friendship with Madrid after 1775.[33] Mansfield continued to cultivate the senior Spanish diplomat in London, Escarano, who was now acting as chargé d'affaires, and emphasized British pacifism. He also sought to explain away Britain's accelerating naval preparations.[34] The efficacy of such private initiatives—like Weymouth's official attempts to remain on good terms with Spain—was limited. The increasing Anglo-French tension was accompanied by a deterioration in relations with Madrid. This was, for the moment, a lower priority in London than Anglo-French diplomacy. Equally, Spain was still undecided about war and was certainly not yet committed to intervention on France's side. She continued to hope that her neutrality might produce some British concessions, particularly in the long-running commercial disputes. By the closing months of 1777, however, the seeds of future conflict had been sown.

The final crisis in Anglo-French relations began in December 1777. It was both brief and decisive: within two months a colonial rebellion had become a world war. The transformation was precipitated in early December by news of Burgoyne's surrender at Saratoga.[35] This

[30] SP 94/204 fos. 3, 259–60; cf. SP 78/305, fo. 76.

[31] See, in particular, SP 94/204, fo. 105.

[32] The ambassador was to die in Nov. 1777: CP (Angleterre) 525, fo. 360.

[33] Mansfield subsequently spoke of Masserano as 'his intimate friend': E 6998, fo. 9. For the ambassador's trust in North's pacifism and good intentions, see ibid., fo. 13.

[34] Ibid., fos. 8, 9–13.

[35] News reached Paris first and had to be confirmed by Stormont: SP 78/305, fos. 150, 173–4.

was a shattering blow to the North Ministry, which until then had believed that the rebellion might still be defeated. No doubt there was always an element of bravado in the continual assertions of ministers and diplomats that Britain anticipated victory in America; there was certainly more than a dash of hyberbole about Mansfield's boast to the Spanish chargé d'affaires at the beginning of October, that the 'total ruin' of the rebels was to be expected.[36] Yet they were justified in terms of the news which ministers were receiving of military operations across the Atlantic. The campaigns of 1776 and 1777 appeared to leave Britain substantially ahead on points.[37] Whatever the long-term problems involved in the re-establishment of British authority over the colonies, the cabinet was correct to believe a purely military victory was possible and perhaps likely. Such hopes were utterly destroyed by Burgoyne's surrender.[38] Saratoga was probably the turning-point in the American War, the hinge on which the whole conflict revolved.

Burgoyne's capitulation was decisive in three distinct ways. It totally undermined British strategy since the outbreak of the rebellion and forced ministers, during the sombre winter of 1777–8, to produce a new plan for military operations in America.[39] Secondly, it precipitated a domestic political crisis: the scale of the reverse stung the opposition into a fierce parliamentary assault while Lord North, who throughout 1777 had been discouraged by the increasing French preparations, now lost heart completely and tried to resign. The first half of 1778 was a period of political turmoil in England and this diverted ministerial attention from foreign affairs, particularly after the ending of Anglo-French diplomacy in March. Finally, the news produced an immediate deterioration in relations with France, which moved rapidly to their final crisis. Little more than three months elapsed before ambassadors were withdrawn and war began in fact, if not in law.

Burgoyne's surrender was particularly decisive because of its impact at the French court. Once again, as since 1775, the key to

---

[36] E 6998, fo. 10.

[37] Cf. the verdict of the most authoritative historian of the war, Mackesy, *War for America*, 141. Accounts of the campaigns of 1776–7 written by North American scholars often fall victim to a sense of the inevitability of Britain's eventual defeat and therefore exaggerate the achievements of rebel arms: see e.g. the otherwise admirable study by D. Higginbotham, *The War of American Independence: Military Attitudes, Policies and Practice 1763–1789* (Bloomington, Ind., 1971), chs. 7 and 8. This is even true of the penetrating essay by D. Syrett, 'The Failure of the British Effort in America, 1777', in J. Black and P. Woodfine, eds., *The British Navy and the Use of Naval Power in the Eighteenth Century* (Leicester, 1988), 171–90.

[38] For an exaggerated but evocative French description of the British reaction, see CP (Angleterre) 526, fos. 157–74.

[39] For the efforts to do so see Mackesy, *War for America*, 154–6.

relations was not British policy but French strategy. The news of Saratoga was the occasion for Vergennes to move finally to open support of the Americans and war with Britain.[40] The sensation caused by their success was skilfully exploited by the American commissioners in Paris, who began to press for a formal political alliance between Congress and the French King. Saratoga was also used by Vergennes to overcome Louis XVI's hesitation. By 12 December 1777—barely a fortnight after news had first reached Paris—formal Franco-American negotiations were under way. Their progress was materially assisted by reports of secret talks in the French capital for an Anglo-American reconciliation. North had initiated these after he heard of Burgoyne's surrender. It was always improbable these discussions would lead anywhere, since it was widely recognized that one immediate result of French intervention would be that the Americans would not settle for anything less than independence, which Britain was not yet prepared to grant.[41] But the existence of the talks was used by the Americans to increase pressure on Vergennes, and they certainly smoothed the path to the conclusion of Franco-American treaties of commerce and alliance, signed formally on 6 February 1778.

The French ministry recognized that these treaties amounted to a declaration of war on Britain. Since fighting in America was still viewed in London as a civil war, no third party could intervene without becoming a belligerent. By the close of 1777 Stormont had concluded it was only a matter of time before fighting began.[42] He had already noted that French ministers were abandoning their attempts to persuade him that France would remain at peace, and that the veil of neutrality was slipping. By January 1778 meetings between the ambassador and members of Louis XVI's government had all but ceased.[43] Vergennes and Maurepas recognized that the time for pretence had passed, and were in any case preoccupied with the Franco-American talks at Versailles. Stormont, from his base in Paris and deprived of regular audiences with French ministers, was unable to penetrate these discussions, though he was certainly aware of them in general terms. He also knew of the considerable naval

[40] The conventional view is that it alone propelled France into open intervention. For a convincing rebuttal, which emphasizes that the success of Sartine's naval reconstruction and the defeats suffered by Washington's forces were at least as important, see Dull, *French Navy*, 89 ff.

[41] W. A. Brown, *Empire or Independence? A Study in the Failure of Reconciliation 1774–1783* (Baton Rouge, La., 1941), 183–93; Ritcheson, *British Politics*, 234–41; Mackesy, *War for America*, 159.   [42] SP 78/305, *passim.*

[43] The British ambassador did not see either Vergennes or Maurepas, except on formal state occasions, until 22 Jan. 1778: SP 78/306, fos. 113–8; cf. Doniol, *Participation*, ii. 744 n. 3.

preparations, as France commissioned her fleet for war. British intelligence penetration of the American mission in Paris ensured that the cabinet was fully cognisant with the rapid progress of the negotiations during January, and received copies of the actual treaties immediately after their conclusion.[44]

Britain's official diplomacy accepted that a French war had become unavoidable.[45] Weymouth certainly assumed that a wider conflict was inevitable; but it is remarkable how little attention he devoted to relations with France in the early weeks of 1778.[46] Such realism did not extend to the secret diplomacy pursued by North, who maintained his strictly private and futile efforts to postpone hostilities. His emissary, Forth, continued to post back and forward to Paris in early 1778.[47] As late as March—the same month that ambassadors were finally withdrawn—the Prime Minister was still trying to preserve peace through his private correspondence with Maurepas.[48] But most members of the cabinet were realistic enough to accept that the time for compromise and negotiation had passed.[49] In these circumstances diplomacy simply stopped. Stormont, like his counterpart Noailles in London, had become redundant. Accepting that peace would soon end, he redoubled his efforts to collect intelligence about the French armed forces and devoted his dispatches to France's likely strategy in the coming war. The final breach came in March 1778, when Vergennes formally communicated the Franco-American treaties to the British government through his ambassador in London.[50] Stormont was immediately told to depart from Paris without taking leave; Noailles also asked for his passports; and by mid-March diplomatic relations had ceased.

[44] S. F. Bemis, 'British Secret Service and the French-American Alliance', *American Historical Review*, 29 (1923–4), 490–1. Stormont, it should be added, was able to send word that France had signed treaties with the Americans on the actual day they were concluded: SP 78/306, fos. 169–70.

[45] See e.g. William Eden (Under-Secretary of State in the Northern Department) to Stormont, 6 Jan. 1778, Stormont Papers, Box 52.

[46] This led Stormont to complain in thinly veiled terms: SP 78/306, fos. 133–4.

[47] For North's view that it might still be possible to delay hostilities, see *Sandwich Papers*, i. 261–2; cf. *Journal de l'abbé de Véri*, ii. 69–70, and *Corr. Geo. III*, iv. 6, 40, 45–6, for his efforts at Paris. For Forth's repeated journeys, see CP (Angleterre) 528, fo. 232; *Corr. Geo. III*, iv. 13; and, more generally, Ward, *Forth*, chs. 5 and 6. His negotiations were accompanied by secret and unofficial efforts, in which the Prime Minister was also involved, to negotiate a settlement with the Americans: see Ritcheson, *British Politics*, 234–41. Forth's standing at the French court and especially with Maurepas was high after his success in suppressing a particularly scurrilous pamphlet libelling the French Queen which was about to be published in London: Ward, *Forth*, 38–49.   [48] *Journal de l'abbé de Véri*, ii. 83.

[49] This was apparent, for example, in the cabinet's decision on 18 Feb. 1778 to attack convoys sailing to America even if these were protected by French or other foreign ships: *Sandwich Papers*, i. 270; cf. *Corr. Geo. III*, iv. 5, 13, 23, 30, 34, 36, etc., for the general expectation of an early war in these months.   [50] SP 78/306, fos. 345–6, 365–6.

The breach was deliberately provoked by Vergennes, who understood that it would inevitably follow the communication of the Franco-American treaties. His aim was to increase pressure on Madrid. Charles III's rebuilt navy had become a central factor in British and French calculations and hence in the diplomacy of each state from 1777 until 1779, when Madrid finally entered the war. Vergennes's decision to fight Britain had been based, to a significant extent, on detailed calculations of naval strength. Sartine's work in the dockyards, together with Britain's already extensive commitments in the American hemisphere, ensured that in January 1778 France enjoyed 'effective naval parity'.[51] This situation was temporary and might only last for one campaign. British naval resources were always potentially far greater, and France's temporary advantage would soon be eroded as Britain commissioned more ships. The Spanish navy was a vital part of French strategic planning, if not for 1778 then certainly for 1779. However, Spain was proving distinctly reluctant to join in the long-awaited *revanche* and to commit her powerful fleet. In December, at the same time that serious negotiations with the Americans began, Vergennes had stepped up pressure on Madrid. Floridablanca refused to be stampeded. He and his colleagues remained reluctant to support American independence and in any case hoped, through skilful diplomacy, to exploit Spain's favourable position.

Madrid's independent stance was a major threat to French strategy and this was clearly understood at Versailles. In provoking the formal breach with Britain in March 1778, Vergennes hoped that the imminent war would overcome Spanish hesitation. Yet the withdrawal of ambassadors was not immediately followed by declarations of war, or by actual hostilities between Britain and France. The severing of diplomatic relations was normally the signal for fighting to begin, but in 1778 several months elapsed before the first shots were fired: it was July before France declared war, after naval clashes in the Channel. During these months each government regarded itself as engaged in hostilities, but neither wished to strike the first blow.[52]

The explanation for this phoney war is to be found in the broader political and strategic objectives of each state. In the case of France Vergennes's aim of involving Spain was, once again, crucial. Madrid was particularly alarmed that a precipitate declaration of war might expose the highly vulnerable annual Spanish fleet from South America to interception by the British navy. French ministers,

[51] Dull, *French Navy*, 97, and figures there cited; cf., more generally, ibid. 89–105.
[52] *Documents of the American Revolution*, xv, nos. 72–4; *Sandwich Papers*, i. 367; *Corr. Geo. III*, iii. 74.

moreover, were still anxious to complete the final disposition of their forces before fighting began: they were haunted by memories of the Seven Years War, when a sudden British attack had trapped France's ships and troops in Europe and contributed significantly to Britain's eventual victory overseas. Vergennes's primary concern was to avoid being labelled the aggressor. France's diplomatic position would be significantly strengthened if Britain declared war or committed an obviously belligerent act first.

Louis XVI had two major defensive alliances: with the Spanish Bourbons and with the Austrian Habsburgs. Madrid's resistance to suggestions that Spain should fight on the American side made Vergennes anxious not to be seen as the aggressor. This would allow Charles III to evade his treaty obligations on the grounds that French provocation rendered the defensive alliance of 1761 void. In the case of the Austrian alliance Vergennes's aims were rather different. This was due to the emergence of a serious crisis over the Bavarian succession during the early months of 1778.[53] By the spring an Austro-Prussian war in Germany appeared probable. This seriously threatened Vergennes's strategy against Britain, which demanded peace in Europe. Austria was France's ally and could demand military assistance if Prussia attacked. But the French foreign minister had already warned Vienna in March that he believed Austria to be the real aggressor over Bavaria and therefore not entitled to aid under the defensive alliance signed in 1756. Though this reduced the likelihood of a general European conflict, it did not remove it completely, particularly as a Russo-Turkish confrontation over the Crimea also threatened to erupt into war. By delaying Anglo-French hostilities Vergennes believed that he was also preserving peace in Europe. In particular, a British attack would make it easier to ignore Austrian demands for support. France could then argue that she was not seeking aid over the American War and expected Vienna to do likewise should Prussia attack.[54]

It was principally Vergennes's actions which delayed open warfare until summer 1778, but Britain was also anxious not to start fighting. There were two principal reasons for this: the desire not to impede London's own search for an alliance and the hope that it might be possible to stay on good terms with Spain. In these months the British government was scouring Europe for an ally, and ministers had no

[53] A fuller account of the Bavarian question and its international repercussions is provided below, pp. 267–70.

[54] O. T. Murphy, 'The View from Versailles', in R. Hoffman and P. J. Albert, eds., *Diplomacy and Revolution: The Franco-American Alliance of 1778* (Charlottesville, Va., 1981), 122–3.

wish to undermine these efforts by appearing the aggressor.[55] Any defensive alliance they might secure would be inoperative if Britain declared war first. Furthermore, the cabinet was all but paralysed by a serious dispute between the advocates of a 'European' and an 'American' strategy.[56] This made any decisive naval action, such as an attack on the French fleet commanded by d'Estaing, which was sent to the American hemisphere, very difficult. In this way Britain successfully avoided being labelled the aggressor until Admiral Keppel's encounter in the Channel with the *Belle-Poule* in June.[57] The clashes between the British and French ships signalled the real beginning of the Anglo-French War, which was formally declared by France on 10 July.[58] Britain immediately put her own forces on a war footing and, early in August, launched her campaign against French trade.

The rapid deterioration in Anglo-French relations was accompanied by an unsuccessful search for an ally. These efforts originated in Britain's increasingly desperate situation, with the prospect of continued fighting in America and war in Europe, perhaps even against the 'united House of Bourbon'.[59] Familiar threats were

[55] Cf. below, pp. 265–72, for this search.

[56] For this clash, see G. S. Brown, 'The Anglo-French Naval Crisis, 1778: A Study of Conflict in the North Cabinet', *William and Mary Quarterly*, 3rd series, 13 (1956), 3–25, and the somewhat fuller account in his *The American Secretary: The Colonial Policy of Lord George Germain 1775–1778* (Ann Arbor, 1963), 149–73, though Sandwich has a better case than Dr Brown allows from his viewpoint of Germain.

[57] For details of the naval clashes see *Burke Corr.* iii. 461.

[58] Brown, 'The Anglo-French Naval Crisis', 4 n. 4.

[59] See Suffolk to Keith, Most Secret and Most Confidential, 6 Jan. 1778, SP 80/220. By Mar. 1778, ministers believed that Britain might be attacked by either France or Spain: *Documents of the American Revolution*, xiii, no. 1499. D. A. Baugh, in a stimulating and original survey, has recently taken up the whole question of the necessity or otherwise of alliances at this time: 'Why did Britain Lose Command of the Sea during the War for America?', in Black and Woodfine, eds., *The British Navy and Naval Power*, 149–69. His perspective is that of the 20th-c. strategist, rather than that of the 18th-c. statesman or foreign minister. Though he rightly cautions against seeing any automatic link between the lack of an ally and the loss of naval supremacy in the middle years of the war, his conclusion that Britain 'was better off without Continental allies in the 1778–83 war' (158) misses the point. Prof. Baugh ignores the extent to which British strategy and policy at this time were conditioned by the experiences of previous successful wars against France and especially that of 1756–63, and these memories suggested the value of allies. So too did the fact that, from the early months of 1778 onwards, Britain's war with France displaced the fighting in America at the top of the cabinet's agenda. His statement (158) that 'The diplomatic situation on the Continent was not alarming to Britain between 1775 and 1783, mainly because the policy of France (which aimed only at a limited reduction of British power) was directed towards maintaining a quiet Europe' is simply wrong for the period after 1778. Ministers believed that only by diverting French resources to a European continental war could they again defeat her. They were here applying the prescription of earlier wars, which suggested that both Hanover and the British war effort would be at risk unless France could be tied down on the European continent, as Suffolk was trying to do in the spring of 1778.

countered by the time-honoured response, for Suffolk's views on foreign policy ran in very traditional grooves. During the first half of 1778 he made determined efforts to find an ally. This reversed Britain's diplomatic strategy since 1773, when the prolonged Anglo-Russian negotiations had finally broken down.[60] The prospects might appear dim, and indeed the cupboard soon proved to be bare; yet such initiatives were now the only option open to the North Ministry. Though Suffolk knew that France aimed to neutralize the European continent, he hoped the Anglo-French war could still be forced back into the familiar pattern and America could in effect be reconquered in Germany. He recognized Hanover had been weakened by the departure of the troops taken into British service, and he believed his wish for a continental war forced him to provide in the traditional way for the Electorate's defence, whether or not it was actually threatened by France.

These efforts were inevitably directed towards the three eastern powers. During the first half of 1778 British diplomacy resembled Rip Van Winkle. Since the first partition of Poland ministers had shown next to no interest in eastern Europe. Britain's representatives in St Petersburg, Berlin, and Vienna had for several years enjoyed an untroubled existence. They were now abruptly reawakened by demands for immediate reports on the prospects for an alliance. Britain's relations with the three eastern powers in fact remained very much in the state in which they had been in the early 1770s, the point at which the impossibility of concluding alliances had been acknowledged in London. But the desperate situation which the British government faced gave impetus to the new search for support.

Suffolk believed the most likely partner to be Russia, still viewed as a natural friend and ally.[61] Relations had been cooled by the failure of previous negotiations and by Catherine II's refusal in 1775 to loan Russian regiments. Russia believed Britain had become a marginal factor in European politics and St Petersburg's interest in an English alliance had therefore all but vanished.[62] Anglo-Russian diplomacy was at its lowest point in the entire age of the American Revolution. The gulf between the states was apparent in the fact that in 1776–7 relations had been maintained for over eighteen months at the level

---

[60] There is one partial exception to this statement: the unsuccessful attempt to hire Russian soldiers for America during the second half of 1775 (see above, pp. 217–20); but this did not involve a full defensive alliance.

[61] See e.g. the 'Instructions' for Hugh Elliot, 3 Mar. 1777, SP 90/101.

[62] This is strongly suggested by the very few references to Britain in the Russian foreign policy documents for the 1770s: *Sbornik*, cxviii, cxxxv, and cxlv *passim*. For an explicit confirmation, see ibid. cxxxv. 238.

of chargé d'affaires and that there had been a minor dispute over the resumption of full representation.[63]

Anglo-Prussian relations were still very poor in 1778, as they had been since the Seven Years War. In the first half of the 1770s Britain's youthful minister, James Harris, had won the plaudits of the court and the esteem of the King himself, but there had been no parallel improvement in relations, which remained cool and distant. Britain continued to regard Frederick II as her implacable foe, especially after the clash over Danzig, and the reception unofficially given to American agents at Berlin had made matters worse.[64] The 1770s had, in fact, seen a softening in the Prussian King's hostility, but Britain was blind to this and continued to give a low priority to relations with him. Instead the cabinet, and particularly Suffolk, tried to cultivate Vienna, hoping for a future revival of an Austrian alliance. Though the mid-1770s had seen some tension between Vienna and George III's Hanoverian ministry, this did little permanent damage to Anglo-Austrian diplomacy, which remained friendly and harmonious. Britain's hopes were still focused on Joseph II.[65] Ministers believed an alliance would not be concluded until the Emperor became sole ruler on Maria Theresa's death. Though Suffolk remained personally devoted to the Old System, he acknowledged that its revival was for the moment impossible.[66]

The Northern Secretary instead concentrated on Russia. In the previous autumn Britain's new envoy, James Harris, had at last set off for St Petersburg. His instructions had been drawn up against the background of a rapid deterioration in Anglo-French relations. They had envisaged future alliance negotiations, though for the moment Harris was simply to listen to any Russian proposals.[67] In the closing months of 1777, as war with France came ever closer, Suffolk had begun to hope that Britain could benefit from the menacing situation in the Balkans. Russian military intervention in the Crimea appeared to threaten a full-scale war between Catherine II and the Turks, and

[63] SP 91/100–1 *passim*.

[64] See A. Toborg, 'Frederick II of Prussia and his Relations with Great Britain during the American Revolution' (unpublished Ph.D. thesis, Columbia University, 1965), 42–73; London also resented the Prussian King's prohibition in 1777 of mercenary troops hired by Britain from passing through his territories on the way to embark for America: ibid. 74–97; see also SP 90/101.

[65] For example, in the official attention given by the British government to hints that the Emperor wished to visit England: see the 'Paper . . . received from Sir Robt. M. Keith during his Residence in England in the Winter *1775*', in SP 80/218; cf. Suffolk to Keith, Confidential, 4 Feb. 1777, SP 80/219.

[66] See, in particular, Suffolk to Keith, Most Secret and Most Confidential, 6 Jan. 1778, SP 80/220. His preference would have been for alliances with Austria and Russia.

[67] These are dated 3 Oct. 1777 and are in SP 91/101, fos. 168–75.

the Empress might therefore listen to British proposals. Though he was aware of the likely obstacles to any treaty, he set in motion the formal approach to St Petersburg early in 1778.[68]

This initiative aimed to secure Russian support against France. Specifically, Britain hoped that Catherine II would provide much-needed ships to transport soldiers and supplies across the Atlantic, since the British government now faced a critical shortage of shipping.[69] The rebellion had multiplied the demand for vessels, while removing the opportunity to hire transports in North America, as in previous wars, and Britain was now facing France as well. In more general terms Suffolk hoped to conclude a conventional defensive alliance, based on the familiar British view of France as the universal bogyman, stirring up the Turks against Catherine II, while aiding the Americans in their struggle with Britain.

This bid was briefly assisted by the growing crisis over Bavaria. The death of the last and childless Wittelsbach Elector at the very end of 1777 had been followed by an apparently striking success for Austrian diplomacy. Early in 1778 Vienna had announced an agreement with the heir, Charles Theodore of the Palatinate. By this the Habsburgs occupied Lower Bavaria, and they also appeared on the point of obtaining the remainder of the Electorate. Superficially this appeared a considerable Austrian triumph, but it was widely unpopular within the *Reich* and also in France, and it was opposed by Vienna's arch-enemy, Prussia.

The importance for British diplomacy was considerable. The first half of 1778 saw a growing threat of war over Bavaria. Austria's defensive alliance with France and Prussia's treaty with Russia meant that the dispute might grow into a general European conflict. This prospect was welcomed in London as a way out of Britain's predicament.[70] To British ministers the parallels with the situation in 1756 were, at least superficially, very striking. Then, as in 1778, Britain had faced an Anglo-French war in the colonies without a major ally in Europe. The fortuitous outbreak of a continental conflict, together with links with Prussia, had enabled Britain to tie

---

[68] His realism is apparent from his two dispatches to Keith, 6 Jan. 1778, SP 80/220. A discriminating study of the alliance negotiations in the early months of 1778 is provided by Madariaga, *Armed Neutrality*, 22–40, on which the following account is largely based; some relevant documents are printed in *Malmesbury Diaries*, i.

[69] Madariaga, *Armed Neutrality*, 21–2 and, more generally, D. Syrett, *Shipping and the American War* (London, 1970).

[70] North to [William Eden], undated but clearly Jan. or Feb. 1778, Stevens, *Facsimiles*, no. 1854. Here the cabinet may have been following Stormont's lead: SP 78/306, fo. 30. As late as July 1778, Germain was still hoping that France would be dragged into a continental war: *HMC Knox*, 144.

down France in Europe and defeat her overseas. During the early months of 1778 ministers clearly hoped that this pattern might recur and that, once again, a European war might be Britain's salvation. The approach to Russia thus came to have a broader purpose: that of securing leverage at St Petersburg and in this way contributing to a widening of any war in Germany or around the Black Sea.

It was not an unreasonable diplomatic strategy; more important, it was the only one open to Britain as she struggled to escape from her isolation. Success was always improbable, however, and her efforts were never wholehearted. In the event her hopes were dashed by Vergennes's shrewd diplomacy. France's foreign minister also understood the lessons of the Seven Years War and was determined that French strategy would never again be undermined by a division of resources between the continent and the colonies. He was therefore careful to keep France out of either of the European conflicts. Vergennes sought to restrain the Turks and refused to aid Austria.

These permutations denied Britain either an ally or the general European war for which ministers craved. For several months, however, there was an illusion of life in the corpse of British hopes for an alliance. Catherine II was particularly afraid she might be drawn into simultaneous wars over Bavaria and against the Turks. In the early months of 1778 this gave Britain a transient importance in Russian calculations. This was why Suffolk's initial approach was not rejected out of hand when it arrived in St Petersburg early in February. Panin's reply was cool, but Britain was invited to submit a formal treaty project: at this point Russia's predicament appeared so threatening that no possibility of aid could be dismissed. Suffolk duly forwarded an alliance project to the Russian court and, for a time, British hopes rose. His proposals were not aided by the fact that the draft treaty was essentially one that had previously been rejected by Catherine II. Remarkably, it retained the 'Turkish Clause', though ministers were prepared to pay a subsidy: the one substantive change from earlier projects.

The proposal to offer a subsidy and not military aid in any Russo-Turkish War was a poor recommendation against a background of tension over the Crimea, of which Suffolk was certainly aware. This was one reason why Britain's approach was rejected. More important, by the time her proposal reached St Petersburg, Catherine II's anxieties had been allayed. She had come to appreciate that her aims coincided with those of Vergennes. Both desired peace in Europe, and the Empress knew that France had actually informed Austria she would not aid her over Bavaria, which ensured that any German war would remain localized. This ended any Russian interest in new links with London, particularly as Catherine II was aware that Britain and France had withdrawn their ambassadors in mid-March, demonstrating war was imminent.[71] Towards the end of May, Britain's offer of an alliance was formally rejected.

British diplomacy had meanwhile undergone a quite sudden and dramatic volte-face. By 7 April 1778 Suffolk had performed a political somersault. Abandoning his own preference for an immediate Russian alliance, to be followed by *rapprochement* with Austria, he convinced himself that Britain's security demanded adherence to the 'Northern System': the alliance of Catherine II and Frederick II which was in fact close to dissolution![72] He therefore proposed nothing less than a new treaty with Berlin and a subsidy to Frederick II, to be paid in return for Prussian protection of Hanover.[73] This was apparently necessary, since the Electorate had provided Britain with troops and was now extremely vulnerable to attack. Suffolk's traditionalism partly explained his growing concern with Hanover. His wish for an enlarged conflict to commit French resources to a continental war forced him to consider how the Electorate could be defended if—as he wrongly assumed—France tried to overrun it and retain it as a bargaining counter in the peace negotiations. This dictated that Britain take steps to protect Hanover, as she had during the last two Anglo-French wars. One obvious way was through co-operation with Prussia, as in the Seven Years War. In the early months of 1778 Anglo-Prussian relations remained poor and there was no obvious reason to anticipate renewed overtures to Berlin.[74] Suffolk's initiative had more immediate causes. He threw British foreign policy into reverse because he had fallen victim both to Frederick II's byzantine diplomacy and to the insistent demands of George III as Elector rather than as King.

Frederick had been circulating wild stories of his own decisive influence in Russia, as part of his general strategy over Bavaria. These were reported from St Petersburg and from Berlin, and this encouraged Suffolk to look towards Prussia for assistance in Britain's search for a Russian alliance.[75] The most immediate influence on British diplomacy was the King, George III. Frederick II was also angling for Hanoverian support over Bavaria, since he was still anxious about the attitudes of France and Russia.[76] This involved a more friendly stance towards Britain as well and his minister

---

[71] *Malmesbury Diaries*, i. 183.
[72] For this misjudgement, see Madariaga, *Armed Neutrality*, 31.
[73] Suffolk to Elliot, nos. 8 and 11, 7 Apr. 1778, SP 90/102.
[74] See e.g., *Malmesbury Diaries*, i. 159.
[75] Toborg, 'Frederick II of Prussia and his relations with Great Britain', 111.
[76] Ibid. 98–125, for this strategy.

Finckenstein therefore made some overtures to Hugh Elliot towards the end of March 1778.[77] When Elliot's dispatches arrived on 6 April with news of the Prussian approach, George III insisted that a cabinet be held the very next day and that new instructions be sent immediately to Berlin.[78] In a similar way it was principally the King's wishes which persuaded Suffolk to overturn the established diplomatic strategy and propose a Prussian alliance.

George II abandoned his own anti-Prussian attitude out of concern for his defenceless Electorate and, more generally, his anxiety at Habsburg expansion in Germany, which he felt only Frederick II could challenge. British and Electoral interests appeared to coincide. A revival of the Anglo-Prussian alliance would protect Hanover and help check Austria; it might also trap France into a continental war. In fact George III was reluctant to commit Hanover to outright opposition to Vienna; he could not be induced to join the kind of *Fürstenbund* (League of Princes) which the Prussian King was trying to sponsor. But the Elector-King had no such compunction in committing Britain to Prussia's cause. He prevailed upon Suffolk and the cabinet, by now clutching at straws, to switch to a Prussian alliance.[79] The extent of the Northern Secretary's political conversion was striking; only a few days before he had reaffirmed his established preference for the Old System and for a pro-Habsburg stance over Bavaria.[80] Though his latest initiative was startling it foundered very quickly, for by the time the British offer reached Berlin, Frederick II's fears about the attitudes of France and Russia had been dispelled. The Prussian King therefore turned confidently to attack Austria, and Britain's half-initiative over a Prussian alliance led nowhere.[81] By the summer Britain found the doors at St Petersburg, Berlin, and Vienna bolted against her:[82] as, indeed, they had been since the early

---

[77] Elliot to Suffolk, no. 21, 28 Mar. 1778, SP 90/102. Britain's minister in Berlin was, in fact, more realistic than his superior proved to be: see his second, private letter of the same date, ibid.

[78] *Corr. Geo. III*, iv. 98. The clearest evidence of George III's influence as Elector is not the approach to Prussia but a remarkable letter also sent on 7 Apr. 1778 by Suffolk to Britain's representative in Bavaria, Morton Eden. This adopted a firmly anti-Austrian line over the Bavarian question, upheld the constitution of the *Reich* and the interests of the smaller states against Habsburg expansion, and instructed Eden to take his orders from the *Hanoverian* minister in Munich, with whom he was to co-operate; the whole dispatch reads as though it had been written by an Electoral minister rather than by a British Secretary of State: SP 81/113. More research is needed on the revival of Hanoverian influence on British foreign policy in the later 1770s.

[79] This desperation is apparent in the fact that Suffolk wrote *four* separate dispatches to Elliot on 7 Apr. (all in SP 90/102) and in the speed of the British reply: the letters from Berlin had only arrived on the 6th, yet a cabinet discussed them the next day (*Corr. Geo. III*, iv. 98) and they were answered later that day.   [80] Suffolk to Keith, 3 Apr. 1778, SP 80/220.

[81] See, in particular, Elliot to Suffolk, 28 Apr. and 4 May 1778, SP 90/102.

[82] Suffolk to Elliot, 19 June 1778, ibid.

1770s. Though ministers continued intermittently to pursue a Russian alliance, the cabinet had to face the enlarged American War without allies.

Suffolk's search for an alliance possesses broader significance. His efforts highlighted the continuing insularity of British diplomacy and the new and acute problems which it faced. The approach to Catherine II had assumed that the Anglo-French struggle was still the dominant concern of all Europe. But to Russia, as to the other continental states, it ranked third after the menacing situation in the Crimea and the threat of an enlarged conflict over Bavaria. Britain's approach had demonstrated her usual indifference to Catherine II's priorities. It had also revealed the extent to which British foreign policy had been undermined by the new political pattern in Europe. This theme was taken up by Charles Jenkinson (the future Lord Liverpool) in the course of a statesmanlike, if pessimistic, analysis of Britain's plight. During the debate on the Franco-American treaties he declared that

The great military powers in the interior parts of Europe, who have amassed together their great treasures, and have modelled their subjects into great armies, will in the next and succeeding period of time, become the predominant powers. France and Great Britain, which have been the first and second-rate powers of the European world will perhaps for the future be but of the third and fourth rate.[83]

His conclusions were endorsed by other observers and were well founded.[84] The political centre of gravity was to be found not in London or even Versailles, but in Potsdam and especially in St Petersburg. Britain's diplomatic isolation during the American War—as throughout the age of the American Revolution—owed less to the deficiencies of her own policies than to this realignment. Her traditional diplomatic strategy had been destroyed by political changes on the continent. Then, Britain's effort to manipulate continental alliances in her own interest demonstrated that this time-honoured ploy had been undermined by events. The political situation now appeared similar to that in 1756. In 1778, however, efforts to exploit the crises over Bavaria and the Crimea were unsuccessful. They failed not only because France now appreciated the importance of neutralizing the continent in any war with Britain, but also because Russia and Prussia were fully fledged great powers in their own right and not auxiliaries of the western states. Their resources, self-confidence, and political maturity ensured that after

---

[83] *Parl. Hist.* xix, col. 948 (17 Mar. 1778).
[84] e.g. *Walpole Corr.* xxiv. 498, 516.

1778 the Anglo-French war did not extend to Germany, and that Britain was left alone to fight the Americans and the Bourbons. This was the real consequence of Britain's failure to conclude an alliance during the decade after the Seven Years War. Isolation was acceptable in peacetime and even during either a war in America, or against one or both Bourbon powers; it was to prove more dangerous when Britain faced simultaneous wars in Europe and on the other side of the Atlantic.

A desire not to damage relations with Madrid had been an additional reason for Britain's reluctance to begin war against France during the spring and summer of 1778.[85] Spanish neutrality remained a significant British objective during the next twelve months and was doggedly pursued by the cabinet.[86] Yet the motives behind this strategy were changing as official policy became even more opportunistic. Britain now aimed merely to delay Spain's intervention for as long as possible. During the first half of 1778 the scale of Spanish naval preparations, reported by Britain's intelligence network, destroyed lingering hopes of Madrid's neutrality. By October the cabinet had accepted Spain would eventually declare war.[87] Thereafter Britain's policy was entirely tactical.[88] Charles III's rebuilt navy would be a formidable addition to Britain's enemies and any delay in its deployment would be welcome. Superficially Britain's strategy appeared successful.[89] It was summer 1779, fifteen months after Stormont's return from Paris, before Grantham was recalled from Madrid, and this delay was of some help to the hard-pressed British navy. Yet the postponement owed less to Britain's own diplomacy than to Spain's objectives. The real key to Charles III's intervention in the American War was not Anglo-Spanish relations, but Franco-Spanish diplomacy.

Spain's foreign minister Floridablanca had resented the way in which France had concluded her treaties with the Americans without

[85] Cf. above, pp. 263–4.

[86] Escarano to Floridablanca, 23 and 26 June 1778, E 7001; *Documents of the American Revolution*, xv, nos. 178–9. In Aug. 1778, in order to preserve the existing 'peace and friendship' with Madrid, Britain was very moderate over a clash on the Mississippi: cf. J. W. Caughey, *Bernardo de Gálvez in Louisiana 1776–1783* (Berkeley, 1934), 124.

[87] By the end of Oct., North believed that Spain's neutrality would only last another 2 months: B. D. Bargar, *Lord Dartmouth and the American Revolution* (Columbia, SC, 1965), 179–80. A few days later, Germain was expecting Spanish intervention: 4 Nov. 1778, *Documents of the American Revolution*, xv, nos. 238–9; cf. *HMC Knox*, 151–2; and *Sandwich Papers*, ii. 179.

[88] British aims after autumn 1778 are outlined in Germain to William Knox, 29 Oct. 1778, *HMC Knox*, 152; cf. *Corr. Geo. III*, iii. 208, and *Sandwich Papers*, ii. 179–83.

[89] For a time, the French ambassador in Madrid, Montmorin, even believed that Spain might be won over: Doniol, *Participation*, iii. 26, 48.

consulting Madrid, and he was determined not to be stampeded into a world war on their behalf.[90] He therefore resisted all Vergennes's pleas that Spain should intervene immediately, while at the same time secretly discussing Bourbon strategy in any conflict with Britain.[91] This caution was, at one level, realistic: Spain still needed to build up her navy and strengthen her defences, while her ministers had no wish to endanger the return of the South American fleet by declaring war. The main reason for the delay, however, was to extract the maximum advantages for Madrid. Floridablanca's astute diplomacy in 1777–9 exemplified the new attitude to the Family Compact and the growing freedom from French direction apparent at the Spanish court since the crisis over Port Egmont.

By 1778 Spain's immediate territorial objectives were clear. Though she wished to expel the British from Florida and from the Bay of Honduras, her principal goals lay in Europe, where she hoped to recover Gibraltar and Minorca. Floridablanca was always prepared to fight for these gains, but he was first anxious to see if territorial concessions might be secured by negotiation. With the rupture of Anglo-French diplomacy in March 1778, the initiative passed to Madrid. Ministers in London never fully appreciated that Britain was a pawn in Floridablanca's diplomatic tug-of-war with Vergennes.[92] Spain played off Britain against France with some skill and evident profit. When Bourbon objectives in the American War were fixed in April 1779, France was forced to promise to fight until Charles III had recovered Gibraltar: a substantial concession by Louis XVI and a significant triumph for Floridablanca.[93]

In 1778–9 it was therefore in the interests of both Britain and Spain that Madrid did not immediately enter the war. This was the origin of Spanish attempts to mediate, which began in April 1778 and continued for almost a year.[94] The idea of a Spanish diplomatic initiative to restore peace had occasionally been floated by Britain during the previous winter. These hints had been part of her established strategy of encouraging Spanish neutrality. Floridablanca's

[90] A good summary of Franco-Spanish relations in 1778–9 is provided by Dull, *French Navy*, 126–43; a more detailed account can be excavated from Doniol, *Participation*, ii–iii, *passim*.

[91] For these discussions, see A. Temple Patterson, *The Other Armada: The Franco-Spanish Attempt to Invade Britain in 1779* (Manchester, 1960), 37–58.

[92] Britain was not helped by the inadequacy of her ambassador in Madrid, the notably gullible Grantham, who took Spanish assurances almost at face value: e.g. SP 94/205, fos. 110–12, 119–20, and *passim*. For British dissatisfaction with his conduct, see *HMC Knox*, 152; for Weymouth's implied rebuke, see his letter to Grantham, Confidential, 29 Dec. 1778, SP 94/206.   [93] Conn, *Gibraltar*, 188.

[94] For a brief account of this initiative, see ibid. 182–7; it can be followed in detail in SP 94/205–8 *passim*.

adoption of mediation was equally opportunistic. He would have been delighted if the prize of Gibraltar could have been secured by negotiation, but his initiative was principally an attempt to reinforce Spain's diplomacy towards France.[95]

It was soon clear that success was improbable. Madrid's hints that Gibraltar was the expected price met with a frosty reception in London. Both Mansfield and North made clear that while the cabinet wanted peace and would be grateful if Spain could bring this about, there could be no question of the fortress's cession. Britain's insistence that Spanish mediation could only cover the Anglo-French war was an equally fundamental obstacle. A second impasse quickly emerged when it became clear that one of France's conditions for peace was British recognition of American independence, which Louis XVI had committed himself to secure in February 1778. Floridablanca's wish to use the mediation against Vergennes led Spain to ignore these fundamental obstacles and instead press ahead with the scheme. Madrid's offer to mediate was immediately accepted by France, but it was at first turned down by Britain. The cabinet, however, changed its mind when a new Spanish ambassador, the diminutive Almodóvar, reached London in mid-July 1778.[96]

Almodóvar's arrival was welcomed by the British government as evidence of Madrid's good faith.[97] Ministers were still emphasizing their desire for peace and for continued good relations. Weymouth, predictably, portrayed the outbreak of Anglo-French hostilities as the simple consequence of France's aggression, which he urged should not damage the existing friendship between Madrid and London.[98] He also sought to play on Spain's anxieties that a successful American revolt might imperil her own authority over her colonies.[99] Though Britain's diplomatic strategy towards Spain was crude and quite transparent, it was the only option available.

The Spanish mediation proposal occasionally spluttered into life during the summer and autumn of 1778. It was notably revived towards the end of September when the British Secretary at War, Viscount Barrington, contrived to leave the Spanish ambassador with the impression that the cabinet would be prepared to cede Gibraltar

---

[95] See, e.g. Dull, *French Navy*, 128, for one example of the way in which British hints of concessions during the Anglo-Spanish talks were used by Floridablanca in an attempt to extract similar concessions from France.

[96] Horace Walpole declared that his 'size makes him look as if he represented the King of Lilliput': *Walpole Corr.* xxiv. 413.

[97] In fact, the new ambassador was continually deceived over the Franco-Spanish discussions that were under way: Patterson, *Other Armada*, 46.

[98] E 7001, fos. 24–5, 30–1; cf. Weymouth to Grantham, 25 Aug. 1778, SP 94/206.

[99] e.g. Weymouth to Grantham, 27 Oct. 1778, ibid.

and Minorca if peace could be concluded.[100] In fact Britain's attitude was hardening, as the pace of Spanish naval preparations revealed that Madrid would soon declare war.[101] In mid-October Sandwich's fears about Britain's naval defences had led the cabinet to keep the negotiations going.[102] Even more than before these were a simple ploy to gain time.[103] In response to a Spanish request Britain duly submitted her terms for peace, but these demonstrated that the British and French positions were irreconcilable, particularly over American independence.[104] Floridablanca, who appreciated that Britain was simply playing for time and was himself now prepared for war, forced the issue in the early months of 1779. Spain tried to impose a settlement of her own, but her proposals were immediately rejected by London. Madrid's response was to sign the Convention of Aranjuez (April 1779) with France, which set out Bourbon war-aims and strategy and made an Anglo-Spanish war inevitable.

Britain continued her efforts to delay Spanish intervention until the end of the 1779 campaigning season, although this was not assisted by Weymouth's volcanic outburst against Almodóvar early in May.[105] Britain's diplomatic strategy was always weakened by the Southern Secretary's poor relations with Spanish representatives in London.[106] Perhaps inspired by reports of the signature of the Franco-Spanish convention he had blended anger and threats in equal proportion, apparently destroying a year's careful diplomacy in one ill-considered outburst: a month later, a chastened Weymouth was still seeking to repair the supposed damage.[107] In reality his tirade made no difference as the time for diplomatic pretence was over. Floridablanca, with France's guarantee to fight until Gibraltar had been recovered in his pocket, was finally prepared to enter the war. Franco-Spanish talks had agreed on a common strategy for the 1779 campaign, the centrepiece of which was an attempted invasion of England, and preparations for this were almost complete. Almodóvar was therefore told to ask for his passports.[108] In mid-June diplomatic relations were severed by his departure from

---

[100] Dull, *French Navy*, 129–30. It is not clear whether this was a private initiative by Barrington or simply Almodóvar's misunderstanding after a conversation.

[101] See North to Dartmouth, 31 Oct. 1778, summarized in *HMC Dartmouth*, 470.

[102] Mackesy, *War for America*, 249–50.

[103] This is particularly apparent from a comparison of Weymouth's ostensible letter to Grantham of 27 Oct. 1778 with his 'Most Confidential' dispatch of the same date: both are in SP 94/206.

[104] This is clearly evident in Weymouth to Grantham, 27 Oct. 1778, ibid.

[105] For this, see E 7005, fos. 8–9; *HMC Knox*, 157.

[106] E 7001, fos. 30–1.

[107] E 7020, fos. 68–73; cf. Weymouth to Grantham, 11 June 1779, SP 94/208.

[108] E 7020, fos. 64–5.

London.[109] Even now ministers were trying to patch up relations with Spain. During his final weeks in London, the ambassador was approached by several emissaries, all suggesting further negotiations. On 12 June a determined effort had been made by 'a friend and relative' of North to convince him that war could still be avoided, but it was too late. Britain's strategy for the war with Spain was now implemented; in particular, attacks were to be mounted against her sprawling and vulnerable American empire.[110] Bourbon strategy posed a more direct challenge. Little more than a month after Almodóvar's departure the first ships in the Franco-Spanish invasion force were sighted in the Channel.

[109] The Spanish ambassador left on 20 June; for an account of his final weeks in London, see E 7020, fos. 71–7. Grantham was immediately recalled and left Madrid on 6 July: SP 94/ 208.
[110] *Documents of the American Revolution*, xvi, nos. 640, 641; xvii, nos. 149, 153.

11

War in Europe, 1778–1780

BOURBON intervention transformed the American War. The defeat of the rebellion was now secondary to victory over Britain's established rivals, and this changed London's diplomatic priorities. The fighting with France revived the familiar disputes over neutral rights and these dominated foreign policy until the winter of 1780–1. In one sense Britain's diplomacy continued to be essentially anti-French, for it aimed principally to deny France items of strategic value and in particular the all-important naval stores, seen as the key to the expanded war. For their part, the neutrals were anxious to exploit the commercial opportunities created by the conflict and resented attempts to control their trade.

In summer 1778 serious clashes over neutral commerce were widely expected.[1] It was assumed these would be caused principally by Britain. In previous eighteenth-century conflicts, and especially during the Seven Years War, London's high-handed behaviour had aroused lasting resentment. Britain's problem after 1778 was partly one of credibility. Few contemporaries believed she would observe relevant treaty provisions or even her own maritime rules, and most feared that political expediency and *force majeure* would again decide the issue of neutral rights.[2] This fear was strengthened by Britain's rhetoric. Though British policy would prove to be less intransigent than expected, ministers always adopted a high tone with the neutral states and rejected, often peremptorily, all their claims. The continuing violence of Britain's language did much to conceal the periodic moderation of her policy. London's view of a 'reasonable' concession proved different from that of the neutrals. Their anxieties were increased by the realization that the English Channel, the principal artery of Europe's maritime trade, was also a magnet for British privateers and cruisers, which were the cutting edge of official policy. Clashes were inevitable and by 1780 these had produced a serious deterioration in Anglo-Dutch diplomacy and had exacerbated relations with the states around the Baltic. This reflected Dutch domination of the carrying trade and northern Europe's pre-eminence as a source of naval stores.

[1] See e.g. *Bernstorffsche Papiere*, iii. 573.
[2] C. L. Roslund-Mercurio, 'The Problem of Neutral Rights in Swedish Relations with Great Britain, 1775–1780' (unpublished Ph.D. thesis, Syracuse University, 1972), 129, 178, 204.

The fundamental problem was the absence of an established legal framework regulating the position of neutrals in wartime.[3] Instead the situation was very fluid, and any dispute was likely to be resolved by naval might and political will. Nevertheless, some rules had become established. There were two principal sources for these. Certain customary laws governing wartime commerce had evolved since the Middle Ages, while in the seventeenth and eighteenth centuries there had been a growing tendency for such trade to be regulated by specific and usually bilateral agreements. Though the doctrines in these two sources were somewhat contradictory, together they provided such framework as existed for neutral trade after 1778.

The most important was the *Consolato del Mare*, originally a medieval compilation which had some later modifications. It favoured a relatively harsh view of neutral rights and decreed that the flag did not cover the cargo. This meant that enemy goods on a neutral ship could be seized and condemned and, as a corollary, neutral property on an enemy ship was free. With the expansion of European trade and the development of national merchant fleets from the middle of the seventeenth century onwards, a more liberal maritime code had evolved. Its principal tenet was embodied in the celebrated formula 'free ships make free goods': that is to say, during wartime neutrals could trade in non-contraband items with belligerents. This doctrine was considerably simpler and more generous towards neutral commercial nations and was therefore rapidly adopted by them.[4] Though relatively small states, these often had sizeable merchant fleets: this was true of Denmark and, in particular, the Dutch Republic. The new doctrine of 'free ships' rather than the framework of the *Consolato* was championed by commercial Europe and incorporated into its treaties. Fifty-one conventions regulating trade had been concluded between 1650 and 1780: thirty-six contained the 'free ships, free goods' principle, while only fifteen retained the harsher provisions of the *Consolato*.[5] During the second half of the eighteenth century this trend was encouraged by the liberal economic ideas of the Enlightenment.

[3] The standard authority on neutral commerce during the American War is Madariaga, *Armed Neutrality*, on which much of the following discussion is based: see, in particular, pp. 57–95; there is also a useful outline in S. F. Bemis, *The Diplomacy of the American Revolution* (Bloomington, Ind., 1957), chs. 10 and 11; while D. Syrett, *Neutral Rights and the War in the Narrow Seas, 1778–82* (Fort Leavenworth, Kan., [1985]), provides a sharply focused discussion. (I am grateful to Dr R. J. B. Knight for drawing this last publication to my attention and for supplying me with a copy of it.)

[4] Though the Baltic states only formally adopted the doctrine of 'free ships' in the Armed Neutrality of 1780: Roslund-Mercurio, 'The Problem of Neutral Rights', 107.

[5] Ibid. 103.

Britain was the principal opponent of the liberalization of wartime commerce. Her position was unique, for she alone possessed a large merchant fleet to supply her own needs during war and a powerful fighting navy. Whereas both France and Spain needed neutral shipping to meet their strategic and commercial requirements after 1778, Britain was less dependent. On the contrary, it was in her interest to weaken her enemies economically and in particular to deprive them of *matériel de guerre*: by the 1770s naval stores, especially from the Baltic, were all important. Where bilateral treaties did not exist, the British government took its stand on the *Consolato del Mare* and seized and condemned enemy goods found on neutral ships. During previous eighteenth-century wars Britain's supremacy at sea had enabled her to impose her own interpretation of international law, often in an arbitrary way. This, together with the proverbial slowness of the Admiralty Courts, had led to considerable friction, and it was clear that it would again do so after 1778.

The second area of difficulties was the question of contraband. The very definition of 'contraband' was a fertile source of tension and disputes during the American War, for there was no agreement over what could be carried during hostilities. Most governments accepted there were certain obvious items which neutrals could not transport to belligerents: soldiers, guns, gunpowder, and suchlike. Beyond this limited consensus lay endless disagreement. Where treaties existed they were frequently vague or ambiguous, or listed only obvious contraband. One particular problem was that many such conventions pre-dated the development of a large-scale trade in Baltic naval stores, which had often not been included in the lists of contraband items.

This was an immediate source of tension during an Anglo-French conflict primarily fought at sea. Once again Britain found herself ranged against the whole of Europe. It was in her interest to insist on the widest possible definition of contraband to deny her enemies commodities of strategic importance, above all naval stores. The British government therefore argued that items listed in treaties were definitely outlawed, but that other goods which were not mentioned could also be deemed contraband provided they could be used for warlike purposes. This attitude was determined by political and strategic considerations. By contrast, commercial factors were always most important for the neutral states, who upheld a narrow definition of contraband in the same way that they championed a liberal regime over wartime commerce.

The issue of neutral rights was highlighted as soon as the war spread to Europe. Traditionally, France had upheld the severe attitude of the *Consolato* and in late June 1778 duly issued an extremely restrictive *Ordonnance*. But the French government believed its maritime strategy against Britain depended on the all-important Baltic naval stores being imported in neutral bottoms. Vergennes was also anxious to pose as the patron of the neutrals, to help turn Europe against Britain. France therefore reversed her strict attitude almost immediately and on 26 July 1778 issued a more liberal *Ordonnance*. This championed the doctrine of 'free ships' and permitted neutrals to trade with the enemy except in contraband goods, which were defined very narrowly and did not include naval stores. These concessions were accompanied by a clear threat. To put pressure on Britain, Vergennes made clear that France would abandon these liberal commercial principles if they were not also adopted by the British government within six months. Among the neutrals the permissive July *Ordonnance* was predictably popular. Equally predictably it was immediately condemned in London.

Britain's actions were rather different, but proved even more provocative. The cabinet responded to the outbreak of war in Europe by an Order in Council of 5 August 1778 which launched a privateering war against France. It permitted the government to issue letters of marque empowering British privateers to seize French ships and property, but it was vague and imprecise in certain crucial respects. Existing treaty rights were not mentioned and no attempt was made to regulate the seizure of enemy property found on neutral ships. Secondly, the Order in Council provided no definition or even guidance over what constituted contraband. This inaugurated a British offensive in the Channel and North Sea, conducted by privateers and Royal Navy vessels. During the late summer and autumn numerous ships were brought into British ports and submitted to the jurisdiction of the Admiralty Courts. These seizures aroused the fury of the neutral states, who were soon protesting in London. By autumn 1778 neutral rights were a significant dimension of British foreign policy.

Wartime trade was primarily an issue in Britain's relations with Sweden, Denmark, and, above all, the Dutch Republic. Though Russia was to assume increasing importance during the next two years and was to be the major force behind the Armed Neutrality of 1780, at this stage Catherine II was still preoccupied with the Bavarian War and her own relations with the Turks over the Crimea. The rights of neutrals were of more immediate concern to France, and Vergennes sought to encourage opposition to Britain. His efforts were more obvious than his influence. British ministers assumed that the hand of France's foreign minister lay behind the protests of the commercial states. This was one reason for their suspicion and hostility towards the neutrals during the American War. Yet they exaggerated Vergennes's influence. The neutral powers were always far more independent of French direction than was recognized in London.

Britain's relations with Sweden were inflamed by a series of captures in autumn 1778.[6] Between 9 August and 28 September fifteen Swedish merchant ships were taken prize, and Stockholm protested vigorously. Wartime trade was regulated by the Treaty of Whitehall signed in 1661. Based on the *Consolato*, it incorporated a narrow view of neutral rights. Naval stores had not been mentioned in the treaty, but their importance had subsequently made them a focal point of dispute. British Prize Courts had ruled that they were contraband, and in previous wars Britain had imposed this interpretation upon Sweden. Matters had been complicated, however, by a contradictory decision by the Lords of Admiralty. Towards the end of the War of the Austrian Succession they had ruled that naval stores found on Swedish ships were not to be confiscated, but forcibly purchased from their owners. The precise legal situation remained uncertain when Anglo-French hostilities began.

From spring 1778, as tension rose in Europe, Sweden's foreign minister Ulrik Scheffer had tried to clarify this confused situation. Aware of the problems war would bring, he sought to negotiate a new framework and to secure far more favourable treatment for Swedish merchants than that conferred by the 1661 treaty. His efforts were not based on legal niceties but on political expediency. He argued that Sweden was entitled to favourable treatment because of her vigorous opposition to the American rebellion after 1775. Scheffer clearly hoped Britain would accept the principle of 'free ships', but it was explicitly rejected by London, as were attempts to exclude naval stores from the definition of contraband. Britain's attitude was determined by broader political considerations.[7] Ministers were for a time alarmed by the Franco-Swedish defensive alliance and even feared that Gustav III might intervene. When they realized that Sweden would not enter the war and that her navy was in a poor condition, no reason for concessions remained.

---

[6] For Anglo-Swedish diplomacy in 1778 and early 1779 see Roslund-Mercurio, 'The Problem of Neutral Rights', 96–225, on which the following account is largely based. Events during the second half of 1778 are more sharply focused in the same author's 'The American Colonial Rebellion and Swedish-British Diplomacy 1775 to 1778', [Swedish] *Historisk tidskrift*, 94 (1974), 482–9.

[7] See, in particular, the 'Instructions' for Sir Thomas Wroughton, 19 June 1778, *BDI* v: *Sweden 1727–89*, ed. J. F. Chance, 235.

Sweden's protests in autumn 1778 over the seizures of her merchantmen were more successful. Her experienced representative in London, Baron Nolcken, argued that since these had commenced immediately after the Order of Council of 5 August and since there had also been no formal British declaration of war, Swedish traders had had no opportunity to conform to the new regulations. This was accepted by Britain and, at the end of September, all the ships were released and compensation paid. Any hopes that this might signal a more liberal British attitude were soon dashed, however. A circular of 19 October 1778 set out Britain's position on neutral rights for the rest of the American War, and it was immediately apparent that London intended to enforce her usually strict approach. Britain would uphold the principles of the *Consolato* and would have no truck with the doctrine of 'free ships'. A further short period of leeway was given to the neutrals; thereafter the fate of captured merchantmen was to be decided in Britain's Prize Courts on the established principles, which were rehearsed in the circular. Foremost among these was the view that the cargo's ownership, rather than its flag, would determine the fate of captured goods. This was diametrically opposed to the neutral states' claim of 'free ships' and highlighted Britain's isolation.

The winter of 1778–9 witnessed a parting of the ways between London and Stockholm. Sweden's hopes for preferential treatment were finally abandoned, as her government adopted a tougher stance. This was accelerated by two particular circumstances. Gustav III was anxious that his wide-ranging legislative plans at the forthcoming Riksdag should not be imperilled by opposition from the merchants, who were complaining loudly about British seizures, while France's threat to suspend her liberal *Ordonnance* if Britain did not follow suit was renewed in November, to Sweden's discomfort. Stockholm's dependence on French subsidies—a new treaty was concluded towards the end of the year—increased Vergennes's leverage on Gustav III. A series of meetings between Suffolk and Nolcken meanwhile confirmed that no concessions were to be had over naval stores. Swedish ships continued to be seized by British privateers and condemned before the Admiralty Courts, enraging Sweden's merchants and her government.[8] By February 1779 Stockholm had abandoned efforts to secure favourable treatment from Britain: negotiation now gave way to an aggressive neutrality policy. As early as autumn 1778 Sweden had begun to

---

[8] Roslund-Mercurio, 'The Problem of Neutral Rights', 234. By the end of Feb. 1779, no less than 32 ships had been formally condemned as prizes.

sound the other Baltic states about co-operation to defend neutral trade. During the following winter she moved slowly, but inexorably towards instituting the convoys demanded by her own commercial community. In February 1779 Stockholm announced an armament of ten ships of the line, together with six frigates, for convoy duty. The decision contained a strong element of propaganda, because of Gustav III's chronic financial weakness and the equally serious shortage of sailors. It was a gesture for internal and international opinion, and it demonstrated the new Swedish attitude. Though they lacked the naval muscle to defend their trade effectively, they would listen sympathetically to suggestions of co-operation against Britain.

Anglo-Danish diplomacy followed broadly similar paths in 1778–9. Denmark had traditionally claimed that her 1670 treaty with England regulating neutral trade had conferred the privilege of carrying enemy goods in wartime, but this had never been accepted in London. In 1778, against the background of a new Anglo-French war, Copenhagen again asserted that this treaty incorporated the principle of 'free ships', but in September its claim was explicitly and forcefully rejected by Britain and thereafter relations deteriorated. Denmark's trade with Britain's enemies was small and, crucially, did not involve substantial quantities of naval stores, unlike Dutch and, to a lesser extent, Swedish commerce. This ensured that Anglo-Danish relations did not deteriorate as sharply, though disputes did still arise. Copenhagen found the British Circular of 19 October 1778 to be as unsatisfactory as did Stockholm and was similarly outraged by British seizures and condemnations during the following winter.[9] Her protests had little impact, however, and her efforts to obtain support from her ally Russia were equally unsuccessful. Though Panin mentioned it to Harris, he did not press the issue. At this stage, Catherine II's interest in neutral rights extended only to a proposal for joint naval patrols to protect ships trading to Russia against privateers.

Britain's intransigence and Russia's lukewarm support together forced Denmark to abandon her claim that the flag covered the cargo.[10] Copenhagen was no more successful in securing a broad definition of contraband. During the first two years of the European conflict, naval inferiority forced Denmark to acquiesce in a British decision that her exports of foodstuffs were contraband, since they could be important during a war. Yet the failure of such formal challenges was only part of the story. After autumn 1778 Denmark

[9] *Bernstorffsche Papiere*, iii. 584.
[10] O. Feldbaek, *Dansk neutralitetspolitik under krigen 1778–1783* (Copenhagen, 1971), 148–9.

fell back on her familiar defensive neutrality policy, which had served her well during previous conflicts.[11] While carefully avoiding any public challenge over neutral trade, her government and her merchants skilfully exploited the political and commercial opportunities and won some significant if tacit concessions. Britain welcomed Bernstorff's evident sympathy for her plight and, in return, respected Danish convoys and acquiesced in the development of Danish trade with the French West Indian islands, though this was a flagrant breach of the 'Rule of 1756'.[12]

This *via media* suited both states. Denmark secured real economic advantages at the price of public compliance, while Britain obtained more support and assistance from Copenhagen than from any other neutral power and, in return, was surprisingly sensitive to Danish interests.[13] Yet this harmony rested upon insecure foundations. To a significant extent it depended on the pro-British sympathies of the Danish foreign minister, A. P. von Bernstorff, whose policies were already unpopular in Copenhagen and who was isolated within the government. More fundamentally, Denmark's international outlook was determined by the wishes of her Russian ally. Any shift in Catherine II's priorities would immediately be apparent in Anglo-Danish diplomacy.

The Dutch Republic was at this stage the most important neutral and, during the second half of 1778, Britain concentrated on the problems posed by its commerce. The Anglo-French War fundamentally altered British objectives at The Hague. Hitherto, ministers had accepted Dutch neutrality in return for token support against the Americans, but they required a more benevolent and pro-British stance from the Dutch authorities. The Republic was Europe's leading commercial nation among the neutrals and its merchants hoped to expand their trade; indeed, the Dutch economy as a whole experienced a mini-boom during the first half of the American War. The spread of fighting to Europe, moreover, found the Dutch in a uniquely favourable legal position. Towards Sweden and Denmark, Britain had upheld her own interpretation of treaty terms and had insisted on a broad definition of contraband. Such a strategy was impossible with the Republic because the relevant treaty, dating from 1674, unambiguously incorporated the principle of 'free ships': in

---

[11] For which see O. Feldbaek, 'Eighteenth-Century Danish Neutrality: Its Diplomacy, Economics and Law', *Scandinavian Journal of History*, 8 (1983), 3–21, and the same author's *Dansk neutralitetspolitik*.

[12] See e.g. SP 75/135, fo. 87. The 'Rule of 1756' prohibited the establishment in wartime of any trade which had been closed in time of peace.

[13] See e.g. *Documents of the American Revolution*, xvi, nos. 1028, 1349.

other words Dutch merchants were legally entitled to continue trading with Britain's enemies after war had begun. The position over naval stores was even worse from a British point of view. The treaty of 1674 specifically declared these not to be contraband: that is to say they could be carried to Britain's enemies by Dutch ships during hostilities. Since the Seven Years War, Yorke had been pressing his government to force a renegotiation of this treaty, but nothing had been done. The European war made the two treaties of commerce and political alliance central issues in Anglo-Dutch diplomacy.

From the very beginning of the Anglo-French conflict ministers were determined to undermine the Republic's privileged status.[14] Ignoring the rights guaranteed by treaty, they set out to force it to give up the privileges conferred by the convention of 1674. The doctrine of 'free ships' and the specific exclusion of naval stores from the list of contraband goods were equally damaging to British interests. They were important because of the expansion of Franco-Dutch trade since the Seven Years War, with the Republic's merchants carrying naval stores to France and returning with manufactured goods.[15] The French government hoped to continue importing these stores in Dutch ships. Britain was determined to cut off the supply of such *matériel*.[16] The problem, however, was that her objectives demanded the Republic's co-operation, whereas Vergennes's strategy required only Dutch neutrality.[17]

In the spring of 1778 the British cabinet had faced up to the problems Dutch privileges would create in the coming war.[18] A possible solution had been suggested by Yorke, already exerting significant influence, and taken up by the Northern Secretary, Suffolk. This was that Britain should link the commercial treaty to the alliance and argue that the Dutch could only enjoy the benefits of the former, if she shouldered the obligations of the latter. The idea was not new. It had been put forward in identical circumstances during the last war, and its revival indicated Britain's similar

---

[14] See e.g. Suffolk to Yorke, Quite Private, 29 Sept. 1778, SP 84/562.

[15] F. Edler, *The Dutch Republic and the American Revolution* (Baltimore, Md., 1911), 95.

[16] British policy was always based on a misconception. Britain clearly exaggerated the importance of this trade for French naval strength (France's supplies of timber were greater than British observers realized): Dull, *French Navy*, 176 and n. 15. Moreover, as the situation in the Channel deteriorated in 1779–80, the French successfully transported some masts (which were needed) via an inland route which ran from the Dutch Republic through the rivers of the Austrian Netherlands into northern France: ibid. 208 n. 7.

[17] See C. Ch. Goslinga, *The Dutch in the Caribbean and in the Guianas 1680–1791* (Assen-Maastricht and Dover, NH, 1985), 140–1, for a similar conclusion; cf. Yorke to Suffolk, 21 Apr. 1778, SP 84/561.   [18] See the correspondence in SP 84/561.

problems after 1778.[19] In a very real sense the American conflict saw the pattern of relations during the Seven Years War repeat itself, while Yorke's established preference for firm measures reflected his earlier experiences in dealing with a neutral Republic between 1756 and 1763. It was not that the British government actually wanted to bring the defensive alliance into operation.[20] Ministers were aware of Dutch weakness and always believed the Republic would be a liability as an ally. For their part, the Dutch understood they were in no position to provide assistance.[21] By the later 1770s the Republic's military establishment had totally decayed after the long and indecisive struggle over the 'Augmentation', while the navy on paper was twenty-nine ships of the line, only eleven mounting more than sixty guns and the newest a quarter of a century old.[22] Nevertheless, the threat to demand the aid specified by the alliance might be employed to remove the 'awkward privileges' enjoyed by the Dutch under the commercial treaty.[23] The Republic, argued Suffolk, could support Britain by concessions over wartime trade rather than by actual military assistance.[24]

This was Britain's strategy by May 1778, but it was only applied in the autumn when disputes arose over neutral rights.[25] The Republic's shipping had suffered most from the attack on neutral trade unleashed by the Order in Council of 5 August 1778. By late September as many as a hundred Dutch merchantmen may have been seized; in October alone, according to one estimate, another forty-two became British prizes.[26] Though some were promptly released and their owners compensated, others were detained and began their

[19] R. Middleton, *The Bells of Victory: The Pitt–Newcastle Ministry and the Conduct of the Seven Years' War 1757–1762* (Cambridge, 1985), 93, and more generally R. Pares, *Colonial Blockade and Neutral Rights 1739–1763* (Oxford, 1938), 242–79.

[20] See e.g. Suffolk to Yorke, 14 Apr. 1778, SP 84/561. Indeed, a formal request for aid under the treaty could be counter-productive and might give an opening for France to increase her influence within the Republic: Yorke to Suffolk, 28 Apr. 1778, ibid.

[21] See e.g. *Archives . . . Orange-Nassau*, 5th series, i. 602.

[22] Edler, *Dutch Republic*, 95; S. Schama, *Patriots and Liberators: Revolution in the Netherlands 1780–1813* (London, 1977), 58; for the decline and fall of the Republic as a naval power, see more generally F.-P. Renaut, *Le Crépuscule d'une puissance navale: La marine hollandaise de 1776 à 1783* (Paris, 1932). Yorke declared in Feb. 1779 that 'Dutch fleets . . . are like Sir John Falstaff's Men in Buckram and don't exist *even upon paper*': Add MSS 35434, fo. 65.

[23] The phrase was Suffolk's: to Yorke, 14 Apr. 1778, SP 84/561.

[24] Suffolk to Yorke, 8 May 1778, ibid.

[25] Contrary to the arguments of Bemis (*Diplomacy of the American Revolution*, 35–9), there was no attempt in the spring to force the Dutch to give up their privileges under the 1674 treaty in whole or part. Suffolk's dispatch of 14 Apr. does not bear the construction placed on it by Bemis and, indeed, the Northern Secretary explicitly denied (to Yorke, 8 May 1778, SP 84/561) that any such approach would be made.

[26] *Walpole Corr.* xxiv, 424; Bemis, *Diplomacy of the American Revolution*, 139.

slow procession through the Prize Courts. Dutch protests followed, and in her answer Britain formally linked the commercial treaty of 1674 to the defensive alliance of 1678.[27]

The question of wartime trade dominated Anglo-Dutch diplomacy throughout the autumn and winter of 1778–9.[28] The Republic's legal position was very strong: the treaty of 1674 conferred an indisputable right to continue trading and declared naval stores were not contraband. But the political will to defend these privileges was lacking at The Hague. By the mid-point of the American War the weakness of the stadtholderian regime and its inability to withstand pressure, either from domestic opponents or foreign rivals, were clear. William V and his ministers were under more direct pressure from France than Britain could ever bring to bear. The Republic's vulnerable southern frontier was highlighted by its own military weakness and by the massive French standing army, while the thriving Dutch trade with France was an easy target for French economic reprisals. Anglo-Dutch discussions took place against a background of repeated French threats to replace the liberal July *Ordonnance* with a harsher maritime code. This directly threatened Dutch trade and prosperity, and it ensured the Anglo-French struggle within the Republic was always an unequal contest. Dutch opinion was turning against Britain, as numerous seizures antagonized the merchants and the public at large, with the resulting protests being skilfully encouraged by the French ambassador.[29] The trading cities, led by Amsterdam, urged a vigorous response to the British onslaught and, in particular, demanded convoys to protect|the Dutch merchant fleet. Already the battle-lines of future conflict within the Republic were drawn.

Britain's diplomacy during the second half of 1778 was surprisingly moderate, in itself the clearest guide to her weak legal position. Instead of the usual exposition of British 'rights' with which neutrals were customarily regaled, ministers tried to calm Dutch protests.[30] London's attitude was even more moderate towards the Republic than towards Denmark and Sweden. Captured Dutch ships were

---

[27] *Dépêches van Thulemeyer*, 196, 197; Suffolk to Yorke, 25 and 29 Sept. 1778, SP 84/562.
[28] These exchanges can be followed in SP 84/562 and 565; and in *Archives . . . Orange-Nassau*, 5th series, i.
[29] Yorke to Suffolk, Most Private, 25 Aug. 1778, SP 84/561; *Archives . . . Orange-Nassau*, 5th series, i. 569; F. C. Spooner, *Risks at Sea: Amsterdam Insurance and Maritime Europe 1766–1780* (Cambridge, 1983), 107. By Nov. the situation was so bad that neither ships nor cargoes could be insured on the Amsterdam Bourse at any price: ibid. 106.
[30] Suffolk to Yorke, 29 Sept. 1778, SP 84/562. Even the Admiralty Court in London was showing partiality towards the Republic in a series of decisions in Dec. 1778: Spooner, *Risks at Sea*, 107; cf. *Archives . . . Orange-Nassau*, 5th series, i. 616–17.

released and compensation paid, while naval stores were compulsorily purchased without any distinction between enemy and neutral property.[31] Suffolk intended this as a concession, since ordinarily such *matériel* owned by the enemy would simply have been seized. He went even further in his attempt to appease the Republic, for by October 1778 he was actually prepared to allow the Dutch to trade with the enemy except in naval stores. In the middle of that month Suffolk, on very bad terms with the Dutch ambassador since the previous year, made a determined effort both to patch things up with Welderen and to promote a negotiated settlement of neutral rights.[32] He hoped that, in return for concessions over trade with the enemy, the Dutch would voluntarily give up their right to carry naval stores. This was exactly the point on which Dutch merchants were most insistent, since they could obviously hope to expand this profitable commerce during the Anglo-French war. Suffolk's absolute refusal to allow *matériel* to be carried wrecked any chance of an agreement. The problem was that Dutch privileges under the 1674 treaty were so great that there was no incentive to accept the kind of compromise sponsored by Suffolk, whose concessions appeared paltry to the Republic's merchants and even its government.

During the winter of 1778–9 relations were simultaneously exacerbated by continuing British seizures and by a series of Prize Court decisions condemning Dutch vessels and goods.[33] The Republic's government continued to be broadly sympathetic towards Britain, though William V and his advisers found Suffolk's conduct less moderate than the latter intended.[34] What was fondly believed in London to be a concession appeared at The Hague to be merely another piece of British intransigence. The gulf between the two states was widening all the time.[35] In mid-November the Dutch government sponsored a compromise of its own, suggesting that naval stores be excluded from the proposed convoys. This proved as unacceptable to Britain as Suffolk's earlier offers had been to the Dutch. In any case, the proposal to exclude *matériel* from the convoys was soon overthrown by the towns of Holland, led by Amsterdam.

[31]   Edler, *Dutch Republic*, 107.
[32]   *Archives . . . Orange-Nassau*, 5th series, i. 525, 560–2.
[33]   Ibid. i. 578–9, 601–2, 617. Particular problems arose in Nov. when, in defiance of Suffolk's recent declaration, English privateers seized ships not carrying naval stores: SP 84/562 *passim*.
[34]   e.g. the view of Prince Louis of Brunswick: *Archives . . . Orange–Nassau*, 5th series, i. 587–90.
[35]   One example of this was the series of clashes in West Indian waters in 1778–9 between a squadron under Bylandt which had been sent to protect Dutch shipping and the British privateers which infested the area: Goslinga, *Dutch in the Caribbean and in the Guianas*, 146.

This made clear the weakness of the Stadtholder's government. William V and his ministers were rapidly losing control and even influence over events. Impotent in foreign affairs, they were now unable to check the anti-British tide within the Republic. This was partly due to Britain's unrealistic expectations over naval stores. Suffolk's failure to appreciate that the Republic would never abandon its profitable privileges created insuperable problems for the Orangist government and helped make its position untenable.[36] It was powerless to resist the clamour for measures to defend the Republic's maritime commerce. Dutch merchants feared their dominance of the European carrying trade would be lost forever unless effective protection were forthcoming, and their demands were reinforced by growing economic difficulties and encouraged by French diplomacy.[37]

The call for convoys was now hard to resist, and in 1779–80 the Stadtholder and his ministers merely sought to postpone their implementation. They did so with some skill, exploiting the same unwieldy and decentralized political system which had so often frustrated their own objectives to win a series of tactical victories. This delayed the introduction of convoys, but the government's weakness was more significant than its minor tactical successes. Already its domestic enemies were gathering strength and the very survival of the Stadtholderate was being questioned.[38] In particular it was unable to check the growth of French influence; indeed, William V and his ministers believed that Britain's actions were driving the Republic into the arms of France.[39] In the longer view these developments were vital for Dutch domestic politics; at the time they were no less important for relations with Britain whose traditional control had been maintained through the pre-eminent position of the House of Orange. Now that ascendancy lay in ruins, and the Stadtholder and his advisers were exasperated by what seemed to them Britain's continuing intransigence. Suffolk's efforts to force a renegotiation of the 1674 treaty were not simply unsuccessful; they also worsened relations and weakened pro-British feeling within the Republic's governing élite.[40]

[36] *Archives . . . Orange–Nassau*, 5th series, i. 650, 689–91.
[37] Edler, *Dutch Republic*, 104.
[38] *Archives . . . Orange–Nassau*, 5th series, i. 588, for Prince Louis of Brunswick's sombre analysis. The prince was said to believe that this was the real objective of French policy: *Dépêches van Thulemeyer*, 203.
[39] *Archives . . . Orange–Nassau*, 5th series, i. 607–8; cf. *Dépêches van Thulemeyer*, 204.
[40] See William V's comments in Mar. 1779: *Archives . . . Orange–Nassau*, 5th series, ii. 6–7.

Anglo-Dutch relations were an immediate casualty of the lack of direction in foreign policy, which became evident early in 1779 and continued until late autumn. Its immediate cause was Suffolk's final illness. By late January he was unable to see foreign diplomats or to conduct correspondence, and at the beginning of March he died.[41] The Southern Secretary Weymouth assumed responsibility for the Northern Department: until October 1779 he was *de facto* foreign minister. These months made his strengths and weaknesses glaringly apparent.[42] He was not unintelligent, and his dispatches contain occasional glimpses of his potential. But his undoubted ability was usually hidden behind the personal failings which troubled his contemporaries and flawed his career. Above all he was notoriously lazy and given to neglecting the routine correspondence on which the smooth running of diplomacy depended.[43] Dispatches would lie unanswered for days and sometimes weeks on end; an answer would then be cobbled together just before the post was due to leave.[44] British diplomats would, at critical moments, find themselves without instructions from London.[45] Weymouth at first followed Suffolk's policies. In relations with the Dutch, for example, he was content to endorse the moderate policy adopted during 1778–9. Even Yorke was surprisingly restrained during these months.[46] Yet while such continuity might, in itself, be welcome, it was always likely to be overtaken by events. For much of 1779 Weymouth allowed Britain to drift along in the face of a deteriorating situation, as the neutrals' resentment mounted with each new British seizure.

The responsibility should not be laid entirely at Weymouth's door. The North Ministry faced serious problems during that year, and from the summer onwards these dwarfed foreign affairs.[47] Diplomacy

---

[41] Ibid. i. 681; HMC *Stopford-Sackville*, i. 140. In Dec. 1778, he had unsuccessfully tried to retire on grounds of ill health: *Corr. Geo. III*, iv. 239–41.

[42] Cf. above, Ch. 5, for Weymouth's notorious personal shortcomings. For a particularly damning verdict on the Southern Secretary, see *Corr. Geo. III*, iv. 452–3.

[43] William Eden to Stormont, 25 Oct. 1779, Stormont Papers, Box 52; cf. above, Ch. 6, for his earlier neglect in this respect. He was equally deficient in carrying out other official correspondence: see e.g. the repeated complaints of Buckinghamshire from Dublin, Sir Herbert Butterfield, *George III, Lord North and the People 1779–80* (London, 1949), 35.

[44] See George III to Stormont, 1 Nov. 1779, Stormont Papers, Box 14.

[45] Cf. above p. 261, for one such example. Weymouth was equally casual over the keeping of cabinet minutes: William Eden to Stormont, 25 Oct. 1779, Stormont Papers, Box 52.

[46] *Archives . . . Orange–Nassau*, 5th series, i. 619–21, and, more generally, SP 84/562 and 568.

[47] The classic account of these difficulties is Butterfield, *George III, Lord North and the People*, though the picture which he presented is overdrawn. For the problems encountered in finding a new secretary of state, see *Corr. Geo. III*, iv. 330–42, 349; for the intrigues which

was just another victim of the government's growing paralysis. In the first place the discontent in Ireland, simmering since the early stages of the American War, reached boiling point. In March the commercial classes adopted a non-importation agreement against British goods; by the summer Irish resentment crystalized around the formidable Volunteer movement. Even more serious, and certainly more direct, was the threat posed by the attempted Franco-Spanish invasion in the summer and autumn of 1779.[48] The danger was not dispelled until early September, when it was replaced by a new ministerial crisis, as Lord North once again tried to resign.[49] These urgent problems and that of waging a world war pushed relations with the neutrals into the background for much of 1779. The framework of official policy remained that established in the previous year, though Weymouth's stubbornness occasionally made difficult situations even worse.[50] British diplomacy with the commercial states continued to be dominated by the actions of the Royal Navy and of British privateers. Their seizures of neutral shipping, together with the decisions—and the delays—of the Prize Courts were further turning Europe against Britain.

Foreign policy was now monopolized by Anglo-Dutch relations. Between 1775 and 1778 Britain's traditional influence in the Republic had been undermined; during 1779 and 1780 it was destroyed completely. Two new factors complicated the situation. France's influence within the Republic and her pressure on its government were both increasing, as was her support for the Stadtholder's domestic opponents. French ministers were anxious to guarantee a regular supply of naval stores and, when the Dutch authorities appeared slow to adopt armed convoys to protect this trade, Vergennes stepped up his pressure. The face of Dutch internal politics was also changing, as a serious political conflict developed. The opponents of the House of Orange, led by Amsterdam and encouraged by the skilful French ambassador, de la Vauguyon, were

hindered this search, Butterfield, *George III, Lord North and the People*, 34, and, more generally, pp. 35–70.

[48] Though this did not stop most of the cabinet except Weymouth from going to the country in Aug. for their holidays: Butterfield, *George III, Lord North and the People*, 59. The standard account of the invasion scare is A. Temple Patterson, *The Other Armada: The Franco-Spanish Attempt to Invade Britain in 1779* (Manchester, 1960).

[49] For the paralysis which overtook the cabinet, see George III's trenchant comments: *Sandwich Papers*, iii. 164; cf. Butterfield, *George III, Lord North and the People*, 117–38, for the autumn crisis.

[50] For example, he inflamed Anglo-Swedish relations by reviving British protests over American trade with the free port of Marstrand: Roslund-Mercurio, 'The Problem of Neutral Rights', 256–9.

moving on to the offensive. By the end of 1779 the contours of the Republic's politics were still recognizable, though they were being eroded by the emerging crisis. In particular the Grand Pensionary, van Bleiswijk, was moving towards Holland and the French party; even more significantly his influence on William V was increasing. In 1779–80 Anglo-French diplomacy struggled for control over the Republic's commercial and foreign policies. It was a contest which the arrogant Yorke was ill equipped to enter and probably bound to lose.

During the closing months of 1778 and the following year, the question of convoys dominated Dutch politics and relations with London.[51] Throughout these exchanges Britain's position remained intransigent: she was determined to prevent Dutch merchants supplying France with naval stores and therefore tried to stop the Republic from taking measures to protect its trade.[52] By the spring of 1779 the British government, convinced the Republic would soon adopt unlimited convoys, had decided to attack any such fleet and actually informed William V's government of this. In the event the decision to protect Dutch commerce was delayed by the federal constitution. Throughout 1779 the question of convoys ground its way through the various provincial assemblies and then on to the States-General. There was evident reluctance to take such a major step, and the Orangist party and Yorke mounted a successful delaying operation, but Dutch resentment against British maritime policy rose with each new seizure or condemnation. French pressure on the Republic also increased, and it proved decisive.

France's supply of naval stores would be secured if unlimited convoys were adopted, and Vergennes therefore tried to force this through by measures against Dutch trade.[53] The privileges which the Republic's merchants enjoyed in France were revoked early in 1779; in March the liberal French *Ordonnance* was finally suspended; an additional tariff of fifteen per cent was imposed on all Dutch shipping calling at French ports; while in September the import of Dutch cheese into France was prohibited. First Amsterdam and then Haarlem were exempted from this assault, and their commerce flourished, while Franco-Dutch trade as a whole collapsed. The prosperity which the Dutch economy had enjoyed during the first half of the American War had ended by the summer of 1779. Instead the Republic's commerce lay in ruins. As Vergennes had calculated, this increased demands from the merchant community for unlimited

---

[51] Events can be followed in SP 84/565–6, and in *Archives . . . Orange–Nassau*, 5th series, i–ii. [52] Weymouth to Yorke, 30 Mar. 1779, SP 84/565.
[53] Spooner, *Risks at Sea*, 107–9.

convoys, and Holland took the lead in pressing for this within the States-General.

In July 1779 Britain tried to check the momentum which had built up for convoys. At Yorke's suggestion, Britain's war with Spain (with whom diplomatic relations had just been severed) was used to demand Dutch aid.[54] Such action had long been considered in London as a way to force The Hague to abandon its privileged position over neutral trade. The clear message was that the Dutch must either furnish this aid or forfeit the privileges conferred by the commercial treaty.[55] This move encouraged Britain's remaining friends in the Republic and it helped to delay the final adoption of convoys. The formal request for aid met with a stony silence and for a time paralysed both the Dutch government and its political opponents.[56] But the combined pressure of France and of the commercial towns was irresistible; by the time of Weymouth's closing weeks in office, the States-General was close to adopting convoys.

Stormont's appointment as Northern Secretary towards the end of October 1779 ended the drift in foreign policy.[57] After a further period of uncertainty, Weymouth abandoned the ailing North Ministry and was replaced at the Southern Department by the Earl of Hillsborough, who had been a thoroughly unsatisfactory American Secretary from 1768 until 1772. Hillsborough was to exert little influence on British diplomacy during the next two and a half years. The war against the Bourbons deprived him of his principal duty: conducting relations with France and Spain. Britain's foreign policy concentrated on the Dutch Republic, Denmark, and Sweden, and to a lesser extent on the three eastern powers. The geographical division between the two senior Secretaries meant that Stormont was responsible for relations with all these states. There was, however, rather more to the Northern Secretary's dominance. Hillsborough had no diplomatic experience and owed his advancement to North's friendship, while Stormont was the leading British diplomat of his generation: in the Prime Minister's view this was an important reason for his appointment when Britain's need for allies was greater

[54] Yorke to Weymouth, 6 July 1779, and Weymouth to Yorke, 16 July 1779, both in SP 84/566.   [55] Madariaga, *Armed Neutrality*, 143.
[56] For its impact, *Archives . . . Orange–Nassau*, 5th series, ii. 49–50.
[57] There are signs that the King was influential in securing his appointment, both because of Stormont's 'distinction' (as George III described it) as a diplomat and because of his value as a government speaker in the Lords: *Corr. Geo. III*, iv. 209, 444, 450, 456. In the event, the new Northern Secretary was to become chief government spokesman in the House of Lords: ibid. v. 131.

than ever.[58] It was always intended that Stormont should take the leading part in foreign affairs, with Hillsborough as a makeweight, responsible only for some minor domestic parts of the Secretaries' duties and for the routine correspondence with Portugal, the Italian states, and the Ottoman Empire.[59] Their partnership looked forward to the rather different pattern created by the formal establishment of the Foreign Secretaryship in 1782.

Stormont clearly enjoyed greater control over foreign policy than most of his recent predecessors. This was assisted by the disappearance, after summer 1779, of the inner group headed by the King and North, whose intervention had complicated Britain's diplomacy in the early stages of the American War.[60] Stormont's attention was not deflected by the two major domestic problems which his harassed colleagues faced in 1779–80: the continuing unrest in Ireland and the County Movement in England. Only once during his three years in office was he obliged to neglect foreign affairs, and that was during the great crisis of the Gordon Riots in June 1780.[61] Then the government temporarily lost control of London to anti-Catholic mobs. Hillsborough's weakness forced Stormont to play a prominent part in restoring order, and diplomacy, like all government business, was for a time suspended, but this was wholly exceptional.

Stormont had significantly greater diplomatic experience when he entered office than any other Secretary of State in the entire age of the American Revolution. He had spent more than two decades abroad, serving first at Dresden and Warsaw, then in Vienna, and finally in Paris. His dedication matched his experience. While ambassador to France Stormont had endured Weymouth's periodic silences and cursory instructions. He himself was always punctilious in observing a regular correspondence with British diplomats. He was equally dedicated to keeping the King regularly and minutely informed and, in sharp contrast to Weymouth, to taking cabinet minutes.[62]

[58] *HMC Stopford–Sackville*, ii. 138. Stormont and North, it should be added, were not on the best of terms: *Corr. Geo. III*, iv. 500; Butterfield, *George III, Lord North and the People*, 133.

[59] For Stormont's seniority, though Hillsborough had greater ministerial experience, see *Corr. Geo. III*, v. 130–1.

[60] The last evidence of such intervention is in June 1779 when North at least was trying to avert the outbreak of war with Spain: above, Ch. 10; in the autumn of the same year, Mansfield was said to have stopped attending cabinet meetings and he was certainly less involved subsequently in the making of policy: J. H. Jesse, ed., *George Selwyn and His Contemporaries* (4 vols.; London, 1844), iv. 259.

[61] For this unrest, see T. Hayter, *The Army and the Crowd in Mid-Georgian England* (London, 1978), 147–59 and 180–6; for Stormont's role, see ibid. 148–9 and Mackesy, *War for America*, 360–2.

[62] See the correspondence in Stormont Papers, Boxes 14 and 16; cf. *Corr. Geo. III*, v–vi *passim*. The collection of cabinet minutes in the Northern Secretary's handwriting (Stormont

Stormont was painstaking and businesslike, and his devotion unquestioned and probably unequalled. But his long diplomatic apprenticeship was not without its dangers. Though he possessed two decades' experience of Europe, he also had twenty years of exposure to British ideas about foreign policy: as Secretary of State he was to exhibit less pragmatism than Suffolk and less imagination than Rochford. Stormont was to display the same qualities as *de facto* foreign minister that he had revealed as an ambassador: he never made the transition from diplomat to statesman. His ideas were traditional and sometimes dangerously inflexible. First and foremost he supported the Old System. He wrote in 1780 that, since the destruction of the Austrian alliance at the beginning of the Seven Years War, 'all our foreign politics have been nothing more than the little expedients of the day'.[63] Britain's eventual salvation, he believed, would be new treaties with Austria and Russia. Yet if his inflexibility and occasional dogmatism would become apparent during his secretaryship, in autumn 1779 it was his knowledge and experience of Europe which Britain most needed and which her hard-pressed diplomats welcomed.[64]

Stormont was immediately confronted by a new Anglo-Dutch crisis and this dominated his early months in office. It concerned not the question of convoy, which rumbled on in the background, but the presence at the Texel of John Paul Jones, the celebrated American privateer who had been forced to seek sanctuary after his famous if costly victory off Flamborough Head.[65] Several of his vessels were in urgent need of repair, and his squadron also contained two captured British vessels (the *Serapis* and the *Scarborough*) and some five hundred British prisoners. The motley flotilla was pursued by a British fleet which immediately blockaded the Texel.

The arrival of Paul Jones in Dutch waters at the beginning of October 1779 precipitated a serious diplomatic confrontation. Yorke bombarded the Dutch government and the States-General with demands that the American captain should be arrested and his British

<hr/>

Papers, Box 13) is considerably more extensive than the minutes available in print or in other manuscript collections.

[63] Quoted by Madariaga, *Armed Neutrality*, 197.

[64] Yorke to Harris, 12 Nov. 1779, Add. MSS 35434, fo. 74; cf. the view of Harris himself: Madariaga, *Armed Neutrality*, 123 n. 8. N. Wraxall, *Historical Memoirs of My Own Time (1772–1784)* (2 vols.; London, 1815). i. 509–10, is a notably shrewd contemporary assessment of the new Northern Secretary.

[65] S. E. Morison, *John Paul Jones: A Sailor's Biography* (Boston, 1959), 251–65, provides a colourful account of his stay; for its political implications, see F.-P. Renaut, *De la neutralité à la belligérance (1775–1780)* (Paris, 1924), 259–82, and J. W. Schulte Nordholt, *The Dutch Republic and American Independence* (1979; Eng. trans., Chapel Hill, NC, 1982), 70–88.

prizes and prisoners released.[66] He argued that since Paul Jones was a notorious privateer, and since the Dutch authorities had refused to recognize Congress, he could claim no legal immunity and should simply be arrested as a pirate. The precise legal status of the American squadron was less clear-cut than Yorke implied. Rumours circulated that Paul Jones was operating under a French commission, and they were given some credence by the arrival of two French frigates which anchored close to his squadron.[67] If true, this would have changed everything: French ships were entitled to temporary sanctuary as belligerents in distress. Both the privateer and the French ambassador initially stayed silent on the question of the flotilla's flag. Paul Jones always knew that he was operating under an American commission, but he was happy to exploit the ambiguity surrounding the squadron.

His presence had a broader political purpose. Franklin, masterminding American diplomacy in Europe from Paris, intended his stay should imply Dutch recognition for Congress and should further strain Anglo-Dutch relations. For their part the Stadtholder and his advisers simply wanted to evict the troublesome American and make the problem disappear. They were fearful that he might possess or acquire a French commission, and uncomfortably aware of the problems posed by two indisputably French vessels. Britain might have a stronger legal case, but French sanctions against Dutch trade were always a more potent threat.[68] The Republic's reply to Yorke's demands was inevitably a compromise: Paul Jones was to be allowed to leave, but his British prizes and prisoners were to be released. Equally predictably, this satisfied no one. Throughout November and most of December 1779, he remained at the Texel, carrying out essential repairs to his ships and defying Dutch attempts to evict him, while Yorke's fury reached new heights.

This was the impasse which confronted Stormont when he became Northern Secretary. He quickly imparted a new firmness to Britain's diplomacy. There was nothing particularly novel about British policy, but it was pursued with greater vigour and consistency, and this was soon apparent to Yorke. In the past the ambassador had sometimes exceeded the letter of his instructions and had made British policy at The Hague more combative. He now found that he

---

[66] His activities can be followed in SP 84/566.

[67] They seem to have reached the Texel 2 weeks after the arrival of the Americans: Edler, *Dutch Republic*, 64.

[68] For William V's frank inability to do what Britain was demanding, see *Archives . . . Orange–Nassau*, 5th series, ii. 114, 121.

had Stormont's whole-hearted support for his firm and even inflammatory approach.

Yorke's own influence increased significantly. Throughout the American War ministers had frequently consulted the ambassador, and on occasions he had helped to shape Britain's diplomacy because of his unique experience and knowledge. This influence was to grow throughout the next year, and he was to contribute directly to the Anglo-Dutch War which began in December 1780. Stormont had no personal experience of the bewildering complexities of Anglo-Dutch diplomacy and the Republic's domestic politics. He therefore looked to Yorke both for guidance about details and for a lead over general policy. While himself an ambassador, Stormont had been consulted by his superiors and had shaped British diplomacy.[69] He was therefore well disposed towards advice from a fellow career diplomat, particularly one with Yorke's long experience.[70] He was not to be disappointed: indeed, within his first fortnight in office, Stormont received a lengthy jeremiad on Anglo-Dutch relations and the Republic's own politics, together with a plea for more vigorous measures.[71] This inaugurated an extensive private, and to some extent secret correspondence, which continued until Yorke left The Hague in December 1780. This provides a more accurate picture of Britain's policy than the official dispatches and was the means by which the ambassador influenced British diplomacy.[72]

Stormont quickly agreed about the need for a more vigorous stance.[73] By mid-November the cabinet had reaffirmed British policy: Dutch ships were to be searched for naval stores even if protected by convoy and Yorke was to renew demands for aid under the 1678 treaty.[74] Ministers were now firmly resolved to use Dutch failure to fulfil their obligation to provide assistance as an excuse to

[69] H. M. Scott, 'Anglo-Austrian Relations after the Seven Years War: Lord Stormont in Vienna, 1763–1772' (unpublished Ph.D. thesis, University of London, 1977), 254–9; *BDI* vii: *France, part iv, 1745–1789*; ed. L. G. Wickham Legg; 128.

[70] Stormont was similarly guided by Harris's dispatches in drawing up a new policy towards Russia: Madariaga, *Armed Neutrality*, 125.

[71] Yorke to Stormont, Private, 9 Nov. 1779, Stormont Papers, Box 59: this letter included the reflection that, legal niceties notwithstanding, British ships should simply have violated Dutch territorial waters and seized John Paul Jones at the Texel!

[72] It is to be found ibid., Boxes 59 and 113. The scale of this private correspondence was remarkable: usually 2 substantial letters from Yorke each week, with 1 reply from Stormont. Its purpose seems clearly to have been to avoid any danger that the discussions out of which British policy emerged would have to be laid before parliament in the event of a 'call' for papers. It was conducted with the knowledge and seeming approbation of the King: see e.g. *Corr. Geo. III*, iv. 487, 519, 539.

[73] See, in particular, Stormont to Yorke, Private, 30 Nov. 1779, Stormont Papers, Box 113; cf. *Corr. Geo. III*, iv. 487.

[74] *Sandwich Papers*, iii. 106; cf. Edler, *Dutch Republic*, 129.

suspend the commercial treaty. In a similar way the Republic's conduct over Paul Jones increased Britain's resentment.[75] Ministers agreed with Yorke that the whole episode simply confirmed Dutch weakness: at the height of the affair a British observer had referred contemptuously to the 'miserable shuffling temporizing system of the Mynheers'.[76] There was no understanding of the complex problems posed by the American's presence, or of the real difficulties which Dutch ministers faced.

The failure to act effectively over Paul Jones severely weakened Britain's assumption that the Republic was still her client, at least when the House of Orange was in power.[77] The episode was seen as further proof of William V's diminished authority and, with it, British influence.[78] Indeed, Yorke declared that during his three decades in the Dutch capital, 'nothing had mortified and vexed him so much . . . because nothing has showed the timidity and anarchy of the Republic so strongly, or sunk the Stadtholder so low'.[79] In time, the collapse of confidence in William V would change British policy. Already the view was gaining ground that the Republic was more use to France as a neutral, given her role in transporting naval stores, than it would be as an ally.[80] At the very end of 1779, however, the principal issue in relations suddenly changed. On 27 December Paul Jones slipped away from the Texel and ran the British blockade, leaving his captives to be exchanged for French prisoners of war and relieving the harassed Dutch authorities of their unwelcome guest. He had left under cover of a Dutch convoy. The immediate arrest of some of these vessels by the British navy produced a new and even more serious crisis.

In mid-November 1779 the States-General had finally decided to give armed protection to Dutch merchant ships.[81] Britain had meanwhile resolved to intercept the first convoy, in the spirit of discouraging the others, and this was duly done.[82] On 29 December

---

[75] e.g. *Sandwich Papers*, iii. 97, 99, 107–8.

[76] William Eden to Morton Eden, 29 Oct. 1779, Stevens, *Facsimiles*, no. 1031.

[77] See Lord North's comments to the Dutch ambassador: *Archives . . . Orange–Nassau*, 5th series, ii. 105; cf. George III to Stormont, 16 Nov. 1779, Stormont Papers, Box 14.

[78] British resentment was increased by the fact that three other British prizes captured by Paul Jones's squadron which took refuge in Bergen were handed over to Britain by the Danish authorities: see S. J. M. P. Fogdall, *Danish-American Diplomacy 1776–1920* (Iowa, 1922), 11–18.   [79] Yorke to Stormont, Private, 23 Nov. 1779, Stormont Papers, Box 113.

[80] D. A. Miller, *Sir Joseph Yorke and Anglo-Dutch Relations 1774–1780* (The Hague, 1970), 90–1.

[81] Though in an unsuccessful attempt to be even-handed, ship's timber was not to be protected: Renaut, *De la neutralité*, 308–9. Inevitably, such a rigorous exclusion could not be enforced.

[82] *Corr. Geo. III*, iv. 487; George III to Stormont, 16 Nov. 1779, Stormont Papers, Box 14. For the exemplary nature of British action, see SP 84/569, fo. 21.

Bylandt's convoy was stopped and eight Dutch merchantmen were carried into port, to await the verdict of the British Prize Courts.[83] For Britain this was a simple matter of depriving France of the all-important naval stores.[84] The Republic's merchants were outraged at this latest blow to their depressed trade, and their protests were immediate and loud.[85] Britain was predictably intransigent, insisting the ships were lawful prize and continuing to press for aid under the 1678 treaty.[86] Stormont's inflexibility and Yorke's familiar arrogance together pushed up the diplomatic temperature.[87] The early months of 1780 were to see some particularly corrosive exchanges, Yorke even telling William V to his face that Britain wanted to support the Republic, but not with the French ambassador as Stadtholder![88] This was an extraordinary outburst, even for the volatile British ambassador, and it emphasized the massive deterioration in relations. The roots of this lay in London. Britain's attitude was quite inflexible: as Stormont wrote, 'ministers never can nor will suffer the Dutch to be nominal allies of Great Britain but the real auxiliaries of France and Spain'.[89] Dutch resentment, in its turn, was fanned by French diplomacy and it flared up when, early in March, the British Admiralty Courts condemned the ships captured from the convoy.[90]

In the same month, Britain once again formally demanded aid. The request was more determined than hitherto. It was presented in a Memorial, drawn up by Yorke and, at his instigation, imposing a time-limit of three weeks on the Dutch reply.[91] Britain knew that assistance would not be forthcoming; the period of twenty-one days was intended to prevent further prevarication. Stormont had resolved shortly after taking office to suspend all Anglo-Dutch treaties, and in April this policy was duly implemented.[92] By the

---

[83] Madariaga, *Armed Neutrality*, 153–4.

[84] *Sandwich Papers*, iii. 114; Walpole, *Last Journals*, ii. 262; *Walpole Corr.* xxv. 3–4.

[85] Spooner, *Risks at Sea*, 111.

[86] Britain's attitude is set out in Stormont's long dispatch of 11 Jan. 1780, SP 84/569, fos. 35–40: a forceful restatement of a familiar position; cf. ibid., fos. 84–7.

[87] SP 84/569 *passim*. Cf. the comments of the French ambassador: CP (Hollande) 540, fo. 297.   [88] Yorke to Stormont, Private, 21 Mar. 1780, Stormont Papers, Box 59.

[89] SP 84/569, fo. 38.

[90] Edler, *Dutch Republic*, 132; cf. Yorke to Stormont, Private, 14 Mar. 1780, Stormont Papers, Box 59, for the impact of these decisions. The increased role of de la Vauguyon during 1780 can be followed in CP (Hollande) 540–2 *passim*.

[91] The correspondence in Stormont Papers, Box 59, makes clear that Yorke drafted this British Memorial.

[92] The formal demand for aid, and the British declaration with which it would be followed that all treaties were null and void, had, in fact, been delayed until Mar. because of the seizure of the Dutch convoy. At this point, Britain did not want war and feared that a second hostile action might bring this on: Stormont to Yorke, Private, 4 Jan. 1780, Stormont Papers, Box 113. For the outrage which this declaration caused within the Republic, see CP (Hollande) 541, fo. 5.

spring of 1780 Britain had deprived the Republic of its cherished and profitable privileges in wartime.[93] The gap between the two countries widened rapidly, for in the same month the States-General adopted unlimited convoys.[94] Simultaneously, a new and explosive element was added to relations. In the early months of 1780 the Republic drew closer to Catherine II of Russia, who was emerging as the patron of a league of neutral states. It had always been a British aim to isolate the Republic and separate Anglo-Dutch diplomacy from relations with other neutrals, but by the spring of 1780 the two dimensions of Britain's European policy were converging. During 1779 and the early months of 1780, British observers had ignored Russia's growing interest in maritime trade and had also failed to appreciate the transformation which her foreign policy was undergoing.

The later 1770s saw a fundamental realignment of Russian diplomacy.[95] It had several distinct though interrelated dimensions. In the first place the 'Northern System', the basis of Catherine II's policy since the early years of her reign, was coming under severe pressure. Panin and his Prussian alliance were being superseded by Potemkin and his dreams for territorial conquests from the Ottoman Empire. Ideas of southern expansion replaced a desire for the stability of the Baltic region, and this in turn suggested an Austrian alliance. Catherine II's established ally, Frederick II, had shown himself unwilling to provide active support against the Turks, whereas St Petersburg's traditional eighteenth-century alliance with Vienna had been based on co-operation against the Ottoman Empire. An Austro-Russian *rapprochement* was improbable as long as Maria Theresa lived, in view of her memories of Russia's desertion of Austria in the final stages of the Seven Years War and her own distaste for the Russian Empress. By the later 1770s, however, the Empress-Queen appeared about to die and her successor, Joseph II, was known to be more favourable to a revival of the alliance.

The second element in the transformation was Catherine II's search for prestige, which had been stimulated by the successful Russo-French mediation in the War of the Bavarian Succession, which was ended by the Peace of Teschen in May 1779. The

---

[93] Cf. *Documents of the American Revolution*, xvi, no. 2005.ii, and J. B. Scott, ed., *The Armed Neutralities of 1780 and 1800* (London, 1918), 281.

[94] This was done on 24 Apr. 1780: Edler, *Dutch Republic*, 136.

[95] The standard authority is Madariaga, *Armed Neutrality*; Panin's attitude is brought into sharper focus by D. M. Griffiths, 'Nikita Panin, Russian Diplomacy and the American Revolution', *Slavic Review*, 28 (1969), 1–24.

Empress's dominant role in this led her both to think in terms of an eventual mediation of the American War and to seize the opportunity to become the patron of the neutrals. It also strengthened a third development within Russian foreign policy: that of *rapprochement* with France. This was the most revolutionary component in the diplomatic realignment of the later 1770s. Since the end of the Seven Years War, as for much of the eighteenth century, Russo-French rivalry had been automatic. Panin's 'Northern System' had been directed principally against France's threat in the vulnerable regions along Catherine's western frontier. During the 1770s, however, tension had declined, and by the end of 1778 a Russo-French *rapprochement* was under way, which would endure until 1782. This was deliberately encouraged by Vergennes, as part of his strategy of turning Europe against Britain. It was gratefully accepted in St Petersburg, for France was also the ally of Austria, a principal objective of Russian foreign policy.

The implications for Britain were serious, for by summer 1779 Russia's new attitude to France was frankly admitted.[96] This completed the long decline of Britain's standing in St Petersburg, and placed a considerable barrier in the way of all her attempts to enlist Catherine's support during the second half of the American War. The Empress professed her personal regard for the English nation, but she adopted a strict neutrality between the western powers and now rejected any thought of alliance with London. Her growing interest in neutral trade was in any case putting the two states on a collision course. During the first year of the European war, Catherine was preoccupied with the fighting in Germany and then with a Russo-Turkish confrontation over the Crimea, which was only settled early in 1779 by the convention of Ainalikawak. Though the Empress was anxious to stimulate trade, Russia's own merchant fleet remained very small and the activities of British privateers at first caused little friction. It was principally the pleas of the commercial states, together with her own quest for prestige, which increased Russia's concern with neutral rights during 1779 and 1780.

The twin changes in St Petersburg's foreign policy were not immediately apparent in London, where a very traditional view of Russia remained supreme. To a significant extent the explanation is to be found in the confusing court politics of the Russian capital, where Panin was now on the defensive, as his great rival Potemkin moved towards complete ascendancy. The principal problem lay in

[96] Madariaga, *Armed Neutrality*, 104–5, citing the 'Instructions' for Simolin, 26 July 1779; 2 weeks later a long report drawn up by the Russian college of foreign affairs endorsed and embroidered this basic conclusion: ibid. 108–10.

the distorting view of those struggles, filtered through the dispatches of Britain's gullible representative, James Harris, and in the inflexibility of British thinking. Harris was undoubtedly able, and in his subsequent career was to show himself to be the greatest British ambassador of his generation. At this point, however, he was a young, relatively inexperienced minister, given to private initiatives and dangerously prone to snap judgements. He also shared the familiar British illusion that the Anglo-French struggle was Europe's principal concern, and this coloured all his views. Soon after his arrival he decided Panin was irrevocably anti-British. This rapid verdict, together with his warm personal relations with Potemkin, led him to throw in his lot with the rising star at Catherine's court and, more important, to transmit the favourite's view of men and events back to London. The confusing struggles in the Empress's entourage, together with the hothouse atmosphere which they engendered, created problems for all foreign diplomats and Harris was no exception. He was often deceived by the wily Potemkin and used as a pawn in the struggle for ascendancy. Yet these miscalculations were always less important than the persistence in London of the idea that the Russian state remained Britain's natural friend and ally. Official policy towards Russia during the middle years of the American War was to provide a particularly graphic illustration of the static thinking which shaped Britain's diplomacy.

The gulf between the two states became particularly noticeable during the winter of 1779–80.[97] Shortly after he entered office, Stormont had launched a fresh diplomatic initiative. During the previous summer Harris, privately and unofficially, had tried through Potemkin to revive the idea of an armed mediation by which the Empress would end the American War, in the same way that she had triumphantly concluded the Bavarian conflict. Neither this, nor Weymouth's belated and blinkered bid in September for an alliance had produced any tangible result. Yet in November 1779 Stormont, guided and misled by Harris's over-optimistic dispatches, revived the idea of Russian mediation and even empowered the ambassador to offer a full alliance for the present war, if it seemed it might be accepted. Harris pursued this approach with his usual energy, but no success. Catherine II understood its real objective was to draw Russia into the American War and wanted to avoid this. By the end of January 1780 the initiative had been decisively rejected.

Stormont and Harris were both blind to the Empress's growing interest in neutral rights. They were convinced of Russia's enduring friendship and encouraged by periodic expressions of goodwill from

[97] Ibid. 105–13 and 121–39, on which this paragraph is based.

both Catherine and Potemkin, and they could not conceive that the Empress would ever join the ranks of their enemies. Yet this is exactly what happened during the early months of 1780. Throughout the first two years of the European war, neutral rights had been a low priority in St Petersburg. In the spring of 1779, in co-operation with Denmark, the Empress had instituted patrols to protect Russia's trade routes, and she had been periodically irritated by privateering activities: occasional complaints had been lodged with London over British seizures of Russian ships and goods, though Harris and his superiors were inclined to dismiss such protests as mere form. During the winter of 1779–80, however, Catherine II took up the cause of the neutrals, who were anxious for the leadership of a major power in their struggle with Britain. Concern at the growing number of attacks on Russia's own trade,[98] together with thoughts of the prestige and political influence which might accrue, induced Catherine to issue her celebrated Declaration of Neutral Rights in March 1780.[99] Commercial states were invited to co-operate under Russia's leadership to enforce a liberal maritime code and specifically the principle of 'free ships'.[100] This, together with the narrow definition of contraband adopted, gave the League of Armed Neutrality a distinctly anti-British appearance and certainly the main opponent of its principles was Britain.

Catherine II's Declaration dominated London's relations with the neutral maritime states for a year after its promulgation. Ministers were surprised and outraged at the Empress's action and naturally attempted to uphold their own ideas in relations with the neutrals.[101] Their efforts were to enjoy very limited success. Sweden had already begun to co-operate with St Petersburg in defence of neutral trade and moved towards the proposed league during the spring and

[98] Ibid. 156, 158, for the way in which seizures of Russian ships by Spain were the 'last straw'.

[99] This can be found in Scott, ed., *The Armed Neutralities*, 273–4; part II of this valuable anthology contains extracts from many important documents bearing on the Armed Neutrality and on Anglo-Dutch diplomacy.

[100] The impetus for the League of Armed Neutrality came from Catherine II who, at this time, was on very poor terms with Panin, whom she did not see for 2 entire months. But it was Panin who provided the 5 principles of the Armed Neutrality, which were, in fact, the principles put forward by A. P. von Bernstorff in 1778 and were now appropriated for Russia's use: Madariaga, *Armed Neutrality*, 162, 173–5. Russia had traditionally supported a liberal maritime code (to enable trade to continue in wartime and to encourage the growth of her own merchant fleet) and the doctrine of 'free ships' was enshrined in Russia's one commercial treaty, that of 1766 with Britain. What was new about the Armed Neutrality was the Empress's attempt to enforce these principles by placing herself at the head of a league of neutrals: ibid. 175–84 *passim*.

[101] France, by contrast, supported the Armed Neutrality, since its aims were identical to French objectives over neutral rights, and even Spain, despite her own severe maritime code, answered the Russian declaration in moderate terms.

summer of 1780. Her own relations with Britain had been exacerbated during 1779 by a series of disputes over the free port of Marstrand and over the inevitable British seizures of Swedish shipping.[102] Though Weymouth's replacement by Stormont had improved relations, it was insufficient to prevent Gustav III accepting Catherine II's Declaration on 21 July 1780, thereby making Sweden the second state to join the Armed Neutrality.[103] Yet the more favourable British policy which Stormont had established continued after mid-1780. It recognized Sweden's right to carry non-contraband goods to France (which Britain had hitherto denied) and ensured that, while Stockholm was nominally part of the Armed Neutrality, Anglo-Swedish disputes over neutral rights were relatively few for the rest of the war.

A similar pattern was evident in Britain's relations with Denmark. The Danish foreign minister, A. P. von Bernstorff, found it difficult to oppose the Armed Neutrality outright since its principles were his own.[104] He was, however, alarmed by the wider implications of the Russian proposals.[105] By 1780 he had given Danish neutrality a pro-British tone, though his moderation was criticized by his domestic opponents. He feared the principal benefactor of the Armed Neutrality would be Denmark's main commercial rival, the Dutch Republic, and this strengthened his reservations about the Russian initiative.[106] British policy towards Denmark was equally moderate.[107] Ministers had successfully prevented the Admiralty Court from pronouncing on the treaty of 1670 and thereby averted a clash over the substantive question of the legality of wartime commerce, particularly in naval stores. Stormont was prepared for further minor concessions, allowing Copenhagen to trade freely in salt beef (Denmark was a major producer of this) in return for the exclusion of *matériel*. Once again, Britain's idea of a concession proved to be very different from that of the neutral powers.

The uneasy equilibrium ended with the Empress's Declaration. The Royal Council forced Bernstorff to negotiate Denmark's accession to the Armed Neutrality, signed on 9 July 1780. At the same time he began to negotiate privately with London, which was prepared to compromise over neutral rights. In the autumn an

---

[102] For Anglo-Swedish relations in 1779–80, see Roslund-Mercurio, 'The Problem of Neutral Rights', 226–71.

[103] Denmark's accession preceded that of Sweden by 12 days.

[104] Madariaga, *Armed Neutrality*, 185–9.

[105] Feldbaek, *Dansk neutralitetspolitik*, 152–3.

[106] *Bernstorffsche Papiere*, iii. 603.

[107] See, in particular, Stormont to Lord Chancellor Thurlow, 28 Mar. 1780, Stormont Papers, Box 17.

agreement was signed, by which Copenhagen gave up the right to carry naval stores in return for freedom of commerce in foodstuffs. Though only ratified early in October, this was backdated to 4 July, in a vain attempt to make it appear to precede Denmark's accession to the neutral league.[108] This agreement immediately undermined the Armed Neutrality. Bernstorff had given way on one of its fundamental doctrines, a narrow definition of contraband, and his actions aroused outrage in St Petersburg and in Copenhagen, where his domestic enemies forced him to resign in November 1780. Britain thus secured an agreement of sorts with Denmark, but at the exceptionally high cost of losing the one neutral observer who exhibited much sympathy for London's difficulties.

The Russian declaration was of greatest importance in Anglo-Dutch diplomacy. Since Catherine II's five principles embodied the doctrine of 'free ships' which Britain was still denying to the Dutch, her initiative challenged the whole basis of British policy at The Hague. In spring 1780, against a background of Britain's suspension of all treaties with the Dutch and their own adoption of unlimited convoy, the Republic was ready for closer co-operation with Catherine II. The Russian minister at The Hague, Galitzin, had begun to work unofficially for this in February and, early in April, the Empress's Declaration was presented to the States-General. For the next six months, Dutch accession to the Armed Neutrality dominated relations between The Hague and London. William V and his ministers were interested, but feared a conflict with Britain: in July, Stormont, continuing his hard-line approach, threatened war if the Republic joined the neutral league. By the late autumn of 1780, however, this appeared imminent.

It was a clear and immediate threat. If the Republic could secure the Armed Neutrality's protection and support for the privileges claimed under the 1674 treaty, then Britain would probably be unable to prevent the Dutch carrying naval stores to France. London's response was war, decided upon by the end of October:[109] at which point William V's authority collapsed totally.[110] Thereafter, Britain was only determined to ensure that the actual breach in relations preceded the Republic's inevitable accession to the Armed Neutrality, since otherwise not merely the Dutch but the far more considerable might of Russia, would be added to the swelling ranks

[108] Madariaga, *Armed Neutrality*, 189 n. 57.
[109] Stormont to Yorke, Private, 31 Oct. 1780, Stormont Papers, Box 113; cf. the Northern Secretary's official dispatch of the same date: SP 84/572, fos. 166–8. By 10 Nov., Yorke was announcing his own imminent departure, with the clear implication that war would immediately follow: *Archives . . . Orange–Nassau*, 5th series, ii. 313.
[110] Yorke to Hardwicke, 31 Oct. and 7 Nov. 1780, Add. MSS 35372, fo. 267, 270.

of her enemies. The timetable of war was determined by the absolute
necessity of avoiding a conflict with Russia as well.[111]

An admirable pretext had been provided in September when an
American agent, Henry Laurens, was captured on the high seas.[112]
His papers included a copy of a draft and strictly unofficial 'treaty',
between representatives of Congress and of Amsterdam, drawn up in
1778. Its aim had been to reserve a privileged position for
Amsterdam in the trade of an independent America. The 'treaty' was
a piece of commercial opportunism rather than political premeditation,
and its precise legal status was, at best, uncertain; it was really no
more than an unofficial set of proposals.[113] However, it was
certainly indiscreet and could be used to provoke war. Laurens's
papers, especially the infamous 'treaty', were communicated to The
Hague, together with a demand that the signatories be punished.[114]
The Dutch government, recognizing the agreement was indefensible,
began an enquiry into the circumstances of its conclusion. This was
viewed in London as further evidence of its weakness and evasiveness,
and completed British disillusionment.[115] During the second half of
November, the States-General voted to join the neutral league.
Britain immediately ended relations: on Boxing Day 1780, Yorke left
The Hague and the fighting began.[116]

The Fourth Anglo-Dutch War (1780–4) has usually been seen as a
natural and even inevitable consequence of the burgeoning maritime
disputes during the American War, which culminated in Dutch
moves to join the Armed Neutrality.[117] This verdict is substantially
correct. The British 'Manifesto' which accompanied the ending of
diplomatic relations listed London's ostensible grievances:[118] Dutch

[111] *Corr. Geo. III*, v. 152; cf. SP 84/572, fo. 103.
[112] The Laurens affair can be followed in the documents assembled in Stevens, *Facsimiles*, nos. 920–80.
[113] J. Osinga, *Frankrijk, Vergennes en de Amerikaanse Onafhankelijkheid 1776–1783* (Amsterdam, 1982), 166; Schulte Nordholt, *Dutch Republic*, 64–6 for its conclusion.
[114] Yorke's behaviour at this point was predictably arrogant and high-handed: CP (Hollande) 542, fo. 284, 429. He was already behaving in a haughty manner over Dutch negotiations at St Petersburg his conduct over the 'treaty' was said to have antagonized even those who were still sympathetic to Britain: *Archives . . . Orange–Nassau*, 5th series, ii. 275, 307; cf. Schulte Nordholt, *Dutch Republic*, 150, for an outburst against the stadtholder early in Nov.
[115] See e.g. SP 80/223, fo. 107. In mid-Nov. Stormont was canvassing, apparently in all seriousness, the idea that Austria should annex the Dutch province of Zealand and join it to the Austrian Netherlands! Ibid., fos. 122–3. This was to be accompanied by the reopening of the Scheldt and was intended to pave the way for a revival of the Anglo-Austrian alliance, but Vienna rejected any idea of attempting such a plan.
[116] SP 84/573, fos. 264–7 for an account of his departure.
[117] This interpretation can be found, for example, in Madariaga, *Armed Neutrality*, 234–8; Miller, *Yorke*, 88–105; Schulte Nordholt, *Dutch Republic*, 146–54 and *passim*; Mackesy, *War for America*, 377–9; and Syrett, *Neutral Rights*, 38.
[118] It is printed in *Parl. Hist.* xxi, cols. 968–72.

trade with the enemy in Europe and at St Eustatius;[119] the Republic's failure to provide the aid specified in the treaty of 1678; and the secret agreement between Amsterdam and Congress, together with the failure to punish its signatories. The 'Manifesto' could not, of course, express the immediate reason why Britain rushed into war in late 1780: the need to anticipate formal Dutch accession to the Armed Neutrality, with the threat that the Republic would receive the support of the neutral states and in particular Russia, for its claim to supply France with naval stores. The obvious danger was that Britain would either have to become reconciled to this trade or face a greatly enlarged war when her situation was already desperate.

Two further factors contributed significantly to the deterioration in Anglo-Dutch relations in 1779–80: the Republic's failure to act effectively against Paul Jones and its attempts to prevent Dutch merchants continuing to supply the garrison at Gibraltar after Spain blockaded the British fortress.[120] These episodes confirmed the prevailing view in London that Dutch neutrality, far from being pro-English as British ministers expected, or simply even-handed, was, in fact, pro-French. In the broadest sense, the Fourth Anglo-Dutch War was the logical consequence of the Republic's drift into the French camp. During the American War, British ministers believed the Dutch had moved from being allies to become enemies, and for this reason they attacked at the very end of 1780.

These arguments are perfectly valid, at least as far as they go. One principal cause of the Fourth Anglo-Dutch War is to be found in the maritime disputes produced by the American rebellion which intensified after 1778. But it had a further, unexpected dimension, not hitherto appreciated, which only fully emerges in the extensive secret correspondence between Stormont and Yorke.[121] Remarkably enough, Britain attacked her traditional friend and ally in an attempt to revive the Stadtholder's power and to save the House of Orange. British resentment at Dutch perfidy also reflected exasperation at the declining fortunes of the Orange party and at the corresponding collapse of London's control over the Republic. Yorke, struggling to

[119] Some indication of Britain's resentment at the continuing role of this Dutch West Indian island is provided by Stormont's remark in Jan. 1781 that 'we should never have been in our present situation, were it our good fortune that St. Eustatia [*sic*] had been destroyed, or sunk in the ocean': *Parl. Hist.* xxi, col. 1004. For trade between St Eustatius and the French West Indian Islands, in defiance of the 'Rule of 1756', see *Sandwich Papers*, iii. 167, 188.

[120] Renaut, *De la neutralité*, 283–97; *Archives . . . Orange Nassau*, 5th series, ii. 172.

[121] For this correspondence, see above, n. 72. This dimension is explored in H. M. Scott, 'Sir Joseph Yorke, Dutch Politics and the Origins of the Fourth Anglo-Dutch War', *Historical Journal* 31 (1988), 571–89, on which the subsequent analysis is largely based; cf. H. H. Rowen, *The Princes of Orange: The Stadholders in the Dutch Republic* (Cambridge, 1988), 207.

uphold British interests, had long been convinced of the need to restore Britain's influence and therefore to revive the flagging fortunes of the Orangists. He had even urged William V to emulate Sweden's Gustav III and carry out a *coup d'état* to restore his own authority, though the Stadtholder dismissed this suggestion. Though the ambassador pressed his views on Stormont from the moment he took office in October 1779, and exerted considerable influence on policy during the next fourteen months, he could not, at first, win over the Northern Secretary to his plan of attack on the Republic to restore William V's authority. The cautious Stormont hesitated for much of 1780, accepting the ambassador's basic analysis, but fearing—correctly—that war might instead exacerbate the Stadt-holder's difficulties. The Northern Secretary was finally persuaded by William V's seemingly irresolute behaviour when presented with the 'treaty' between Amsterdam and the Americans in October 1780, which convinced him Yorke was correct, and war followed two months later.

This analysis was characteristically Anglocentric. Britain's approach to relations, in the 1770s as throughout the eighteenth century, was based on the expectation that the Republic's ministers, and especially the Stadtholder, would follow her lead and do her bidding. The longer the American War continued, the more this was shown to be false.[122] In 1778–80, London actually expected the Dutch authorities to take action to prevent naval stores being carried to France and to arrest John Paul Jones. Ministers were both disappointed and let down by the Republic's failure to comply with their wishes, as it had usually done during the first half of the American War. They were also highly critical of the weakness and irresolution of Dutch policy. Stormont's view was shaped by Yorke's prejudices. The ambassador was by this stage openly contemptuous of William V and also on exceedingly bad terms with Prince Louis of Brunswick. Yorke recognized that the Grand Pensionary van Bleiswijk was firmly in the French camp, and he pessimistically believed the *Griffier* Fagel was the only 'true friend' to Britain. In fact, the Stadtholder did try, with his usual dim integrity, to uphold Dutch neutrality and at the same time to defend England's cause.[123] By 1779–80, it was a difficult and perhaps impossible task, and his efforts received little thanks in London, where Dutch neutrality increasingly appeared favourable to France. British observers saw only William V's glaring personal failings and his regime's political bankruptcy.

[122] Yet as late as Sept. and Oct. 1780, Britain was unsuccessfully trying to hire transports from the Dutch: *Documents of the American Revolution*, xviii, no. 180.

[123] Spooner, *Risks at Sea*, 107–9, for his efforts to prevent the adoption of convoys.

This led Yorke and Stormont to a sombre analysis of the Republic's plight. Money and the profit motive, together with French intrigues, had brought the decline, with Holland and, in particular, Amsterdam, acting as the agents of Dutch collapse.[124] Their blinkered view of the Republic's history provided an answer to its predicament, historically dubious, but politically attractive. The fortunes of the Republic and of the House of Orange, which were identical, should be restored by war. A British attack would bring about Dutch salvation. In Britain's eyes, the events of 1780 were to follow the pattern of the Orange restorations of 1672 and 1747. On both of these occasions, war had rescued the Stadtholderate, as it was hoped to do again: the established formula would be repeated, with the single difference that the Republic's principal foreign enemy would now be England and not France. By a curious, misplaced logic, Britain had come to believe that she could only save the Dutch state, and her own position within it, by attacking her traditional friend and ally. It rested upon the assumption that war had revived the political fortunes and increased the authority of the Orangist party in the past and if applied would do so in the present. There was, however, a remarkable vagueness as to precisely how this would be achieved. William V was written off: little was expected from the man who had himself contributed to the decline of the Republic and of the Stadtholderate. Instead, the glorious traditions of the House of Orange were invoked. In particular, the career of William III, the Stadtholder-King, who had first saved the Republic, then England, and finally Europe, provided some solace to Britain's increasingly beleaguered government in the dark winter of 1780–1.[125]

This analysis of Anglo-Dutch relations and of the domestic impact of war does not survive close examination. Neither Yorke nor Stormont ever faced the central question of who could play the key role of the new William III, for which there was an embarrassing shortage of candidates. Both men recognized the present Stadtholder was not the stuff of which heroes were made. But their ideas never proceeded beyond generalities. They hoped that, in some mysterious way, a war would again rejuvenate the House of Orange and, eventually, restore an Anglo-Dutch alliance dominated by Britain. Their view of the Republic's history lacked precision and their analysis of its contemporary politics was woefully deficient. It was evocative of Britain's plight by the end of 1780 that her policy at The Hague had so lost contact with reality.

---

[124] See e.g. Stormont's comments: *Parl. Hist.* xxi, cols. 644, 1006.
[125] See Stormont's remarks: ibid. xxi, col. 1001.

12

The Coming of Peace, 1781–1783

THE Anglo-Dutch War appeared to make Britain's situation critical.[1] The spectacle of a traditional ally joining her enemies demonstrated her plight. British domestic politics wore a forlorn face. The Gordon Riots, besides revealing the North Ministry's weakness, had been accompanied by attacks on embassy chapels, a traditional source of distrust and resentment to Protestant Englishmen.[2] These damaged Britain's standing in Europe: the failure to protect foreign diplomats was a particularly serious matter. The mounting parliamentary onslaught on Lord North was also widely reported on the continent and further dented Britain's already damaged prestige. Yet the appearance of collapse and of the final decline of British power was exaggerated. Though Britain's situation in 1780–1 was serious, it was not yet terminal.

One likely source of difficulties was Catherine II's Armed Neutrality, but in 1781–2 its impact proved less damaging than feared.[3] It came to be joined by Austria, Prussia, and even the Kingdom of the Two Sicilies, as well as Denmark, Sweden, and the Dutch Republic. These states all had distinct and usually diverse motives and the neutral league was never a coherent, far less unified, force. Politically it reinforced Britain's isolation: by uniting the neutral states against her, it helped to defeat every British attempt to find allies. Economically its impact proved to be less than anticipated. The accession of Austria and Prussia allowed Dutch ships to use their flags as flags of convenience, and this undermined one aim of Britain's war against the Republic. The Armed Neutrality certainly pushed London on to the defensive over neutral rights, but the government was not forced to make any substantial or permanent concessions. Britain's attitude in 1781–2 proved more moderate. Fewer neutral vessels were seized, and though several Russian ships were captured, they were usually released very quickly and damages

---

[1] Cf. Sandwich's sombre survey in mid-Jan. 1781: *Sandwich Papers*, iv. 23–6.
[2] For these, and for British attempts to compensate the embassies involved, see *Corr. Geo. III*, v. 70, 72.
[3] Madariaga, *Armed Neutrality*, 361–86; A. Toborg, 'Frederick II of Prussia and his Relations with Great Britain during the American Revolution' (unpublished Ph.D. thesis, Columbia University, 1965), 195–228.

paid. This cumbersome procedure was necessary because the cabinet, fearful of erecting a legal precedent, would not publicly admit Russian claims that the doctrine of 'free ships' had been established by the Commercial Treaty of 1766. Ministers privately accepted this was so, but refused a formal concession on the substantive issue.

By 1780–1 British resources were stretched to the limit, particularly the all-important ships of the line. It may be that the balance of naval and military forces was by now so decisively tilted against Britain that defeat had become inevitable. Such judgements rest principally on hindsight. Britain's overall strategic position did not markedly deteriorate until the second half of 1781. Ministers certainly found it increasingly difficult to support the war effort and encountered severe problems in distributing available resources. There was no reason, until news arrived of Cornwallis's surrender at Yorktown, for the cabinet to believe Britain would be defeated.

This is at first sight surprising, in view of the forces which were now ranged against her and the unparalleled scale of the operations. It was partly due to the success of British strategy. In 1779–80 Britain had gone on the offensive at sea and particularly in America. In May 1780 her troops had captured Charlestown, a significant and potentially decisive gain in a purely American context. By 1781, however, an aggressive strategy was becoming less feasible, as Britain was forced on to the defensive. Yet if her difficulties were undoubted, they were paralleled and even eclipsed by those facing her enemies. Franco-Spanish co-operation, the foundation of Vergennes's strategy, was proving difficult, and Bourbon efforts were hampered by a resulting inability to co-ordinate operations against Britain. Their difficulties were increased after December 1780 by the need to take the Dutch into their strategic calculations. The feeble Republic, as British ministers had forseen, proved of greater use as a neutral than as an ally. Across the Atlantic the situation of the Americans was also becoming desperate by the closing months of 1780.

The very nature of the conflict militated against a decisive victory. Eighteenth-century wars were seldom won on the battlefield or on the high seas: limited warfare produced small-scale changes in the military or naval balance. Instead financial strength and political will usually determined the outcome, and here Britain's renowned economic power appeared to give her an advantage. In September 1780 George III had prophesied that 'this war like the last will prove one of Credit', a verdict which Vergennes endorsed, styling the American conflict a *'guerre d'écus'*.[4] By 1780 France's mounting

[4] *Corr. Geo. III*, v. 136; R. D. Harris, *Necker: Reform Statesman of the Ancien Régime* (Berkeley and Los Angeles, 1979), 209.

financial problems were certainly alarming her ministry. These difficulties were known in London, where they inspired the hope that another campaign, or perhaps two, might force a bankrupt France to terms.[5] The North Ministry was also becoming aware of the weakness and divisions of the Americans and these reports, though exaggerated, encouraged similar hopes that the rebellion might yet collapse, particularly if French support should diminish or even disappear.[6] In the light of subsequent events such hopes may appear foolhardy. Yet there was little in the fighting during 1780 or the first half of 1781 to suggest that the stalemate was about to be broken. Though the anti-British coalition had 'a thin margin of superiority', neither side had the resources or the opportunity for a decisive victory.[7]

This stalemate was accompanied by attempts, beginning in 1779, to negotiate peace. These initiatives, however, do not represent the beginnings of the eventual peace settlement. At this stage no government wanted an early treaty and, more important, was willing to make the necessary concessions. The various attempts at mediation and at direct negotiations in 1779–81 were a means of waging war, not of achieving peace. All the states involved had broader political purposes, and none expected that these talks would end the fighting. By exploring attitudes and assessing territorial and political demands, every government hoped to learn something about their enemies' resolve and morale. In Britain's case, this objective was accompanied by a wish to probe the weak points in the opposing alliance and principally the flawed co-operation between France and Spain.

The purpose of such secret diplomacy was well illustrated by the earliest and most prolonged initiative in which London became involved. This was the celebrated Hussey–Cumberland negotiations, an extended series of Anglo-Spanish peace discussions which began in November 1779 and was only terminated by Britain in March 1781.[8] These were initiated by Thomas Hussey, the former chaplain of the Spanish Embassy in London and head of its intelligence network. In June 1780 Germain's secretary, Richard Cumberland, was sent to Madrid, where he remained until the following March. But it was never intended that these negotiations should produce peace. London hoped to sow discord between Madrid and Versailles,

---

[5] *Corr. Geo. III.* v. 144, 187; cf. Mackesy, *War for America*, 384.
[6] *Corr. Geo. III*, v. 256; Mackesy, *War for America*, 385.
[7] Dull, *French Navy*, 210.
[8] A good brief account is Conn, *Gibraltar*, 190–7; S. F. Bemis, *The Hussey–Cumberland Mission and American Independence* (Princeton, 1931) provides more detail, though it neglects important British sources and exaggerates the importance of the discussions, particularly for London.

and these talks were accompanied by increased British naval and military pressure on Spain's vulnerable empire.[9] In a very important sense these were a logical extension of earlier British policy: that of driving a wedge between the Bourbon allies, playing on Spanish doubts about fighting for American independence, and purchasing Madrid's neutrality through British concessions. Spain also used these talks (as she had done in 1778–9) for her own purposes. Floridablanca understood Britain's real motives and was circumspect in his own discussions with London. He also employed the talks against France, to further Madrid's interests within the Bourbon alliance.[10]

Spain's price for a settlement was made clear at the outset: the cession of Gibraltar, for a territorial equivalent. This demand was predictably a major stumbling block. The British government was prepared to cede territory, but ministers were thinking in terms of West Florida rather than Britain's citadel at the entrance to the Mediterranean.[11] Though North and Germain at least were prepared to consider handing over the fortress, the cabinet's collective view was that this was impossible without a far larger 'equivalent' than Madrid would contemplate. British public opinion was believed to be so strongly attached to Gibraltar that no ministry dare cede it without securing substantial territory in return.[12] Cumberland was therefore expressly forbidden to discuss the fortress and, at one point, was even told not to enter Spain until he was assured by Floridablanca it would not be brought up in the discussions. Since Madrid's principal objective was Gibraltar, these talks were condemned to failure. A second, equally fundamental problem, was that Britain remained unwilling to discuss the future position of the Americans with any third party. Even Spain, at best lukewarm over colonial independence, recognized this would have to be part of any peace settlement.

Britain's refusal to discuss North America immediately wrecked secret Anglo-French discussions during the second half of 1780. In July and August of that year, and again in December, a group on the French council made peace overtures to London.[13] These approaches were the work of Necker and Maurepas, with Louis XVI's knowledge and approval, and they appear to have been concealed

[9] Mackesy, *War for America*, 317.

[10] Dull, *French Navy*, 186, 204.

[11] *HMC Knox*, 290.

[12] The fear of public opinion is apparent from Stormont's 'Memorandum', drawn up in Jan. 1781 at the height of the debate in cabinet: Stormont Papers, Bundle 1384.

[13] Harris, *Necker*, 208–16; Necker had always been hostile to the American War, which delayed his reform programme. Maurepas revived his earlier links with Forth to pass on the overtures to London: M. Ward, *Forth* (Chichester, 1982), 103–4.

from Vergennes. The foreign minister shared his colleagues' alarm at France's deteriorating financial position and was also worried by Spain's evident weakness: in September he was warned from Madrid that famine and financial problems might prevent Charles III from continuing the war after the next campaign.[14] Vergennes shrewdly wanted to avoid direct negotiations with Britain in case these were viewed as a sign of French weakness: which was exactly how Necker's overtures were interpreted in London. The cabinet continued to hope for eventual victory, and France's approaches were bluntly rejected. Britain's attitude to peace remained dismissive until the closing weeks of 1781. Her optimism, and her determination to fight on, were made clear by Stormont when he told the Austrian minister Belgioioso

that the King of England would recognise the independence of the colonies when the French were masters of the Tower of London, and that with respect to Gibraltar, only Madrid would be recognised as an equivalent for that place.[15]

This confidence, however misplaced in retrospect, destroyed these negotiations.

Vergennes was always more flexible, and also less confident about the war's outcome. Rejecting direct talks, he instead explored possible diplomatic intervention by other states and principally by Austria and Russia, both of whom were anxious to contribute to a settlement.[16] Britain's response in 1780–1 was opportunistic.[17] The cabinet was suspicious of any mediation since it would have taken the settlement out of its own hands. As in the earlier discussions with Spain, ministers would have been prepared for peace on their own terms, but they did not seriously believe these would be acceptable and refused to make major concessions. Austrian and Russian intervention was not expected to produce a settlement, and indeed Britain was determined that it should fail.[18] Yet it could not be ignored. Stormont's response was dictated by Britain's broader objectives and in particular by her search for an alliance.

The military and naval stalemate, together with his knowledge of American and Bourbon difficulties, induced Stormont to believe that

---

[14] Dull, *French Navy*, 197.   [15] Quoted by Conn, *Gibraltar*, 198.

[16] Kaunitz had actively tried to mediate in the summer and autumn of 1779 (SP 80/221 *passim*) while Catherine II had long been hinting in similar vein (e.g. Madariaga, *Armed Neutrality*, 98–9, 136).

[17] A full and masterly account is provided by Madariaga, *Armed Neutrality*, 264–360.

[18] In Sept. 1780, Gustav III's offer to mediate was rejected out of hand, partly because he was believed to be acting in league with France: *Corr. Geo. III*, v. 117–9.

if Britain could secure an ally she might yet defeat her enemies. His own preferences were clear. He wanted to revive the Old System and, during the second half of 1780 and the early months of 1781, tried unsuccessfully to conclude an Anglo-Austrian alliance.[19] He did this principally by suggesting Vienna should open the river Scheldt, officially closed since 1648, and even annex the Dutch province of Zealand and join it to the Austrian Netherlands. Maria Theresa's death in November 1780 and Joseph II's accession to sole authority briefly strengthened British hopes, which for over a decade had been focused on the Emperor, but these expectations were soon dashed. Habsburg foreign policy aimed at a *rapprochement* with Russia, and not even the lure of opening the Scheldt and reviving the prosperity of the Southern Netherlands could tempt Austria back to its British alliance.

Britain's plight, as the Anglo-Dutch War began, was evident both in these proposals and in the offer, early in 1781, to cede Minorca to Russia in return for an immediate alliance. This too was unsuccessful, for Catherine II appreciated that its real purpose was to draw her state into a European war which she was determined to avoid and might also, in the longer term, drive a wedge between Russia and Britain's enemies.[20] The hope of involving the Empress was also the principal reason why Britain accepted St Petersburg's offers to mediate in 1780–1, though a more immediate purpose was fear of Russian retaliation over the Dutch War. Ministers were anxious to avoid conflict with the formidable power of Russia, yet the Dutch Republic was on the point of joining Catherine II's Armed Neutrality. Requesting Russian mediation was an obvious way of trying to placate the Empress.[21]

Russia and Austria also had their own objectives in pursuing a mediated settlement. European diplomacy in 1780–1 was dominated not by Britain's American War but by the Russo-Austrian *rapprochement*. This had been facilitated first by Russia's own diplomatic realignment in the later 1770s and then by Maria Theresa's death in November 1780. By the following spring Catherine II and Joseph II had secretly signed an alliance, though the familiar problems over the imperial title ensured that this took the unusual form of an exchange

---

[19] SP 80/223 and FO 7/1, *passim; Joseph II., Leopold II. und Kaunitz: Ihr Briefwechsel*, ed. A. Beer (Vienna, 1873), 29–34.

[20] Madariaga, *Armed Neutrality*, 239–312, *passim*. Britain believed Russian possession of Minorca would be 'an everlasting cause of jealousy' between the Empress and the Bourbons: *HMC Knox*, 291.

[21] See, in particular, the interesting 'Note to be read to the Cabinet' drawn up by Stormont in Sept. 1781: Stormont Papers, Box 64.

of letters between the two rulers and not a formal convention.[22] Austria's attitude to mediation reflected her desire to strengthen her links with Russia and her determination that the Russian Empress should not dominate the new alliance. For her part, Catherine II had long seen mediation as a means of increasing her own prestige and political influence and that of her state.

In 1780–1 the idea of a mediated settlement was kept alive by its broader political context, rather than by any real expectation of peace.[23] In fact the various proposals soon foundered because of the attitudes of the belligerents. All had their own objectives, often pursued with scant regard to military or political reality. Spain, for example, had failed to capture Gibraltar and had even been unable to prevent Britain reinforcing it in April 1781, but this did not prevent Floridablanca demanding the fortress as a *sine qua non* of any settlement. France, despite her mounting financial problems and lack of decisive victories, made American independence a precondition. Until autumn 1781 Britain refused to consider either of these demands. Indeed British ministers made their own contribution to the stalemate by continuing to insist that the war in America was still a domestic matter and that any settlement, or even a suspension of arms, must exclude this struggle.[24] These irreconcilable attitudes guaranteed that the various peace initiatives in 1780–1 would all fail.

The diplomatic impasse was the product of a continuing military and naval stalemate. During the second half of 1781, however, news of a series of British reverses reached London. Tobago was lost; then Pensacola and with it West Florida; Bourbon troops landed on Minorca; and finally Britain's southern offensive against the Americans was turned back. The climax was Cornwallis's disastrous surrender at Yorktown in mid-October. This resulted from the success of the American-Bourbon axis in co-ordinating its operations for one campaign, and it brought not merely a strategic breakthrough, but an end to the diplomatic stalemate as well. Yorktown did not on its own end the American War, far less determine the peace settlement. Britain's notable recovery during 1782 was almost as

[22] Isabel de Madariaga, 'The Secret Austro-Russian Treaty of 1781', *Slavonic and East European Review*, 38 (1959–60), 114–45.
[23] Britain kept the mediation going in 1781 despite believing Kaunitz favoured France: see, in particular, Stormont to Keith, Very Private, 16 Mar. 1781, Stormont Papers, Box 58.
[24] See e.g. the emphatic statement of this doctrine by Stormont: to Keith, Secret, 27 Feb. 1781, FO 7/1. The decisive voice here was probably that of George III, who wrote in Mar. 1781 that 'no Advice or Difficulty shall ever make me permit any foreign [state] to interfere in the terms for bringing my Rebellious Subjects to a sense of their Crimes': to Stormont, 14 Mar. 1781, Stormont Papers, Box 16.

significant an influence on the final treaties. Cornwallis's surrender was principally decisive in the context of domestic British politics.[25] It broke the failing North Ministry and, more generally, undermined Britain's morale. After the news of Yorktown arrived on 25 November 1781 there was widespread recognition that America at least had been lost. Only the King remained defiant, rejecting the arguments of his ministers that colonial independence was inevitable and refusing to accept that the rebellion had succeeded. The North Ministry had been so closely identified with the war in America that it was difficult and perhaps impossible for it to concede defeat, but a new administration would be less constrained by the ghosts of its own political past. Three months after the news of Yorktown arrived, North's long ascendancy was over. During February 1782 his majority in the Commons was gradually whittled away, as the country gentlemen deserted him, and on the 27th he was finally defeated when Conway's motion against 'offensive war' in America was carried by almost twenty votes. North made one final, futile attempt to negotiate peace directly with France. In early March 1782 N. P. Forth was sent to Paris and offered the French government a separate peace.[26] This was rejected, and after some equally unproductive political manœuvring at home, North resigned on 20 March.

The North Ministry was immediately replaced by an administration nominally headed by the elderly Rockingham, but dominated by two bitter rivals, Charles James Fox and the Earl of Shelburne. This political hybrid was agreed on the need for an early peace settlement, but divided on every other important issue, and these fissures soon spilled over into British diplomacy. Formally, greater unity was given to foreign policy by the replacement of the established framework of two Secretaries of State by a new office of Foreign Secretary, who was solely responsible for the conduct of diplomacy. But administrative unity was accompanied by acute personal rivalry between Fox and Shelburne and by a dispute over their precise spheres of influence. The foreign policy of the short-lived Rockingham Administration, and particularly its attempts to conclude peace, were soon weakened by its internecine strife.

The new Foreign Secretary was Charles James Fox, a diplomatic

[25] I. R. Christie, *The End of North's Ministry 1780–1782* (London, 1958), 267–369. For the devastating initial effect on North himself, see N. Wraxall, *Historical Memoirs of My Own Time (1772–1784)* (2 vols.; London, 1815), ii. 102–3.
[26] Ward, *Forth*, 104–6; R. R. Crout, 'In Search of a "Just and Lasting Peace": The Treaty of 1783, Louis XVI, Vergennes, and the Regeneration of the Realm', *International History Review*, 5 (1983), 381; *Walpole Corr.* xxxiii. 331 nn. 9–10.

novice, but a man of determination and restless activity. His ignorance of European affairs did not prevent him from holding some distinctive and implacable views. Foremost among these was a conviction that everything the previous government had done was misguided or simply wrong, and he set to work to correct the mistakes of his predecessor Stormont. Fox's tenure of the Foreign Secretaryship was brief, but eventful: little more than three months later he was out of office. His 'Hundred Days' were marked by frenetic activity in all areas of Britain's diplomacy.[27] This activity, however, was not accompanied by coherent direction or by an overall plan—apart from a general desire to bring about an early peace settlement. Indeed the various strands in Fox's strategy proved irreconcilable and only his swift departure from office prevented his policy blowing up in his face.

Fox inherited a series of unresolved problems. Foremost among these were the continuing Russo-Austrian mediation, Catherine II's separate offer to mediate in the Anglo-Dutch War, and the minor problems which arose from the Armed Neutrality and from the Empress's desire to secure European recognition for her maritime principles. Stormont had been reluctant to confront any of these problems directly, particularly during the final year of the North Ministry, but such passive diplomacy was not to his successor's taste. Fox first rushed towards peace with the Dutch, abandoning overnight Britain's established insistence on a renegotiation of the commercial treaty of 1674 and, instead, accepting the Republic's demand that the principle of 'free ships' should govern wartime commerce. This completely reversed Britain's attitude towards neutral rights. It had been one source of the war which Fox now unsuccessfully tried to end, both by direct negotiations with The Hague and through Russian mediation. These efforts were frustrated principally by France's influence within the Republic. Vergennes opposed any separate peace and therefore exerted pressure to prevent an Anglo-Dutch settlement. Simultaneously, Fox began to seek Catherine II's friendship and also to move towards a *rapprochement* with Frederick II. By his final weeks in office he was aiming at nothing less than a full-blown 'Northern Alliance' of Britain, Russia, and Prussia, to which Denmark might even be added. The new league

---

[27] Madariaga, *Armed Neutrality*, 387–412, provides an excellent introduction; Toborg, 'Frederick II and Great Britain', 240–54, contains important details on his Prussian policy, but the overall perspective is unsatisfactory. A considerable amount of relevant correspondence is to be found in *Memorials and Correspondence of Charles James Fox*, ed. Lord J. Russell (4 vols.; London, 1853), i, and in Duke of Buckingham and Chandos, *Memoirs of the Court and Cabinets of George III* (2 vols.; rev. edn., London, 1853), i.

would then throw its massive diplomatic weight behind Britain and thereby facilitate a satisfactory peace.[28]

This grandiose vision had one fatal flaw: it ignored the inconvenient reality that Russia was now the ally of Austria and not, as hitherto, Prussia. The European realignment of the early 1780s meant that a new Russo-Prussian alliance was impossible and Fox's schemes were doomed. His miscalculation was particularly striking since he actually knew of the secret Russo-Austrian alliance. Britain's minister in St Petersburg, Harris—alone among all the foreign diplomats in the Russian capital—had discovered its existence by bribery and had reported it to London.[29] Though Harris subsequently contributed to Fox's failed initiative by greatly exaggerating Prussia's residual influence at St Petersburg, the Foreign Secretary's miscalculation was largely his own work. He was also misled by Frederick II. Though the Prussian King was prepared to consider an English alliance as a way out of his own dangerous isolation, his principal motive in encouraging Britain was purely tactical. Fox's approach might enable Frederick to insinuate his way into the joint mediation by Catherine II and Joseph II, to weaken or even wreck the Russo-Austrian *rapprochement*, and to restore his own standing in St Petersburg.

Fox's ignorance of European affairs and his naïvety as a foreign minister were apparent in this futile pursuit of Russia and Prussia. These overtures also exhibited the other characteristic of his diplomacy: its secrecy. Britain's approach to Frederick II was pursued through his resident in London and was not communicated to Elliot in Berlin; while Harris in St Petersburg was left in ignorance when Britain abandoned the Russo-Austrian mediation for direct negotiations with France, an oversight which strengthened Catherine II's resentment.[30] But the main victims were his cabinet colleagues and Britain's negotiations at Paris. Fox's grandiose diplomacy was intended to bolster Britain's international position and to bring about a satisfactory peace settlement. He also came to be involved in overtures for peace in the French capital, as was his colleague and bitter rival Shelburne. The fissures within British diplomacy simply reflected the more fundamental ones within the Rockingham

---

[28] *Memorials of Fox*, ed. Russell, i. 338–43; cf. Fox to Keith, 10 May 1782, FO 7/4.

[29] Madariaga, *Armed Neutrality*, 316.

[30] The first letter of any importance which Elliot received from Fox was written on 14 June 1782 (some two and a half weeks before the Foreign Secretary resigned) and simply informed him of his recall! FO 64/3. The Austrian Chancellor Kaunitz was also put out by these direct Anglo-French negotiations: see Keith's bitter complaints, to Fox, Secret and Confidential, 15 May 1782, FO 7/4.

Administration.[31] George III had been extremely reluctant to accept the new ministry and had always intended that Shelburne would counteract the influence of the Rockinghams; indeed the King wanted the Earl to be 'joint first minister'.[32] By assiduously cultivating George III Shelburne was able to strengthen his own position. In the view of some contemporaries and subsequent historians, he spent Fox's 'Hundred Days' preparing and conspiring for a ministry which he himself would dominate.

Fox and Shelburne were established political rivals and personal enemies; their respective posts in the Rockingham Ministry were a further source of conflict. Fox as Foreign Secretary claimed to monopolize the forthcoming peace negotiations. Shelburne, who was Home and Colonial Secretary, contended that until formal independence the American negotiations lay within his department, and in logic at least he had a plausible case. The two men, moreover, viewed Britain's prospects in North America and in Europe in distinct and contradictory ways. Though by spring 1782 Shelburne was coming to accept Fox's view that American independence would have to be conceded, the two ministers were at loggerheads over the timing. The Foreign Secretary favoured an immediate grant of independence, not least because this would facilitate his own undivided control of the peace negotiations. By contrast Shelburne, influenced by the King's wishes, favoured granting independence only as part of a general settlement. Their views on Britain's European policy were also diametrically opposed. Fox believed in the traditional strategy, that of unquestioned opposition to France, pursued by means of alliances with the great powers in eastern Europe. Only his preference for links with Prussia rather than Austria, in addition to Russia, set him apart from the overwhelming majority of his contemporaries. By contrast Shelburne's approach was radical and even revolutionary. He wished to lay the ground for future co-operation with France against the hegemony of the three eastern powers, and this strongly influenced his approach to the making of peace.

Shelburne's habitual secrecy and willingness to deceive his colleagues were clearly apparent during the Rockingham Administration. His previous contacts with Benjamin Franklin—the two men

[31] For the domestic political situation, see J. Cannon, *The Fox–North Coalition: Crisis of the Constitution 1782–84* (Cambridge, 1969), 1–37; O'Gorman, *Rise of Party*, 446–66; and L. G. Mitchell, *Charles James Fox and the Disintegration of the Whig Party 1782–1794* (Oxford, 1971), 9–24.

[32] Cannon, *Fox–North Coalition*, 5. The King was extremely hostile towards Fox because of his dissolute friendship with the Prince of Wales, and not surprisingly also disliked his foreign policy: see e.g. *Corr. Geo. III*, vi. 21.

had met frequently in 1767 and remained in touch thereafter—induced America's leading diplomat to write to him in the final days of the North Ministry. This inaugurated a private negotiation at Paris which continued throughout the spring and early summer of 1782.[33] Shelburne sent a most unlikely agent to negotiate with the crafty Franklin.[34] This was Richard Oswald, a septuagenarian Scottish merchant and banker who was innocent of the ways of diplomacy and also hostile to the American rebellion. He spoke no French, an additional drawback as Vergennes soon became involved in the Anglo-American talks. Oswald was hard-headed and pragmatic, however, and retained important commercial connections in North America, where he had lived for six years. At this point the purpose of the Oswald mission was exploratory. Shelburne wondered if the Americans could be detached from their French allies. Fox's approach to the making of peace was broadly similar. In April 1782 he sent his crony Thomas Grenville to Paris to probe France's attitude to the negotiations which everyone acknowledged would soon begin. Thereafter Britain had two diplomats in the French capital: or, rather, the two wings of the Rockingham Administration were each represented in France.[35]

The unusual spectacle of two separate and potentially rival diplomacies aroused amusement and even ridicule at the French court, but had no impact on the eventual settlement. All sides viewed the talks in Paris as a means of probing their opponents' attitudes before actual negotiations finally began.[36] This was certainly Vergennes's view. Though France's financial plight was worsening, he wished to delay serious talks until he knew the outcome of the latest French initiative, an attack on British India. For her part, Spain refused to negotiate until she had captured Gibraltar, which her forces were besieging. The Spanish ambassador in Paris, Aranda, could not even discuss a possible settlement until fresh orders arrived from Madrid, and these could not be expected as long as Spain believed the fortress might be taken.

The principal impact of Britain's dual diplomacy at Paris was on

[33] Shelburne simultaneously approached the Americans directly through Britain's military and naval commanders in North America, but these overtures for a separate peace were rejected outright: E. Wright, 'The British Objectives, 1780–1783: "If not Dominion then Trade" ', in R. Hoffman and P. J. Albert, eds., *Peace and Peacemakers: The Treaty of 1783* (Charlottesville, Va., 1986), 17–8.

[34] For Franklin's skill see J. R. Dull, *Franklin the Diplomat: The French Mission* (*Transactions of the American Philosophical Society*, 72/1, Philadelphia, Pa, 1982), 53–64.

[35] For the resulting problems, see the comments of Fox's emissary, Thomas Grenville: *Memorials of Fox*, ed. Russell, i. 372–5.

[36] Towards the end of June, in the final days of the Rockingham Ministry, peace with France was still believed unlikely: *Grafton Autobiography*, 321.

the Rockingham Administration itself. Initially Oswald and Grenville had co-operated uneasily. But early in June 1782 Oswald's revelation that he was receiving proposals from Franklin concerning Canada's future status and might even be provided with a formal commission to negotiate increased the rivalry between Fox and Shelburne. Over the negotiations as over Ireland the cabinet was already divided: as indeed, it had been since its first day in office. This struggle intensified during June. Shelburne's low political cunning, always a useful adjunct to his proclaimed high idealism, ensured that a majority in the cabinet supported him; perhaps more crucially he possessed and cultivated the King's support. Fox was not permitted either to monopolize the peace negotiations or to grant immediate American independence. He was also prevented from abandoning Britain's maritime principles, which the cabinet insisted should only be given up in return for a full alliance with Russia and not simply as part of a general peace settlement. By the end of June Fox's initiatives in foreign policy had all been rejected by his fellow ministers and he was ready to resign.

The matter was resolved by the death of the ailing Rockingham at the very beginning of July. The King now asked Shelburne to lead the ministry, and the Earl secured the full authority which he craved. When Fox heard of this promotion he immediately resigned, being replaced as Foreign Secretary by Lord Grantham, ambassador at Madrid between 1771 and 1779. Grantham's diplomatic experience was greater than his abilities, and he was to be a cipher in the months that followed.[37] The peace negotiations were monopolized by Shelburne as Prime Minister. The Earl's government was insecurely grounded and, in particular, lacked a natural majority in the Commons. The Rockinghams' determined opposition and Fox's inveterate hostility made Shelburne's tenure of power precarious and perhaps short-lived. He was initially sustained by the fallen Prime Minister, Lord North, and by the convenient fact that he did not have to meet parliament until the closing months of the year.[38] His own political survival was always linked to the coming peace settlement. Shelburne believed that in order to establish his government and secure his own power, he must conclude a treaty which both the country and the Commons deemed satisfactory. His dogged attempts to end the war during the second half of 1782 were inspired

[37] For the limited expectations of Shelburne and the King, and Grantham's own reluctance, *Corr. Geo. III*, vi. 82–3.

[38] Both Houses were sitting during the early days of the Shelburne Ministry, but parliament was prorogued on 11 July and did not reassemble until 5 Dec. 1782. Cf. *Grafton Autobiography*, 349.

by shrewd political calculation as well as by lofty vision. His hope was that a war-weary parliament and nation would reward him by supporting his administration and thereby enable him to implement his wide-ranging plans for reform.

The settlement of 1783 was Shelburne's peace, the one positive achievement of his political career.[39] His ideas shaped the American and European treaties; he personally conducted the crucial negotiations with France; and his short-lived ministry was brought down over the settlement. This in itself is a source of considerable difficulty, for Shelburne was, and to a significant extent remains, the greatest enigma in eighteenth-century British politics.[40] He puzzled his contemporaries and continues to baffle historians. Shelburne was a man of enormous and unresolved contradictions. In private he could be charming and genial, but in public he was aloof, sarcastic, and mysterious. The reforming ideas which he espoused were at variance with his reputation for evasiveness and double-dealing. Politically he was an outsider: he had been Chatham's lieutenant and then his political executor. This association did nothing to recommend him to contemporaries. He had briefly held office immediately after the Seven Years War and had then served as Southern Secretary in the ill-fated Chatham Administration, but had been in the political wilderness since 1768. By 1782 his views had changed dramatically. The Chathamite Francophobe who had urged war over Corsica had become the advocate of reconciliation with France; the relatively orthodox mercantilist had turned into the supporter of free trade; the declared opponent of American independence was fast being reconciled to the loss of the colonies.[41] The flexibility of Shelburne's principles, together with the ease with which they were adopted and then discarded, partly explains the suspicion and hostility of his contemporaries, to whom he appeared merely a cynical opportunist. It was certainly true that, in the early 1780s, many of his ideas were

---

[39] See, e.g., J. R. Dull, 'Vergennes, Rayneval and the Diplomacy of Trust', in Hoffman and Albert, eds., *Peace and Peacemakers*, 106–7; cf. B. Perkins, 'The Peace of Paris: Patterns and Legacies', ibid. 229.

[40] A short, sympathetic study is provided by C. Stuart, 'Lord Shelburne' in H. Lloyd-Jones, V. Pearl, and B. Worden, eds., *History and Imagination: Essays in Honour of H. R. Trevor-Roper* (London, 1981), 243–53 and an interesting if discursive discussion by P. Brown, *The Chathamites* (London, 1967), 34–108; his reforming ideas are examined by J. Norris, *Shelburne and Reform* (London, 1963). The importance of European influences is made clear by C. R. Ritcheson, 'The Earl of Shelburne and Peace with America 1782–1783: Vision and Reality', *International History Review*, 5 (1983), 322–45, esp. 329–30. The old study by Fitzmaurice, *Life of Shelburne*, i–ii, remains a valuable source of information.

[41] Shelburne subsequently claimed that he had been convinced that independence was inevitable by the Conway motions in Feb. 1782: *Corr. Geo. III*, vi. 128.

the exact opposite of those he had held two decades before. But appearances were deceptive. The Earl was not indifferent to principles; on the contrary he collected them enthusiastically and sought doggedly to implement them.

In his intellectual range Shelburne was one of the most impressive of all British prime ministers and a man of the European Enlightenment. Continental influences on his thinking were important, particularly in his conversion to free trade. Here the principal influence was not British theorists such as Adam Smith and Dean Tucker, but the French *philosophes*. Through his friendship with the Abbé Morellet, whom he first met in 1771, the Earl became a convert to the liberal economic doctrines of the French Enlightenment. Morellet was a minor *philosophe* and popularizer of Turgot's theories, and during the 1770s he was the major intellectual influence on Shelburne. Yet the Earl's grasp of economic doctrines, like much of his thinking, was superficial. He was in reality an intellectual magpie. Shelburne picked up ideas and championed them without either digesting their principles or defining their implications. He saw issues in large-scale terms and was apt to be impatient over details.[42] His thinking was not systematic but impressionistic, a matter of impulse and enthusiasm, and it was far from consistent. Shelburne's views were often far-sighted: on many of Britain's problems in the early 1780s he had original and often imaginative solutions to offer, whether for Ireland, parliamentary reform, or, above all, the making of peace. But visionary statesmanship was not accompanied by a necessary grasp of reality: too often his ideas ran ahead of what was possible in the context of the time.

In many ways Shelburne appears out of place as a British Prime Minister. His ideas closely resemble many of the policies pursued by the enlightened absolutists of later eighteenth-century Europe, and he might have been better cast as the all-powerful first minister of a reforming continental monarch. The marriage of politics and economics, on which his approach to the peace negotiations was based, and his general ideas were in tune with the 'new diplomacy' of the age of the Enlightenment.[43] This sought to replace confrontation in international relations by co-operation, political as well as economic, and was extremely critical of the naked competitiveness of the European states-system. Shelburne's conduct of British foreign policy during the second half of 1782 sought to translate such ideas into practice. Though many of his specific proposals had to be

---

[42] Cf. Rayneval's view: Bancroft/Circourt, iii. 52.

[43] For which see F. Gilbert, 'The "New Diplomacy" of the Eighteenth Century' in his *History: Choice and Commitment* (Cambridge, Mass., 1977), 323–49.

abandoned, his general approach determined Britain's stance during the peace negotiations.

Yet there was a much darker and less attractive side to the Earl's character. To his contemporaries he was Malagrida, the 'Jesuit of Berkeley Square'. 'His falsehood', proclaimed Walpole, 'was so constant and notorious, that it was rather his profession than his instrument.' It was symptomatic of the universal distrust, loathing, and hatred which he inspired, that many contemporaries believed he was Junius, the anonymous and acerbic critic of ministers and their policies whose attacks, in the form of letters in the newspapers, had created such a stir in the late 1760s and early 1777s. No other politician in eighteenth-century British history was so intensely disliked, or universally distrusted. One of his Under-Secretaries of State, who had suffered at his hands, told him to his face on leaving office, 'God be thanked I am not to be under you again.' The principal reason for this deep, abiding, and universal distrust was the Earl's inability to inform, far less consult, other ministers: as one colleague caustically observed, he maintained the unanimity of his cabinets 'by never meeting them at all', while his conduct of the peace negotiations drove half the ministry to mutiny. It is astonishing that at a crucial stage the Foreign Secretary, Grantham, had to be told by a member of the parliamentary opposition that a French emissary had arrived in England and was negotiating secretly with Shelburne.[44] Such conduct makes it easier to understand why the Earl was so hated and distrusted. His habitual secrecy, together with an evasiveness in personal relations and a widely held view that he adjusted his language to the needs of the moment, were to undermine his ministry and destroy his career. Shelburne's handling of the peace negotiations revealed both sides of his personality, the statesmanship of Dr Jekyll and the political knavery of Mr Hyde. He was to demonstrate considerable tactical skill, particularly during the all-important talks with France's emissary, Rayneval, and his role in persuading George III to accept peace was crucial.[45]

---

[44] Malagrida was the Portuguese Jesuit tried and executed by Pombal during his campaign against the Society of Jesus. Shelburne's London house was in Berkeley Square, and this was the origin of the epithet coined by George III during the 1760s: Walpole, *Last Journals*, ii. 465; cf. ibid. ii. 465–8, for a vitriolic 'Character of Lord Shelburne'; Mackesy, *War for America*, 472; Buckingham and Chandos, *Memoirs of the Court and Cabinets of George III*, i. 76; Cannon, *Fox–North Coalition*, 37. This disregard was probably caused by the opposition to concessions which Shelburne had already encountered at cabinet: *Grafton Autobiography*, 345; *Memorials of Fox*, ed. Russell, ii. 9. Grantham knew in general terms of the negotiations and twice met Rayneval (*Corr. Geo. III*, vi. 133, 169), but this was after the French emissary's detailed discussions with Shelburne. The Foreign Secretary exerted next to no influence on the settlement.   [45] This is suggested by *Corr. Geo. III*, vi *passim*.

The peace negotiations were to a certain extent a triangular struggle between Britain, the Americans, and their Bourbon allies. Both Britain and France recognized the points of contact between the two sets of discussions. London's willingness to concede independence, and Vergennes's recognition of this, made it more difficult for France to play off one set of negotiations against the other. Indeed Shelburne's diplomacy during the second half of 1782 falls naturally into two parts: the settlement with the Americans and the parallel discussions with France and Spain.[46] The Anglo-American talks

---

[46] This literature on the peace of 1783 and on Britain's part in it is still dominated by V. T. Harlow. His detailed study of the negotiations and Shelburne's decisive role (*The Founding of the Second British Empire 1763–1793* (2 vols.; London, 1952–64), i. 223–447) remains the essential starting-point and is the basis of the account which follows. His arguments had, in some measure, been anticipated by C. W. Alvord: see his 1925 Raleigh Lecture in History, 'Lord Shelburne and the Founding of British-American Goodwill', *Proceedings of the British Academy*, 11 (1924–5), 369–93. Harlow's account is not without its drawbacks. It rightly emphasizes Shelburne's statesmanship and magnanimity, but underestimates his tactical skill; it owes too much to Harlow's overriding theme, the reorientation and revision of British imperial ambitions; and it tends to see Shelburne as a visionary vindicated by 19th- and even 20th-c. developments. It also errs in ascribing definite 'free trade' ideas to Shelburne and in identifying Adam Smith as the principal source of these. The most important recent contributions are two overlapping articles by C. R. Ritcheson: 'The Earl of Shelburne and Peace with America, 1782–1783', 322–45 and 'Britain's Peacemakers 1782–1783: "To an Astonishing Degree Unfit for the Task"?', in Hoffman and Albert, eds., *Peace and Peacemakers*, 70–100. Ritcheson presents an important critique of Harlow's interpretation, while upholding its main arguments; he is more convincing on the sources of Shelburne's ideas; and he makes the important point that the Earl was not as politically inept as Harlow's portrait suggests. But Ritcheson perhaps reacts too strongly against the picture of these negotiations contained in *Founding of the Second British Empire*; he exaggerates Shelburne's isolation during the Rockingham Ministry; and he is wrong to regard strategic vision and tactical flair as opposed: Shelburne exhibited both in considerable measure. A less critical approach is apparent in Wright's survey, 'The British Objectives, 1780–1783', 3–29, which is dominated by Harlow's perspectives and contributes some errors of its own, though it contains occasional acute remarks. Norris, *Shelburne and Reform*, contains some important material, but presents a narrow and one-dimensional view. The most comprehensive and detailed account of the negotiations is by the distinguished North American historian R. B. Morris, *The Peacemakers: The Great Powers and American Independence* (New York, 1965), based on massive archival research. But it must be used with caution. It displays limited knowledge of the ways of diplomacy and diplomats, and this is the source of some significant errors; it is also too narrowly American in its focus, and can on occasions seem chauvinist and even triumphalist. This is even more true of Morris's brief survey, 'The Treaty of Paris of 1783', *Fundamental Testaments of the American Revolution* (Washington, DC, 1973), 83–107. There are some valuable studies from a French perspective, notably Crout, 'In search of a "Just and Lasting Peace" ', 364–98, and Dull, 'Vergennes, Rayneval and the Diplomacy of Trust', 101–31. Spain's part is outlined by Conn, *Gibraltar*, 199–236. But while individual parts of the negotiations have been thoroughly studied, there is no satisfactory monograph on the settlement as a whole. Such a study, which gives equal attention to the European and the American dimensions, is urgently needed. The account which follows is based on these studies and on the two principal British printed sources: Fitzmaurice, *Life of Shelburne*, ii. and *Corr. Geo. III*, vi. It is impossible, in the space available, to follow all the twists and turns, and I have therefore emphasized Shelburne's ideas and their contribution to the final settlement. I have also given more attention to the Anglo-Bourbon negotiations, which were more important at the time, than to the better-known Anglo-American talks.

which took place in Paris and were conducted first by Oswald and then by Henry Strachey were facilitated by the widespread acceptance within Britain that the colonies had been lost forever. This view had quickly become established after news arrived of Yorktown. Shelburne's conduct from the very beginning of his own ministry revealed his acceptance of American independence, and he also deserves more credit than he has received for reconciling its arch-opponent, George III, to the loss of the colonies. Britain's negotiations with the American Commissioners were facilitated by her recognition of colonial independence and by Shelburne's determination to have an early settlement, in order to put more pressure on Vergennes. The main problems concerned the precise territorial extent of the new Republic and its retrospective financial obligations.

Shelburne had the imagination to conceive of the American negotiations as more than a negative surrender, a simple concession of independence to Britain's former colonies. Instead he hoped to establish a new and enduring relationship. The Earl's views are complex and not a little elusive: he never defined the kind of Anglo-American links he hoped would emerge. His premiss was the essential unity of the English-speaking peoples. This led him to hope that some kind of federal union would emerge, with Britain and an independent Republic as permanent allies. Such links would accomplish one further British objective: to ensure that the Franco-American wartime alliance did not survive the coming of peace and that the new state was instead completely independent of France. Shelburne believed that his own record as an opponent of coercion in the early 1770s would enable him to promote reconciliation during the 1780s, but he was soon disillusioned.

These new political links were to be cemented by economic ties. The Earl intended that the Americans should be given commercial advantages within Britain, with the clear expectation that the economic bonds which had existed before 1775 could be re-established. This vision was expressed in the language of lofty idealism. Yet it was a Trojan Horse, for hidden inside Shelburne's rhetoric was shrewd economic self-interest. His intention was that the newly independent Republic should retain its former colonial role: it was to be an expanding market and a source of raw materials for industrial Britain. This was why he favoured a generous western frontier, which he had opposed twenty years before. By encouraging the expansion of American territory and population, he now hoped to promote the growth of new markets for British goods to conquer.

Shelburne's ideas were never worked out in detail, and largely came to be abandoned once their impracticality became clear. His vision of an Anglo-American community, a political and economic union which would guarantee the security and prosperity of each nation, stayed firmly on the drawing board. He greatly under-estimated the enmity caused by seven years of fighting and civil war. It was impossible—on either side of the Atlantic—to wipe away the bitterness and bloodshed by one apparently magnanimous gesture. This soon became clear when serious negotiations began in Paris in summer 1782, and Shelburne was forced to modify his approach. Acknowledging that a political and economic union could not be created overnight, but would take time, he instead aimed to cultivate American goodwill and to do nothing which might prevent the eventual realization of his schemes. Yet if the time-scale had changed, Shelburne's fundamental goal remained. He was therefore prepared to make considerable concessions, though these fell far short of a total surrender. Britain retained Canada, though the Americans secured a more advantageous north-western frontier than they had expected, and also extracted significant concessions over two vexed questions.[47] These were the extent of the new Republic's respons-ibility for debts to British subjects contracted before 1775, and the thorny question of the Loyalists, those colonists who had continued to support Britain and had had their property and wealth confiscated by the American authorities. Parliamentary supervision of the peace settlement, together with Shelburne's vulnerable position in the Commons, ensured that Britain upheld the interests of her subjects on these two issues. The final treaty, at least on paper, contained American commitments over these debts and over the Loyalists. Apart from these two questions, the American Commissioners secured as much as they could reasonably have expected and more than their Bourbon allies intended.[48] Anglo-American peace pre-liminaries were signed in Paris at the end of November 1782. By these the independence of America was acknowledged; no barriers were placed in the path of future westward expansion by the new Republic; the Americans were admitted to the Newfoundland Fisheries; and they secured an advantageous frontier with Canada.

The emergence and subsequent importance of an independent American Republic, together with the enduring significance of the settlement for constitutional questions within the United States, had

[47] For the very limited success of these provisions and the subsequent struggles over the Loyalists and the debts see C. R. Ritcheson, *Aftermath of Revolution: British Policy towards the United States 1783–1795* (Dallas, 1969), 49–69.

[48] Indeed, as B. Perkins has recently demonstrated, in one important area (the so-called 'Nipissing Boundary') the Americans settled for significantly less than Britain was prepared to grant: 'The Peace of Paris: Patterns and Legacies', 194–221.

ensured that this dimension of Shelburne's peace has received most attention from later historians, and this emphasis has been strengthened by the recent Bicentennial.[49] Yet whatever the subsequent importance of the American settlement, the European peace negotiations were more significant for contemporaries. The simple fact of American independence, remarkable as it was at the time and for the future history of the western world, should not obliterate the contemporary pre-eminence of the Anglo-Bourbon negotiations. There were several reasons for this. The settlement's acknowledged importance for Shelburne's political survival made the treaty with the Bourbons all-important. Since 1778 the American War had been primarily a struggle between Britain and her established rivals, France and Spain, and this was equally true of the peace. Parliament's response to the final treaty would be determined principally by the terms secured from the Bourbons. Once the Commons had tacitly accepted independence in the Conway resolutions of February 1782, the detailed terms negotiated with the Americans were less important than the European settlement.

Shelburne's task was made more difficult by the revival of Britain's fortunes during 1782, and in particular by Rodney's great victory at the Saints in April and by the successful relief of Gibraltar in the autumn. These successes aroused hopes in Britain that, even if America had been lost, the war with the Bourbons could be fought to a finish and some recompense obtained from the national enemies, rather than peace purchased by British concessions. The mood of national humiliation occasioned by the loss of the American colonies was accompanied by a desire for revenge on the agents of independence, France and Spain: which was, of course, the opposite of what Shelburne intended. Such thinking had its adherents within the cabinet, and this certainly complicated his task: as did the strength of opinion, in parliament and in the country at large, against concessions to either Bourbon power. Once again foreign policy was circumscribed by the extent of British hatred of France.

[49] This remains true of even the most recent accounts: Morris, *The Peacemakers*; Hoffman and Albert, eds., *Peace and the Peacemakers*; and the articles in the special issue devoted to the 1783 settlement by *International History Review*, 5:3 (1983). This concentration has been further strengthened by the nature of the available evidence. Since the American settlement was negotiated in Paris, both the Public Record Office and Shelburne's own papers contain ample material on this dimension of the peace. But the Anglo-Bourbon negotiations were largely conducted in secret by Shelburne himself, and his views on the European settlement therefore have to be reconstructed primarily from French sources. For the principal of these, Rayneval's account of the discussions in September 1782, see H. Doniol, 'La Première Négociation de la paix de 1783 entre la France et la Grande-Bretagne', *Revue d'histoire diplomatique*, 6 (1892), 56–89, while important extracts from his dispatches during all three visits to England are contained in Bancroft/Circourt, iii, 29–63.

The European peace was negotiated in a distinctly unusual way. Though Anglo-French talks were held in Paris, between Vergennes and Britain's representative Alleyne Fitzherbert, the real negotiations took place in England.[50] The Anglo-Bourbon settlement was largely drawn up at Shelburne's country seat, Bowood Park in Wiltshire, and at his London home in Berkeley Square. Vergennes sent his trusted subordinate Gérard de Rayneval on three 'secret' trips to England during the second half of 1782.[51] It was in private discussions between Shelburne and Rayneval that the contours of a settlement were hammered out. This was highly unusual, for Britain's established practice was to conduct important diplomacy abroad. Shelburne's own obsessive secrecy and his determination to mould the final treaty himself partly explain why his peace was drawn up in England. More important were the concessions which he was determined to offer and the prevailing political climate in England.[52] There was always the risk of a 'call' for papers, a particularly serious threat when Shelburne's parliamentary position was insecure, and this made the Earl commit very little of his thoughts on the European settlement to paper, and instead trust to his discussions with Rayneval.

Shelburne's approach to the Anglo-Bourbon negotiations was equally distinctive. As in the parallel American talks his objectives went far beyond the obvious aim of escaping from a bad situation with minimum losses. His thinking was imaginative, and his approach again united politics and economics. Shelburne hoped to make the settlement a new dawn in Anglo-French relations.[53] He aimed to bring about a political *rapprochement*, and to cement this by a commercial treaty: the needs of industrial Britain and the lure of opening up the massive French internal market to British penetration, and even domination, can once again be glimpsed behind the heady rhetoric. Though this was in some measure to be achieved by the Eden Treaty negotiated in 1786, it was the political reconciliation which came to be his most immediate objective during the second half of 1782.

Shelburne's overriding aim was nothing less than the restoration of Anglo-French hegemony in Europe. He had correctly identified the central political development since the Seven Years War to be the loss

[50] Fitzherbert arrived in Paris in early Aug. 1782 and remained there until the following June.

[51] For J. M. G. de Rayneval, a *premier commis* (approximately an under-secretary) in the French foreign office, see Dull, 'Vergennes, Rayneval and the Diplomacy of Trust', 113–6.

[52] For the political situation, see Cannon, *Fox–North Coalition*, 20–56.

[53] Doniol, 'La Première Négociation', 70, 81. One of the clearest statements of his objectives came during a subsequent conversation with the new French ambassador in June 1783: Bancroft/Circourt, iii. 61.

of leadership by the traditional western rivals. By fighting one another Britain and France had contributed both to their own decline and to the rise of the 'predatory Powers': the dominant eastern states of Russia, Prussia, and Austria, with their formidable armies and established appetite for the territory of their weaker neighbours. This was the trend which Shelburne hoped to halt and even to reverse. It was to be achieved through close Anglo-French co-operation: as he remarked to a startled Rayneval in September, Britain and France should become allies, 'and let us lay down the law to the rest of Europe . . . If we agree, we shall regain our former place and we shall direct all the changes in Europe.' George III, who came to share and endorse Shelburne's objectives, subsequently tried to persuade Rayneval that such co-operation would prevent any second partition of Poland.[54]

The Earl had long been attraced by an Anglo-French *rapprochement*. He may have been initially involved in the secret negotiations in 1772–3 and subsequently denounced their failure in thinly veiled terms, as a missed opportunity.[55] Shelburne's analysis of the shift in European power was acute and his solution was attractive. But it was also, in the context of peace negotiations, impractical: once again his ideas were dangerously remote from political reality, and he was notably vague as to exactly how the 'predatory Powers' might be checked. He failed in particular to grasp the significance of the crisis over the Crimea, which he does not seem to have mentioned to Rayneval, though it represented a potential route to co-operation with France and was central to Vergennes's thinking at this time.

The fundamental problem was that, at the end of the long and costly American War, France was anxious to secure visible rewards for her financial and military sacrifices. Vergennes fully shared Shelburne's concern with the rise of the eastern powers and was also attracted by political co-operation.[56] He believed this should follow the peace settlement rather than be part of it. Britain must first give

---

[54] Doniol, 'La Première Négociation', 81; Bancroft/Circourt, iii. 47. The phrase 'predatory Powers' was coined by V. T. Harlow (e.g. *Founding of the Second British Empire*, i. 228, 312) but it well characterizes Shelburne's attitude: see e.g. his hostile comments in June 1780: *Parl. Hist.* xxi, cols. 638–9; cf. Doniol, 'La Première Négociation', 70; Crout, 'In Search of a "Just and Lasting Peace" ', 388; Bancroft/Circourt, iii. 56. Since the King had favoured an Anglo-French *rapprochement* in 1772–3, the question arises as to whether the prime minister was dancing to a royal tune. This seems improbable: Shelburne's own interest in such a realignment was undoubted and in 1782–3, George III was initially reluctant to accept peace, far less a reconciliation, and had to be won over by Shelburne.

[55] M. Roberts, 'Great Britain and the Swedish Revolution, 1772–3', in his *Essays in Swedish History* (London, 1967), 337 n. 73; *Parl. Hist.* xxi, col. 638: a remarkable sentiment given that Britain and France were then at war.

[56] Crout, 'In Search of a "Just and Lasting Peace" ', 396.

up the commanding position secured in 1763. The balance between the western powers must be restored before they could work together against the Leviathans in the east. This had been Vergennes's strategy when he intervened in the American War and it remained his objective in 1782–3. His priorities were understandable in the context of French domestic politics, but at the same time they were an obstacle to the kind of progress desired by Shelburne. In the negotiations with France, as in the American settlement, the Earl's grandiose initial objectives had to be scaled down to politically acceptable proportions. If his ideas were not reflected in the final settlement with the Bourbons, they clearly influenced his attitude during the negotiations with Rayneval: this was why Shelburne's distinctive approach was the principal influence on the final treaty.

The talks with France began in summer 1782, during the early weeks of the Shelburne Ministry. The Earl opened up direct negotiations through the captured French admiral, de Grasse, who first forwarded a letter through his nephew to Vergennes and then himself travelled back to Paris. The French foreign minister was initially amazed and suspicious, not least because of Shelburne's long association with the anti-French Chatham and celebrated willingness for war, over Corsica, in 1768. Yet this approach represented a breakthrough and France's own need for peace was considerable. There was also the lurking danger that a separate Anglo-American peace might be signed. Vergennes therefore sent Rayneval to England on three occasions between September and December 1782. Shelburne was certainly prepared for concessions, but he was also anxious to defend Britain's interests in India and the Caribbean, areas he believed crucial for future imperial development. This conflicted with France's insistence on recovering some of her losses sustained in 1763. Vergennes was particularly anxious to secure a territorial, rather than a merely commercial position in India, which he believed was central to any future French economic recovery. It was an ambition which could not easily be reconciled with Shelburne's own imperial dreams.

In the event, the negotiations during the final months of 1782 were not seriously delayed by these competing aspirations. This was principally because France's territorial ambitions and those of her Spanish ally had to be scaled down as the strategic, financial, and diplomatic situation of the Bourbon powers worsened. In particular, their military situation deteriorated significantly during 1782. The great offensive in India did not produce the anticipated victories, while de Grasse's defeat at the Saints and the failure to capture Gibraltar were important reverses. Simultaneously, Vergennes was becoming anxious about the Crimea, where Russia was intervening to support the puppet Khan whom she had imposed but who had subsequently been driven from his throne. During the second half of 1782, he wished to be free of the American imbroglio so he could throw France's diplomatic influence against any further extension of Russian power.

These factors forced France to reduce her initial territorial demands to secure an early peace. This pressure was increased by the separate Anglo-American preliminaries at the very end of November. Vergennes also appreciated that Shelburne's hold on power was precarious and came to fear his government might fall before a treaty had been concluded, and would be replaced by a ministry prepared to seek popularity, by continuing the war against the Bourbons. In particular, he knew peace preliminaries must be agreed before parliament reassembled in late November, otherwise the war party might exploit the absence of a settlement to sweep to power. During the final stages of the negotiations Shelburne skilfully played on these fears to extract some significant concessions.[57] He himself had always been prepared to make sacrifices to secure a settlement and to plant the seeds of future reconciliation. Vergennes, by contrast, was obliged by the pressure of events to settle for less than he had hoped for and, indeed, expected. The French minister also paved the way for the signature of preliminaries by prevailing on the Spaniards to make concessions.

Spain had only begun to negotiate directly with Britain when her ambassador in Paris, Aranda, presented the British negotiator Fitzherbert with a long list of demands early in October 1782.[58] Though this was after the failure of the assault on Gibraltar, Spain continued to expect substantial British concessions—in defiance of the Bourbons' military and financial plight—and these demands were supported by Vergennes throughout October and November. The demand for Gibraltar was not rejected out of hand by Britain. George III and Shelburne would have been happy to part with it in return for an equivalent, and their preferred target was Puerto Rico. The Earl's hopes of re-establishing Britain's commercial power after the loss of the American colonies can clearly be seen in this search for gains in the Caribbean. On 3 December 1782 the British cabinet actually agreed to cede Gibraltar. Two ministers, Keppel and Richmond, vigorously contested this decision and continued their opposition by resigning from the government. The public and

---

[57] See e.g. Bancroft/Circourt, iii. 51.
[58] See Conn, *Gibraltar*, 210.

parliamentary clamour which followed might itself have prevented any exchange involving the fortress, but Gibraltar's future and that of the entire peace settlement was soon resolved not in England, but in France.[59]

By the final weeks of 1782 Vergennes was worried that peace might elude him altogether. This was the context of Rayneval's second and third journeys to England in late November and early December and of the postponement of the parliamentary session until 5 December. But the crucial breakthrough came in Paris. In mid-December Vergennes prevailed on Aranda to abandon Spain's demand for Gibraltar. This involved the ambassador ignoring or—at best—liberally interpreting his instructions, and it has attracted much comment. One established interpretation is that this had, all along, been the objective of the crafty Vergennes, who recognized that British possession of the fortress guaranteed Franco-Spanish friendship in the future and was an obstacle to any Anglo-Spanish reconciliation.[60] This seems improbable, particularly given his strenuous support for the Spanish demand throughout October and the first half of November. His abandonment of Spain was spontaneous and not the product of a deeply concealed diplomatic strategy.[61] By December the demand for Gibraltar had become the principal obstacle to peace, which Vergennes believed to be imperative, and he therefore induced Aranda to give it up. Britain's inflexibility, rather than France's perfidy, was the principal reason why Madrid's lingering hopes of securing the fortress were dashed.

This paved the way for the signature of Anglo-Bourbon peace preliminaries in Paris on 20 January 1783. The final treaty was not to be signed until eight months later, but in all important respects it was the settlement obtained by Shelburne. By then he was back in his familiar habitat, the political wilderness. Shelburne himself professed to believe that the peace terms were, in the circumstances, favourable and would therefore be supported in parliament. He was soon shown to be mistaken. In February 1783, when the preliminaries were presented to parliament, his ministry was twice defeated in the Commons. These votes, and the emergence of the Fox–North coalition which they announced, persuaded Shelburne to resign.[62]

---

[59] There had evidently been a considerable struggle at this cabinet, which lasted for eight and a half hours: *Grafton Autobiography*, 349–50. Wraxall, a well-placed and shrewd observer, believed that the outcry in the Commons against the cession persuaded Shelburne to drop the idea: *Historical Memoirs*, ii. 275.

[60] Conn, *Gibraltar*, 234, 236.

[61] Cf. Crout, 'In Search of a "Just and Lasting Peace" ', 391–2.

[62] For an admirable account of Shelburne's decline and fall, see Cannon, *Fox–North Coalition*, 44–64.

On 24 February he duly submitted his resignation, though it was another month before the King accepted it.

No other eighteenth-century British government was defeated in parliament over the terms of a peace settlement. The debates in the Commons on 17 and 21 February had really been about Shelburne's political survival and not the fine print of the actual preliminaries.[63] The opposition attack concentrated on those aspects of the treaties which had attracted most opprobrium: the weak provisions for the Loyalists and British debts, the generous western frontier, and so on.[64] But this was tactical, and the future coalition of Charles James Fox and Lord North largely endorsed the settlement negotiated by Shelburne. Indeed, the new partners had been obliged, during the debates in February, to signal their support for the preliminaries to avoid the charge that they wanted to continue fighting.

The definitive peace with the Bourbons, together with the final American settlement, was signed at Versailles on 3 September 1783. By this treaty France secured the West Indian island of Tobago and retrieved that of St Lucia, but returned all her other Caribbean conquests to Britain. In Africa, she recovered her former colony of Senegal, but in India secured only a minor improvement in her position. A similar improvement was obtained in the Newfoundland Fisheries: France recovered the islands of St Pierre and Miquelon (captured by Britain during the war) and her fishermen received an enlarged and more clearly defined right of access. Finally, she at last secured British consent to the fortification of Dunkirk and the removal of Britain's commissioner at the port, thereby ending a diplomatic dispute that had rumbled on for three-quarters of a century. The other member of the Bourbon alliance, Spain, did not secure Gibraltar but still made substantial gains, receiving the Mediterranean island of Minorca (held by Britain since 1713) and both West and East Florida. The other main point of the Anglo-Spanish settlement concerned the running sore of the Bay of Honduras.[65] The Peace of Versailles fixed and also reduced the limits of British activities there; in return Spain acknowledged fully for the first time that Britain had a legal right to occupy part of this region.

The final settlement was with the Dutch Republic. The definitive Anglo-Dutch treaty was not signed until May 1784 in Paris, where it had also been negotiated. These discussions had been notably slow as

[63] *The Political Memoranda of Francis, Fifth Duke of Leeds*, ed. O. Browning (London, 1884), 78.   [64] The debates are in *Parl. Hist.* xxiii, cols. 373–571.
[65] For the detailed negotiations, see C. A. Anderson, 'Anglo-Spanish Negotiations Involving Central America in 1783' in E. R. Huck and E. H. Moseley, eds., *Militarists, Merchants and Missionaries: United States Expansion in Middle America* (Alabama, 1970), 23–37.

well as difficult. The central problem had been Dutch reluctance to accept that their disastrous performance during the war should be reflected in the peace terms. Though the Dutch had fought bravely, their weakened navy had been no match for Britain's superior sea-power. The fighting had dealt a severe blow to the Republic's commerce and seaborne empire, as the British fleet mopped up Dutch colonies in the Caribbean and in the Far East and expelled their merchants from the Indian subcontinent. Though French forces subsequently recovered two of the most important Dutch losses, the island of St Eustatius and the naval base of Trincomalee in Ceylon, as well as occupying the colony at the Cape, this only emphasized that the Republic was equally at the mercy of its British enemy and its French ally.

Initially the Dutch government had asked Vergennes to negotiate on its behalf. France's friends in the Republic, the Patriots, hoped that this might be a way of minimizing losses.[66] Only in September 1782 did Dutch diplomats begin direct discussions with Fitzherbert in Paris, and even then the French foreign minister continued to negotiate on their behalf. The disasters of the war did not prevent the Republic from demanding that Britain accept the principles of the Armed Neutrality and restore all conquests at the peace. Vergennes regarded such claims as absurd and pressed the Dutch to accept more realistic terms. He was also determined that the Republic should not obstruct a general settlement and, when its representatives continued to put forward impossible demands, he simply made concessions on their behalf and drew up a preliminary Anglo-Dutch settlement. This the Dutch plenipotentiaries refused to accept, though they did put their initials to a truce with Britain in January 1783. Peace preliminaries were not to be signed until September 1783, and a further eight months elapsed before the definitive treaty was finalized.

These delays were partly caused by the Republic's cumbersome political structure, and this familiar problem was accentuated by the growing strife between the Orangists and the Patriots. The domestic party struggle mirrored a diplomatic tug-of-war between Britain and France for future ascendancy within the Republic, which was to continue and indeed intensify during the early years of peace. Britain's dislike of growing French influence in Dutch life had contributed to the war of 1780–4, and ministers sought to use the

---

[66] Brief accounts of the Anglo-Dutch negotiations are provided by N. Tarling, *Anglo-Dutch Rivalry in the Malay World 1780–1824* (St Lucia, Queensland, 1962), 7–11, and Harlow, *Founding of the Second British Empire*, i. 384–93.

peace negotiations to disrupt the Franco-Dutch alliance and to restore their own traditional authority:[67] this was why the terms secured by the Republic were relatively moderate after the severe defeats it had suffered. These considerations delayed the final Anglo-Dutch settlement until 20 May 1784, when the definitive treaty was signed at Paris. Its terms were identical to those drawn up by Vergennes sixteen months before. Britain secured Negapatam, a minor port and trading station on the south-eastern coast of India, and the potentially important concession that British subjects could 'navigate' in the Dutch East Indian archipelago, hitherto closed to other European nations. This was the first acknowledged breach in the Republic's strict monopoly of its colonial commerce and was to be a fertile source of disputes in the future. These gains were less than the scale of Britain's victory had seemed to justify. In particular Shelburne had been forced to abandon his hope of securing the significant naval base of Trincomalee: a victory for French diplomacy rather than for Dutch procrastination. Yet these were Britain's only tangible gains at the end of a long and expensive war. The only other success for British diplomacy was the absence of any mention of neutral rights in either the Anglo-Dutch treaty or the Anglo-Bourbon settlement. This was pricipally due to Catherine II's preoccupation with the Crimea in 1782–4. This distracted her from the peace negotiations and also made her anxious not to offend Britain, whose support Russia might need if she encountered active French opposition to her annexation of the Khanate.

The final settlement has often seemed a significant defeat for Britain, particularly when measured against the commanding peace concluded two decades before. In August 1782, while the negotiations were at an early stage, Horace Walpole had pronounced himself 'mortified at the fall of England' and added for good measure that he saw 'little or no prospect of its ever being a great nation again'. The peace settlement of 1783–4 does not deserve to be seen in such a gloomy light, and Britain salvaged more from the American War than might have been expected. George III, who had for long opposed both treaties, was eventually forced to concede that they could have been a great deal worse. 'The more I reflect,' the King wrote in January 1783, '. . . the more I thank Providence for having through so many difficulties . . . enabled so good a peace . . . to be concluded.'[68] Britain's two principal enemies, France and Spain,

---

[67] In the early months of 1782, France's influence had been decisive in frustrating a British attempt to conclude a separate peace: J. H. Hutson, *John Adams and the Diplomacy of the American Revolution* (Lexington, 1980), 105–7.

[68] *Walpole Corr.* xxv. 310; *Corr. Geo. III*, vi. 222.

certainly made some territorial gains. In the context of Anglo-Bourbon relations, however, the Peace of Versailles did not completely undermine the supremacy which Britain had secured at the end of the victorious Seven Years War. These territorial losses were in any case less important than the massive damage done to British prestige by the success of the American colonial rebellion. Britain's reputation was an important element in her foreign policy, and it had been severely dented by American independence. In other respects the Peace of Versailles was a less serious defeat than it might have been, and certainly the terms were rather better than could have been anticipated given Britain's unequal struggle since 1778 and her plight by the winter of 1781–2.

Conclusion

IN 1763 Britain's supremacy had been complete. Her triumphant empire had seemed at its zenith, while her wealth and power had impressed and awed all Europe. Two decades later it was a very different story. Britain, declared Joseph II in March 1783, had ceased to be a great power and was instead a second-rank state comparable to Sweden or Denmark. Frederick II was quick to join in the chorus of political obituaries, sneering in a familiar way at British 'exhaustion and weakness'. Britain's extinction as a great power had been feared in London as well: in 1781 both George III and Sandwich had prophesied that this would be the consequence of defeat in the American War.[1]

The King, characteristically, was disposed to blame his domestic opponents rather than his foreign enemies, and it is certainly true that the bitter political and constitutional strife which followed North's resignation in March 1782 was one source of Britain's difficulties.[2] The re-emergence of the kind of ministerial instability which had undermined British diplomacy after the Seven Years War seemed likely to immobilize her once again during the 1780s: the administration headed by the Younger Pitt was not at first given much chance of survival. The loss of America and the financial burdens of defeat were seen as more fundamental causes of British decline. The recognition of American independence was widely viewed as the first act in a political tragedy, the denouement of which would be the final disintegration of Britain's empire. Yet if Britain's political obituaries had been written in 1783, within a few years they were shown to have been premature.

This is not to diminish the severe defeat represented by the independence of the North American colonies. Reputation was still the basis of success in foreign policy and Britain's reputation had been severely damaged by the recognition of colonial independence. The American Revolution was the first successful colonial rebellion

---

[1] T. C. W. Blanning, ' "That Horrid Electorate" or "Ma Patrie Germanique"? George III, Hanover and the *Fürstenbund* of 1785', *Historical Journal*, 20 (1977), 314–5 and n. 12; *Corr. Geo. III*, v. 247, 297, cf. Sandwich's jeremiad: 'We shall never again figure as a leading power in Europe, but think ourselves happy if we can drag on for some years a contemptible existence as a commercial state' (*Sandwich Papers*, iv. 26).

[2] *Corr. Geo. III*, vi. 147.

in modern history, and this considerably increased its contemporary impact and the damage it did to British prestige. Britain's situation was certainly bleak in 1783. The new Prime Minister, William Pitt, was confronted by a wide-ranging series of problems, not the least urgent of which was his own political survival. Yet within a few years a recovery was under way and by the end of the 1780s it was not Britain but France whose very existence appeared to be imperilled. France's victory in 1783 was more apparent to contemporaries than it has been to posterity. American independence certainly boosted her flagging prestige and made her diplomacy pre-eminent in western Europe during the early years of peace, yet it was soon revealed as a pyrrhic victory. Its costs far outran the short-term benefits which accrued to Louis XVI's state. In particular the American War completed the destruction of French finances and further weakened France's position in Europe: several years before the calling of the Estates-General in 1789 mounting financial problems had removed France temporarily from the ranks of the great powers. Even in 1783 Britain's potential for recovery was greater, and within a few years the internal problems of the victor were to be more important than those of the vanquished.

In any case the balance of power between the two western states had become peripheral: Joseph II's relegation of Britain to the rank of a second-class state also testified to the new maturity and predominance of the eastern powers. Russia's annexation of the Crimea in 1783–4 provided a further demonstration of the diminished importance of Britain and France in this new political order.[3] Catherine II, skilfully exploiting the alliance she had secretly concluded with the Emperor in 1781, carried through the formal incorporation of the Khanate into the Russian state, and Vergennes was powerless to resist this encroachment. He unsuccessfully hinted to Britain that she might join in a diplomatic *démarche* designed to prevent Russian annexation. Such co-operation was difficult at the end of a bitter conflict. British hostility towards the Bourbon powers, and France in particular, had been strengthened by the war of 1778–83. Though Pitt at least was briefly interested in *rapprochement* with Versailles, the main theme of Britain's diplomacy during the 1780s continued to be that of opposition to France, particularly in the Dutch Republic after 1785.[4] This was pursued—as before—by

[3] There is an admirable introduction by M. S. Anderson, 'The Great Powers and the Russian Annexation of the Crimea, 1783–4', *Slavonic and East European Review*, 37 (1958–9), 17–41.

[4] Black, *Natural and Necessary Enemies*, 194 and, more generally, 64–92 *passim*; id., 'The Marquis of Carmarthen and Relations with France 1784–1787', *Francia*, 12 (1984), 283–303; id., 'Sir Robert Ainslie: His Majesty's *agent-provocateur*? British Foreign Policy and the International Crisis of 1787', *European History Quarterly*, 14 (1984), 253–83.

building up the navy and seeking to conclude continental alliances.

The political pattern on the continent was a formidable obstacle to a successful diplomacy by Britain. The American War's principal legacy for British foreign policy was a strengthened appreciation of the vital importance of a European ally. Diplomatic isolation did not, in itself, lead to the loss of the American colonies: there were far more profound political, strategic, and logistical reasons for this. Yet it certainly contributed to this defeat. Britain's failure to secure an ally during the first decade after the Peace of Paris helped to ensure that after 1778 France could concentrate her resources on the struggle overseas and give important assistance to the American cause. This in turn was an important source of Britain's strategic problems during her war for America, especially after 1778. To this extent that conflict appeared to confirm established British thinking about the necessity of allies. This doctrine rested primarily on the Duke of Newcastle's assertion of the importance of continental alliances, rather than on their actual contribution to British strategy in previous wars. Yet such thinking appeared to be confirmed by the American War, during which Britain had been condemned to fight the Bourbons without a continental ally. After 1783 ministers were determined that this would never happen again. A central component in Britain's diplomacy after the Peace of Versailles came to be a renewed quest for alliances.[5] Yet, as the Foreign Secretary, Carmarthen, was soon forced to recognize, the prospects were poor indeed. Britain's preferred targets were still Austria and Russia, but both powers were preoccupied with their own political objectives and had been indifferent to a British alliance. The Austro-French alliance survived but the initiative had now passed decisively to Vienna, while France retained her alliance with Spain. Only Prussia among the major continental states was isolated, and the ageing Frederick II was being forced to consider an alliance with Britain, though the *rapprochement* was to be delayed until after the old King's death. In 1787–8 events in the Dutch Republic would serve as the catalyst for a Triple Alliance linking London, The Hague, and Berlin, and this would temporarily end Britain's quarter-century of diplomatic isolation.

The enduring prejudice against Prussia, like the continuing preference for alliances with Austria and Russia, revealed the traditional thinking and mental inflexibility which was an important dimension of British diplomacy throughout the generation after the

---

[5] The best introduction is J. Ehrman, *The Younger Pitt: The Years of Acclaim* (London, 1969), chs. 16 and 17.

Seven Years War. In 1772 Panin made the significant remark that 'by endeavouring to patch and to mend old projects Britain had lost sight of the present state and connections of the powers of Europe'.[6] His comments neatly encapsulate one principal charge against British diplomacy in the age of the American Revolution. The minds of British statesmen ran along familiar grooves: Old System, 'liberties of Europe', and so on. Their established assumptions were rapidly becoming outdated in the new political circumstances of the 1760s and 1770s. Yet it is by no means clear how Britain's diplomacy could have been adjusted to take account of the changing circumstances on the continent. In retrospect it is clear that British foreign policy was undermined by France's decline as a European power, by her stable and enduring alliance with Austria, and by the rise of Prussia and Russia. Britain's eighteenth-century diplomacy had been based on an ability to exploit fear of French power and to conscript the other continental states into alliances against the supposed threat of France. After 1763 such a strategy was impossible. Yet the continuation and intensification of Anglo-French rivalry after the Peace of Paris confirmed British ministers in their belief that continental alliances were essential. Herein lay the central problem for policy-makers in London for a generation after the Seven Years War. Britain, they believed, still needed alliances; yet, as they gradually appreciated, the new political pattern on the continent was a considerable obstacle to their conclusion. The framework of British foreign policy remained traditional, but the relations of the continental states had been transformed. The Austrian Chancellor Kaunitz put the point with characteristic precision in 1785, after another futile British attempt to restore the old alliance with Vienna.

It is well known [he told the Austrian minister in London] that a foundation-stone of English policy is the destruction of the Bourbon power; it is no less true that its continuance is a foundation-stone of our policy and must continue to serve as such. This is an anachronism, that the English government has for too long overlooked and to this day still overlooks.[7]

Britain's own rise to pre-eminence, along with the corresponding decline of France, had undermined her foreign policy. This first became fully apparent during the age of the American Revolution. The success of British diplomacy ultimately depended on the existence of a strong and aggressive French state which was—or could be portrayed as—a threat to the other continental powers. This was lacking for three decades after the Seven Years War, when

---

[6] SP 91/90, fo. 31.
[7] Quoted in translation in Spencer, *Sandwich Corr.* 11.

Britain's problems were compounded by the emergence of the eastern powers and, at times, by her own internal upheavals. This generation was a period of acute difficulties for British foreign policy. The revival of French military imperialism in the early 1790s, albeit under the very different banner of the Revolution, restored the traditional pattern and opened the way for the further expansion of British power and of Britain's empire.

Bibliography

1. MANUSCRIPT SOURCES

Public Record Office, London

SP 75/125–6, 135
SP 78/256–306
SP 79/24
SP 80/199–223
SP 81/113, 143
SP 82/90
SP 84/501, 542–73
SP 88/92, 118
SP 89/71, 80–2
SP 90/81–104
SP 91/70–101
SP 92/73
SP 94/179, 184–6, 197–208
SP 98/73
SP 103/63
SP 104/224, 240
SP 105/284
SP 110/1

FO 7/1–7
FO 64/1–5

ADM 1/240, 4130, 4131, 4132, 4133, 4134
ADM 2/97, 241

PRO 30/29/1/14–15; 30/29/3/1–2   (Granville Papers)

British Library, London

Add. MSS 6809, 6810, 6826, 6828   (Mitchell Papers)
Add. MSS 9234, 9242   (Coxe Transcripts)
Add. MSS 22359
Add. MSS 24157, 24158, 24159, 24160, 24170, 24174   (Grantham
      Papers)
Add. MSS 32919, 32921, 32931
Add. MSS 34412   (Auckland Papers)
Add. MSS 35370, 35371, 35372, 35434, 35503, 35504, 35505, 35506,
      35507, 35508, 35510, 35511, 35517, 35518, 35519, 35520,
      35521, 35522, 35547, 35554, 35555, 35556, 35570, 35571,
      35572, 35580, 35581   (Hardwicke Papers)
Add. MSS 37054   (Letter Book of Henry Shirley)

Add. MSS 37833, 37834   (Robinson Papers)
Add. MSS 61860, 61863   (North Papers)
Egerton 215–62   (Cavendish Debates)
Egerton 982
Egerton 2701, 2702, 2703   (Gunning Papers)
Stowe 142, 257, 258, 259

Private Collections

Buckinghamshire Papers, Norfolk County Record Office, Norwich
Cathcart Papers, in the Possession of the Earl Cathcart
Grafton Papers, Suffolk Record Office, Bury St Edmunds
Stormont Papers, Scone Palace, Perthshire
Thynne Papers, Longleat House, Wiltshire

Archives du Ministère des Relations Extérieures, Paris

CP (Angleterre) 450–529
MD (Angleterre) 6
CP (Danemark) 157
CP (Espagne) 538–47, 560–3
CP (Hollande) 540–2
CP (Russie) 98

Archives Nationales, Paris

Archives de la Marine: AM B^5
AM B^7

Österreichische Staatsarchiv, Vienna (Abteilung: Haus-, Hof- und Staatsarchiv)

England-Korrespondenz 109–16, 128
England-Varia 11
Familienarchiv Sammelbände 88
DD.B

Archivo General de Simancas

E 6978, 6979, 6980, 6981, 6990, 6991, 6995, 6996, 6998, 7001, 7005, 7020

2. PRINTED SOURCES

(Printed sources are generally listed under the author or subject rather than the editor.)

The Armed Neutralities of 1780 and 1800, ed. J. B. Scott (London, 1918).
BANCROFT, GEORGE *Histoire de l'action commune de la France et de*

l'Amérique pour l'indépendance des États-Unis, ed. and trans. A. de Circourt (3 vols.; Paris, 1876).

Beaumarchais Correspondance, ed. B. N. Morton and D. C. Spinelli (4 vols. to date, Paris, 1969–).

Correspondence of John, Fourth Duke of Bedford, ed. Lord J. Russell (3 vols.; London, 1842–6).

Bernstorffsche Papiere, ed. A. Friis (3 vols.; Copenhagen, 1904–13).

Correspondance ministérielle du comte J. H. E. von Bernstorff 1751–1770, ed. P. Vedel (2 vols.; Copenhagen, 1882).

British Diplomatic Instructions 1689–1789, ed. J. F. Chance and L. G. Wickham Legg (7 vols.; London, 1922–34).

Correspondance secrète du comte de Broglie avec Louis XV, 1756–1774, ed. D. Ozanam and M. Antoine (2 vols.; Paris, 1956–61).

BUCKINGHAM and CHANDOS, Duke of, *Memoirs of the Court and Cabinets of George III* (2 vols., rev. edn., London, 1853).

The Despatches and Correspondence of John, Second Earl of Buckinghamshire, Ambassador to the Court of Catherine II 1762–1765, ed. A. D'A. Collyer (2 vols.; London, 1900–2).

The Correspondence of Edmund Burke, ed. T. W. Copeland (9 vols.; Cambridge, 1958–70).

The Writings and Speeches of Edmund Burke, ii: *Party, Parliament and the American Crisis 1766–1774*, ed. P. Langford (Oxford, 1981).

Byron's Journal of His Circumnavigation 1764–1766, ed. R. E. Gallagher (Cambridge, 1964).

Carteret's Voyage around the World 1766–1769, ed. H. Wallis (2 vols.; Cambridge, 1965).

Sir Henry Cavendish's Debates of the House of Commons, during the Thirteenth Parliament of Great Britain, ed. J. Wright (2 vols.; London, 1841–3).

Mémoires du duc de Choiseul 1719–1785, ed. F. Calmettes (Paris, 1904).

The Devonshire Diary: William Cavendish, Fourth Duke of Devonshire— Memoranda on State Affairs 1759–1762, ed. P. D. Brown and K. W. Schweizer (London, 1982).

Documents of the American Revolution 1770–1783 (Colonial Office Series), ed. K. G. Davies (21 vols.; Shannon, Ireland, 1972–81).

A Memoir of the Rt. Hon. Hugh Elliot, ed. Countess of Minto (Edinburgh, 1868).

FLAMMERMONT, J., ed., *Les Correspondances des agents diplomatiques étrangers en France avant la Révolution* (Paris, 1896).

Fort William—India House Correspondence, v: *1767–69*, ed. N. K. Sinha (Delhi, 1949); vi: *1770–72*, ed. B. Prasad (Delhi, 1960).

Memorials and Correspondence of Charles James Fox, ed. Lord John Russell (4 vols.; London, 1853).

The Papers of Benjamin Franklin, ed. L. W. Labaree, W. B. Willcox, *et al.* (27 vols. to date; New Haven, Conn., 1959–).

Œuvres de Frédéric le Grand, ed J. D. E. Preuss (30 vols.; Berlin, 1846–56).

Politische Correspondenz Friedrichs des Grossen, ed. J. G. Droysen *et al.* (46 vols., Berlin, etc., 1879–1939).

Die Politischen Testamente Friedrichs des Grossen, ed. G. B. Volz (Berlin, 1920).

The Correspondence of King George III from 1760 to December 1783, ed. Sir J. Fortescue (6 vols.; London, 1927–8).

NAMIER, SIR L., *Additions and Corrections to Sir John Fortescue's Edition of the Correspondence of King George III* (vol. i) (Manchester, 1937).

Letters from George III to Lord Bute 1756–1766, ed. R. R. Sedgwick (London, 1939).

The Correspondence of George III with Lord North from 1768 to 1783, ed. W. Bodham Donne (2 vols.; London, 1867).

The Autobiography and Political Correspondence of Augustus Henry, Third Duke of Grafton, ed. Sir W. R. Anson (London, 1898).

The Grenville Papers, ed. W. J. Smith (4 vols.; London, 1852–3).

Additional Grenville Papers 1763–1765, ed. J. R. G. Tomlinson (Manchester, 1962).

Historical Manuscripts Commission Reports:
  HMC III
  Abergavenny (1887)
  Dartmouth (1887–96)
  Eglinton (1885)
  Knox (1909: 'Various Collections', vi)
  Lothian
  Stopford-Sackville (1904).
  Various VI

Calendar of Home Office Papers of the Reign of George III, ed. J. Redington and R. A. Roberts (4 vols.; London, 1878–99).

The Jenkinson Papers 1760–1766, ed. N. S. Jucker (London, 1949).

Joseph II., Leopold II. und Kaunitz: Ihr Briefwechsel, ed. A. Beer (Vienna, 1873).

The Letters of Junius, ed. J. Cannon (Oxford, 1978).

The Letters of Junius, ed. C. W. Everett (London, 1927).

Memoirs and Correspondence of Sir Robert Murray Keith, ed. Mrs Gillespie Smyth (2 vols.; London, 1849).

The Political Memoranda of Francis, Fifth Duke of Leeds, ed. O. Browning (London, 1884).

Correspondance secrète inédite de Louis XV sur la politique étrangère, ed. M. Boutaric (2 vols.; Paris, 1866).

Some Account of the Public Life, and a Selection from the Unpublished Writings, of the Earl of Macartney, ed. J. Barrow (2 vols.; London, 1807).

MACPHERSON, D. *Annals of Commerce, Manufactures, Fisheries, and Navigation* . . . (4 vols.; London, 1805).

Diaries and Correspondence of James Harris, First Earl of Malmesbury, ed. Earl of Malmesbury (4 vols.; London, 1844).

Correspondance inédite du général-major de Martange, ed. C. Bréard (Paris, 1898).

Bibliography 349

MARTENS, F. VON, *Recueil des traités et conventions conclus par la Russie avec les puissances étrangères* (15 vols.; St Petersburg, 1874–1909).

Correspondance secrète du comte de Mercy-Argenteau avec l'empereur Joseph II et le prince de Kaunitz, ed. A. von Arneth and J. Flammermont (2 vols.; Paris, 1889).

A Narrative of the Changes in the Ministry, 1765–1767, As Told by the Duke of Newcastle in a Series of Letters to John White, M.P., ed. M. Bateson (London, 1898).

Archives ou correspondance inédite de la Maison d'Orange-Nassau
4th series (Leiden, 1909–14)
5th series (Leiden, 1910–15).

Österreichische Staatsverträge: England, ed. A. F. Pribram (2 vols.; Vienna, 1907–13)

The Parliamentary History of England from the Earliest Period to the Year 1803 (36 vols.; London, 1806–20).

Proceedings and Debates of the British Parliaments respecting North America 1754–1783, ed. R. C. Simmons and P. D. G. Thomas (6 vols. to date; New York, 1982–).

Correspondence of William Pitt, Earl of Chatham, ed. W. S. Taylor and J. H. Pringle (4 vols.; London, 1838–40).

Recueil des instructions données aux ambassadeurs et ministres de France, depuis les traités de Westphalie jusqu'a la Révolution française (30 vols. to date; Paris, 1884–).

Struensée et la cour de Copenhague 1760–1772: Mémoires de Reverdil, ed. A. Roger (Paris, 1858).

Memoirs of the Marquis of Rockingham and his Contemporaries, ed. Earl of Albermarle (2 vols.; London, 1852).

The Fourth Earl of Sandwich: Diplomatic Correspondence 1763–1765, ed. F. Spencer (Manchester, 1961).

The Sandwich Papers, ed. G. R. Barnes and J. H. Owen (4 vols.; Navy Records Society; London, 1932–8).

Sbornik imperatorskogo russkogo istorischeskogo obshchestva (148 vols.; St Petersburg, 1867–1916).

Papers Illustrating the History of the Scots Brigade in the Service of the United Netherlands 1572–1782, ed. J. Ferguson (3 vols.; Scottish History Society; Edinburgh, 1899–1901).

SÉGUR, L. P. de, *Politique de tous les cabinets de l'Europe pendant les règnes de Louis XV et Louis XVI* (3 vols.; 2nd ed., Paris, 1801).

Colonel St. Paul of Ewart, Soldier and Diplomat, ed. G. Grey Butler (2 vols.; London, 1911).

STEVENS, B. F., *Facsimiles of Manuscripts in European Archives Relating to America 1773–1783* (25 vols.; London, 1889–98).

The Quest and Occupation of Tahiti by Emissaries of Spain during the years 1772–1776, ed. B. Glanvill Corney (3 vols.; London, 1913–15).

Dépêches van Thulemeyer 1763–1788, ed. H. T. Colenbrander (Werken uitgegeven door het Historisch Genootschap, 3rd series, vol. 30; Amsterdam,1912).

Ambasciatori veneti in Inghilterra, ed. L. Firpo (Turin, 1978).
Journal de l'abbé de Véri, ed. Baron J. de Witte (2 vols.; Paris, 1928–30).
Arkhiv Kniazia Vorontsova, ed. P. Bartenev (40 vols.; Moscow, 1870–95).
Horace Walpole's Correspondence, ed. W. S. Lewis (48 vols.; New Haven, Conn., 1937–83).
Horace Walpole: Memoirs of the Reign of King George III, ed. G. F. R. Barker (4 vols.; London, 1894).
The Last Journals of Horace Walpole during the Reign of George III, from 1771–1783, ed. A. F. Steuart (2 vols.; London, 1910).
WHITWORTH, Sir CHARLES, *State of the Trade of Great Britain in its Imports and Exports, Progressively from the Year 1697* (London, 1776).
WRAXALL, Sir NATHANIEL, *Historical Memoirs of My Own Time (1772–1784)* (2 vols.; London, 1815).

3. SECONDARY STUDIES

ABARCA, R. E., 'Classical Diplomacy and Bourbon "Revanche" Strategy, 1763–70', *Review of Politics*, 32 (1970), 313–37.
AITON, A. S., 'Spain and the Family Compact, 1770–1773', in A. Curtis Wilgus, ed., *Hispanic American Essays* (North Carolina, 1942; New York, 1970 repr.), 135–49.
—— 'Spanish Colonial Reorganisation under the Family Compact', *Hispanic American Historical Review*, 12 (1932), 269–80.
ALBION, R. G., *Forests and Sea Power: The Timber Problem of the Royal Navy 1652–1862* (Cambridge, Mass., 1926).
ALDEN, D., 'The Marquis of Pombal and the American Revolution', *The Americas*, 17 (1961), 369–82.
—— *Royal Government in Colonial Brazil: With Special Reference to the Administration of the Marquis of Lavradio, Viceroy, 1769–1779* (Berkeley and Los Angeles, 1968).
—— 'The Undeclared War of 1773–1777: Climax of Luso-Spanish Platine Rivalry', *Hispanic American Historical Review*, 41 (1961), 55–74.
ALVORD, C. W., 'Lord Shelburne and the Founding of British-American Goodwill', *Proceedings of the British Academy*, 11 (1924–5), 369–93.
AMBURGER, E., *Russland und Schweden 1762–1772* (Berlin, 1934).
ANDERSON, C. A., 'Anglo-Spanish Negotiations Involving Central America in 1783', in Eugene R. Huck and Edward H. Moseley, eds., *Militarists, Merchants and Missionaries: United States Expansion in Middle America* (Alabama, 1970), 23–37.
ANDERSON, M. S., *Britain's Discovery of Russia 1553–1815* (London, 1958).
—— *The Eastern Question 1774–1923: A Study in International Relations* (London, 1966).
—— 'Great Britain and the Barbary States in the Eighteenth Century', *Bulletin of the Institute of Historical Research*, 29 (1956), 87–107.

—— 'Great Britain and the Russian Fleet, 1769–70', *Slavonic and East European Review*, 31 (1952–3), 148–63.

—— 'Great Britain and the Russo-Turkish War of 1768–74', *English Historical Review*, 69 (1954), 39–58.

—— 'The Great Powers and the Russian Annexation of the Crimea, 1783–4', *Slavonic and East European Review*, 37 (1958–9), 17–41.

ARNETH, A. VON, *Geschichte Maria Theresias* (10 vols.; Vienna, 1863–79).

ARUGA, T., 'The Diplomatic Thought of the American Revolution', *Hitotsubashi Journal of Law and Politics*, 9 (1981), 26–41.

—— 'The Franco-American Treaties of 1778: The Diplomacy of the American Revolution and the French and Spanish Responses', *Hitotsubashi Journal of Law and Politics*, 10 (1981), 28–50.

ASKENAZY, S., *Dantzig and Poland* (London, 1921).

—— *Die letzte polnische Königswahl* (Göttingen, 1894).

ATHERTON, H. M., *Political Prints in the Age of Hogarth* (Oxford, 1974).

ATWOOD, R., *The Hessians: Mercenaries from Hessen-Kassel in the American Revolution* (Cambridge, 1980).

AYLING, S., *George the Third* (London, 1972).

BARGAR, B. D., *Lord Dartmouth and the American Revolution* (Columbia, SC, 1965).

BARTON, H. A., 'Sweden and the War of American Independence', *William and Mary Quarterly*, 23 (1966), 408–30.

BAUGH, D. A., 'Why Did Britain Lose Command of the Sea during the War for America?', in Black and Woodfine, eds., *British Navy and Naval Power* (q.v.).

BAXTER, S. B., 'The Conduct of the Seven Years War', in S. Baxter, ed., *England's Rise to Greatness 1660–1763* (Berkeley and Los Angeles, 1983).

—— 'The Myth of the Grand Alliance in the Eighteenth Century', in S. Baxter and P. Sellin, eds., *Anglo-Dutch Cross Currents in the Seventeenth and Eighteenth Centuries* (Los Angeles, 1976), 42–59.

BEER, A., *Die erste Theilung Polens* (3 vols.; Vienna, 1873).

—— *Die Orientalische Politik Österreichs seit 1774*, i (Prague and Leipzig, 1883).

BEMIS, S. F., 'British Secret Service and the French-American Alliance', *American Historical Review*, 29 (1923–4), 474–95.

—— *The Diplomacy of the American Revolution* (New Haven, Conn., 1935; repr. Bloomington, Ind., 1957).

—— *The Hussey–Cumberland Mission and American Independence* (Princeton, 1931).

BERNARD, P. P., *Joseph II and Bavaria: Two Eighteenth-Century Attempts at German Unification* (The Hague, 1965).

BLACK, J., 'Anglo-Russian Relations after the Seven Years War', *Scottish Slavonic Review*, 9 (1987), 27–37.

—— *British Foreign Policy in the Age of Walpole* (Edinburgh, 1985).

—— 'British Foreign Policy in the Eighteenth Century: A Survey', *Journal of British Studies*, 26 (1987), 26–53.

BLACK, J., 'The British State and Foreign Policy in the Eighteenth Century', *Trivium*, 23 (1988), 127–48.
—— *The English Press in the Eighteenth Century* (London, 1987).
—— 'Jacobitism and British Foreign Policy under the First Two Georges 1714–1760', *Royal Stuart Papers*, 32 (1988), 1–18.
—— ed., *Knights Errant and True Englishmen: British Foreign Policy 1660–1800* (Edinburgh, 1989).
—— 'The Marquis of Carmarthen and Relations with France 1784–1787', *Francia*, 12 (1984), 283–303.
—— *Natural and Necessary Enemies: Anglo-French Relations in the Eighteenth Century* (London, 1986).
—— 'Sir Robert Ainslie: His Majesty's *agent-provocateur*? British Foreign Policy and the International Crisis of 1787', *European History Quarterly*, 14 (1984), 253–83.
—— and WOODFINE, PHILIP, eds., *The British Navy and the Use of Naval Power in the Eighteenth Century* (Leicester, 1988).
BLANNING, T. C. W., ' "That Horrid Electorate" or "Ma Patrie Germanique"? George III, Hanover and the *Fürstenbund* of 1785', *Historical Journal*, 20 (1977), 311–44.
BLART, L., *Les rapports de la France et de l'Espagne après le pacte de famille, jusqu'à la fin du ministère du duc de Choiseul* (Paris, 1915).
BOLKHOVITINOV, N. N., *Russia and the American Revolution* (Eng. trans., Tallahassee, Fla., 1976).
BOSHER, J. F., 'The French Crisis of 1770', *History*, 57 (1972), 17–30.
BOURGUET, A., *Le duc de Choiseul et l'Alliance Espagnole* (Paris, 1906).
—— *Études sur la politique étrangère du duc de Choiseul* (Paris, 1907).
BOXER, C. R., *The Portuguese Seaborne Empire, 1425–1815* (London, 1969).
BRANDT, O., *Caspar von Saldern und die nordeuropäische Politik im Zeitalter Katharinas II.* (Erlangen and Kiel, 1932).
BREWER, J., 'Commercialization and Politics', in N. McKendrick *et al.*, *Birth of a Consumer Society* (q.v.).
—— 'The Misfortunes of Lord Bute: A Case-Study of Eighteenth-Century Political Argument and Public Opinion', *Historical Journal*, 16 (1973), 3–43.
—— *Party Ideology and Popular Politics at the Accession of George III* (Cambridge, 1976).
—— *The Sinews of Power: War, Money and the English State, 1688–1783* (London, 1989).
BROMLEY, J. S., 'The Second Hundred Years' War (1689–1815)', in D. Johnson *et al.*, eds., *Britain and France: Ten Centuries* (Folkestone, 1980).
BROOKE, J., *The Chatham Administration 1766–1768* (London, 1956).
—— *King George III* (London, 1972; repr. 1974).
BROWN, G. S., *The American Secretary: The Colonial Policy of Lord George Germain 1775–1778* (Ann Arbor, 1963).
—— 'The Anglo-French Naval Crisis, 1778: A Study of Conflict in the

North Cabinet', *William and Mary Quarterly*, 3rd series, 13 (1956), 3–25.

BROWN, P., *The Chathamites* (London, 1967).

BROWN, V. L., 'Anglo-Spanish Relations in America in the Closing Years of the Colonial Era', *Hispanic American Historical Review*, 5 (1922), 327–483.

BROWN, W., *Empire or Independence? A Study in the Failure of Reconciliation, 1774–1783* (Baton Rouge, 1941).

BROWNING, R., *The Duke of Newcastle* (New Haven, Conn., 1975).

BULLION, J. L., 'Securing the Peace: Lord Bute, the Plan for the Army, and the Origins of the American Revolution', in Schweizer, ed., *Lord Bute: Essays in Re-interpretation* (q.v.).

BUTTERFIELD, SIR H., 'British Foreign Policy 1762–65', *Cambridge Historical Journal* 6 (1963), 131–40.

—— *George III, Lord North and the People 1779–80* (London, 1949).

The Cambridge History of British Foreign Policy 1783–1919, i: *1783–1815*, ed. A. W. Ward and G. P. Gooch (Cambridge, 1922).

CANNON, JOHN, *The Fox–North Coalition: Crisis of the Constitution 1782–84* (Cambridge, 1969).

CASTRIES, duc de, 'Le Pacte de Famille et la guerre d'Indépendance Américaine', *Revue d'histoire diplomatique*, 75 (1961), 254–306.

CAUGHEY, J. W., *Bernardo de Gálvez in Louisiana 1776–1783* (Berkeley, 1934).

CEDERGREEN BECH, S., *Struensee og hans tid* (Copenhagen, 1972).

CHILDS, J., 'The Scottish Brigade in the Service of the Dutch Republic, 1689–1782', *Documentatieblad Werkgroep Achttiende Eeuw*, 16 (1984), 59–75.

CHRISTELOW, A., 'French Interests in the Spanish Empire during the Ministry of the duc de Choiseul, 1759–1771', *Hispanic American Historical Review*, 21 (1941), 513–37.

—— 'Great Britain and the Trades from Cadiz and Lisbon to Spanish America and Brazil, 1759–1783', *Hispanic American Historical Review*, 27 (1947), 2–29.

CHRISTIE, I. R., 'British Politics and the American Revolution', *Albion*, 9 (1977), 205–26.

—— *The End of North's Ministry 1780–1782* (London, 1958).

—— 'George III and the Historians—Thirty Years On', *History*, 71 (1986), 205–21.

—— *Myth and Reality in Late Eighteenth Century British Politics and Other Papers* (London, 1970).

—— *Wars and Revolutions: Britain 1760–1815* (London, 1982).

—— *Wilkes, Wyvill and Reform: the Parliamentary Reform Movement in British Politics, 1760–1785* (London, 1962).

CLENDENNING, P. H., 'The Background and Negotiations for the Anglo-Russian Commercial Treaty of 1766', in A. G. Cross, ed., *Great Britain and Russia in the Eighteenth Century: Contacts and Comparisons* (Newtonville, Mass., 1979), 145–63.

CLENDENNING, P. H., 'The Economic Awakening of Russia in the Eighteenth Century', *Journal of European Economic History*, 14 (1985), 443–72.

COBBAN, ALFRED, *Ambassadors and Secret Agents: The Diplomacy of the First Earl of Malmesbury at The Hague* (London, 1954).

CONN, S., *Gibraltar in British Diplomacy in the Eighteenth Century* (New Haven, 1942).

CONRADY, S., 'Die Wirksamkeit König Georgs III. für die hannoverschen Kurlande', *Niedersächsisches Jahrbuch für Landesgeschichte*, 39 (1967), 150–91.

COQUELLE, P., *Le Comte de Guerchy, ambassadeur de France à Londres (1763–1767)* (Paris, n.d. but ?1908; repr. from the *Revue des études historiques*, 1908).

—— *Le Comte Duchâtelet, ambassadeur de France à Londres (1768–1770)* (Paris, 1910; repr. from the *Bulletin historique et philologique*, 1909).

CORWIN, E., 'The French Objective in the American Revolution', *American Historical Review*, 21 (1915), 33–62.

—— *French Policy and the American Alliance of 1778* (Princeton, 1916).

CROUT, R. R., 'In Search of a "Just and Lasting Peace": The Treaty of 1783, Louis XVI, Vergennes, and the Regeneration of the Realm', *International History Review*, 5 (1983), 364–98.

DANN, U., *Hannover und England 1740–1760: Diplomatie und Selbsterhaltung* (Hildesheim, 1986).

DAWSON, F. G., 'William Pitt's Settlement at Black River on the Mosquito Shore: A Challenge to Spain in Central America', *Hispanic American Historical Review*, 63 (1983), 677–706.

DAUBIGNY, E., *Choiseul et la France d'outre-mer après le Traité de Paris* (Paris, 1897).

DAVIES, N., *God's Playground: A History of Poland* (2 vols.; Oxford, 1981).

DE CONDE, A., 'The French Alliance in Historical Speculation', in Hoffman and Albert, eds., *Diplomacy and Revolution* (q.v.).

—— 'Historians, the War of American Independence, and the Persistence of the Exceptionalist Ideal', *International History Review*, 5 (1983), 399–430).

DICKINSON, H. T., 'Party, Principle and Public Opinion in Eighteenth Century Politics', *History*, 61 (1976), 231–7.

DIPPEL, H., 'Prussia's English Policy after the Seven Years' War', *Central European History*, 4 (1971), 195–214.

DONIOL, H., *Histoire de la participation de la France à l'établissement des États-Unis d'Amérique* (5 vols.; Paris, 1886–92).

—— 'La Première Négociation de la paix de 1783 entre la France et la Grande-Bretagne', *Revue d'histoire diplomatique*, 6 (1892), 56–89.

DONOUGHUE, B., *British Politics and the American Revolution: The Path to War 1773–75* (London, 1964).

DORAN, P. F., *Andrew Mitchell and Anglo-Prussian Diplomatic Relations during the Seven Years War* (New York and London, 1986).

DORN, W., 'Frederick the Great and Lord Bute', *Journal of Modern History*, 1 (1929), 529–60.

DULL, J. R., 'Benjamin Franklin and the Nature of American Diplomacy', *International History Review* 5 (1983), 346–63.

—— *A Diplomatic History of the American Revolution* (New Haven, Conn., 1985).

—— *Franklin the Diplomat: The French Mission* (Philadelphia: *Transactions of the American Philosophical Society* 72/1 (1982)).

—— *The French Navy and American Independence: A Study of Arms and Diplomacy 1774–87* (Princeton, 1975).

—— 'Vergennes, Rayneval and the Diplomacy of Trust', in Hoffman and Albert, eds., *Peace and Peacemakers* (q.v.).

EDLER, F., *The Dutch Republic and the American Revolution* (Baltimore, Md., 1911).

EHRMAN, J., *The Younger Pitt: The Years of Acclaim* (London, 1969).

ELDON, C. W., *England's Subsidy Policy towards the Continent during the Seven Years' War* (Philadelphia, 1938).

ELLIS, K. L., 'The Administrative Connections between Britain and Hanover', *Journal of the Society of Archivists*, 3 (1969), 546–66.

—— 'British Communications and Diplomacy in the Eighteenth Century', *Bulletin of the Institute of Historical Research*, 31 (1958), 159–67.

—— *The Post Office in the Eighteenth Century* (London, 1958).

FAUCHILLE, P., *La Diplomatie française et la Ligue des Neutres de 1780* (Paris, 1893).

FELDBAEK, O., *Dansk neutralitetspolitik under krigen 1778–1783* (Copenhagen, 1971).

—— 'Eighteenth-Century Danish Neutrality: Its Diplomacy, Economics and Law', *Scandinavian Journal of History*, 8 (1983), 3–21.

FISHER, A. W., *The Russian Annexation of the Crimea 1772–1783* (Cambridge, 1970).

FISHER, H. E. S., *The Portugal Trade: A Study of Anglo-Portuguese Commerce 1700–1770* (London, 1971).

FITZMAURICE, LORD, *Life of William, Earl of Shelburne* (2nd, rev. ed., 2 vols., London, 1912).

FOGDALL, S. J. M. P., *Danish-American Diplomacy 1776–1920* (Iowa, 1922).

FRAGUIER, B. du, 'Le Duc d'Aiguillon et l'Angleterre', *Revue d'histoire diplomatique*, 26 (1912), 607–27.

GERHARD, D., *England und der Aufstieg Russlands* (Munich and Berlin, 1933).

—— 'Kontinentalpolitik und Kolonialpolitik im Frankreich des ausgehenden "ancien régime" ', *Historische Zeitschrift*, 148 (1933), 21–31.

GIBBS, G. C., 'English Attitudes towards Hanover and the Hanoverian Succession in the First Half of the Eighteenth Century', in A. M. Birke and K. Kluoen, eds., *England und Hannover: England and Hanover* (Munich, 1986), 33–5.

—— 'Laying Treaties before Parliament in the Eighteenth Century', in

Hatton and Anderson, eds., *Studies in Diplomatic History* (q.v.), 116–37.
—— 'Parliament and Foreign Policy in the Age of Stanhope and Walpole', *English Historical Review*, 77 (1962), 18–37.
—— 'The Revolution in Foreign Policy', in G. Holmes, ed., *Britain after the Glorious Revolution*, (London, 1969), 59–79.
GILBERT, F., 'The "New Diplomacy" of the Eighteenth Century', *History: Choice and Commitment* (Cambridge, Mass., 1977), 323–49.
GOEBEL, D. B., 'The "New England Trade" and the French West Indies, 1763–1774: A Study in Trade Policies', *William and Mary Quarterly*, 3rd series, 20 (1963), 331–72.
GOEBEL, J., *The Struggle for the Falkland Islands* (New Haven, Conn., 1927; repr. 1982).
GOSLINGA, C. CH., *The Dutch in the Caribbean and in the Guianas 1680–1791* (Assen-Maastricht and Dover, NH, 1985).
GRIFFITHS, D. M., 'Catherine the Great, the British Opposition and the American Revolution', in L. S. Kaplan, ed., *The American Revolution and a 'Candid World'* (q.v.).
—— 'The Rise and Fall of the Northern System', *Canadian-American Slavic Studies*, 4 (1970), 547–69.
—— 'Nikita Panin, Russian Diplomacy and the American Revolution', *Slavic Review*, 28 (1969), 1–24.
GRUBER, I. D., *The Howe Brothers and the American Revolution* (Chapel Hill, NC, 1972).
HALL, T. E., *France and the Eighteenth-Century Corsican Question* (New York, 1971).
HAMMER, J. DE., *Histoire de l'Empire Ottoman, depuis son origine jusqu'à nos jours* (18 vols.; Paris, 1835–41).
HARLOW, V. T., *The Founding of the Second British Empire 1763–1793* (2 vols.; London, 1952–64).
HARRIS, R. D., *Necker: Reform Statesman of the Ancien Regime* (Berkeley and Los Angeles, 1979).
HATTON, R. M., *The Anglo-Hanoverian Connection 1714–1760* (London, 1982).
—— and ANDERSON, M. S., eds., *Studies in Diplomatic History: Essays in Memory of David Bayne Horn* (London, 1970).
HAYTER, T., *The Army and the Crowd in Mid-Georgian England* (London, 1978).
HIGGINBOTHAM, D., *The War of American Independence: Military Attitudes, Policies and Practice 1763–1789* (Bloomington, Ind., 1971).
HOFFMAN, R., and ALBERT, P. J., eds., *Diplomacy and Revolution: the Franco-American Alliance of 1778* (Charlottesville, V., 1981).
—— and —— eds., *Peace and Peacemakers: The Treaty of 1783* (Charlottesville, V., 1986).
HOLM, E., *Danmark-Norges Historie 1720–1814* (Copenhagen, 1902).
—— *Danmarks Riges Historie 1699–1814* (Copenhagen, 1897), vol. v of J. C. M. R. Steenstrup *et al.*, *Danmarks Riges Historie* (6 vols.; Copenhagen, 1897–1907).

HORN, D. B., ed., *British Diplomatic Representatives 1689–1789* (London, 1932).
—— *The British Diplomatic Service 1689–1789* (Oxford, 1961).
—— *British Public Opinion and the First Partition of Poland* (Edinburgh, 1945).
—— 'The Diplomatic Experience of Secretaries of State, 1660–1852', *History*, 41 (1956), 88–99.
—— *Great Britain and Europe in the Eighteenth Century* (Oxford, 1967).
—— *Scottish Diplomatists 1689–1789* (London, 1944).
HOTBLACK, K., 'The Peace of Paris, 1763', *Transactions of the Royal Historical Society*, 3rd series, 2 (1908), 235–69.
HUTSON, J., *John Adams and the Diplomacy of the American Revolution* (Lexington, 1980).
IRVINE, D., 'The Newfoundland Fisheries: A French Objective in the War of American Independence', *Canadian Historical Review*, 13 (1932), 268–85.
JAMESON, J. F., 'St. Eustatius in the American Revolution', *American Historical Review*, 8 (1903), 683–708.
JARRETT, D., *The Begetters of Revolution: England's Involvement with France, 1759–1789* (London, 1973).
JESSE, J. H., ed., *George Selwyn and His Contemporaries* (4 vols.; London, 1844).
JOHNSTON, R. Y., 'American Privateers in French Ports, 1776–1778', *Pennsylvania Magazine of History and Biography*, 53 (1929), 352–74.
JONES, J. R., *Britain and the World 1649–1815* (London, 1980).
KAPLAN, H. H., *The First Partition of Poland* (New York, 1962).
KAPLAN, L. S., ed., *The American Revolution and 'A Candid World'* (Kent, Oh., 1977).
—— 'The American Revolution in an International Perspective: Views from Bicentennial Symposia', *International History Review*, 1 (1979), 408–26.
—— *Colonies into Nations: American Diplomacy 1763–1801* (New York, 1972).
—— 'The Treaty of Paris, 1783: A Historiographical Challenge', *International History Review*, 5 (1983), 431–42.
KENNEDY, P. M., *The Rise and Fall of British Navy Mastery* (London, 1976).
KENT, H. S. K., *War and Trade in Northern Seas: Anglo-Scandinavian Economic Relations in the Mid-Eighteenth Century* (Cambridge, 1973).
KONOPCZYNSKI, W., 'England and the First Partition of Poland', *Journal of Central European Affairs*, 8 (1948–9), 1–23.
LACOUR-GAYET, G., *La Marine Militaire de la France sous le règne de Louis XV* (Paris, 1910).
—— *La Marine Militaire de la France sous le règne de Louis XVI* (Paris, 1905).
LA MORANDIÈRE, C. DE, *Histoire de la pêche française de la morue dans l'Amérique septentrionale* (3 vols.; Paris, 1962–6).
LANGFORD, P., *The Eighteenth Century 1688–1815* (London, 1976).

LANGFORD, P., *The First Rockingham Administration 1765–1766* (Oxford, 1973).

LAUGIER, L., *Un ministère réformateur sous Louis XV: Le Triumvirat (1770–1774)* (Paris, 1975).

LAWSON, P., *George Grenville: A Political Life* (Oxford, 1984).

LINDGREN, R. E., 'The League of Armed Neutrality', in Carl. F. Bayerschmidt and Erik J. Friis, eds., *Scandinavian Studies: Essays presented to Henry Goddard Leach* (New York, 1965).

LODGE, SIR. R., *Great Britain and Prussia in the Eighteenth Century* (Oxford, 1923).

McCURRY, A. J., 'The North Government and the Outbreak of the American Revolution', *Huntington Library Quarterly*, 34 (1970–1), 141–57.

MACKAY, R. F., *Admiral Hawke* (Oxford, 1965).

MACKESY, P., 'British Strategy in the War of American Independence', *Yale Review*, 52 (1963), 539–57.

—— *The War for America 1775–1783* (London, 1964).

McKENDRICK, N., BREWER, J., and PLUMB, J. H., *The Birth of a Consumer Society: The Commercialisation of Eighteenth-Century England* (London, 1982; repr. 1983).

MADARIAGA, I. DE, *Britain, Russia and the Armed Neutrality of 1780* (London, 1962).

—— *Russia in the Age of Catherine the Great* (London, 1981).

—— 'The Secret Austro-Russian Treaty of 1781', *Slavonic and East European Review*, 38 (1959–60), 114–45.

—— 'The Use of British Secret Funds at St. Petersburg, 1777–1782', *Slavonic and East European Review*, 32 (1953–4), 464–74.

MARSHALL, P. J., 'British Expansion in India in the Eighteenth Century: A Historical Revision', *History*, 60 (1975), 28–43.

MARSHALL, PETER, 'The British Empire and the American Revolution', *Huntington Library Quarterly*, 27 (1963–4), 135–44.

—— 'The First and Second British Empires: A Question of Demarcation', *History*, 49 (1964), 13–23.

MARTELLI, G., *Jemmy Twitcher: A Life of the Fourth Earl of Sandwich* (London, 1962).

MARTIN, G., 'Commercial Relations between Nantes and the American Colonies during the War of Independence', *Journal of Economic and Business History*, 4 (1931–2), 812–29.

MAXWELL, K. R., 'Pombal and the Nationalisation of the Luso-Brazilian Economy', *Hispanic American Historical Review*, 48 (1968), 608–31.

MEDIGER, W., 'Great Britain, Hanover and the Rise of Prussia', in Hatton and Anderson, eds., *Studies in Diplomatic History* (q.v.).

MENG, J. J., *The Comte de Vergennes: European Phases of His American Diplomacy, 1774–1780* (Washington, 1932).

METCALF, M. F., *Russia, England and Swedish Party Politics 1762–1766* (Stockholm and Totowa, 1977).

MEYER, J., and BROMLEY, J., 'The Second Hundred Years' War (1689–

1815)', in D. Johnson, F. Bédarida, and F. Crouzet, eds., *Britain and France: Ten Centuries* (London, 1980), 139–72.

MICHAEL, W., *Englands Stellung zur Ersten Teilung Polens* (Hamburg and Leipzig, 1890).

MIDDLETON, C. R., *The Administration of British Foreign Policy 1782–1846* (Durham, NC, 1977).

MIDDLETON, R. *The Bells of Victory: The Pitt–Newcastle Ministry and the Conduct of the Seven Years' War 1757–1762* (Cambridge, 1985).

MILLER, D. A., *Sir Joseph Yorke and Anglo-Dutch Relations 1774–1780* (The Hague, 1970).

MITCHELL, L. G., *Charles James Fox and the Disintegration of the Whig Party 1782–1794* (Oxford, 1971).

MOORE, J. P., 'Anglo-Spanish Rivalry on the Louisiana Frontier, 1763–68', in J. F. McDermott, ed., *The Spanish in the Mississippi Valley, 1762–1804* (Urbana, 1974), 72–86.

MORISON, S. E., *John Paul Jones: A Sailor's Biography* (Boston, 1959).

MORRIS, R. B., *The Peacemakers: The Great Powers and American Independence* (New York, 1963; 2nd ed., Boston, 1984).

—— 'The Treaty of Paris of 1783', *Fundamental Testaments of the American Revolution* (Washington, DC, 1973), 83–107.

MURPHY, O. T., *Charles Gravier, Comte de Vergennes: French Diplomacy in the Age of Revolution 1719–1787* (Albany, NY, 1982).

—— 'Charles Gravier de Vergennes: Profile of an Old Regime Diplomat', *Political Science Quarterly*, 83 (1968), 400–18.

—— 'The Comte de Vergennes, the Newfoundland Fisheries and the Peace Negotiations of 1783: A Reappraisal', *Canadian Historical Review*, 46 (1965), 32–46.

—— 'The View from Versailles', in Hoffman and Albert, eds., *Diplomacy and Revolution* (q.v.).

NAMIER, Sir L., *England in the Age of the American Revolution* (2nd edn., London, 1963).

—— and BROOKE, J., eds., *The House of Commons 1754–1790* (3 vols.; London, 1964).

NIEDHART, G., *Handel und Krieg in der britischen Weltpolitik 1738–1763* (Munich, 1979).

NORRIS, J., *Shelburne and Reform* (London, 1963).

OAKLEY, S. P., *The Story of Denmark* (London, 1972).

O'GORMAN, F., *The Rise of Party in England: The Rockingham Whigs 1760–82* (London, 1975).

OLSON, A. G., *The Radical Duke: The Career and Correspondence of Charles Lennox, Third Duke of Richmond* (Oxford, 1961).

OSINGA, J., *Frankrijk, Vergennes en de Amerikaanse Onafhankelijkheid 1776–1783* (Amsterdam, 1982).

OUTREY, A., *L'Administration française des affaires étrangères: Histoire et principes* (Paris, 1954).

OZANAM, D., 'Les Origines du troisième Pacte de Famille (1761)', *Revue d'histoire diplomatique*, 75 (1961), 307–40.

PARES, R., 'American versus Continental Warfare 1739–63', *English Historical Review*, 51 (1936), 429–65; repr. in Pares, *The Historian's Business and Other Essays* (Oxford, 1961), 130–72.
—— *Colonial Blockade and Neutral Rights 1739–1763* (Oxford, 1938).
—— *King George III and the Politicians* (Oxford, 1953; repr. 1967).
—— *War and Trade in the West Indies 1739–1763* (Oxford, 1936).
PATTERSON, A. T., *The Other Armada: The Franco-Spanish Attempt to Invade Britain in 1779* (Manchester, 1960).
PERKINS, B., 'The Peace of Paris: Patterns and Legacies', in Hoffman and Albert, eds., *Peace and Peacemakers* (q.v.).
PETERSSON, B., ' "The Correspondent in Paris": En engelsk informations-källa under 1700-talet', *Scandia*, 28 (1962), 387–99.
POTTLE, F. A., *James Boswell: The Earlier Years 1740–1769* (London, 1966).
PRITCHARD, J., *Louis XV's Navy 1748–1762: A Study of Organization and Administration* (Kingston and Montreal, 1987).
REA, R. R., *The English Press in Politics 1760–1774* (Lincoln, Nebr., 1963).
RAMSEY, J. F., *Anglo–French Relations 1763–1770: A Study of Choiseul's Foreign Policy* (Berkeley, 1939).
RASHED, Z. E., *The Peace of Paris 1763* (Liverpool, 1951).
REDDAWAY, W. F., 'Great Britain and Poland, 1762–72', *Cambridge Historical Journal*, 4 (1932–4), 233–62.
—— 'Macartney in Russia, 1765–67', *Cambridge Historical Journal*, 3 (1929–31), 260–94.
RENAUT, F.-P., *Le Crépuscule d'une puissance navale: la marine hollandaise de 1776 à 1783* (Paris, 1932).
—— *De la neutralité à la belligérance (1775–1780)*, vol. i of *Les Provinces Uniés et la Guerre d'Amérique* (Paris, 1924).
—— *Le Pacte de famille et l'Amérique: la politique franco-espagnole de 1760 à 1792* (Paris, 1922).
—— *Le Secret Service de l'Amirauté britannique au temps de la guerre d'Amérique 1776–1783* (*L'Espionnage naval au XVIIIᵉ siècle*, i) (Paris, 1936).
RICE, G. W., 'Great Britain, the Manila Ransom and the First Falkland Islands Dispute with Spain, 1766', *International History Review*, 2 (1980), 386–409.
RICHMOND, SIR H., *The Navy in India 1763–1783* (London, 1931).
—— *Statesmen and Sea Power* (Oxford, 1946).
RILEY, J. C., *The Seven Years War and the Old Regime in France: The Economic and Financial Toll* (Princeton, 1986).
RITCHESON, C. R., *Aftermath of Revolution: British policy towards the United States 1783–1795* (Dallas, 1969).
—— 'Britain's Peacemakers 1782–1783: "To an Astonishing Degree Unfit for the Task"?', in Hoffman and Albert, eds., *Peace and Peacemakers* (q.v.).
—— *British Politics and the American Revolution* (Norman, Okla., 1954).

—— 'The Earl of Shelburne and Peace with America, 1782–1783: Vision and Reality', *International History Review*, 5 (1983), 322–45.

ROBERTS, M., *British Diplomacy and Swedish Politics 1758–1773* (London, 1980).

—— 'Great Britain, Denmark and Russia, 1763–1770', in Hatton and Anderson, eds., *Studies in Diplomatic History* (q.v.).

—— 'Great Britain and the Swedish Revolution, 1772–3', *Essays in Swedish History* (London, 1967), 286–347.

—— *Macartney in Russia* (*English Historical Review*, Supplement 7 (London, 1974)).

—— *Splendid Isolation 1763–1780* (Reading, 1970).

ROSLUND-MERCURIO, C. L., 'The American Colonial Rebellion and Swedish-British Diplomacy, 1775–1778', [Swedish] *Historisk tidskrift*, 94 (1974), 475–89.

ROUZEAU, L., 'Aperçus du rôle de Nantes dans la guerre d'indépendance d'Amérique', *Annales de Bretagne*, 74 (1967), 217–78.

ROWEN, H. H., *The Princes of Orange: The Stadholders in the Dutch Republic* (Cambridge, 1988).

RUDÉ, G., *Wilkes and Liberty: A Social Study of 1763–1774* (Oxford, 1965 edn.).

RUVILLE, A. VON., *William Pitt, Earl of Chatham* (3 vols.; London, 1907).

SAVORY, SIR R., *His Britannic Majesty's Army in Germany during the Seven Years War* (Oxford, 1966).

SCHAMA, S., *Patriots and Liberators: Revolution in the Netherlands 1780–1813* (London, 1977).

SCHLENKE, M. *England und das friderizianische Preussen 1740–1763* (Freiburg and Munich, 1963).

SCHMIDT, K. R., 'Problems Connected with the Last Polish Royal Election: A Study in the Development of Count Panin's Northern System', *Scando-Slavica*, 2 (1956), 134–48.

—— 'The Treaty of Commerce between Great Britain and Russia in 1766: A Study in the Development of Count Panin's Northern System', *Scando-Slavica*, 1 (1954), 115–34.

—— 'Wie ist Panins Plan zu einem Nordischen System entstanden?', *Zeitschrift für Slawistik*, 2 (1957), 406–22.

SCHROEDER, P. W., 'Old Wine in New Bottles: Recent Contributions to British Foreign Policy and European International Politics, 1789–1848', *Journal of British Studies*, 26 (1987), 1–25.

SCHWEIZER, K. W., ed., *Lord Bute: Essays in Re-interpretation* (Leicester, 1988).

—— 'Lord Bute, Newcastle, Prussia and the Hague Overtures: A Re-examination', *Albion*, 9 (1977), 72–97.

—— 'The Non-Renewal of the Anglo-Prussian Subsidy Treaty, 1761–62: A Historical Revision', *Canadian Journal of History*, 13 (1978), 383–96.

—— 'Scotsmen and the British Diplomatic Service, 1714–1789', *Scottish Tradition*, 7–8 (1977–8), 115–36.

SCHWEIZER, K. W., 'William Pitt, Lord Bute, and the Peace Negotiations with France, May–September 1761', *Albion*, 13 (1981), 262–75.

—— and LEONARD, C. S., 'Britain, Prussia, Russia and the Galitzin Letter: a Reassessment', *Historical Journal*, 26 (1983), 531–56.

SCOTT, H. M., 'Great Britain, Poland and the Russian Alliance, 1763–1767', *Historical Journal*, 19 (1976), 53–74.

—— 'The Importance of Bourbon Naval Reconstruction to the Strategy of Choiseul after the Seven Years War', *International History Review*, 1 (1979), 17–35.

—— 'Sir Joseph Yorke, Dutch Politics and the Origins of the Fourth Anglo-Dutch War', *Historical Journal* 31 (1988), 571–89.

—— ' "The True Principles of the Revolution": the Duke of Newcastle and the Idea of the Old System', in J. Black, ed., *Knights Errant and True Englishmen* (Edinburgh, 1989), 55–91.

SEN, S. P., *The French in India, 1763–1816* (Calcutta, 1958).

SHELTON, W. J., *English Hunger and Industrial Disorders: A Study of Social Conflict During the First Decade of George III's Reign* (London, 1973).

SINGH, R. J., *French Diplomacy in the Caribbean and the American Revolution* (Hicksville, NY, 1977).

SOREL, A., *The Eastern Question in the Eighteenth Century* (Eng. trans. London, 1898).

SPECTOR, M. M., *The American Department of the British Government 1768–82* (New York, 1940).

SPENCER, F., 'The Anglo-Prussian Breach of 1762: An Historical Revision', *History*, 41 (1956), 100–12.

—— 'Lord Sandwich, Russian Masts and American Independence', *The Mariner's Mirror*, 44 (1958), 116–27.

SPOONER, F. C., *Risks at Sea: Amsterdam Insurance and Maritime Europe 1766–1780* (Cambridge, 1983).

STEPHENSON, O. W., 'The Supply of Gunpowder in 1776', *American Historical Review*, 30 (1924–5), 271–81.

STIEGUNG, H., *Den engeleska underrättelseverksamheten rörande Sverige under 1700-talet* (Stockholm, 1961).

STINCHCOMBE, W. C., *The American Revolution and the French Alliance* (Syracuse, NY, 1969).

STOURZH, G. S., *Benjamin Franklin and American Foreign Policy* (Chicago, 1954; 2nd ed., 1969).

STUART, C., 'Lord Shelburne', in H. Lloyd-Jones, V. Pearl, and B. Worden, eds., *History and Imagination: Essays in Honour of H. R. Trevor-Roper* (London, 1981), 243–53.

SUTHERLAND, L. S., *The East India Company in Eighteenth-century Politics* (Oxford, 1952).

—— 'The East India Company and the Peace of Paris', *English Historical Review*, 62 (1947), 179–90.

SYRETT, D., 'Defeat at Sea: The Impact of American Naval Operations upon the British, 1775–1778', *Maritime Dimensions of the American Revolu-*

tion (Naval History Division, Department of the Navy; Washington, 1977), 13–22.

—— 'The Failure of the British Effort in America, 1777', in Black and Woodfine, eds., *British Navy and Naval Power* (q.v.).

—— *Neutral Rights and the War in the Narrow Seas 1778–82* (Fort Leavenworth, Kan., [1985]).

—— *Shipping and the American War* (London, 1970).

TARLING, N., *Anglo-Dutch Rivalry in the Malay World 1780–1824* (St Lucia, Queensland, 1962).

TEMPERLEY, H. W. V. *Frederic the Great and Kaiser Joseph* (London, 1915; repr. 1968).

THOMAS, P. D. G., *British Politics and the Stamp Act Crisis: The First Phase of the American Revolution, 1763–1767* (Oxford, 1975).

—— 'George III and the American Revolution', *History*, 70 (1985), 16–31.

—— *The House of Commons in the Eighteenth Century* (Oxford, 1971).

—— *Lord North* (London, 1976).

—— *The Townshend Duties Crisis: The Second Phase of the American Revolution 1767–73* (Oxford, 1987).

THOMSON, B. P., *Spain: Forgotten Ally of the American Revolution* (North Quincy, Mass., 1976).

THOMSON, M. A., *The Secretaries of State, 1681–1782* (Oxford, 1932).

TRACY, N., 'The Administration of the Duke of Grafton and the French Invasion of Corsica', *Eighteenth-Century Studies*, 8 (1974–5), 169–82.

—— 'British Assessments of French and Spanish Naval Reconstruction, 1763–68', *The Mariner's Mirror*, 61 (1975), 73–85.

—— 'The Falkland Islands crisis of 1770: Use of Naval Force', *English Historical Review*, 90 (1975), 40–75.

—— 'The Gunboat Diplomacy of the Government of George Grenville, 1764–65: The Honduras, Turks' Island and Gambian Incidents', *Historical Journal*, 17 (1974), 711–31.

—— *Navies, Deterrence and American Independence: Britain and Seapower in the 1760s and 1770s* (Vancouver, 1988).

—— 'Parry of a Threat to India, 1768–1774', *The Mariner's Mirror*, 59 (1973), 35–48.

TRAMOND, J., 'La Marine et les réformes de M. de Boynes', *La Revue maritime*, 61 (1925).

TUCKER, R. W., and HENDRICKSON, D. C., *The Fall of the First British Empire: Origins of the War of American Independence* (Baltimore, Md., 1983).

TUNSTALL, B., *William Pitt, Earl of Chatham* (London, 1938).

TUXEN, O., 'Principles and Priorities: The Danish View of Neutrality during the Colonial War of 1755–63', *Scandinavian Journal of History*, 13 (1988).

UNZER, A., *Der Friede von Teschen* (Kiel, 1903).

VAN ALSTYNE, R. W., *Empire and Independence: The International History of the American Revolution* (New York, 1965).

—— 'Europe, the Rockingham Whigs and the War for American Independence: Some Documents', *Huntington Library Quarterly*, 25 (1961–2), 1–28.

—— 'Great Britain, the War for Independence and the "Gathering Storm" in Europe 1775–1778', *Huntington Library Quarterly*, 27 (1964), 311–46.

VINCITORIO, G. L., 'Edmund Burke and the First Partition of Poland', in id., ed., *Crisis in the 'Great Republic': Essays Presented to Ross J. S. Hoffman* (New York, 1969), 14–46.

WADDINGTON, R., *Louis XV et le renversement des alliances* (Paris, 1896).

WARD, M., *Forth* (Chichester, 1982).

WATSON, J. S., *The Reign of George III, 1760–1815* (Oxford, 1960).

WILKINS, W. H., *A Queen of Tears: Caroline Mathilda, Queen of Denmark* (2 vols.; London, 1904).

WILLIAMS, B., *The Life of William Pitt, Earl of Chatham* (2 vols.; London, 1913).

WOOD, A. C., *A History of the Levant Company* (Oxford, 1935).

WRIGHT, E., 'The British Objectives, 1780–1783: ' "If not Dominion then Trade" ', in Hoffman and Albert, eds., *Peace and Peacemakers* (q.v.).

4. UNPUBLISHED DISSERTATIONS

ABARCA, R. E., 'Bourbon "Revanche" against England: The Balance of Power, 1763–1770' (Ph.D., University of Notre Dame, 1965).

ANDERSON, M. S., 'British Diplomatic Relations with the Mediterranean, 1763–1778' (Ph.D., University of Edinburgh, 1952).

BAGIS, A. I., 'The Embassy of Sir Robert Ainslie at Istanbul' (Ph.D., University of London, 1974).

CROUT, R. R., 'The Diplomacy of Trade: The Influence of Commercial Considerations on French Involvement in the Angloamerican War of Independence, 1775–78' (Ph.D., University of Georgia, 1977).

DANN, U., 'Hanover and Great Britain 1740–1760' (D.Phil., University of Oxford, 1980).

DORAN, P. F., 'Andrew Mitchell and Anglo-Prussian Diplomatic Relations during the Seven Years War' (Ph.D., University of London, 1972).

DURRANT, P., 'A Political Life of Augustus Henry Fitzroy, Third Duke of Grafton (1735–1811)' (Ph.D., University of Manchester, 1978).

ESCOTT, M. M., 'Britain's Relations with France and Spain, 1763–1771' (Ph.D., University of Wales, 1988).

GRIFFITHS, D. M., 'Russian Court Politics and the Question of an Expansionist Foreign Policy under Catherine II, 1762–1783' (Ph.D., Cornell University, 1967).

HAMER, M. T., 'From the Grafton Administration to the Ministry of North 1768–1772' (Ph.D., University of Cambridge, 1970).

HARDMAN, J. D., 'Ministerial Politics from the Accession of Louis XVI to the Assembly of Notables, 1774–1787' (D.Phil., University of Oxford, 1973).

JULIAN, E. A., 'British Projects and Activities in the Philippines: 1759–1805' (Ph.D., University of London, 1963).

KENNEDY, B. E., 'Anglo-French Rivalry in India and in the Eastern Seas, 1763–93: A Study of Anglo-French Tensions and of Their Impact on the Consolidation of British Power in the Region' (Ph.D., Australian National University, 1969).

LALAGUNA LASALA, J. A., 'England, Spain and the Family Compact, 1763–83' (Ph.D., University of London, 1968).

MCLEISH, J., 'British Activities in Yucatan and on the Moskito Shore in the Eighteenth Century' (MA, University of London, 1926).

MISIUNAS, R. J., 'Russia and Sweden 1772–1778' (Ph.D., Yale University, 1971).

RICE, G. W., 'An Aspect of European Diplomacy in the Mid-Eighteenth Century: The Diplomatic Career of the Fourth Earl of Rochford at Turin, Madrid and Paris, 1749–1768' (Ph.D., University of Canterbury, New Zealand, 1973).

ROSLUND-MERCURIO, C. L., 'The Problem of Neutral Rights in Swedish Relations with Great Britain, 1775–1780' (Ph.D., Syracuse University, 1972).

ROTHNEY, G. O., 'British Policy in the North American Cod Fisheries, with Special Reference to Foreign Competition 1775–1819' (Ph.D., University of London, 1939).

SCOTT, H. M., 'Anglo-Austrian Relations after the Seven Years War: Lord Stormont in Vienna, 1763–1772' (Ph.D., University of London, 1977).

SCOTT, L., 'Under Secretaries of State, 1755–1775' (MA, University of Manchester, 1950).

SORSBY, W. S., 'The British Superintendency of the Mosquito Shore 1749–1787' (Ph.D., University of London, 1969).

SPENCER, F., 'The Diplomatic Correspondence of John, Fourth Earl of Sandwich, during his Secretaryship of State in the Northern Department, September 9, 1763–July 10, 1765' (Ph.D., University of Manchester, 1953).

TOBORG, A., 'Frederick II of Prussia and his Relations with Great Britain during the American Revolution' (Ph.D., Columbia University, 1965).

WILLIAMS, M. J., 'The Naval Administration of the Fourth Earl of Sandwich, 1771–82' (D.Phil., University of Oxford, 1962).

Index

Passing references to countries have not generally been indexed.